# THIS BIBLE BELONGS TO:

. . . . . . . . . . . . . . . . . . . . . . . . . . . . .

## GIVEN BY:

. . . . . . . . . . . . . . . . . . . . . . . . . . . . .

## DATE:

. . . . . . . . . . . . . . . . . . . . . . . . . . . . .

## OCCASION:

. . . . . . . . . . . . . . . . . . . . . . . . . . . . .

**"Tell the greatness of the Lord with me. Let us praise his name together."** *Psalm 34:3*

# MAGNiFY ™

## THE COMPLETE NEW TESTAMENT

A Nelson Biblezine™

International Children's Bible®

A Division of Thomas Nelson, inc.
www.tommynelson.com

# TABLE OF CONTENTS

# INTRODUCTION

The title says it—Magnify™—both in discovering the secrets and truths of the Bible and in magnifying and honoring God!

This newest Biblezine™ gives you a super-cool new way to read the Bible so you can have a blast while learning about God's Word. You'll be surprised at how fun getting to know the Bible can be!

The Complete New Testament of the International Children's Bible® will come

alive as you uncover facts that help you learn how the Bible is meaningful in your life today. There's even a secret decoder to help you discover amazing secrets found in the Bible.

## JUMP IN AND EXPLORE GREAT FEATURES LIKE:

### WILD WORLD FACTS

Awesome and true facts about God's wonderful creation. Sometimes gross, often weird, but always amazing to see how God's hand is in everything in the world around us!

### BIBLE BASICS

Just the facts—pure and simple—about great Bible truths that you need to know.

### LIVIN' IT!

Great articles to show you how to live your life based on the wisdom, promises, and truths from the Bible. Livin' your life according to God's Word will help you be the best you can be!

### CALENDARS

One for January through December... each one with its own focus on a special Christian trait such as Forgiveness, Friendship, Honesty, and many more. Also included are suggestions for fun activities you can do to help others!

### GET CONNECTED

Ever wonder how to get along with others or how to have strong relationships with family and friends? Read the Get Connected articles to learn "tried and true" ways to help you live a happy life with the people around you.

## GAMES & QUIZZES

Tons of creative and fun games and quizzes to color, decipher, decode, and solve. Find out things you may have never known before, and have a great time learning them!

## TOP TEN

Cool lists of things to do or trivia facts for you to know, like the top 10 ways to bless your family, top 10 favorite sundae toppings, or top 10 places to pray.

## REAL SUPER HEROES

Yep, that's right! There were Super Heroes in the Bible...people like John, Paul, Mary, and of course Jesus! Learn about some of these awesome people that made a difference.

## Going Global

Have you ever wondered about kids on the other side of the world (or even in your own community)? How do they dress? What do they eat? Do they go to school? How can you help them? This feature connects you to websites around the world to help you do just that...learn about "global" kids and the ways you can help them!

## Gotta Know

Do you have a question? Wanna know the answer? Well here are some questions that were asked by kids your age, and the answers are found right in the Bible. Maybe some things you've been longing to know are right here inside these pages!

## KIDS SPEAK UP!

Kids were asked questions about silly, wacky, funny...even serious things...and you'll laugh at some of the things they said!

## DECODER SECRETS!

Do you like being a detective? Do you like solving mysteries or finding hidden messages? Use your free Magnify™ secret decoder to uncover the hidden messages found throughout the Bible pages. If you're a real "undercover agent," you can read the Bible verses to find the answer, too!

# FROM THE PUBLISHERS OF

# MAGNiFY™

**God never intended for the Bible to be too difficult for his people to understand.** To make sure God's message was clear, the authors of the Bible wrote it down in everyday language. These books brought a message that the original readers could understand. These first readers knew that God spoke through these books. Down through the centuries, many people wanted a Bible so badly that they copied different Bible books by hand!

Today, now that the Bible is so easy to get, many Christians do not read it every day. Many people feel that it is too hard to understand or doesn't have any answers for their life.

The International Children's Bible® translation speaks in a clear and simple message that even young readers can understand. The ICB presents God's Word in a clear and dynamic way.

A team of scholars from the World Bible Translation Center worked together with twenty-one other experienced Bible scholars from around the world to translate the verses from the best available Hebrew and Greek texts. You can trust that this Bible accurately presents God's Word as it came to us in the original languages.

Translators kept sentences short and simple. They tried to stay away from difficult words and worked hard to make the verses easier to read. They used more modern words for places and measurements. They put figures of speech and expressions in language that even children could understand. Also included within the text are small "d's" (to refer you to a dictionary in the back of full ICB versions) and small "n's" that refer you to a footnote found at the bottom of the Bible page.

It is with great humility and prayerfulness that this Bible is presented to God's children. We acknowledge the infallibility of God's Word and our own human frailty. We pray that God will use this Bible to help you understand his rich truth for your life. We magnify God's holy name, and for his glory this Bible is given.

The Publisher

Matthew quit his job to follow Jesus.

Written around A.D. 58-68 by Matthew, a former tax collector.

# THE GOSPEL ACCORDING TO MATTHEW

First book of the New Testament.

You'll find the Sermon on the Mount in Matthew (chapter 5).

Originally written in Hebrew then later copied in Greek.

Matthew tells the Jews about Jesus.

# BiBLE BasiCS

## WHO IS GOD?

It might be a little hard to understand the idea of who God is since you can't see him. You can't see him because he is a spirit and doesn't have a body like we do. But because he isn't limited by a body, he is everywhere and sees everything that is going on all the time. Because he made everything that exists, he also controls all that he has made.

## THE FAMILY HISTORY OF JESUS

**1** This is the family history of Jesus Christ. He came from the family of David. David came from the family of Abraham.

[2] Abraham was the father[n] of Isaac. Isaac was the father of Jacob. Jacob was the father of Judah and his brothers.

[3] Judah was the father of Perez and Zerah.
(Their mother was Tamar.)
Perez was the father of Hezron. Hezron was the father of Ram.

[4] Ram was the father of Amminadab. Amminadab was the father of Nahshon.
Nahshon was the father of Salmon.

[5] Salmon was the father of Boaz.
(Boaz's mother was Rahab.)
Boaz was the father of Obed.
(Obed's mother was Ruth.)
Obed was the father of Jesse.

[6] Jesse was the father of King David. David was the father of Solomon.
(Solomon's mother had been Uriah's wife.)

[7] Solomon was the father of Rehoboam. Rehoboam was the father of Abijah. Abijah was the father of Asa.

[8] Asa was the father of Jehoshaphat. Jehoshaphat was the father of Jehoram. Jehoram was the ancestor of Uzziah.

[9] Uzziah was the father of Jotham. Jotham was the father of Ahaz. Ahaz was the father of Hezekiah.

[10] Hezekiah was the father of Manasseh. Manasseh was the father of Amon. Amon was the father of Josiah.

[11] Josiah was the grandfather of Jehoiachin and his brothers.
(This was at the time that the people were taken to Babylon.)

[12] After they were taken to Babylon:
Jehoiachin was the father of Shealtiel. Shealtiel was the grandfather of Zerubbabel.

[13] Zerubbabel was the father of Abiud. Abiud was the father of Eliakim. Eliakim was the father of Azor.

[14] Azor was the father of Zadok. Zadok was the father of Akim. Akim was the father of Eliud.

[15] Eliud was the father of Eleazar. Eleazar was the father of Matthan. Matthan was the father of Jacob.

[16] Jacob was the father of Joseph. Joseph was the husband of Mary, and Mary was the mother of Jesus. Jesus is called the Christ.[d]

[17] So there were 14 generations from Abraham to David. And there were 14 generations from David until the time when the people were taken to Babylon. And there were 14 generations from the time when the people were taken to Babylon until Christ was born.

## THE BIRTH OF JESUS CHRIST

[18] The mother of Jesus Christ was Mary. And this is how the birth of Jesus came about. Mary was engaged to marry Joseph. But before they married, she learned that she was going to have a baby. She was pregnant by the power of the Holy Spirit.[d] [19] Mary's husband, Joseph, was a good man. He did not want to disgrace her in public, so he planned to divorce her secretly.

[20] While Joseph thought about this, an angel of the Lord came to him in a dream. The angel said, "Joseph, descendant[d] of David, don't be afraid to take Mary as your wife. The baby in her is from the Holy Spirit. [21] She will give birth to a son. You will name the son Jesus.[n] Give him that name because he will save his people from their sins."

[22] All this happened to make clear the full meaning of what the Lord had said through the prophet:[d] [23] "The virgin[d] will be pregnant. She will have a son, and they will name him Immanuel."[n] This name means "God is with us."

[24] When Joseph woke up, he did what the Lord's angel had told him to do. Joseph married Mary. [25] But he did not have sexual relations with her until she gave birth to the son. And Joseph named the son Jesus.

## WISE MEN COME TO VISIT JESUS

**2** Jesus was born in the town of Bethlehem in Judea during the time when Herod was king. After Jesus was born, some wise men from the east came to Jerusalem. [2] They asked, "Where is the baby who was born to be the king of the Jews? We saw his star in the east. We came to worship him."

[3] When King Herod heard about this new king of the Jews, he was troubled. And all the people in Jerusalem were worried too. [4] Herod called a meeting of all the leading priests and teachers of the law. He asked them where the Christ[d] would be born. [5] They answered, "In the town of Bethlehem in Judea. The prophet[d] wrote about this in the Scriptures:[d]

**DECODE THIS!**

*Jesus Christ came from the family of _____.*

1:2 **father** "Father" in Jewish lists of ancestors can sometimes mean grandfather or more distant relative.
1:21 **Jesus** The name Jesus means "salvation." 1:23 **"The virgin . . . Immanuel."** Quotation from Isaiah 7:14.

⁶"'But you, Bethlehem, in the land of
    Judah,
        you are important among the
            rulers of Judah.
    A ruler will come from you.
        He will be like a shepherd for my
            people, the Israelites.'" *Micah 5:2*

⁷Then Herod had a secret meeting with the wise men from the east. He learned from them the exact time they first saw the star. ⁸Then Herod sent the wise men to Bethlehem. He said to them, "Go and look carefully to find the child. When you find him, come tell me. Then I can go worship him too."

⁹The wise men heard the king and then left. They saw the same star they had seen in the east. It went before them until it stopped above the place where the child was. ¹⁰When the wise men saw the star, they were filled with joy. ¹¹They went to the house where the child was and saw him with his mother, Mary. They bowed down and worshiped the child. They opened the gifts they brought for him. They gave him treasures of gold, frankincense,*ᵈ* and myrrh.*ᵈ* ¹²But God warned the wise men in a dream not to go back to Herod. So they went home to their own country by a different way.

## JESUS' PARENTS TAKE HIM TO EGYPT

¹³After they left, an angel of the Lord came to Joseph in a dream. The angel said, "Get up! Take the child and his mother and escape to Egypt. Herod will start looking for the child to kill him. Stay in Egypt until I tell you to return."

¹⁴So Joseph got up and left for Egypt during the night with the child and his mother. ¹⁵Joseph stayed in Egypt until Herod died. This was to make clear the full meaning of what the Lord had said through the prophet.*ᵈ* The Lord said, "I called my son out of Egypt."*ⁿ*

## SEEING STARS

We all know that the wise men found Jesus by following a star. But the story becomes even more amazing when we realize what stars are.

Stars are huge masses of burning gases. The closest one to us is the sun, which is 93 million miles away. Other stars are so far away that scientists use a special measurement called light-years to describe it. One light-year is 6 trillion miles. The next closest star, Proxima Centauri, is a little over 4 light-years away. Today we have the Hubble Space Telescope that lets us see stars that are over 12 billion light-years away!

No matter how far the universe stretches, God is still there. Instead of a star, God now uses the light of Scripture to lead us to Jesus.

[Yahooligans: Ask Earl]

## HEROD KILLS THE BABY BOYS

¹⁶When Herod saw that the wise men had tricked him, he was very angry. So he gave an order to kill all the baby boys in Bethlehem and in all the area around Bethlehem. He said to kill all the boys who were two years old or younger. This was in keeping with the time he learned from the wise men. ¹⁷So what God had said through the prophet*ᵈ* Jeremiah came true:

¹⁸"A sound was heard in Ramah.
        It was painful crying and much
            sadness.
    Rachel cries for her children,
        and she cannot be comforted,
        because her children are dead."
                                        *Jeremiah 31:15*

## JOSEPH AND MARY RETURN

¹⁹After Herod died, an angel of the Lord came to Joseph in a dream. This happened while Joseph was in Egypt. ²⁰The angel said, "Get up! Take the child and his mother and go to Israel. The people who were trying to kill the child are now dead." ²¹So Joseph took the

child and his mother and went to Israel. ²²But he heard that Archelaus was now king in Judea. Archelaus became king when his father Herod died. So Joseph was afraid to go there. After being warned in a dream, he went to the area of Galilee. ²³He went to a town called Nazareth and lived there. And so what God had said through the prophets*ᵈ* came true: "He will be called a Nazarene."*ⁿ*

## THE WORK OF JOHN THE BAPTIST

**3** About that time John the Baptist*ᵈ* came and began preaching in the desert area of Judea. ²John said, "Change your hearts and lives because the kingdom of heaven is coming soon." ³John the Baptist is the one Isaiah the prophet*ᵈ* was talking about. Isaiah said:

    "This is a voice of a man
        who calls out in the desert:
    'Prepare the way for the Lord.
        Make the road straight for him.'"
                                        *Isaiah 40:3*

## DECODE THIS!

*Who ordered the baby boys to be killed in Bethlehem?*

2:15 **"I called . . . Egypt."** Quotation from Hosea 11:1. 2:23 **Nazarene** A person from the city of Nazareth, a name probably meaning "branch" (see Isaiah 11:1).

# JANUARY FORGIVENESS

**1** Watch football with your dad, and make his favorite snack.

**2** ROMANS 3:23: All people have sinned and are not good enough for God's glory.

**3** Prayer Pointer: Take time to praise God for loving and forgiving you.

**4**

**5**

**6** Make a list of all the fun things you'd like to do this year.

**7** My LiST!

**8** ROMANS 5:8: But Christ died for us while we were still sinners. In this way God shows his great love for us.

**9**

**10** Take the first step to rebuild a friendship that was broken last year.

**11**

**12**

**13** Prayer Pointer: Ask God to search your heart, and see if there is any sin you need to confess to him.

**14**

**15** PSALM 103:12: He has taken our sins away from us as far as the east is from west.

**16**

**17**

**18** Write a note to your mom telling her how glad you are to be her kid.

**19**

**20**

**21** Put on your warmest clothes, and go for a walk with a friend.

**22** I JOHN 1:9: But if we confess our sins, he will forgive our sins. We can trust God. He does what is right. He will make us clean from all the wrongs we have done.

**23**

**24** Prayer Pointer: Pray for your family to grow closer to God and each other this year.

**25**

**26** Cut out paper into snowflakes, and hang them from your ceiling.

**27**

**28**

**29** MATTHEW 6:15: But if you don't forgive the wrongs of others, then your Father in heaven will not forgive the wrong things you do.

**30**

**31** Prayer Pointer: Pray for your pastor to speak the Good News clearly and for the church to listen.

*The Lord's love never ends. His mercies never stop (Lamentations 3:22).*

⁴John's clothes were made from camel's hair. He wore a leather belt around his waist. For food, he ate locusts[d] and wild honey. ⁵Many people went to hear John preach. They came from Jerusalem and all Judea and all the area around the Jordan River. ⁶They told of the sins they had done, and John baptized them in the Jordan River.

⁷Many of the Pharisees[d] and Sadducees[d] came to the place where John was baptizing people. When John saw them, he said: "You are all snakes! Who warned you to run away from God's anger that is coming? ⁸You must do the things that show that you have really changed your hearts and lives. ⁹And don't think that you can say to yourselves, 'Abraham is our father.' I tell you that God could make children for Abraham from these rocks. ¹⁰The ax is now ready to cut down the trees. Every tree that does not produce good fruit will be cut down and thrown into the fire.[n]

¹¹"I baptize you with water to show that your hearts and lives have changed. But there is one coming later who is greater than I am. I am not good enough to carry his sandals. He will

should be baptized by you!"

¹⁵Jesus answered, "Let it be this way for now. We should do all things that are right." So John agreed to baptize Jesus.

¹⁶Jesus was baptized and came up out of the water. Heaven opened, and he saw God's Spirit[d] coming down on him like a dove. ¹⁷And a voice spoke from heaven. The voice said, "This is my Son and I love him. I am very pleased with him."

### THE TEMPTATION OF JESUS

**4** Then the Spirit[d] led Jesus into the desert to be tempted by the devil. ²Jesus ate nothing for 40 days and nights. After this, he was very hungry. ³The devil came to Jesus to tempt him. The devil said, "If you are the Son of God, tell these rocks to become bread."

⁴Jesus answered, "It is written in the Scriptures,[d] 'A person does not live only by eating bread. But a person lives by everything the Lord says.'"[n]

⁵Then the devil led Jesus to the holy city of Jerusalem. He put Jesus on a very

**"it is written in the Scriptures,'A person does not live only by eating bread. But a person lives by everything the Lord says.'"**     *Matthew 4:4*

baptize you with the Holy Spirit[d] and with fire. ¹²He will come ready to clean the grain. He will separate the good grain from the chaff.[d] He will put the good part of the grain into his barn. And he will burn the chaff with a fire that cannot be put out."[n]

### JESUS IS BAPTIZED BY JOHN

¹³At that time Jesus came from Galilee to the Jordan River. He came to John and wanted John to baptize him. ¹⁴But John tried to stop him. John said, "Why do you come to me to be baptized? I

high place of the Temple.[d] ⁶The devil said, "If you are the Son of God, jump off. It is written in the Scriptures,

'He has put his angels in charge of you.
They will catch you with their hands.
And you will not hit your foot on a rock.'"     *Psalm 91:11-12*

⁷Jesus answered him, "It also says in the Scriptures, 'Do not test the Lord your God.'"[n]

⁸Then the devil led Jesus to the top of a very high mountain. He showed Jesus all the kingdoms of the world and all the great things that are in those kingdoms. ⁹The devil said, "If you will bow down and worship me, I will give you all these things."

¹⁰Jesus said to the devil, "Go away from me, Satan! It is written in the Scriptures, 'You must worship the Lord your God. Serve only him!'"[n]

¹¹So the devil left Jesus. And then some angels came to Jesus and helped him.

### JESUS BEGINS WORK IN GALILEE

¹²Jesus heard that John had been put in prison. So Jesus went back to Galilee. ¹³He left Nazareth and went and lived in Capernaum, a town near Lake Galilee.

## ？ DECODE THIS!
*Who tempted Jesus in the desert?*

★ **3:10 The ax . . . fire.** This means that God is ready to punish his people who do not obey him. **3:12 He will . . . out.** This means that Jesus will come to separate the good people from the bad people, saving the good and punishing the bad. **4:4 'A person . . . says.'** Quotation from Deuteronomy 8:3. **4:7 'Do . . . God.'** Quotation from Deuteronomy 6:16. **4:10 'You . . . him!'** Quotation from Deuteronomy 6:13.

Capernaum is in the area near Zebulun and Naphtali. [14]Jesus did this to make true what the prophet[d] Isaiah said:

[15]"Land of Zebulun and land of Naphtali
 are on the way to the sea.
They are along the Jordan River.
 This is Galilee where the
  non-Jewish people live.
[16]These people who live in darkness
 will see a great light.
They live in a place that is
 very dark.
But a light will shine on them."

*Isaiah 9:1-2*

### JESUS CHOOSES SOME FOLLOWERS

[17]From that time Jesus began to preach, saying, "Change your hearts and lives, because the kingdom of heaven is coming soon."

[18]Jesus was walking by Lake Galilee. He saw two brothers, Simon (called Peter) and Simon's brother Andrew. The brothers were fishermen, and they were fishing in the lake with a net. [19]Jesus said, "Come follow me. I will make you fishermen for men." [20]At once Simon and Andrew left their nets and followed him.

[21]Jesus continued walking by Lake Galilee. He saw two other brothers, James and John, the sons of Zebedee. They were in a boat with their father Zebedee, preparing their nets to catch fish. Jesus told them to come with him. [22]At once they left the boat and their father, and they followed Jesus.

### JESUS TEACHES AND HEALS PEOPLE

[23]Jesus went everywhere in Galilee. He taught in the synagogues[d] and preached the Good News[d] about the kingdom of heaven. And he healed all the people's diseases and sicknesses. [24]The news about Jesus spread all over Syria, and people brought all the sick to him. These sick people were suffering from different kinds of diseases and pain. Some were suffering very great pain, some had demons,[d] some were epileptics,[n] and some were paralyzed. Jesus healed all of them. [25]Many people followed him. They came from Galilee, the Ten Towns,[n] Jerusalem, Judea, and the land across the Jordan River.

### JESUS TEACHES THE PEOPLE

**5** Jesus saw the crowds who were there. He went up on a hill and sat down. His followers came to him. [2]Jesus taught the people and said:

[3]"Those people who know they have
 great spiritual needs are
 happy.
 The kingdom of heaven
  belongs to them.
[4]Those who are sad now are
 happy.
 God will comfort them.
[5]Those who are humble are happy.
 The earth will belong to them.
[6]Those who want to do right
 more than anything else
 are happy.
 God will fully satisfy them.

[7]Those who give mercy to others
 are happy.
 Mercy will be given to them.
[8]Those who are pure in their
 thinking are happy.
 They will be with God.
[9]Those who work to bring peace are
 happy.
 God will call them his sons.
[10]Those who are treated badly for doing
 good are happy.
 The kingdom of heaven belongs
 to them.
[11]"People will say bad things about you and hurt you. They will lie and say all kinds of evil things about you because you follow me. But when they do these things to you, you are happy. [12]Rejoice

## Ways to Remember Scripture

1. Buy a verse-a-day calendar.

2. Write your favorite verse on a note card, and put it on the bathroom mirror.

3. Put your verse to a tune, and sing it.

4. Repeat your verse before every meal.

5. Pray your verse back to God.

6. Start a memory club with your friends.

7. Memorize a verse for every letter of the alphabet.

8. Draw pictures that help you remember the verse.

9. Memorize a verse at the dinner table with your family.

10. Write it down in a notebook as many times as you can.

**4:24 epileptics** People with a disease that causes them sometimes to lose control of their bodies, and maybe faint, shake strongly, or not be able to move. **4:25 Ten Towns** In Greek, called "Decapolis." It was an area east of Lake Galilee that once had ten main towns.

and be glad. You have a great reward waiting for you in heaven. People did the same evil things to the prophets[d] who lived before you.

## SECRET SUCCESS

You've been to the prayer meetings before—the kind where the kids who seem so spiritual pray these incredible, long prayers. And then it's your turn—and you forget how to speak English, let alone talk to God.

Don't worry. God doesn't need or even want a spectacular prayer. In fact, he says that it's great to pray in secret so the conversation is just between you and God. He doesn't want us to care what others think—just what he thinks. And he loves to hear from our hearts, whether the words come out right or not.

## YOU ARE LIKE SALT AND LIGHT

[13]"You are the salt of the earth. But if the salt loses its salty taste, it cannot be made salty again. It is good for nothing. It must be thrown out for people to walk on.

[14]"You are the light that gives light to the world. A city that is built on a hill cannot be hidden. [15]And people don't hide a light under a bowl. They put the light on a lampstand. Then the light shines for all the people in the house. [16]In the same way, you should be a light for other people. Live so that they will see the good things you do. Live so that they will praise your Father in heaven.

## THE IMPORTANCE OF THE LAW

[17]"Don't think that I have come to destroy the law of Moses or the teaching of the prophets.[d] I have not come to destroy their teachings but to do what they said. [18]I tell you the truth. Nothing will disappear from the law until heaven and earth are gone. The law will not lose even the smallest letter or the smallest part of a letter until all has happened. [19]Whoever refuses to obey any command and teaches other people not to obey that command will be the least important in the kingdom of heaven. But who-

ever obeys the law and teaches other people to obey the law will be great in the kingdom of heaven. [20]I tell you that you must do better than the teachers of the law and the Pharisees.[d] If you are not better than they are, you will not enter the kingdom of heaven.

## JESUS TEACHES ABOUT ANGER

[21]"You have heard that it was said to our people long ago, 'You must not murder anyone.[n] Anyone who murders another will be judged.' [22]But I tell you, if you are angry with your brother, you will be judged. And if you say bad things to

"**But i tell you, love your enemies. Pray for those who hurt you.**" *Matthew 5:44*

your brother, you will be judged by the Jewish council. And if you call your brother a fool, then you will be in danger of the fire of hell.

[23]"So when you offer your gift to God at the altar, and you remember that your brother has something against you, [24]leave your gift there at the altar. Go and make peace with him. Then come and offer your gift.

[25]"If your enemy is taking you to court, become friends with him quickly. You should do that before you go to court. If

you don't become his friend, he might turn you over to the judge. And the judge might give you to a guard to put you in jail. [26]I tell you that you will not leave that jail until you have paid everything you owe.

## JESUS TEACHES ABOUT SEXUAL SIN

[27]"You have heard that it was said, 'You must not be guilty of adultery.'[n] [28]But I tell you that if anyone looks at a woman and wants to sin sexually with her, then he has already done that sin with the woman in his mind. [29]If your right eye causes you to sin, then take it out and throw it away. It is better to lose one part of your body than to have your whole body thrown into hell. [30]If your right hand causes you to sin, then cut it off and throw it away. It is better to lose one part of your body than for your whole body to go into hell.

## JESUS TEACHES ABOUT DIVORCE

[31]"It was also said, 'Anyone who divorces his wife must give her a written divorce paper.'[n] [32]But I tell you that anyone who divorces his wife is causing his wife to be guilty of adultery.[d] The only reason for a man to divorce his wife is if

she has sexual relations with another man. And anyone who marries that divorced woman is guilty of adultery.

## MAKE PROMISES CAREFULLY

[33]"You have heard that it was said to our people long ago, 'When you make a promise, don't break your promise. Keep the promises that you make to the Lord.'[n] [34]But I tell you, never make an oath. Don't make an oath using the name of heaven, because heaven is God's throne. [35]Don't make an oath using the name of

**5:21 You . . . anyone.** Quotation from Exodus 20:13; Deuteronomy 5:17. **5:27 'You . . . adultery.'** Quotation from Exodus 20:14; Deuteronomy 5:18. **5:31 'Anyone . . . divorce paper.'** Quotation from Deuteronomy 24:1. **5:33 'When . . . Lord.'** Quotation from Leviticus 19:12; Numbers 30:2; Deuteronomy 23:21.

# LiViN' iT!

## THE POWER OF LOVE
### MATTHEW 5:43

Imagine this: Another kid at school has been saying mean things about you behind your back. Now other kids are starting to make fun of you, too. What should you do? Our normal reaction is to get mad. Maybe even say ugly things back to them or behind their backs. But that's not what Jesus says to do.

Jesus says that we should actually love our enemies and pray for those who hurt us. Even people who don't know Jesus at all love the people who are nice to them. There's nothing really special about that. But when we love people who are unlovely and unkind to us, then everyone else can see the special love of God shining through us. They know that we are different from the world, and we have a special power that they don't. By loving others God's way, we can help even our enemies come to know God.

the earth, because the earth belongs to God. Don't make an oath using the name of Jerusalem, because that is the city of the great King. ³⁶And don't even say that your own head is proof that you will keep your oath. You cannot make one hair on your head become white or black. ³⁷Say only 'yes' if you mean 'yes,' and say only 'no' if you mean 'no.' If you must say more than 'yes' or 'no,' it is from the Evil One.

## DON'T FIGHT BACK

³⁸"You have heard that it was said, 'An eye for an eye, and a tooth for a tooth.'ⁿ ³⁹But I tell you, don't stand up against an evil person. If someone slaps you on the right cheek, then turn and let him slap the other cheek too. ⁴⁰If someone wants to sue you in court and take your shirt, then let him have your coat too. ⁴¹If a soldier forces you to go with him one mile, then go with him two miles. ⁴²If a person asks you for something, then give it to him. Don't refuse to give to a person who wants to borrow from you.

## LOVE ALL PEOPLE

⁴³"You have heard that it was said, 'Love your neighborⁿ and hate your enemies.' ⁴⁴But I tell you, love your enemies. Pray for those who hurt you. ⁴⁵If you do this, then you will be true sons of your Father in heaven. Your Father causes the sun to rise on good people and on bad people. Your Father sends rain to those who do good and to those who do wrong. ⁴⁶If you love only the people who love you, then you will get no reward. Even the tax collectors do that. ⁴⁷And if you are nice only to your friends, then you are no better than other people. Even people without God are nice to their friends. ⁴⁸So you must be perfect, just as your Father in heaven is perfect.

## JESUS TEACHES ABOUT GIVING

**6** "Be careful! When you do good things, don't do them in front of people to be seen by them. If you do that, then you will have no reward from your Father in heaven.

²"When you give to the poor, don't be like the hypocrites.ᵈ They blow trumpets before they give so that people will see them. They do that in the synagoguesᵈ and on the streets. They want other people to honor them. I tell you the truth. Those hypocrites already have their full reward. ³So when you give to the poor, give very secretly. Don't let anyone know what you are doing. ⁴Your giving should be done in secret. Your Father can see what is done in secret, and he will reward you.

## JESUS TEACHES ABOUT PRAYER

⁵"When you pray, don't be like the hypocrites.ᵈ They love to stand in the synagoguesᵈ and on the street corners and pray loudly. They want people to see them pray. I tell you the truth. They already have their full reward. ⁶When you pray, you should go into your room and close the door. Then pray to your Father who cannot be seen. Your Father can see what is done in secret, and he will reward you.

⁷"And when you pray, don't be like those people who don't know God. They continue saying things that mean nothing. They think that God will hear them because of the many things they say. ⁸Don't be like them. Your Father knows the things you need before you ask him. ⁹So when you pray, you should pray like this:

'Our Father in heaven,
we pray that your name will always be
kept holy.
¹⁰We pray that your kingdom will
come.
We pray that what you want will
be done,
here on earth as it is in heaven.
¹¹Give us the food we need for
each day.
¹²Forgive the sins we have done,
just as we have forgiven those who
did wrong to us.

## DECODE THIS!

*What destroys treasures here on earth?*

---

5:38 'An eye . . . tooth.' Quotation from Exodus 21:24; Leviticus 24:20; Deuteronomy 19:21. 5:43 Love your neighbor Quotation from Leviticus 19:18.

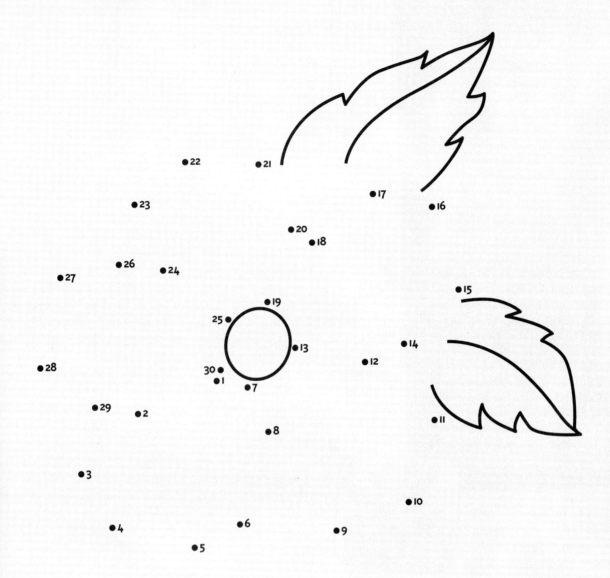

READ THE FOLLOWING PASSAGE
AND CONNECT THE DOTS.
THEN COLOR IT IN!

# MATTHEW 6:27-29

V. 28  AND WHY DO YOU WORRY ABOUT CLOTHES?
LOOK AT THE FLOWERS IN THE FIELD. SEE HOW THEY GROW.

[13]Do not cause us to be tested;
but save us from the Evil One.'

[14]Yes, if you forgive others for the things they do wrong, then your Father in heaven will also forgive you for the things you do wrong. [15]But if you don't forgive the wrongs of others, then your Father in heaven will not forgive the wrong things you do.

### JESUS TEACHES ABOUT WORSHIP

[16]"When you give up eating,[n] don't put on a sad face like the hypocrites.[d] They make their faces look strange to show people that they are giving up eating. I tell you the truth, those hypocrites already have their full reward. [17]So when you give up eating, comb your hair and wash your face. [18]Then people will not know that you are giving up eating. But your Father, whom you cannot see, will see you. Your Father sees what is done in secret, and he will reward you.

### GOD IS MORE IMPORTANT THAN MONEY

[19]"Don't store treasures for yourselves here on earth. Moths and rust will destroy treasures here on earth. And thieves can break into your house and steal the things you have. [20]So store your treasure in heaven. The treasures in heaven cannot be destroyed by moths or rust. And thieves cannot break in and steal that treasure. [21]Your heart will be where your treasure is.

[22]"The eye is a light for the body. If your eyes are good, then your whole body will be full of light. [23]But if your eyes are evil, then your whole body will be full of darkness. And if the only light you have is really darkness, then you have the worst darkness.

[24]"No one can be a slave to two masters. He will hate one master and love the other. Or he will follow one master and refuse to follow the other. So you cannot serve God and money at the same time.

### DON'T WORRY

[25]"So I tell you, don't worry about the food you need to live. And don't worry about the clothes you need for your body. Life is more important than food. And the body is more important than clothes. [26]Look at the birds in the air. They don't plant or harvest or store food in barns. But your heavenly Father feeds the birds. And you know that you are worth much more than the birds. [27]You cannot add any time to your life by worrying about it.

[28]"And why do you worry about clothes? Look at the flowers in the field. See how they grow. They don't work or make clothes for themselves. [29]But I tell you that even Solomon with his riches was not dressed as beautifully as one of these flowers. [30]God clothes the grass in the field like that. The grass is living today, but tomorrow it is thrown into the fire to be burned. So you can be even more sure that God will clothe you. Don't have so little faith! [31]Don't worry and say, 'What will we eat?' or 'What will we drink?' or 'What will we wear?' [32]All the people who don't know God keep trying to get these things. And your Father in heaven knows that you need them. [33]The thing you should want most is God's kingdom and doing what God wants. Then all these other things you need will be given to you. [34]So don't worry about tomorrow. Each day has enough trouble of its own. Tomorrow will have its own worries.

### LIVIN' IT!

**KINGDOM SEEKERS**
**MATTHEW 6:33**

When you get home from school, do you ask your parents if they've paid the bills? Do you try to find work so you can pay for your food? Do you check to make sure what they've brought home from the store is healthy? No, of course not. You know your parents love you and are going to take care of you. You are free to think about other things, because you know they've taken care of your basic needs.

Whatever kind of parents you have, God is a million times better. He knows everything we truly need, and loves to provide us with it. So we don't have to worry about money or clothes or food. We trust him to meet our needs. We need to be looking for ways we can help spread God's love with his world, making his friendship with us and others the most important part of our lives.

### DECODE THIS!

*What was wrong with the man Jesus healed in Matthew 8?*

**6:16 give up eating** This is called "fasting." The people would give up eating for a special time of prayer and worship to God. It was also done to show sadness.

### BE CAREFUL ABOUT JUDGING OTHERS

**7** "Don't judge other people, and you will not be judged. ²You will be judged in the same way that you judge others. And the forgiveness you give to others will be given to you.

## LiViN' iT!

### ONLY ONE GATE
### MATTHEW 7:13-14

The Bible talks about the road to hell being wide and easy to travel, while the road to heaven is narrow and difficult. What's so hard about getting into heaven?

The truth is, it isn't difficult if you're trusting Jesus to take you there. In fact, the "gate" this passage talks about is another word for Jesus. He is all we need to get into heaven.

What makes this hard for people is that many just don't believe it. They would rather try to do enough good deeds to earn their way inside. Or maybe try a different god that they like better. But like the Bible says, their road ends in destruction.

Obeying Jesus may not always be easy, but it is the only right thing we can do. Stay strong in the truth, and ask him for help so you can stay on the right road your whole life.

³"Why do you notice the little piece of dust that is in your brother's eye, but you don't notice the big piece of wood that is in your own eye? ⁴Why do you say to your brother, 'Let me take that little piece of dust out of your eye'? Look at yourself first! You still have that big piece of wood in your own eye. ⁵You are a hypocrite!ᵈ First, take the wood out of your own eye. Then you will see clearly enough to take the dust out of your brother's eye.

⁶"Don't give holy things to dogs. Don't throw your pearls before pigs. Pigs will only trample on them. And the dogs will only turn to attack you.

### ASK GOD FOR WHAT YOU NEED

⁷"Continue to ask, and God will give to you. Continue to search, and you will find. Continue to knock, and the door will open for you. ⁸Yes, everyone who continues asking will receive. He who continues searching will find. And he who continues knocking will have the door opened for him.

⁹"What would you do if your son asks for bread? Which of you would give him a stone? ¹⁰Or if your son asks for a fish, would you give him a snake? ¹¹Even though you are bad, you know how to give good gifts to your children. So surely your heavenly Father will give good things to those who ask him.

### THE MOST IMPORTANT RULE

¹²"Do for other people the same things you want them to do for you. This is the meaning of the law of Moses and the teaching of the prophets.ᵈ

### THE WAY TO HEAVEN IS HARD

¹³"Enter through the narrow gate. The road that leads to hell is a very easy road. And the gate to hell is very wide. Many people enter through that gate. ¹⁴But the gate that opens the way to true life is very small. And the road to true life is very hard. Only a few people find that road.

### PEOPLE KNOW YOU BY YOUR ACTIONS

¹⁵"Be careful of false prophets.ᵈ They come to you and look gen-tle like sheep. But they are really dangerous like wolves. ¹⁶You will know these people because of the things they do. Good things don't come from bad people, just as grapes don't come from thornbushes. And figs don't come from thorny weeds. ¹⁷In the same way, every good tree produces good fruit. And bad trees produce bad fruit. ¹⁸A good tree cannot produce bad fruit. And a bad tree cannot produce good fruit. ¹⁹Every tree that does not produce good fruit is cut down and thrown into the fire. ²⁰You will know these false prophets by what they produce.

²¹"Not everyone who says that I am his Lord will enter the kingdom of heaven. The only people who will enter the kingdom of heaven are those who do the things that my Father in heaven wants. ²²On the last day many people will say to me, 'You are our Lord! We spoke for you. And through you we

> **"Do for other people the same things you want them to do for you."**
> *Matthew 7:12*

forced out demonsᵈ and did many miracles.'ᵈ ²³Then I will tell them clearly, 'Get away from me, you who do evil. I never knew you.'

### TWO KINDS OF PEOPLE

²⁴"Everyone who hears these things I say and obeys them is like a wise man. The wise man built his house on rock. ²⁵It rained hard and the water rose. The winds blew and hit that house. But the house did not fall, because the house was built on rock. ²⁶But the person who hears the things I teach and does not obey them is like a foolish man. The

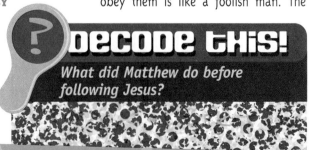

### DECODE THiS!
*What did Matthew do before following Jesus?*

# HOW'S YOUR FRUIT?

## Read Matthew 7:15-20.

Jesus says that others will know we belong to him by the fruit we bear. Take a look at each of these events, and answer honestly how you would respond. If you score a 7-8: Fantastic! If you're being honest, this shows that God is at work in your heart. Keep praying that you'll stay obedient to him. Score 5-6: Keep up the good work, and pray for more growth. Score 4 or below: Think again about how your attitude reveals your heart. Ask God to help you be more like him.

1. Your parents just brought home a new game, and your little brother takes it first. You:
   a. Grab it out of his hands and tell him that older kids go first.
   b. Complain to your parents that he has the game.
   c. Thank your parents for the gift, and ask if you can see it when your brother is finished.

2. You see a new kid at school. You:
   a. Tease her about her clothes.
   b. Ask your friends what they know about her.
   c. Ask her to join your friends for lunch.

3. Your sister just won the school spelling bee. You:
   a. Give her a hug and tell her "congratulations."
   b. Get quiet and pretend she didn't win anything.
   c. Try to do something to get your parents' attention.

4. Your mom is sick. You:
   a. Ask her to make you breakfast.
   b. Tell her you hope you don't get it.
   c. Fight with your siblings since she's not watching.
   d. Ask her how you can help.

5. Your class has a party, and you come home with candy. You:
   a. Hide it from your brothers and sisters and keep it for yourself.
   b. Let your sister have a bite.
   c. Offer to let your siblings choose which pieces they want.

6. The cool kids at school start making fun of your friend behind his back. You:
   a. Laugh with them.
   b. Pretend like you didn't hear what they said.
   c. Get in a fight about it.
   d. Tell them why your friend is really great.

7. Your parents tell you you're not allowed to watch the movie all your friends are seeing. You:
   a. Have a tantrum and yell.
   b. Tell your parents they're not being fair.
   c. Tell them you're disappointed, but that you will obey.
   d. Argue with your parents.

# LIVIN' IT!

**BRICKS IN THE SAND
MATTHEW 7:24**

You've probably heard this story lots of times since you were a child and even know a song about it. But when it comes to really building your life on a rock and not sand, what does it mean?

You'll find in life how good sand can look. Money, the right clothes, the right friends, the way you look—there's so many things out there that we can be tempted to make important. To think, "If I just had that, I'd be happy." As soon as we start wanting and hoping for things instead of God, we've just laid another brick on the sand.

Instead, realize that real joy only comes from God. Work to strengthen your friendship with him by reading and memorizing his Word and worshiping him. Then, no matter what comes your way, you will have him as your best friend to help you.

foolish man built his house on sand. ²⁷It rained hard, the water rose, and the winds blew and hit that house. And the house fell with a big crash."

²⁸When Jesus finished saying these things, the people were amazed at his teaching. ²⁹Jesus did not teach like their teachers of the law. He taught like a person who had authority.

## JESUS HEALS A SICK MAN

**8** When Jesus came down from the hill, great crowds followed him. ²Then a man sick with a harmful skin disease came to Jesus. The man bowed down before him and said, "Lord, you have the power to heal me if you want."

³Jesus touched the man and said, "I want to heal you. Be healed!" And immediately the man was healed from his skin disease. ⁴Then Jesus said to him, "Don't tell anyone about what happened. But go and show yourself to the priest." And offer the gift that Moses commanded" for people who are made well. This will show people that you are healed."

## JESUS HEALS A SOLDIER'S SERVANT

⁵Jesus went to the city of Capernaum. When he entered the city, an army officer came to Jesus and begged for help. ⁶The officer said, "Lord, my servant is at home in bed. He can't move his body and is in much pain."

⁷Jesus said to the officer, "I will go and heal him."

⁸The officer answered, "Lord, I am not good enough for you to come into my house. All you need to do is command that my servant be healed, and he will be healed. ⁹I myself am a man under the authority of other men. And I have soldiers under my command. I tell one soldier, 'Go,' and he goes. I tell another soldier, 'Come,' and he comes. I say to my servant, 'Do this,' and my servant obeys me."

¹⁰When Jesus heard this, he was amazed. He said to those who were with him, "I tell you the truth. This man has more faith than any other person I have found, even in Israel. ¹¹Many people will come from the east and from the west. They will sit and eat with Abraham, Isaac, and Jacob in the kingdom of heaven. ¹²And those people who should have the kingdom will be thrown outside into the darkness. In that place people will cry and grind their teeth with pain."

¹³Then Jesus said to

the officer, "Go home. Your servant will be healed just as you believed he would." And at that same time his servant was healed.

## JESUS HEALS MANY PEOPLE

¹⁴Jesus went to Peter's house. There Jesus saw that Peter's mother-in-law was in bed with a high fever. ¹⁵Jesus touched her hand, and the fever left her. Then she stood up and began to serve Jesus.

¹⁶That evening people brought to Jesus many who had demons.ᵈ Jesus spoke and the demons left them. Jesus healed all the sick. ¹⁷He did these things to make come true what Isaiah the prophetᵈ said:

"He took our suffering on him.
And he felt our pain for us."

*Isaiah 53:4*

## PEOPLE WANT TO FOLLOW JESUS

¹⁸When Jesus saw the crowd around him, he told his followers to go to the other side of the lake. ¹⁹Then a teacher of the law came to Jesus and said, "Teacher, I will follow you any place you go."

²⁰Jesus said to him, "The foxes have holes to live in. The birds have nests to live in. But the Son of Manᵈ has no place where he can rest his head."

²¹Another man, one of Jesus' followers, said to Jesus, "Lord, let me go and bury my father first."

²²But Jesus said to him, "Follow me, and let the people who are dead bury their own dead."

## JESUS STOPS A STORM

²³Jesus got into a boat, and his followers went with him. ²⁴A very bad storm arose on the lake. The waves covered the boat. But Jesus was sleeping. ²⁵The followers went to Jesus and woke him. They said, "Lord, save us! We will drown!"

# DECODE THIS!

*God knows how many of these you have.*

**8:4 show . . . priest** The law of Moses said a priest must say when a Jew who had a harmful skin disease was well. **8:4 Moses commanded** Read about this in Leviticus 14:1–32.

# Gotta Know!

## Why doesn't everybody believe the Bible?

Believing the Bible requires more than just reading words and agreeing with them. To believe what the Bible says means that you have to admit you're a sinner, and you must have Jesus to save you from your sins. Many people don't want to surrender to God because of the sin in their hearts. That same sin keeps them from actually understanding what the Bible says. Unless God changes their hearts and gives them understanding (faith), they cannot see the truth. That's why it's so important to pray for the lost, that God himself would open their eyes to his truth.

of cloth that is not yet shrunk. If he does, the patch will shrink and pull away from the coat. Then the hole will be worse. [17]Also, people never pour new wine into old leather bags for holding wine. If they do, the old bags will break. The wine will spill, and the wine bags will be ruined. But people always pour new wine into new wine bags. Then the wine and the wine bags will continue to be good."

### JESUS GIVES LIFE TO A DEAD GIRL AND HEALS A SICK WOMAN

[18]While Jesus was saying these things, a ruler of the synagogue[d] came to him. The ruler bowed down before Jesus and said, "My daughter has just died. But come and touch her with your hand, and she will live again."

[19]So Jesus stood up and went with the ruler. Jesus' followers went too.

[20]Then a woman who had been bleeding for 12 years came behind Jesus and touched the edge of his coat. [21]She was thinking, "If I can touch his coat, then I will be healed."

[22]Jesus turned and saw the woman. He said, "Be happy, dear woman. You are made well because you believed." And the woman was healed at once.

[23]Jesus continued along with the ruler and went into the ruler's house. Jesus saw people there who play music for funerals.

And he saw many people there crying. [24]Jesus said, "Go away. The girl is not dead. She is only asleep." But the people laughed at Jesus. [25]After the crowd had been put outside, Jesus went into the girl's room. He took her hand, and she stood up. [26]The news about this spread all around the area.

### JESUS HEALS MORE PEOPLE

[27]When Jesus was leaving there, two blind men followed him. They cried out, "Show kindness to us, Son of David!"[d]

[28]Jesus went inside, and the blind men went with him. He asked the men, "Do you believe that I can make you see again?"

They answered, "Yes, Lord."

[29]Then Jesus touched their eyes and said, "You believe that I can make you see again. So this will happen." [30]Then the men were able to see. But Jesus warned them very strongly, saying, "Don't tell anyone about this." [31]But the blind men left and spread the news about Jesus all around that area.

[32]When the two men were leaving, some people brought another man to Jesus.

This man could not talk because he had a demon[d] in him. [33]Jesus forced the demon to leave the man. Then the man who couldn't talk was able to speak. The crowd was amazed and said, "We have never seen anything like this in Israel."

[34]But the Pharisees[d] said, "The leader of demons is the one that gives him power to force demons out."

[35]Jesus traveled through all the towns and villages. He taught in their synagogues[d] and told people the Good News[d] about the kingdom. And he healed all kinds of diseases and sicknesses. [36]He saw the crowds of people and felt sorry for them because they were worried and helpless. They were like sheep without a shepherd. [37]Jesus said to his followers, "There are many people to harvest, but there are only a few workers to help harvest them. [38]God owns the harvest. Pray to him that he will send more workers to help gather his harvest."[n]

### JESUS SENDS OUT HIS APOSTLES

**10** Jesus called his 12 followers together. He gave them power to drive out evil spirits and to heal every kind of disease and sickness. [2]These are the names of the 12 apostles:[d] Simon (also called Peter) and his brother Andrew; James son of Zebedee, and his brother John; [3]Philip and Bartholomew;

### "The crowd was amazed and said, 'We have never seen anything like this in Israel.'"

*Matthew 9:33*

Thomas and Matthew, the tax collector; James son of Alphaeus, and Thaddaeus; [4]Simon the Zealot[d] and Judas Iscariot. Judas is the one who turned against Jesus.

[5]These 12 men he sent out with the following order: "Don't go to the non-Jewish people. And don't go into any town where the Samaritans[d] live. [6]But go to the people of Israel. They are like sheep

9:37-38 "There are . . . harvest." As a farmer sends workers to harvest the grain, Jesus sends his followers to bring people to God.

[26]Jesus answered, "Why are you afraid? You don't have enough faith." Then Jesus got up and gave a command to the wind and the sea. The wind stopped, and the sea became very calm.

[27]The men were amazed. They said, "What kind of man is this? Even the wind and the sea obey him!"

## JESUS HEALS TWO MEN WITH DEMONS

[28]Jesus arrived at the other side of the lake in the country of the Gadarene[n] people. There, two men came to Jesus. They had demons[d] in them. These men lived in the burial caves. They were so dangerous that people could not use the road by those caves. [29]The two men came to Jesus and shouted, "What do you want with us, Son of God? Did you come here to punish us before the right time?"

[30]Near that place there was a large herd of pigs feeding. [31]The demons begged Jesus, "If you make us leave these men, please send us into that herd of pigs."

[32]Jesus said to them, "Go!" So the demons left the men and went into the pigs. Then the whole herd of pigs ran down the hill into the lake and were drowned. [33]The men who were caring for the pigs ran away and went into town. They told about all of this and what had happened to the men who had demons.

[34]Then the whole town went out to see Jesus. When they saw him, they begged him to leave their area.

## JESUS HEALS A PARALYZED MAN

**9** Jesus got into a boat and went back across the lake to his own town. [2]Some people brought to Jesus a man who was paralyzed. The man was lying on his mat. Jesus saw that these people had great faith, so he said to the paralyzed man, "Be happy, young man. Your sins are forgiven."

[3]Some of the teachers of the law heard this. They said to themselves, "This man speaks as if he were God—that is blasphemy!"[n]

[4]Jesus knew what they were thinking. So he said, "Why are you thinking evil thoughts? [5]Which is easier: to tell this paralyzed man, 'Your sins are forgiven,' or to tell him, 'Stand up and walk'? [6]But I will prove to you that the Son of Man[d] has power on earth to forgive sins." Then Jesus said to the paralyzed man, "Stand up. Take your mat and go home." [7]And the man stood up and went home. [8]The people saw this and were amazed. They praised God for giving power like this to men.

## JESUS CHOOSES MATTHEW

[9]When Jesus was leaving, he saw a man named Matthew. Matthew was sitting in the tax office. Jesus said to him, "Follow me." And Matthew stood up and followed Jesus.

[10]Jesus had dinner at Matthew's house. Many tax collectors and "sinners" came and ate with Jesus and his followers. [11]The Pharisees[d] saw this and asked Jesus' followers, "Why does your teacher eat with tax collectors and 'sinners'?"

[12]Jesus heard the Pharisees ask this. So he said, "Healthy people don't need a doctor. Only the sick need a doctor. [13]Go and learn what this means: 'I want faithful love more than I want animal sacrifices.'[n] I did not come to invite good people. I came to invite sinners."

## JESUS IS NOT LIKE OTHER JEWS

[14]Then the followers of John[n] came to Jesus. They said to Jesus, "We and the Pharisees[d] often give up eating.[n] But your followers don't. Why?"

[15]Jesus answered, "The friends of the bridegroom are not sad while he is with them. But the time will come when the bridegroom will leave them. Then his friends are sad, and they will give up eating.

[16]"When someone sews a patch over a hole in an old coat, he never uses a piece

8:28 **Gadarene** From Gadara, an area southeast of Lake Galilee. 9:3 **blasphemy** Saying things against God. 9:13 **'I want . . . sacrifices.'** Quotation from Hosea 6:6. 9:14 **John** John the Baptist, who preached to people about Christ's coming (Matthew 3, Luke 3). 9:14 **give up eating** This is called "fasting." The people would give up eating for a special time of prayer and worship to God. It was also done to show sadness.

## REAL SUPER HEROES

# JOHN THE BAPTIST

He didn't look too cool. John the Baptist was famous for his camel-hair clothes and unusual diet of locusts (like big grasshoppers) and wild honey. But people came to him where he lived out in the wilderness, anyway. Why? He had a message they wanted to hear. He told them they needed to repent of their sins if they wanted to be forgiven.

John had a special job. The Bible had told about his coming long before he was born. He was the special prophet who prepared the way for Jesus, helping the people to understand the new ideas Jesus was about to teach them. When Jesus arrived, John baptized him and told the people that the attention must now turn to Jesus, not to him anymore. John lived to serve the Lord.

John teaches us a couple of things. One, we don't need to worry about what we look like. And second, we need to do what God asks us to do and remember that God's glory is what's important, not our own.

that are lost. [7]When you go, preach this: 'The kingdom of heaven is coming soon.' [8]Heal the sick. Give dead people life again. Heal those who have harmful skin diseases. Force demons[d] to leave people. I give you these powers freely. So help other people freely. [9]Don't carry any money with you—gold or silver or copper. [10]Don't carry a bag. Take for your trip only the clothes and sandals you are wearing. Don't take a walking stick. A worker should be given the things he needs.

[11]"When you enter a city or town, find some worthy person there and stay in his home until you leave. [12]When you enter that home, say, 'Peace be with you.' [13]If the people there welcome you, let your peace stay there. But if they don't welcome you, take back the peace you wished for them. [14]And if a home or town refuses to welcome you or listen to you, then leave that place. Shake its dust off your feet.[n] [15]I tell you the truth. On the Judgment Day it will be worse for that town than for the towns of Sodom and Gomorrah.[n]

## JESUS WARNS HIS APOSTLES

[16]"Listen! I am sending you out, and you will be like sheep among wolves. So be as smart as snakes. But also be like doves and do nothing wrong. [17]Be careful of people. They will arrest you and take you to court. They will whip you in their synagogues.[d] [18]Because of me you will be taken to stand before governors and kings. You will tell them and the non-Jewish people about me. [19]When you are arrested, don't worry about what to say or how you should say it. At that time you will be given the things to say. [20]It will not really be you speaking. The Spirit of your Father will be speaking through you.

[21]"Brothers will turn against their own brothers and give them over to be killed. Fathers will turn against their own children and give them to be killed. Children will fight against their own parents and have them killed. [22]All people will hate you because you follow me. But the person who continues strong until the end will be saved. [23]When you are treated badly in one city, go to another city. I tell you the truth. You will not finish going through all the cities of Israel before the Son of Man[d] comes.

[24]"A student is not better than his teacher. A servant is not better than his master. [25]A student should be satisfied to become like his teacher. A servant should be satisfied to become like his master. If the head of the family is called Beelzebul,[d] then the other members of the family will be called worse names!

## FEAR GOD, NOT PEOPLE

[26]"So don't be afraid of those people. Everything that is hidden will be shown. Everything that is secret will be made known. [27]I tell you these things in the dark, but I want you to tell them in the light. I speak these things only to you, but you should tell them to everyone. [28]Don't be afraid of people. They can only kill the body. They cannot kill the soul. The only one you should fear is the One who can destroy the body and the soul in hell. [29]When birds are sold, two small birds cost only a penny. But not even one of the little birds can die without your Father's knowing it. [30]God even knows how many hairs are on your head. [31]So don't be afraid. You are worth much more than many birds.

## TELL PEOPLE ABOUT YOUR FAITH

[32]"If anyone stands before other people and says he believes in me, then I will say that he belongs to me. I will say this before my Father in heaven. [33]But if

## Going Global

### Wycliffe Bible Translators

Where would you be without God's Word in your language? Did you know there are more than 6,800 languages and about 270 of them still need to have the Bible translated?

Get the scoop from your new buds, KC and Lynnk at http://www.wycliffe.org/kids/home.htm. A friendly suitcase (KC) and PDA (Lynnk) will tell you how you can be part of Bible translation right now. Wycliffe was founded in 1942 by William Cameron Townsend, a missionary to the Cakchiquel Indians of Guatemala. Townsend caught the vision for translation when a man challenged him: "If your God is so smart; why can't he speak my language?"

Wycliffe Bible Translators is a missionary organization that works together with partners all over the world translating God's Word into languages that do not have it yet. Their goal within the next 20 years is to see translation started in every language that still needs a Bible! KC and Lynnk can show you how to help!

## DECODE THIS!

*What is no good if it loses its taste?*

 10:14 Shake . . . feet. A warning. It showed that they were finished talking to these people. 10:15 Sodom and Gomorrah Two cities that God destroyed because the people were so evil.

anyone stands before people and says he does not believe in me, then I will say that he does not belong to me. I will say this before my Father in heaven.

³⁴"Don't think that I have come to bring peace to the earth. I did not come to bring peace, but a sword. ³⁵I have come to make this happen:

'A son will be against his father,
   a daughter will be against her
      mother,
   a daughter-in-law will be against her
      mother-in-law.
³⁶    A person's enemies will be members
      of his own family.'        *Micah 7:6*
³⁷"Whoever loves his father or mother more than he loves me is not worthy to be my follower. Whoever loves his son or daughter more than he loves me is not worthy to be my follower. ³⁸Whoever is not willing to die on a cross and follow

me is not worthy of me. ³⁹Whoever tries to hold on to his life will give up true life. Whoever gives up his life for me will hold on to true life. ⁴⁰Whoever accepts you also accepts me. And whoever accepts me also accepts the One who sent me.

⁴¹"Whoever meets a prophet*ᵈ* and accepts him will receive the reward of a prophet. And whoever accepts a good man because that man is good will receive the reward of a good man. ⁴²Whoever helps one of these little ones because they are my followers will truly get his reward. He will get his reward even if he only gave my follower a cup of cold water."

## JESUS AND JOHN THE BAPTIST

**11** Jesus finished telling these things to his 12 followers. Then he left there and went to the towns in Galilee to teach and preach.

²John the Baptist*ᵈ* was in prison, but he heard about the things Christ was doing. So John sent some of his followers to Jesus. ³They asked Jesus, "Are you the man who John said was coming, or should we wait for another one?"

⁴Jesus answered, "Go back to John and tell him about the things you hear and see: ⁵The blind can see. The crippled can walk. People with harmful skin diseases are healed. The deaf can hear. The dead are raised to life. And the Good News*ᵈ* is told to the poor. ⁶The person who does not lose faith because of me is blessed."

⁷As John's followers were leaving, Jesus began talking to the people about John. Jesus said, "What did you go out to the desert to see? A reed*ⁿ* blown by the wind? No. ⁸Really, what did you go out to see? A man dressed in fine clothes? No. Those people who wear fine clothes live in kings' palaces. ⁹So what did you go out to see? A prophet?*ᵈ* Yes, and I tell you, John is more than a prophet. ¹⁰This was written about John in the Scriptures:*ᵈ*

'I will send my messenger ahead of
   you.
He will prepare the way for you.'
                            *Malachi 3:1*

¹¹"I tell you the truth: John the Baptist is greater than any other man who has ever lived. But even the least important person in the kingdom of heaven is greater than John. ¹²Since the time John the Baptist came until now, the kingdom of heaven has been going forward in strength. People using force have been trying to take the kingdom. ¹³All the prophets and the law of Moses spoke until the time John came. They told about the things that would happen. ¹⁴And if you will believe the things the law and the prophets said, then you will believe that John is Elijah. The law and the prophets said he would come. ¹⁵You people who hear me, listen!

¹⁶"What can I say about the people who live today? What are they like? They are like children sitting in the marketplace. One group calls to the other,

¹⁷'We played music for you, but you did
      not dance;
   we sang a sad song, but you did
      not cry.'

¹⁸John came, and he did not eat like other people or drink wine. And people say, 'He has a demon.'*ᵈ* ¹⁹The Son of Man*ᵈ*

> **"Go back to John and tell him about the things you hear and see: The blind can see. The crippled can walk."**
>
> *Matthew 11:4-5*

## DECODE THIS!
*What does Jesus offer tired and weary people?*

came, eating and drinking wine, and people say, 'Look at him! He eats too much and drinks too much. He is a friend of tax collectors and "sinners."' But wisdom is proved to be right by the things it does."

## JESUS WARNS UNBELIEVERS

20 Then Jesus criticized the cities where he did most of his miracles.[d] He criticized them because the people there did not change their lives and stop sinning. 21 Jesus said, "How terrible for you, Korazin! How terrible for you, Bethsaida! I did many miracles in you. If those same miracles had happened in Tyre and Sidon,[n] then the people there would have changed their lives a long time ago. They would have worn rough cloth and put ashes on themselves to show that they had changed. 22 But I tell you, on the Judgment Day it will be worse for you than for Tyre and Sidon. 23 And you, Capernaum,[n] will you be lifted up to heaven? No. You will be thrown down to the depths. I did many miracles in you. If those same miracles had happened in Sodom,[n] its people would have stopped sinning, and it would still be a city today. 24 But I tell you it will be worse for you on the Judgment Day than for Sodom."

## JESUS OFFERS REST TO PEOPLE

25 Then Jesus said, "I thank you, Father, Lord of heaven and earth. I praise you because you have hidden these things from the people who are wise and smart. But you have shown them to those who are like little children. 26 Yes, Father, this is what you really wanted.

27 "My Father has given me all things. No one knows the Son—only the Father knows the Son. And no one knows the Father—only the Son knows the Father. And the only people who will know about the Father are those whom the Son chooses to tell.

28 "Come to me, all of you who are tired and have heavy loads. I will give you rest. 29 Accept my work and learn from me. I am gentle and humble in spirit. And you will find rest for your souls. 30 The work that I ask you to accept is easy. The load I give you to carry is not heavy."

## JESUS IS LORD OF THE SABBATH

**12** About that same time, Jesus was walking through some fields of grain on a Sabbath[d] day. His followers were with him, and they were hungry. So they began to pick the grain and eat it. 2 The Pharisees[d] saw this, and they said to Jesus, "Look! Your followers are doing something that is against the Jewish law to do on the Sabbath day."

3 Jesus answered, "Have you not read what David did when he and the people with him were hungry? 4 David went into God's house. He and those with him ate the bread that was made holy for God. It was against the law for them to eat that bread. Only the priests were allowed to eat it. 5 And have you not read in the law of Moses that on every Sabbath day the priests in the Temple[d] break this law about the Sabbath day? But the priests are not wrong for doing that. 6 I tell you that there is something here that is greater than the Temple. 7 The Scripture[d] says, 'I want faithful love more than I want animal sacrifices.'[n] You don't really know what those words mean. If you understood them, you would not judge those who have done nothing wrong.

8 "The Son of Man[d] is Lord of the Sabbath day."

## JESUS HEALS A MAN'S CRIPPLED HAND

9 Jesus left there and went into their synagogue.[d] 10 In the synagogue, there was a man with a crippled hand. Some Jews there were looking for a reason to accuse Jesus of doing wrong. So they asked him, "Is it right to heal on the Sabbath[d] day?"[n]

11 Jesus answered, "If any of you has a sheep, and it falls into a ditch on the Sabbath day, then you will take the sheep and help it out of the ditch. 12 Surely a man is more important than a sheep. So the law of Moses allows people to do good things on the Sabbath day." 13 Then Jesus said to the man with the crippled hand, "Let me see your hand." The man put his hand out, and the hand became well again, the same as the other hand. 14 But the Pharisees[d] left and made plans to kill Jesus.

## JESUS IS GOD'S CHOSEN SERVANT

15 Jesus knew what the Pharisees[d] were

---

# Gotta Know!

## If God can do anything, why can't he make people believe in him?

If you wanted someone to really love you, would you rather they *want* to love you or be *forced* to love you? Forced love isn't real. God wants us to choose to love him. Of course, he has to change our hardened hearts and help us to want him. But when he draws us to himself and opens our minds so we can understand how much he loves us, we want to believe in him and love him back.

---

doing, so he left that place. Many people followed him, and he healed all who were sick. ¹⁶But Jesus warned the people not to tell who he was. ¹⁷He did these things to make come true what Isaiah the prophet*d* had said:

¹⁸"Here is my servant whom I have
chosen.
I love him, and I am pleased
with him.
I will put my Spirit*d* in him.
Then he will tell how I will judge
all people fairly.
¹⁹He will not argue or shout.
No one will hear his voice in
the streets.
²⁰He will not break a crushed blade
of grass.
He will not put out even a
weak flame.
He will continue until he makes fair
judgment win the victory.
²¹    In him will the nations find hope."

*Isaiah 42:1-4*

**Q. If you could ask God a question, what would it be?**

**A. What's it like in heaven?**

## JESUS' POWER IS FROM GOD

²²Then some people brought a man to Jesus. This man was blind and could not talk, because he had a demon.*d*

Jesus healed the man, and the man could talk and see. ²³All the people were amazed. They said, "Perhaps this man is the Son of David!"*d*

²⁴The Pharisees*d* heard the people saying this. The Pharisees said, "Jesus uses the power of Beelzebul*d* to force demons out of people. Beelzebul is the ruler of demons."

²⁵Jesus knew what the Pharisees were thinking. So he said to them, "Every kingdom that is fighting against itself will be destroyed. And every city that is divided will fall. And every family that is divided cannot succeed. ²⁶So if Satan forces out his own demons, then Satan is divided, and his kingdom will not continue. ²⁷You say that I use the power of Satan when I force out demons. If that is true, then what power do your people use when they force out demons? So your own people prove that you are wrong. ²⁸But if I use the power of God's Spirit*d* to force out demons, this shows that the kingdom of God has come to you.

²⁹"If anyone wants to enter a strong man's house and steal his things, first he must tie up the strong man. Then he can steal the things from the strong man's house.

³⁰"If anyone is not with me, then he is against me. He who does not work with me is working against me. ³¹So I tell you, people can be forgiven for every sin they do. And people can be forgiven for every bad thing they say. But if anyone speaks against the Holy Spirit, then he will not be forgiven. ³²Anyone who says things against the Son of Man*d* can be forgiven. But anyone who says things against the Holy Spirit will not be forgiven. He will not be forgiven now or in the future.

## PEOPLE KNOW YOU BY YOUR WORDS

³³"If you want good fruit, you must make the tree good. If your tree is not good, then it will have bad fruit. A tree is known by the kind of fruit it produces. ³⁴You snakes! You are evil people! How can you say anything good? The mouth speaks the things that are in the heart. ³⁵A good person has good things in his heart. And so he speaks the good things that come from his heart. But an evil person has evil in his heart. So he speaks the evil things that come from his heart. ³⁶And I tell you that people will have to explain about every careless thing they have said. This will happen on the Judgment Day. ³⁷The words you have said will be used to judge you. Some of your words will prove you right, but some of your words will prove you guilty."

## THE LEADERS ASK FOR A MIRACLE

³⁸Then some of the Pharisees*d* and teachers of the law answered Jesus. They said, "Teacher, we want to see you work a miracle*d* as a sign."

³⁹Jesus answered, "Evil and sinful people are the ones who want to see a miracle for a sign. But no sign will be given to them. The only sign will be what happened to the prophet*d* Jonah. ⁴⁰Jonah was in the stomach of the big fish for three days and three nights. In the same way, the Son of Man*d* will be in the grave three days and three nights. ⁴¹And on the Judgment Day the men from Nineveh*n* will stand up with you people who live today. They will show that you are guilty because when Jonah preached to them, they were sorry and changed their lives. And I tell you that someone greater than Jonah is here! ⁴²On the Judgment Day, the Queen of the South*n* will stand up with

**DECODE THIS!**

*Jesus helped people understand God's Word how?*

12:41 **Nineveh** The city where Jonah preached to warn the people. Read Jonah 3.   12:42 **Queen of the South** The Queen of Sheba. She traveled 1,000 miles to learn God's wisdom from Solomon. Read 1 Kings 10:1-13.

## BiBLe BasiCS

### WHAT iS THE BiBLE?

Although the word *Bible* means "book," it is a book like no other. The words were written down by men who were filled with the Holy Spirit and only wrote what God told them to write. The Bible has two parts, the Old Testament and the New Testament. The Old Testament has 39 books, and the New Testament has 27 books.

you people who live today. She will show that you are guilty because she came from far away to listen to Solomon's wise teaching. And I tell you that someone greater than Solomon is here!

### PEOPLE TODAY ARE FULL OF EVIL

⁴³"When an evil spirit comes out of a man, it travels through dry places looking for a place to rest. But it finds no place to rest. ⁴⁴So the spirit says, 'I will go back to the home I left.' When the spirit comes back to the man, the spirit finds the home still empty. The home is swept clean and made neat. ⁴⁵Then the evil spirit goes out and brings seven other spirits even more evil than it is. Then all the spirits go into the man and live there. And that man has even more trouble than he had before. It is the same way with the evil people who live today."

### JESUS' TRUE FAMILY

⁴⁶While Jesus was talking to the people, his mother and brothers stood outside. They wanted to talk to him. ⁴⁷Someone told Jesus, "Your mother and brothers are waiting for you outside. They want to talk to you."

⁴⁸He answered, "Who is my mother? Who are my brothers?" ⁴⁹Then he pointed to his followers and said, "See! These people are my mother and my brothers. ⁵⁰My true brothers and sisters and mother are those who do the things that my Father in heaven wants."

### A STORY ABOUT PLANTING SEED

**13** That same day Jesus went out of the house and sat by the lake. ²Large crowds gathered around him. So Jesus got into a boat and sat, while the people stayed on the shore. ³Then Jesus used stories to teach them many things. He said: "A farmer went out to plant his seed. ⁴While he was planting, some seed fell by the road. The birds came and ate all that seed. ⁵Some seed fell on rocky ground, where there wasn't enough dirt. That seed grew very fast, because the ground was not deep. ⁶But when the sun rose, the plants dried up because they did not have deep roots. ⁷Some other seed fell among thorny weeds. The weeds grew and choked the good plants. ⁸Some other seed fell on good ground where it grew and became grain. Some plants made 100 times more grain. Other plants made 60 times more grain, and some made 30 times more grain. ⁹You people who hear me, listen!"

### WHY JESUS USED STORIES TO TEACH

¹⁰The followers came to Jesus and asked, "Why do you use stories to teach the people?"

¹¹Jesus answered, "Only you can know the secret truths about the kingdom of heaven. Other people cannot know these secret truths. ¹²The person who has something will be given more. And he will have all he needs. But the person who does not have much, even what he has will be taken from him. ¹³This is why I use stories to teach the people: They see, but they don't really see. They hear, but they don't really understand. ¹⁴So they show that the things Isaiah said about them are true:

'You will listen and listen, but you
        will not understand.
    You will look and look, but you
        will not learn.
¹⁵For these people have become
        stubborn.
    They do not hear with their ears.
    And they have closed their eyes.
Otherwise they might really
        understand
    what they see with their eyes
    and hear with their ears.
They might really understand in
        their minds.
    If they did this, they would come
        back to me and be forgiven.'

*Isaiah 6:9-10*

¹⁶But you are blessed. You understand the things you see with your eyes. And you understand the things you hear with your ears. ¹⁷I tell you the truth. Many prophets<sup>d</sup> and good people wanted to see the things that you now see. But they did not see them. And many prophets and good people wanted to hear the things that you now hear. But they did not hear them.

> "My true brothers and sisters and mother are those who do the things that my Father in heaven wants."
>
> *Matthew 12:50*

## JESUS EXPLAINS THE SEED STORY

[18]"So listen to the meaning of that story about the farmer. [19]What is the seed that fell by the road? That seed is like the person who hears the teaching

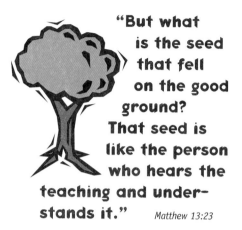

**"But what is the seed that fell on the good ground? That seed is like the person who hears the teaching and under-stands it."**   *Matthew 13:23*

about the kingdom but does not understand it. The Evil One comes and takes away the things that were planted in that person's heart. [20]And what is the seed that fell on rocky ground? That seed is like the person who hears the teaching and quickly accepts it with joy. [21]But he does not let the teaching go deep into his life. He keeps it only a short time. When trouble or persecution comes because of the teaching he accepted, then he quickly gives up. [22]And what is the seed that fell among the thorny weeds? That seed is like the person who hears the teaching but lets worries about this life and love of money stop that teaching from growing. So the teaching does not produce fruit[n] in that person's life. [23]But what is the seed that fell on the good ground? That seed is like the person who hears the teaching and understands it. That person grows and produces fruit, sometimes 100 times more, sometimes 60 times more, and sometimes 30 times more."

## A STORY ABOUT WHEAT AND WEEDS

[24]Then Jesus told them another story.

He said, "The kingdom of heaven is like a man who planted good seed in his field. [25]That night, when everyone was asleep, his enemy came and planted weeds among the wheat. Then the enemy went away. [26]Later, the wheat grew and heads of grain grew on the wheat plants. But at the same time the weeds also grew. [27]Then the man's servants came to him and said, 'You planted good seed in your field. Where did the weeds come from?' [28]The man answered, 'An enemy planted weeds.' The servants asked, 'Do you want us to pull up the weeds?' [29]The man answered, 'No, because when you pull up the weeds, you might also pull up the wheat. [30]Let the weeds and the wheat grow together until the harvest time. At harvest time I will tell the workers this: First gather the weeds and tie them together to be burned. Then gather the wheat and bring it to my barn.'"

## STORIES OF MUSTARD SEED AND YEAST

[31]Then Jesus told another story: "The kingdom of heaven is like a mustard seed. A man plants the seed in his field. [32]That seed is the smallest of all seeds. But when it grows, it is one of the largest garden plants. It becomes a tree, big enough for the wild birds to come and make nests in its branches."

[33]Then Jesus told another story: "The kingdom of heaven is like yeast that a woman mixes into a big bowl of flour. The yeast makes all the dough rise."

[34]Jesus used stories to tell all these things to the people. He always used stories to teach people. [35]This is as the prophet[d] said:

"I will speak using stories;
   I will tell things that
      have been secret
      since the world
      was made."

*Psalm 78:2*

## JESUS EXPLAINS ABOUT THE WHEAT AND WEEDS

[36]Then Jesus left the crowd and went into the house. His followers came to him and said, "Explain to us the meaning of the story about the weeds in the field."

[37]Jesus answered, "The man who planted the good seed in the field is the Son of Man.[d] [38]The field is the world. And the good seed are all of God's children in the kingdom. The weeds are those people who belong to the Evil One. [39]And the enemy who planted the bad seed is the devil. The harvest time is the end of the world. And the workers who gather are God's angels.

[40]"The weeds are pulled up and burned in the fire. It will be this way at the end of the world. [41]The Son of Man will send out his angels. They will gather out of his kingdom all who cause sin and all who do evil. [42]The angels will throw them into the blazing furnace. There the people will cry and grind their teeth with pain. [43]Then the good people will shine like the sun in the kingdom of their Father. You people who hear me, listen!

## STORIES OF A TREASURE AND A PEARL

[44]"The kingdom of heaven is like a treasure hidden in a field. One day a man found the treasure, and then he hid it in the field again. The man was very happy to find the treasure. He went and sold everything that he owned to buy that field.

[45]"Also, the kingdom of heaven is like a man looking for fine pearls. [46]One day he found a very valuable pearl. The man went and sold everything he had to buy that pearl.

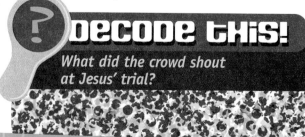

**DECODE THIS!**
*What did the crowd shout at Jesus' trial?*

---

⭐ **13:22 produce fruit** To produce fruit means to have in your life the good things God wants.

# NEW TESTAMENT SCRA-MBLE

Try to unscramble these New Testament words:

1. **E C R G A** _____

2. **E L V O** _____

3. **D P S I C E L I** _____

4. **E E L A G I L** _____

5. **Y C A A L V R** _____

## A STORY OF A FISHING NET

[47]"Also, the kingdom of heaven is like a net that was put into the lake. The net caught many different kinds of fish. [48]When it was full, the fishermen pulled the net to the shore. They sat down and put all the

good fish in baskets. Then they threw away the bad fish. [49]It will be this way at the end of the world. The angels will come and separate the evil people from the good people. [50]The angels will throw the evil people into the blazing furnace. In that place the people will cry and grind their teeth with pain."

[51]Jesus asked his followers, "Do you understand all these things?"

They answered, "Yes, we understand."

[52]Then Jesus said to them, "So every teacher of the law who has been taught about the kingdom of heaven is like the owner of a house. He has both new things and old things saved in his house. And he brings out both those new things and old things."

## JESUS GOES TO HIS HOMETOWN

[53]When Jesus finished teaching with these stories, he left there. [54]He went to the town where he grew up. He taught the people in the synagogue,[d] and they were amazed. They said, "Where did this man get this wisdom and this power to

do miracles?[d] [55]He is only the son of the carpenter. And his mother is Mary. His brothers are James, Joseph, Simon and Judas. [56]And all his sisters are here with us. So where does this man get all these things?" [57]And the people refused to accept Jesus.

But Jesus said to them, "A prophet[d] is honored everywhere except in his own town or in his own home."

[58]The people there did not believe in Jesus. So Jesus did not do many miracles there.

## HOW JOHN THE BAPTIST WAS KILLED

**14** At that time Herod, the ruler of Galilee, heard the reports about Jesus. [2]So Herod said to his servants, "Jesus is really John the

Baptist.[d] He has risen from death. That is why he is able to do these miracles."[d]

[3]Sometime before this, Herod had arrested John, tied him up, and put him into prison. Herod did this because of Herodias. Herodias was the wife of Philip, Herod's brother. [4]Herod arrested John because he told Herod: "It is not right for you to have Herodias." [5]Herod wanted to kill John, but he was afraid of the people. They believed that John was a prophet.[d]

[6]On Herod's birthday, the daughter of Herodias danced for Herod and his guests. Herod was very pleased with her, [7]so he promised he would give her anything she wanted. [8]Herodias told her daughter what to ask for. So she said to Herod, "Give me the head of John the Baptist here on a platter." [9]King Herod was very sad. But he had promised to give her anything she wanted, and the people eating with him had heard his promise. So Herod ordered that what she asked for be done. [10]He sent men to the prison to cut off John's head. [11]And the men brought John's head on a platter and gave it to the girl. She took it to her mother, Herodias. [12]John's followers came and got his body and buried it. Then they went and told Jesus what happened.

## MORE THAN 5,000 PEOPLE FED

[13]When Jesus heard what happened to John, Jesus left in a boat. He went to a lonely place by himself. But when the crowds heard about it, they followed him on foot from the towns. [14]When Jesus arrived, he saw a large crowd. He felt sorry for them and healed those who were sick.

[15]Late that afternoon, his followers came to Jesus and said, "No one lives in this place. And it is already late. Send the

## WILD WORLD FACTS

### MiND ALSO MATTERS

Many of the sick people who came to Jesus to be healed had epilepsy. Back then, they didn't know what epilepsy was or what caused it, but now we do. The word "epilepsy" is a Greek word which means "to hold or seize." People with epilepsy have seizures which are caused by too much electrical activity happening in the brain. Basically, the brain cells tell the rest of the body to move, even when the person doesn't want to. Seizures can cause people to lose consciousness, shake all over, drool, throw up, or stiffen. Sometimes they make people simply stare. Once the seizure is over, the person usually feels tired and needs to rest.

The people in Jesus' day didn't realize it, but when he healed the epileptics, he actually healed their brain. Nothing is too difficult for God!

[Kidshealth.org]

## DECODE THIS!
*How was John the Baptist killed?*

people away so they can go to the towns and buy food for themselves."

[16]Jesus answered, "They don't need to go away. You give them some food to eat."

[17]The followers answered, "But we have only five loaves of bread and two fish."

[18]Jesus said, "Bring the bread and the fish to me." [19]Then he told the people to sit down on the grass. He took the five loaves of bread and the two fish. Then he looked to heaven and thanked God for the food. Jesus divided the loaves of bread. He gave them to his followers, and they gave the bread to the people. [20]All the people ate and were

> "Between three and six o'clock in the morning, Jesus' followers were still in the boat. Jesus came to them. He was walking on the water."
>
> *Matthew 14:25*

satisfied. After they finished eating, the followers filled 12 baskets with the pieces of food that were not eaten. [21]There were about 5,000 men there who ate, as well as women and children.

### JESUS WALKS ON THE WATER

[22]Then Jesus made his followers get into the boat. He told them to go ahead of him to the other side of the lake. Jesus stayed there to tell the people they could go home. [23]After he said good-bye to them, he went alone up into the hills to pray. It was late, and Jesus was there alone. [24]By this time, the boat was already far away on the lake. The boat was having trouble because of the waves, and the wind was blowing against it.

[25]Between three and six o'clock in the morning, Jesus' followers were still in the boat. Jesus came to them. He was walking on the water. [26]When the followers saw him walking on the water, they were afraid. They said, "It's a ghost!" and cried out in fear.

[27]But Jesus quickly spoke to them. He said, "Have courage! It is I! Don't be afraid."

[28]Peter said, "Lord, if that is really you, then tell me to come to you on the water."

[29]Jesus said, "Come."

And Peter left the boat and walked on the water to Jesus. [30]But when Peter saw the wind and the waves, he became afraid and began to sink. He shouted, "Lord, save me!"

[31]Then Jesus reached out his hand and caught Peter. Jesus said, "Your faith is small. Why did you doubt?"

[32]After Peter and Jesus were in the boat, the wind became calm. [33]Then those who were in the boat worshiped Jesus and said, "Truly you are the Son of God!"

[34]After they crossed the lake, they came to the shore at Gennesaret. [35]The people there saw Jesus and knew who he was. So they told people all around there that Jesus had come. They brought all their sick to him. [36]They begged Jesus to let them just touch the edge of his coat to be healed. And all the sick people who touched it were healed.

### OBEY GOD'S LAW NOT MEN'S

**15** Then some Pharisees[d] and teachers of the law came to Jesus from Jerusalem. They asked him, [2]"Why do your followers not obey the rules given to us by the great people who lived before us? Your followers don't wash their hands before they eat!"

[3]Jesus answered, "And why do you refuse to obey God's command so that you can follow those rules you have? [4]God said, 'Honor your father and mother.'[n] And God also said, 'Anyone who says cruel things to his father or mother must be put to death.'[n] [5]But you say that a person can tell his father or mother, 'I have something I could use to help you. But I will not use it for you. I will give it to God.' [6]You teach that person not to honor his father. You teach that it is not important to do what God said. You think that it is more important to follow the rules you have. [7]You are hypocrites![d] Isaiah was right when he spoke about you:

[8]'These people show honor to me
    with words.
But their hearts are far from me.
[9]Their worship of me is worthless.
    The things they teach are nothing
    but human rules they have
    memorized.'"    *Isaiah 29:13*

[10]Jesus called the crowd to him. He said, "Listen and understand what I am saying. [11]It is not what a person puts into his mouth that makes him unclean.[d] It is what comes out of his mouth that makes him unclean."

[12]Then his followers came to Jesus and asked, "Do you know that the Pharisees are angry because of what you said?"

[13]Jesus answered, "Every plant that my Father in heaven has not planted himself will be pulled up by the roots. [14]Stay away from the Pharisees. They are blind leaders. And if a blind man leads another blind man, then both men will fall into a ditch."

[15]Peter said, "Explain the story to us."

---

15:4 'Honor . . . mother.' Quotation from Exodus 20:12; Deuteronomy 5:16.   15:4 'Anyone . . . death.' Quotation from Exodus 21:17.

[16]Jesus said, "You still have trouble understanding? [17]Surely you know that all the food that enters the mouth goes into the stomach. Then that food goes out of the body. [18]But what a person says with his mouth comes from the way he thinks. And these are the things that make him unclean. [19]Out of his mind come evil thoughts, murder, adultery,[d] sexual sins, stealing, lying, and saying bad things against other people. [20]These things make a person unclean. But eating with unwashed hands does not make him unclean."

### JESUS HELPS A NON-JEWISH WOMAN

[21]Jesus left that place and went to the area of Tyre and Sidon. [22]A Canaanite woman from that area came to Jesus. The woman cried out, "Lord, Son of David,[d] please help me! My daughter has a demon,[d] and she is suffering very much."

[23]But Jesus did not answer the woman. So the followers came to Jesus and begged him, "Tell the woman to go away. She is following us and shouting."

[24]Jesus answered, "God sent me only to the lost sheep, the people of Israel."

[25]Then the woman came to Jesus again.

[28]Then Jesus answered, "Woman, you have great faith! I will do what you asked me to do." And at that moment the woman's daughter was healed.

### JESUS HEALS MANY PEOPLE

[29]Then Jesus left that place and went to the shore of Lake Galilee. He went up on a hill and sat there.

[30]Great crowds came to Jesus. They brought their sick with them: the lame, the blind, the crippled, the dumb and many others. They put them at Jesus' feet, and he healed them. [31]The crowd was amazed when they saw that people who could not speak were able to speak again. The crippled were made strong again. Those who could not walk were able to walk again. The blind were able to see again. And they praised the God of Israel for this.

### MORE THAN 4,000 PEOPLE FED

[32]Jesus called his followers to him and said, "I feel sorry for these people. They have been with me three days, and now they have nothing to eat. I don't want to send them away hungry. They might faint while going home."

### Places to Pray

1. On your bed in the morning before you get up
2. While you're taking a shower or bath
3. In the car on the way to school
4. At your desk after you've finished your work
5. Taking a walk outside
6. At the table before meals
7. In your favorite chair during your devotionals
8. While waiting in line at the grocery store
9. Kneeling beside your bed at night
10. Wherever you are—all throughout the day!

[35]Jesus told the people to sit on the ground. [36]He took the seven loaves of bread and the fish and gave thanks to God for the food. Then Jesus divided the food and gave it to his followers. They gave the food to the people. [37]All the people ate and were satisfied. After this, the followers filled seven baskets with the pieces of food that were not eaten. [38]There were about 4,000 men there who ate, besides women and children. [39]After they ate, Jesus told the people to go home. He got into the boat and went to the area of Magadan.

> **"it is not what a person puts into his mouth that makes him unclean. it is what comes out of his mouth that makes him unclean."**
> *Matthew 15:11*

She bowed before him and said, "Lord, help me!"

[26]Jesus answered, "It is not right to take the children's bread and give it to the dogs."

[27]The woman said, "Yes, Lord, but even the dogs eat the pieces of food that fall from their masters' table."

[33]His followers asked him, "Where can we get enough bread to feed all these people? We are far away from any town."

[34]Jesus asked, "How many loaves of bread do you have?"

They answered, "We have seven loaves and a few small fish."

### THE LEADERS ASK FOR A MIRACLE

**16** The Pharisees[d] and Sadducees[d] came to Jesus. They wanted to trap him. So they asked him to show them a miracle[d] to prove that he was from God. [2]Jesus answered, "When you see the sunset, you know what the weather will be. If the sky is red, then you say we will have good weather. [3]And in the morning if the sky is dark and red, then you say that it will be a rainy day. You see these signs in the sky, and you know what they mean. In the same way, you see the things that are happening now. But you don't know their meaning. [4]Evil and sinful people ask for a miracle as a sign. But they will have no sign—only the sign of Jonah."[n] Then Jesus left them and went away.

### GUARD AGAINST WRONG TEACHINGS

[5]Jesus and his followers went across the lake. But the followers forgot to bring bread. [6]Jesus said to them, "Be careful! Guard against the yeast of the Pharisees[d] and the Sadducees."[d]

[7]The followers discussed the meaning of this. They said, "Did Jesus say this because we forgot to bring bread?"

[8]Jesus knew that they were talking about this. So he asked them, "Why are you talking about not having bread? Your faith is small. [9]You still don't understand? Remember the five loaves of bread that fed the 5,000 people? And remember that you filled many baskets with bread after the people finished eating? [10]And remember the seven loaves of bread that fed the 4,000 people? Remember that you filled many baskets then also? [11]So I was not talking to you about bread. Why don't you understand that? I am telling you to be careful and guard against the yeast of the Pharisees and the Sadducees." [12]Then the followers understood what Jesus meant. He was not telling them to guard against the yeast used in bread. He was telling them to guard against the teaching of the Pharisees and the Sadducees.

### PETER SAYS JESUS IS THE CHRIST

[13]Jesus went to the area of Caesarea Philippi. He said to his followers, "I am the Son of Man.[d] Who do the people say I am?"

[14]They answered, "Some people say you are John the Baptist.[d] Others say you are Elijah. And others say that you are Jeremiah or one of the prophets."[d]

[15]Then Jesus asked them, "And who do you say I am?"

[16]Simon Peter answered, "You are the Christ,[d] the Son of the living God."

[17]Jesus answered, "You are blessed, Simon son of Jonah. No person taught you that. My Father in heaven showed you who I am. [18]So I tell you, you are Peter.[n] And I will build my church on this rock. The power of death will not be able to defeat my church. [19]I will give you the keys of the kingdom of heaven. The things you don't allow on earth will be the things that God does not allow. The things you allow on earth will be the things that God allows." [20]Then Jesus warned his followers not to tell anyone that he was the Christ.

### JESUS SAYS THAT HE MUST DIE

[21]From that time on Jesus began telling his followers that he must go to Jerusalem. He explained that the older Jewish leaders, the leading priests, and the teachers of the law would make him suffer many things. And he told them that he must be killed. Then, on the third day, he would be raised from death.

[22]Peter took Jesus aside and began to criticize him. Peter said, "God save you from those things, Lord! Those things will never happen to you!"

[23]Then Jesus said to Peter, "Go away from me, Satan![n] You are not helping me! You don't care about the things of God. You care only about things that men think are important."

[24]Then Jesus said to his followers, "If anyone wants to follow me, he must say 'no' to the things he wants. He must be willing even to die on a cross, and he must follow me. [25]Whoever wants to save his life will give up true

## GET CONNECTED

### THE ART OF FORGIVENESS

Jesus talked about it a lot. Forgiveness is such an important part of building and keeping friendships with God and other people. So what exactly does a real apology look like?

True repentance starts in the heart, when you realize you really goofed up. Then, with a humble attitude, you go to the person you hurt and tell them what a bad thing you did, and take the blame for the problem. Then, simply say, "I'm sorry for [whatever it is that you did]," followed with, "Will you please forgive me?" No matter how they respond, you can rest knowing you're forgiven by God and have done all that you can do.

## DECODE THIS!

*If the blind leads the blind they will fall where?*

★ **16:4 sign of Jonah** Jonah's three days in the big fish are like Jesus' three days in the tomb. The story about Jonah is in the book of Jonah. **16:18 Peter** The Greek name "Peter," like the Aramaic name "Cephas," means "rock." **16:23 Satan** Name for the devil, meaning "the enemy." Jesus means that Peter was talking like Satan.

> "The Son of Man will come again with his Father's glory and with his angels."
>
> *Matthew 16:27*

life. And whoever gives up his life for me will have true life. ²⁶It is worth nothing for a man to have the whole world if he loses his soul. He could never pay enough to buy back his soul. ²⁷The Son of Man[d] will come again with his Father's glory and with his angels. At that time, he will reward everyone for what he has done. ²⁸I tell you the truth. There are some people standing here who, before they die, will see the Son of Man coming with his kingdom."

## JESUS WITH MOSES AND ELIJAH

**17** Six days later, Jesus took Peter, James, and John the brother of James up on a high mountain. They were all alone there. ²While they watched, Jesus was changed. His face became bright like the sun. And his clothes became white as light. ³Then two men were there, talking with him. The men were Moses and Elijah.[n]

⁴Peter said to Jesus, "Lord, it is good that we are here. If you want, I will put three tents here—one for you, one for Moses, and one for Elijah."

⁵While Peter was talking, a bright cloud covered them. A voice came from the cloud. The voice said, "This is my Son and I love him. I am very pleased with him. Obey him!"

⁶The followers with Jesus heard the voice. They were so frightened that they fell to the ground. ⁷But Jesus went to them and touched them. He said, "Stand up. Don't be afraid." ⁸When the followers looked up, they saw Jesus was now alone.

⁹When Jesus and the followers were coming down the mountain, Jesus commanded them, "Don't tell anyone about the things you saw on the mountain. Wait until the Son of Man[d] has been raised from death. Then you may tell."

¹⁰The followers asked Jesus, "Why do the teachers of the law say that Elijah must come first, before the Christ[d] comes?"

¹¹Jesus answered, "They are right to say that Elijah is coming. And it is true that Elijah will make everything the way it should be. ¹²But I tell you, Elijah has already come. People did not know who he was. They did to him everything they wanted to do. It will be the same with the Son of Man. Those same people will make the Son of Man suffer." ¹³Then the followers understood that Jesus was talking about John the Baptist.[d]

## JESUS HEALS A SICK BOY

¹⁴Jesus and his followers went back to the crowd. A man came to Jesus and bowed before him. ¹⁵The man said, "Lord, please help my son. He has epilepsy[n] and is suffering very much. He often falls into the fire or into the water. ¹⁶I brought him to your followers, but they could not cure him."

¹⁷Jesus answered, "You people have no faith. Your lives are all wrong. How long must I stay with you? How long must I continue to be patient with you? Bring the boy here." ¹⁸Jesus gave a strong command to the demon[d] inside the boy. Then the demon came out, and the boy was healed.

¹⁹The followers came to Jesus when he was alone. They said, "Why couldn't we force the demon out?"

²⁰Jesus answered, "You were not able to drive out the demon because your faith is too small. I tell you the truth. If your faith is as big as a mustard seed,[n] you can say to this mountain, 'Move from here to there.' And the mountain will move. All things will be possible for you." ²¹ [n]

## JESUS TALKS ABOUT HIS DEATH

²²Later, the followers met together in Galilee. Jesus said to them, "The Son of Man[d] will be given into the control

**KIDS SPEAK UP!**

Q. What do you think is in outer space?

A. Black holes with millions of galaxies.

 **17:3 Moses and Elijah** Two of the most important Jewish leaders in the past. **17:15 epilepsy** A disease that causes a person sometimes to lose control of his body, and maybe faint, shake strongly, or not be able to move. **17:20 mustard seed** This seed is very small, but the plant grows taller than a man. **17:21 Verse 21** Some Greek copies add verse 21: "That kind of spirit comes out only if you use prayer and give up eating."

28

## WILD WORLD FACTS

### A DONKEY'S STORY

Jesus chose a colt to make his big entry into Jerusalem. Mary rode one all the way to Bethlehem. People don't celebrate donkeys much, but they do keep popping up in Scripture. So what's up with all the donkeys?

Well, for one thing, they have been domesticated (tamed for people to use them) for thousands of years. (The first one tamed was a Nubian wild ass in the Nile Valley in 4000 B.C.). The donkeys we see now in America are hybrid animals, meaning they come from a blend of three other kinds: the Nubian, Somali, and North African. And really, they're great creatures. They are very social and need to be with other animals. Though stubborn, they are very smart and healthy, often living as long as 40 years.

Even if your parents won't let you have one for a pet, you can now appreciate the simple beauty God created in donkeys.

[WildWNC.org]

of some men. ²³They will kill him, but on the third day he will be raised from death." And the followers were filled with sadness.

### JESUS TALKS ABOUT PAYING TAXES

²⁴Jesus and his followers went to Capernaum. There some men came to Peter. They were the men who collected the Temple[d] tax. They asked, "Does your teacher pay the Temple tax?"

²⁵Peter answered, "Yes, Jesus pays the tax."

Peter went into the house where Jesus was. Before Peter could speak, Jesus said to him, "The kings on the earth collect different kinds of taxes. But who are the people who pay the taxes? Are they the king's children? Or do others pay the taxes? What do you think?"

²⁶Peter answered, "Other people pay the taxes."

Jesus said to Peter, "Then the children of the king don't have to pay taxes. ²⁷But we don't want to make these tax collectors angry. So go to

the lake and fish. After you catch the first fish, open its mouth. Inside its mouth you will find a coin. Take that coin and give it to the tax collectors. That will pay the tax for you and me."

### WHO IS THE GREATEST?

**18** At that time the followers came to Jesus and asked, "Who is greatest in the kingdom of heaven?"

²Jesus called a little child to him. He stood the child before the followers. ³Then he said, "I tell you the truth. You must change and become like little children. If you don't do this, you will never enter the kingdom of heaven. ⁴The greatest person in the kingdom of heaven is the one who makes himself humble like this child.

⁵"Whoever accepts a little child in my name accepts me. ⁶If one of these little children believes in me, and someone causes that child to sin, then it will be very bad for that person. It would be better for him to have a large

stone tied around his neck and be drowned in the sea. ⁷How terrible for the people of the world because of the things that cause them to sin. Such things will happen. But how terrible for the one who causes them to happen. ⁸If your hand or your foot causes you to sin, cut it off and throw it away. It is better for you to have only part of your body but have life forever. That is much better than to have two hands and two feet but be thrown into the fire that burns forever. ⁹If your eye causes you to sin, take it out and throw it away. It is better for you to have only one eye but have life forever. That is much better than to have two eyes but be thrown into the fire of hell.

### A LOST SHEEP

¹⁰"Be careful. Don't think these little children are worth nothing. I tell you that they have angels in heaven who are always with my Father in heaven." [n]

¹²"If a man has 100 sheep, but 1 of the sheep gets lost, he will leave the other 99 sheep on the hill. He will go to look for the lost sheep. ¹³And if he finds it, he is happier about that 1 sheep than about the 99 that were never lost. I tell you the truth. ¹⁴In the same way, your Father in heaven does not want any of these little children to be lost.

### WHEN A PERSON SINS AGAINST YOU

¹⁵"If your brother sins against you, go and tell him what he did wrong. Do this in private. If he listens to you, then you have helped him to be your brother again. ¹⁶But if he refuses to listen, then go to him again and take one or two other people with you. 'Every case may be proved by two or three witnesses.'[n] ¹⁷If he refuses to listen to them, then tell it to the church. If he refuses to listen to

 18:11 **Verse 11** Some Greek copies add verse 11: "The Son of Man came to save lost people."
18:16 **'Every . . . witnesses.'** Quotation from Deuteronomy 19:15.

## DECODE THIS!
*What did Jesus feed the crowds?*

# FEBRUARY LOVE

**1** MATTHEW 22:37: Jesus answered, "Love the Lord your God with all your heart, soul, and mind."

**2** Make hot chocolate for your brothers and sisters.

**3**

**4**

**5** Prayer Pointer: Ask God to help you love your brothers and sisters better.

**6**

**7** Call someone from your class today that you've never called before just to talk.

**8** JOHN 3:16: For God loved the world so much that he gave his only Son. God gave his Son so that whoever believes in him may not be lost, but have eternal life.

**9**

**10** See how many designs you can make by gluing hearts together.

**11**

**12**

**13** Prayer Pointer: Pray that God would help parents to stay together and show God's love to each other and their children.

**14** Let your parents sleep late while you make breakfast for the family.

**15** 1 JOHN 3:18: My children, our love should not be only words and talk. Our love must be true love. And we should show that love by what we do.

**16**

**17**

**18** Ask your parents how they met and what they love about each other the most.

**19**

**20** Prayer Pointer: Ask God to show you some ways that you can show others you love them.

**21**

**22** JOHN 15:12: This is my command: Love each other as I have loved you.

**23**

**24** Write a poem or note to God thanking him for his love.

**25**

**26** Prayer Pointer: Pray for your friends to understand how much God loves them.

**27**

**28** Go to the gym with your family, and exercise with them.

*The greatest love a person can show is to die for his friends (John 15:13).*

## "i tell you, you must forgive him more than 7 times. You must forgive him even if he does wrong to you 70 times 7." *Matthew 18:22*

the church, then treat him as you would one who does not believe in God. Treat him as if he were a tax collector.

[18]"I tell you the truth. The things you don't allow on earth will be the things God does not allow. The things you allow on earth will be the things that God allows.

[19]"Also, I tell you that if two of you on earth agree about something, then you can pray for it. And the thing you ask for will be done for you by my Father in heaven. [20]This is true because if two or three people come together in my name, I am there with them."

### AN UNFORGIVING SERVANT

[21]Then Peter came to Jesus and asked, "Lord, when my brother sins against me, how many times must I forgive him? Should I forgive him as many as 7 times?"

[22]Jesus answered, "I tell you, you must forgive him more than 7 times. You must forgive him even if he does wrong to you 70 times 7.

[23]"The kingdom of heaven is like a king who decided to collect the money his servants owed him. [24]So the king began to collect his money. One servant owed him several million dollars. [25]But the servant did not have enough money to pay his master, the king. So the master ordered that everything the servant owned should be sold, even the servant's wife and children. The money would be used to pay the king what the servant owed.

[26]"But the servant fell on his knees and begged, 'Be patient with me. I will pay you everything I owe.' [27]The master felt sorry for his servant. So the master told the servant he did not have to pay. He let the servant go free.

[28]"Later, that same servant found another servant who owed him a few dollars. The servant grabbed the other servant around the neck and said, 'Pay me the money you owe me!'

[29]"The other servant fell on his knees and begged him, 'Be patient with me. I will pay you everything I owe.'

[30]"But the first servant refused to be patient. He threw the other servant into prison until he could pay everything he owed. [31]All the other servants saw what happened. They were very sorry. So they went and told their master all that had happened.

[32]"Then the master called his servant in and said, 'You evil servant! You begged me to forget what you owed. So I told you that you did not have to pay anything. [33]I had mercy on you. You should have had the same mercy on that other servant.' [34]The master was very angry, and he put the servant in prison to be punished. The servant had to stay in prison until he could pay everything he owed.

[35]"This king did what my heavenly Father will do to you if you do not forgive your brother from your heart."

### JESUS TEACHES ABOUT DIVORCE

**19** After Jesus said all these things, he left Galilee. He went into the area of Judea on the other side of the Jordan River. [2]Large crowds followed Jesus, and he healed them there.

[3]Some Pharisees[d] came to Jesus and tried to trick him. They asked, "Is it right for a man to divorce his wife for any reason he chooses?"

[4]Jesus answered, "Surely you have read in the Scriptures:[d] When God made the world, 'he made them male and female.'[n] [5]And God said, 'So a man will leave his father and mother and be united with his wife. And the two people will become one body.'[n] [6]So the two are not two, but one. God joined the two people together. No person should separate them."

[7]The Pharisees asked, "Why then did Moses give a command for a man to divorce his wife by giving her divorce papers?"

[8]Jesus answered, "Moses allowed you to divorce your wives because you refused to accept God's teaching. But divorce was not allowed in the beginning. [9]I tell you that anyone who divorces his wife and marries another woman is guilty of adultery.[d] The only reason for a man to divorce and marry again is if his first wife has sexual relations with another man."

[10]The followers said to him, "If that is the only reason a man can divorce his wife, then it is better not to marry."

[11]Jesus answered, "Not everyone can accept this truth about marriage. But God has made some able to accept it. [12]There are different reasons why some men cannot marry. Some men were born without the ability to become fathers. Others were made that way later in life by other people. And other men have given up marriage because of the kingdom of heaven. But the person who can marry should accept this teaching about marriage."[n]

**?** DECODE THIS!
*Your faith should be like what?*

19:4 'he made . . . female.' Quotation from Genesis 1:27 or 5:2. 19:5 'So . . . body.' Quotation from Genesis 2:24. 19:12 But . . . marriage. This may also mean, "The person who can accept this teaching about not marrying should accept it."

## JESUS WELCOMES CHILDREN

[13]Then the people brought their little children to Jesus so that he could put his hands on them[n] and pray for them. When his followers saw this, they told the people to stop bringing their children to Jesus. [14]But Jesus said, "Let the little children come to me. Don't stop them, because the kingdom of heaven belongs to people who are like these children." [15]After Jesus put his hands on the children, he left there.

## A RICH YOUNG MAN'S QUESTION

[16]A man came to Jesus and asked, "Teacher, what good thing must I do to have life forever?"

[17]Jesus answered, "Why do you ask me about what is good? Only God is good. But if you want to have life forever, obey the commands."

[18]The man asked, "Which commands?"

Jesus answered, "'You must not murder anyone. You must not be guilty of adultery.[d] You must not steal. You must not tell lies about your neighbor in court. [19]Honor your father and mother.[n] Love your neighbor as you love yourself.'"[n]

[20]The young man said, "I have obeyed all these things. What else do I need to do?"

[21]Jesus answered, "If you want to be perfect, then go and sell all the things you own. Give the money to the poor. If you do this, you will have a treasure in heaven. Then come and follow me!"

[22]But when the young man heard this, he became very sad because he was very rich. So he left Jesus.

[23]Then Jesus said to his followers, "I tell you the truth. It will be very hard for a rich person to enter the kingdom of heaven. [24]Yes, I tell you that it is easier for a camel to go through the eye of a needle than for a rich person to enter the kingdom of God."

[25]When the followers heard this, they were very surprised. They asked, "Then who can be saved?"

[26]Jesus looked at them and said, "This is something that men cannot do. But God can do all things."

[27]Peter said to Jesus, "We left everything we had and followed you. So what will we have?"

[28]Jesus said to them, "I tell you the truth. When the new age comes, the Son of Man[d] will sit on his great throne. And all of you who followed me will also sit on 12 thrones. And you will judge the 12 tribes[d] of Israel. [29]And everyone who has left houses, brothers, sisters, father, mother, children, or farms to follow me will get much more than he left. And he will have life forever. [30]Many who have the highest place in life now will have the lowest place in the future. And many who have the lowest place now will have the highest place in the future.

## A STORY ABOUT VINEYARD WORKERS

**20** "The kingdom of heaven is like a man who owned some land. One morning, he went out very early to hire some people to work in his vineyard. [2]The man agreed to pay the workers one silver coin[n] for working that day. Then he sent them into the vineyard to work. [3]About nine o'clock the man went to the marketplace and saw some other people standing there, doing nothing. [4]So he said to them, 'If you go and work in my vineyard, I will pay you what your work is worth.' [5]So they went to work in the vineyard. The man went out again about twelve o'clock and again at three o'clock. Both times he hired people to work in his vineyard. [6]About five o'clock the man went to the marketplace again. He saw others standing there. He asked them, 'Why did you stand here all day doing nothing?' [7]They answered, 'No one gave us a job.' The man said to them, 'Then you can go and work in my vineyard.'

[8]"At the end of the day, the owner of the vineyard said to the boss of all the workers, 'Call the workers and pay them. Start by paying the last people I hired. Then pay all of them, ending with the workers I hired first.'

## WILD WORLD FACTS

### HEALING TOUCH

It's easy to see why lepers longed for Jesus' healing touch.

Leprosy is a very bad skin disease that is caused by a slow-growing bacteria. Once it spreads, it can cause damage to the skin, nerves, limbs, and eyes, and it will not go away. It is not very contagious, but lepers are usually not allowed to be near well people. That's why it was so amazing that Jesus allowed lepers to come to him to heal them. Leprosy is still a problem today in the poorer countries of Asia, Africa, and Latin America, but we do have a medicine now that can treat and cure the disease.

[World Health Organization]

## DECODE THIS!

*Jesus said "Let the _____ come to me."*

19:13 **put his hands on them** Showing that Jesus gave special blessings to these children.
19:18-19 **'You . . . mother.'** Quotation from Exodus 20:12-16; Deuteronomy 5:16-20. 19:19 **'Love . . . yourself.'** Quotation from Leviticus 19:18. 20:2 **silver coin** A Roman denarius. One coin was the average pay for one day's work.

# Gotta Know!

## When will the world come to an end?

The world won't come to an end until after Jesus returns for the second time to take all of his people up to heaven with him. Up until that point, the Bible says that people will be living just like they are today—getting married, having babies, working, and so on. The day Jesus returns will be a huge surprise, so we need to live each day as if it's the one when Jesus will come back. Only God the Father knows the last day, and he will tell Jesus when to return.

⁹"The workers who were hired at five o'clock came to get their pay. Each worker received one silver coin. ¹⁰Then the workers who were hired first came to get their pay. They thought they would be paid more than the others. But each one of them also received one silver coin. ¹¹When they got their silver coin, they complained to the man who owned the land. ¹²They said, 'Those people were hired last and worked only one hour. But you paid them the same as you paid us. And we worked hard all day in the hot sun.' ¹³But the man who owned the vineyard said to one of those workers, 'Friend, I am being fair to you. You agreed to work for one silver coin. ¹⁴So take your pay and go. I want to give the man who was hired last the same pay that I gave you. ¹⁵I can do what I want with my own money. Are you jealous because I am good to those people?'

¹⁶"So those who have the last place now will have the first place in the future. And those who have the first place now will have the last place in the future."

## JESUS TALKS ABOUT HIS OWN DEATH

¹⁷Jesus was going to Jerusalem. His 12 followers were with him. While they were on the way, Jesus gathered the followers together and spoke to them privately. He said to them, ¹⁸"We are going to Jerusalem. The Son of Man[d] will be turned over to the leading priests and the teachers of the law. They will say that he must die. ¹⁹They will give the Son of Man to the non-Jewish people. They will laugh at him and beat him with whips, and then they will kill him on a cross. But on the third day after his death, he will be raised to life again."

## A MOTHER ASKS JESUS A FAVOR

²⁰Then the wife of Zebedee came to Jesus. Her sons were with her. The mother bowed before Jesus and asked him to do something for her.

²¹Jesus asked, "What do you want?"

She said, "Promise that one of my sons will sit at your right side in your kingdom. And promise that the other son will sit at your left side."

²²But Jesus said, "You don't understand what you are asking. Can you accept the kind of suffering that I must suffer?"[n]

The sons answered, "Yes, we can!"

²³Jesus said to them, "Truly you will suffer the same things that I will suffer. But I cannot choose who will sit at my right side or my left side. Those places belong to those for whom my Father has prepared them."

²⁴The other ten followers heard this and were angry with the two brothers.

²⁵Jesus called all the followers together. He said, "You know that the rulers of the non-Jewish people love to show their power over the people. And their important leaders love to use all their authority. ²⁶But it should not be that way among you. If one of you wants to become great, then he must serve the rest of you like a servant. ²⁷If one of you wants to become first, then he must serve the rest of you like a slave. ²⁸So it is with the Son of Man.[d] The Son of Man did not come for other people to serve him. He came to serve others. The Son of Man came to give his life to save many people."

## JESUS HEALS TWO BLIND MEN

²⁹When Jesus and his followers were leaving Jericho, a great many people followed Jesus. ³⁰There were two blind men sitting by the road. The blind men heard that Jesus was going by, so they shouted, "Lord, Son of David,[d] please help us!"

³¹All the people criticized the blind men. They told them to be quiet. But the blind men shouted more and more, "Lord, Son of David, please help us!"

³²Jesus stopped and said to the blind men, "What do you want me to do for you?"

³³They answered, "Lord, we want to be able to see."

³⁴Jesus felt sorry for the blind men. He touched their eyes, and at once they were able to see. Then the men followed Jesus.

## JESUS ENTERS JERUSALEM AS A KING

**21** Jesus and his followers were coming closer to Jerusalem. But first they stopped at Bethphage at the hill called the Mount of Olives.[d] From there Jesus sent two of his followers into the town. ²He said to them, "Go to the town you can see there. When you

20:22 accept . . . suffer Literally, "drink the cup that I must drink." Jesus used the idea of drinking from a cup to mean accepting the terrible things that would happen to him.

33

enter it, you will find a donkey tied there with its colt. Untie them and bring them to me. [3]If anyone asks you why you are taking the donkeys, tell him, 'The Master needs them. He will send them back soon.'"

[4]This was to make clear the full meaning of what the prophet[d] said:

[5]"Tell the people of Jerusalem,

'Your king is coming to you.

He is gentle and riding on a donkey.

He is on the colt of a donkey.'"

*Isaiah 62:11; Zechariah 9:9*

> ## "The children were saying, 'Praise to the Son of David.'"
> *Matthew 21:15*

[6]The followers went and did what Jesus told them to do. [7]They brought the donkey and the colt to Jesus. They laid their coats on the donkeys, and Jesus sat on them. [8]Many people spread their coats on the road before Jesus. Others cut branches from the trees and spread them on the road. [9]Some of the people were walking ahead of Jesus. Others were walking behind him. All the people were shouting,

"Praise[n] to the Son of David![d]

God bless the One who comes in the name of the Lord! *Psalm 118:26*

Praise to God in heaven!"

[10]Then Jesus went into Jerusalem. The city was filled with excitement. The people asked, "Who is this man?"

"The crowd answered, "This man is Jesus. He is the prophet from the town of Nazareth in Galilee."

## JESUS GOES TO THE TEMPLE

[12]Jesus went into the Temple.[d] He threw out all the people who were buying and selling there. He turned over the tables that belonged to the men who were exchanging different kinds of money. And he upset the benches of those who were selling doves. [13]Jesus said to all the people there, "It is written in the Scriptures,[d] 'My Temple will be a house where people will pray.'[n] But you are changing God's house into a 'hideout for robbers.'"[n]

[14]The blind and crippled people came to Jesus in the Temple, and Jesus healed them. [15]The leading priests and the teachers of the law saw that Jesus was doing wonderful things. They saw the children praising him in the Temple. The children were saying, "Praise[n] to the Son of David."[d] All these things made the priests and the teachers of the law very angry.

[16]They asked Jesus, "Do you hear the things these children are saying?"

Jesus answered, "Yes. Haven't you read in the Scriptures, 'You have taught children and babies to sing praises'?"[n]

[17]Then Jesus left and went out of the city to Bethany, where he spent the night.

## THE POWER OF FAITH

[18]Early the next morning, Jesus was going back to the city. He was very hungry. [19]He saw a fig tree beside the road. Jesus went to it, but there were no figs on the tree. There were only leaves. So Jesus said to the tree, "You will never again have fruit!" The tree immediately dried up.

[20]His followers saw this and were amazed. They asked, "How did the fig tree dry up so quickly?"

[21]Jesus answered, "I tell you the truth. If you have faith and do not doubt, you will be able to do what I did to this tree. And you will be able to do more. You will be able to say to this mountain, 'Go, mountain, fall into the sea.' And if you have faith, it will happen. [22]If you believe, you will get anything you ask for in prayer."

## LEADERS DOUBT JESUS' AUTHORITY

[23]Jesus went to the Temple.[d] While he was teaching there, the leading priests and the older leaders of the people came to Jesus. They said to him, "Tell us! What authority do you have to do these things? Who gave you this authority?"

[24]Jesus answered, "I will ask you a question, too. If you answer me, then I will tell you what authority I have to do these things. [25]Tell me: When John baptized people, did that come from God or from man?"

The priests and the leaders argued about Jesus' question. They said to each other, "If we answer, 'John's baptism was from God,' then Jesus will say, 'Then why didn't you believe John?' [26]But if we say, 'It was from man,' we are afraid of what the people will do because they all believe that John was a prophet."[d]

[27]So they answered Jesus, "We don't know."

Then Jesus said, "Then I won't tell you what authority I have to do these things!

## A STORY ABOUT TWO SONS

[28]"Tell me what you think about this: There was a man who had two sons. He went to the first son and said, 'Son, go and work today in my vineyard.' [29]The son answered, 'I will not go.' But later the son decided he should go, and he went. [30]Then the father went to the other son and said, 'Son, go and work today in my vineyard.' The son answered, 'Yes, sir, I will go and work.' But he did not go. [31]Which of the two sons obeyed his father?"

The priests and leaders answered, "The first son."

Jesus said to them, "I tell you the

**21:9, 15 Praise** Literally, "Hosanna," a Hebrew word used at first in praying to God for help. At this time it was probably a shout of joy used in praising God or his Messiah. **21:13 'My Temple . . . pray.'** Quotation from Isaiah 56:7. **21:13 'hideout for robbers.'** Quotation from Jeremiah 7:11. **21:16 'You . . . praises'** Quotation from the Septuagint (Greek) version of Psalm 8:2.

34

truth. The tax collectors and the prostitutes[d] will enter the kingdom of God before you do. [32]John came to show you the right way to live. And you did not believe him. But the tax collectors and prostitutes believed John. You saw this, but you still refused to change and believe him.

# Gotta Know!

## Who made God?

Nobody. God was not ever created. He does not have a beginning at all. He has always been in existence, and he will always be here. It's hard—really, impossible—for us to understand because everything else we know of had a beginning. But not God. He's the Alpha and Omega, the beginning and the end. Everything that is has come from him.

### GOD SENDS HIS SON

[33]"Listen to this story: There was a man who owned a vineyard. He put a wall around the vineyard and dug a hole for a winepress.[d] Then he built a tower. He leased the land to some farmers and left for a trip. [34]Later, it was time for the grapes to be picked. So the man sent his servants to the farmers to get his share of the grapes. [35]But the farmers grabbed the servants, beat one, killed another, and then killed a third servant with stones. [36]So the man sent some other servants to the farmers. He sent more servants than he sent the first time. But the farmers did the same thing to the servants that they had done before. [37]So the man decided to send his son to the farmers. He said, 'The farmers will respect my son.' [38]But when the farmers saw the son, they said to each other, 'This is the owner's son. This vineyard will be his. If we kill him, then his vineyard will be ours!' [39]So the farmers grabbed the son, threw him out of the vineyard, and killed him. [40]So what will the owner of the vineyard do to these farmers when he comes?"

[41]The priests and leaders said, "He will surely kill those evil men. Then he will lease the vineyard to some other farmers. They will give him his share of the crop at harvest time."

[42]Jesus said to them, "Surely you have read this in the Scriptures:[d]

'The stone that the builders did
   not want
   became the cornerstone.[d]
The Lord did this,
   and it is wonderful to us.'
*Psalm 118:22-23*

[43]"So I tell you that the kingdom of God will be taken away from you. It will be given to people who do the things God wants in his kingdom. [44]The person who falls on this stone will be broken. But if the stone falls on him, he will be crushed."

[45]The leading priests and the Pharisees[d] heard these stories that Jesus told. They knew he was talking about them. [46]They wanted to arrest him. But they were afraid of the people, because the people believed that Jesus was a prophet.[d]

### A STORY ABOUT A WEDDING FEAST

**22** Jesus used stories to tell other things to the people. He said, [2]"The kingdom of heaven is like a king who prepared a wedding feast for his son. [3]The king invited some people to the feast. When the feast was ready, the king sent his servants to tell the people to come. But they refused to come to the feast.

[4]"Then the king sent other servants. He said to them, 'Tell those who have been invited that my feast is ready. I have killed my best bulls and calves for the dinner. Everything is ready. Come to the wedding feast.'

[5]"But the people refused to listen to the servants. They went to do other things. One went to work in his field, and another went to his business. [6]Some of the other people grabbed the servants, beat them, and killed them. [7]The king was very angry. He sent his army to kill the people who had killed his servants. And the army burned their city.

> "i tell you the truth. if you have faith and do not doubt, you will be able to do what i did to this tree." *Matthew 21:21*

[8]"After that, the king said to his servants, 'The wedding feast is ready. I invited those people, but they were not worthy to come. [9]So go to the street corners and invite everyone you see. Tell them to come to my feast.' [10]So the

## Decode this!

*How did Jesus enter Jerusalem?*

## GET CONNECTED

### LOVING GOD

How can we love a spirit? We can't see God or touch him, and we certainly can't put our arms around him to give him a big hug. So how do we really love God?

We love God with our lives. The way we show concern for others. The way we feed the poor and make friends with those who are lonely. When we care for the sick, or when we obey our parents. When we spend time thinking about God and his Word, and when we sing praises to him or pray. Everything we do in life can be a way to love him, if we make him the focus and the reason behind why we do what we do.

servants went into the streets. They gathered all the people they could find, both good and bad. And the wedding hall was filled with guests.

[11]"Then the king came in to see all the guests. He saw a man there who was not dressed in the right clothes for a wedding. [12]The king said, 'Friend, how were you allowed to come in here? You are not wearing the right clothes for a wedding.' But the man said nothing. [13]So the king told some servants, 'Tie this man's hands and feet. Throw him out into the darkness. In that place, people will cry and grind their teeth with pain.'

[14]"Yes, many people are invited. But only a few are chosen."

### THE PHARISEES TRY TO TRAP JESUS

[15]Then the Pharisees[d] left the place where Jesus was teaching. They made plans to trap Jesus with a question. [16]They sent some of their own followers and some men from the group called Herodians.[n] These men said, "Teacher, we know that you are an honest man. We know that you teach the truth about God's way. You are not afraid of what other people think about you. All men are the same to you. [17]So tell us what you think. Is it right to pay taxes to Caesar[d] or not?"

[18]But Jesus knew that these men were try-

ing to trick him. So he said, "You hypocrites![d] Why are you trying to trap me? [19]Show me a coin used for paying the tax." The men showed him a silver coin.[n] [20]Then Jesus asked, "Whose picture is on the coin? And whose name is written on the coin?"

[21]The men answered, "Caesar's."

Then Jesus said to them, "Give to Caesar the things that are Caesar's. And give to God the things that are God's."

[22]The men heard what Jesus said, and they were amazed. They left him and went away.

### SADDUCEES TRY TO TRICK JESUS

[23]That same day some Sadducees[d] came to Jesus. (Sadducees believe that no person will rise from death.) The Sadducees asked Jesus a question. [24]They said, "Teacher, Moses told us that a married man might die without having children. Then his brother must marry the widow and have children for him. [25]There were seven brothers among us. The first one married but died. He had no children. So his brother married the widow. [26]Then the second brother also died. The same thing happened to the third brother and all the other broth-

ers. [27]The woman was last to die. [28]But all seven men had married her. So when people rise from death, whose wife will she be?"

[29]Jesus answered, "You don't understand because you don't know what the Scriptures[d] say. And you don't know about the power of God. [30]When people rise from death, there will be no marriage. People will not be married to each other. They will be like the angels in heaven. [31]Surely you have read what God said to you about the rising from death? [32]God said, 'I am the God of Abraham, the God of Isaac, and the God of Jacob.'[n] God is the God of living people, not dead people."

[33]All the people heard this. They were amazed at Jesus' teaching.

> "Yes, many people are invited. But only a few are chosen." *Matthew 22:14*

### THE MOST IMPORTANT COMMAND

[34]The Pharisees[d] learned that the Sadducees[d] could not argue with Jesus' answers to them. So the Pharisees met together. [35]One Pharisee was an expert in the law of Moses. That Pharisee asked Jesus a question to test him. [36]The Pharisee asked, "Teacher, which command in the law is the most important?"

[37]Jesus answered, "'Love the Lord your God with all your heart, soul and mind.'[n] [38]This is the first and most important command. [39]And the second command is like the first: 'Love your neighbor as you love yourself.'[n] [40]All the law and the writings of the prophets[d] depend on these two commands."

## ? DECODE THIS!

*What sort of tree did Jesus cause to dry up?*

 22:16 **Herodians** A political group that followed Herod and his family. 22:19 **silver coin** A Roman denarius. One coin was the average pay for one day's work. 22:32 **'I am . . . Jacob.'** Quotation from Exodus 3:6. 22:37 **'Love . . . mind.'** Quotation from Deuteronomy 6:5. 22:39 **'Love . . . yourself.'** Quotation from Leviticus 19:18.

Games & Quizzes

# HOW'S YOUR SERVE?

## READ MATTHEW 20:24-28.

Jesus said that if we want to be great, we must be great servants. How many words about service can you find here?

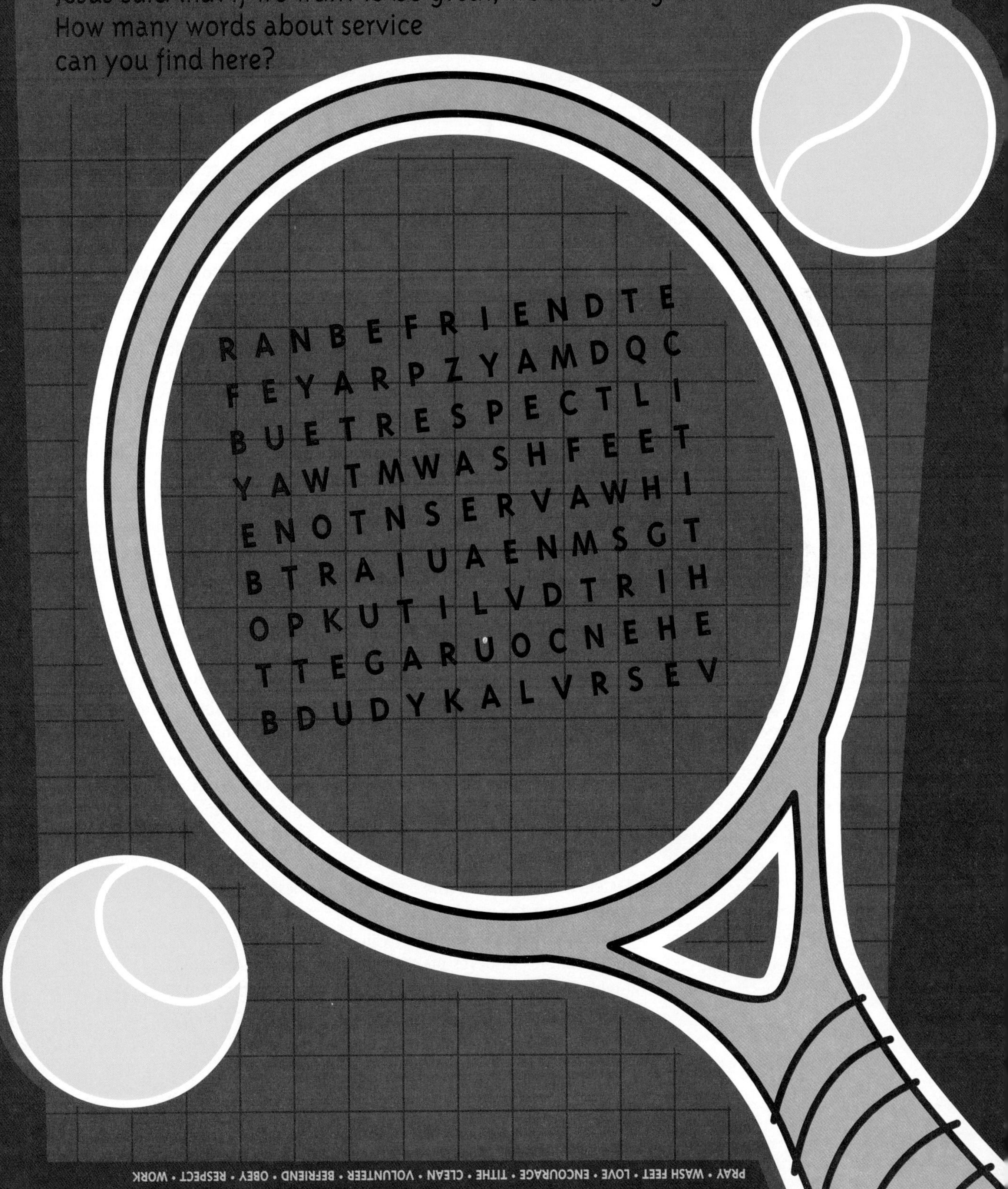

R A N B E F R I E N D T E
F E Y A R P Z Y A M D Q C
B U E T R E S P E C T L I
Y A W T M W A S H F E E T
E N O T N S E R V A W H I
B T R A I U A E N M S G T
O P K U T I L V D T R I H
T T E G A R U O C N E H E
B D U D Y K A L V R S E V

PRAY • WASH FEET • LOVE • ENCOURAGE • TITHE • CLEAN • VOLUNTEER • BEFRIEND • OBEY • RESPECT • WORK

## JESUS QUESTIONS THE PHARISEES

[41]"While the Pharisees[d] were together, Jesus asked them a question. [42]He asked, "What do you think about the Christ?[d] Whose son is he?"

The Pharisees answered, "The Christ is the Son of David."[d]

[43]Then Jesus said to them, "Then why

> **"Jesus answered, 'Love the Lord your God with all your heart, soul and mind.'"** *Matthew 22:37*

did David call him 'Lord'? David was speaking by the power of the Holy Spirit.[d] David said,

[44]'The Lord said to my Lord:
Sit by me at my right side,
until I put your enemies under
your control.' *Psalm 110:1*

[45]David calls the Christ 'Lord.' So how can he be David's son?"

[46]None of the Pharisees could answer Jesus' question. And after that day no one was brave enough to ask Jesus any more questions.

**Q. What did Jesus do when he was my age?**

**A. I think he probably played ball.**

## JESUS ACCUSES THE LEADERS

**23** Then Jesus spoke to the crowds and to his followers. Jesus said, [2]"The teachers of the law and the Pharisees[d] have the authority to tell you what the law of Moses says. [3]So you should obey and follow whatever they tell you. But their lives are not good examples for you to follow. They tell you to do things, but they don't do the things themselves. [4]They make strict rules and try to force people to obey them. But they themselves will not try to follow any of those rules.

[5]"The reason they do good things is so other people will see them. They make the boxes[n] of Scriptures[d] that they wear bigger and bigger. And they make their special prayer clothes very long so that people will notice them. [6]Those Pharisees and teachers of the law love to have the most important seats at the feasts. And they love to have the most important seats in the synagogues.[d] [7]They love people to show respect to them in the marketplaces. And they love to have people call them 'Teacher.'

[8]"But you must not be called 'Teacher.' You are all brothers and sisters together. You have only one Teacher. [9]And don't call any person on earth 'Father.' You have one Father. He is in heaven. [10]And you should not be called 'Master.' You have only one Master, the Christ.[d] [11]He who serves you as a servant is the greatest among you. [12]Whoever makes himself great will be made humble. Whoever makes himself humble will be made great.

[13]"How terrible for you, teachers of the law and Pharisees! You are hypocrites![d]

You close the door for people to enter the kingdom of heaven. You yourselves don't enter, and you stop others who are trying to enter. [14] [n]

[15]"How terrible for you, teachers of the law and Pharisees! You are hypocrites! You travel across land and sea to find one person who will follow your ways. When you find that person, you make him more fit for hell than you are.

[16]"How terrible for you, teachers of the law and Pharisees! You guide the people, but you are blind. You say, 'If anyone swears by the Temple[d] when he makes a promise, that means nothing. But if anyone swears by the gold that is in the Temple, then he must keep that promise.' [17]You are blind fools! Which is greater: the gold or the Temple? The Temple makes that gold holy. [18]And you say, 'If anyone swears by the altar when he makes a promise, that means nothing. But if he swears by the gift on the altar, then he must keep his promise.' [19]You are blind! Which is greater: the gift or the altar? The altar makes the gift holy. [20]The person who swears by the altar is really using the altar and also everything on the altar. [21]And the person who uses the Temple to make a promise is really using the Temple and also everything in the Temple. [22]The person who uses heaven to make a promise is also using God's throne and the One who sits on that throne.

[23]"How terrible for you, teachers of the law and Pharisees! You are hypocrites! You give to God one-tenth of everything you earn—even your mint, dill, and cummin.[n] But you don't obey the really important teachings of the law—being fair, showing mercy, and being loyal. These are the things you should do, as well as those other things. [24]You guide the people, but you are blind! You are like a person who picks a fly out of his drink and then swallows a camel![n]

[25]"How terrible for you, teachers of the law and Pharisees! You are hypocrites!

**23:5 boxes** Small leather boxes containing four important Scriptures. Some Jews tied these to the forehead and left arm, probably to show they were very religious. **23:14 Verse 14** Some Greek copies add verse 14: "How terrible for you, teachers of the law and Pharisees. You are hypocrites. You take away widows' houses, and you make long prayers so that people can see you. So you will have a worse punishment." **23:23 mint, dill, and cummin** Small plants grown in gardens and used for spices. Only very religious people would be careful enough to give a tenth of these plants. **23:24 You . . . camel!** Meaning, "You worry about the smallest mistakes but commit the biggest sin."

## WILD WORLD FACTS

### FOR THE BIRDS

Want to be an ornithologist? (You know—someone who studies birds.) God says we should be. He tells us that whenever we're worried about our clothes or where we live, we need to look at the birds to see how God provides for them.

Right now there are more than 9,000 different kinds of birds (species) in the world. But what they all have in common are wings, feathers, a beak, strong hollow bones, powerful flight muscles, and they are warm blooded. Most of them can fly, and they have strong hearts and breathing systems. The peregrine falcon is so fast it can fly up to 90 miles an hour!

Even though there are lots of different birds with different needs, God is able to care for them by providing the food and materials they need for nests. If he can do it for them, he can do it for his people, too—whom he loves much more than the birds!

[Yahooligans]

You wash the outside of your cups and dishes. But inside they are full of things that you got by cheating others and pleasing only yourselves. ²⁶Pharisees, you are blind! First make the inside of the cup clean and good. Then the outside of the cup can be truly clean.

²⁷"How terrible for you, teachers of the law and Pharisees. You are hypocrites! You are like tombs that are painted white. Outside, those tombs look fine. But inside, they are full of the bones of dead people, and all kinds of unclean things are there. ²⁸It is the same with you. People look at you and think you are good. But on the inside you are full of hypocrisy and evil.

²⁹"How terrible for you, teachers of the law and Pharisees! You are hypocrites! You build tombs for the prophets.ᵈ You show honor to the graves of people who lived good lives. ³⁰And you say, 'If we had lived during the time of our fathers, we would not have helped them kill the prophets.' ³¹But you give proof that you are children of those people who murdered the prophets.

³²And you will complete the sin that your fathers started!

³³"You are snakes! A family of poisonous snakes! You will not escape God. You will all be judged guilty and be sent to hell! ³⁴So I tell you this: I am sending to you prophets and wise men and teachers. You will kill some of these people. You will nail some of them to crosses. You will beat some of them in your synagogues. You will chase them from town to town. ³⁵So you will be guilty for the death of all the good people who have been killed on earth. You will be guilty for the murder of that good man Abel. And you will be guilty for the murder of Zechariahⁿ son of Berakiah. He was murdered when he was between the Temple and the altar. ³⁶I tell you the truth. All of these things will happen to you people who are living now.

### JESUS FEELS SORRY FOR JERUSALEM

³⁷"Jerusalem, Jerusalem! You kill the prophetsᵈ and kill with stones those men God sent to you. Many times I wanted to help your people! I wanted to gather them together as a hen gathers her chicks under her wings. But you did not let me. ³⁸Now your home will be left completely empty. ³⁹I tell you, you will not see me again until that time when you will say, 'God bless the One who comes in the name of the Lord.'"ⁿ

### THE TEMPLE WILL BE DESTROYED

**24** Jesus left the Templeᵈ and was walking away. But his followers came to show him the Temple's buildings. ²Jesus asked, "Do you see all these buildings? I tell you the truth. Every stone will be thrown down to the ground. Not one stone will be left on another."

³Later, Jesus was sitting on the Mount of Olives.ᵈ His followers came to be alone with him. They said, "Tell us when these things will happen. And what will happen to show us that it is time for you to come again and for the world to end?"

⁴Jesus answered: "Be careful that no one fools you. ⁵Many people will come in my name. They will say, 'I am the Christ.'ᵈ And they will fool many people. ⁶You will hear about wars and stories of wars that are coming. But don't be afraid. These things must happen before the end comes. ⁷Nations will fight against other nations. Kingdoms will fight against other kingdoms. There will be times when there is no food for people to eat. And there will be earthquakes in different places. ⁸These things are like the first pains when something new is about to be born.

⁹"Then men will arrest you and hand

23:35 **Abel . . . Zechariah** In the Hebrew Old Testament, the first and last men to be murdered.
23:39 **'God . . . Lord'** Quotation from Psalm 118:26.

## DECODE THIS!

*What 3 things should you love the Lord with?*

# Gotta Know!

## How can I get to know my brothers and sisters better?

It might seem tough if they want to bother you all the time, but if you make the effort, you'll find great reward. Ask them questions about what they do for fun or how they feel about things in their school. Ask them about their relationship with God. And just hang out with them when they will let you. Let them know you really care about them. They might not tell you, but they will appreciate it.

you over to be hurt and kill you. They will hate you because you believe in me. [10]At that time, many who believe will lose their faith. They will turn against each other and hate each other. [11]Many false prophets[d] will come and cause many people to believe false things. [12]There will be more and more evil in the world. So most people will stop showing their love for each other. [13]But the person who continues to be strong until the end will be saved. [14]The Good News[d] about God's kingdom will be preached in all the world, to every nation. Then the end will come.

[15]"Daniel the prophet spoke about 'the horrible thing that destroys.'[n] You will see this terrible thing standing in the holy place." (You who read this should understand what it means.) [16]"At that time, the people in Judea should run away to the mountains. [17]If a person is on the roof[n] of his house, he must not go down to get anything out of his house. [18]If a person is in the field, he must not go back to get his coat. [19]At that time, it will be hard for women who are pregnant or have nursing babies! [20]Pray that it will not be winter or a Sabbath[d] day when these things happen and you have to run away. [21]This is because at that time there will be

much trouble. There will be more trouble than has ever happened since the beginning of the world. And nothing as bad as that will ever happen again. [22]God has decided to make that terrible time short. If that time were not made short, then no one would go on living. But God will make that time

> "They will see the Son of Man coming on clouds in the sky. He will come with great power and glory."
>
> *Matthew 24:30*

short to help the people he has chosen. [23]At that time, someone might say to you, 'Look, there is the Christ!' Or

another person might say, 'There he is!' But don't believe them. [24]False Christs and false prophets will come and perform great things and miracles.[d] They will do these things to the people God has chosen. They will fool them, if that is possible. [25]Now I have warned you about this before it happens.

[26]"If people tell you, 'The Christ is in the desert'—don't go there. If they say, 'The Christ is in the inner room'—don't believe it. [27]When the Son of Man[d] comes, he will be seen by everyone. It will be like lightning flashing in the sky that can be seen everywhere. [28]Wherever there is a dead body, there the vultures will gather.

[29]"Soon after the trouble of those days, this will happen:

'The sun will grow dark.
  And the moon will not give
    its light.
The stars will fall from the sky.
  And everything in the sky will be
    changed.'    *Isaiah 13:10; 34:4*

[30]"At that time, there will be something in the sky that shows the Son of Man is coming. All the peoples of the world will cry. They will see the Son of Man coming on clouds in the sky. He will come with great power and glory. [31]He will use a loud trumpet to send his angels all around the earth. They will gather his chosen people from every part of the world.

[32]"The fig tree teaches us a lesson: When its branches become green and soft, and new leaves begin to grow, then you know that summer is near. [33]So also, when you see all these things happening, you will know that the time is near, ready to come. [34]I tell you the truth. All these things will happen while the people of this time are still living! [35]The whole world, earth and sky, will be destroyed, but the words I have said will never be destroyed!

24:15 'the horrible . . . destroys.' Mentioned in Daniel 9:27; 12:11 (cf. Daniel 11:31). 24:17 roof In Bible times houses were built with flat roofs. The roof was used for drying things such as flax and fruit. And it was used as an extra room, as a place for worship and as a place to sleep in the summer.

### WHEN WILL JESUS COME AGAIN?

[36]"No one knows when that day or time will be. Even the Son and the angels in heaven don't know. Only the Father knows. [37]When the Son of Man[d] comes, it will be the same as what happened during Noah's time. [38]In those days before the flood, people were eating and drinking. They were marrying and giving their children to be married. They were still doing those things until the day Noah entered the boat. [39]They knew nothing about what was happening. But then the flood came, and all those people were destroyed. It will be the same when the Son of Man comes. [40]Two men will be working together in the field. One man will be taken and the other left. [41]Two women will be grinding grain with a hand mill.[n] One woman will be taken and the other will be left.

[42]"So always be ready. You don't know the day your Lord will come. [43]Remember this: If the owner of the house knew what time a thief was coming, then the owner would be ready for him. The owner would watch and not let the thief enter his house. [44]So you also must be ready. The Son of Man will come at a time you don't expect him.

[45]"Who is the wise and trusted servant? The master trusts one servant to give the other servants their food at the right time. [46]When the master comes and finds the servant doing his work, the servant will be very happy. [47]I tell you the truth. The master will choose that servant to take care of everything the master owns. [48]But what will happen if the servant is evil and thinks his master will not come back soon? [49]Then that servant will begin to beat the other servants. He will feast and get drunk with others like him. [50]And the master will come when the servant is not ready and is not expecting him. [51]Then the master will punish that servant. He will send him away to be among the hypocrites.[d]

There people will cry and grind their teeth with pain.

### A STORY ABOUT TEN GIRLS

**25** "At that time the kingdom of heaven will be like ten girls who went to wait for the bridegroom. They took their lamps with them. [2]Five of the girls were foolish and five were wise. [3]The five foolish girls took their lamps, but they did not take more oil for the lamps to burn. [4]The wise girls took their lamps and more oil in jars. [5]The bridegroom was very late. All the girls became sleepy and went to sleep.

[6]"At midnight someone cried out, 'The bridegroom is coming! Come and meet him!' [7]Then all the girls woke up and got their lamps ready. [8]But the foolish girls said to the wise, 'Give us some of your oil. Our lamps are going out.' [9]The wise girls answered, 'No! The oil we have might not be enough for all of us. Go to the people who sell oil and buy some for yourselves.'

[10]"So the five foolish girls went to buy oil.

### "So always be ready. You don't know the day or the time the Son of Man will come."
*Matthew 25:13*

While they were gone, the bridegroom came. The girls who were ready went in with the bridegroom to the wedding feast. Then the door was closed and locked.

[11]"Later the others came back. They called, 'Sir, sir, open the door to let us in.' [12]But the bridegroom answered, 'I tell you the truth, I don't know you.'

[13]"So always be ready. You don't know the day or the time the Son of Man[d] will come.

### A STORY ABOUT THREE SERVANTS

[14]"The kingdom of heaven is like a man who was going to another place for a visit. Before he left, he talked with his servants. The man told them to take care of his things while he was gone. [15]He decided how much each servant would be able to care for. He gave one servant five bags of money. He gave another servant two bags of money. And he gave a third servant one bag of money. Then the man left. [16]The servant who got five bags went quickly to invest the money. The five bags of money earned five more. [17]It was the same with the servant who had two bags of money. He invested the money and earned two more. [18]But the servant who got one bag of money went out and dug a hole in the ground. Then he hid his master's money in the hole.

[19]"After a long time the master came home. He asked the servants what they did with his money. [20]The servant who got five bags of money brought five more bags to the master. The servant said, 'Master, you trusted me to care for five bags of money. So I used your five bags to earn five more.' [21]The master answered, 'You did well. You are a good servant who can be trusted. You did well with small things. So I will let you care for much greater things. Come and share my happiness with me.'

[22]"Then the servant who got two bags of money came to the master. The servant said, 'Master, you gave me two bags of money to care for. So I used your two bags to earn two more.' [23]The master answered, 'You did well. You are a good servant who can be trusted. You did well with small things. So I will

24:41 **mill** Two large, round, flat rocks used for grinding grain to make flour.

### DECODE THIS!
*Jesus wanted to gather Jerusalem's people like what?*

# MIRACLES OF JESUS

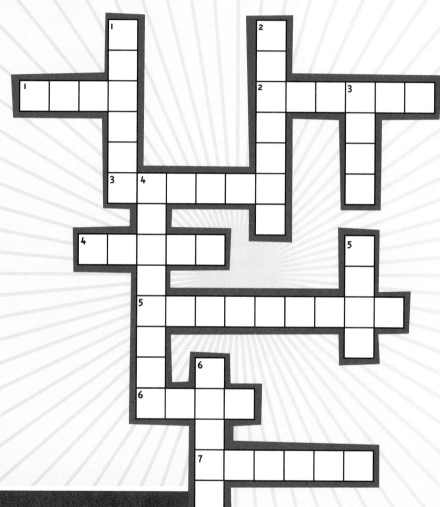

## ACROSS:

1. Location of first miracle
2. Were fed by the thousands
3. Fell from the blind man's eyes
4. Can't see
5. Can't move
6. No life
7. Day of Resurrection

## DOWN:

1. A young boy's donation
2. Skin issues
3. Ran off a cliff and drowned
4. Another word for lame
5. Cursed by Jesus and died
6. Obeyed Jesus

let you care for much greater things. Come and share my happiness with me.'

24"Then the servant who got one bag of money came to the master. The servant said, 'Master, I knew that you were a hard man. You harvest things you did not plant. You gather crops where you did not sow any seed. 25So I was afraid. I went and hid your money in the ground. Here is the bag of money you gave me.'

26The master answered, 'You are a bad and lazy servant! You say you knew that I harvest things I did not plant, and that I gather crops where I did not sow any seed? 27So you should have put my money in the bank. Then, when I came home, I would get my money back with interest.'

28"So the master told his other servants, 'Take the bag of money from that servant and give it to the servant who has ten bags of money. 29Everyone who uses what he has will get more. He will have much more than he needs. But the one who does not use what he has will have everything taken away from him.' 30Then the master said, 'Throw that useless servant outside, into the darkness! There people will cry and grind their teeth with pain.'

## THE KING WILL JUDGE ALL PEOPLE

31"The Son of Man[d] will come again in his great glory. All his angels will come with him. He will be King and sit on his great throne. 32All the people of the world will be gathered before him. Then he will separate them into two groups as a shepherd separates the sheep from the goats. 33The Son of Man will put the sheep, the good people, on his right and the goats, the bad people, on his left.

34"Then the King will say to the good people on his right, 'Come. My Father has given you his blessing. Come and receive the kingdom God has prepared for you since the world was made. 35I was hungry, and you gave me food. I was thirsty, and you gave me something to drink. I was alone and away from home, and you invited me into your house. 36I was without clothes, and you gave me something to wear. I was sick, and you cared for me. I was in prison, and you visited me.'

37"Then the good people will answer, 'Lord, when did we see you hungry and give you food? When did we see you thirsty and give you something to drink? 38When did we see you alone and away from home and invite you into our house? When did we see you without clothes and give you something to wear? 39When did we see you sick or in prison and care for you?'

40"Then the King will answer, 'I tell you the truth. Anything you did for any of my people here, you also did for me.'

41"Then the King will say to those on his left, 'Go away from me. God has said that you will be punished. Go into the fire that burns forever. That fire was prepared for the devil and his helpers. 42I was hungry, and you gave me nothing to eat. I was thirsty, and you gave me nothing to drink. 43I was alone and away from home, and you did not invite me into your house. I was without clothes, and you gave me nothing to wear. I was sick and in prison, and you did not care for me.'

44"Then those people will answer, 'Lord, when did we see you hungry or thirsty? When did we see you alone and away from home? Or when did we see you without clothes or sick or in prison? When did we see these things and not help you?'

45"Then the King will answer, 'I tell you the truth. Anything you refused to do for any of my people here, you refused to do for me.'

46"These people will go off to be punished forever. But the good people will go to live forever."

## THE PLAN TO KILL JESUS

**26** After Jesus finished saying all these things, he told his followers, 2"You know that the day after tomorrow is the day of the Passover[d] Feast. On that day the Son of Man[d] will be given to his enemies to be killed on a cross."

3Then the leading priests and the older Jewish leaders had a meeting at the palace of the high priest. The high priest's name was Caiaphas. 4At the meeting, they planned to set a trap to arrest Jesus and kill him. 5But they said, "We must not do it during the feast. The people might cause a riot."

## A WOMAN WITH PERFUME FOR JESUS

6Jesus was in Bethany. He was at the house of Simon, who had a harmful skin disease. 7While Jesus was there, a

> "i tell you the truth. Anything you did for any of my people here, you also did for me." *Matthew 25:40*

## DECODE THIS!

*How many bridesmaids were foolish and wise?*

woman came to him. She had an alabaster[d] jar filled with expensive perfume. She poured this perfume on Jesus' head while he was eating.

[8]His followers saw the woman do this and were upset. They asked, "Why waste that perfume? [9]It could be sold for a great deal of money, and the money could be given to the poor."

[10]But Jesus knew what happened. He said, "Why are you troubling this woman? She did a very beautiful thing for me. [11]You will always have the poor with you. But you will not always have me. [12]This woman poured perfume on my body to prepare me for burial. [13]I tell you the truth. The Good News[d] will be told to people in all the world. And in every place where it is preached, what this woman has done will be told. And people will remember her."

## JUDAS BECOMES AN ENEMY OF JESUS

[14]Then 1 of the 12 followers went to talk to the leading priests. This was the follower named Judas Iscariot. [15]He said, "I will give Jesus to you. What will you pay me for doing this?" The priests gave Judas 30 silver coins. [16]After that, Judas waited for the best time to give Jesus to the priests.

## JESUS EATS THE PASSOVER FEAST

[17]On the first day of the Feast[d] of Unleavened Bread, the followers came to Jesus. They said, "We will prepare everything for you to eat the Passover[d] Feast. Where do you want to have the feast?"

[18]Jesus answered, "Go into the city to a certain man. Tell him that the Teacher says, 'The chosen time is near. I will have the Passover Feast with my followers at your house.'" [19]The followers did what Jesus told them to do, and they prepared the Passover Feast.

[20]In the evening Jesus was sitting at the table with his 12 followers. [21]They were all eating. Then Jesus said, "I tell you the truth. One of you 12 will turn against me."

[22]This made the followers very sad. Each one said to Jesus, "Surely, Lord, I am not the one who will turn against you. Am I?"

[23]Jesus answered, "The man who has dipped his hand with me into the bowl is the one who will turn against me. [24]The Son of Man[d] will die. The Scriptures[d] say this will happen. But how terrible it will be for the person who gives the Son of Man to be killed. It would be better for him if he had never been born."

[25]Then Judas said to Jesus, "Teacher, surely I am not the one. Am I?" (Judas is the one who would give Jesus to his enemies.)

Jesus answered, "Yes, it is you."

## THE LORD'S SUPPER

[26]While they were eating, Jesus took some bread. He thanked God for it and broke it. Then he gave it to his followers and said, "Take this bread and eat it. This bread is my body."

[27]Then Jesus took a cup. He thanked God for it and gave it to the followers. He said, "Every one of you drink this. [28]This is my blood which begins the new agreement that God makes with his people. This blood is poured out for many to forgive their sins. [29]I tell you this: I will not drink of this fruit of the vine[n] again until that day when I drink it new with you in my Father's kingdom."

[30]They sang a hymn.

Q. What is one of the worst messes you've ever made?

A. I spilled red punch all over a school book, and I couldn't get it out.

Then they went out to the Mount of Olives.[d]

## JESUS' FOLLOWERS WILL ALL LEAVE HIM

[31]Jesus told the followers, "Tonight you will lose your faith because of me. It is written in the Scriptures:[d]

'I will kill the shepherd,
and the sheep will scatter.'

*Zechariah 13:7*

[32]But after I rise from death, I will go ahead of you into Galilee."

[33]Peter said, "All the other followers may lose their faith because of you. But I will never lose my faith."

[34]Jesus said, "I tell you the truth. Tonight you will say you don't know me. You will say this three times before the rooster crows."

[35]But Peter said, "I will never say that I don't know you! I will even die with you!" And all the other followers said the same thing.

## JESUS PRAYS ALONE

[36]Then Jesus went with his followers to a place called Gethsemane. He said to

## ? DECODE THIS!

*What meal is the Feast of Unleavened Bread?*

 26:29 fruit of the vine Product of the grapevine; this may also be translated "wine."

them, "Sit here while I go over there and pray." [37]He told Peter and the two sons of Zebedee to come with him. Then Jesus began to be very sad and troubled. [38]He said to Peter and the two sons of Zebedee, "My heart is full of sorrow and breaking with sadness. Stay here with me and watch."

[39]Then Jesus walked a little farther away from them. He fell to the ground and prayed, "My Father, if it is possible, do not give me this cup[n] of suffering. But do what you want, not what I want." [40]Then Jesus went back to his followers and found them asleep. Jesus said to Peter, "You men could not stay awake with me for one hour? [41]Stay awake and pray for strength against temptation. Your spirit wants to do what is right. But your body is weak."

[42]Then Jesus went away a second time. He prayed, "My Father, if it is not possible for this painful thing to be taken from me, and if I must do it, then I pray that what you want will be done."

[43]Then Jesus went back to the followers. Again he found them asleep, because their eyes were heavy. [44]So Jesus left them and went away one more time and prayed. This third time he prayed, he said the same thing.

[45]Then Jesus went back to the followers and said, "You are still sleeping and resting? The time has come for the Son of Man[d] to be given to sinful people. [46]Get up. We must go. Here comes the man who has turned against me."

## JESUS IS ARRESTED

[47]While Jesus was still speaking, Judas came up. Judas was 1 of the 12 followers. He had many people with him. They had been sent from the leading priests and the older leaders of the people. They carried swords and clubs. [48]Judas had planned to give them a signal. He had said, "The man I kiss is Jesus. Arrest him." [49]At once Judas went to Jesus and said, "Greetings, Teacher!" Then Judas kissed him.

[50]Jesus answered, "Friend, do the thing you came to do."

Then the men came and grabbed Jesus and arrested him. [51]When that happened, one of Jesus' followers reached for his sword and pulled it out. The follower struck the servant of the high priest with the sword and cut off his ear.

[52]Jesus said to the man, "Put your sword back in its place. All who use swords will be killed with swords. [53]Surely you know I could ask my Father, and he would give me more than 12 armies of angels. [54]But this thing must happen this way so that it will be as the Scriptures[d] say."

[55]Then Jesus said to the crowd, "You came to get me with swords and clubs as if I were a criminal. Every day I sat in the Temple[d] teaching. You did not arrest me there. [56]But all these things have happened so that it will be as the prophets[d] wrote." Then all of Jesus' followers left him and ran away.

## JESUS BEFORE THE LEADERS

[57]Those men who arrested Jesus led him to the house of Caiaphas, the high priest. The teachers of the law and the older Jewish leaders were gathered there. [58]Peter followed Jesus but did not go near him. He followed Jesus to the courtyard of the high priest's house. He sat down with the guards to see what would happen to Jesus.

[59]The leading priests and the Jewish council tried to find something false against Jesus so that they could kill him. [60]Many people came and told lies about him. But the council could find no real reason to kill Jesus. Then two people came and said, [61]"This man said, 'I can destroy the Temple[d] of God and build it again in three days.'"

[62]Then the high priest stood up and said to Jesus, "Aren't you going to answer? Don't you have something to say about their charges against you?" [63]But Jesus said nothing.

Again the high priest said to Jesus, "You must swear to this. I command you by the power of the living God to tell us the truth. Tell us, are you the Christ,[d] the Son of God?"

[64]Jesus answered, "Yes, I am. But I tell you, in the future you will see the Son of Man[d] sitting at the right hand of God, the Powerful One. And you will see him coming in clouds in the sky."

[65]When the high priest heard this, he was very angry. He tore his clothes and said, "This man has said things that are against God! We don't need any more witnesses. You all heard him say these things against God. [66]What do you think?"

The people answered, "He is guilty, and he must die."

[67]Then the people there spit in Jesus' face and beat him with their fists. Others slapped Jesus. [68]They said, "Prove to us that you are a prophet,[d] you Christ! Tell us who hit you!"

> **"My Father, if it is possible, do not give me this cup of suffering. But do what you want, not what I want."** *Matthew 26:39*

**26:39 cup** Jesus is talking about the bad things that will happen to him. Accepting these things will be very hard, like drinking a cup of something that tastes very bitter.

## PETER SAYS HE DOESN'T KNOW JESUS

[69]At that time, Peter was sitting in the courtyard. A servant girl came to him and said, "You were with Jesus, that man from Galilee."

[70]But Peter said that he was never with Jesus. He said this to all the people there. Peter said, "I don't know what you are talking about."

[71]Then he left the courtyard. At the gate, another girl saw him. She said to the people there, "This man was with Jesus of Nazareth."

[72]Again, Peter said that he was never with Jesus. Peter said, "I swear that I don't know this man Jesus!"

[73]A short time later, some people standing there went to Peter. They said, "We know you are one of those men who followed Jesus. We know this because of the way you talk."

[74]Then Peter began to curse. He said, "May a curse fall on me if I'm not telling the truth. I don't know the

man." After Peter said this, a rooster crowed. [75]Then he remembered what Jesus had told him: "Before the rooster crows, you will say three times that you don't know me." Then Peter went outside and cried painfully.

## JESUS IS TAKEN TO PILATE

**27** Early the next morning, all the leading priests and older leaders of the people decided to kill Jesus. [2]They tied him, led him away, and turned him over to Pilate, the governor.

## JUDAS KILLS HIMSELF

[3]Judas saw that they had decided to kill Jesus. Judas was the one who gave Jesus to his enemies. When Judas saw what happened, he was very sorry for what he had done. So he took the 30 silver coins back to the priests and the leaders. [4]Judas said, "I sinned. I gave you an innocent man to be killed."

The leaders answered, "What is that to us? That's your problem, not ours."

[5]So Judas threw the money into the Temple.[d] Then he went off and hanged himself.
[6]The leading priests picked up the silver coins in the Temple. They said, "Our law does not allow us to keep this money with the Temple money. This money has paid for a man's death." [7]So they decided to use the coins to buy a field called Potter's Field. This field would be a place to bury strangers who died while visiting Jerusalem. [8]That is why that field is still called the Field of Blood. [9]So the thing came true that Jeremiah the prophet[d] had said: "They took 30 silver coins. That is

how little the Israelites thought he was worth. [10]They used those 30 silver coins to buy the potter's field, as the Lord commanded me."[n]

## PILATE QUESTIONS JESUS

[11]Jesus stood before Pilate the governor. Pilate asked him, "Are you the King of the Jews?"

Jesus answered, "Yes, I am."

[12]When the leading priests and the older leaders accused Jesus, he said nothing.

[13]So Pilate said to Jesus, "Don't you hear these people accusing you of all these things?"

[14]But Jesus said nothing in answer to Pilate. Pilate was very surprised at this.

## PILATE TRIES TO FREE JESUS

[15]Every year at the time of Passover[d] the governor would free one person from prison. This was always a person the people wanted to be set free. [16]At that time there was a man in prison who was known to be very bad. His name was Barabbas. [17]All the people gathered at Pilate's house. Pilate said, "Which man do you want me to free: Barabbas, or Jesus who is called the Christ?"[d] [18]Pilate knew that the people gave Jesus to him because they were jealous.

[19]Pilate said these things while he was sitting on the judge's seat. While he was sitting there, his wife sent a message to him. The message said, "Don't do anything to that man. He is not guilty. Today I had a dream about him, and it troubled me very much."

[20]But the leading priests and older leaders told the crowd to ask for Barabbas to be freed and for Jesus to be killed.

[21]Pilate said, "I have Barabbas and Jesus. Which do you want me to set free for you?"

The people answered, "Barabbas!"

[22]Pilate asked, "What should I do with Jesus, the one called the Christ?"

They all answered, "Kill him on a cross!"

> "Pilate asked him, 'Are you the King of the Jews?' Jesus answered, 'Yes, I am.'"
>
> *Matthew 27:11*

27:10 "They . . . commanded me." See Zechariah 11:12-13 and Jeremiah 32:6-9.

**46**

# BiBLe BasiCS

## WHAT IS THE GREAT COMMISSION?

God wants the world to know about the incredible gift of salvation he offers through his Son. Before Jesus went back to heaven, he told his disciples to go into all the world and tell the gospel to every person. The Great Commission is every Christian's instruction to spread the Good News of God's forgiveness through Jesus Christ.

²³Pilate asked, "Why do you want me to kill him? What wrong has he done?"

But they shouted louder, "Kill him on a cross!"

²⁴Pilate saw that he could do nothing about this, and a riot was starting. So he took some water and washed his hands[n] in front of the crowd. Then he said, "I am not guilty of this man's death. You are the ones who are causing it!"

²⁵All the people answered, "We will be responsible. We accept for ourselves and for our children any punishment for his death."

²⁶Then Pilate freed Barabbas. Pilate told some of the soldiers to beat Jesus with whips. Then he gave Jesus to the soldiers to be killed on a cross.

²⁷Pilate's soldiers took Jesus into the governor's palace. All the soldiers gathered around Jesus. ²⁸They took off his clothes and put a red robe on him. ²⁹Then the soldiers used thorny branches to make a crown. They put this crown of thorns on Jesus' head. They put a stick in his right hand. Then the soldiers bowed before Jesus and made fun of him. They said, "Hail, King of the Jews!" ³⁰They spit on Jesus. Then they took his stick and hit him on the head many times. ³¹After they finished making fun of Jesus, the soldiers took off the robe and put his own clothes on him again. Then they led Jesus away to be killed on a cross.

### JESUS IS KILLED ON A CROSS

³²The soldiers were going out of the city with Jesus. They forced another man to carry the cross to be used for Jesus. This man was Simon, from Cyrene. ³³They all came to the place called Golgotha. (Golgotha means the Place of the Skull.) ³⁴At Golgotha, the soldiers gave Jesus wine to drink. This wine was mixed with gall.[n] He tasted the wine but refused to drink it. ³⁵The soldiers nailed Jesus to a cross. They threw lots[d] to decide who would get his clothes. ³⁶The soldiers sat there and continued watching him. ³⁷They put a sign above Jesus' head with the charge against him written on it. The sign read: "THIS IS JESUS THE KING OF THE JEWS." ³⁸Two robbers were nailed to crosses beside Jesus, one on the right and the other on the left. ³⁹People walked by and insulted Jesus. They shook their heads, ⁴⁰saying, "You said you could destroy the Temple[d] and build it again in three days. So save yourself! Come down from that cross, if you are really the Son of God!"

⁴¹The leading priests, the teachers of the law, and the older Jewish leaders were also there. These men made fun of Jesus ⁴²and said, "He saved other people, but he can't save himself! People say he is the King of Israel! If he is the King, then let him come down now from the cross. Then we will believe in him. ⁴³He trusts in God. So let God save him now, if God really wants him. He himself said, 'I am the Son of God.'" ⁴⁴And in the same way, the robbers who were being killed on crosses beside Jesus also insulted him.

### JESUS DIES

⁴⁵At noon the whole country became dark. This darkness lasted for three hours. ⁴⁶About three o'clock Jesus cried out in a loud voice, "Eli, Eli, lama sabachthani?" This means, "My God, my God, why have you left me alone?"

⁴⁷Some of the people standing there heard this. They said, "He is calling Elijah."

⁴⁸Quickly one of them ran and got a sponge. He filled the sponge with vinegar and tied it to a stick. Then he used the stick to give the sponge to Jesus to drink from it. ⁴⁹But the others said, "Don't bother him. We want to see if Elijah will come to save him."

⁵⁰Again Jesus cried out in a loud voice. Then he died.

> **"The soldiers nailed Jesus to a cross. They threw lots to decide who would get his clothes."** *Matthew 27:35*

⁵¹Then the curtain in the Temple[n] split into two pieces. The tear started at the top and tore all the way down to the bottom. Also, the earth shook and rocks broke apart. ⁵²The graves opened, and many of God's people who had died were raised from death. ⁵³They came out of the graves after Jesus was raised from death. They went into the holy city, and many people saw them.

⁵⁴The army officer and the soldiers guarding Jesus saw this earthquake and everything else that happened. They

## DECODE THIS!

*With what did Judas betray Jesus?*

27:24 **washed his hands** He did this as a sign to show that he wanted no part in what the people did. 27:34 **gall** Probably a drink of wine mixed with drugs to help a person feel less pain. 27:51 **curtain in the Temple** A curtain divided the Most Holy Place from the other part of the Temple. That was the special building in Jerusalem where God commanded the Jews to worship him.

were very frightened and said, "He really was the Son of God!"

[55]Many women were standing at a distance from the cross, watching. These were women who had followed Jesus from Galilee to care for him. [56]Mary Magdalene, and Mary the mother of James and Joseph, and the mother of James and John were there.

## JESUS IS BURIED

[57]That evening a rich man named Joseph came to Jerusalem. He was a follower of Jesus from the town of Arimathea. [58]Joseph went to Pilate and asked to have Jesus' body. Pilate gave orders for the soldiers to give it to Joseph. [59]Then Joseph took the body and wrapped it in a clean linen cloth. [60]He put Jesus' body in a new tomb that he had cut in a wall of rock. He rolled a very large stone to block the entrance of the tomb. Then Joseph went away. [61]Mary Magdalene and the other woman named Mary were sitting near the tomb.

## THE TOMB OF JESUS IS GUARDED

[62]That day was the day called Preparation[d] Day. The next day, the leading priests and the Pharisees[d] went to Pilate. [63]They said, "Sir, we remember that while that liar was still alive he said, 'After three days I will rise from death.' [64]So give the order for the tomb to be guarded closely till the third day. His followers might come and steal the body. Then they could tell the people that he has risen from death. That lie would be even worse than the first one."

[65]Pilate said, "Take some soldiers and go guard the tomb the best way you know." [66]So they all went to the tomb and made it safe from thieves. They did

this by sealing the stone in the entrance and then putting soldiers there to guard it.

## JESUS RISES FROM DEATH

**28** The day after the Sabbath[d] day was the first day of the week. At dawn on the first day, Mary Magdalene and another woman named Mary went to look at the tomb. [2]At that time there was a strong earthquake. An angel of the Lord came down from heaven.

### "He has risen from death as he said he would." Matthew 28:6

The angel went to the tomb and rolled the stone away from the entrance. Then he sat on the stone. [3]He was shining as bright as lightning. His clothes were white as snow. [4]The soldiers guarding the tomb were very frightened of the angel. They shook with fear and then became like dead men.

[5]The angel said to the women, "Don't be afraid. I know that you are looking for Jesus, the one who was killed on the cross. [6]But he is not here. He has risen from death as he said he would. Come and see the place where his body was. [7]And go quickly and tell his followers. Say to them: 'Jesus has risen from death. He is going into Galilee. He will be there before you. You will see him there.'" Then the angel said, "Now I have told you."

[8]The women left the tomb quickly. They were afraid, but they were also very happy. They ran to tell Jesus' followers what had happened. [9]Suddenly, Jesus met them and

said, "Greetings." The women came up to Jesus, took hold of his feet, and worshiped him. [10]Then Jesus said to them, "Don't be afraid. Go and tell my brothers to go on to Galilee. They will see me there."

## THE SOLDIERS REPORT TO THE JEWISH LEADERS

[11]The women went to tell Jesus' followers. At the same time, some of the soldiers who had been guarding the tomb went into the city. They went to tell the leading priests everything that had happened. [12]Then the priests met with the older Jewish leaders and made a plan. They paid the soldiers a large amount of money. [13]They said to the soldiers, "Tell the people that Jesus' followers came during the night and stole the body while you were asleep. [14]If the governor hears about this, we will satisfy him and save you from trouble." [15]So the soldiers kept the money and obeyed the priests. And that story is still spread among the Jews even today.

## JESUS TALKS TO HIS FOLLOWERS

[16]The 11 followers went to Galilee. They went to the mountain where Jesus told them to go. [17]On the mountain they saw Jesus and worshiped him. But some of them did not believe that it was really Jesus. [18]Then Jesus came to them and said, "All power in heaven and on earth is given to me. [19]So go and make followers of all people in the world. Baptize them in the name of the Father and the Son and the Holy Spirit.[d] [20]Teach them to obey everything that I have told you. You can be sure that I will be with you always. I will continue with you until the end of the world."

**DECODE THIS!**
*Who first found Jesus' tomb empty?*

# HOW WELL DO YOU KNOW THE WORD?

**Y**ou've heard the stories, but how well do you remember them? Test your Bible knowledge and see. Score 9-10: You're a Bible scholar. Keep up the good work! Score 7-8: You're a Bible student, learning and growing. Score 5-6: You're a Bible beginner; keep studying! Score 4 or below: Bible baby. Grow in your knowledge by spending more time in God's Word!

**1.** Which of the following names is not one of the twelve disciples?

 a. John

 b. Matthew

 c. Bartholomew

 d. Jacob

**2.** Jesus was born in what city?

 a. Nazareth

 b. Bethlehem

 c. Samaria

 d. Galilee

**3.** Which miracle did Jesus perform?

 a. Raising a dead girl to life

 b. Healing a blind man's eyes

 c. Casting out a legion of demons

 d. Turning water into wine

 e. All of the above

**4.** In Acts, God got Saul's attention through

 a. a blaring trumpet.

 b. another person.

 c. a disease.

 d. a blinding light.

**5.** In the parable of the seeds, how many kinds of soil were there?

 a. 1

 b. 2

 c. 3

 d. 4

**6.** John the Baptist had an interesting diet of

 a. steak and fries.

 b. locust and honey.

 c. olives and bread.

 d. lentils and barley.

**7.** When the children came to Jesus, Jesus said,

 a. "Send them away; my work is for adults."

 b. "I'm too tired for this."

 c. "Bring them to me, and let me bless them."

 d. "Where are their parents?"

**8.** Judas betrayed Jesus

 a. for free.

 b. for a position in the Sanhedrin.

 c. for 30 gold coins.

 d. for 30 silver coins.

**9.** After Jesus rose again, he first appeared to

 a. Peter.

 b. James.

 c. John.

 d. Mary Magdalene.

**10.** What is Jesus doing now?

 a. sitting on his throne

 b. praying for us

 c. preparing a place in heaven for us

 d. all of the above

ANSWER KEY: 1. D; 2. B; 3. E; 4. D; 5. D; 6. B; 7. C; 8. D; 9. D; 10. D

Only 16 chapters—the shortest of the Gospels.

Many scholars believe Mark was the first of the 4 Gospels to be written.

# THE GOSPEL ACCORDING TO MARK

Tells us more about what Jesus did and less about what he taught.

Mark's mother's house was used often as a place for meetings in Jerusalem.

Mark portrays the life of Jesus the Servant.

### JOHN PREPARES FOR JESUS

**1** This is the beginning of the Good News[d] about Jesus Christ, the Son of God,[n] [2]as the prophet[d] Isaiah wrote:

"I will send my messenger ahead
of you.
He will prepare your way."

*Malachi 3:1*

[3]"There is a voice of a man who
calls out in the desert:
'Prepare the way for the Lord.
Make the road straight for him.'"

*Isaiah 40:3*

[4]John was baptizing people in the desert. He preached a baptism of changed hearts and lives for the forgiveness of sins. [5]All the people from Judea and Jerusalem were going out to John. They told about the sins they had done. Then they were baptized by him in the Jordan River. [6]John wore clothes made from camel's hair and had a leather belt around his waist. He ate locusts[d] and wild honey. [7]This is what John preached to the people: "There is one coming later who is greater than I. I am not good enough even to kneel down and untie his sandals. [8]I baptize you with water. But the one who is coming will baptize you with the Holy Spirit."[d]

### JESUS IS BAPTIZED

[9]At that time Jesus came from the town of Nazareth in Galilee to the place where John was. John baptized Jesus in the Jordan River. [10]When Jesus was coming up out of the water, he saw heaven open. The Holy Spirit[d] came down on him like a dove. [11]A voice came from heaven and said: "You are my Son and I love you. I am very pleased with you."

[12]Then the Spirit sent Jesus into the desert alone. [13]He was in the desert 40 days and was there with the wild animals. While he was in the desert, he was tempted by Satan. Then angels came and took care of Jesus.

### JESUS CHOOSES SOME FOLLOWERS

[14]After John was put in prison, Jesus went into Galilee and preached the Good News[d] from God. [15]Jesus said, "The right time has come. The kingdom of God is near. Change your hearts and lives and believe the Good News!"

[16]When Jesus was walking by Lake Galilee, he saw Simon[n] and Simon's brother, Andrew. They were fishermen and were throwing a net into the lake to catch fish. [17]Jesus said to them, "Come and follow me. I will make you fishermen for men." [18]So Simon and Andrew immediately left their nets and followed him.

[19]Jesus continued walking by Lake Galilee. He saw two more brothers, James and John, the sons of Zebedee. They were in their boat, preparing their nets to catch fish. [20]Their father Zebedee and the men who worked for him were in the boat with the brothers. When Jesus saw the brothers, he called them to come with him. They left their father and followed Jesus.

### JESUS REMOVES AN EVIL SPIRIT

[21]Jesus and his followers went to Capernaum. On the Sabbath[d] day Jesus went to the synagogue[d] and began to teach. [22]The people there were amazed at his teaching. He did not teach like their teachers of the law. He taught like a person who had authority.

### "Jesus said, 'The right time has come. The kingdom of God is near. Change your hearts and lives and believe the Good News!'"

*Mark 1:15*

[23]While he was in the synagogue, a man was there who had an evil spirit in him. The man shouted, [24]"Jesus of Nazareth! What do you want with us? Did you come to destroy us? I know who you are—God's Holy One!" [25]Jesus said strongly, "Be quiet! Come out of the man!" [26]The evil spirit made the man shake violently. Then the spirit gave a loud cry and came out of him.

[27]The people were amazed. They asked each other, "What is happening here? This man is teaching something new. And he teaches with authority. He even gives commands to evil spirits, and they obey him." [28]And the news about Jesus spread quickly everywhere in the area of Galilee.

### JESUS HEALS MANY PEOPLE

[29]Jesus and his followers left the synagogue.[d] They all went at once with

## DECODE THIS!

*What did John the Baptist eat?*

 **1:1 the Son of God** Some Greek copies omit these words. **1:16 Simon** Simon's other name was Peter.

51

James and John to the home of Simon[n] and Andrew. [30]Simon's mother-in-law was sick in bed with a fever. The people there told Jesus about her. [31]So Jesus went to her bed, took her hand, and helped her up. Immediately the fever left her, and she was healed. Then she began serving them.

[32]That night, after the sun went down, the people brought to Jesus all who were sick. They also brought those who had demons[d] in them. [33]The whole town gathered at the door of the house. [34]Jesus healed many who had different kinds of sicknesses. He also forced many demons to leave people. But he would not allow the demons to speak, because they knew who he was.

[35]Early the next morning, Jesus woke and left the house while it was still dark. He went to a place to be alone and pray. [36]Later, Simon and his friends went to look for Jesus. [37]They found him and said, "Everyone is looking for you!"

[38]Jesus answered, "We should go somewhere else, to other towns around here. Then I can preach there too. That is the reason I came." [39]So he traveled everywhere in Galilee. He preached in the synagogues and forced demons to leave people.

**Q. What secret do you keep from your parents?**

**A. I keep a pet rat in my room, and my parents don't know about it.**

### JESUS HEALS A SICK MAN

[40]A man who had a harmful skin disease came to Jesus. The man fell to his knees and begged Jesus, "I know that you can heal me if you will."

[41]Jesus felt sorry for the man. So he touched him and said, "I want to heal you. Be healed!" [42]At once the disease left the man, and he was healed.

[43]Jesus told the man to go at once. But Jesus warned him strongly, [44]"Don't tell anyone about what I did for you. But go and show yourself to the priest. And offer a gift to God because you have been healed. Offer the gift that Moses commanded.[n] This will

show the people that you are healed." [45]The man left there, but he told everyone he saw that Jesus had healed him. So the news about Jesus spread. That is the reason Jesus could not enter a town if people saw him. He stayed in places where nobody lived. But people came from all the towns to wherever he was.

### JESUS HEALS A PARALYZED MAN

**2** A few days later, Jesus came back to Capernaum. The news spread that he was home. [2]So many people gathered to hear him preach that the house was full. There was no place to stand, not even outside the door. Jesus was teaching them. [3]Some people came, bringing a paralyzed man to Jesus. Four of them were carrying the paralyzed man. [4]But they could not get to Jesus because of the crowd. So they went to the roof above Jesus and made a hole in the roof. Then they lowered the mat with the paralyzed man on it. [5]Jesus saw that these men had great faith. So he said to the paralyzed man, "Young man, your sins are forgiven."

[6]Some of the teachers of the law were sitting there. They saw what Jesus did, and they said to themselves, [7]"Why does this man say things like that? He is saying things that are against God. Only God can forgive sins."

[8]At once Jesus knew what these teachers of the law were thinking. So he said to them, "Why are you thinking these things? [9]Which is easier: to tell this paralyzed man, 'Your sins are forgiven,' or to tell him, 'Stand up. Take your mat and walk'? [10]But I will prove to you that the Son of Man[d] has authority on earth to forgive sins." So Jesus said to the paralyzed man, [11]"I tell you, stand up. Take your mat and go home." [12]Immediately the paralyzed man stood up. He took his mat and walked out while everyone was watching him.

# Gotta Know!

## Why does God allow sickness and death?

As long as we're on this earth, we may never know why God chooses to allow the things to happen in our lives that he allows. We need to trust his goodness and love, even when life looks very bad. We also know that God doesn't like sickness and death, either. That's why he was willing to give up his own Son to death in order to beat it once and for all. Heaven—eternal life spent with him without pain, sadness, or death—is God's final answer to the hurt we feel in this life.

The people were amazed and praised God. They said, "We have never seen anything like this!"

[13]Jesus went to the lake again. A crowd followed him there, and he taught them. [14]While he was walking beside the lake, he saw a tax collector named Levi son of Alphaeus. Levi was sitting in the tax office. Jesus said to him, "Follow me." And Levi stood up and followed Jesus.

[15]Later that day, Jesus ate at Levi's house. There were many tax collectors and "sinners" eating there with Jesus and his followers. Many people like this followed Jesus. [16]The teachers of the law who were Pharisees[d] saw Jesus eating with the tax collectors and "sinners." They asked his followers, "Why does he eat with tax collectors and sinners?"

[17]Jesus heard this and said to them, "Healthy people don't need a doctor. It is the sick who need a doctor. I did not come to invite good people. I came to invite sinners."

## JESUS' FOLLOWERS ARE CRITICIZED

[18]One day the followers of John[n] and the Pharisees[d] were giving up eating.[n] Some people came to Jesus and said, "John's followers and the followers of the Pharisees give up eating. But your followers don't. Why?"

[19]Jesus answered, "When there is a wedding, the friends of the bridegroom are not sad while he is with them. They do not give up eating while the bridegroom is still there. [20]But the time will come when the bridegroom will leave them. Then the friends will be sad and will give up eating.

[21]"When a person sews a patch over a hole on an old coat, he never uses a piece of cloth that is not yet shrunk. If he does, the patch will shrink and pull away from the coat. Then the hole will be worse. [22]Also, no one ever pours new wine into old leather bags for holding wine. If he does, the new wine will break the bags, and the wine will be ruined along with the bags for the wine. People always put new wine into new leather bags."

## JESUS IS LORD OF THE SABBATH

[23]On the Sabbath[d] day, Jesus was walking through some grainfields. His followers were with him and picked some grain to eat. [24]The Pharisees[d] saw this and said to Jesus, "Why are your followers doing what is not lawful on the Sabbath?"

[25]Jesus answered, "You have read what David did when he and those with him were hungry and needed food. [26]It was during the time of Abiathar the high priest. David went into God's house and ate the bread that was made holy for God. The law of Moses says that only priests may eat that bread. But David also gave some of the bread to those who were with him."

[27]Then Jesus said to the Pharisees, "The Sabbath day was made to help people. They were not made to be ruled by the Sabbath day. [28]The Son of Man[d] is Lord even of the Sabbath."

## JESUS HEALS A MAN'S CRIPPLED HAND

**3** Another time when Jesus went into a synagogue,[d] a man with a crippled hand was there. [2]Some people there wanted to see Jesus do something wrong so they could accuse him. They watched him closely to see if he would heal the man on the Sabbath[d] day.

[3]Jesus said to the man with the crippled hand, "Stand up here in front of everyone."

[4]Then Jesus asked the people, "Which is right on the Sabbath day: to do good, or to do evil? Is it right to save a

## WILD WORLD FACTS

### BROKEN DOWN

Many paralytics came to Jesus for healing because doctors didn't know how to help. Even today, many people become paralyzed through accidents, or they are born with the problem—and doctors can't always help.

When you are paralyzed, you are unable to move certain parts of your body because the connection between those muscles and the nerves in your brain has been broken. Your spinal column (backbone) holds very delicate bands of nerves that send messages to and from the brain to every area of your body. If the backbone gets damaged and the nerves inside it are also hurt, often the brain can no longer tell the rest of the body what to do. Scientists today are trying to find ways to help the broken nerves grow back together and heal, but they still have more work to do.

Jesus didn't need a doctor because he is the Great Physician. He healed the people just by speaking the word.

## DECODE THIS!

*How did the paralyzed man get to Jesus for healing?*

 **2:18 John** John the Baptist who preached to the Jews about Christ's coming (Mark 1:4–8). **2:18 giving up eating** This is called "fasting." The people would give up eating for a special time of prayer and worship to God. It was also done to show sadness.

life or to destroy one?" But they said nothing to answer him.

[5]Jesus was angry as he looked at the people. But he felt very sad because they were stubborn. Then he said to the man, "Let me see your hand." The man put his hand out for Jesus, and it was healed. [6]Then the Pharisees[d] left and began making plans with the Herodians[n] about a way to kill Jesus.

### MANY PEOPLE FOLLOW JESUS

[7]Jesus left with his followers for the lake. A large crowd from Galilee followed him. [8]Also many people came from Judea, from Jerusalem, from Idumea, from the lands across the Jordan River, and from the area of Tyre and Sidon. They came because they had heard about all the things Jesus was doing. [9]Jesus saw the crowds. So he told his followers to get a boat ready for him. He wanted the boat so that the many people would not crowd themselves against him. [10]He had healed many people. So all the sick were pushing toward him to touch him. [11]Some had evil spirits in them. When the evil spirits saw Jesus, they fell down before him and shouted, "You are the Son of God!" [12]But Jesus strongly commanded the spirits not to tell who he was.

### JESUS CHOOSES HIS 12 APOSTLES

[13]Then Jesus went up on a hill and called some men to come to him. These were the men Jesus wanted, and they went up to him. [14]Jesus chose 12 men and called them apostles.[d] He wanted these 12 to be with him, and he wanted to send them to other places to preach. [15]He also wanted them to have the power to force demons[d] out of people. [16]These are the 12 men he chose: Simon (Jesus gave him the name Peter); [17]James and John, the sons of Zebedee (Jesus gave them the name Boanerges, which means "Sons of Thunder"); [18]Andrew, Philip, Bartholomew, Matthew, Thomas, James the son of Alphaeus, Thaddaeus, Simon the Zealot,[d] [19]and Judas Iscariot. Judas is the one who gave Jesus to his enemies.

### PEOPLE SAY JESUS HAS A DEVIL

[20]Then Jesus went back home. But again a crowd gathered. There were so many people that Jesus and his followers could not eat. [21]His family heard about all these things. They went to get him because people were saying that Jesus was out of his mind. [22]And the teachers of the law from Jerusalem were saying, "Beelzebul[d] is living inside him! He uses power from the ruler of demons[d] to force demons out."

[23]So Jesus called the people together and used stories to teach them. He said, "Satan will not force his own demons out of people. [24]A kingdom that fights against itself cannot continue. [25]And a family that is divided cannot continue. [26]And if Satan is against himself and fights against his own people, then he cannot continue. And that is the end of Satan. [27]If a person wants to enter a strong man's house and steal his things, first he must tie up the strong man. Then the thief can steal the things from the strong man's house. [28]I tell you the truth. All sins that people do can be forgiven. And all the bad things people say against God can be forgiven. [29]But any person who says bad things against the Holy Spirit[d] will never be forgiven. He is guilty of a sin that continues forever."

[30]Jesus said this because the teachers of the law said that Jesus had an evil spirit inside him.

> **"Jesus chose 12 men and called them apostles. He wanted these 12 to be with him, and he wanted to send them to other places to preach."**
>
> *Mark 3:14*

## REAL SUPER HEROES

# JAMES & JOHN
## THE SONS OF THUNDER

Their name says it all. Sons of Thunder. Loud. Strong. People you'd remember. They were brothers, and they were fishermen together, mending nets with their father when they heard Jesus' call to follow him. Without a second thought, they left their nets, and they obeyed Jesus.

Throughout Jesus' ministry, James and John were close by his side. They, along with Peter, were the chosen 3 who got to see Jesus show his glory, proving he was God. Like Peter, they often said the wrong things. But their hearts were good and strong for the Lord—even until their death when Herod Agrippa murdered them for what they believed.

God isn't concerned that we always have our act together. What he does want is for us to be passionate about him—to really love him with all our hearts, no matter what the cost, just like James and John.

# HOW WELL DO YOU KNOW YOUR SIBLING?

Take this test yourself, and then have your brother or sister circle the right answer. Count up how many you got right. If you scored an 8 or above, you guys are tight! Keep up the close connection. If you scored between 5 and 7, you are good friends, but there's more to each other you could get to know. If you scored 4 or below, your friendship needs work. Tell him/her that you want to get to know him/her better, and make time to hang out together more on a daily basis.

**1.** It's a beautiful day and you're ready to play. Your sibling is most likely to want to

A. Grab a ball and go outside.

B. Test out the bike.

C. Stay inside and play on the computer.

D. Call up a friend.

E. None of the above.

**2.** Someone is mean to you at school, so you ask your sibling for advice. They would probably say,

A. "You should show them who's boss and start a fight."

B. "You should think of a good insult."

C. "You should tell the teacher or your parent."

D. "You should talk it out with that person."

**3.** Your sibling spends most of his/her time feeling

A. Happy.

B. Sad.

C. Worried.

D. Laid back.

E. None of the above.

**4.** Your sibling's best talent is

A. Knowing how to get out of trouble.

B. Making friends.

C. School work.

D. Sports.

E. All of the above.

F. None of the above.

**5.** What's most important to your sibling?

A. Appearance

B. Grades

C. Athletic ability

D. Friends

E. God

**6.** What's your sibling's favorite type of book?

A. Comic

B. Novel

C. Mystery

D. Biography

**7.** Your sibling has more friends who are

A. Girls.

B. Boys.

**8.** Your sibling's greatest strength would probably be

A. Sense of humor.

B. Courage.

C. Kindness.

D. Intellect.

E. Strength.

**9.** Your sibling's favorite flavor of ice cream is

A. Vanilla.

B. Chocolate.

C. Anything with nuts.

D. Sherbet.

E. None of the above.

## JESUS' TRUE FAMILY

³¹Then Jesus' mother and brothers arrived. They stood outside and sent someone in to tell him to come out. ³²Many people were sitting around Jesus. They said to him, "Your mother and brothers are waiting for you outside."

³³Jesus asked, "Who is my mother? Who are my brothers?" ³⁴Then Jesus looked at those sitting around him. He said, "Here are my mother and my brothers! ³⁵My true brother and sister and mother are those who do the things God wants."

## A STORY ABOUT PLANTING SEED

**4** Another time Jesus began teaching by the lake. A great crowd gathered around him. So he got into a boat and went out on the lake. All the people stayed on the shore close to the water. ²Jesus used many stories to teach them. He said, ³"Listen! A farmer went out to plant his seed. ⁴While the farmer was planting, some seed fell by the road. The birds came and ate all that seed. ⁵Some seed fell on rocky ground where there wasn't much dirt. The seed grew very fast there because the ground was not deep. ⁶But when the sun rose, the plants withered. The plants died because they did not have deep roots. ⁷Some other seed fell among thorny weeds. The weeds grew and choked the good plants. So those plants did not make grain. ⁸Some other seed fell on good ground. In the good ground, the seed began to grow. It grew and made a crop of grain. Some plants made 30 times more grain, some 60 times more grain, and some 100 times more grain."

⁹Then Jesus said, "You people who hear me, listen!"

## Ways to Bless Your Mother

1. Obey her.

2. Help her clean the house.

3. Tell her you love her.

4. Go as long as you can without asking for something.

5. Make up your bed, and clean your room.

6. Write her a love poem.

7. Draw a picture for her.

8. Rub her shoulders.

9. Remember to say "Ma'am."

10. Be kind to your brothers and sisters.

## JESUS TELLS WHY HE USED STORIES

¹⁰Later, when Jesus was alone, the 12 apostles^d and others around him asked him about the stories. ¹¹Jesus said, "Only you can know the secret truth about the kingdom of God. But to other people I tell everything by using stories. ¹²I do this so that:

'They will look and look, but they will not learn.
    They will listen and listen, but they will not understand.
If they did learn and understand, they would come back to me and be forgiven.'" *Isaiah 6:9-10*

## JESUS EXPLAINS THE SEED STORY

¹³Then Jesus said to the followers, "Do you understand this story? If you don't, then how will you understand any story? ¹⁴The farmer is like a person who plants God's teaching in people. ¹⁵Sometimes the teaching falls on the road. This is like some people. They hear the teaching of God. But Satan quickly comes and takes away the teaching that was planted in them. ¹⁶Others are like the seed planted on rocky ground. They hear the teaching and quickly accept it with joy. ¹⁷But they don't allow the teaching to go deep into

their lives. They keep it only a short time. When trouble or persecution comes because of the teaching, they quickly give up. ¹⁸Others are like the seed planted among the thorny weeds. They hear the teaching. ¹⁹But then other things come into their lives: worries, the love of money, and wanting all kinds of other things. These things stop the teaching from growing. So that teaching does not produce fruit^n in their lives. ²⁰Others are like the seed planted in the good ground. They hear the teaching and accept it. Then they grow and produce fruit—sometimes 30 times more, sometimes 60 times more, and sometimes 100 times more."

## DECODE THIS!

*How many apostles did Jesus choose?*

 **4:19 produce fruit** To produce fruit means to have in your life the good things God wants.

## USE WHAT YOU HAVE

[21]Then Jesus said to them, "Do you hide a lamp under a bowl or under a bed? No! You put the lamp on a lampstand. [22]Everything that is hidden will be made clear. Every secret thing will be made known. [23]You people who hear me, listen!

[24]"Think carefully about the things you hear. The way you give to others is the

plant in the ground. [32]But when you plant this seed, it grows and becomes the largest of all garden plants. It produces large branches. Even the wild birds can make nests in it and be protected from the sun."

[33]Jesus used many stories like these to teach them. He taught them all that they could understand. [34]He always used sto-

care about us? We will drown!"

[39]Jesus stood up and commanded the wind and the waves to stop. He said, "Quiet! Be still!" Then the wind stopped, and the lake became calm.

[40]Jesus said to his followers, "Why are you afraid? Do you still have no faith?"

[41]The followers were very afraid and asked each other, "What kind of man is this? Even the wind and the waves obey him!"

# Gotta Know!

## Will God keep me safe all the time?

If you belong to God, he promises to never let anything separate you from him. He also promises to watch over you and never allow anything to come into your life that isn't for your good. However, his promise does not mean you will never get hurt. The Bible says we will face trials and troubles in this life. But even the things that look bad have a purpose for changing our lives for the good. So trust God—through the good times and the bad!

## A MAN WITH DEMONS INSIDE HIM

**5** Jesus and his followers went across the lake to the region of the Gerasene people. [2]When Jesus got out of the boat, a man came to him from the caves where dead people were buried. This man, who lived in the caves, had an evil spirit living in him. [3]No one could tie him up, not even with a chain. [4]Many times people had used chains to tie the man's hands and feet. But he always broke the chains off. No one was strong enough to control him. [5]Day and night he would wander around the burial caves and on the hills, screaming and cutting himself with stones. [6]While Jesus was still far away, the man saw him. He

way God will give to you. But God will give you more than you give. [25]The person who has something will be given more. But the person who does not have much, even what he has will be taken from him."

## JESUS USES A STORY ABOUT SEED

[26]Then Jesus said, "The kingdom of God is like a man who plants seed in the ground. [27]The seed comes up and grows night and day. It doesn't matter whether the man is asleep or awake; the seed still grows. The man does not know how it grows. [28]Without any help, the earth produces grain. First the plant grows, then the head, and then all the grain in the head. [29]When the grain is ready, the man cuts it. This is the harvest time."

## A STORY ABOUT MUSTARD SEED

[30]Then Jesus said, "How can I show you what the kingdom of God is like? What story can I use to explain it? [31]The kingdom of God is like a mustard seed. The mustard seed is the smallest seed you

ries to teach them. But when he and his followers were alone together, Jesus explained everything to them.

**"Jesus stood up and commanded the wind and the waves to stop. He said, 'Quiet! Be still!' Then the wind stopped, and the lake became calm."** *Mark 4:39*

## JESUS STOPS A STORM

[35]That evening, Jesus said to his followers, "Come with me across the lake." [36]He and the followers left the people there. They went in the boat that Jesus was already sitting in. There were also other boats with them. [37]A very strong wind came up on the lake. The waves began coming over the sides and into the boat. It was almost full of water. [38]Jesus was at the back of the boat, sleeping with his head on a pillow. The followers went to him and woke him. They said, "Teacher, do you

ran to Jesus and knelt down before him. [7-8]Jesus said to the man, "You evil spirit, come out of that man."

But the man shouted in a loud voice, "What do you want with me, Jesus, Son of the Most High God? I beg you, promise God that you will not punish me!"

[9]Then Jesus asked the man, "What is your name?"

The man answered, "My name is Legion," because I have many spirits in

## DECODE THIS!

*Where was Jesus sleeping when he calmed the storm?*

5:9 **Legion** Means very many. A legion was about 5,000 men in the Roman army.

me." [10]The man begged Jesus again and again not to send the spirits out of that area.

[11]"A large herd of pigs was eating on a hill near there. [12]The evil spirits begged Jesus, "Send us to the pigs. Let us go into them." [13]So Jesus allowed them to do this. The evil spirits left the man and went into the pigs. Then the herd of pigs rushed down the hill into the lake and were drowned. There were about 2,000 pigs in that herd.

[14]The men who took care of the pigs ran away. They went to the town and to the countryside, telling everyone about this. So people went out to see what had happened. [15]They came to Jesus and saw the man who had had the many evil spirits. The man was sitting there, clothed and in his right mind. The people were frightened. [16]Some people were there who saw what Jesus had done. They told the others what had happened to the man who had the demons[d] living in him. And they also told about

## BiBLE BASiCS

### WHAT DOES "BELIEVE" MEAN?

In the Bible, *believe* means "to be firm and trust." It means that we need to trust God when he tells us in his Word that Jesus really is his Son, and that he is the only way we can get to heaven. But belief has an even deeper meaning. God says that even the demons believe that Jesus is God's Son. We need to not only believe the facts, but also let them touch our hearts in such a way that we obey him. If we really believe what he's told us, our lives will be different from the rest of the world's.

---

> ## "Tell them how much the Lord has done for you and how he has had mercy on you."
>
> *Mark 5:19*

---

the pigs. [17]Then the people began to beg Jesus to leave their area.

[18]Jesus was getting ready to leave in the boat. The man who was freed from the demons begged to go with him.

[19]But Jesus would not allow the man to go. Jesus said, "Go home to your family and friends. Tell them how much the Lord has done for you and how he has had mercy on you." [20]So the man left and told the people in the Ten Towns[n] about the great things Jesus had done for him. All the people were amazed.

### JESUS GIVES LIFE TO A DEAD GIRL AND HEALS A SICK WOMAN

[21]Jesus went in the boat back to the other side of the lake. There, a large crowd gathered around him. [22]A ruler from the synagogue,[d] named Jairus, came to that place. Jairus saw Jesus and bowed before him. [23]The ruler begged Jesus again and again. He said, "My little daughter is dying. Please come and put your hands on

her. Then she will be healed and will live." [24]So Jesus went with the ruler, and many people followed Jesus. They were pushing very close around him.

[25]A woman was there who had been bleeding for the past 12 years. [26]She had suffered very much. Many doctors had tried to help her. She had spent all the money she had, but she was not improving. She was getting worse. [27]When the woman heard about Jesus, she followed him with the people and touched his coat. [28]The woman thought, "If I can even touch his coat, that will be enough to heal me." [29]When she touched his coat, her bleeding stopped. She could feel in her body that she was healed.

[30]At once Jesus felt power go out from him. So he stopped and turned around. Then he asked, "Who touched my clothes?"

[31]The followers said, "There are so many people pushing against you! And you ask, 'Who touched me?'"

[32]But Jesus continued looking around to see who had touched him. [33]The woman knew that she was healed. So she came and bowed at Jesus' feet. Shaking with fear, she told him the whole story. [34]Jesus said to the woman, "Dear woman, you are made well because you believed. Go in peace. You will have no more suffering."

[35]Jesus was still speaking to her when some men came from the house of Jairus, the synagogue ruler. The men said, "Your daughter is dead. There is now no need to bother the teacher."

[36]But Jesus paid no attention to what the men said. He said to the synagogue ruler, "Don't be afraid; only believe."

---

5:20 **Ten Towns** In Greek, called "Decapolis." It was an area east of Lake Galilee that once had ten main towns.

## KIDS SPEAK UP!

**Q. If you could talk to Moses, what would you ask him?**

**A. "Hey Moses, what was it like to talk to a burning bush?"**

### JESUS GOES TO HIS HOMETOWN

**6** Jesus left there and went back to his hometown. His followers went with him. [2]On the Sabbath[d] day he taught in the synagogue.[d] Many people heard him and were amazed. They said, "Where did this man get these teachings? What is this wisdom that has been given to him? And where did he get the power to work miracles?[d] [3]He is only the carpenter. His mother is Mary. He is the brother of James, Joseph, Judas, and Simon. And his sisters are here with us." The people did not accept Jesus.

[4]Jesus said to them, "Other people give honor to a prophet.[d] But in his own town with his own people and in his own home, a prophet does not receive honor." [5]Jesus was not able to work many miracles there. The only miracles he did were to heal some sick people by putting his hands on them. [6]Jesus was amazed that they had no faith.

Then Jesus went to other villages in that area and taught. [7]He called the 12 followers together and sent them out in groups of 2. He gave them authority over evil spirits. [8]This is what Jesus told them: "Take nothing for your trip except a walking stick. Take no bread, no bag, and no money in your pockets. [9]Wear sandals, and take only the clothes you are wearing. [10]When you enter a house, stay there until you leave that place. [11]If any town refuses to accept you or its people refuse to listen to you, then leave that town. Shake its dust off your feet.[n] This will be a warning to them."

[12]The followers went out and preached to the people to change their hearts and lives. [13]The followers forced many demons[d] out and poured olive oil on many sick people and healed them.

### HOW JOHN THE BAPTIST WAS KILLED

[14]King Herod heard about Jesus, because Jesus was now well-known. Some people said, "He is John the Baptist.[d] He is risen from death. That is the reason he can work these miracles."[d] [15]Others said, "He is Elijah."[n]

Other people said, "Jesus is a prophet.[d] He is like the prophets who lived long ago."

[16]Herod heard all these things about Jesus. He said, "I killed John by cutting off his head. Now he has been raised from death!"

[17]Herod himself had ordered his soldiers to arrest John, and John was put in prison. Herod did this to please his wife, Herodias. Herodias was the wife of Philip, Herod's brother. But then Herod married her. [18]John told Herod that it was not lawful for him to be married to his brother's wife. [19]So Herodias hated John and wanted to kill him. But she could not because of Herod. [20]Herod was afraid to kill John because he knew John was a good and holy man. So Herod protected John. Also, Herod enjoyed listening to John preach. But John's preaching always bothered him.

[21]Then the perfect time came for Herodias to cause John's death. It happened on Herod's birthday. Herod gave

[37]Jesus let only Peter, James, and John the brother of James go with him to Jairus's house. [38]They came to the house of the synagogue ruler, and Jesus found many people there crying loudly. There was much confusion. [39]Jesus entered the house and said to the people, "Why are you crying and making so much noise? This child is not dead. She is only asleep." [40]But they only laughed at Jesus. He told all the people to leave. Then he went into the room where the child was. He took the child's father and mother and his three followers into the room with him. [41]Then he took hold of the girl's hand and said to her, "Talitha, koum!" (This means, "Little girl, I tell you to stand up!") [42]The girl stood right up and began walking. (She was 12 years old.) The father and mother and the followers were amazed. [43]Jesus gave the father and mother strict orders not to tell people about this. Then he told them to give the girl some food.

**"The followers went out and preached to the people to change their hearts and lives."**

*Mark 6:12*

**DECODE THIS!**

*What was Jesus' occupation?*

6:11 **Shake . . . feet** A warning. It showed that they were finished talking to these people.
6:15 **Elijah** A man who spoke for God. He lived hundreds of years before Christ.

a dinner party for the most important government leaders, the commanders of his army, and the most important people in Galilee. ²²The daughter of Herodias came to the party and danced. When she danced, Herod and the people eating with him were very pleased.

So King Herod said to the girl, "I will give you anything you want." ²³He promised her, "Anything you ask for I will give to you. I will even give you half of my kingdom."

²⁴The girl went to her mother and asked, "What should I ask the king to give me?"

gathered around him and told him about all the things they had done and taught. ³¹Crowds of people were coming and going. Jesus and his followers did not even have time to eat. He said to them, "Come with me. We will go to a quiet place to be alone. There we will get some rest."

³²So they went in a boat alone to a place where there were no people. ³³But many people saw them leave and recognized them. So people from all the towns ran to the place where Jesus was going. They got there before Jesus arrived. ³⁴When he landed, he saw a

sat in groups of 50 or groups of 100. ⁴¹Jesus took the five loaves and two fish. He looked up to heaven and thanked God for the bread. He divided the bread and gave it to his followers for them to give to the people. Then he divided the two fish among them all. ⁴²All the people ate and were satisfied. ⁴³The followers filled 12 baskets with the pieces of bread and fish that were not eaten. ⁴⁴There were about 5,000 men there who ate.

## JESUS WALKS ON THE WATER

⁴⁵Then Jesus told his followers to get into the boat and go to Bethsaida on the other side of the lake. Jesus said that he would come later. He stayed there to tell the people they could go home. ⁴⁶After sending them away, he went into the hills to pray.

**"And everywhere he went, the people brought the sick to the marketplaces. They begged him to let them just touch the edge of his coat. And all who touched him were healed."** *Mark 6:56*

Her mother answered, "Ask for the head of John the Baptist."ᵈ

²⁵Quickly the girl went back to the king. She said to him, "Please give me the head of John the Baptist. Bring it to me now on a platter."

²⁶The king was very sad. But he had promised to give the girl anything she wanted. And the people eating there with him had heard his promise. So Herod could not refuse what she asked. ²⁷Immediately the king sent a soldier to bring John's head. The soldier went and cut off John's head in the prison ²⁸and brought it back on a platter. He gave it to the girl, and the girl gave it to her mother. ²⁹John's followers heard about what happened. So they came and got John's body and put it in a tomb.

### MORE THAN 5,000 PEOPLE FED
³⁰The apostlesᵈ that Jesus had sent out to preach returned. They

great crowd waiting. Jesus felt sorry for them, because they were like sheep without a shepherd. So he taught them many things.

³⁵It was now late in the day. Jesus' followers came to him and said, "No one lives in this place. And it is already very late. ³⁶Send the people away. They need to go to the farms and towns around here to buy some food to eat."

³⁷But Jesus answered, "You give them food to eat."

They said to him, "We can't buy enough bread to feed all these people! We would all have to work a month to earn enough money to buy that much bread!"

³⁸Jesus asked them, "How many loaves of bread do you have now? Go and see."

When they found out, they came to him and said, "We have five loaves and two fish."

³⁹Then Jesus said to the followers, "Tell all the people to sit in groups on the green grass." ⁴⁰So all the people sat in groups. They

⁴⁷That night, the boat was in the middle of the lake. Jesus was alone on the land. ⁴⁸He saw the followers working hard to row the boat because the wind was blowing against them. At some time between three and six o'clock in the morning, Jesus came to them, walking on the water. He continued walking until he was almost past the boat. ⁴⁹But when his followers saw him walking on the water, they thought he was a ghost and cried out. ⁵⁰They all saw him and were terrified. But Jesus spoke to them and said, "Have courage! It is I! Do not be afraid." ⁵¹Then he got into the boat with them. And the wind became calm. The followers were greatly amazed. ⁵²They had seen Jesus make more bread from the five loaves. But they did not understand what it meant. Their minds were closed.

⁵³When they had crossed the lake, they came to shore at Gennesaret. They tied the boat there. ⁵⁴When they got out of the boat, the people saw

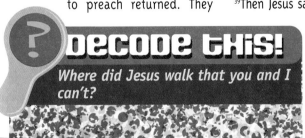

## DECODE THIS!
*Where did Jesus walk that you and I can't?*

Jesus and immediately recognized him. [55]They ran to tell others everywhere in that area that Jesus was there. They brought sick people on mats to every place Jesus went. [56]Jesus went into towns and cities and farms around that area. And everywhere he went, the people brought the sick to the marketplaces. They begged him to let them just touch the edge of his coat. And all who touched him were healed.

## OBEY GOD'S LAW NOT MEN'S

**7** Some Pharisees[d] and some teachers of the law came from Jerusalem. They gathered around Jesus. [2]They saw that some of Jesus' followers ate food with hands that were not clean.[d] ("Not

# LIVIN' IT!

## THAT THING YOU DO
## MARK 7

Why do you do the things you do? Is it just so you won't get into trouble? So people will like you better?

Jesus had an interesting talk with the Pharisees (religious leaders) of his day. They did a lot of things that made them look like really good people on the outside. They said and did all the right things in the eyes of others. But there was a big problem. They didn't really love God with all their hearts. They looked good on the outside following all the rules, but on the inside they didn't really care what God thought. Jesus wasn't fooled. He told them their rules were useless because God cares about our heart attitude more than anything else.

Why do you do what you do? Ask God to search your heart. If you do it for any reason other than serving God, it's not real obedience.

## GET CONNECTED

## WHAT'S IN YOUR HEART?

The day has hardly begun, and you've already had an argument with your parents. Hurt and angry, you are more than happy to tell your friend all about it. And at first you feel a little better—but then, a little worse. Why?

God wants us to always honor our parents—when they're around and when they're not. We've really got to control our tongues, so we don't say ugly things about our parents when we're angry. Instead, we should thank God for them and ask him to help us love and obey them more. Make sure your heart is right before God, because whatever's in our hearts is what eventually comes out in our talk.

clean" means that they did not wash their hands in the way the Pharisees said people must. [3]The Pharisees and all the Jews never eat before washing their hands in this special way. They do this to follow the teaching given to them by their great people who lived before them. [4]And when the Jews buy something in the market, they never eat it until they wash it in a special way. They also follow other rules of their great people who lived before them. They follow rules about the washing of cups, pitchers, and pots.)

[5]The Pharisees and the teachers of the law said to Jesus, "Your followers don't follow the rules given to us by our great people who lived before us. Your followers eat their food with hands that are not clean. Why do they do this?"

[6]Jesus answered, "You are all hypocrites![d] Isaiah was right when he spoke about you. Isaiah wrote,

'These people show honor to me with words.

But their hearts are far from me.

[7]Their worship of me is worthless.

The things they teach are nothing

but human rules they have memorized.'     *Isaiah 29:13*

[8]You have stopped following the commands of God. Now you only follow the teachings of men."

[9]Then Jesus said to them: "You think you are clever! You ignore the commands of God so that you can follow your own teachings! [10]Moses said, 'Honor your father and mother.'[n] Then Moses also said, 'Anyone who says cruel things to his father or mother must be put to death.'[n] [11]But you teach that a person can say to his father or mother, 'I have something I could use to help you. But I will not use it for you. I will give it to God.' [12]You are telling that person that he does not have to do anything for his father or mother. [13]So you are teaching that it is not important to do what God said. You think that it is more important to follow your own rules, which you teach people. And you do many things like that."

[14]Jesus called the people to him again. He said, "Every person should listen to me and understand what I am saying. [15]There is nothing a person puts into his body that makes him unclean. A person is made unclean by the things that come out of him." [16] [n]

[17]When Jesus left the people and went inside, his followers asked him about

7:10 'Honor your father and mother.' Quotation from Exodus 20:12; Deuteronomy 5:16. 7:10 'Anyone . . . death.' Quotation from Exodus 21:17. 7:16 Verse 16 Some Greek copies add verse 16: "You people who hear me, listen!"

61

# WHAT'S IN A DOZEN?

The number 12 appears several times throughout the Gospels. Solve the equations in the code chart below. Then write the letter from each sum in the matching blanks to find out how Jesus taught and ministered with 12.

Jesus gave authority to 12 __ __ __ __ __ __ __ __ __. (Matthew 10:1)
15  21  18  18  21  25  14  22  23

After the 5,000 were fed, the disciples had 12 leftover __ __ __ __ __ __ __. (Mark 8:19)
13  12  23  17  14  24  23

The daughter of Jairus had lived for 12 __ __ __ __ __ when Jesus healed her. (Mark 5:42)
26  14  12  22  23

Jesus could have used 12 __ __ __ __ __ __ of angels in the Garden of Gethsemane. (Matthew 26:53)
12  22  19  16  14  23

Jesus told his followers that they would judge 12 __ __ __ __ __ __ and sit
24  22  16  13  14  23

on 12 __ __ __ __ __ __ __. (Matthew 19:28)
24  27  22  21  20  14  23

12 + 0 = ____ (a)      12 + 4 = ____ (i)      12 + 6 = ____ (l)      12 + 5 = ____ (k)

12 + 13 = ____ (w)     12 + 2 = ____ (e)      12 + 9 = ____ (o)      12 + 1 = ____ (b)

12 + 7 = ____ (m)      12 + 11 = ____ (s)     12 + 12 = ____ (t)     12 + 14 = ____ (y)

12 + 15 = ____ (h)     12 + 8 = ____ (n)      12 + 10 = ____ (r)     12 + 3 = ____ (f)

this story. [18]Jesus said, "Do you still have trouble understanding? Surely you know that nothing that enters a man from the outside can make him unclean. [19]Food does not go into a person's mind. Food goes into his stomach. Then that food goes out of his body." (When Jesus said this, he meant that there is no food that is unclean for people to eat.)

[20]And Jesus said, "The things that come out of a man are the things that make him unclean. [21]All these evil things begin inside a person, in his mind: evil thoughts, sexual sins, stealing, murder, adultery,[d] [22]selfishness, doing bad things to other people, lying, doing sinful things, jealousy, saying bad things about people, pride, and foolish living. [23]All these evil things come from within a person. These things make a person unclean."

## JESUS HELPS A NON-JEWISH WOMAN

[24]Jesus left that place and went to the area around Tyre. He went into a house and did not want anyone to know he was there. But Jesus could not stay hidden. [25]A woman heard that he was there. Her little daughter had an evil spirit in her. So the woman quickly came to Jesus and fell at his feet. [26]She was not Jewish. She was Greek, born in Phoenicia, in Syria. She begged Jesus to force the demon[d] out of her daughter.

[27]Jesus told the woman: "It is not right to take the children's bread and give it to the dogs. First let the children eat all they want."

[28]She answered, "That is true, Lord. But the dogs under the table can eat the pieces of food that the children don't eat."

[29]Then Jesus said, "That is a very good answer. You may go. The demon has left your daughter."

[30]The woman went home and found her daughter lying in bed. The demon was gone.

## JESUS HEALS A DEAF MAN

[31]Then Jesus left the area around Tyre. He went through Sidon to Lake Galilee, to the area of the Ten Towns.[n] [32]While he was there, some people brought a man to him. This man was deaf and could not talk. The people begged Jesus to put his hand on the man to heal him.

[33]Jesus led the man away from the crowd, to be alone with him. Jesus put his fingers in the man's ears. Then Jesus spit and touched the man's tongue. [34]Jesus looked up to heaven and took a deep breath. He said to the man, "Ephphatha!" (This means, "Be opened.") [35]When Jesus did this, the man was able to hear. He was also able to use his tongue, and he spoke clearly.

[36]Jesus commanded the people not to tell anyone about what happened. But the more he commanded them, the more they told about it. [37]They were really amazed. They said, "Jesus does everything well. He makes the deaf hear! And those who can't talk—Jesus makes them able to speak."

## MORE THAN 4,000 PEOPLE FED

**8** Another time there was a great crowd with Jesus. They had nothing to eat. So Jesus called his followers to him. He said, [2]"I feel sorry for these people. They have been with me for three days, and now they have nothing to eat. [3]I cannot send them home hungry. If they leave without eating, they will faint on the way home. Some of them live a long way from here."

[4]Jesus' followers answered, "But we are far away from any towns. Where can we get enough bread to feed all these people?"

[5]Jesus asked, "How many loaves of bread do you have?"

They answered, "We have seven loaves."

[6]Jesus told the people to sit on the ground.

> "When Jesus did this, the man was able to hear. He was also able to use his tongue, and he spoke clearly."
>
> *Mark 7:35*

Then he took the seven loaves and gave thanks to God. Jesus divided the bread and gave the pieces to his followers. He told them to pass out the bread to the people, and they did so. [7]The followers also had a few small fish. Jesus gave thanks for the fish and told his followers to give the fish to the people. [8]All the people ate and were satisfied. Then the followers filled seven baskets with the pieces of food that were not eaten. [9]There were about 4,000 men who ate. After they had eaten, Jesus told them to go home. [10]Then he went in a boat with his followers to the area of Dalmanutha.

## THE LEADERS ASK FOR A MIRACLE

[11]The Pharisees[d] came to Jesus and asked him questions. They wanted to trap him. So they asked Jesus to do a miracle[d] to show that he was from God.

**? DECODE THIS!**

*How did Jesus heal the blind man in Mark 8:22-26?*

7:31 **Ten Towns** In Greek, called "Decapolis." It was an area east of Lake Galilee that once had ten main towns.

[12]Jesus sighed deeply. He said, "Why do you people ask for a miracle as proof? I tell you the truth. No miracle will be given to you." [13]Then Jesus left the Pharisees. He went in the boat to the other side of the lake.

## GUARD AGAINST WRONG TEACHINGS

[14]The followers had only one loaf of bread with them in the boat. They had forgotten to bring more bread. [15]Jesus warned them, "Be careful! Guard against the yeast of the Pharisees[d] and the yeast of Herod."

[16]Among themselves, his disciples discussed the meaning of this. They said, "He said this because we have no bread."

[17]Jesus knew what his followers were talking about. So he asked them, "Why are you talking about having no bread? You still don't see or understand? Are your minds closed? [18]You have eyes, but you don't really see. You have ears, but you don't really listen. Remember what I did before, when we did not have enough bread? [19]I divided five loaves of bread for 5,000 people. Remember how many baskets you filled with pieces of food that were not eaten?"

They answered, "We filled 12 baskets."

[20]"And remember that I divided seven loaves of bread for 4,000 people. Remember how many baskets you filled

## SALT SHAKERS

Salt is a mixture of 2 elements, sodium and chloride. Salt can be found in both the surface and underground parts of the earth and in the oceans, of which 2.6% are salt. Salt has even arrived to earth by meteors that brought it in from space. More than 225 million metric tons of salt are produced around the world each year. Even before history was written down, people have used salt for many things. It is vital to health in humans, animals, and even some plants. It can keep dead bodies from decaying, and it keeps meat and other foods fresh. It is used as a medicine and even in pottery—in addition to all the cooking uses it has.

When God says we are the salt of the world, he's telling us that we have the hope of Jesus in us, which can heal, preserve, and bring spiritual life to others around us. So shake some out wherever you go!

[Yahooligans: Ask Earl]

remember these things I did, but you still don't understand?"

## JESUS HEALS A BLIND MAN

[22]Jesus and his followers came to Bethsaida. Some people brought a blind man to Jesus and begged him to touch the man. [23]So Jesus took the blind man's hand and led him out of the village. Then he spit on the man's eyes. He put his hands on the blind man and asked, "Can you see now?"

[24]The man looked up and said, "Yes, I see people, but they look like trees walking around."

[25]Again Jesus put his hands on the man's eyes. Then the man opened his eyes wide. His eyes were healed, and he was able to see everything clearly. [26]Jesus told him to go home, saying, "Don't go into the town."

## PETER SAYS JESUS IS THE CHRIST

[27]Jesus and his followers went to the towns around Caesarea Philippi. While they were traveling, Jesus asked them, "Who do people say I am?"

[28]They answered, "Some people say you are John the Baptist.[d] Others say you are Elijah.[n] And others say that you are one of the prophets."[d]

[29]Then Jesus asked, "Who do you say I am?"

Peter answered, "You are the Christ."[d]

[30]Jesus ordered his followers, "Don't tell anyone who I am."

[31]Then Jesus began to teach them that the Son of Man[d] must suffer many things. He taught that the Son of Man would not be accepted by the older Jewish leaders, the leading priests, and the teachers of the law. He taught that the Son of Man must be killed and then rise from death after three days. [32]Jesus told them plainly what would happen. Then Peter took Jesus aside and began to criticize him. [33]But Jesus turned and looked at his followers. Then he criticized Peter and said, "Go away from me, Satan!"[n] You don't care about the things of God. You care only about things men think are important."

> ## "if anyone wants to follow me, he must say 'no' to the things he wants." Mark 8:34

with pieces of food that were not eaten?"

They answered, "We filled 7 baskets."

[21]Then Jesus said to them, "You

## DECODE THIS!

Who appeared on the high mountain with Jesus?

8:28 Elijah A man who spoke for God. He lived hundreds of years before Christ.
8:33 Satan Name for the devil meaning "the enemy." Jesus means that Peter was talking like Satan.

> "A voice came
> from the cloud.
> The voice said,
> 'This is my Son,
> and i love him.
> Obey him!'"
>
> *Mark 9:7*

[34]Then Jesus called the crowd to him, along with his followers. He said, "If anyone wants to follow me, he must say 'no' to the things he wants. He must be willing to die on a cross, and he must follow me. [35]Whoever wants to save his life will give up true life. But whoever gives up his life for me and for the Good News[d] will have true life forever. [36]It is worth nothing for a person to have the whole world, if he loses his soul. [37]A person could never pay enough to buy back his soul. [38]The people who live now are living in a sinful and evil time. If anyone is ashamed of me and my teaching, then I will be ashamed of him. I will be ashamed of him when I come with the glory of my Father and the holy angels."

**9** Then Jesus said to the people, "I tell you the truth. Some of you standing here will see the kingdom of God come with power before you die."

### JESUS WITH MOSES AND ELIJAH

[2]Six days later Jesus took Peter, James, and John and went up on a high mountain. They were all alone there. While these followers watched, Jesus was changed. [3]His clothes became shining white, whiter than any person could make them. [4]Then two men appeared, talking with Jesus. The men were Moses and Elijah.[n]

[5]Peter said to Jesus, "Teacher, it is good that we are here. We will put three tents here—one for you, one for Moses, and one for Elijah." [6]Peter did not know what to say, because he and the others were so frightened.

[7]Then a cloud came and covered them. A voice came from the cloud. The voice said, "This is my Son, and I love him. Obey him!"

[8]Then Peter, James, and John looked around, but they saw only Jesus there alone with them.

[9]As Jesus and his followers were walking back down the mountain, he commanded them, "Don't tell anyone about the things you saw on the mountain. Wait till the Son of Man[d] rises from death. Then you may tell."

[10]So the followers obeyed Jesus and said nothing about what they had seen. But they discussed what Jesus meant about rising from death.

[11]They asked Jesus, "Why do the teachers of the law say that Elijah must come first?"

[12]Jesus answered, "They are right to say that Elijah must come first. Elijah makes all things the way they should be. But why does the Scripture[d] say that the Son of Man will suffer much and that people will treat him as if he were nothing? [13]I tell you that Elijah has already come. And people did to him whatever they wanted to do. The Scriptures said this would happen to him."

### JESUS HEALS A SICK BOY

[14]Then Jesus, Peter, James, and John went to the other followers. They saw a great crowd around them. The teachers of the law were arguing with them. [15]But when the crowd saw Jesus, they were surprised and ran to welcome him.

[16]Jesus asked, "What are you arguing about with the teachers of the law?"

[17]A man answered, "Teacher, I brought my son to you. He has a spirit from the devil in him. This spirit stops him from talking. [18]The spirit attacks him and throws him on the ground. My son foams at the mouth, grinds his teeth, and becomes very stiff. I asked your followers to force the evil spirit out, but they couldn't."

[19]Jesus answered, "You people don't

## LIVIN' IT!

**REVERSED RULES**
**MARK 9:35**

★EXTRA★
WHO'S #1?

All this talk about a kingdom had gotten the disciples excited. They began secretly wondering how important they were going to be when Jesus was officially made king. Soon, their sinful thoughts broke the silence, and they began arguing over who was the greatest.

But Jesus' kingdom is like no other. His correction was gentle. He said that if they wanted to be great in his kingdom, they must become the servant of all.

Servant of all? What kind of power is that? It's the kind of kingdom Jesus himself brought to earth when he gave up so many of his rights to become a human like us. This King of the universe—the very Creator of the earth he walked on—humbly healed the hurts of his people and offered his own life to wash away their sin. If Jesus, the greatest person, showed his importance through his love and service, then we, his followers, should do the same.

 9:4 **Moses and Elijah** Two of the most important Jewish leaders in the past.

believe! How long must I stay with you? How long must I go on being patient with you? Bring the boy to me!"

²⁰So the followers brought him to Jesus. As soon as the evil spirit saw Jesus, it attacked the boy. He fell down and rolled on the ground, foaming from his mouth.

²¹Jesus asked the boy's father, "How long has this been happening?"

The father answered, "Since he was very young. ²²The spirit often throws him into a fire or into water to kill him. If you can do anything for him, please have pity on us and help us."

²³Jesus said to the father, "You said, 'If you can!' All things are possible for him who believes."

²⁴Immediately the father cried out, "I do believe! Help me to believe more!"

²⁵Jesus saw that a crowd was running there to see what was happening. So he spoke to the evil spirit, saying, "You deaf and dumb spirit—I command you to come out of this boy and never enter him again!"

## Going Global

### Feed The Children

Can I have some more please? Feed The Children helps with nearly 500,000 meals a day worldwide. They are not run like drive-through restaurants, but their system is fast and efficient. Here's their setup: They deliver food to partner organizations that quickly get the food to over 60,000 groups who work with the hungry. Get this: There's no charge to children, families, or persons in need!

Feed The Children has created and organized one of the world's largest private organizations dedicated to feeding hungry people in the United States and around the world. Find out how you can help at www.feedthechildren.org.

²⁶The evil spirit screamed and caused the boy to fall on the ground again. Then the spirit came out. The boy looked as if he were dead. And many people said, "He is dead!" ²⁷But Jesus took hold of the boy's hand and helped him to stand up.

²⁸Jesus went into the house. His followers were alone with him there. They said, "Why couldn't we force that evil spirit out?"

²⁹Jesus answered, "That kind of spirit can only be forced out by prayer."

### JESUS TALKS ABOUT HIS DEATH

³⁰Then Jesus and his followers left that place and went through Galilee. Jesus did not want anyone to know where he was ³¹because he wanted to teach his followers alone. He said to them, "The Son of Man[d] will be given to men who will kill him. After three days, he will rise from death." ³²But the followers did not understand what Jesus meant. And they were afraid to ask.

### WHO IS THE GREATEST?

³³Jesus and his followers went to Capernaum and went into a house there.

Then Jesus said to them, "What were you arguing about on the road?" ³⁴But the followers did not answer, because their argument on the road was about which one of them was the greatest.

³⁵Jesus sat down and called the 12 apostles[d] to him. He said, "If anyone wants to be the most important, then he must be last of all and servant of all."

³⁶Then Jesus took a small child and had him stand among them. He took the child in his arms and said, ³⁷"If anyone accepts children like these in my name, then he is also accepting me. And if he accepts me, then he is also accepting the One who sent me."

### ANYONE NOT AGAINST US IS FOR US

³⁸Then John said, "Teacher, we saw a man using your name to force demons[d] out of a person. We told him to stop, because he does not belong to our group."

³⁹Jesus said, "Don't stop him. Anyone who uses my name to do powerful things will not say evil things about me. ⁴⁰He who is not against us is with us. ⁴¹I tell you the truth. If anyone helps you by giving you a drink of water because you

> "Jesus sat down and called the 12 apostles to him. He said, 'if anyone wants to be the most important, then he must be last of all and servant of all.'" *Mark 9:35*

belong to the Christ,[d] then he will truly get his reward.

[42]"If one of these little children believes in me, and someone causes that child to sin, then it will be very bad for him. It would be better for him to have a large stone tied around his neck and be drowned in the sea. [43]If your hand causes you to sin, cut it off. It is better for you to lose part of your body but have life forever. That is much better than to have two hands and go to hell. In that place the fire never goes out. [44][n] [45]If your foot causes you to sin, cut it off. It is better for you to lose part of your body but have life forever. That is much better than to have two feet and be thrown into hell. [46][n] [47]If your eye causes you to sin, take it out. It is better for you to have only one eye but have life forever. That is much better than to have two eyes and be thrown into hell. [48]In hell the worm does not die; the fire is never stopped. [49]Every person will be salted with fire.

[50]"Salt is good. But if the salt loses its salty taste, then you cannot make it salty again. So, be full of goodness. And have peace with each other."

## JESUS TEACHES ABOUT DIVORCE

**10** Then Jesus left that place. He went into the area of Judea and across the Jordan River. Again, crowds came to him. And Jesus taught them as he always did.

[2]Some Pharisees[d] came to Jesus and tried to trick him. They asked, "Is it right for a man to divorce his wife?"

[3]Jesus answered, "What did Moses command you to do?"

[4]They said, "Moses allowed a man to write out divorce papers and send her away."[n]

[5]Jesus said, "Moses wrote that command for you because you refused to accept God's teaching. [6]But when God made the world, 'he made them male

and female.'[n] [7]'So a man will leave his father and mother and be united with his wife. [8]And the two people will become one body.'[n] So the people are not two, but one. [9]God has joined the two people together. So no one should separate them."

[10]Later, the followers and Jesus were in the house. They asked Jesus again about the question of divorce. [11]He

answered, "Anyone who divorces his wife and marries another woman is guilty of adultery[d] against her. [12]And the woman who divorces her husband and marries another man is also guilty of adultery."

## JESUS ACCEPTS CHILDREN

[13]Some people brought their small children to Jesus so he could touch them. But his followers told the people to stop bringing their children to him. [14]When Jesus saw this, he was displeased. He said to them, "Let the little children come to me. Don't stop them. The kingdom of God belongs to people who are like these little children. [15]I tell you the truth. You must accept the kingdom of God as a little child accepts things, or you will never enter it." [16]Then Jesus took the children in his

arms. He put his hands on them and blessed them.

## A RICH YOUNG MAN'S QUESTION

[17]Jesus started to leave, but a man ran to him and fell on his knees before Jesus. The man asked, "Good teacher, what must I do to get the life that never ends?"

[18]Jesus answered, "Why do you call me good? No one is good except God alone. [19]You know the commands: 'You must not murder anyone. You must not be guilty of adultery.[d] You must not steal. You must not tell lies about your neighbor in court. You must not cheat. Honor your father and mother.'"[n]

[20]The man said, "Teacher, I have obeyed all these commands since I was a boy."

**"He said to them, 'Let the little children come to me. Don't stop them.'"**

*Mark 10:14*

[21]Jesus looked straight at the man and loved him. Jesus said, "There is still one more thing you need to do. Go and sell everything you have, and give the money to the poor. You will have a reward in heaven. Then come and follow me."

[22]He was very sad to hear Jesus say this, and he left. The man was sad because he was very rich.

[23]Then Jesus looked at his followers and said, "How hard it will be for those who are rich to enter the kingdom of God!"

[24]The followers were amazed at what Jesus said. But he said again, "My children, it is very hard to enter the kingdom of God! [25]And it will be very hard for a rich person to enter the kingdom of God. It would be easier for a camel to go through the eye of a needle!"

## DECODE THIS!

*When Jesus took the children in his arms, what did he do?*

 9:44 Verse 44 Some Greek copies of Mark add verse 44, which is the same as verse 48. 9:46 Verse 46 Some Greek copies of Mark add verse 46, which is the same as verse 48. 10:4 "Moses . . . away." Quotation from Deuteronomy 24:1. 10:6 'he made . . . female.' Quotation from Genesis 1:27. 10:7-8 'So . . . body.' Quotation from Genesis 2:24. 10:19 'You . . . mother.' Quotation from Exodus 20:12-16; Deuteronomy 5:16-20.

# Gotta Know!

## How can I know if my siblings are Christians?

The best way is to ask. Ask them, "If something were to happen today and you died, would you go to heaven?" If they say "Yes," or "I think so," then follow with, "If God asked you why he should let you into heaven, what would you say?" If they say because Jesus died for their sins, then they are Christians. If they answer anything like, "Because I'm a pretty good person," or "I thought everybody went to heaven," then they need to know the truth. You can tell them the Good News of what Jesus has done for them, and invite them to receive his gift of forgiveness and eternal life through prayer.

26The followers were even more amazed and said to each other, "Then who can be saved?"

27Jesus looked straight at them and said, "This is something that men cannot do. But God can do it. God can do all things."

28Peter said to Jesus, "We left everything to follow you!"

29Jesus said, "I tell you the truth. Everyone who has left his home, brothers, sisters, mother, father, children, or fields for me and for the Good News[d] 30will get a hundred times more than he left. Here in this world he will have more homes, brothers, sisters, mothers, children, and fields. And with those things, he will also suffer for his belief. But in the age that is coming he will have life forever. 31Many who have the highest place now will have the lowest place in the future. And those who have the lowest place now will have the highest place in the future."

### JESUS TALKS ABOUT HIS OWN DEATH

32Jesus and the people with him were on the road to Jerusalem. Jesus was leading the way. The followers were amazed, but those who followed behind them were afraid. Jesus took the 12 apostles[d] aside and talked with them alone. He told them what would happen in Jerusalem. 33He said, "We are going to Jerusalem. The Son of Man[d] will be given to the leading priests and teachers of the law. They will say that he must die. They will give him to the non-Jewish people, 34who will laugh at him and spit on him. They will beat him with whips and kill him. But on the third day after his death, he will rise to life again."

### TWO FOLLOWERS ASK JESUS A FAVOR

35Then James and John, sons of Zebedee, came to Jesus. They said, "Teacher, we want to ask you to do something for us."

36Jesus asked, "What do you want me to do for you?"

37They answered, "You will have glory in your kingdom. Let one of us sit at your right, and let one of us sit at your left."

38Jesus said, "You don't understand what you are asking. Can you drink the cup that I must drink? And can you be baptized with the same kind of baptism that I must have?"[n]

39They answered, "Yes, we can!"

Jesus said to them, "You will drink the same cup that I will drink. And you will be baptized with the same baptism that I must have. 40But I cannot choose who will sit at my right or my left. These places are for those for whom they are prepared."

41The ten followers heard this. They began to be angry with James and John. 42Jesus called all the followers together. He said, "The non-Jewish people have men they call rulers. You know that those rulers love to show their power over the people. And their important leaders love to use all their authority. 43But it should not be that way among you. If one of you wants to become great, then he must serve you like a ser-vant. 44If one of you wants to become the most important, then he must serve all of you like a slave. 45In the same way, the Son of Man[d] did not come to be served. He came to serve. The Son of Man came to give his life to save many people."

### JESUS HEALS A BLIND MAN

46Then they came to the town of Jericho. As Jesus was leaving there with his followers and a large crowd, a blind beggar named Bartimaeus (son of Timaeus) was sitting by the road. 47He

> " Jesus said, 'Go. You are healed because you believed.' " *Mark 10:52*

## DECODE THIS!

*What building did Jesus throw people out of?*

10:38 Can you . . . have? Jesus was asking if they could suffer the same terrible things that would happen to him.

# MARCH FRIENDSHIP

*A friend loves you all the time. A brother is always there to help you (Proverbs 17:17).*

**1** MATTHEW 28:20: You can be sure that I will be with you always. I will continue with you until the end of the world.

**2**

**3** Ask your friend if he or she has any prayer requests.

**4** Prayer Pointer: Ask God to show you who needs a friend and for wisdom to know how to become a good friend.

**5**

**6** Call up a group of friends, and go to the science museum together.

**7**

**8** JOHN 15:14: You are my friends if you do what I command you.

**9**

**10**

**11**

**12** Put on a jacket, and go fly a kite.

**13**

**14** Prayer Pointer: Ask God to help you make your parents your best friends.

**15**

**16** MATTHEW 7:12: Do for other people the same things you want them to do for you.

**17**

**18**

**19** See how many sit-ups you can do in 3 minutes.

**20**

**21** Prayer Pointer: Pray for missionary children in other countries to find friends who will help them know God better.

**22**

**23** HEBREWS 10:24: Let us think about each other and help each other to show love and do good deeds.

**24**

**25**

**26** Make a healthy snack for you and your siblings to enjoy.

**27**

**28**

**29** Have a spend-the-night party, and play video games together.

**30** James 4:4: If a person wants to be a friend of the world, he makes himself God's enemy.

**31**

heard that Jesus from Nazareth was walking by. The blind man cried out, "Jesus, Son of David,ᵈ please help me!"

⁴⁸Many people scolded the blind man and told him to be quiet. But he shouted more and more, "Son of David, please help me!"

## GET CONNECTED

### HEALED HURTS

Take a minute and think about all the friendships you have in your life right now. Has anyone of those people hurt your feelings or made you angry toward them? Has the problem been fixed?

If not, it's time for you to forgive them. To forgive them means to no longer think of the bad thing they did when you think of them. It means to forget it and go on. Forgiving isn't always easy because sometimes our hurts are very deep. But ask Jesus to heal your heart. Ask him to help you forgive others the same way he forgives you, and he will.

⁴⁹Jesus stopped and said, "Tell the man to come here."

So they called the blind man. They said, "Cheer up! Get to your feet. Jesus is calling you." ⁵⁰The blind man stood up quickly. He left his coat there and went to Jesus.

⁵¹Jesus asked him, "What do you want me to do for you?" The blind man answered, "Teacher, I want to see again."

⁵²Jesus said, "Go. You are healed because you believed." At once the man was able to see again, and he followed Jesus on the road.

### JESUS ENTERS JERUSALEM AS A KING

**11** Jesus and his followers were coming closer to Jerusalem. They came to the towns of Bethphage and Bethany near the Mount of Olives.ᵈ There Jesus sent two of his followers. ²He said to them, "Go to the town you see there.

When you enter it, you will find a colt tied which no one has ever ridden. Untie it and bring it here to me. ³If anyone asks you why you are doing this, tell him, 'The Master needs the colt. He will send it back soon.'"

⁴The followers went into the town. They found a colt tied in the street near the door of a house, and they untied it. ⁵Some people were standing there and asked, "What are you doing? Why are you untying that colt?" ⁶The followers answered the way Jesus told them to

## "Jesus said, 'Go. You are healed because you believed.' At once the man was able to see again, and he followed Jesus on the road."

*Mark 10:52*

answer. And the people let them take the colt.

⁷The followers brought the colt to Jesus. They put their coats on the colt, and Jesus sat on it. ⁸Many people spread their coats on the road. Others cut branches in the fields and spread the branches on the road. ⁹Some of the people were walking ahead of Jesus. Others were following him. All of them were shouting,

"Praiseⁿ God! God bless the One who comes in the name of the Lord! *Psalm 118:26*

¹⁰God bless the kingdom of our father David! That kingdom is coming! Praise to God in heaven!"

¹¹Jesus entered Jerusalem and went into the Temple.ᵈ When he had looked at everything, and since it was already late, he went out to Bethany with the 12 apostles.ᵈ

¹²The next day as Jesus was leaving Bethany, he was hungry. ¹³He saw a fig tree in leaf. So he went to the tree to see if it had any figs on it. But he found no figs, only leaves. It was not the right season for figs to grow. ¹⁴So Jesus said to the tree, "May no one ever eat fruit from you again." Jesus' followers heard him say this.

### JESUS GOES TO THE TEMPLE

¹⁵Jesus returned to Jerusalem and went into the Temple.ᵈ He began to throw out those who were buying and selling things there. He overturned the tables that belonged to the men who were exchanging different kinds of money. And he turned over the benches of the men who were selling doves. ¹⁶Jesus refused to allow anyone to carry goods through the Temple courts. ¹⁷Then Jesus taught the people. He said, "It is written in the Scriptures,ᵈ 'My Temple will be a house where people from all nations will pray.'ⁿ But you are changing God's house into a 'hideout for robbers.'"ⁿ

¹⁸The leading priests and the teachers of the law heard all this. They began trying to find a way to kill Jesus. They were afraid of him because all the people were amazed at his teaching. ¹⁹That night, Jesus and his followers left the city.

11:9 **Praise** Literally, "Hosanna," a Hebrew word used at first in praying to God for help, but at this time it was probably a shout of joy used in praising God or his Messiah. 11:17 **'My Temple . . . pray.'** Quotation from Isaiah 56:7. 11:17 **'hideout for robbers.'** Quotation from Jeremiah 7:11.

70

## THE POWER OF FAITH

²⁰The next morning, Jesus was passing by with his followers. They saw the fig tree, and it was dry and dead, even to the roots. ²¹Peter remembered the tree and said to Jesus, "Teacher, look! Yesterday, you cursed the fig tree. Now it is dry and dead!"

²²Jesus answered, "Have faith in God. ²³I tell you the truth. You can say to this mountain, 'Go, mountain, fall into the sea.' And if you have no doubts in your mind and believe that the thing you say will happen, then God will do it for you. ²⁴So I tell you to ask for things in prayer. And if you believe that you have received those things, then they will be yours. ²⁵When you are praying, and you remember that you are angry with another person about something, then forgive him. If you do this, then your Father in heaven will also forgive your sins." ²⁶ ⁿ

## LEADERS DOUBT JESUS' AUTHORITY

²⁷Jesus and his followers went again to Jerusalem. Jesus was walking in the Temple.ᵈ The leading priests, the teachers of the law, and the older Jewish leaders came to him. ²⁸They said to him, "Tell us! What authority do you have to do these things? Who gave you this authority?"

²⁹Jesus answered, "I will ask you one question. You answer it. Then I will tell you whose authority I use to do these things. ³⁰Tell me: When John baptized people, was that from God or from man? Answer me!"

³¹They argued about Jesus' question. They said to each other, "If we answer, 'John's baptism was from God,' then Jesus will say, 'Then why didn't you believe John?' ³²But if we say, 'From man,' then the people will be against us." (These leaders were afraid of the people. All the people believed that John was a prophet.ᵈ)

³³So the leaders answered Jesus, "We don't know."

Jesus said, "Then I will not tell you what authority I use to do these things."

## GOD SENDS HIS SON

**12** Jesus used stories to teach the people. He said, "A man planted a vineyard. He put a wall around it and dug a hole for a winepress.ᵈ Then he built a tower. He leased the vineyard to some farmers and left for a trip. ²Later, it was time for the grapes to be picked. So the man sent a servant to the farmers to get his share of the grapes. ³But the farmers grabbed the servant and beat him. They sent him away with nothing. ⁴Then the man sent another servant. They hit him on the head and showed no respect for him. ⁵So the man sent another ser-vant. They killed this servant. The man sent many other servants. The farmers beat some of them and killed others. ⁶The man had one person left to send, his son whom he loved. He sent him last of all, saying, 'The farmers will respect my son.'

⁷"But they said to each other, 'This is the owner's son. This vineyard will be his. If we kill him, then it will be ours.' ⁸So they took the son, killed him, and threw him out of the vineyard.

⁹"So what will the man who owns the vineyard do? He will go to the vineyard and kill those farmers. Then he will give the vineyard to other farmers. ¹⁰Surely you have read this Scripture:ᵈ

'The stone that the builders did not want
　became the cornerstone.ᵈ

"The Lord did this,
　and it is wonderful to us.'"

*Psalm 118:22-23*

¹²The Jewish leaders knew that the story was about them. So they wanted to find a way to arrest Jesus, but they were afraid of the people. So the leaders left him and went away.

## THE LEADERS TRY TO TRAP JESUS

¹³Later, the Jewish leaders sent some Phariseesᵈ and some men from the group called Herodiansⁿ to Jesus. They wanted to catch Jesus saying something wrong. ¹⁴They came to him and said, "Teacher, we know that you are an honest man. You are not afraid of what other people think about you. All men are the same to you. And you teach the truth about God's

**"So I tell you to ask for things in prayer. And if you believe that you have received those things, then they will be yours."**

*Mark 11:24*

## DECODE THIS!

*If you are angry with someone, what should you do?*

11:26 **Verse 26** Some early Greek copies add verse 26: "But if you don't forgive other people, then your Father in heaven will not forgive your sins." 12:13 **Herodians** A political group that followed Herod and his family.

71

> "Love the Lord your God. Love him with all your heart, all your soul, all your mind, and all your strength."
>
> *Mark 12:30*

way. Tell us: Is it right to pay taxes to Caesar?[d] Should we pay them, or not?"

[15]But Jesus knew what these men were really trying to do. He said, "Why are you trying to trap me? Bring me a silver coin. Let me see it." [16]They gave Jesus a coin, and he asked, "Whose picture is on the coin? And whose name is written on it?"

They answered, "Caesar's."

[17]Then Jesus said to them, "Give to Caesar the things that are Caesar's. And give to God the things that are God's." The men were amazed at what Jesus said.

## SADDUCEES TRY TO TRICK JESUS

[18]Then some Sadducees[d] came to Jesus. (Sadducees believe that no person will rise from death.) The Sadducees asked Jesus a question. [19]They said, "Teacher, Moses wrote that a man's brother might die. He leaves a wife but no children. Then that man must marry the widow and have children for the dead brother.

[20]There were seven brothers. The first brother married but died. He had no children. [21]So the second brother married the widow. But he also died and had no children. The same thing happened with the third brother. [22]All seven brothers married her and died. None of the brothers had any children. The woman was last to die. [23]But all seven brothers had married her. So at the time people rise from death, whose wife will the woman be?"

[24]Jesus answered, "Why did you make this mistake? Is it because you don't know what the Scriptures[d] say? Or is it because you don't know about the power of God? [25]When people rise from death, there will be no marriage. People will not be married to each other but will be like angels in heaven. [26]Surely you have read what God said about people rising from death.

In the book in which Moses wrote about the burning bush,[n] it says that God told Moses this: 'I am the God of Abraham, the God of Isaac, and the God of Jacob.'[n] [27]God is the God of living people, not dead people. You Sadducees are wrong!"

## THE MOST IMPORTANT COMMAND

[28]One of the teachers of the law came to Jesus. He heard Jesus arguing with the Sadducees[d] and the Pharisees.[d] He saw that Jesus gave good answers to their questions. So he asked Jesus, "Which of the commands is most important?"

[29]Jesus answered, "The most important command is this: 'Listen, people of Israel! The Lord our God, he is the only Lord. [30]Love the Lord your God. Love him with all your heart, all your soul, all your mind, and all your strength.'[n] [31]The second most important command is this: 'Love your neighbor as you love yourself.'[n] These two commands are the most important commands."

[32]The man answered, "That was a good answer, Teacher. You were right when you said these things. God is the only

## Ways to Share Your Faith

1. By the way you play with your friends
2. By apologizing when you've offended someone
3. By the way you treat your siblings
4. By obeying your parents
5. By putting others first
6. By the way you spend your time
7. By giving more than getting
8. By knowing and telling what you believe
9. By using your time to serve others
10. By loving God's people

12:26 **burning bush** Read Exodus 3:1-12 in the Old Testament. 12:26 'I am . . . Jacob.' Quotation from Exodus 3:6. 12:29-30 'Listen . . . strength.' Quotation from Deuteronomy 6:4-5. 12:31 'Love . . . yourself.' Quotation from Leviticus 19:18.

72

Lord, and there is no other God besides him. [33]One must love God with all his heart, all his mind, and all his strength. And one must love his neighbor as he loves himself. These commands are more important than all the animals and sacrifices we offer to God."

[34]Jesus saw that the man answered him wisely. So Jesus said to him, "You are close to the kingdom of God." And after that, no one was brave enough to ask Jesus any more questions.

[35]Jesus was teaching in the Temple.[d] He asked, "Why do the teachers of the law say that the Christ[d] is the son of David? [36]David himself, speaking by the Holy Spirit,[d] said:

'The Lord said to my Lord:
Sit by me at my right side,
until I put your enemies
under your control.' *Psalm 110:1*

[37]David himself calls the Christ 'Lord.' So how can the Christ be David's son?" The large crowd listened to Jesus with pleasure.

[38]Jesus continued teaching. He said, "Beware of the teachers of the law. They like to walk around wearing clothes that look important. And they love for people to show respect to them in the marketplaces. [39]They love to have the most important seats in the synagogues.[d] And they love to have the most important seats at the feasts. [40]They cheat widows and steal their homes. Then they try to make themselves look good by saying long prayers. God will punish these people terribly."

## TRUE GIVING

[41]Jesus sat near the Temple[d] money box where people put their gifts. He watched the people put in their money. Many rich people gave large sums of money. [42]Then a poor widow came and gave two very small copper coins. These coins were not worth even a penny.

[43]Jesus called his followers to him. He said, "I tell you the truth. This poor widow gave only two small coins. But she really gave more than all those rich people. [44]The rich have plenty; they gave only what they did not need. This woman is very poor. But she gave all she had. And she needed that money to help her live."

## THE TEMPLE WILL BE DESTROYED

**13** Jesus was leaving the Temple.[d] One of his followers said to him, "Look, Teacher! This Temple has beautiful buildings with very big stones."

[2]Jesus said, "Do you see all these great buildings? Every stone will be thrown to the ground. Not one stone will be left on another."

[3]Later, Jesus was sitting on the Mount of Olives.[d] He was alone with Peter, James, John, and Andrew. They could all see the Temple. They asked Jesus, [4]"Tell us, when will all these things happen? And what will show us that the time has come for them to happen?"

[5]Jesus said to them: "Be careful that no one fools you. [6]Many people will come and use my name. They will say, 'I am the One.' And they will fool many. [7]You will hear about wars and stories of wars that are coming. But don't be afraid. These things must happen before the end comes. [8]Nations will fight against other nations. Kingdoms will fight against other kingdoms. There will be times when there is no food for people to eat. And there will be earthquakes in different places. These things are like the first pains when something new is about to be born.

[9]"You must be careful. People will arrest you and take you to court. They will beat you in their synagogues.[d] You will be forced to stand before kings and

# LIVIN' IT!

**THE BIG DEAL**
**MARK 12:42**

Two small coins! Big deal! Did you see what that guy gave in front of her? Now we're talking m-o-n-e-y!

But it wasn't the rich person's gift that caught Jesus' attention. His eyes were focused on the widow and her gift of 2 small coins. So why was Jesus so amazed? Everyone else who had given money only gave what they had left over. The poor widow had only those 2 coins to begin with. She needed that money in order to live, but she gave it anyway.

How we give shows what's going on in our hearts. If we hold back from what God has asked of us, we know we have placed people or things as more important than God in our lives, and we don't trust him to provide what we need. When we give with a joyful heart, it strengthens our trust and friendship with God and honors him.

governors, to tell them about me. This will happen to you because you follow me. [10]But before these things happen, the Good News[d] must be told to all people. [11]When you are arrested and judged, don't worry about what you should say. Say the things God gives you to say at that time. It will not really be you

**? DECODE THIS!**

*Who should you love as yourself?*

## BiBLe BASiCS

### WHAT iS THE LORD'S SUPPER?

The last night before Jesus' death, he had a special dinner for his disciples. He broke bread and offered a cup of wine to the 11 (Judas had already left), saying that his people should "drink his blood" and "eat his body." It might sound weird, but it was a way for his disciples to remember the special union they had in Christ through his death and resurrection. We still have communion today in obedience to Christ and to remember what he did for us on the cross.

speaking. It will be the Holy Spirit.[d]

12"Brothers will turn against their own brothers and give them over to be killed. Fathers will turn against their own children and give them over to be killed. Children will fight against their own parents and cause their parents to be killed. 13All people will hate you because you follow me. But the person

anything out of his house. 16If a person is in the field, he must not go back to get his coat. 17At that time, it will be hard for women who are pregnant or have nursing babies. 18Pray that these things will not happen in winter. 19This is because those days will be full of trouble. There will be more trouble than there has ever been since the begin-

ning, when God made the world. And nothing as bad will ever happen again. 20God has decided to make that terrible time short. If that time were not made short, then no one would go on living. But God will make that time short to help his special people whom he has chosen. 21At that time, someone might say to you, 'Look, there is the Christ!'[d] Or another person might say, 'There he is!' But don't believe them. 22False Christs and false prophets[d] will come and perform great wonders and miracles.[d] They will do these things to the people God has chosen. They will do these things to

25The stars will fall from the sky.
    And everything in the sky will be changed.'        *Isaiah 13:10; 34:4*

26"Then people will see the Son of Man[d] coming in clouds with great power and glory. 27The Son of Man will send his angels all around the earth. They will gather his chosen people from every part of the earth.

28"The fig tree teaches us a lesson: When its branches become green and soft, and new leaves begin to grow, then you know that summer is near. 29So also when you see all these things happening, then you will know that the time is near, ready to come. 30I tell you the truth. All these things will happen while the people of this time are still living. 31The whole world, earth and sky, will be destroyed, but the words I have said will never be destroyed.

32"No one knows when that day or time will be. The Son and the angels in heaven don't know. Only the Father knows. 33Be careful! Always be ready! You don't know when that time will be. 34It is like a man who goes on a trip. He leaves his house and lets his servants take care of it. He gives each servant a special job to do. One servant has the work of guarding the door. The man tells this servant always to be watchful.

> "Then people will see the Son of Man coming in clouds with great power and glory."
> *Mark 13:26*

who continues to be strong until the end will be saved.

14"You will see 'the horrible thing that destroys.'[n] You will see this thing standing in the place where it should not be." (You who read this should understand what it means.) "At that time, the people in Judea should run away to the mountains. 15If a person is on the roof[n] of his house, he must not go down to take

try to fool them, if that is possible. 23So be careful. For I have warned you about all this before it happens.

24"During the days after this trouble comes,

'The sun will grow
        dark.
    And the moon
        will not give
        its light.

This is what I am now telling you. 35You must always be ready. You don't know when the owner of the house will come back. He might come in the evening, or at midnight, or in the early morning, or when the sun rises. 36He might come

### ? DECODE THIS!

*Which apostle betrayed Jesus?*

13:14 'the horrible . . . destroys.' Mentioned in Daniel 9:27; 12:11 (cf. Daniel 11:31). 13:15 roof In Bible times houses were built with flat roofs. The roof was used for drying things such as flax and fruit. And it was used as an extra room, as a place for worship and as a place to sleep in the summer.

# GET CONNECTED

## PERFECT PLAN

The earth was dark and empty. No light. No trees. No life—just God. Know what was on his mind? You! God says that even before the world began, he knew every person who would one day become his child. He carefully planned the details of your life. When the right time came, he crafted you into the person you are. But you know what that means, don't you? You are not a mistake. Nothing about you is. Not even your parents or your brothers and sisters. God has placed you in your family for a special reason: Your family was the best way he could use to bring you closer to him.

back quickly. If you are always ready, then he will not find you sleeping. ³⁷I tell you this, and I say this to everyone: 'Be ready!'"

### THE PLAN TO KILL JESUS

**14** It was now only two days before the Passoverᵈ and the Feastᵈ of Unleavened Bread. The leading priests and teachers of the law were trying to find a way to use some trick to arrest Jesus and kill him. ²But they said, "We must not do it during the feast. The people might cause a riot."

### A WOMAN WITH PERFUME FOR JESUS

³Jesus was in Bethany. He was at dinner in the house of Simon, who had a harmful skin disease. While Jesus was there, a woman came to him. She had an alabasterᵈ jar filled with very expensive perfume, made of pure nard.ᵈ The woman opened the jar and poured the perfume on Jesus' head.

⁴Some of those who were there saw this and became angry. They complained to each other, saying, "Why waste that perfume? ⁵It was worth a full year's work. It could be sold, and the money could be given to the poor." They spoke to the woman sharply.

⁶Jesus said, "Don't bother the woman. Why are you troubling her? She did a beautiful thing for me. ⁷You will always

have the poor with you. You can help them anytime you want. But you will not always have me. ⁸This woman did the only thing she could do for me. She poured perfume on my body. She did this before I die to prepare me for

burial. ⁹I tell you the truth. The Good Newsᵈ will be told to people in all the world. And in every place it is preached, what this woman has done will be told. And people will remember her."

### JUDAS BECOMES AN ENEMY OF JESUS

¹⁰One of the 12 followers, Judas Iscariot, went to talk to the leading priests. Judas

offered to give Jesus to them. ¹¹The leading priests were pleased about this. They promised to pay Judas money. So he waited for the best time to give Jesus to them.

### JESUS EATS THE PASSOVER FEAST

¹²It was now the first day of the Feastᵈ of Unleavened Bread. This was a time when the Jews always sacrificed the Passoverᵈ lambs. Jesus' followers came to him. They said, "We will go and prepare everything for the Passover Feast. Where do you want to eat the feast?"

¹³Jesus sent two of his followers and said to them, "Go into the city. A man carrying a jar of water will meet you. Follow him. ¹⁴He will go into a house. Tell the owner of the house, 'The Teacher

> "i tell you the truth. The Good News will be told to people in all the world. And in every place it is preached, what this woman has done will be told. And people will remember her."
>
> Mark 14:9

asks that you show us the room where he and his followers can eat the Passover Feast.' ¹⁵The owner will show you a large room upstairs. This room is ready. Prepare the food for us there."

¹⁶So the followers left and went into the city. Everything happened as Jesus had said. So they prepared the Passover Feast.

¹⁷In the evening, Jesus went to that house with the 12. ¹⁸While they were all eating, Jesus said, "I tell you the truth. One of you will give me to my enemies—one of you eating with me now."

¹⁹The followers were very sad to hear this. Each one said to Jesus, "I am not the one, am I?"

²⁰Jesus answered, "The man who is against me is 1 of the 12. He is the 1 who dips his bread into the bowl with me. ²¹The Son of Manᵈ must go and die. The Scripturesᵈ say this will happen. But how

terrible it will be for the person who gives the Son of Man to be killed. It would be better for that person if he had never been born."

## THE LORD'S SUPPER

[22]While they were eating, Jesus took some bread. He thanked God for it and broke it. Then he gave it to his followers and said, "Take it. This bread is my body."

[23]Then Jesus took a cup. He thanked God for it and gave it to the followers. All the followers drank from the cup. [24]Then Jesus said, "This is my blood which begins the new agreement that God makes with his people. This blood is poured out for many. [25]I tell you the truth. I will not drink of this fruit of the vine[n] again until that day when I drink it new in the kingdom of God."

[26]They sang a hymn and went out to the Mount of Olives.[d]

**"This is my blood which begins the new agreement that God makes with his people. This blood is poured out for many."** *Mark 14:24*

## JESUS' FOLLOWERS WILL ALL LEAVE HIM

[27]Then Jesus told the followers, "You will all lose your faith in me. It is written in the Scriptures:[d]

'I will kill the shepherd,
  and the sheep will scatter.'

*Zechariah 13:7*

[28]But after I rise from death, I will go ahead of you into Galilee."

[29]Peter said, "All the other followers may lose their faith. But I will not."

[30]Jesus answered, "I tell you the truth. Tonight you will say you don't know me. You will say this three times before the rooster crows twice."

[31]But Peter answered strongly, "I will never say that I don't know you! I will even die with you!" And all the other followers said the same thing.

## JESUS PRAYS ALONE

[32]Jesus and his followers went to a place called Gethsemane. He said to his followers, "Sit here while I pray." [33]Jesus told Peter, James, and John to come with him. Then Jesus began to be very sad and troubled. [34]He said to them, "I am full of sorrow. My heart is breaking with sadness. Stay here and watch."

[35]Jesus walked a little farther away from them. Then he fell on the ground and prayed. He prayed that, if possible, he would not have this time of suffering. [36]He prayed, "Abba,[n] Father! You can do all things. Let me not have this cup[n] of suffering. But do what you want, not what I want."

[37]Then Jesus went back to his followers. He found them asleep. He said to Peter, "Simon, why are you sleeping? You could not stay awake with me for one hour? [38]Stay awake and pray that you will not be tempted. Your spirit wants to do what is right, but your body is weak."

[39]Again Jesus went away and prayed the same thing. [40]Then he went back to the followers. Again he found them asleep because their eyes were very heavy. And they did not know what to say to Jesus.

[41]After Jesus prayed a third time, he went back to his followers. He said to them, "You are still sleeping and resting? That's enough! The time has come for the Son of Man[d] to be given to sinful people. [42]Get up! We must go. Here comes the man who has turned against me."

## JESUS IS ARRESTED

[43]While Jesus was still speaking, Judas came up. Judas was 1 of the 12 followers. He had many people with him. They were sent from the leading priests, the teachers of the law, and the older Jewish leaders. Those with Judas had swords and clubs.

[44]Judas had planned a signal for them. He had said, "The man I kiss is Jesus. Arrest him and guard him while you lead him

## LIVIN' IT!

### OUR LIFELINE
### MARK 14:38

Have you ever wondered why Jesus prayed? Jesus said that he only did the things his Father told him to do. The many times we see Jesus waking up early in the morning, or escaping the crowds to pray, shows how important it was to Jesus to stay connected to the Father. Even in the Garden of Gethsemane, Jesus worked so hard in prayer that he sweated blood.

Prayer is not just a nice idea or something we do when we want God to give us something. It's the main way we stay connected with our heavenly Father, just like Jesus did. He gives us prayer to help us see the sin we need to confess. It also helps us do unseen work by lifting up other people's needs to God—as well as our own. Prayer keeps us listening to God's direction for our lives. The Bible says we should always be in an attitude of prayer to God.

## DECODE THIS!

*What happened to the high priest's servant at Jesus' arrest?*

14:25 **fruit of the vine** Product of the grapevine; this may also be translated "wine."
14:36 **Abba** Name that a child called his father. 14:36 **cup** Jesus is talking about the bad things that will happen to him. Accepting these things will be very hard, like drinking a cup of something that tastes very bitter.

> "He prayed, 'Abba Father! You can do all things. Let me not have this cup of suffering. But do what you want, not what i want.'"
>
> *Mark 14:36*

away." ⁴⁵So Judas went to Jesus and said, "Teacher!" and kissed him. ⁴⁶Then the men grabbed Jesus and arrested him. ⁴⁷One of the followers standing near drew his sword. He struck the servant of the high priest with the sword and cut off his ear.

⁴⁸Then Jesus said, "You came to get me with swords and clubs as if I were a criminal. ⁴⁹Every day I was with you teaching in the Temple.ᵈ You did not arrest me there. But all these things have happened to make the Scripturesᵈ come true." ⁵⁰Then all of Jesus' followers left him and ran away.

⁵¹A young man, wearing only a linen cloth, was following Jesus. The people also grabbed him. ⁵²But the cloth he was wearing came off, and he ran away naked.

## JESUS BEFORE THE LEADERS

⁵³The people who arrested Jesus led him to the house of the high priest. All the leading priests, the older Jewish leaders, and the teachers of the law were gathered there. ⁵⁴Peter followed far behind and entered the courtyard of the high priest's house. There he sat with the guards, warming himself by the fire.

⁵⁵The leading priests and all the Jewish council tried to find something that Jesus had done wrong so they could kill him. But the council could find no proof against him. ⁵⁶Many people came and told false things about him. But all said different things—none of them agreed.

⁵⁷Then some men stood up and lied about Jesus. They said, ⁵⁸"We heard this man say, 'I will destroy this Templeᵈ that men made. And three days later, I will build another Temple—a Temple not made by men.'" ⁵⁹But even the things these men said did not agree.

⁶⁰Then the high priest stood before them and said to Jesus, "Aren't you going to answer the charges these men bring against you?" ⁶¹But Jesus said nothing. He did not answer.

The high priest asked Jesus another question: "Are you the Christ,ᵈ the Son of the blessed God?"

⁶²Jesus answered, "I am. And in the future you will see the Son of Manᵈ sitting at the right side of the Powerful One. And you will see the Son of Man coming on clouds in the sky."

⁶³When the high priest heard this, he was very angry. He tore his clothes and said, "We don't need any more witnesses! ⁶⁴You all heard him say these things against God. What do you think?"

They all said that Jesus was guilty and should be killed. ⁶⁵Some of the people there spit at Jesus. They covered his eyes and hit him with their fists. They said, "Prove that you are a prophet!"ᵈ Then the guards led Jesus away and beat him.

## PETER SAYS HE DOESN'T KNOW JESUS

⁶⁶Peter was still in the courtyard when a servant girl of the high priest came

## GLOBAL INTERESTS

When Jesus went back to heaven, he told us to go into all of the world to tell others his Good News. So how many countries are in the whole world?

Right now there are 190 independent countries in the world, with Russia being the largest. Vatican City in Rome is less than a half mile wide, making it the smallest one. It might sound like we should have been able to get the gospel around to everybody by now, but don't let the numbers fool you. There are many more territories and groups that exist, but they are not yet considered independent countries. In addition, each year the number of independent countries changes as new ones are added to the list.

You may not be able to visit all the countries in the world, but you can pray for all of them. Pray for missionaries, too, who will leave home and try to reach all the peoples of the world.

[Yahooligans: Ask Earl]

there. ⁶⁷She saw Peter warming himself at the fire. She looked closely at him.

Then the girl said, "You were with Jesus, that man from Nazareth."

⁶⁸But Peter said that he was never with Jesus. He said, "I don't know or understand what you are talking about." Then Peter left and went toward the entrance of the courtyard."

⁶⁹The servant girl saw Peter there. Again she said to the people who were standing there, "This man is one of those who followed Jesus." ⁷⁰Again Peter said that it was not true.

A short time later, some people were standing near Peter. They said, "We

## "Some of the people there spit at Jesus. They covered his eyes and hit him with their fists." *Mark 14:65*

know you are one of those who followed Jesus. You are from Galilee, too."

⁷¹Then Peter began to curse. He said, "I swear that I don't know this man you're talking about!"

⁷²As soon as Peter said this, the rooster crowed the second time. Then Peter remembered what Jesus had told him: "Before the rooster crows twice, you will say three times that you don't know me." Then Peter was very sad and began to cry.

### PILATE QUESTIONS JESUS

**15** Very early in the morning, the leading priests, the older Jewish leaders, the teachers of the law, and all the Jewish council decided what to do with Jesus. They tied him, led him away, and turned him over to Pilate, the governor.

²Pilate asked Jesus, "Are you the king of the Jews?"

Jesus answered, "Yes, I am."

³The leading priests accused Jesus of many things. ⁴So Pilate asked Jesus

another question. He said, "You can see that these people are accusing you of many things. Why don't you answer?"

⁵But Jesus still said nothing. Pilate was very surprised at this.

### PILATE TRIES TO FREE JESUS

⁶Every year at the Passover*d* time the governor would free one person from prison. He would free any person the people wanted him to free. ⁷At that time, there was a man named Barabbas in prison. He was a rebel and had committed murder during a riot. ⁸The crowd came to Pilate and asked him to free a prisoner as he always did.

⁹Pilate asked them, "Do you want me to free the king of the Jews?" ¹⁰Pilate knew that the leading priests had given Jesus to him because they were jealous of Jesus. ¹¹And the leading priests had persuaded the people to ask Pilate to free Barabbas, not Jesus.

¹²Pilate asked the crowd again, "So what should I do with this man you call the king of the Jews?"

¹³They shouted, "Kill him on a cross!"

¹⁴Pilate asked, "Why? What wrong has he done?"

But they shouted louder and louder, "Kill him on a cross!"

¹⁵Pilate wanted to please the crowd. So he freed Barabbas for them. And Pilate told the soldiers to beat Jesus with whips. Then he gave Jesus to the soldiers to be killed on a cross.

¹⁶Pilate's soldiers took Jesus into the governor's palace (called the Praetorium). They called all the other

soldiers together. ¹⁷They put a purple robe on Jesus. Then they used thorny branches to make a crown. They put it on his head. ¹⁸Then they called out to him, "Hail, King of the Jews!" ¹⁹The soldiers beat Jesus on the head many times with a stick. They also spit on him. Then they made fun of him by bowing on their knees and worshiping him. ²⁰After they finished making fun of him, the soldiers took off the purple robe and put his own clothes on him again. Then they led Jesus out of the palace to be killed on a cross.

## LIVIN' iT!

### MISSION POSSIBLE
### MARK 16:15

Did you know that God created you just as you are and just where you live for a reason? Mark 16:15 tells us what that reason is: to share the Good News of Jesus' work on the cross and the hope of forgiveness and eternal life.

Look around you. Your neighbors. Your friends. Your family members. Is there anyone who doesn't belong to Jesus? Begin today to do the work of the Great Commission, right in your own bedroom. Begin praying for all the people God brings into your life who do not know God's love. Pray for chances to tell them the Good News. Then when the time comes, don't be shy. Tell them what an incredible gift God has for them. Invite them to your church to find out more. Discover the tremendous joy of working with God to build his kingdom.

---

 **14:68 Verse 68** Many Greek copies add: "And the rooster crowed."

## JESUS IS KILLED ON A CROSS

[21]There was a man from Cyrene coming from the fields to the city. The man was Simon, the father of Alexander and Rufus. The soldiers forced Simon to carry the cross for Jesus. [22]They led Jesus to the place called Golgotha. (Golgotha means the Place of the Skull.) [23]At Golgotha the soldiers tried to give Jesus wine to drink. This wine was mixed with myrrh.[d] But he refused to drink it. [24]The soldiers nailed Jesus to a cross. Then they divided his clothes among themselves. They threw lots[d] to decide which clothes each soldier would get.

[25]It was nine o'clock in the morning when they nailed Jesus to the cross. [26]There was a sign with the charge against Jesus written on it. The sign read: "THE KING OF THE JEWS." [27]They also put two robbers on crosses beside Jesus, one on the right, and the other on the left. [28] [n] [29]People walked by and

insulted Jesus. They shook their heads, saying, "You said you could destroy the Temple[d] and build it again in three days. [30]So save yourself! Come down from that cross!"

[31]The leading priests and the teachers of the law were also there. They made fun of Jesus just as the other people did. They said among themselves, "He saved other people, but he can't save himself. [32]If he is really the Christ,[d] the king of Israel, then let him come down from the cross now. We will see this, and then we will believe in him." The robbers who were being killed on the crosses beside Jesus also insulted him.

## JESUS DIES

[33]At noon the whole country became dark. This darkness lasted for three hours. [34]At three o'clock Jesus cried in a loud voice, "Eloi, Eloi, lama sabachthani." This means, "My God, my God, why have you left me alone?"

[35]Some of the people standing there heard this. They said, "Listen! He is calling Elijah."

[36]One man there ran and got a sponge. He filled the sponge with vinegar and tied it to a stick. Then he used the stick to give the sponge to Jesus to drink from it. The man said, "We should wait now and see if Elijah will come to take him down from the cross."

[37]Then Jesus cried in a loud voice and died.

[38]When Jesus died, the curtain in the Temple[n] split into two pieces. The tear started at the top and tore all the way

> **"Then Jesus cried in a loud voice and died."**
> Mark 15:37

to the bottom. [39]The army officer that was standing there before the cross saw what happened when Jesus died. The officer said, "This man really was the Son of God!"

[40]Some women were standing at a distance from the cross, watching. Some of these women were Mary Magdalene, Salome, and Mary the mother of James and Joseph. (James was her youngest son.) [41]These were the women who followed Jesus in Galilee and cared for him. Many other women were also there who had come with Jesus to Jerusalem.

> **"The army officer that was standing there before the cross saw what happened when Jesus died. The officer said, 'This man really was the Son of God!'"**
> Mark 15:39

## JESUS IS BURIED

[42]This was Preparation[d] Day. (That means the day before the Sabbath[d] day.) It was becoming dark. [43]A man named Joseph from Arimathea was brave enough to go to Pilate and ask for Jesus' body. Joseph was an important member of the Jewish council. He was one of the people who wanted the kingdom of God to come. [44]Pilate wondered if Jesus was already dead. Pilate called the army officer who guarded Jesus and asked him if Jesus had already died. [45]The officer told Pilate that he was dead. So Pilate told Joseph he could have the body. [46]Joseph bought some linen cloth, took the body down from the cross and wrapped it in the linen. He put the body in a tomb that was cut in a wall of rock. Then he closed the tomb by

**DECODE THIS!**
Whose tomb was Jesus buried in?

15:28 Verse 28 Some Greek copies add verse 28: "And the Scripture came true that says, 'They put him with criminals.'" 15:38 curtain in the Temple A curtain divided the Most Holy Place from the other part of the Temple. That was the special building in Jerusalem where God commanded the Jews to worship him.

rolling a very large stone to cover the entrance. ⁴⁷And Mary Magdalene and Mary the mother of Joseph saw the place where Jesus was laid.

## JESUS RISES FROM DEATH

**16** The day after the Sabbath^d day, Mary Magdalene, Mary the mother of James, and Salome bought some sweet-smelling spices to put on Jesus' body. ²Very early on that day, the first day of the week, the women were on their way to the tomb. It was soon after sunrise. ³They said to each other, "There is a large stone covering the entrance of the tomb. Who will move the stone for us?"

⁴Then the women looked and saw that the stone was already moved. The stone was very large, but it was moved away from the entrance. ⁵The women entered the tomb and saw a young man wearing a white robe. He was sitting on the right side, and the women were afraid.

> **"Don't be afraid. You are looking for Jesus from Nazareth, the one who was killed on a cross. He has risen from death."**
>
> *Mark 16:6*

⁶But the man said, "Don't be afraid. You are looking for Jesus from Nazareth, the one who was killed on a cross. He has risen from death. He is not here. Look, here is the place they laid him. ⁷Now go and tell his followers and Peter, 'Jesus is going into Galilee. He will be there before you. You will see him there as he told you before.'"

> **"Jesus said to the followers, 'Go everywhere in the world. Tell the Good News to everyone.'"** *Mark 16:15*

⁸The women were confused and shaking with fear. They left the tomb and ran away. They did not tell anyone about what happened, because they were afraid."

## SOME FOLLOWERS SEE JESUS

⁹Jesus rose from death early on the first day of the week. He showed himself first to Mary Magdalene. One time in the past, he had forced seven demons^d to leave Mary. ¹⁰After Mary saw Jesus, she went and told his followers. They were very sad and were crying. ¹¹But Mary told them that Jesus was alive. She said that she had seen him, but the followers did not believe her.

¹²Later, Jesus showed himself to two of his followers while they were walking in the country. But Jesus did not look the same as before. ¹³These followers went back to the others and told them what had happened. Again, the followers did not believe them.

## JESUS TALKS TO THE APOSTLES

¹⁴Later Jesus showed himself to the 11 followers while they were eating. He criticized them because they had little faith. They were stubborn and refused to believe those who had seen him after he had risen from death.

¹⁵Jesus said to the followers, "Go everywhere in the world. Tell the Good News^d to everyone. ¹⁶Anyone who believes and is baptized will be saved. But he who does not believe will be judged guilty. ¹⁷And those who believe will be able to do these things as proof: They will use my name to force demons^d out of people. They will speak in languages they never learned. ¹⁸They will pick up snakes without being hurt. And they will drink poison without being hurt. They will touch the sick, and the sick will be healed."

¹⁹After the Lord Jesus said these things to the followers, he was carried up into heaven. There, Jesus sat at the right side of God. ²⁰The followers went everywhere in the world and told the Good News to people. And the Lord helped them. The Lord proved that the Good News they told was true by giving them power to work miracles.^d

16:8 **Verse 8** Some early Greek copies end the book with verse 8.

DECODE THIS!
*Jesus wanted his followers to go to the world and tell what?*

# HIDE AND SEEK

You love the eggs, the candy, and the hunts—but how much do you know about the events that led to the first Easter? Test your Bible knowledge and see! Score a 9-10: Well done! You know the real reason for Easter! Score 7-8: Good, but seek a little harder for the truth. Score 5-6: Average—study the Gospels for better understanding. Score 4 or below: Eat less candy, and read a lot more!

**1.** We know Jesus was truly dead because

A. a soldier speared his side to make sure.

B. everyone around saw him die.

C. he was dead for 3 days.

D. all of the above.

**2.** When Jesus was dying on the cross, the soldiers standing below

A. played games to win his clothes.

B. made fun of him.

C. realized he was God.

D. all of the above.

**3.** How many women named Mary were at the foot of the cross?

A. 1

B. 2

C. 3

D. 4

HELLO
MY NAME IS
Mary ☺

**4.** How many of Jesus' bones were broken?

A. 1

B. 2

C. most of them

D. none of them

**5.** The name of the man who gave his tomb to Jesus was

A. John of Athens

B. Jacob of Nazareth

C. Joseph of Arimathea

D. Matthew of Judea

**6.** Jesus first appeared to

A. Peter

B. James

C. John

D. Mary Magdalene

**7.** Jesus rose from the dead on a

A. Friday

B. Saturday

C. Sunday

D. Monday

**8.** How did Jesus prove to Thomas he was alive?

A. He appeared to him.

B. He let him touch his wounds.

C. He told him it's even better to believe without seeing.

D. All of the above.

**9.** When Jesus left the earth, how did he go to heaven?

A. Angels came and got him.

B. He instantly disappeared.

C. He rose to the sky in a cloud.

D. A fiery chariot took him away.

**10.** Before he left, Jesus promised to give the disciples a gift. What was it?

A. money

B. God's Spirit

C. an easy life

D. new shoes

Luke served jail time with Paul.

Luke worked extra hard writing the story of Christ, beginning with the birth of John the Baptist.

# THE GOSPEL ACCORDING TO

# LUKE

Luke was probably not a Jew.

Look for the Lord's Prayer in chapter 11.

Paul calls Luke "the beloved physician."

Luke tells the non-Jews about Jesus.

## LUKE WRITES ABOUT JESUS' LIFE

**1** To Theophilus:
Many have tried to give a history of the things that happened among us. ²They have written the same things that we learned from others—the people who saw those things from the beginning and served God by telling people his message. ³I myself studied everything carefully from the beginning, your Excellency.ⁿ I thought I should write it out for you. So I put it in order in a book. ⁴I write these things so that you can know that what you have been taught is true.

# BiBLe BaSiCS

## WHAT iS THE GOOD NEWS?

It's easiest to understand the good news when you know what the bad news is. The bad news is that everyone is a sinner and deserves to die as the punishment for their sins. The good news is that Jesus took our punishment on himself when he died on the cross. If we believe he alone can save us from our sins and we give our lives to him, we will be forgiven and will live in heaven with him forever.

## ZECHARIAH AND ELIZABETH

⁵During the time Herod ruled Judea, there was a priest named Zechariah. He belonged to Abijah's group.ⁿ Zechariah's wife came from the family of Aaron. Her name was Elizabeth. ⁶Zechariah and Elizabeth truly did what God said was good. They did everything the Lord commanded and told people to do. They were without fault in keeping his law. ⁷But Zechariah and Elizabeth had no children. Elizabeth could not have a baby; and both of them were very old.

⁸Zechariah was serving as a priest before God for his group. It was his group's time to serve. ⁹According to the custom of the priests, he was chosen to go into the Temple*ᵈ* of the Lord and burn incense.*ᵈ* ¹⁰There were a great many people outside praying at the time the incense was offered. ¹¹Then, on the right side of the incense table, an angel of the Lord came and stood before Zechariah. ¹²When he saw the angel, Zechariah was confused and frightened. ¹³But the angel said to him, "Zechariah, don't be afraid. Your prayer has been heard by God. Your wife, Elizabeth, will give birth to a son. You will name him John. ¹⁴You will be very happy. Many people will be happy because of his birth. ¹⁵John will be a great man for the Lord. He will never drink wine or beer. Even at the time John is born, he will be filled with the Holy Spirit.*ᵈ* ¹⁶He will help many people of Israel return to the Lord their God. ¹⁷He himself will go first before the Lord. John will be powerful in spirit like Elijah. He will make peace between fathers and their children. He will bring those who are not obeying God back to the right way of thinking. He will make people ready for the coming of the Lord."

¹⁸Zechariah said to the angel, "How can I know that what you say is true? I am an old man, and my wife is old, too."

¹⁹The angel answered him, "I am Gabriel. I stand before God. God sent me to talk to you and to tell you this good news. ²⁰Now, listen! You will not be able to talk until the day these things happen. You will lose your speech because you did not believe what I told you. But these things will really happen."

²¹Outside, the people were still waiting for Zechariah. They were surprised that he was staying so long in the Temple. ²²Then Zechariah came outside, but he could not speak to them. So they knew that he had seen a vision in the Temple. Zechariah could not speak. He could only make signs to them. ²³When his time of service as a priest was finished, he went home.

²⁴Later, Zechariah's wife, Elizabeth, became pregnant. She did not go out of her house for five months. Elizabeth said, ²⁵"Look what the Lord has done for me! My people were ashamedⁿ of me, but now the Lord has taken away that shame."

## THE VIRGIN MARY

²⁶⁻²⁷During Elizabeth's sixth month of pregnancy, God sent the angel Gabriel to a virgin*ᵈ* who lived in Nazareth, a town in Galilee. She was engaged to marry a man named Joseph from the family of David. Her name was Mary. ²⁸The angel came to her and said, "Greetings! The Lord has blessed you and is with you."

> **"You will give birth to a son, and you will name him Jesus. He will be great, and people will call him the Son of the Most High."** *Luke 1:31-32*

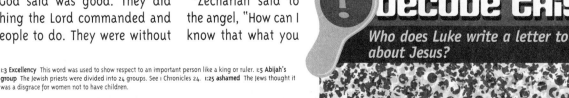

# DECODE THIS!

*Who does Luke write a letter to about Jesus?*

**1:3 Excellency** This word was used to show respect to an important person like a king or ruler. **1:5 Abijah's group** The Jewish priests were divided into 24 groups. See 1 Chronicles 24. **1:25 ashamed** The Jews thought it was a disgrace for women not to have children.

²⁹But Mary was very confused by what the angel said. Mary wondered, "What does this mean?"

³⁰The angel said to her, "Don't be afraid, Mary, because God is pleased with you. ³¹Listen! You will become pregnant. You will give birth to a son, and you will name him Jesus. ³²He will be great, and people will call him the Son of the Most High. The Lord God will give him the throne of King David, his ancestor. ³³He will rule over the people of Jacob forever. His kingdom will never end."

³⁴Mary said to the angel, "How will this happen? I am a virgin!"

³⁵The angel said to Mary, "The Holy Spirit[d] will come upon you, and the power of the Most High will cover you. The baby will be holy. He will be called the Son of God. ³⁶Now listen! Elizabeth, your relative, is very old. But she is also pregnant with a son. Everyone thought she could not have a baby, but she has been pregnant for six months. ³⁷God can do everything!"

³⁸Mary said, "I am the servant girl of the Lord. Let this happen to me as you say!" Then the angel went away.

> "You are blessed because you believed what the Lord said to you would really happen."
>
> *Luke 1:45*

### MARY'S VISIT

³⁹Mary got up and went quickly to a town in the mountains of Judea. ⁴⁰She went to Zechariah's house and greeted Elizabeth. ⁴¹When Elizabeth heard Mary's greeting, the unborn baby inside Elizabeth jumped. Then Elizabeth was filled with the Holy Spirit.[d] ⁴²She cried out in a loud voice, "God has blessed you more than any other woman. And God has blessed the baby which you will give birth to. ⁴³You are the mother of my Lord, and you have come to me! Why has something so good happened to me? ⁴⁴When I heard your voice, the baby inside me jumped with joy. ⁴⁵You are blessed because you believed what the Lord said to you would really happen."

### MARY PRAISES GOD

⁴⁶Then Mary said,
 "My soul praises the Lord;
⁴⁷    my heart is happy because
        God is my Savior.
⁴⁸I am not important, but God has
        shown his care for me, his
        servant girl.
 From now on, all people will say
        that I am blessed,
⁴⁹    because the Powerful One has
        done great things for me.
 His name is holy.
⁵⁰God will always give mercy
        to those who worship him.
⁵¹God's arm is strong.
 He scatters the people who
        are proud
 and think great things about
        themselves.
⁵²God brings down rulers from their
        thrones,
 and he raises up the humble.
⁵³God fills the hungry
        with good things,
 but he sends the rich
        away with nothing.

### DECODE THIS!

What did Elizabeth's unborn baby do when he heard Mary speak?

## TOP TEN

### Commandments to Remember

1. Love the Lord your God with all your heart.
2. Don't bow down to idols.
3. Don't take God's name in vain.
4. Keep the Sabbath holy.
5. Honor your father and mother.
6. Don't kill.
7. Stay with the one to whom you are married.
8. Don't take anything that doesn't belong to you.
9. Don't lie.
10. Don't covet (want what your neighbor has).

⁵⁴God has helped his people Israel who
        serve him.
 He gave them his mercy.
⁵⁵God has done what he promised to
        our ancestors,
        to Abraham and to his children
        forever."
⁵⁶Mary stayed with Elizabeth for about three months and then returned home.

### THE BIRTH OF JOHN

⁵⁷When it was time for Elizabeth to give birth, she had a boy. ⁵⁸Her neighbors and relatives heard how good the Lord was to her, and they rejoiced.

⁵⁹When the baby was eight days old, they came to circumcise[d] him. They

wanted to name him Zechariah because this was his father's name. ⁶⁰But his mother said, "No! He will be named John."

⁶¹The people said to Elizabeth, "But no one in your family has this name!" ⁶²Then they made signs to his father, "What would you like to name him?" ⁶³Zechariah asked for something to write on. Then he wrote, "His name is John." Everyone was surprised. ⁶⁴Then Zechariah could talk again. He began to praise God. ⁶⁵And all their neighbors became alarmed. In all the mountains of Judea people continued talking about all these things. ⁶⁶The people who heard about these things wondered about them. They thought, "What will this child be?" They said this because the Lord was with him.

## ZECHARIAH PRAISES GOD

⁶⁷Then Zechariah, John's father, was filled with the Holy Spirit.ᵈ He told the people what would happen:
⁶⁸"Let us thank the Lord, the God
  of Israel.
  God has come to help his people
    and has given them freedom.
⁶⁹God has given us a powerful Savior
  from the family of God's servant
  David.
⁷⁰God said that he would do this.
  He said it through his holy
    prophetsᵈ who lived long ago.
⁷¹God will save us from our enemies
  and from the power of all those
    who hate us.
⁷²God said he would give mercy to
  our fathers.
  And he remembered his holy
    promise.
⁷³God promised Abraham, our father,
⁷⁴  that he would free us from the
    power of our enemies,
  so that we could serve him
    without fear.

⁷⁵We will be righteous and holy before
  God as long as we live.

⁷⁶"Now you, child, will be called a
    prophet of the Most High God.
  You will go first before the Lord
    to prepare the people for his
    coming.
⁷⁷You will make his people know that
    they will be saved.
  They will be saved by having
    their sins forgiven.
⁷⁸With the loving mercy of our God,
  a new day from heaven will
    shine upon us.
⁷⁹God will help those who live in
    darkness,
  in the fear of death.
  He will guide us into the path that
    goes toward peace."
⁸⁰And so the child grew up and became strong in spirit. John lived away from other people until the time when he came out to preach to Israel.

## THE BIRTH OF JESUS

**2** At that time, Augustus Caesarᵈ sent an order to all people in the countries that were under Roman rule. The order said that they must list their names in a register. ²This was the first registrationⁿ taken while Quirinius was governor of Syria. ³And everyone went to their own towns to be registered.

⁴So Joseph left Nazareth, a town in Galilee. He went to the town of Bethlehem in Judea. This town was known as the town of David. Joseph went there because he was from the family of David. ⁵Joseph registered with Mary because she was engaged to marry him. (Mary was now pregnant.) ⁶While Joseph and Mary were in Bethlehem, the time came for her to have the baby. ⁷She gave birth to her first son. There were no rooms left in the inn. So she wrapped the baby with cloths and laid him in a box where animals are fed.

> "All the angels were praising God saying, 'Give glory to God in heaven, and on earth let there be peace to the people who please God.'"
>
> *Luke 2:13-14*

## SOME SHEPHERDS HEAR ABOUT JESUS

⁸That night, some shepherds were in the fields nearby watching their sheep. ⁹An angel of the Lord stood before them. The glory of the Lord was shining around them, and suddenly they became very frightened. ¹⁰The angel said to them, "Don't be afraid, because I am bringing you some good news. It will be a joy to all the people. ¹¹Today your Savior was born in David's town. He is Christ,ᵈ the Lord. ¹²This is how you will know him: You will find a baby wrapped in cloths and lying in a feeding box."

¹³Then a very large group of angels from heaven joined the first angel. All the angels were praising God, saying:
¹⁴"Give glory to God in heaven,
  and on earth let there be peace to
    the people who please God."

¹⁵Then the angels left the shepherds and went back to heaven. The shepherds said to each other, "Let us go to Bethlehem and see this thing that has happened. We will see this thing the Lord told us about."

¹⁶So the shepherds went quickly and found Mary and Joseph. ¹⁷And the

2:2 **registration** Census. A counting of all the people and the things they own.

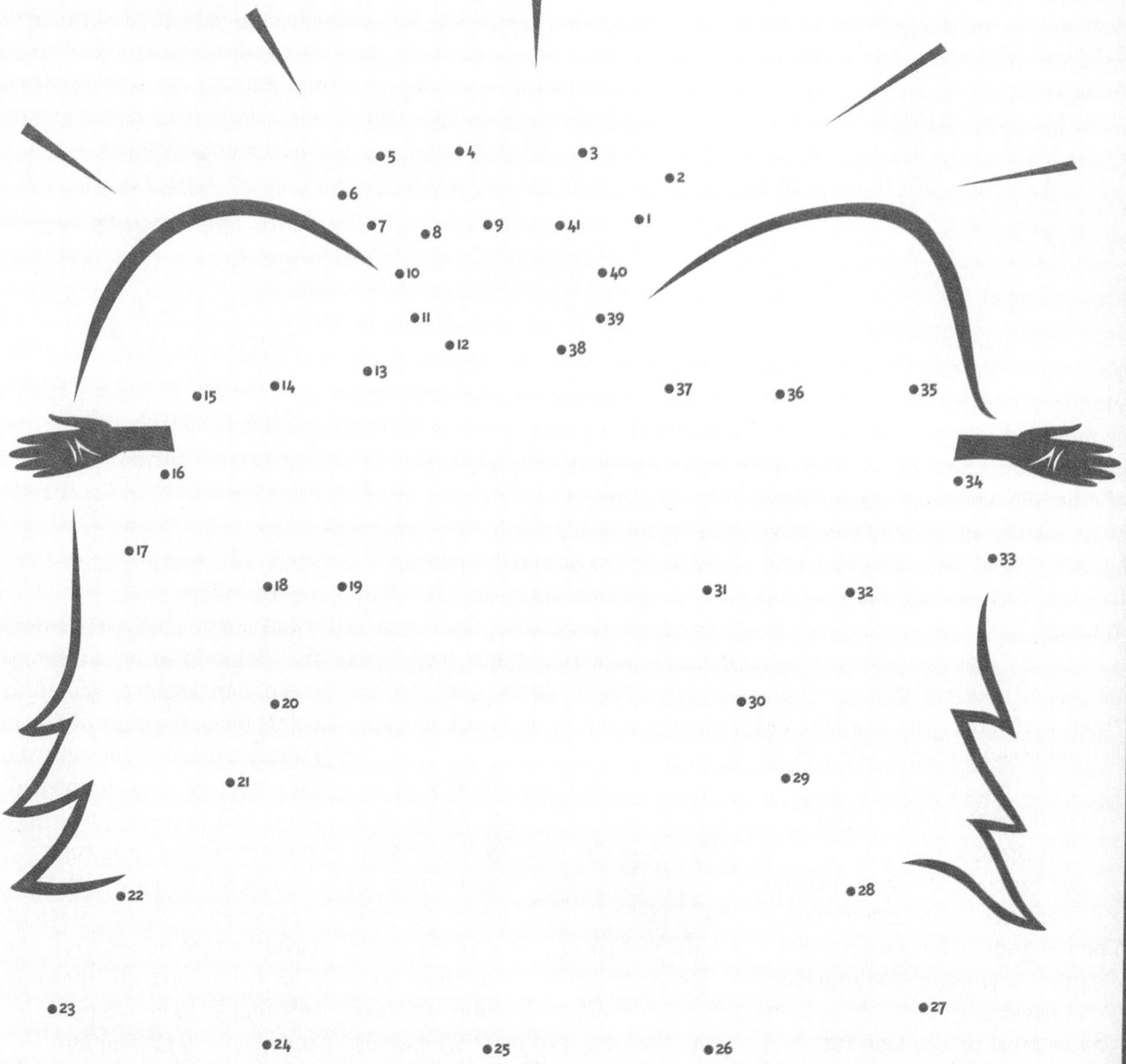

•5  •4  •3
•2
•6
•7  •8  •9  •41  •1
•10  •40
•11  •39
•12  •38
•13  •37  •36  •35
•15  •14
•16  •34
•17  •33
•18  •19  •31  •32
•20  •30
•21  •29
•22  •28
•23  •27
•24  •25  •26

**WRITE OUT THE VERSE AND CONNECT THE DOTS.**

## LUKE 2:10

_____

_____

_____

_____

_____

# GET CONNECTED

## BEST FRIENDS FOR LIFE

They were there when you were born. Stayed up with you through countless nights. Fed you, changed your diapers, played silly games with you, and watched you grow. Your parents know more about you than you do, and if they're like most parents, they love you more than you'll ever know. Your parents are a precious gift from God.

So don't take his gift and throw it away. Don't reject it because it's not "cool." If you let them, your parents can become your very best friends, who will encourage you and love you through the rest of your life.

*Best Friends*

shepherds saw the baby lying in a feeding box. Then they told what the angels had said about this child. [18]Everyone was amazed when they heard what the shepherds said to them. [19]Mary hid these things in her heart; she continued to think about them. [20]Then the shepherds went back to their sheep, praising God and thanking him for everything that they had seen and heard. It was just as the angel had told them.

[21]When the baby was eight days old, he was circumcised,[d] and he was named Jesus. This name had been given by the angel before the baby began to grow inside Mary.

## JESUS IS PRESENTED IN THE TEMPLE

[22]The time came for Mary and Joseph to do what the law of Moses taught about being made pure.[n] They took Jesus to Jerusalem to present him to the Lord. [23]It is written in the law of the Lord: "Give every firstborn[d] male to the Lord."[n] [24]Mary and Joseph also went to offer a sacrifice, as the law of

the Lord says: "You must sacrifice two doves or two young pigeons."[n]

## SIMEON SEES JESUS

[25]A man named Simeon lived in Jerusalem. He was a good man and very religious. He was waiting for the time when God would help Israel. The Holy Spirit[d] was in him. [26]The Holy Spirit told Simeon that he would not die before he saw the Christ[d] promised by the Lord. [27]The Spirit led Simeon to the Temple.[d] Mary and Joseph brought the baby Jesus to the Temple to do what the law said they must do. [28]Then

Simeon took the baby in his arms and thanked God:
[29]"Now, Lord, you can let me, your servant,
    die in peace as you said.
        [30]I have seen your
            Salvation[n] with my
            own eyes.

[31]    You prepared him before all people.
[32]He is a light for the non-Jewish people to see.
    He will bring honor to your people, the Israelites."

[33]Jesus' father and mother were amazed at what Simeon had said about him. [34]Then Simeon blessed them and said to Mary, "Many in Israel will fall and many will rise because of this child. He will be a sign from God that many people will not accept. [35]The things they think in secret will be made known. And the things that will happen will make your heart sad, too."

## ANNA SEES JESUS

[36]Anna, a prophetess,[d] was there at the Temple.[d] She was from the family of Phanuel in the tribe[d] of Asher. Anna was very old. She had once been married for seven years. [37]Then her husband died and she lived alone. She was now 84 years old. Anna never left the Temple. She worshiped God by going without food and praying day and night. [38]She was standing there at that time, thanking God. She talked about Jesus to all who were waiting for God to free Jerusalem.

> "i have seen your Salvation with my own eyes." *Luke 2:30*

## JOSEPH AND MARY RETURN HOME

[39]Joseph and Mary finished doing everything that the law of the Lord commanded. Then they went home to Nazareth, their own town in Galilee. [40]The little child began to grow up. He became stronger and wiser, and God's blessings were with him.

# DECODE THIS!

*Who sent the order that all people had to register?*

2:22 **pure** The law of Moses said that 40 days after a Jewish woman gave birth to a baby, she must be cleansed by a ceremony at the Temple. Read Leviticus 12:2–8. 2:23 **"Give . . . Lord."** Quotation from Exodus 13:2. 2:24 **"You . . . pigeons."** Quotation from Leviticus 12:8. 2:30 **Salvation** Simeon was talking about Jesus. The name Jesus means "salvation."

### JESUS AS A BOY

⁴¹Every year Jesus' parents went to Jerusalem for the Passover[d] Feast. ⁴²When Jesus was 12 years old, they went to the feast as they always did. ⁴³When the feast days were over, they went home. The boy Jesus stayed behind in Jerusalem, but his parents did not know it. ⁴⁴Joseph and Mary traveled for a whole day. They thought that Jesus was with them in the group. Then they began to look

> **"All who heard him were amazed at his understanding and wise answers."** *Luke 2:47*

for him among their family and friends, ⁴⁵but they did not find him. So they went back to Jerusalem to look for him there. ⁴⁶After three days they found him. Jesus was sitting in the Temple[d] with the religious teachers, listening to them and asking them questions. ⁴⁷All who heard him were amazed at his understanding and wise answers. ⁴⁸When Jesus' parents saw him, they were amazed. His mother said to him, "Son, why did you do this to us? Your father and I were very worried about you. We have been looking for you."

⁴⁹Jesus asked, "Why did you have to look for me? You should have known that I must be where my Father's work is!" ⁵⁰But they did not understand the meaning of what he said.

⁵¹Jesus went with them to Nazareth and obeyed them. His mother was still thinking about all that had happened. ⁵²Jesus continued to learn more and more and to grow physically. People liked him, and he pleased God.

### THE PREACHING OF JOHN

**3** It was the fifteenth year of the rule of Tiberius Caesar.[d] These men were under Caesar: Pontius Pilate was the ruler of Judea. Herod was the ruler of Galilee. Philip, Herod's brother, was the ruler of Iturea and Trachonitis. And Lysanias was the ruler of Abilene. ²Annas and Caiaphas were the high priests. At this time, a command from God came to John son of Zechariah. John was living in the desert. ³He went all over the area around the Jordan River and preached to the people. He preached a baptism of changed hearts and lives for the forgiveness of their sins. ⁴As it is written in the book of Isaiah the prophet:[d]

"This is a voice of a man
  who calls out in the desert:

'Prepare the way for the Lord.
  Make the road straight for him.
⁵Every valley should be filled in.
  Every mountain and hill should be made flat.
Roads with turns should be made straight,
  and rough roads should be made smooth.
⁶And all people will know about the salvation of God!'" *Isaiah 40:3-5*

⁷Crowds of people came to be baptized by John. He said to them, "You poisonous snakes! Who warned you to run away from God's anger that is coming? ⁸You must do the things that will show that you really have changed your hearts. Don't say, 'Abraham is our father.' I tell you that God can make children for Abraham from these rocks here. ⁹The ax is now ready to cut down the

## HOPPY MEALS

John the Baptist was known for his unusual diet of honey and locusts. Of course, that might not sound so bad—until you hear what locusts are.

Locusts are a kind of grasshopper. In fact, they actually look the same as grasshoppers, but they act differently. Grasshoppers like to live alone. Sometimes locusts live alone, but when they get together, everything changes. Their body shape and color, where and how they migrate, even how they reproduce changes. They join together into a swarm and eat so much that they can destroy entire crops.

So maybe it's a good thing John ate them. (Might have even cut down on the swarming problem.) Whenever your mom cooks something you don't like, just remember what John ate. It could always be worse.

[Australian Government: Department of Agriculture, Fisheries, & Forestry]

> **"You are my Son and i love you. i am very pleased with you."** *Luke 3:22*

trees. Every tree that does not produce good fruit will be cut down and thrown into the fire."[n]

[10]The people asked John, "What should we do?"

[11]John answered, "If you have two shirts, share with the person who does not have one. If you have food, share that too."

[12]Even tax collectors came to John to be baptized. They said to John, "Teacher, what should we do?"

[13]John said to them, "Don't take more taxes from people than you have been ordered to take."

[14]The soldiers asked John, "What about us? What should we do?"

John said to them, "Don't force people to give you money. Don't lie about them. Be satisfied with the pay you get."

[15]All the people were hoping for the Christ[d] to come, and they wondered about John. They thought, "Maybe he is the Christ."

[16]John answered everyone, "I baptize you with water, but there is one coming later who can do more than I can. I am not good enough to untie his sandals. He will baptize you with the Holy Spirit[d] and with fire. [17]He will come ready to clean the grain. He will separate the good grain from the chaff.[d] He will put the good part of the grain into his barn. Then he will burn the chaff with a fire that cannot be put out."[n] [18]And John continued to preach the Good News,[d] saying many other things

to encourage the people.

[19]But John spoke against Herod, the governor, because of his sin with Herodias, the wife of Herod's brother. John also criticized Herod for the many other evil things Herod did. [20]So Herod did another evil thing: He put John in prison.

## JESUS IS BAPTIZED BY JOHN

[21]When all the people were being baptized by John, Jesus also was baptized. While Jesus was praying, heaven opened and [22]the Holy Spirit[d] came down on him. The Spirit was in the form of a dove. Then a voice came from heaven and said, "You are my Son and I love you. I am very pleased with you."

## THE FAMILY HISTORY OF JESUS

[23]When Jesus began to teach, he was about 30 years old. People thought that Jesus was Joseph's son. Joseph was the son[n] of Heli. [24]Heli was the son of Matthat. Matthat was the son of Levi. Levi was the son of Melki. Melki was the son of Jannai. Jannai was the son of Joseph. [25]Joseph was the son of Mattathias. Mattathias was the son of Amos.

Amos was the son of Nahum. Nahum was the son of Esli. Esli was the son of Naggai. [26]Naggai was the son of Maath. Maath was the son of Mattathias. Mattathias was the son of Semein. Semein was the son of Josech. Josech was the son of Joda. [27]Joda was the son of Joanan. Joanan was the son of Rhesa. Rhesa was the son of Zerubbabel. Zerubbabel was the grandson of Shealtiel. Shealtiel was the son of Neri. [28]Neri was the son of Melchi. Melchi was the son of Addi. Addi was the son of Cosam. Cosam was the son of Elmadam. Elmadam was the son of Er. [29]Er was the son of Joshua. Joshua was the son of Eliezer. Eliezer was the son of Jorim. Jorim was the son of Matthat. Matthat was the son of Levi. [30]Levi was the son of Simeon. Simeon was the son of Judah. Judah was the son of Joseph. Joseph was the son of Jonam. Jonam was the son of Eliakim. [31]Eliakim was the son of Melea. Melea was the son of Menna. Menna was the son of Mattatha. Mattatha was the son of Nathan. Nathan was the son of David. [32]David was the son of Jesse. Jesse was the son of Obed. Obed was the son of Boaz. Boaz was the son of Salmon.

## JESUS' FAMILY TREE

## DECODE THIS!

Who were the two people who saw baby Jesus in the temple?

**3:9 The ax . . . fire.** This means that God is ready to punish his people who do not obey him. **3:17 He will . . . out.** This means that Jesus will come to separate the good people from the bad people, saving the good and punishing the bad. **3:23 son** "Son" in Jewish lists of ancestors can sometimes mean grandson or more distant relative.

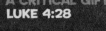

Salmon was the son of Nahshon.
[33]Nahshon was the son of Amminadab.
Amminadab was the son of Admin.
Admin was the son of Arni.
Arni was the son of Hezron.
Hezron was the son of Perez.
Perez was the son of Judah.
[34]Judah was the son of Jacob.
Jacob was the son of Isaac.
Isaac was the son of Abraham.
Abraham was the son of Terah.
Terah was the son of Nahor.
[35]Nahor was the son of Serug.
Serug was the son of Reu.
Reu was the son of Peleg.
Peleg was the son of Eber.
Eber was the son of Shelah.
[36]Shelah was the son of Cainan.
Cainan was the son of Arphaxad.
Arphaxad was the son of Shem.
Shem was the son of Noah.
Noah was the son of Lamech.
[37]Lamech was the son of Methuselah.
Methuselah was the son of Enoch.
Enoch was the son of Jared.
Jared was the son of Mahalalel.
Mahalalel was the son of Kenan.
[38]Kenan was the son of Enosh.
Enosh was the son of Seth.
Seth was the son of Adam.
Adam was the son of God.

## JESUS IS TEMPTED BY THE DEVIL

**4** Jesus, filled with the Holy Spirit,[d] returned from the Jordan River. The Spirit led Jesus into the desert [2]where the devil tempted Jesus for 40 days. Jesus ate nothing during that time. When those days were ended, he was very hungry.

### "Jesus answered,...'A person does not live only by eating bread.'"
*Luke 4:4*

[3]The devil said to Jesus, "If you are the Son of God, tell this rock to become bread."

[4]Jesus answered, "It is written in the Scriptures:[d] 'A person does not live only by eating bread.'"[n]

[5]Then the devil took Jesus and showed him all the kingdoms of the world in a moment of time. [6]The devil said to Jesus, "I will give you all these kingdoms and all their power and glory. It has all been given to me, and I can give it to anyone I wish. [7]If you worship me, all will be yours."

[8]Jesus answered, "It is written in the Scriptures: 'You must worship the Lord your God. Serve only him!'"[n]

[9]Then the devil led Jesus to Jerusalem and put him on a high place of the Temple.[d] He said to Jesus, "If you are the Son of God, jump off! [10]It is written in the Scriptures:

'He has put his angels in charge of you.
    They will watch over you.'
*Psalm 91:11*

[11]'They will catch you with their hands.
    And you will not hit your foot on
    a rock.'"    *Psalm 91:12*

[12]Jesus answered, "But it also says in the Scriptures: 'Do not test the Lord your God.'"[n]

[13]After the devil had tempted Jesus in every way, he went away to wait until a better time.

## JESUS TEACHES THE PEOPLE

[14]Jesus went back to Galilee with the power of the Holy Spirit.[d] Stories about Jesus spread all through the area. [15]He

began to teach in the synagogues,[d] and all the people praised him.

[16]Jesus traveled to Nazareth, where he had grown up. On the Sabbath[d] day he went to the synagogue as he always did. Jesus stood up to read. [17]The book of Isaiah the prophet[d] was given to him. He opened the book and found the place where this is written:

[18]"The Spirit of the Lord is in me.
    This is because God chose me to
        tell the Good News[d] to the poor.
God sent me to tell the prisoners of
        sin that they are free,
    and to tell the blind that they
        can see again.    *Isaiah 61:1*

### LIVIN' IT!

**A CRITICAL GIFT**
**LUKE 4:28**

Jesus wasn't telling them anything they didn't already know. Really, he was just giving them a history lesson, reminding them how Israel had always treated her prophets so badly. But the Pharisees and Jewish leaders got his point. He was talking about them, showing their sinful hearts. And they got mad—so mad that they wanted to kill Jesus.

It's never easy to hear someone tell us we're doing something wrong. We would rather make them be quiet or ignore them than think about what they are saying. But God wants us to have teachable, humble hearts. If we can remember that we are sinners who need correction, then we won't be so surprised when we hear we've done something wrong. We can be thankful that someone cared enough to show us our sin. Then we can confess it, repent, and grow even closer to Jesus.

4:4 'A person . . . bread.' Quotation from Deuteronomy 8:3.  4:8 'You . . . him!' Quotation from Deuteronomy 6:13.  4:12 'Do . . . God.' Quotation from Deuteronomy 6:16.

God sent me to free those who have
been treated unfairly,

*Isaiah 58:6*

[19] and to announce the time when
the Lord will show kindness to
his people."

*Isaiah 61:2*

[20]Jesus closed the book, gave it back, and sat down. Everyone in the synagogue was watching Jesus closely. [21]He began to speak to them. He said, "While you heard these words just now, they were coming true!"

[22]All the people praised Jesus. They were amazed at the beautiful words he spoke. They asked, "Isn't this Joseph's son?"

[23]Jesus said to them, "I know that you will tell me the old saying: 'Doctor, heal yourself.' You want to say, 'We heard about the things you did in Capernaum. Do those things here in your own town!'" [24]Then Jesus said, "I tell you the truth. A prophet is not accepted in his own town. [25]What I say is true. During the time of Elijah it did not rain in Israel for three and a half years. There was no food anywhere in the whole country. And there were many widows in Israel during that time. [26]But Elijah was sent to none of those widows. He was sent only to a widow in Zarephath, a town in Sidon. [27]And there were many with a harmful skin disease living in Israel during the time of the prophet Elisha. But none of them were healed except Naaman, who was from the country of Syria."

[28]When all the people in the synagogue heard these things, they became very angry. [29]They got up and forced Jesus out of town. The town was built on a hill. They took Jesus to the edge of the hill and wanted to throw

him off. [30]But Jesus walked through the crowd and went on his way.

## JESUS REMOVES AN EVIL SPIRIT

[31]Jesus went to Capernaum, a city in Galilee. On the Sabbath[d] day, Jesus taught the people. [32]They were amazed at his teaching, because he spoke with authority. [33]In the synagogue[d] there was a man who had an evil spirit from the devil inside him. The man shouted in a loud voice, [34]"Jesus of Nazareth! What do you want with us? Did you come here to destroy us? I know who you are—God's Holy One!"

[35]But Jesus warned the evil spirit to stop. He said, "Be quiet! Come out of the man!" The evil spirit threw the man down to the ground before all the people. Then the evil spirit left the man and did not hurt him.

[36]The people were amazed. They said to each other, "What does this mean? With authority and power he commands evil spirits, and they come out." [37]And so the news about Jesus spread to every place in the whole area.

## JESUS HEALS MANY PEOPLE

[38]Jesus left the synagogue[d] and went to Simon's[n] house. Simon's mother-in-law was very sick with a high fever. They asked Jesus to do something to help her. [39]He stood very close to her and commanded the fever to leave. It left her immediately, and she got up and began serving them.

[40]When the sun went down, the people brought their sick to Jesus. They had many different diseases. Jesus put his hands on each sick

person and healed every one of them. [41]Demons[d] came out of many people. The demons would shout, "You are the Son of God." But Jesus gave a strong command for the demons not to speak. They knew Jesus was the Christ.[d]

[42]At daybreak, Jesus went to a place to be alone, but the people looked for him. When they found him, they tried to keep him from leaving. [43]But Jesus said to them, "I must tell the Good News[d] about God's kingdom to other towns, too. This is why I was sent."

[44]Then Jesus kept on preaching in the synagogues[d] of Judea.

> **"What does this mean? With authority and power he commands evil spirits, and they come out."**
>
> *Luke 4:36*

## JESUS' FIRST FOLLOWERS

**5** One day Jesus was standing beside Lake Galilee. Many people were pressing all around him. They wanted to hear the word of God. [2]Jesus saw two boats at the shore of the lake. The fishermen had left them and were

## DECODE THIS!

*In what form did the Holy Spirit come down at Jesus' baptism?*

4:38 Simon Simon's other name was Peter.

washing their nets. ³Jesus got into one of the boats, the one which belonged to Simon." Jesus asked Simon to push off a little from the land. Then Jesus sat down in the boat and continued to teach the people on the shore.

⁴When Jesus had finished speaking, he said to Simon, "Take the boat into deep water. If you will put your nets in the water, you will catch some fish."

⁵Simon answered, "Master, we worked hard all night trying to catch fish, but we caught nothing. But you say to put the nets in the water; so I will." ⁶The fishermen did as Jesus told them. And they caught so many fish that the nets began to break. ⁷They called to their friends in the other boat to come and help them. The friends came, and both boats were filled so full that they were almost sinking.

⁸⁻⁹The fishermen were all amazed at the many fish they caught. When Simon Peter saw what had happened, he bowed down before Jesus and said, "Go away from me, Lord. I am a sinful man!" ¹⁰James and John, the sons of Zebedee, were amazed too. (James and John were Simon's partners.) Jesus said to Simon, "Don't be afraid.

> **"The fishermen did as Jesus told them. And they caught so many fish that the nets began to break."** *Luke 5:6*

From now on you will be fishermen for men." ¹¹When the men brought their boats to the shore, they left everything and followed Jesus.

## JESUS HEALS A SICK MAN

¹²One time Jesus was in a town where a very sick man lived. The man was

**Q. What is one of the worst foods you've ever tasted?**

**A. Liver**

covered with a harmful skin disease. When he saw Jesus, he bowed before Jesus and begged him, "Lord, heal me. I know you can if you want to."

¹³Jesus said, "I want to. Be healed!" And Jesus touched the man. Immediately the disease disappeared. ¹⁴Then Jesus said, "Don't tell anyone about what happened. But go show yourself to the priest." And offer a gift to God for your healing as Moses commanded." This will prove to everyone that you are healed."

¹⁵But the news about Jesus was spreading more and more. Many people came to hear Jesus and to be healed of their sicknesses. ¹⁶But Jesus often slipped away to other places to be alone so that he could pray.

## JESUS HEALS A PARALYZED MAN

¹⁷One day Jesus was teaching the people. The Pharisees⁴ and teachers of the law were there, too. They had come from every town in Galilee and from Judea and Jerusalem. The Lord was giving Jesus the power to heal people. ¹⁸There was a man who was paralyzed. Some men were carrying him

on a mat. They tried to bring him in and put him down before Jesus. ¹⁹But because there were so many people there, they could not find a way to Jesus. So the men went up on the roof and made a hole in the ceiling. They lowered the mat so that the paralyzed man was lying right before Jesus. ²⁰Jesus saw that these men believed. So he said to the sick man, "Friend, your sins are forgiven."

²¹The Jewish teachers of the law and the Pharisees thought to themselves, "Who is this man? He is saying things that are against God! Only God can forgive sins."

²²But Jesus knew what they were thinking. He said, "Why do you have thoughts like that in your hearts? ²³Which is easier: to tell this paralyzed man, 'Your sins are forgiven,' or to tell him, 'Stand up and walk'? ²⁴But I will prove to you that the Son of Man⁴ has authority on earth to forgive sins." So Jesus said to the paralyzed man, "I tell you, stand up! Take your mat and go home."

²⁵Then the man stood up before the people there. He picked up his mat and went home, praising God. ²⁶All the people were fully amazed and began to praise God. They were filled with much respect and said, "Today we have seen amazing things!"

## LEVI FOLLOWS JESUS

²⁷After this, Jesus went out and saw a tax collector named Levi sitting in the tax office. Jesus said to him, "Follow me!" ²⁸Levi got up, left everything, and followed Jesus.

²⁹Then Levi gave a big dinner for Jesus. The dinner was at Levi's house. At the table there were many tax

**DECODE THIS!**
*The man in Capernaum that Jesus healed had what?*

**5:3 Simon** Simon's other name was Peter. **5:14 show . . . priest** The law of Moses said a priest must say when a Jew with a harmful skin disease was well. **5:14 Moses commanded** Read about this in Leviticus 14:1-32.

# A SAVIOR IS BORN

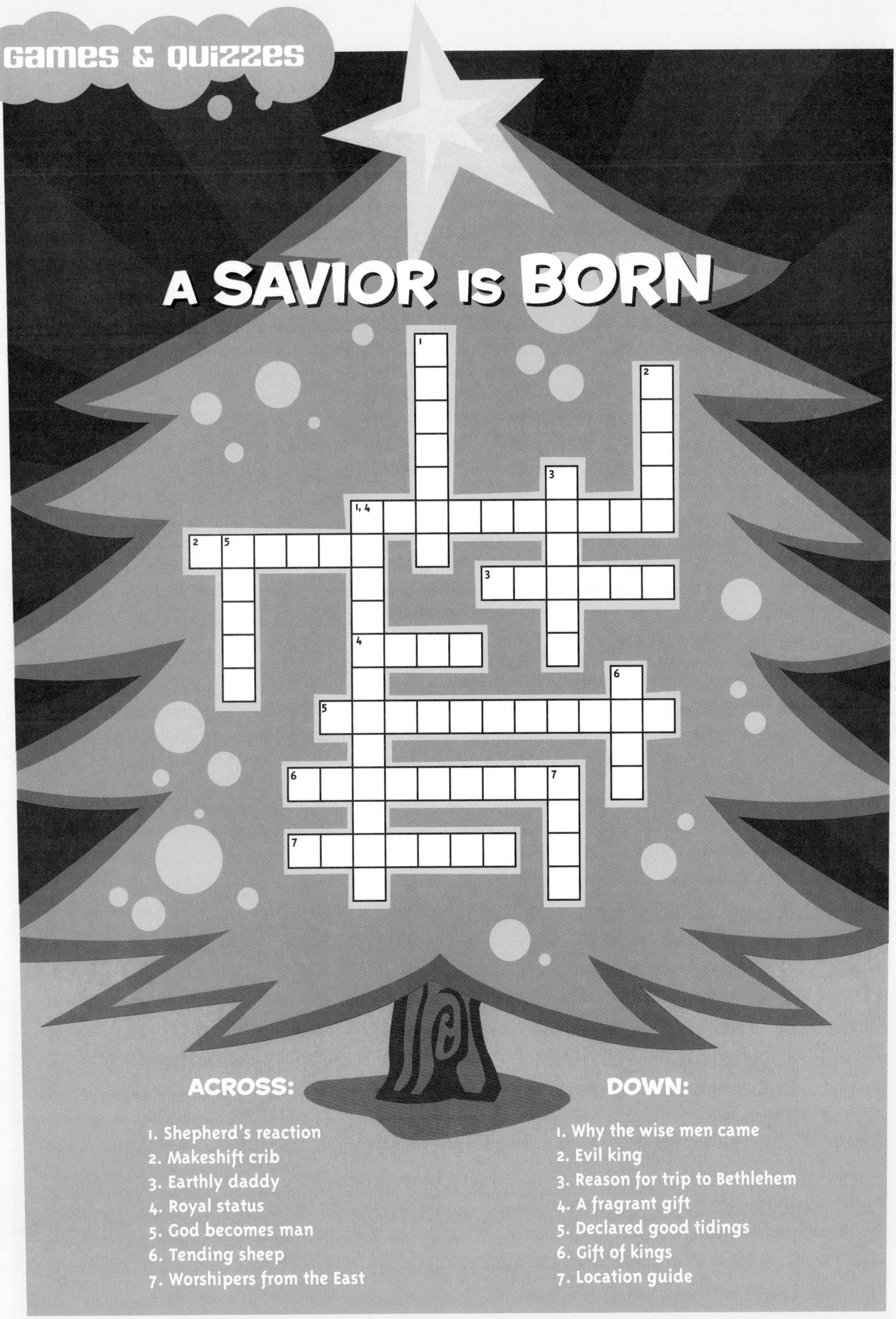

## ACROSS:

1. Shepherd's reaction
2. Makeshift crib
3. Earthly daddy
4. Royal status
5. God becomes man
6. Tending sheep
7. Worshipers from the East

## DOWN:

1. Why the wise men came
2. Evil king
3. Reason for trip to Bethlehem
4. A fragrant gift
5. Declared good tidings
6. Gift of kings
7. Location guide

ANSWER KEY: ACROSS: 1. FRIGHTENED; 2. MANGER; 3. JOSEPH; 4. KING; 5. INCARNATION; 6. SHEPHERDS; 7. WISE MEN
DOWN: 1. WORSHIP; 2. HEROD; 3. CENSUS; 4. FRANKINCENSE; 5. ANGEL; 6. GOLD; 7. STAR

> **"i have come to invite sinners to change their hearts."** *Luke 5:32*

collectors and other people, too. ³⁰But the Pharisees*ᵈ* and the men who taught the law for the Pharisees began to complain to the followers of Jesus. They said, "Why do you eat and drink with tax collectors and 'sinners'?"

³¹Jesus answered them, "Healthy people don't need a doctor. It is the sick who need a doctor. ³²I have not come to invite good people. I have come to invite sinners to change their hearts and lives!"

### JESUS ANSWERS A QUESTION

³³They said to Jesus, "John's followers often give up eating*ⁿ* and pray, just as the Pharisees*ᵈ* do. But your followers eat and drink all the time."

³⁴Jesus said to them, "When there is a wedding, you cannot make the friends of the bridegroom give up eating while he is still with them. ³⁵But the time will come when he will be taken away from them. Then his friends will give up eating."

³⁶Jesus told them this story: "No one takes cloth off a new coat to cover a hole in an old coat. If he does, he ruins the new coat, and the cloth from the new coat will not be the same as the old cloth. ³⁷People never pour new wine into old leather bags for holding wine. If they do, the new wine will break the bags, and the wine will spill out. Then the leather bags for holding wine will be ruined. ³⁸People always put new wine into new leather bags. ³⁹No one after drinking old wine wants new wine because he says, 'The old wine is better.'"

### JESUS IS LORD OVER THE SABBATH

**6** One Sabbath*ᵈ* day Jesus was walking through some grainfields. His followers picked the heads of grain, rubbed them in their hands, and ate them. ²Some Pharisees*ᵈ* said, "Why are you doing that? It is against the law of Moses to do that on the Sabbath day."

³Jesus answered, "Haven't you read about what David did when he and those with him were hungry? ⁴David went into God's house. He took the bread that was made holy for God and ate it. And he gave some of the bread to the people with him. This was against the law of Moses. It says that only priests can eat that bread." ⁵Then Jesus said to the Pharisees, "The Son of Man*ᵈ* is Lord of the Sabbath day."

### JESUS HEALS A MAN'S CRIPPLED HAND

⁶On another Sabbath*ᵈ* day Jesus went into the synagogue*ᵈ* and was teaching. A man with a crippled right hand was there. ⁷The teachers of the law and the Pharisees*ᵈ* were watching to see if Jesus would heal on the Sabbath day. They wanted to see Jesus do something wrong so that they could accuse him. ⁸But he knew what they were thinking. He said to the man with the crippled hand, "Get up and stand before these people." The man got up and stood there. ⁹Then Jesus said to them, "I ask you, which is it right to do on the Sabbath day: to do good, or to do evil? Is it right to save a life or to destroy one?" ¹⁰Jesus looked around at all of them. He said to the man, "Let me see your hand." The man stretched out his hand, and it was completely healed.

¹¹The Pharisees and the teachers of the law became very angry. They

**5:33 give up eating** This is called "fasting." The people would give up eating for a special time of prayer and worship to God. It was also done to show sadness.

# REAL SUPER HEROES

## ELIZABETH

Elizabeth wanted to have a baby, but her body just couldn't. She could have become angry and turned against God, but she didn't. She still loved God and trusted in his goodness. She and her husband, Zechariah the priest, continued to obey and serve God every day.

Then an angel appeared to Zechariah. Elizabeth, though she was now old, would have a special son who would lead many Israelites back to God. Just as God promised through the angel, Elizabeth had a son and named him John—the chosen prophet who would prepare the way for Jesus. God blessed Elizabeth, and she played a part in God's plan of salvation for his people.

When times are hard, it's easy to question God's goodness. But believe, like Elizabeth, and remember that God's ways are best. Wait on his perfect timing, and remember to thank him for all his great gifts!

said to each other, "What can we do to Jesus?"

## JESUS CHOOSES HIS APOSTLES

[12]At that time Jesus went off to a mountain to pray. He stayed there all night, praying to God. [13]The next morning, Jesus called his followers to him. He chose 12 of them, whom he named "apostles."[d] They were [14]Simon (Jesus named him Peter) and Andrew, Peter's brother; James and John, Philip and Bartholomew; [15]Matthew, Thomas, James son of Alphaeus, and Simon (called the Zealot[d]), [16]Judas son of James and Judas Iscariot. This Judas was the one who gave Jesus to his enemies.

## JESUS TEACHES AND HEALS

[17]Jesus and the apostles[d] came down from the mountain. Jesus stood on level ground where there was a large group of his followers. Also, there were many people from all around Judea, Jerusalem, and the seacoast cities of Tyre and Sidon. [18]They all came to hear Jesus teach and to be healed of their sicknesses. He healed those who were troubled by evil spirits. [19]All the people were trying to touch Jesus, because power was coming from him and healing them all!

[20]Jesus looked at his followers and said,
"Poor people, you are happy,
    because God's kingdom belongs
        to you.
[21]You people who are now hungry are
    happy,
    because you will be satisfied.
You people who are now crying are
    happy,
    because you will laugh with joy.
[22]"You are happy when people hate you and are cruel to you. You are happy when they say that you are evil because you belong to the Son of Man.[d] [23]At that time be full of joy, because you have a

great reward in heaven. Their fathers were cruel to the prophets[d] in the same way these people are cruel to you.
[24]"But how terrible it will be for you
    who are rich,
    because you have had your easy
        life.
[25]How terrible it will be for you who
    are full now,
    because you will be hungry.
How terrible it will be for you who are
    laughing now,
    because you will be sad and cry.
[26]"How terrible when all people say only good things about you. Their fathers always said good things about the false prophets.

> "i say to you who are listening to me, love your enemies. Do good to those who hate you."
>
> Luke 6:27

## LOVE YOUR ENEMIES

[27]"I say to you who are listening to me, love your enemies. Do good to those who hate you. [28]Ask God to bless those who say bad things to you. Pray for those who are cruel to you. [29]If anyone slaps you on one cheek, let him slap the other cheek too. If someone takes your coat, do not stop him from taking your shirt. [30]Give to everyone who asks you. When a person takes something that is yours, don't ask for it back. [31]Do for other people what you want them to do for you. [32]If you love only those who love you, should you get some

special praise for doing that? No! Even sinners love the people who love them! [33]If you do good only to those who do good to you, should you get some special praise for doing that? No! Even sinners do that! [34]If you lend things to people, always hoping to get something back, should you get some special praise for that? No! Even sinners lend to other sinners so that they can get back the same amount! [35]So love your enemies. Do good to them, and lend to them without hoping to get anything back. If you do these things, you will have a great reward. You will be sons of the Most High God. Yes, because God is kind even to people who are ungrateful and full of sin. [36]Show mercy just as your father shows mercy.

## LOOK AT YOURSELVES

[37]"Don't judge other people, and you will not be judged. Don't accuse others of being guilty, and you will not be accused of being guilty. Forgive other people, and you will be forgiven. [38]Give, and you will receive. You will be given much. It will be poured into your hands—more than you can hold. You will be given so much that it will spill into your lap. The way you give to others is the way God will give to you."

[39]Jesus told them this story: "Can a blind man lead another blind man? No! Both of them will fall into a ditch. [40]A student is not better than his teacher. But when the student has fully learned all that he has been taught, then he will be like his teacher. [41]"Why do you notice the little piece of dust that is in your brother's eye, but you don't see the big piece of

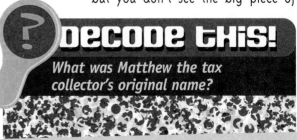

**Oecooe this!**

*What was Matthew the tax collector's original name?*

wood that is in your own eye? [42]You say to your brother, 'Brother, let me take that little piece of dust out of your eye.' Why do you say this? You cannot see that big piece of wood in your own eye! You are a hypocrite![d] First, take the piece of wood out of your own eye. Then you will see clearly to take the dust out of your brother's eye.

## TWO KINDS OF FRUIT

[43]"A good tree does not produce bad fruit. Also, a bad tree does not produce good fruit. [44]Each tree is known by its fruit. People don't gather figs from thornbushes. And they don't get grapes from bushes. [45]A good person has good things saved up in his heart. And so he brings good things out of his heart. But an evil person has evil things saved up in his heart. So he brings out bad things. A person speaks the things that are in his heart.

## TWO KINDS OF PEOPLE

[46]"Why do you call me, 'Lord, Lord,' but do not do what I say? [47]Everyone who comes to me and listens to my words and obeys [48]is like a man building a house. He digs deep and lays his foundation on rock. The floods come, and the water tries to wash the house away. But the flood cannot move the house, because the house was built well. [49]But the one who hears my words and does not obey is like a man who builds his house on the ground without a foundation. When the floods come, the house quickly falls down. And that house is completely destroyed."

> **"First, take the piece of wood out of your own eye. Then you will see clearly to take the dust out of your brother's eye."**
>
> *Luke 6:42*

## JESUS HEALS A SOLDIER'S SERVANT

**7** When Jesus finished saying all these things to the people, he went to Capernaum. [2]In Capernaum there was an army officer. He had a servant who was so sick he was nearly dead. The officer loved the servant very much. [3]When the officer heard about Jesus, he sent some older Jewish leaders to him. The officer wanted the leaders to ask Jesus to come and heal his servant. [4]The men went to Jesus and begged him saying, "This officer is worthy of your help. [5]He loves our people, and he built us a synagogue."[d]

[6]So Jesus went with the men. He was getting near the officer's house when the officer sent friends to say, "Lord, you don't need to come into my house. I am not good enough for you to be under my roof. [7]That is why I did not come to you myself. You only need to say the word, and my servant will be healed. [8]I, too, am a man under the authority of other men. And I have soldiers under my command. I tell one soldier, 'Go,' and he goes. And I tell another soldier, 'Come,' and he comes. And I say to my servant, 'Do this,' and my servant obeys me."

[9]When Jesus heard this, he was amazed. He turned to the crowd following him and said, "I tell you, this is the greatest faith I have seen anywhere, even in Israel."

[10]The men who had been sent to Jesus went back to the house. There they found that the servant was healed.

## JESUS BRINGS A MAN BACK TO LIFE

[11]The next day Jesus went to a town called Nain. His followers and a large crowd were traveling with him. [12]When he came near the town gate, he saw a funeral. A mother, who was a widow, had lost her only son. A large crowd from the town was with the mother while her son was being carried out. [13]When the Lord saw her, he felt very sorry for her. Jesus said to her, "Don't cry." [14]He went up to the coffin and touched it. The men who were carrying it stopped. Jesus said, "Young man, I tell you, get up!" [15]And the son sat up and began to talk. Then Jesus gave him back to his mother.

[16]All the people were amazed. They began praising God. They said, "A great prophet[d] has come to us! God is taking care of his people."

[17]This news about Jesus spread through all Judea and into all the places around there.

## JOHN ASKS A QUESTION

[18]John's followers told him about all these things. He called for two of his followers. [19]He sent them to the Lord to ask, "Are you the One who is coming, or should we wait for another?"

[20]So the men came to Jesus. They said, "John the Baptist[d] sent us to you with this question: 'Are you the One who is coming, or should we wait for another?'"

[21]At that time, Jesus healed many people of their sicknesses, diseases, and evil spirits. He healed many blind people so that they could see again.

## ? DECODE THIS!

*Who does Jesus tell us to love when we may not want to?*

# LIVIN' IT!

**BROKEN HEARTS HEAL**
**LUKE 7:47**

We're not sure what she had done, but it was something bad—and something the whole town knew. Simon thought this woman was a "sinner," a totally different kind of person than he, a religious leader, was.

And he was right; they were different. But not in the way he thought. The woman loved Jesus. She bathed his feet with her tears and kisses. Simon? Well, he liked talking about religious issues, but his heart was cold to God. Jesus said that if we try to hide our sin to make us look perfect to everyone else, then we can't know the love and joy that comes from forgiveness. If we think we don't need Jesus' help, we won't help other people, either. We need to be like the woman who knew her sin and was so grateful to be forgiven. Out of our thanks to God, we are free to show our love to him and to others.

²²Then Jesus said to John's followers, "Go tell John the things that you saw and heard here. The blind can see. The crippled can walk. People with a harmful skin disease are healed. The deaf can hear, and the dead are given life. And the Good News^d is told to the poor. ²³The person who does not lose faith is blessed!"

²⁴When John's followers left, Jesus began to tell the people about John: "What did you go out into the desert to see? A reed^n blown by the wind? ²⁵What did you go out to see? A man dressed in fine clothes? No. People who have fine clothes live in kings' palaces. ²⁶But what did you go out to

see? A prophet?^d Yes, and I tell you, John is more than a prophet. ²⁷This was written about John:

'I will send my messenger
    ahead of you.
He will prepare the way for
    you.'          *Malachi 3:1*

²⁸I tell you, John is greater than any other man ever born. But even the least important person in the kingdom of God is greater than John."

²⁹(When the people heard this, they all agreed that God's teaching was good. Even the tax collectors agreed. These were people who were already baptized by John. ³⁰But the Pharisees^d and teachers of the law refused to accept God's plan for themselves; they did not let John baptize them.)

³¹Then Jesus said, "What shall I say about the people of this time? What are they like? ³²They are like children sitting in the marketplace. One group of children calls to the other group and says,

'We played music for you, but
    you did not dance.
We sang a sad song, but you
    did not cry.'

³³John the Baptist came and did not eat like other people

## "The deaf can hear, and the dead are given life. And the Good News is told to the poor."

*Luke 7:22*

or drink wine. And you say, 'He has a demon^d in him.' ³⁴The Son of Man^d came eating like other people and drinking wine. And you say, 'Look at him! He eats too much and drinks too much wine! He is a friend of the tax collectors and "sinners"!' ³⁵But wisdom is shown to be right by the things it does."

**SIMON THE PHARISEE**

³⁶One of the Pharisees^d asked Jesus to eat with him. Jesus went into the Pharisee's house and sat at the table. ³⁷A sinful woman in the town learned that Jesus was eating at the Pharisee's house. So she brought an alabaster^d jar of perfume. ³⁸She stood at Jesus' feet, crying, and began to wash his feet with her tears. She dried his feet with her hair, kissed them many times and rubbed them with the perfume. ³⁹The Pharisee who asked Jesus to come to his house saw this. He thought to himself, "If Jesus were a prophet,^d he would know that the woman who is touching him is a sinner!"

⁴⁰Jesus said to the Pharisee, "Simon, I have something to say to you."

Simon said, "Teacher, tell me."

⁴¹Jesus said, "There were two men. Both men owed money to the same banker. One man owed the banker 500 silver coins.^n The other man owed the banker 50 silver coins. ⁴²The men had no money; so they could not pay what they owed. But the banker told the men that they did not have to pay him. Which one of the two men will love the banker more?"

⁴³Simon, the Pharisee, answered, "I think it would be the one who owed him the most money."

Jesus said to Simon, "You are right." ⁴⁴Then Jesus turned toward the woman and said to Simon, "Do you see this woman? When I came into your house, you gave me no water for my feet. But she washed my feet with her tears and dried my feet with her hair. ⁴⁵You did not kiss me, but she has been kissing my feet since I came

---

**7:24 reed** It means that John was not weak like grass blown by the wind. **7:41 silver coins** A Roman denarius. One coin was the average pay for one day's work.

## Gotta Know!

### Why are there mosquitoes and bugs?

Imagine if suddenly, one day, all the insects were gone. What would happen? We'd probably be thrilled—but just for awhile. Then, when all of the animals that depend on insects for food died, and all the animals that depended on those animals for food died, we'd see just why the pesky bugs are such an important part of the earth. Each creature is a part of God's incredible creativity and serves the purpose of bringing him glory!

in! <sup>46</sup>You did not rub my head with oil, but she rubbed my feet with perfume. <sup>47</sup>I tell you that her many sins are forgiven. This is clear because she showed great love. But the person who has only a little to be forgiven will feel only a little love."

<sup>48</sup>Then Jesus said to her, "Your sins are forgiven."

<sup>49</sup>The people sitting at the table began to think to themselves, "Who is this man? How can he forgive sins?"

<sup>50</sup>Jesus said to the woman, "Because you believed, you are saved from your sins. Go in peace."

### THE GROUP WITH JESUS

**8** The next day, while Jesus was traveling through some cities and small towns, he preached and told the Good News<sup>d</sup> about God's kingdom. The 12 apostles<sup>d</sup> were with him. <sup>2</sup>There were also some women with him who had been healed of sicknesses and evil spirits. One of the women was Mary, called Magdalene, from whom seven demons<sup>d</sup> had gone out. <sup>3</sup>Also among the women were Joanna, the wife of Chuza (Herod's helper), Susanna, and many other women. These women used their own money to help Jesus and his apostles.

### A STORY
### ABOUT PLANTING SEED

<sup>4</sup>A great crowd gathered. People were coming to Jesus from every town. He told them this story:

<sup>5</sup>"A farmer went out to plant his seed. While he was planting, some seed fell beside the road. People walked on the seed, and the birds ate all this seed. <sup>6</sup>Some seed fell on rock. It began to grow but then died because it had no water. <sup>7</sup>Some seed fell among thorny weeds. This seed grew, but later the weeds choked the good plants. <sup>8</sup>And some seed fell on good ground. This seed grew and made 100 times more grain."

Jesus finished the story. Then he called out, "You people who hear me, listen!"

<sup>9</sup>Jesus' followers asked him, "What does this story mean?"

<sup>10</sup>Jesus said, "You have been chosen to know the secret truths of the kingdom of God. But I use stories to speak to other people. I do this so that:

'They will look, but they may not see. They will listen, but they may not understand.'    *Isaiah 6:9*

<sup>11</sup>"This is what the story means: The seed is God's teaching. <sup>12</sup>What is the seed that fell beside the road? It is like the people who hear God's teaching, but then the devil comes and takes it away from their hearts. So they cannot believe the teaching and be saved. <sup>13</sup>What is the seed that fell on rock? It is like those who hear God's teaching and accept it gladly. But they don't have deep roots. They believe for a while, but then trouble comes. They stop believing and turn away from God. <sup>14</sup>What is the seed that fell among the thorny weeds? It is like those who hear God's teaching, but they let the worries, riches, and pleasures of this life keep them from growing. So they never produce good fruit. <sup>15</sup>And what is the seed that fell on the good ground? That is like those who hear God's teaching with a good, honest heart. They obey God's teaching and patiently produce good fruit.

### USE WHAT YOU HAVE

<sup>16</sup>"No one lights a lamp and then covers it with a bowl or hides it under a bed. Instead, he puts the lamp on a lampstand so that those who come in will have enough light to see. <sup>17</sup>Everything that is hidden will become clear. Every secret thing will be made known. <sup>18</sup>So be careful how you listen. The person who has something will be given more. But to the person who has nothing, this will

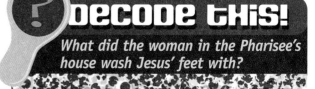

## DECODE THIS!

*What did the woman in the Pharisee's house wash Jesus' feet with?*

happen: Even what he thinks he has will be taken away from him."

## JESUS' TRUE FAMILY

[19]Jesus' mother and brothers came to see him. There was such a crowd that they could not get to him. [20]Someone said to Jesus, "Your mother and your brothers are standing outside. They want to see you."

[21]Jesus answered them, "My mother and my brothers are those who listen to God's teaching and obey it!"

## JESUS STOPS A STORM

[22]One day Jesus and his followers got into a boat. He said to them, "Come with me across the lake." And so they started across. [23]While they were sailing, Jesus fell asleep. A big storm blew up on the lake. The boat began to fill with water, and they were in danger.

[24]The followers went to Jesus and woke him. They said, "Master! Master! We will drown!"

Jesus got up and gave a command to the wind and the waves. The wind stopped, and the lake became calm. [25]Jesus said to his followers, "Where is your faith?"

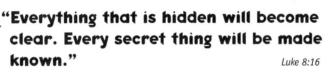

"Everything that is hidden will become clear. Every secret thing will be made known."

*Luke 8:16*

The followers were afraid and amazed. They said to each other, "What kind of man is this? He commands the wind and the water, and they obey him!"

## A MAN WITH DEMONS INSIDE HIM

[26]Jesus and his followers sailed across the lake from Galilee to the area where the Gerasene people live. [27]When Jesus got out of the boat, a man from the town came to Jesus. This man had

demons[d] inside him. For a long time he had worn no clothes. He lived in the burial caves, not in a house. [28]When he saw Jesus, he cried out and fell down before him. The man said with a loud voice, "What do you want with me, Jesus, Son of the Most High God? Please don't punish me!" [29]He said this because Jesus had commanded the evil spirit to come out of him. Many times it had taken hold of him. He had been kept under guard and chained hand and foot. But he had broken his chains and had been driven by the demon out into the desert.

[30]Jesus asked him, "What is your name?"

The man answered, "Legion."[n] (He said his name was "Legion" because many demons were in him.) [31]The demons begged Jesus not to send them into eternal darkness.[n] [32]On the hill there was a large herd of pigs eating. The demons begged Jesus to allow them to go into the pigs. So Jesus allowed them to do this. [33]Then the demons came out of the man and went into the pigs. The herd of pigs ran down the hill and into the lake. All the pigs drowned.

[34]The men who took care of the pigs ran away. They told about this in the town and the countryside. [35]And people went to see what had happened. They came to Jesus and found the man sitting there at Jesus' feet. The man was clothed and in his right mind because the demons were gone. But

the people were frightened. [36]The men who saw these things happen told the others all about how Jesus had made the man well. [37]All the people of the Gerasene country asked Jesus to go away. They were all very afraid. So Jesus got into the boat and went back to Galilee.

[38]The man that Jesus had healed begged to go with him. But Jesus sent him away, saying, [39]"Go back home and tell people what God did for you." So the man went all over town telling how much Jesus had done for him.

## JESUS GIVES LIFE TO A DEAD GIRL AND HEALS A SICK WOMAN

[40]When Jesus got back to Galilee, a crowd welcomed him. Everyone was waiting for him. [41]A man named Jairus came to Jesus. Jairus was a ruler of the synagogue.[d] He bowed down at

> "Jesus got up and gave a command to the wind and the waves. The wind stopped, and the lake became calm."
>
> *Luke 8:24*

8:30 "Legion" Means very many. A legion was about 5,000 men in the Roman army. 8:31 eternal darkness Literally, "the abyss," something like a pit or a hole that has no end.

Jesus' feet and begged him to come to his house. ⁴²Jairus had only one daughter. She was 12 years old, and she was dying.

While Jesus was on his way to Jairus' house, the people were crowding all around him. ⁴³A woman was there who had been bleeding for 12 years. She had spent all her money on doctors, but no doctor was able to heal her. ⁴⁴The woman came up behind Jesus and touched the edge of his coat. At that moment, her bleeding stopped. ⁴⁵Then Jesus said, "Who touched me?"

All the people said they had not touched Jesus. Peter said, "Master, the people are all around you and are pushing against you."

Jesus said, "Don't cry. She is not dead; she is only sleeping."

⁵³The people laughed at Jesus because they knew that the girl was dead. ⁵⁴But Jesus took her by the hand and called to her, "My child, stand up!" ⁵⁵Her spirit came back into her, and she stood up immediately. Jesus said, "Give her something to eat." ⁵⁶The girl's parents were amazed. Jesus told them not to tell anyone about what happened.

## JESUS SENDS OUT THE APOSTLES

**9** Jesus called the 12 apostles*ᵈ* together. He gave them power to heal sicknesses and power over all demons.*ᵈ* ²Jesus sent the apostles out

the Baptist*ᵈ* is risen from death." ⁸Others said, "Elijah has come to us." And still others said, "One of the prophets*ᵈ* from long ago has risen from death." ⁹Herod said, "I cut off John's head. So who is this man I hear these things about?" And Herod kept trying to see Jesus.

## MORE THAN 5,000 PEOPLE FED

¹⁰When the apostles*ᵈ* returned, they told Jesus all the things they had done on their trip. Then Jesus took them away to a town called Bethsaida. There, Jesus and his apostles could be alone together. ¹¹But the people learned where Jesus went and followed him. Jesus welcomed them and

> ## "Dear woman, you are healed because you believed. Go in peace."
>
> *Luke 8:48*

⁴⁶But Jesus said, "Someone did touch me! I felt power go out from me." ⁴⁷When the woman saw that she could not hide, she came forward, shaking. She bowed down before Jesus. While all the people listened, she told why she had touched him. Then, she said, she was healed immediately. ⁴⁸Jesus said to her, "Dear woman, you are healed because you believed. Go in peace."

⁴⁹While Jesus was still speaking, someone came from the house of the synagogue ruler and said to the ruler, "Your daughter has died! Don't bother the teacher now."

⁵⁰When Jesus heard this, he said to Jairus, "Don't be afraid. Just believe, and your daughter will be well."

⁵¹Jesus went to the house. He let only Peter, John, James, and the girl's father and mother go inside with him. ⁵²All the people were crying and feeling sad because the girl was dead. But

to tell about God's kingdom and to heal the sick. ³He said to them, "When you travel, don't take a walking stick. Also, don't carry a bag, or food, or money. Take for your trip only the clothes you are wearing. ⁴When you go into a house, stay there until it is time to leave. ⁵If the people in the town will not welcome you, go outside the town and shake the dust off of your feet.ⁿ This will be a warning to them."

⁶So the apostles went out. They traveled through all the towns. They told the Good News*ᵈ* and healed people everywhere.

## HEROD IS CONFUSED ABOUT JESUS

⁷Herod, the governor, heard about all these things that were happening. He was confused because some people said, "John

talked with them about God's kingdom. He healed those who needed to be healed.

¹²Late in the afternoon, the 12 apostles came to Jesus and said, "No one lives in this place. Send the people away. They need to find food and places to sleep in the towns and countryside around here."

¹³But Jesus said to them, "You give them something to eat."

They said, "We have only five loaves of bread and two fish. Do you want us to go buy food for all these people?" ¹⁴(There were about 5,000 men there.)

Jesus said to his followers, "Tell the people to sit in groups of about 50 people."

¹⁵So the followers did this, and all the

9:5 **shake . . . feet** A warning. It showed that they were finished talking to these people.

DECODE THIS!

*What did the woman touch on Jesus that made her heal instantly?*

# APRIL HONESTY

**1** EPHESIANS 4:25: You must stop telling lies. Tell each other the truth because we all belong to each other in the same body.

**2** Make a card for each brother and sister that tells them how special they are to you.

**3**

**4** Make a date with your parents, and tell them what's on your mind these days.

**5** Prayer Pointer: Ask God to show you any areas in your life where you're not telling the truth—and to give you courage to always speak the truth.

**6**

**7** Get all your friends online for a good chat session.

**8**

**9** JOHN 14:6: Jesus answered, "I am the way. And I am the truth and the life. The only way to the Father is through me."

**10**

**11**

**12** Bake chocolate chip cookies, and give some to your neighbors.

**13**

**14** Prayer Pointer: Ask God to help you and your friends believe what God tells you in his Word.

**15**

**16**

**17** I CORINTHIANS 13:6: Love is not happy with evil, but is happy with the truth.

**18**

**19** Sleep late.

**20**

**21** Go for a walk, and count all the different kinds of flowers you see.

**22**

**23** EPHESIANS 4:15: We will speak the truth with love. We will grow up in every way to be like Christ, who is the head.

**24**

**25** Have a movie night at home with popcorn, soda, and candy.

**26**

**27**

**28** Prayer Pointer: Ask God to stop Satan's lies and help his people speak God's truth clearly to everyone.

**29**

**30**

people sat down. [16]Then Jesus took the five loaves of bread and two fish. He looked up to heaven and thanked God for the food. Then Jesus divided the food and gave it to the followers to give to the people. [17]All the people ate and were satisfied. And there was much food left. Twelve baskets were filled with pieces of food that were not eaten.

**"Whoever wants to save his life will lose it. And whoever gives his life for me will save it."**

*Luke 9:24*

### JESUS IS THE CHRIST

[18]One time when Jesus was praying alone, his followers came together there. Jesus asked them, "Who do the people say I am?"

[19]They answered, "Some say you are John the Baptist.[d] Others say you are Elijah.[n] And others say you are one of the prophets[d] from long ago who has come back to life."

[20]Then Jesus asked, "And who do you say I am?"

Peter answered, "You are the Christ[d] from God."

[21]Jesus warned them not to tell anyone. Then he said, [22]"The Son of Man[d] must suffer many things. He will be rejected by the older Jewish leaders, the leading priests, and the teachers of the law. The Son of Man will be killed. But after three days he will be raised from death."

[23]Jesus went on to say to all of them, "If anyone wants to follow me, he must say 'no' to the things he wants. Every day he must be willing even to die on a cross, and he must follow me. [24]Whoever wants to save his life will

lose it. And whoever gives his life for me will save it. [25]It is worth nothing for a man to have the whole world, if he himself is destroyed or lost. [26]If anyone is ashamed of me and my teaching, then I[n] will be ashamed of him. I will be ashamed of him at the time I come with my glory and with the glory of the Father and the holy angels. [27]I tell you the truth. Some of you people standing here will see the kingdom of God before you die."

### JESUS WITH MOSES AND ELIJAH

[28]About eight days after Jesus said these things, he took Peter, James, and John and went up on a mountain to pray. [29]While Jesus was praying, his face was changed, and his clothes became shining white. [30]Then two men were talking with Jesus. The men were Moses and Elijah.[n] [31]They appeared in heavenly glory, talking with Jesus about his death which would happen in Jerusalem. [32]Peter and the others were asleep. But they woke up and saw the glory of Jesus. They also saw the two men who were standing with him. [33]When Moses and Elijah were about to leave, Peter said, "Master, it is good that we are here. We will put three tents here—one for you, one for Moses, and one for Elijah." (Peter did not know what he was saying.)

[34]While Peter was saying these things, a cloud came down all around them. Peter, James, and John became afraid when the cloud covered them. [35]A voice came from the cloud. The voice said, "This is my Son. He is the One I have chosen. Obey him."

[36]When the voice finished speaking, only Jesus was there. Peter, James, and John said nothing. At that time they told no one about what they had seen.

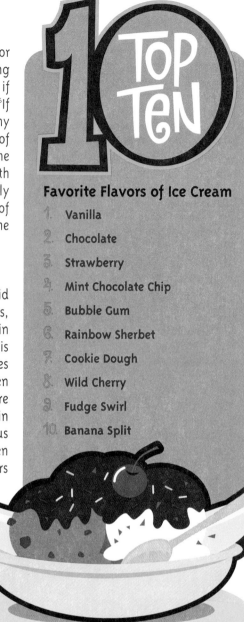

**10 TOP TEN**

### Favorite Flavors of Ice Cream

1. Vanilla
2. Chocolate
3. Strawberry
4. Mint Chocolate Chip
5. Bubble Gum
6. Rainbow Sherbet
7. Cookie Dough
8. Wild Cherry
9. Fudge Swirl
10. Banana Split

### JESUS HEALS A SICK BOY

[37]The next day, Jesus, Peter, James, and John came down from the mountain. A large crowd met Jesus. [38]A man in the crowd shouted to Jesus, "Teacher, please come and look at my son. He is the only child I have. [39]An evil spirit comes into my son, and then he shouts. He loses control of himself, and he foams at the mouth. The evil spirit keeps on hurting him

---

**9:19 Elijah** A man who spoke for God. He lived hundreds of years before Christ. **9:26 I** Literally, "the Son of Man." **9:30 Moses and Elijah** Two of the most important Jewish leaders in the past.

and almost never leaves him. [40]I begged your followers to make the evil spirit leave my son, but they could not do it."

[41]Jesus answered, "You people who live now have no faith. Your lives are all wrong. How long must I be with you and be patient with you?" Then Jesus said to the man, "Bring your son here."

[42]While the boy was coming, the demon[d] threw him on the ground. The boy lost control of himself. But Jesus

little child like this in my name, then he accepts me. And when he accepts me, he accepts the One who sent me. He who is least among you all—he is the greatest."

## ANYONE NOT AGAINST US IS FOR US

[49]John answered, "Master, we saw someone using your name to force demons[d] out of people. We told him to stop because he does not belong to our group."

But the Son of Man[d] has no place to rest his head."

[59]Jesus said to another man, "Follow me!"

But the man said, "Lord, first let me go and bury my father."

[60]But Jesus said to him, "Let the people who are dead bury their own dead! You must go and tell about the kingdom of God."

[61]Another man said, "I will follow you, Lord, but first let me go and say

> ## "if anyone accepts a little child like this in my name, then he accepts me. And when he accepts me, he accepts the One who sent me."
>
> Luke 9:48

gave a strong command to the evil spirit. Then the boy was healed, and Jesus gave him back to his father. [43]All the people were amazed at the great power of God.

## JESUS TALKS ABOUT HIS DEATH

The people were all wondering about the things Jesus did. But he said to his followers, [44]"Don't forget the things I tell you now: The Son of Man[d] will be handed over into the control of men." [45]But the followers did not understand what Jesus meant. The meaning was hidden from them so that they could not understand it. But they were afraid to ask Jesus about what he said.

## THE MOST IMPORTANT PERSON

[46]Jesus' followers began to have an argument about which one of them was the greatest. [47]Jesus knew what they were thinking. So he took a little child and stood the child beside him. [48]Then Jesus said, "If anyone accepts a

[50]Jesus said to him, "Don't stop him. If a person is not against you, then he is for you."

## A SAMARITAN TOWN

[51]The time was coming near when Jesus would leave and be taken to heaven. He was determined to go to Jerusalem [52]and sent some men ahead of him. The men went into a town in Samaria to make everything ready for Jesus. [53]But the people there would not welcome him because he was going toward Jerusalem. [54]James and John, the followers of Jesus, saw this. They said, "Lord, do you want us to call fire down from heaven and destroy those people?"[n]

[55]But Jesus turned and scolded them.[n]

[56]Then he and his followers went to another town.

## FOLLOWING JESUS

[57]They were all going along the road. Someone said to Jesus, "I will follow you any place you go."

[58]Jesus answered, "The foxes have holes to live in. The birds have nests to live in.

good-bye to my family."

[62]Jesus said, "Anyone who begins to plow a field but keeps looking back is of no use in the kingdom of God."

## JESUS SENDS THE 72 MEN

**10** After this, the Lord chose 72[n] others. He sent them out in pairs. He sent them ahead of him into every town and place where he planned to go. [2]He said to them, "There are a great many people to harvest. But there are only a few workers to harvest them. God owns the harvest. Pray to God that he will send more workers to help gather his harvest. [3]You can go now. But listen! I am sending you, and you will be like sheep among wolves. [4]Don't carry a purse, a bag, or sandals. Don't stop to talk with people on the road. [5]Before you go into a house, say, 'Peace be with this house.' [6]If a peaceful man lives there, your blessing of peace will stay with him. If the man is not peaceful, then your blessing of peace will come back to you. [7]Stay in the peaceful house. Eat and drink what the people there give you. A worker should be given his pay.

**DECODE THIS!**
Who killed John the Baptist?

9:54 Verse 54 Here, some Greek copies add: ". . . as Elijah did." 9:55 Verse 55 Here, some copies add: "And Jesus said, 'You don't know what kind of spirit you belong to. [56] The Son of Man did not come to destroy the souls of men but to save them.' " 10:1 72 Many Greek copies read 70.

# LIVIN' IT!

## THE TATTLETALE
### LUKE 10:42

What's the most important thing you can do for God? Martha certainly wanted to know. She had a whole list of to-dos in order to have a nice meal for Jesus and the disciples. She actually got mad at Mary for not helping her, so she tattled on her to Jesus.

But Jesus' answer surprised her. He told her she worried about too many things, and really, there was only one thing she needed to do—and Mary had chosen it. What was it? It was sitting at Jesus' feet, listening to him share what was in his heart. Of all the things in the world we could be doing, there is nothing more important than just spending time with the Savior and learning from him. Then, as we learn his truth, we are better prepared to go do what he says.

Don't move from house to house. [8]If you go into a town and the people welcome you, eat what they give you. [9]Heal the sick who live there. Tell them, 'The kingdom of God is soon coming to you!' [10]But if you go into a town, and the people don't welcome you, then go out into the streets of that town. Say to them, [11]'Even the dirt from your town that sticks to our feet we wipe off against you.[n] But remember that the kingdom of God is coming soon.' [12]I tell you, on the Judgment Day it will be worse for the people of that town than for the people of Sodom.[n]

## JESUS WARNS UNBELIEVERS

[13]"How terrible for you, Korazin! How terrible for you, Bethsaida! I did many miracles[d] in you. If those same miracles had happened in Tyre and Sidon,[n] those people would have changed their lives and stopped sinning long ago. They would have worn rough cloth and put ashes on themselves to show that they had changed. [14]But on the Judgment Day it will be worse for you than for Tyre and Sidon. [15]And you, Capernaum,[n] will you be lifted up to heaven? No! You will be thrown down to the depths!

[16]"He who listens to you is really listening to me. He who refuses to accept you is really refusing to accept me. And he who refuses to accept me is refusing to accept the One who sent me."

## SATAN FALLS

[17]When the 72[n] men came back from their trip, they were very happy. They said, "Lord, even the demons[d] obeyed us when we used your name!"

[18]Jesus said to the men, "I saw Satan falling like lightning from the sky. [19]Listen! I gave you power to walk on snakes and scorpions. I gave you more power than the Enemy has. Nothing will hurt you. [20]You should be happy, but not because the spirits obey you. You should be happy because your names are written in heaven."

## JESUS PRAYS TO THE FATHER

[21]Then the Holy Spirit[d] made Jesus rejoice. He said, "I thank you, Father, Lord of heaven and earth, because you have hidden these things from the people who are wise and smart. But you have shown them to those who are like little children. Yes, Father, you did this because this is what you really wanted.

[22]"My Father has given me all things. No one knows the Son—only the Father knows. And only the Son knows the Father. The only people who will know about the Father are those whom the Son chooses to tell."

[23]Then Jesus turned to his followers and said privately, "You are blessed to see what you now see! [24]I tell you, many prophets[d] and kings wanted to see what you now see. But they did not see these things. And many prophets and kings wanted to hear what you now hear. But they did not hear these things."

## THE GOOD SAMARITAN

[25]Then a teacher of the law stood up. He was trying to test Jesus. He said, "Teacher, what must I do to get life forever?"

[26]Jesus said to him, "What is written in the law? What do you read there?"

[27]The man answered, "Love the Lord your God. Love him with all your heart, all your soul, all your strength, and all your mind."[n] Also, "You must love your neighbor as you love yourself."[n]

[28]Jesus said to him, "Your answer is right. Do this and you will have life forever."

[29]But the man wanted to show that the way he was living was right. So he said to Jesus, "And who is my neighbor?"

[30]To answer this question, Jesus said, "A man was going down the road from Jerusalem to Jericho. Some robbers attacked him. They tore off his clothes and beat him. Then they left him lying there, almost dead. [31]It happened that a Jewish priest was going down that road. When the

10:11 dirt . . . you A warning. It showed that they were finished talking to these people. 10:12 Sodom City that God destroyed because the people were so evil. 10:13 Tyre and Sidon Towns where wicked people lived. 10:13, 15 Korazin . . . Bethsaida . . . Capernaum Towns by Lake Galilee where Jesus preached to the people. 10:17 72 Many Greek copies read 70. 10:27 "Love . . . mind." Quotation from Deuteronomy 6:5. 10:27 "You . . . yourself." Quotation from Leviticus 19:18.

priest saw the man, he walked by on the other side of the road. [32]Next, a Levite[n] came there. He went over and looked at the man. Then he walked by on the other side of the road. [33]Then a Samaritan[n] traveling down the road came to where the hurt man was lying. He saw the man and felt very sorry for him. [34]The Samaritan went to him and poured olive oil and wine[n] on his wounds and bandaged them. He put the hurt man on his own donkey and took him to an inn. At the inn, the Samaritan took care of him. [35]The next day, the Samaritan brought out two silver coins[n] and gave them to the innkeeper. The Samaritan said, 'Take care of this man. If you spend more money on him, I will pay it back to you when I come again.'"

[36]Then Jesus said, "Which one of these three men do you think was a neighbor to the man who was attacked by the robbers?"

[37]The teacher of the law answered, "The one who helped him."

Jesus said to him, "Then go and do the same thing he did!"

## MARY AND MARTHA

[38]While Jesus and his followers were traveling, Jesus went into a town. A woman named Martha let Jesus stay at her house. [39]Martha had a sister named Mary. Mary was sitting at Jesus' feet and listening to him teach. [40]Martha became angry because she had so much work to do. She went in and said, "Lord, don't you care that my sister has left me alone to do all the work? Tell her to help me!"

[41]But the Lord answered her, "Martha, Martha, you are getting worried and upset about too many things. [42]Only one thing is important. Mary has chosen the right thing, and it will never be taken away from her."

## JESUS TEACHES ABOUT PRAYER

**11** One time Jesus was praying in a place. When he finished, one of his followers said to him, "John taught his followers how to pray. Lord, please teach us how to pray, too."

[2]Jesus said to them, "When you pray, say:

'Father, we pray that your name
     will always be kept holy.
We pray that your kingdom will
     come.
[3]Give us the food we need for
     each day.
[4]Forgive us the sins we have done,
     because we forgive every person
     who has done wrong to us.
And do not cause us to be tested.'"

## CONTINUE TO ASK

[5-6]Then Jesus said to them, "Suppose one of you went to your friend's house at midnight and said to him, 'A friend of mine has come into town to visit me. But I have nothing for him to eat. Please loan me three loaves of bread.' [7]Your friend inside the house answers, 'Don't bother me! The door is already locked. My children and I are in bed. I cannot get up and give you the bread now.' [8]I tell you, maybe friendship is not enough to make him get up to give you the bread. But he will surely get up to give you what you need if you continue to ask. [9]So I tell you, continue to ask, and God will give to you. Continue to search, and you will find. Continue to knock, and the door will open for you. [10]Yes, if a person continues asking, he will receive. If he continues searching, he will find. And if he continues knocking, the door will open for him. [11]What would you fathers do if your son asks you for a fish? Would any of you give him a snake? [12]Or, if your son asks for an egg, would you give him a scorpion? [13]Even though you are bad, you know how to give good things to your children. So surely your heavenly Father knows how to give the Holy Spirit[d] to those who ask him."

## JESUS' POWER IS FROM GOD

[14]One time Jesus was sending a demon[d] out of a man who could not talk. When the demon came out, the man was able to speak. The people were amazed. [15]But some of them said,

> "Father, we pray that your name will always be kept holy. We pray that your kingdom will come. Give us the food we need for each day. Forgive us the sins we have done, because we forgive every person who has done wrong to us. And do not cause us to be tested." *Luke 11:2-4*

**DECODE THIS!**
*Who did Jesus heal who foamed at the mouth?*

"Jesus uses the power of Beelzebul[d] to force demons out of people. Beelzebul is the ruler of demons."

[16]Other people wanted to test Jesus. They asked him to give them a sign from heaven. [17]But Jesus knew what they were thinking. So he said to them, "Every kingdom that is divided and fights against itself will be destroyed. And a family that fights against itself will break apart. [18]So if Satan is fighting against himself, then how will his kingdom last? You say that I use the power of Beelzebul

kingdom of God has come to you!

[21]"When a strong man with many weapons guards his own house, then the things in his house are safe. [22]But suppose a stronger man comes and defeats him. The stronger man will take away the weapons that the first man trusted to keep his house safe. Then the stronger man will do what he wants with the first man's things.

[23]"If anyone is not with me, he is against me. He who does not work with me is working against me.

> ## "if anyone is not with me, he is against me. He who does not work with me is working against me." Luke 11:23

to force out demons. [19]But if I use the power of Beelzebul to force out demons, then by what power do your people force out demons? So your own people prove that you are wrong. [20]But if I use the power of God to force out demons, the

### THE EMPTY MAN

[24]"When an evil spirit comes out of a person, it travels through dry places, looking for a place to rest. But that spirit finds no place to rest. So it says, 'I will go back to the home I left.'

[25]When the spirit comes back to that person, it finds that home swept clean and made neat. [26]Then the evil spirit goes out and brings seven other spirits more evil than itself. Then all the evil spirits go into that person and live there. And he has even more trouble than he had before."

### PEOPLE WHO ARE TRULY BLESSED

[27]When Jesus was saying these things, a woman in the crowd spoke out. She said to Jesus, "Your mother is blessed because she gave birth to you and nursed you."

[28]But Jesus said, "Those who hear the teaching of God and obey it—they are the ones who are truly blessed."

### GIVE US PROOF!

[29]The crowd grew larger. Jesus said, "The people who live today are evil. They ask for a miracle[d] as a sign from God. But they will have no sign—only the sign of Jonah.[n] [30]Jonah was a sign for those people who lived in Nineveh. In the same way the Son of Man[d] will be a sign for the people of this time. [31]On the Judgment Day the Queen of the South[n] will stand up with the men who live now. She will show that they are guilty because she came from far away to listen to Solomon's wise teaching. And I tell you that someone greater than Solomon is here! [32]On the Judgment Day the men of Nineveh will stand up with the people who live now. And they will show that you are guilty, because when Jonah preached to those people, they changed their hearts and lives. And I tell you that someone greater than Jonah is here!

### BE A LIGHT FOR THE WORLD

[33]"No one takes a light and puts it under a bowl or hides it. Instead, he puts the light on a lampstand so that

## Going Global

### Kids Around the World

How much time in your lifetime have you spent at playgrounds? Probably adds up to days, months, years!! Did you want to go to every one you saw at school, at church, or at a park? Isn't it great to be a kid and climb . . . slide . . . swing . . . hang out with friends at your favorite playground? Perhaps you're in a situation where you are just an average kid at play.

In 1994 Dennis Johnson met with a group of businessmen. Their goal was to build playgrounds for children who had a hard time just being a kid. Mr. Johnson named that group "Kids Around the World." Today it is a Christian organization that has a network of volunteers from all over the United States. These are people, young and old, who have a common passion—children. They give their time, talents, and money to travel around the U.S. to build playgrounds and train children's workers. They come from all professions, backgrounds, ethnic groups, and income levels. They work hard to put smiles on the faces of as many children as they possibly can, and they help to fill their hearts and lives with joy.

To learn more about helping Mr. Johnson and his volunteers, go to www.kidsaroundtheworld.com.

11:29 sign of Jonah Jonah's three days in the big fish are like Jesus' three days in the tomb. 11:31 Queen of the South The Queen of Sheba. She traveled 1,000 miles to learn God's wisdom from Solomon. Read 1 Kings 10:1-3.

106

the people who come in can see. [34]Your eye is a light for the body. If your eyes are good, then your whole body will be full of light. But if your eyes are evil, then your whole body will be full of darkness. [35]So be careful! Don't let the light in you become darkness. [36]If your whole body is full of light, and none of it is dark, then you will shine bright, as when a lamp shines on you."

> **"Your eye is a light for the body. if your eyes are good, then your whole body will be full of light."** *Luke 11:34*

## JESUS ACCUSES THE PHARISEES

[37]After Jesus had finished speaking, a Pharisee[d] asked Jesus to eat with him. So Jesus went in and sat at the table. [38]But the Pharisee was surprised when he saw that Jesus did not wash his hands[n] before the meal. [39]The Lord said to him, "You Pharisees clean the outside of the cup and the dish. But inside you are full of greed and evil. [40]You are foolish. The same One who made what is outside also made what is inside. [41]So give what is in your cups and dishes to the poor. Then you will be fully clean. [42]But how terrible for you Pharisees! You give God one-tenth of even your mint, your rue, and every other plant in your garden. But you forget to be fair to other people and to love God. These are the things you should do. And you should

also continue to do those other things—like giving one-tenth. [43]How terrible for you Pharisees, because you love to get the most important seats in the synagogues.[d] And you love people to show respect to you in the marketplaces. [44]How terrible for you, because you are like hidden graves. People walk on them without knowing it."

## JESUS TALKS TO TEACHERS OF THE LAW

[45]One of the teachers of the law said to Jesus, "Teacher, when you say these things, you are insulting us, too."

[46]Jesus answered, "How terrible for you, you teachers of the law! You make strict rules that are very hard for people to obey. But you yourselves don't even try to follow those rules. [47]How terrible for you, because you build tombs for the prophets.[d] But these are the prophets that your fathers killed! [48]And now you show that you approve of what your fathers did. They killed the prophets, and you build tombs for the prophets! [49]This is why in his wisdom God said, 'I will send prophets and apostles[d] to them. Some of my prophets and apostles will be killed, and others will be treated cruelly.' [50]So you who live now will be punished for the deaths of all the prophets who were killed since the beginning of the world. [51]You will be punished for the killing of Abel and for the killing of Zechariah.[n] Zechariah was killed between the altar and the Temple.[d] Yes, I tell you that you people who live now will be punished for them all.

[52]"How terrible for you, you teachers of the law. You have hidden the key to learning about God.

You yourselves would not learn, and you stopped others from learning, too."

[53]When Jesus was leaving, the teachers of the law and the Pharisees[d] began to give him trouble, asking him questions about many things. [54]They were trying to catch Jesus saying something wrong.

## DON'T BE LIKE THE PHARISEES

**12** Many thousands of people had gathered. There were so many people that they were stepping on each other. Before Jesus spoke to them, he said to his followers, "Be careful of the yeast of the Pharisees.[d] They are hypocrites.[d] [2]Everything that is hidden will be shown. Everything that is secret will be made known. [3]The things you say in the dark will be told in the light. The things you have whispered in an inner room will be shouted from the top of the house."

## FEAR ONLY GOD

[4]Then Jesus said to the people, "I tell you, my friends, don't be afraid of people. People can kill the body, but after that they can do nothing more to hurt you. [5]I will show you the One to fear. You should fear him who has the power to kill you and also to throw you into hell. Yes, he is the One you should fear.

[6]"When five sparrows are sold, they cost only two pennies. But God does not forget any of them. [7]Yes, God even knows how many hairs you have on your head. Don't be afraid. You are worth much more than many sparrows.

## DON'T BE ASHAMED OF JESUS

[8]"I tell you, if anyone stands before others and says that he believes in me, then I will say that he belongs to me. I will say this before the angels of God. [9]But if anyone stands before others

**oecoOe tHiS!**
*Who stopped to help the man beaten by robbers?*

11:38 **wash his hands** This was a Jewish religious custom that the Pharisees thought was very important.
11:51 **Abel . . . Zechariah** In the Hebrew Old Testament, the first and last men to be murdered.

and says he does not believe in me, then I will say that he does not belong to me. I will say this before the angels of God.

[10]"If a person says something against the Son of Man,[d] he can be forgiven. But a person who says bad things against the Holy Spirit[d] will not be forgiven.

[11]"When men bring you into the synagogues[d] before the leaders and other important men, don't worry about how to defend yourself or what to say. [12]At that time the Holy Spirit will teach you what you must say."

## BiBLe BaSiCS

### WHat Does it mean to repent?

Have you ever walked one direction, realized you were going the wrong way, and turned around and walked back in the opposite direction? To repent means the same thing, only spiritually. Once you realize you're wrong, you confess your sins to God, and you stop doing them. You turn your heart around and start doing the right things again.

### JESUS WARNS AGAINST SELFISHNESS

[13]One of the men in the crowd said to Jesus, "Teacher, tell my brother to divide with me the property our father left us."

[14]But Jesus said to him, "Who said that I should be your judge or decide how to divide the property between you two?" [15]Then Jesus said to them, "Be careful and guard against all kinds of greed. A man's life is not measured by the many things he owns."

[16]Then Jesus used this story: "There was a rich man who had some land, which grew a good crop of food. [17]The rich man thought to himself, 'What will I do? I have no place to keep all my crops.' [18]Then he said, 'I know what I will do. I will tear down my barns and build bigger ones! I will put all my grain and other goods together in my new barns. [19]Then I can say to myself, I have enough good things stored to last for many years. Rest, eat, drink, and enjoy life!'

[20]"But God said to that man, 'Foolish man! Tonight you will die. So who will get those things you have prepared for yourself?'

[21]"This is how it will be for anyone who stores things up only for himself and is not rich toward God."

### DON'T WORRY

[22]Jesus said to his followers, "So I tell you, don't worry about the food you need to live. Don't worry about the clothes you need for your body. [23]Life is more important than food. And the body is more important than clothes. [24]Look at the birds. They don't plant or harvest. They don't save food in houses or barns. But God takes care of them. And you are worth much more than birds. [25]None of you can add any time to your life by worrying about it. [26]If you cannot do even the little things, then why worry about the big things? [27]Look at the wild flowers. See how they grow. They don't work or make clothes for themselves. But I tell you that even Solomon, the great and rich king, was not dressed as beautifully as one of these flowers. [28]God clothes the grass in the field like that. That grass is living today, but tomorrow it will be thrown into the fire. So you know how much more God will clothe you. Don't have so little faith! [29]Don't always think about what you will eat or what you will drink. Don't worry about it. [30]All the people in the world are trying to get those things. Your Father knows that you need them. [31]The thing you should seek is God's kingdom. Then all the other things you need will be given to you.

### DON'T TRUST IN MONEY

[32]"Don't fear, little flock. Your Father wants to give you the kingdom. [33]Sell the things you have and give to the poor. Get for yourselves purses that don't wear out. Get the treasure in heaven that never runs out. Thieves can't steal it in heaven, and moths can't destroy it. [34]Your heart will be where your treasure is.

### ALWAYS BE READY

[35]"Be ready! Be dressed for service and have your lamps shining. [36]Be like servants who are waiting for their master to come home from a wedding party. The master comes and knocks. The servants immediately open the door for him. [37]Those servants will be blessed when their master comes home, because he sees that his servants are ready and wait-

> ## "Your heart will be where your treasure is." *Luke 12:34*

ing for him. I tell you the truth. The master will dress himself to serve and tell the servants to sit at the table. Then the master will serve them. [38]Those servants might have to wait until midnight or later for their master. But they will be happy when he comes in and finds them still waiting.

## WILD WORLD FACTS

### IT JUST KEEPS GOING & GOING . . .

Even when you're sleeping, your heart is still hard at work. As a kid, your heart is the size of your fist and beats about 100,000 times in one day—that's about 35 million times in a year! Each time it beats, it pumps blood through your veins and arteries to the rest of your body so all of your body parts get the oxygen and nutrients they need to live. During a regular lifetime, your heart will beat more than 2.5 billion times, pumping more than 1 million barrels of blood (enough to fill more than 3 super tankers) throughout your body.

Just like our hearts never rest, we need to keep loving God with our spiritual hearts as long as we live. It's what keeps us spiritually alive and strong!

[Yahooligans: Ask Earl]

³⁹"Remember this: If the owner of the house knew what time a thief was coming, then the owner would not allow the thief to enter his house. ⁴⁰So you also must be ready! The Son of Man will come at a time when you don't expect him!"

### WHO IS THE TRUSTED SERVANT?

⁴¹Peter said, "Lord, did you tell this story for us or for all people?"

⁴²The Lord said, "Who is the wise and trusted servant? Who is the servant the master trusts to give the other servants their food at the right time? ⁴³When the master comes and finds his servant doing the work he gave him, that servant will be very happy. ⁴⁴I tell you the truth. The master will choose that servant to take care of everything the master owns. ⁴⁵But what will happen if the servant is evil and thinks that his master will not come back soon? That

servant will begin to beat the other servants, men and women. He will eat and drink and get drunk. ⁴⁶Then the master will come when that servant is not ready. It will be a time when the servant is not expecting him. Then the master will cut him in pieces and send him away to be with the others who don't obey.

⁴⁷"The servant who knows what his master wants but is not ready or does not do what the master wants will be beaten with many blows! ⁴⁸But the servant who does not know what his master wants and does things that should be punished will be beaten with few blows. Everyone who has been given much will be responsible for much. Much more will be expected from the one who has been given more."

### JESUS CAUSES DIVISION

⁴⁹Jesus continued speaking, "I came to set fire to the world. I wish it were already burning! ⁵⁰I

must be baptized with a different kind of baptism." I feel very troubled until it is over. ⁵¹Do you think that I came to give peace to the world? No! I came to divide the world! ⁵²From now on, a family with five people will be divided, three against two, and two against three. ⁵³A father and son will be divided: The son will be against his father. The father will be against his son. A mother and her daughter will be divided: The daughter will be against her mother. The mother will be against her daughter. A mother-in-law and her daughter-in-law will be divided: The daughter-in-law will be against her mother-in-law. The mother-in-law will be against her daughter-in-law."

### UNDERSTANDING THE TIMES

⁵⁴Then Jesus said to the people, "When you see clouds coming up in the west, you say, 'It's going to rain.' And soon it begins to rain. ⁵⁵When you feel the wind begin to blow from the south, you say, 'It will be a hot day.' And you are right. ⁵⁶Hypocrites! You can understand the weather. Why don't you understand what is happening now?

### SETTLE YOUR PROBLEMS

⁵⁷"Why can't you decide for yourselves what is right? ⁵⁸When someone is suing you, and you are going with him to court, try hard to settle it on the way. If you don't settle it, he may take you to the judge. The judge might turn you over to the officer. And the officer might throw you into jail. ⁵⁹You will not get out of there until they have taken everything you have."

 12:50 I . . . baptism. Jesus was talking about the suffering he would soon go through.

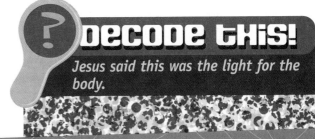

### DECODE THIS!
Jesus said this was the light for the body.

## CHANGE YOUR HEARTS

**13** At that time some people were there with Jesus. They told him about what had happened to some people from Galilee. Pilate[n] killed those people while they were worshiping. He mixed their blood with the blood of the animals they were sacrificing to God. [2]Jesus answered, "Do you think this happened to them because they were more sinful than all others from Galilee? [3]No, they were not! But if all of you don't change your hearts and lives, then you will be destroyed as

## JESUS HEALS ON THE SABBATH

[10]Jesus was teaching in one of the synagogues[d] on the Sabbath[d] day. [11]In the synagogue there was a woman who had an evil spirit in her. This spirit had made the woman a cripple for 18 years. Her back was always bent; she could not stand up straight. [12]When Jesus saw her, he called her over and said, "Woman, your sickness has left you!" [13]Jesus put his hands on her. Immediately she was able to stand up straight and began praising God.

[14]The synagogue leader was angry because Jesus healed on the Sabbath

[20]Jesus said again, "What can I compare God's kingdom with? [21]It is like yeast that a woman mixes into a big bowl of flour. The yeast makes all the dough rise."

## THE NARROW DOOR

[22]Jesus was teaching in every town and village. He continued to travel toward Jerusalem. [23]Someone said to Jesus, "Lord, how many people will be saved? Only a few?"

Jesus said, [24]"Try hard to enter through the narrow door that opens the way to heaven! Many people will

> "Try hard to enter through the narrow door that opens the way to heaven! Many people will try to enter there, but they will not be able." Luke 13:24

they were! [4]What about those 18 people who died when the tower of Siloam fell on them? Do you think they were more sinful than all the others who live in Jerusalem? [5]They were not! But I tell you, if you don't change your hearts and lives, then you will all be destroyed too!"

## THE USELESS TREE

[6]Jesus told this story: "A man had a fig tree planted in his vineyard. He came looking for some fruit on the tree, but he found none. [7]So the man said to his servant who took care of his vineyard, 'I have been looking for fruit on this tree for three years, but I never find any. Cut it down! Why should it waste the ground?' [8]But the servant answered, 'Master, let the tree have one more year to produce fruit. Let me dig up the dirt around it and put on some fertilizer. [9]Maybe the tree will produce fruit next year. If the tree still doesn't produce fruit, then you can cut it down.'"

day. He said to the people, "There are six days for work. So come to be healed on one of those days. Don't come for healing on the Sabbath day."

[15]The Lord answered, "You people are hypocrites![d] All of you untie your work animals and lead them to drink water every day—even on the Sabbath day! [16]This woman that I healed is our Jewish sister. But Satan has held her for 18 years. Surely it is not wrong for her to be freed from her sickness on a Sabbath day!" [17]When Jesus said this, all the men who were criticizing him were ashamed. And all the people were happy for the wonderful things Jesus was doing.

## STORIES OF MUSTARD SEED AND YEAST

[18]Then Jesus said, "What is God's kingdom like? What can I compare it with? [19]God's kingdom is like the seed of the mustard plant.[n] A man plants this seed in his garden. The seed grows and becomes a tree. The wild birds build nests on its branches."

try to enter there, but they will not be able. [25]A man gets up and closes the door of his house. You can stand outside and knock on the door. You can say, 'Sir, open the door for us!' But he will answer, 'I don't know you! Where did you come from?' [26]Then you will say, 'We ate and drank with you. You taught in the streets of our town.' [27]But he will say to you, 'I don't know you! Where did you come from? Go away from me! All of you do evil!' [28]You will see Abraham, Isaac, Jacob, and all the prophets[d] in God's kingdom. But you will be thrown outside. Then you will cry and grind your teeth with pain. [29]People will come from the east, west, north, and south. They will sit down at the table in the kingdom of God. [30]Those who have the lowest place in life now will have the highest place in the future. And those who have the highest place now will have the lowest place in the future."

13:1 **Pilate** Pontius Pilate was the Roman governor of Judea from A.D. 26 to A.D. 36. 13:19 **mustard plant** The seed is very small, but the plant grows taller than a man.

## JESUS WILL DIE IN JERUSALEM

[31]At that time some Pharisees[d] came to Jesus and said, "Go away from here! Herod wants to kill you!"

[32]Jesus said to them, "Go tell that fox Herod, 'Today and tomorrow I am forcing demons[d] out of people and finishing my work of healing. Then, on the third day, I will reach my goal.' [33]Yet I must be on my way today and tomorrow and the next day. Surely it cannot be right for a prophet[d] to be killed anywhere except in Jerusalem.

[34]"Jerusalem, Jerusalem! You kill the prophets. You kill with stones those men that God has sent you. Many times I wanted to help your people. I wanted to gather them together as a hen gathers her chicks under her wings. But you did not let me. [35]Now your home will be left completely empty. I tell you, you will not see me again until that time when you will say, 'God bless the One who comes in the name of the Lord.'"[n]

## IS IT RIGHT TO HEAL ON THE SABBATH?

**14** On a Sabbath[d] day, Jesus went to the home of a leading Pharisee[d] to eat with him. The people there were all watching Jesus very closely. [2]A man with dropsy[n] was brought before Jesus. [3]Jesus said to the Pharisees and teachers of the law, "Is it right or wrong to heal on the Sabbath day?" [4]But they would not answer his question. So Jesus took the man, healed him, and sent him away. [5]Jesus said to the Pharisees and teachers of the law, "If your son or ox falls into a well on the Sabbath day, will you not pull him out quickly?" [6]And they could not answer him.

## DON'T MAKE YOURSELF IMPORTANT

[7]Then Jesus noticed that some of the guests were choosing the best places to sit. So Jesus told this story: [8]"When someone invites you to a wedding feast, don't take the most important seat. The host may have invited someone more important than you. [9]And if you are sitting in the most important seat, the host will come to you and say, 'Give this man your seat.' Then you will begin to move down to the last place. And you will be very embarrassed. [10]So when you are invited, go sit in a seat that is not important. Then the host will come to you and say, 'Friend, move up here to a more important place!' Then all the other guests will respect you. [11]Everyone who makes himself great will be made humble. But the person who makes himself humble will be made great."

## YOU WILL BE REWARDED

[12]Then Jesus said to the man who had invited him, "When you give a lunch or a dinner, don't invite only your friends, brothers, relatives, and rich neighbors. At another time they will invite you to eat with them. Then you will have your reward. [13]Instead, when you give a feast, invite the poor, the crippled, the lame and the blind. [14]Then you will be blessed, because they cannot pay you back. They have nothing. But you will be rewarded when the good people rise from death."

# LIVIN' IT!

**EACH ONE MATTERS**
**LUKE 15**

Come on! You have 99 other sheep. Do you really need to go looking for the one that always wanders off? Or if you have 9 of 10 coins, will you really miss just one? According to Jesus and the way he looks at his people, the answer is yes!

Jesus said that all of heaven rejoices when just one sinner repents and turns to God. But you know what's really amazing about the stories of the lost sheep and the lost coin? Neither the lost sheep nor the lost coin was worried about finding their master. They were simply lost without hope of being found—until the owner got busy looking for them.

Isn't it astounding that God chases after us to show us his love? He finds us, and he changes our hearts. His family is just not complete without all his children in it. Thank God today for finding you and bringing you into his family.

## A STORY ABOUT A BIG BANQUET

[15]One of the men sitting at the table with Jesus heard these things. The man said to Jesus, "The people who will eat a meal in God's kingdom are blessed."

[16]Jesus said to him, "A man gave a big banquet and invited many people. [17]When it was time to eat, the man sent his servant to tell the guests, 'Come! Everything is ready!'

[18]"But all the guests said they could not come. Each man made an excuse. The first one said, 'I have just bought a field, and I must go look at it. Please

 **13:35** 'God . . . Lord.' Quotation from Psalm 118:26. **14:2 dropsy** A sickness that causes the body to swell larger and larger.

excuse me.' ¹⁹Another man said, 'I have just bought five pairs of oxen; I must go and try them. Please excuse me.' ²⁰A third man said, 'I just got married; I can't come.' ²¹So the servant returned. He told his master what had happened. Then the master became angry and said, 'Go at once into the streets and alleys of the town. Bring in the poor, the crippled, the blind, and the lame.' ²²Later the servant said to him, 'Master, I did what you told me to do, but we still have places for more people.' ²³The master said to the servant, 'Go out to the roads and country lanes. Tell the people there to come. I want my house to be full! ²⁴None of those men that I invited first will ever eat with me!'"

### YOU MUST FIRST PLAN

²⁵Large crowds were traveling with Jesus. He turned and said to them, ²⁶"If anyone comes to me but loves his father, mother, wife, children, brothers, or sisters more than he loves me, then he cannot be my follower. A person must love me more than he loves himself! ²⁷If anyone is not willing to die on a cross when he follows me, then he cannot be my follower. ²⁸If you wanted to build a tower, you would first sit down and decide how much it would cost. You must see if you have enough money to finish the job. ²⁹If you don't do that, you might begin the work, but you would not be able to finish. And if you could not finish it, then all who would see it would laugh at you. ³⁰They would say, 'This man began to build but was not able to finish!'

³¹"If a king is going to fight against another king, first he will sit down and plan. If the king has only 10,000 men, he will plan to see if he is able to defeat the other king who has 20,000 men. ³²If he cannot defeat the other king, then he will send some

## "The son was so hungry that he was willing to eat the food the pigs were eating."
*Luke 15:16*

men to speak to the other king and ask for peace. ³³In the same way, you must give up everything you have to follow me. If you don't, you cannot be my follower!

### DON'T LOSE YOUR INFLUENCE

³⁴"Salt is a good thing. But if the salt loses its salty taste, then it is worth nothing. You cannot make it salty again. ³⁵It is no good for the soil or for manure. People throw it away.

"You people who hear me, listen!"

### A LOST SHEEP AND A LOST COIN

**15** Many tax collectors and "sinners" came to listen to Jesus. ²The Pharisees^d and the teachers of the law began to complain: "Look! This man welcomes sinners and even eats with them!"

³Then Jesus told them this story: ⁴"Suppose one of you has 100 sheep, but he loses 1 of them. Then he will leave the other 99 sheep alone and go out and look for the lost sheep. The man will keep on searching for the lost sheep until he finds it. ⁵And when he finds it, the man is very happy. He puts it on his shoulders ⁶and goes home. He calls to his friends and neighbors and says, 'Be happy with me because I found my lost sheep!' ⁷In the

same way, I tell you there is much joy in heaven when 1 sinner changes his heart. There is more joy for that 1 sinner than there is for 99 good people who don't need to change.

⁸"Suppose a woman has ten silver coins,^n but she loses one of them. She will light a lamp and clean the house. She will look carefully for the coin until she finds it. ⁹And when she finds it, she will call her friends and neighbors and say, 'Be happy with me because I have found the coin that I lost!' ¹⁰In the same way, there is joy before the angels of God when 1 sinner changes his heart."

### THE SON WHO LEFT HOME

¹¹Then Jesus said, "A man had two sons. ¹²The younger son said to his father, 'Give me my share of the property.' So the father divided the property between his two sons. ¹³Then the younger son gathered up all that was his and left. He traveled far away to another country. There he wasted his money in foolish living. ¹⁴He spent everything that he had. Soon after that, the land became very dry, and there was no rain. There was not enough food to eat anywhere in the country. The son was hungry and needed money. ¹⁵So he got a job

## "But the father said to his servants, 'Hurry! Bring the best clothes and put them on him. Also, put a ring on his finger and sandals on his feet."
*Luke 15:22*

15:8 silver coins A Roman denarius. One coin was the average pay for one day's work.

# Gotta Know!

## Will friendships last forever?

They don't always, but they can. It depends upon whether or not both people belong to Jesus. If you both love Jesus, then you can enjoy each other's company your whole life, as you both learn more about God and grow closer to him. You will always have Jesus in common. Then, in heaven, everyone will be friends—so it will indeed last forever.

with one of the citizens there. The man sent the son into the fields to feed pigs. ¹⁶The son was so hungry that he was willing to eat the food the pigs were eating. But no one gave him anything. ¹⁷The son realized that he had been very foolish. He thought, 'All of my father's servants have plenty of food. But I am here, almost dying with hunger. ¹⁸I will leave and return to my father. I'll say to him: Father, I have sinned against God and have done wrong to you. ¹⁹I am not good enough to be called your son. But let me be like one of your servants.' ²⁰So the son left and went to his father.

"While the son was still a long way off, his father saw him coming. He felt sorry for his son. So the father ran to him, and hugged and kissed him. ²¹The son said, 'Father, I have sinned against God and have done wrong to you. I am not good enough to be called your son.' ²²But the father said to his servants, 'Hurry! Bring the best clothes and put them on him. Also, put a ring on his finger and sandals on his feet.

²³And get our fat calf and kill it. Then we can have a feast and celebrate! ²⁴My son was dead, but now he is alive again! He was lost, but now he is found!' So they began to celebrate.

²⁵"The older son was in the field. As he came closer to the house, he heard the sound of music and dancing. ²⁶So he called to one of the servants and asked, 'What does all this mean?' ²⁷The servant said, 'Your brother has come back. Your father killed the fat calf to eat because your brother came home safely!' ²⁸The older son was angry and would not go in to the feast. So his father went out and begged him to come in. ²⁹The son said to his father, 'I have served you like a slave for many years! I have always obeyed your commands. But you never even killed a young goat for me to have a feast with my friends. ³⁰But your other son has wasted all your money on prostitutes.ᵈ Then he comes home, and you kill the fat calf for him!' ³¹The father said to him, 'Son, you are always with me. All that I have is yours. ³²We had to celebrate

and be happy because your brother was dead, but now he is alive. He was lost, but now he is found.'"

### TRUE WEALTH

**16** Jesus also said to his followers, "Once there was a rich man. He had a manager to take care of his business. Later, the rich man learned that his manager was cheating him. ²So he called the manager in and said to him, 'I have heard bad things about you. Give me a report of what you have done with my money. You can't be my manager any longer!' ³Later, the manager thought to himself, 'What will I do? My master is taking my job away from me! I am not strong enough to dig ditches. I am too proud to beg. ⁴I know! I'll do something so that when I lose my job, people will welcome me into their homes.'

⁵"So the manager called in everyone who owed the master any money. He said to the first man, 'How much do you owe my master?' ⁶The man answered, 'I owe him 800 gallons of olive oil.' The manager said to him, 'Here is your bill; sit down quickly and make the bill less. Write 400 gallons.' ⁷Then the manager said to another man, 'How much do you owe my master?' The man answered, 'I owe him 1,000 bushels of wheat.' Then the manager said to him, 'Here is your bill; you can make it less. Write 800 bushels.' ⁸Later, the master praised the dishonest manager for being smart. Yes, worldly people are smarter with their own kind than spiritual people are.

⁹"I tell you, make friends for yourselves using worldly riches. Then, when those things are gone, you will

## DECODE THIS!

*Jesus healed a man on the Sabbath day who had_____.*

be welcomed in that home that continues forever. ¹⁰Whoever can be trusted with small things can also be trusted with large things. Whoever is dishonest in little things will be dishonest in large things too. ¹¹If you cannot be trusted with worldly riches, then you will not be trusted with the true riches. ¹²And if you cannot be trusted with the things that belong to someone else, then you will not be given things of your own.

¹³"No servant can serve two masters. He will hate one master and love the other. Or he will follow one master and refuse to follow the other. You cannot serve both God and money."

> **"if your brother sins, tell him he is wrong. But if he is sorry and stops sinning, forgive him."**
>
> *Luke 17:3*

### GOD'S LAW CANNOT BE CHANGED

¹⁴The Pharisees*ᵈ* were listening to all these things. They made fun of Jesus because they all loved money. ¹⁵Jesus said to them, "You make yourselves look good in front of people. But God knows what is really in your hearts. The things that are important to people are worth nothing to God.

¹⁶"God wanted the people to live by the law of Moses and the writings of the prophets.*ᵈ* But ever since John*ⁿ* came, the Good News*ᵈ* about the kingdom of God is being told. Now everyone is trying hard to get into the kingdom. ¹⁷Even the smallest part of a letter in the law cannot be changed. It would be easier for heaven and earth to pass away.

### DIVORCE AND REMARRIAGE

¹⁸"If a man divorces his wife and marries another woman, he is guilty of adultery.*ᵈ* And the man who marries a divorced woman is also guilty of adultery."

### THE RICH MAN AND LAZARUS

¹⁹Jesus said, "There was a rich man who always dressed in the finest clothes. He lived in luxury every day. ²⁰There was also a very poor man named Lazarus, whose body was covered with sores. Lazarus was often placed at the rich man's gate. ²¹He wanted to eat only the small pieces of food that fell from the rich man's table. And the dogs would come and lick his sores! ²²Later, Lazarus died. The angels took Lazarus and placed him in the arms of Abraham.*ᵈ* The rich man died, too, and was buried. ²³But he was sent to where the dead are and had much pain. The rich man saw Abraham far away with Lazarus in his arms. ²⁴He called, 'Father Abraham, have mercy on me! Send Lazarus to me so that he can dip his finger in water and cool my tongue. I am suffering in this fire!' ²⁵But Abraham said, 'My child, remember when you lived? You had all the good things in life, but all the bad things happened to Lazarus. Now Lazarus is comforted here, and you are suffering. ²⁶Also, there is a big pit between you and us. No one can cross over to help you. And no one can leave there and come here.' ²⁷The rich man said, 'Then please send Lazarus to my father's house on earth! ²⁸I have five brothers. Lazarus could warn my brothers so that they will not come to this place of pain.' ²⁹But Abraham said, 'They have the law of Moses and the writings of the prophets*ᵈ* to read; let them learn from them!' ³⁰The rich man said, 'No, father Abraham! If someone came to them from the dead, they

## LIVIN' IT!

**ONE TRUE LOVE**
**LUKE 16:14**

In case you missed it, Jesus draws the battle lines clearly: It's impossible to serve money and God at the same time. What does it mean to serve money? It means to value any possession more than God or to spend your time trying to get it instead of obeying God. It's not wrong to need or want things, but if our desire for something is stronger than our desire to do what God wants, we're sinning.

What Jesus said made the Pharisees mad, and it makes a lot of people angry today, too. People don't want to think they are greedy or that they love money. But if you look at where and how your money is spent, you'll have a good idea of what matters most to you. Ask God to work in your heart to help you appreciate his good gifts, but to always use them in ways that bring him the most glory.

would believe and change their hearts and lives.' ³¹But Abraham said to him, 'No! If your brothers won't listen to Moses and the prophets, then they won't listen to someone who comes back from death.'"

### SIN AND FORGIVENESS

**17** Jesus said to his followers, "Things will surely happen that cause people to sin. But how terrible for

---

 **16:16 John** John the Baptist, who preached to people about Christ's coming (Matthew 3, Luke 3).

the one who causes them to happen. [2]It would be better for him to be thrown into the sea with a large stone around his neck than to cause one of these weak people to sin. [3]So be careful!

"If your brother sins, tell him he is wrong. But if he is sorry and stops sinning, forgive him. [4]If your brother sins against you seven times in one day, but he says that he is sorry each time, then forgive him."

[12]he came into a small town. Ten men met him there. These men did not come close to Jesus, because they all had a harmful skin disease. [13]But they called to him, "Jesus! Master! Please help us!"

[14]When Jesus saw the men, he said, "Go and show yourselves to the priests."[n]

While the ten men were going, they were healed. [15]When one of them saw that he was healed, he went back to

## WHEN JESUS COMES AGAIN

[24]"The Son of Man[d] will come again. On the day he comes he will shine like lightning, which flashes across the sky and lights it up from one side to the other. [25]But first, the Son of Man must suffer many things and be rejected by the people of this time. [26]When the Son of Man comes again, it will be as it was when Noah lived. [27]In the time of Noah, people were eating, drinking, and get-

> **"Whoever tries to keep his life will give up true life. But whoever gives up his life will have true life."** Luke 17:33

## HOW BIG IS YOUR FAITH?

[5]The apostles[d] said to the Lord, "Give us more faith!"

[6]The Lord said, "If your faith is as big as a mustard seed,[n] then you can say to this mulberry tree, 'Dig yourself up and plant yourself in the sea!' And the tree will obey you.

## BE GOOD SERVANTS

[7]"Suppose one of you has a servant who has been plowing the ground or caring for the sheep. When the servant comes in from working in the field, would you say, 'Come in and sit down to eat'? [8]No, you would say to your servant, 'Prepare something for me to eat. Then get yourself ready and serve me. When I finish eating and drinking, then you can eat.' [9]The servant does not get any special thanks for doing what his master told him to do. [10]It is the same with you. When you do everything you are told to do, you should say, 'We don't deserve any special thanks. We have only done the work we should do.'"

## BE THANKFUL

"Jesus was on his way to Jerusalem. Traveling from Galilee to Samaria,

Jesus. He praised God in a loud voice. [16]Then he bowed down at Jesus' feet and thanked him. (This man was a Samaritan.[d]) [17]Jesus asked, "Ten men were healed; where are the other nine? [18]Is this Samaritan the only one who came back to thank God?" [19]Then Jesus said to him, "Stand up and go on your way. You were healed because you believed."

## GOD'S KINGDOM IS WITHIN YOU

[20]Some of the Pharisees[d] asked Jesus, "When will the kingdom of God come?"

Jesus answered, "God's kingdom is coming, but not in a way that you will be able to see with your eyes. [21]People will not say, 'Look, God's kingdom is here!' or, 'There it is!' No, God's kingdom is within you."

[22]Then Jesus said to his followers, "The time will come when you will want very much to see one of the days of the Son of Man.[d] But you will not be able to see it. [23]People will say to you, 'Look, there he is!' or, 'Look, here he is!' Stay where you are; don't go away and search.

ting married even on the day when Noah entered the boat. Then the flood came and killed all the people. [28]It will be the same as during the time of Lot. Those people were eating, drinking, buying, selling, planting, and building. [29]They were doing these things even on the day Lot left Sodom.[n] Then fire and sulfur rained down from the sky and killed them all. [30]This is exactly how it will be when the Son of Man comes again.

[31]"On that day, if a man is on his roof, he will not have time to go inside and get his things. If a man is in the field, he cannot go back home. [32]Remember what happened to Lot's wife?[n] [33]Whoever tries to keep his life will give up true life. But whoever gives up his life will have true life. [34]At the time when I come again, there may be two people sleeping in one bed. One will be taken and the other will be left. [35]There may be two women grinding grain together. One will be taken and the other will be left." [36][n]

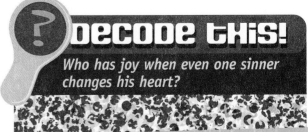

**Who has joy when even one sinner changes his heart?**

17:6 **mustard seed** This seed is very small, but the plant grows taller than a man. 17:14 **show . . . priests** The law of Moses said a priest must say when a Jew with a harmful skin disease became well. 17:29 **Sodom** City that God destroyed because the people were so evil. 17:32 **Lot's wife** A story about what happened to Lot's wife is found in Genesis 19:15-17, 26. 17:36 **Verse 36** A few Greek copies add verse 36: "Two men will be in the same field. One man will be taken, but the other man will be left behind."

[37]The followers asked Jesus, "Where will this be, Lord?"

Jesus answered, "People can always find a dead body by looking for the vultures."

## GOD WILL ANSWER HIS PEOPLE

**18** Then Jesus used this story to teach his followers that they should always pray and never lose hope. [2]"Once there was a judge in a town. He did not care about God. He also did not care what people thought about him. [3]In that same town there was a widow who

kept coming to this judge. She said, 'There is a man who is not being fair to me. Give me my rights!' [4]But the judge did not want to help the widow. After a long time, he thought to himself, 'I don't care about God. And I don't care about what people think. [5]But this widow is bothering me. I will see that

she gets her rights, or she will bother me until I am worn out!'"

[6]The Lord said, "Listen to what the bad judge said. [7]God's people cry to him night and day. God will always give them what is right, and he will not be slow to answer them. [8]I tell you, God will help his people quickly! But when the Son of Man[d] comes again, will he find those on earth who believe in him?"

## BEING RIGHT WITH GOD

[9]There were some people who thought that they were very good and looked down on everyone else. Jesus used this story to teach them: [10]"One day there was a Pharisee[d] and a tax collector. Both went to the Temple[d] to pray. [11]The Pharisee stood alone, away from the tax collector. When the Pharisee prayed, he said, 'God, I thank you that I am not as bad as other people. I am not like men who steal, cheat, or take part in adultery.[d] I thank you that I am better than this tax collector. [12]I give up eating[n] twice a week, and I give one-tenth of everything I earn!'

[13]"The tax collector stood at a distance. When he prayed, he would not even look up to heaven. He beat on his chest because he was so sad. He said, 'God, have mercy on me. I am a sinner!' [14]I tell you, when this man went home, he was right with God. But the Pharisee was not right with God. Everyone who makes himself great will be made humble. But everyone who makes himself humble will be made great."

## WHO WILL ENTER GOD'S KINGDOM?

[15]Some people brought their small

> **"Everyone who makes himself great will be made humble. But everyone who makes himself humble will be made great."** *Luke 18:14*

children to Jesus so that he could touch them. When the followers saw this, they told the people not to do this. [16]But Jesus called the little children to him and said to his followers, "Let the little children come to me. Don't stop them, because the kingdom of God belongs to people who are like these little children. [17]I tell you the truth. You must accept God's kingdom like a little child, or you will never enter it!"

## A RICH MAN'S QUESTION

[18]A Jewish leader asked Jesus, "Good Teacher, what must I do to get the life that continues forever?"

[19]Jesus said to him, "Why do you call me good? Only God is good. [20]You know the commands: 'You must not be guilty of adultery.[d] You must not murder anyone. You must not steal. You must not tell lies about your neighbor in court. Honor your father and mother.'[n]

[21]But the leader said, "I have obeyed all these commands since I was a boy!"

[22]When Jesus heard this, he said to him, "But there is still one more thing you need to do. Sell everything you have and give the money to the poor. You will have a reward in heaven. Then come and follow me!" [23]But when the man heard this, he became very sad because he was very rich.

---

## BIBLE BASICS

### WHAT IS FORGIVENESS?

Meaning "to send away," forgiveness is God's special act toward us when we turn from our sins. His forgiveness takes away the punishment our sins deserve and erases from God's record the fact that we ever sinned in the first place. When God forgives us, he does not remember our sins any more, and he separates them from us "as far as the east is from west" (Psalm 103:12). God promises to forgive us any time we confess our sins to him.

---

## DECODE THIS!

*When Jesus comes again he will shine like what?*

---

★ **18:12 give up eating** This is called "fasting." The people would give up eating for a special time of prayer and worship to God. It was also done to show sadness. **18:20 'You . . . mother.'** Quotation from Exodus 20:12-16; Deuteronomy 5:16-20.

# HELP THE WISE KINGS
# FOLLOW THE STAR
## THAT LEADS THEM TO JESUS.

[24]When Jesus saw that the man was sad, he said, "It will be very hard for rich people to enter the kingdom of God! [25]It would be easier for a camel to go through the eye of a needle than for a rich person to enter the kingdom of God!"

## WHO CAN BE SAVED?

[26]When the people heard this, they asked, "Then who can be saved?"

[27]Jesus answered, "God can do things that are not possible for men to do!"

[28]Peter said, "Look, we left everything we had and followed you!"

[29]Jesus said, "I tell you the truth. Everyone who has left his house, wife, brothers, parents, or children for God's kingdom [30]will get much more than he left. He will receive many times more in this life. And after he dies, he will live with God forever."

## JESUS WILL RISE FROM DEATH

[31]Then Jesus talked to the 12 apostles[d] alone. He said to them, "Listen! We are going to Jerusalem. Everything that God told the prophets[d] to write about the Son of Man[d] will happen! [32]He will be turned over to the non-Jewish people. They will laugh at him, insult him, and spit on him. [33]They will beat him with whips and then kill him. But on the third day after his death, he will rise to life again." [34]The apostles tried to understand this, but they could not; the meaning was hidden from them.

## JESUS HEALS A BLIND MAN

[35]Jesus was coming near the city of Jericho. There was a blind man sitting beside the road, begging for money. [36]When he heard the people coming down the road, he asked, "What is happening?"

[37]They told him, "Jesus, the one from Nazareth, is coming here."

[38]The blind man cried out, "Jesus, Son of David![d] Please help me!"

[39]The people who were in front, leading the group, told the blind man to be quiet. But the blind man shouted more and more, "Son of David, please help me!"

[40]Jesus stopped and said, "Bring the blind man to me!" When he came near, Jesus asked him, [41]"What do you want me to do for you?"

He said, "Lord, I want to see again."

[42]Jesus said to him, "Then see! You are healed because you believed."

[43]At once the man was able to see, and he followed Jesus, thanking God. All the people who saw this praised God.

## ZACCHAEUS

**19** Jesus was going through the city of Jericho. [2]In Jericho there was a man named Zacchaeus. He was a wealthy, very important tax collector. [3]He wanted to see who Jesus was, but he was too short to see above the crowd. [4]He ran ahead to a place where he knew Jesus would come. He climbed a sycamore tree so he could see Jesus. [5]When Jesus came to that place, he looked up and saw Zacchaeus in the tree. He said to him, "Zacchaeus, hurry and come down! I must stay at your house today."

[6]Zacchaeus came down quickly. He was pleased to have Jesus in his house. [7]All the people saw this and began to complain, "Look at the kind of man Jesus stays with. Zacchaeus is a sinner!"

[8]But Zacchaeus said to the Lord, "I will give half of my money to the poor. If I have cheated anyone, I will pay that person back four times more!"

[9]Jesus said, "Salvation has come to this house today. This man truly belongs to the family of Abraham. [10]The Son of Man[d] came to find lost people and save them."

## A STORY ABOUT THREE SERVANTS

[11]Jesus traveled closer to Jerusalem. Some of the people thought that God's kingdom would appear soon. [12]Jesus knew that the people thought this, so he told them this story: "A very important man was preparing to go to a country far away to be made a king. Then he planned to return home and rule his people. [13]So the man

**KIDS SPEAK UP!**

Q. What do you sleep with at night that you wouldn't want your friends to know about?
A. I sleep with a little stuffed bear that I got when I was a baby.

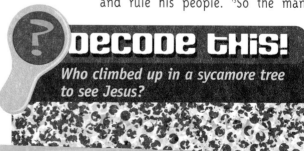

**DECODE THIS!**
Who climbed up in a sycamore tree to see Jesus?

# GET CONNECTED

## FAKE FAITH

### T OR F?

Are you surrounded by Christian friends? Christian family? Been going to church your whole life? Then watch out!

Lots of Christian friends are a huge gift from God. But you need to be careful. You can become very comfortable talking about or learning about God, without ever actually knowing God personally for yourself. Real faith cannot be caught from other Christians, like a cold. You have to decide in your own heart if you are going to give your life to God. He wants to be *your* best friend, *your* father, *your* life. Where do *you* stand in your relationship with God today?

called ten of his servants together. He gave a bag of money[n] to each servant. He said, 'Do business with this money till I get back.' [14]But the people in the kingdom hated the man. So they sent a group to follow him and say, 'We don't want this man to be our king!'

[15]"But the man became king. When he came home, he said, 'Call those servants who have my money. I want to know how much they earned with it.'

[16]"The first servant came and said, 'Sir, I earned ten bags of money with the one bag you gave me!' [17]The king said to the servant, 'Fine! You are a good servant. I see that I can trust you with small things. So now I will let you rule over ten of my cities.'

[18]"The second servant said, 'Sir, with your one bag of money I earned five bags!' [19]The king said to this servant, 'You can rule over five cities.'

[20]"Then another servant came in. The servant said to the king, 'Sir, here is your bag of money. I wrapped it in a piece of cloth and hid it. [21]I was afraid of you because you are a hard man. You even take money that you didn't earn and gather food that you didn't plant.' [22]Then the king said to the servant, 'You evil servant! I will use your own words to condemn you. You said that I am a hard man. You said that I even take money that I didn't earn

and gather food that I didn't plant. [23]If that is true, then you should have put my money in the bank. Then, when I came back, my money would have earned some interest.'

[24]"Then the king said to the men who were watching, 'Take the bag of money away from this servant and give it to the servant who earned ten bags of money.' [25]They said to the king, 'But sir, that servant already has ten bags of money!' [26]The king said, 'The one who uses what he has will get more. But the one who does not use what he has will have everything taken away from him. [27]Now where are my enemies who didn't want me to be king? Bring them here and kill them before me.'"

## JESUS ENTERS JERUSALEM AS A KING

[28]After Jesus said this, he went on toward Jerusalem. [29]Jesus came near Bethphage and Bethany, towns near the hill called the Mount of Olives.[d] Then he sent out two of his followers. [30]He said, "Go into the town you can see there. When you enter it, you will find

a colt tied there. No one has ever ridden this colt. Untie it, and bring it here to me. [31]If anyone asks you why you are taking it, say, 'The Master needs it.'"

[32]The two followers went into town. They found the colt just as Jesus told them. [33]The followers untied it, but the owners of the colt came out. They asked the followers, "Why are you untying our colt?"

[34]The followers answered, "The Master needs it." [35]So they brought it to Jesus. They threw their coats on the colt's back and put Jesus on it. [36]As Jesus rode toward Jerusalem, the followers spread their coats on the road before him.

[37]Jesus was coming close to Jerusalem. He was already near the bottom of the Mount of Olives. The whole crowd of followers was very happy. They began shouting praise to God for all the powerful works they had seen. They said,

[38]"God bless the king who comes in the name of the Lord!
There is peace in heaven and glory to God!" *Psalm 118:26*

[39]Some of the Pharisees[d] said to Jesus, "Teacher, tell your followers not to say these things!"

[40]But Jesus answered, "I tell you, if my followers don't say these things, then the stones will cry out."

> "The Son of Man came to find lost people and save them." *Luke 19:10*

## JESUS CRIES FOR JERUSALEM

[41]Jesus came near Jerusalem. He saw the city and began to cry for it. [42]Jesus said to Jerusalem, "I wish you knew today what would bring you peace! But you can't know it, because it is hidden from you. [43]A time is coming when your enemies will build a wall around you and will hold you in on all sides. [44]They will

19:13 bag of money One bag of money was a Greek "mina." One mina was enough money to pay a person for working three months.

119

destroy you and all your people. Not one stone of your buildings will be left on another. All this will happen because you did not know the time when God came to save you."

## GOOD NiGHT, GOOD MORNiNG

**Jesus was facing death, and he asked his disciples to watch and pray. But what did they do? They fell asleep!**

Why do we spend more than one-third of our lives sleeping? Scientists offer different opinions, but basically they say that it helps us in 2 ways: First, it helps us save up energy by slowing our metabolism and lowering our body temperature for a short time. Second, it gives our bodies time to clean themselves and restore themselves for the next day's activities. People need different amounts of sleep at different ages. At your age, you should get 9-10 hours a night, with occasional naps. When we're well rested, we're better able to do what God has for us to do—and with a better attitude!

**[Oracle Thinkquest]**

### JESUS GOES TO THE TEMPLE

[45]Jesus went into the Temple.[d] He began to throw out the people who were selling things there. [46]He said, "It is written in the Scriptures,[d] 'My Temple will be a house where people will pray.'[n] But you have changed it into a 'hideout for robbers'!"[n]

[47]Jesus taught in the Temple every day. The leading priests, the teachers of the law, and some of the leaders of the people wanted to kill Jesus. [48]But all the people were listening closely to him and were interested in all the things he said. So the leading priests, the teachers of the law, and the leaders did not know how they could kill him.

### THE LEADERS QUESTION JESUS

**20** One day Jesus was in the Temple,[d] teaching the people and telling them the Good News.[d] The leading priests, teachers of the law, and older Jewish leaders came up to talk with him. [2]They said, "Tell us! What authority do you have to do these things? Who gave you this authority?"

[3]Jesus answered, "I will ask you a question too. Tell me: [4]When John baptized people, did that come from God or from man?"

[5]The priests, the teachers of the law, and the Jewish leaders all talked about this. They said to each other, "If we answer, 'John's baptism was from God,' then Jesus will say, 'Then why did you not believe John?' [6]But if we say, 'John's baptism was from man,' then all the people will kill us with stones because they believe that John was a prophet."[d] [7]So they answered,

"We don't know the answer."

[8]So Jesus said to them, "Then I will not tell you by what authority I do these things!"

### GOD SENDS HIS SON

[9]Then Jesus told the people this story: "A man planted a vineyard. The man leased the land to some farmers. Then he went away for a long time. [10]Later, it was time for the grapes to be picked. So the man sent a servant to those farmers to get his share of the grapes. But they beat the servant and sent him away with nothing. [11]Then he sent another servant. They beat this servant too. They showed no respect for him and sent him away with nothing. [12]So the man sent a third servant. The farmers hurt this servant badly and threw him out. [13]The owner of the vineyard said, 'What will I do now? I will send my son whom I love very much. Maybe they will respect him!' [14]When they saw the son, they said to each other, 'This is the owner's son. This vineyard will be his. If we kill him, then it will be ours!' [15]So the farmers threw the son out of the vineyard and killed him.

"What will the owner of this vineyard do? [16]He will come and kill those farmers! Then he will give the vineyard to other farmers."

The people heard this story. They said, "No! Let this never happen!"

[17]But Jesus looked at them and said, "Then what does this verse mean:
'The stone that the builders did not want
became the cornerstone'?[d]

*Psalm 118:22*

[18]Everyone who falls on that stone will be broken. If that stone falls on you, it will crush you!"

[19]The teachers of the law and the priests heard this story that Jesus told. They knew the story was about them. So they wanted to arrest Jesus

---

19:46 'My Temple . . . pray.' Quotation from Isaiah 56:7. 19:46 'hideout for robbers' Quotation from Jeremiah 7:11.

at once. But they were afraid of what the people would do.

### THE LEADERS TRY TO TRAP JESUS

²⁰So they waited for the right time to get Jesus. They sent some spies who acted as if they were good men. They wanted to trap Jesus in what he said so they could hand him over to the authority and power of the governor. ²¹So the spies asked Jesus, "Teacher, we know that what you say and teach is true. You teach the same to all people. You always teach the truth about God's way. ²²Tell us, is it right that we pay taxes to Caesar*d* or not?"

²³But Jesus knew that these men were trying to trick him. He said, ²⁴"Show me a coin. Whose name is on the coin? And whose picture is on it?"

They said, "Caesar's."

> **"We know that what you say and teach is true. You teach the same to all people. You always teach the truth about God's way."**
>
> *Luke 20:21*

²⁵Jesus said to them, "Then give to Caesar the things that are Caesar's. And give to God the things that are God's."

²⁶The men were amazed at his answer.

They could say nothing. They were not able to trap Jesus in anything he said before the people.

### SADDUCEES TRY TO TRICK JESUS

²⁷Some Sadducees*d* came to Jesus. (Sadducees believe that people will not rise from death.) They asked, ²⁸"Teacher, Moses wrote that a man's brother might die. He leaves a wife but no children. Then that man must marry the widow and have children for his dead brother. ²⁹One time there were seven brothers. The first brother married, but died. He had no children. ³⁰Then the second brother married the widow, and he died. ³¹And the third brother married the widow, and he died. The same thing happened with all the other brothers. They all died and had no children. ³²The woman was the last to die. ³³But all seven brothers married her. So when people rise from death, whose wife will the woman be?"

³⁴Jesus said to the Sadducees, "On earth, people marry each other. ³⁵But those who will be worthy to be raised from death and live again will not marry. ³⁶In that life they are like angels and cannot die. They are children of God, because they have been raised from death. ³⁷Moses clearly showed that the dead are raised to life. When Moses wrote about the burning bush,*n* he said that the Lord is 'the God of Abraham, the God of Isaac, and the God of Jacob.'*n* ³⁸God is the God of living people, not dead people. All people are alive to God."

³⁹Some of the teachers of the law said, "Teacher, your answer was good." ⁴⁰No one was brave enough to ask him another question.

### IS THE CHRIST THE SON OF DAVID?

⁴¹Then Jesus said, "Why do people say that the Christ*d* is the Son of David?*d* ⁴²In the book of Psalms, David himself says:

> 'The Lord said to my Lord:
>     Sit by me at my right side,
> ⁴³    until I put your enemies under
>         your control.'*n*          *Psalm 110:1*

⁴⁴David calls the Christ 'Lord.' But the Christ is also the son of David. How can both these things be true?"

### JESUS ACCUSES THE LEADERS

⁴⁵While all the people were listening, Jesus said to his followers, ⁴⁶"Be careful of the teachers of the law. They like to walk around wearing clothes that look important. And they love for people to show respect to them in the marketplaces. They love to have the most important seats in the synagogues*d* and at the feasts. ⁴⁷But they cheat widows and steal their houses. Then they try to make themselves look good by saying long prayers. God will punish these men very much."

### TRUE GIVING

**21** Jesus saw some rich people putting their gifts into the Temple*d* money box.*n* ²Then Jesus saw a poor widow. She put two small copper coins into the box. ³He said, "I tell you the truth. This poor widow gave only two small coins. But she really gave more than all those rich people. ⁴The rich have plenty; they gave only what they did not need. This woman is very poor, but she gave all she had. And she needed that money to live on."

**DECODE THIS!**

*Who gave all she had to the Temple money box?*

20:37 **burning bush** Read Exodus 3:1–12 in the Old Testament. 20:37 **'the God of . . . Jacob'** These words are taken from Exodus 3:6. 20:43 **until . . . control** Literally, "until I make your enemies a footstool for your feet." 21:1 **money box** A special box in the Jewish place for worship where people put their gifts to God.

THE ARMY OFFICER'S
SERVANT IS VERY SICK.

HELP THE ARMY OFFICER
REACH JESUS FOR HELP.

# Gotta Know!

## How does God know everything?

God says that his thoughts are not our thoughts, and his ways are not our ways. He says we can't even begin to understand him. Why? Because he is God! He alone was there when the world first began. Everything that exists stays alive because the Creator God wills it to be. Because he made everything, he knows exactly how everything works. His knowledge is so big he can know your thoughts, even before you think them. He's an amazing God!

## THE TEMPLE WILL BE DESTROYED

[5]Some of the followers were talking about the Temple[d] and how it was decorated with beautiful stones and gifts offered to God.

[6]But Jesus said, "The time will come when all that you see here will be destroyed. Every stone will be thrown down to the ground. Not one stone will be left on another!"

[7]Some followers asked Jesus, "Teacher, when will these things happen? What will show us that it is time for them to take place?"

[8]Jesus said, "Be careful! Don't be fooled. Many people will come using my name. They will say, 'I am the Christ'[d] and, 'The right time has come!' But don't follow them. [9]When you hear about wars and riots, don't be afraid. These things must happen first. Then the end will come later."

[10]Then he said to them, "Nations will fight against other nations. Kingdoms will fight against other kingdoms. [11]There will be great earthquakes, sicknesses, and other terrible things in many places. In some places there will be no food for the people to eat. Fearful events and great signs will come from heaven.

[12]"But before all these things happen, people will arrest you and treat you cruelly. They will judge you in their synagogues[d] and put you in jail. You will be forced to stand before kings and governors. They will do all these things to you because you follow me. [13]But this will give you an opportunity to tell about me. [14]Don't worry about what you will say. [15]I will give you the wisdom to say things so that none of your enemies will be able to show that you are wrong. [16]Even your parents, brothers, relatives and friends will turn against you. They will kill some of you. [17]All people will hate you because you follow me. [18]But none of these things can really harm you. [19]You will save yourselves by continuing strong in your faith through all these things.

## JERUSALEM WILL BE DESTROYED

[20]"When you see armies all around Jerusalem, then you will know that it will soon be destroyed. [21]At that time, the people in Judea should run away to the mountains. The people in Jerusalem must get out. If you are near the city, don't go in! [22]These are the days of punishment to make come true all that is written in the Scriptures.[d] [23]At that time, it will be hard for women who are pregnant or have nursing babies! Great trouble will come upon this land, and God will be angry with these people. [24]Some will be killed by the sword and taken as prisoners to all nations. Jerusalem will be crushed by non-Jewish people until their time is over.

## DON'T FEAR

[25]"Amazing things will happen to the sun, moon, and stars. On earth, nations will be afraid because of the roar and fury of the sea. They will not know what to do. [26]People will be so afraid they will faint. They will wonder what is happening to the whole world. Everything in the sky will be changed. [27]Then people will see the Son of Man[d] coming in a cloud with power and great glory. [28]When these things begin to happen, don't fear. Look up and hold your heads high because the time when God will free you is near!"

## MY WORDS WILL LIVE FOREVER

[29]Then Jesus told this story: "Look at the fig tree and all the other trees.

> "You will save yourselves by continuing strong in your faith through all these things." *Luke 21:19*

## DECODE THIS!

*Where did Jesus go to pray before he was arrested?*

[30]"When their leaves appear, you know that summer is near. [31]In the same way, when you see all these things happening, then you will know that God's kingdom is coming very soon.

[32]"I tell you the truth. All these things will happen while the people of this time are still living! [33]The whole world, earth and sky, will be destroyed; but the words I have said will never be destroyed!

> ## "The whole world, earth and sky, will be destroyed; but the words i have said will never be destroyed!"
>
> *Luke 21:33*

## BE READY ALL THE TIME

[34]"Be careful! Don't spend your time feasting and drinking. Or don't be too busy with worldly things. If you do that, you will not be able to think straight. And then that day might come when you are not ready. [35]It will close like a trap on all people on earth. [36]So be ready all the time. Pray that you will be strong enough to escape all these things that will hap-pen. And pray that you will be able to stand before the Son of Man."[d]

[37]During the day, Jesus taught the people in the Temple.[d] At night he went out of the city and stayed on the Mount of Olives.[d] [38]Every morning all the people got up early to go to the Temple to listen to him.

## PLANS TO KILL JESUS

**22** It was almost time for the Jewish Feast[d] of Un-leavened Bread, called the Passover[d] Feast. [2]The lead-ing priests and teachers of the law were trying to find a way to kill Jesus. But they were afraid of the people.

[3]One of Jesus' 12 apostles[d] was named Judas Iscariot. Satan entered Judas, and he went to [4]the leading priests and some of the soldiers who guarded the Temple.[d] He talked to them about a way to give Jesus to them. [5]They were pleased and promised to give Judas money. [6]Judas agreed. Then he waited for the best time to turn Jesus over to them without the crowd knowing it.

## PREPARATION OF THE PASSOVER MEAL

[7]The Day of Unleavened[d] Bread came. This was the day the Passover[d] lambs had to be sacrificed. [8]Jesus said to Peter and John, "Go and prepare the Passover meal for us to eat."

[9]They asked, "Where do you want us to prepare it?"

Jesus said to them, [10]"Listen! After you go into the city, you will see a man carrying a jar of water. Follow him into the house that he enters. [11]Tell the person who owns that house, 'The Teacher asks that you please show us the room where he and his followers may eat the Passover meal.' [12]Then he will show you a large room upstairs. This room is ready for you. Prepare the Passover meal there."

[13]So Peter and John left. Everything hap-pened as Jesus had said. So they pre-pared the Passover meal.

## THE LORD'S SUPPER

[14]When the time came, Jesus and the apostles[d] were sitting at the table. [15]He said to them, "I wanted very much to eat this Passover[d] meal with you before I die. [16]I will never eat another Passover meal until it is given its true meaning in the king-dom of God."

[17]Then Jesus took a cup. He gave thanks to God for it and said, "Take this cup and give it to everyone here. [18]I will not drink again from the fruit of the vine[n] until God's king-dom comes."

[19]Then Jesus took some bread. He thanked God for it, broke it, and gave it to the apostles. Then Jesus said, "This bread is my body that I am giv-ing for you. Do this to remember me." [20]In the same way, after supper, Jesus took the cup and said, "This cup shows the new agreement that God makes with his people. This new agreement begins with my blood which is poured out for you."[n]

## WHO WILL TURN AGAINST JESUS?

[21]Jesus said, "One of you will turn against me. His hand is by my hand on the table. [22]The Son of Man[d] will do

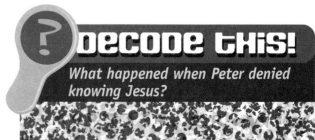

**DECODE THIS!**
*What happened when Peter denied knowing Jesus?*

---

**22:18 fruit of the vine** Product of the grapevine; this may also be translated "wine."
**22:20 Verse 20** A few Greek copies do not have the last part of verse 19 and all of verse 20.

# GET CONNECTED

## BLIND LEADING THE BLIND

The Pharisees had a problem. They were Israel's main leaders, the ones who were supposed to know the best way to get to God. But they didn't really know who God was. When Jesus came, they rejected him, too. Jesus said they were like blind people trying to lead other blind people. Both will end up in the wrong place.

God doesn't want us to be that way. He wants to be our guide, and he wants us to know the truth. But we won't find the truth by making it up ourselves. We need to look for God in the Bible and find out what he says about himself. Then we will know who he is and be able to help others find out the truth, too.

what God has planned. But how terrible it will be for that man who gives the Son of Man to be killed."

²³Then the apostles[d] asked each other, "Which one of us would do that to Jesus?"

## BE LIKE A SERVANT

²⁴Then the apostles[d] began to argue about which one of them was the most important. ²⁵But Jesus said to them, "The kings of the world rule over their people. Men who have authority over others are called 'very important.' ²⁶But you must not be like that. The

³⁰You will eat and drink at my table in my kingdom. You will sit on thrones and judge the 12 tribes[d] of Israel.

## DON'T LOSE YOUR FAITH!

³¹"Satan has asked to test all of you as a farmer tests his wheat. Simon, Simon, ³²I have prayed that you will not lose your faith! Help your brothers be stronger when you come back to me."

³³But Peter said to Jesus, "Lord, I am ready to go to prison with you. I will even die with you!"

have money or a bag, carry that with you. If you don't have a sword, sell your coat and buy one. ³⁷The Scripture[d] says, 'He was treated like a criminal.'[n] This scripture must have its full meaning. It was written about me, and it is happening now."

³⁸The followers said, "Look, Lord, here are two swords!"

He said to them, "That's enough."

## JESUS PRAYS ALONE

³⁹⁻⁴⁰Jesus left the city and went to the Mount of Olives.[d] His followers went with him. (Jesus went there often.) He said to his followers, "Pray for strength against temptation."

⁴¹Then Jesus went about a stone's throw away from them. He kneeled down and prayed, ⁴²"Father, if it is what you want, then let me not have this cup[n] of suffering. But do what you want, not what I want." ⁴³Then an angel from heaven appeared to him to help him. ⁴⁴Jesus was full of pain; he prayed even more. Sweat dripped from his face as if he were bleeding. ⁴⁵When he finished praying, he went to his followers. They were asleep.

> ## "Peter, before the rooster crows tonight, you will say you don't know me. You will say this three times!"
> *Luke 22:34*

greatest among you should be like the youngest, and the leader should be like the servant. ²⁷Who is more important: the one sitting at the table or the one serving him? You think the one at the table is more important. But I am like a servant among you!

²⁸"You men have stayed with me through many struggles. ²⁹My Father has given me the power to rule. I also give you authority to rule with me.

³⁴But Jesus said, "Peter, before the rooster crows tonight, you will say you don't know me. You will say this three times!"

## BE READY FOR TROUBLE

³⁵Then Jesus said to the apostles,[d] "When I sent you out without money, a bag, or sandals, did you need anything?"

They said, "No."

³⁶He said to them, "But now if you

(Their sadness had made them very tired.) ⁴⁶Jesus said to them, "Why are you sleeping? Get up and pray for strength against temptation."

## JESUS IS ARRESTED

⁴⁷While Jesus was speaking, a crowd came up. One of the 12 apostles[d] was leading them. He was Judas. He came close to Jesus so that he could kiss him.

22:37 'He . . . criminal.' Quotation from Isaiah 53:12. 22:42 cup Jesus is talking about the bad things that will happen to him. Accepting these things will be hard, like drinking a cup of something that tastes very bitter.

## Gotta Know!

### Why are big kids mean to little kids?

The reason why big kids are mean to little kids will differ from person to person. It is likely, though, that acting tough makes some feel important. Getting to boss others around makes some people feel like they can control something or someone. When they do this, they are forgetting God's call for them to love others and put their needs before their own. Be patient and remember to forgive those who are mean to you. They may have older kids doing the same thing to them, so they take it out on you. You, however, can stop the cycle of sin by treating younger people with love and respect.

⁴⁸But Jesus said to him, "Judas, are you using the kiss to give the Son of Man*d* to his enemies?"

⁴⁹The followers of Jesus were standing there too. They saw what was happening. They said to Jesus, "Lord, should we use our swords?" ⁵⁰And one of them did use his sword. He cut off the right ear of the servant of the high priest.

⁵¹Jesus said, "Stop!" Then he touched the servant's ear and healed him.

⁵²Those who came to arrest Jesus were the leading priests, the soldiers who guarded the Temple,*d* and the older Jewish leaders. Jesus said to them, "Why did you come out here with swords and sticks? Do you think I am a criminal? ⁵³I was with you every day in the Temple. Why didn't you try to arrest me there? But this is your time—the time when darkness rules."

### PETER SAYS HE DOESN'T KNOW JESUS

⁵⁴They arrested Jesus and took him away. They brought him into the house of the high priest. Peter followed them, but he did not go near Jesus. ⁵⁵The soldiers started a fire in the middle of the courtyard and sat together. Peter sat with them. ⁵⁶A servant girl saw Peter sitting there near the light. She looked closely at Peter's face and said, "This man was also with him!"

⁵⁷But Peter said this was not true. He said, "Girl, I don't know him."

⁵⁸A short time later, another person saw Peter and said, "You are also one of them."

But Peter said, "Man, I am not!"

⁵⁹About an hour later, another man insisted, "It is true! This man was with him. He is from Galilee!"

⁶⁰But Peter said, "Man, I don't know what you are talking about!"

Immediately, while Peter was still speaking, a rooster crowed. ⁶¹Then the Lord turned and looked straight at Peter. And Peter remembered what the Lord had said: "Before the rooster crows tonight, you will say three times that you don't know me." ⁶²Then Peter went outside and cried with much pain in his heart.

### THE PEOPLE LAUGH AT JESUS

⁶³⁻⁶⁴Some men were guarding Jesus. They made fun of him like this: They covered his eyes so that he could not see them. Then they hit him and said, "Prove that you are a prophet,*d* and tell us who hit you!" ⁶⁵The men said many cruel things to Jesus.

### JESUS BEFORE THE LEADERS

⁶⁶When day came, the older leaders of the people, the leading priests, and the teachers of the law came together. They led Jesus away to their highest court. ⁶⁷They said, "If you are the Christ,*d* then tell us that you are!"

Jesus said to them, "If I tell you I am the Christ, you will not believe me. ⁶⁸And if I ask you, you will not answer. ⁶⁹But beginning now, the Son of Man*d* will sit at the right hand of the powerful God."

⁷⁰They all said, "Then are you the Son of God?"

Jesus said to them, "Yes, you are right when you say that I am."

⁷¹They said, "Why do we need witnesses now? We ourselves heard him say this!"

### GOVERNOR PILATE QUESTIONS JESUS

**23** Then the whole group stood up and led Jesus to Pilate.*n* ²They began to accuse Jesus. They told Pilate, "We caught this man telling things that were confusing our people. He says that we should not pay taxes to Caesar.*d* He calls himself the Christ,*d* a king."

³Pilate asked Jesus, "Are you the king of the Jews?"

> **"Jesus said, 'Father, forgive them. They don't know what they are doing.'"**
>
> *Luke 23:34*

---

23:1 **Pilate** Pontius Pilate was the Roman governor of Judea from A.D. 26 to A.D. 36.

Jesus answered, "Yes, that is right."
⁴Pilate said to the leading priests and the people, "I find nothing wrong with this man."
⁵They said again and again, "But Jesus is making trouble with the people! He teaches all around Judea. He began in Galilee, and now he is here!"

**KIDS SPEAK UP!**

Q. What was something really silly that you did?

A. We had chocolate day at school (making stuff with chocolate), and I got chocolate everywhere, even in my ears.

### PILATE SENDS JESUS TO HEROD

⁶Pilate heard this and asked if Jesus was from Galilee. ⁷If so, Jesus was under Herod's authority. Herod was in Jerusalem at that time; so Pilate sent Jesus to him. ⁸When Herod saw Jesus, he was very glad. He had heard about Jesus and had wanted to meet him for a long time. Herod was hoping to see Jesus work a miracle.ᵈ ⁹Herod asked Jesus many questions, but Jesus said nothing. ¹⁰The leading priests and teachers of the law were standing there. They were shouting things against Jesus. ¹¹Then Herod and his soldiers made fun of Jesus. They dressed him in a kingly robe and

then sent him back to Pilate. ¹²In the past, Pilate and Herod had always been enemies. But on that day they became friends.

### JESUS MUST DIE

¹³Pilate called all the people together with the leading priests and the Jewish leaders. ¹⁴He said to them, "You brought this man to me. You said that he was making trouble among the people. But I have questioned him before you all, and I have not found him guilty of the things you say. ¹⁵Also, Herod found nothing wrong with him; he sent him back to us. Look, he has done nothing for which he should die. ¹⁶So, after I punish him, I will let him go free." ¹⁷ ⁿ
¹⁸But all the people shouted, "Kill him! Let Barabbas go free!" ¹⁹(Barabbas was a man who was in prison because he started a riot in the city. He was guilty of murder.)
²⁰Pilate wanted to let Jesus go free. So he told this to the crowd. ²¹But they shouted again, "Kill him! Kill him on a cross!"
²²A third time Pilate said to them, "Why? What wrong has he done? I can find no reason to kill him. So I will have him punished and set him free."
²³But they continued to shout. They demanded that Jesus be killed on the cross. Their yelling became so loud that ²⁴Pilate decided to give them what they wanted. ²⁵They wanted Barabbas to go free, the man who was in jail for starting a riot and for murder. Pilate let Barabbas go free and gave Jesus to them to be killed.

### JESUS IS KILLED ON A CROSS

²⁶The soldiers led Jesus away. At that time, there was a man coming into the city from the fields. His name was Simon, and he was from the city of Cyrene. The soldiers forced Simon to carry Jesus' cross and walk behind him.
²⁷A large crowd of people was following Jesus. Some of the women were sad and crying. ²⁸But Jesus turned and said to them, "Women of Jerusalem, don't cry for me. Cry for yourselves and for your children too! ²⁹The time is coming when people will say, 'Happy are the women who cannot have children! Happy are the women who have no babies to nurse.' ³⁰Then people will say to the mountains, 'Fall on us!' And they will say to the hills, 'Cover us!' ³¹If they act like this now when life is good, what will happen when bad times come?"ⁿ
³²There were also two criminals led out with Jesus to be killed. ³³Jesus and the two criminals were taken to a place called the Skull. There the soldiers nailed Jesus to his cross. They also nailed the criminals to their crosses, one beside Jesus on the right and the other beside Jesus on the left. ³⁴Jesus said, "Father, forgive them. They don't know what they are doing."ⁿ
The soldiers threw lotsᵈ to decide who would get his clothes. ³⁵The people stood there watching. The leaders made fun of Jesus. They said, "If he is God's Chosen One, the Christ,ᵈ then let him save himself. He saved other people, didn't he?"
³⁶Even the soldiers made fun of him. They came to Jesus and offered him

 23:17 **Verse 17** A few Greek copies add verse 17: "Every year at the Passover Feast, Pilate had to release one prisoner to the people." 23:31 **If . . . come?** Literally, "If they do these things in the green tree, what will happen in the dry?" 23:34 **Verse 34** Some early Greek copies do not have this part of the verse.

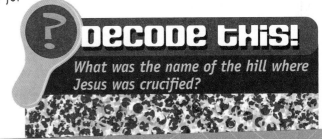

**DECODE THIS!**
*What was the name of the hill where Jesus was crucified?*

> "Why are you looking for a living person here? This is a place for the dead. Jesus is not here. He has risen from death!"
>
> *Luke 24:5-6*

some vinegar. [37]They said, "If you are the king of the Jews, save yourself!" [38](At the top of the cross these words were written: "THIS IS THE KING OF THE JEWS.")

[39]One of the criminals began to shout insults at Jesus: "Aren't you the Christ? Then save yourself! And save us too!"

[40]But the other criminal stopped him. He said, "You should fear God! You are getting the same punishment as he is. [41]We are punished justly; we should die. But this man has done nothing wrong!" [42]Then this criminal said to Jesus, "Jesus, remember me when you come into your kingdom!"

[43]Then Jesus said to him, "Listen! What I say is true: Today you will be with me in paradise!"[n]

### JESUS DIES

[44]It was about noon, and the whole land became dark until three o'clock in the afternoon. [45]There was no sun! The curtain in the Temple[n] was torn into two pieces. [46]Jesus cried out in a loud voice, "Father, I give you my life." After Jesus said this, he died.

[47]The army officer there saw what happened. He praised God, saying, "I know this was a good man!"

[48]Many people had gathered there to watch this thing. When they saw what happened, they returned home. They beat their chests because they were so sad. [49]Those who were close friends of Jesus were there. Some were women who had followed Jesus from Galilee. They all stood far away from the cross and watched.

### JOSEPH OF ARIMATHEA

[50-51]A man from the Jewish town of Arimathea was there, too. His name was Joseph. He was a good, religious man. He wanted the kingdom of God to come. Joseph was a member of the Jewish council, but he had not agreed when the other leaders decided to kill Jesus. [52]Joseph went to Pilate to ask for the body of Jesus. [53]So Joseph took the body down from the cross and wrapped it in cloth. Then he put Jesus' body in a tomb that was cut in a wall of rock. This tomb had never been used before. [54]This was late on Preparation[d] Day. When the sun went down, the Sabbath[d] day would begin.

[55]The women who had come from Galilee with Jesus followed Joseph. They saw the tomb and saw inside where the body of Jesus was laid. [56]Then the women left to prepare perfumes and spices.

On the Sabbath day they rested, as the law of Moses commanded.

### JESUS RISES FROM DEATH

**24** Very early on the first day of the week, the women came to the tomb where Jesus' body was laid. They brought the spices they had prepared. [2]They found that the stone had been rolled away from the entrance of the tomb. [3]They went in, but they did not find the body of the Lord Jesus. [4]While they were wondering about this, two men in shining clothes suddenly stood beside them. [5]The women were very afraid; they bowed their heads to the ground. The men said to the women, "Why are you looking for a living person here? This is a place for the dead. [6]Jesus is not here. He has risen from death! Do you remember what he said in Galilee? [7]He said that the Son of Man[d] must be given to evil men, be killed on a cross, and rise

> "He said that the Son of Man must be given to evil men, be killed on a cross, and rise from death on the third day."
>
> *Luke 24:7*

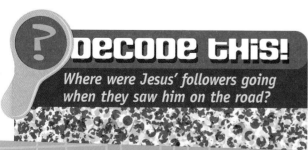

**DECODE THIS!**

*Where were Jesus' followers going when they saw him on the road?*

23:43 **paradise** A place where good people go when they die. 23:45 **curtain in the Temple** A curtain divided the Most Holy Place from the other part of the Temple. This was the special building in Jerusalem where God commanded the Jews to worship him.

# CHRISTMAS COUNTDOWN

You've probably heard the Christmas story a lot of times, but how well do you know the details? Test your Yuletide trivia with the following quiz:

**Score 9-10:** Merry Christmas! You're an expert.
**Score 5-8:** Cool Christmas! You know some stuff and have more to learn.  **Score 4 and below:** Bah Humbug! You need to revisit the trip to Bethlehem!

1. Jesus was from the tribe of
   A. Levi.
   B. Manasseh.
   C. Dan.
   D. Judah.

2. Jesus' parents' names were
   A. John and Elizabeth.
   B. Zechariah and Mary.
   C. Bob and Sue.
   D. Joseph and Mary.

3. At first, Joseph thought he should leave Mary. Why?
   A. He decided she wasn't pretty.
   B. He wanted to marry someone else.
   C. She was pregnant, and it wasn't his child.
   D. Getting married made him nervous.

4. What was different about Mary's pregnancy?
   A. An angel told her it would happen.
   B. She became pregnant through the Holy Spirit.
   C. The baby she was carrying would save the world.
   D. All of the above.

5. How were the shepherds to know they found the right baby?
   A. The star would show the way.
   B. They would hear the birthday music.
   C. The baby would be in a manger.
   D. The baby would tell them.

6. Where did the wise men come from?
   A. the North
   B. the South
   C. the East
   D. the West

7. How did Joseph know where to hide his family for protection?
   A. He guessed.
   B. He relied on information from his relatives.
   C. He used common sense.
   D. God told him through angels in his dreams.

8. How old was Jesus when he was circumcised?
   A. 1 day
   B. 8 days
   C. 1 year
   D. 12 years

9 What was the name of the prophetess who confirmed that Jesus was the promised Christ?
   A. Esther
   B. Deborah
   C. Anna
   D. Rachel

10. What city did Jesus grow up in?
   A. Bethlehem
   B. Nazareth
   C. Jerusalem
   D. None of the above

ANSWER KEY: 1. D; 2. D; 3. C; 4. D; 5. A; 6. C; 7. D; 8. B; 9. C; 10. B

from death on the third day." [8]Then the women remembered what Jesus had said.

> "When Jesus talked to us on the road, it felt like a fire burning in us. it was exciting when he explained the true meaning of the Scriptures."
>
> *Luke 24:32*

[9]The women left the tomb and told all these things to the 11 apostles[d] and the other followers. [10]These women were Mary Magdalene, Joanna, Mary the mother of James, and some other women. The women told the apostles everything that had happened at the tomb. [11]But they did not believe the women. It sounded like nonsense. [12]But Peter got up and ran to the tomb. He looked in, but he saw only the cloth that Jesus' body had been wrapped in. Peter went away to be alone, wondering about what had happened.

## ON THE ROAD TO EMMAUS

[13]That same day two of Jesus' followers were going to a town named Emmaus. It is about seven miles from Jerusalem. [14]They were talking about everything that had happened. [15]While they were discussing these things, Jesus himself came near and began walking with them. [16](They were not allowed to recognize Jesus.) [17]Then he said, "What are these things you are talking about while you walk?"

The two followers stopped. Their faces were very sad. [18]The one named Cleopas answered, "You must be the only one in Jerusalem who does not know what just happened there."

[19]Jesus said to them, "What are you talking about?"

The followers said, "It is about Jesus of Nazareth. He was a prophet[d] from God to all the people. He said and did many powerful things. [20]Our leaders and the leading priests gave him up to be judged and killed. They nailed him to a cross. [21]But we were hoping that he would free the Jews. It is now the third day since this happened. [22]And today some women among us told us some amazing things. Early this morning they went to the tomb, [23]but they did not find his body there. They came and told us that they had seen a vision of angels. The angels said that Jesus was alive! [24]So some of our group went to the tomb, too. They found it just as the women said, but they did not see Jesus."

[25]Then Jesus said to them, "You are foolish and slow to realize what is true. You should believe everything the prophets said.

[26]They said that the Christ[d] must suffer these things before he enters his glory." [27]Then Jesus began to explain everything that had been written about himself in the Scriptures.[d] He started with Moses, and then he talked about what all the prophets had said about him.

[28]They came near the town of Emmaus, and Jesus acted as if he did not plan to stop there. [29]But they begged him, "Stay with us. It is late; it is almost night." So he went in to stay with them.

[30]Jesus sat down with them and took some bread. He gave thanks for the food and divided it. Then he gave it to them. [31]And then, they were allowed to recognize Jesus. But when they saw who he was, he disappeared. [32]They said to each other, "When Jesus talked to us on the road, it felt like a fire burning in us. It was exciting when he explained the true meaning of the Scriptures."

[33]So the two followers got up at once and went back to Jerusalem. There they found the 11 apostles[d] and others gathered. [34]They were saying, "The Lord really has risen from death! He showed himself to Simon."

[35]Then the two followers told what had happened on the road. They talked about how they recognized Jesus when he divided the bread.

> "Then Jesus opened their minds so they could understand the Scriptures." *Luke 24:45*

## JESUS APPEARS TO HIS FOLLOWERS

[36]While the two followers were telling this, Jesus himself stood

**DECODE THIS!**

*What did the followers give Jesus to eat to prove he was alive?*

among those gathered. He said to them, "Peace be with you."

[37]They were fearful and terrified. They thought they were seeing a ghost. [38]But Jesus said, "Why are you troubled? Why do you doubt what you see? [39]Look at my hands and my feet. It is I myself! Touch me. You can see that I have a living body; a ghost does not have a body like this."

[40]After Jesus said this, he showed them his hands and feet. [41]The followers were amazed and very happy. They still could not believe it. Jesus said to them, "Do you have any food here?" [42]They gave him a piece of cooked fish. [43]While the followers watched, Jesus took the fish and ate it.

[44]He said to them, "Remember when I was with you before? I said that everything written about me must happen—everything in the law of Moses, the books of the prophets,[d] and the Psalms."

[45]Then Jesus opened their minds so they could understand the Scriptures.[d] [46]He said to them, "It is written that the Christ[d] would be killed and rise from death on the third day. [47-48]You saw these things happen—you are witnesses. You must tell people to change their hearts and lives. If they do this, their sins will be forgiven. You must start at Jerusalem and preach these things in my name to all nations. [49]Listen! My Father has promised you something; I will send it to you. But you must stay in Jerusalem until you have received that power from heaven."

## WILD WORLD FACTS

### FUNGUS AMONG US

Jesus said that the Pharisees' (religious leaders of Jesus' day) bad teachings were like yeast in dough. So why did he compare them to yeast?

Yeast is a very small fungus that grows by splitting itself in half. Each new piece becomes its own cell and splits again. The fungus is alive and multiplies quickly whenever it can find food, water, and warmth. It eats different kinds of sugars and releases carbon dioxide gas in the process. The gas makes bubbles in the dough, giving bread its light and airy look.

Pharisees were like yeast fungus among the Israelites. Their bad teachings were spreading quickly and infecting the whole community. Jesus told his followers to watch out for their lies and stop the growth.

[Yahooligans: Ask Earl]

### JESUS GOES BACK TO HEAVEN

[50]Jesus led his followers out of Jerusalem almost to Bethany. He raised his hands and blessed them. [51]While he was blessing them, he was separated from them and carried into heaven. [52]They worshiped him and then went back to the city very happy. [53]They stayed in the Temple[d] all the time, praising God.

John was one of the 12 apostles.

This Gospel focuses on 7 miracles and 7 "I am" statements about Jesus.

John tells about Jesus, the Son of God.

THE GOSPEL ACCORDING TO

JOHN

John's father was Zebedee, and his mother was Salome.

John and his brother James were nicknamed by Jesus "the Sons of Thunder."

Key verse to memorize: 3:16

## CHRIST COMES TO THE WORLD

**1** Before the world began, there was the Word.[n] The Word was with God, and the Word was God. [2]He was with God in the beginning. [3]All things were made through him. Nothing was made without him. [4]In him there was life. That life was light for the people of the world. [5]The Light shines in the darkness. And the darkness has not overpowered the Light.

[6]There was a man named John[n] who was sent by God. [7]He came to tell people about the Light. Through him all people could hear about the Light and believe. [8]John was not the Light, but he came to tell people about the Light. [9]The true Light was coming into the world. The true Light gives light to all.

[10]The Word was in the world. The world was made through him, but the world did not know him. [11]He came to the world that was his own. But his own people did not accept him. [12]But some people did accept him. They believed in him. To them he gave the right to become children of God. [13]They did not become his children in the human way. They were not born because of the desire or wish of some man. They were born of God.

[14]The Word became a man and lived among us. We saw his glory—the glory that belongs to the only Son of the Father. The Word was full of grace and truth. [15]John told about him. He said, "This is the One I was talking about. I said, 'The One who comes after me is greater than I am. He was living before me.'"

[16]The Word was full of grace and truth. From him we all received more and more blessings. [17]The law was given through Moses, but grace and truth came through Jesus Christ. [18]No man has ever seen God. But God the only Son is very close to the Father.[n] And the Son has shown us what God is like.

## JOHN TELLS PEOPLE ABOUT JESUS

[19]The Jews in Jerusalem sent some priests and Levites to John.[n] The Jews sent them to ask, "Who are you?"

[20]John spoke freely and did not refuse to answer. He said clearly, "I am not the Christ."[d]

[21]So they asked him, "Then who are you? Are you Elijah?"[n]

He answered, "No, I am not Elijah."

Then they asked, "Are you the Prophet?"[n]

He answered, "No, I am not the Prophet."

[22]Then they said, "Who are you? Give us an answer to tell those who sent us. What do you say about yourself?"

[23]John told them in the words of the prophet Isaiah:

"I am the voice of a man
   calling out in the desert:
'Make the road straight for the Lord.'"

*Isaiah 40:3*

[24]In the group of Jews who were sent, there were some Pharisees.[d] [25]They said to John: "You say you are not the Christ. You say you are not Elijah or the Prophet. Then why do you baptize people?"

[26]John answered, "I baptize people with water. But there is one here with you that you don't know. [27]He is the One who comes after me. I am not good enough to untie the strings of his sandals."

[28]This all happened at Bethany on the other side of the Jordan River. This is where John was baptizing people.

[29]The next day John saw Jesus coming toward him. John said, "Look, the Lamb of God.[n] He takes away the sins of the world! [30]This is the One I was talking about. I said, 'A man will come after me, but he is greater than I am, because he was living before me.' [31]Even I did not know who he was. But I came baptizing with water

> "His own people did not accept him. But some people did accept him. They believed in him. To them he gave the right to become children of God."
>
> *John 1:11-12*

so that the people of Israel could know who he is."

[32-33]Then John said, "I did not know who the Christ was. But God sent me to baptize with water. And God told me, 'You will see the Spirit[d] come down and rest on a man. That man is the One who will baptize with the Holy Spirit.'" John said, "I saw the Spirit come down from heaven. The Spirit looked like a dove and rested on him. [34]I have seen this happen. So I tell people: 'He is the Son of God.'"

## THE FIRST FOLLOWERS OF JESUS

[35]The next day John[n] was there again with two of his followers. [36]He saw Jesus walking by and said, "Look, the Lamb of God!"[n]

[37]The two followers heard John say this. So they followed Jesus. [38]Jesus turned and saw them following him. He asked, "What do you want?"

---

★ **1:1 Word** The Greek word is "logos," meaning any kind of communication. It could be translated "message." Here, it means Christ. Christ was the way God told people about himself. **1:6, 19, 35 John** John the Baptist, who preached to people about Christ's coming (Matthew 3, Luke 3). **1:18 But . . . Father** This could be translated, "But the only God is very close to the Father." Also, some Greek copies say, "But the only Son is very close to the Father." **1:21 Elijah** A man who spoke for God. He lived hundreds of years before Christ. **1:21 Prophet** They probably meant the prophet that God told Moses he would send (Deuteronomy 18:15-19). **1:29, 36 Lamb of God** Name for Jesus. Jesus is like the lambs that were offered for a sacrifice to God.

**DECODE THIS!**
*John said that he was not good enough to untie the strings of Jesus' what?*

They said, "Rabbi, where are you staying?" ("Rabbi" means "Teacher.")

[39]Jesus answered, "Come with me and you will see." So the two men went with Jesus. They saw the place where Jesus was staying and stayed there with him that day. It was then about four o'clock.

[40]These two men followed Jesus after they heard about him from John. One of the men was Andrew. He was Simon Peter's brother. [41]The first thing Andrew did was to find his brother, Simon. He said to Simon, "We have found the Messiah." ("Messiah" means "Christ."[d])

[42]Then Andrew took Simon to Jesus.

coming, and the prophets[d] also wrote about him. We have found him. He is Jesus, the son of Joseph. He is from Nazareth."

[46]But Nathanael said to Philip, "Nazareth! Can anything good come from Nazareth?"

Philip answered, "Come and see."

[47]Jesus saw Nathanael coming toward him. He said, "Here is truly a person of Israel. There is nothing false in him."

[48]Nathanael asked, "How do you know me?"

Jesus answered, "I saw you when you were under the fig tree. That was before Philip told you about me."

## "Jesus said to Nathanael, 'You believe in me because i told you i saw you under the fig tree. But you will see greater things than that!'" *John 1:50*

Jesus looked at Simon and said, "You are Simon son of John. You will be called Cephas." ("Cephas" means "Peter."[n])

[43]The next day Jesus decided to go to Galilee. He found Philip and said to him, "Follow me." [44]Philip was from the town of Bethsaida, where Andrew and Peter lived. [45]Philip found Nathanael and told him, "Remember that Moses wrote in the law about a man who was

[49]Then Nathanael said to Jesus, "Teacher, you are the Son of God. You are the King of Israel."

[50]Jesus said to Nathanael, "You believe in me because I told you I saw you under the fig tree. But you will see greater things than that!" [51]And Jesus said to them, "I tell you the truth. You will all see heaven open. You will see 'angels of God going up and coming down'[n] on the Son of Man."[d]

## THE WEDDING AT CANA

**2** Two days later there was a wedding in the town of Cana in Galilee. Jesus' mother was there. [2]Jesus and his followers were also invited to the wedding. [3]When all the wine was gone, Jesus' mother said to him, "They have no more wine."

[4]Jesus answered, "Dear woman, why come to me? My time has not yet come."

[5]His mother said to the servants, "Do whatever he tells you to do."

[6]In that place there were six stone water jars. The Jews used jars like these in their washing ceremony.[n] Each jar held about 20 or 30 gallons.

[7]Jesus said to the servants, "Fill the jars with water." So they filled the jars to the top.

[8]Then he said to them, "Now take some out and give it to the master of the feast."

So the servants took the water to the master. [9]When he tasted it, the water had become wine. He did not know where the wine came from. But the servants who brought the water knew. The master of the wedding called the bridegroom [10]and said to him, "People always serve the best wine first. Later, after the guests have been drinking a lot, they serve the cheaper wine. But you have saved the best wine till now."

[11]So in Cana of Galilee, Jesus did his first miracle.[d] There he showed his glory, and his followers believed in him.

## JESUS IN THE TEMPLE

[12]Then Jesus went to the town of Capernaum with his mother, brothers and his followers. They all stayed in Capernaum for a few days. [13]But it was almost time for the Jewish Passover[d] Feast. So Jesus went to Jerusalem. [14]In the Temple[d] he found men selling cattle, sheep, and doves. He saw others sitting at tables, exchanging money. [15]Jesus made a whip out of cords. Then

## GETCONNECTED

### BAALIEVE IT

Want to know something interesting about sheep? They're not too smart. They don't know where they are going. They make the same mistakes again and again. And if they fall over, someone else must pick them up. Want to know something else? God says that we are his sheep! He knows that we need help, guidance, and direction. So he gives it to us through his Word—and through our parents. God says that children must obey their parents, just like sheep must follow the shepherd. Obeying your parents not only honors God, but it also keeps you safe.

1:42 **Peter** The Greek name "Peter," like the Aramaic name "Cephas," means "rock." 1:51 **'angels . . . down'** These words are from Genesis 28:12. 2:6 **washing ceremony** The Jews washed themselves in special ways before eating, before worshiping in the Temple, and at other special times.

he forced all these men, with the sheep and cattle, to leave the Temple. He turned over the tables and scattered the money of the men who were exchanging it. [16]Then he said to those who were selling pigeons, "Take these things out of here! Don't make my Father's house a place for buying and selling!"

[17]When this happened the followers remembered what was written in the Scriptures:[d] "My strong love for your Temple completely controls me."[n]

[18]The Jews said to Jesus, "Show us a miracle[d] for a sign. Prove that you have the right to do these things."

[19]Jesus answered, "Destroy this temple, and I will build it again in three days."

[20]The Jews answered, "Men worked 46 years to build this Temple! Do you really believe you can build it again in three days?"

[21](But the temple Jesus meant was his own body. [22]After Jesus was raised from death, his followers remembered that Jesus had said this. Then they believed the Scripture[d] and the words Jesus said.)

[23]Jesus was in Jerusalem for the Passover Feast. Many people believed in him because they saw the miracles he did. [24]But Jesus did not trust himself to

## "Jesus answered, 'I tell you the truth. Unless one is born again, he cannot be in God's kingdom.'"

*John 3:3*

them because he knew them all. [25]He did not need anyone to tell him about people. Jesus knew what was in a person's mind.

### JESUS AND NICODEMUS

**3** There was a man named Nicodemus who was one of the Pharisees.[d] He was an important Jewish leader. [2]One night Nicodemus came to Jesus. He

said, "Teacher, we know that you are a teacher sent from God. No one can do the miracles[d] you do, unless God is with him."

[3]Jesus answered, "I tell you the truth. Unless one is born again, he cannot be in God's kingdom."

[4]Nicodemus said, "But if a man is already old, how can he be born again? He cannot enter his mother's body again. So how can he be born a second time?"

[5]But Jesus answered, "I tell you the truth. Unless one is born from water and the Spirit,[d] he cannot enter God's kingdom. [6]A person's body is born from his human parents. But a person's spiritual life is born from the Spirit. [7]Don't be surprised when I tell you, 'You must all be born again.' [8]The wind blows where it wants to go. You hear the wind blow. But you don't know where the wind comes from or where it is going. It is the same with every person who is born from the Spirit."

[9]Nicodemus asked, "How can all this be possible?"

[10]Jesus said, "You are an important teacher in Israel. But you still don't understand these things? [11]I tell you the truth. We talk about what we know. We tell about what we have seen. But you don't accept what we tell you. [12]I have told you about things here on earth, but you do not believe me. So surely you will not believe me if I tell you about the things of heaven! [13]The only one who has ever gone up to heaven is the One who came down from

heaven—the Son of Man.[d]

[14]"Moses lifted up the snake in the desert.[n] It is the same with the Son of Man. The Son of Man must be lifted up too. [15]Then everyone who believes in him can have eternal life.

[16]"For God loved the world so much that he gave his only Son. God gave his Son so that whoever believes in him may not be lost, but have eternal life. [17]God did not send his Son into the world to judge the world guilty, but to save the world through him. [18]He who believes in God's Son is not judged guilty. He who does not believe has

2:17 "My . . . me." Quotation from Psalm 69:9.
3:14 Moses . . . desert The people of Israel were dying from snake bites. God told Moses to put a brass snake on a pole. The people who looked at the snake were healed (Numbers 21:4-9).

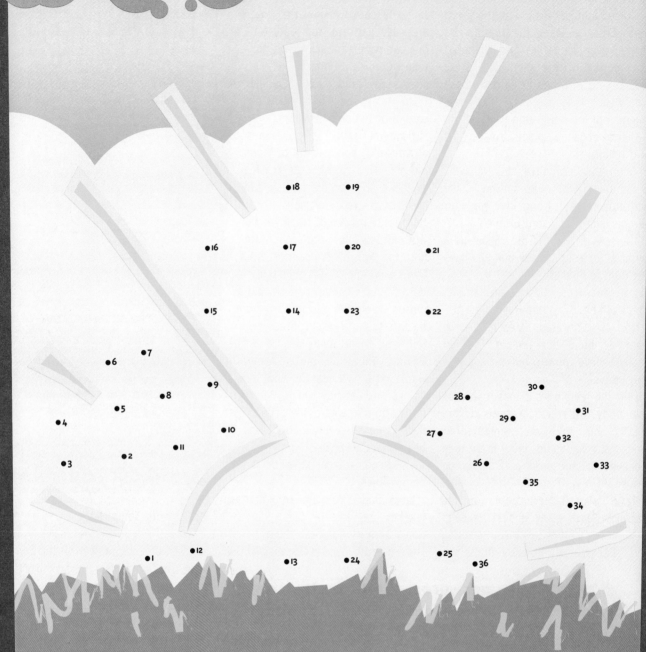

FILL IN THE BLANKS:

FOR ___ _____ THE _____ SO MUCH THAT HE

_____ HIS ONLY ___. GOD ____ HIS ___ SO THAT

_____ _____ IN HIM MAY ___ BE _____,

BUT HAVE _____ LIFE.

JOHN 3:16

already been judged guilty, because he has not believed in God's only Son. [19]People are judged by this fact: I am the

Light from God that has come into the world. But men did not want light. They wanted darkness because they were doing evil things. [20]Everyone who does evil hates the light. He will not come to the light because it will show all the evil things he has done. [21]But he who follows the true way comes to the light. Then the light will show that the things he has done were done through God."

## JESUS AND JOHN THE BAPTIST

[22]After this, Jesus and his followers went into the area of Judea. There Jesus stayed with his followers and baptized people. [23]John was also baptizing in Aenon, near Salim, because there was plenty of water there. People were going there to be baptized. [24](This was before John was put into prison.)

[25]Some of John's followers had an argument with a Jew about religious washing.[n] [26]So they came to John and said, "Teacher, remember the man who was with you on the other side of the Jordan River, the one you spoke about? He is baptizing, and everyone is going to him."

[27]John answered, "A man can get only

what God gives him. [28]You yourselves heard me say, 'I am not the Christ.[d] I am only the one God sent to prepare the way for him.' [29]The bride belongs only to the bridegroom. The friend who

> ## "God did not send his Son into the world to judge the world guilty, but to save the world through him. He who believes in God's Son is not judged guilty." *John 3:17-18*

helps the bridegroom waits and listens for him. He is glad when he hears the bridegroom's voice. That is the same pleasure I have. And my time of joy is now here. [30]He must become greater. And I must become less important.

## THE ONE WHO COMES FROM HEAVEN

[31]"The One who comes from above is greater than all. He who is from the earth belongs to the earth and talks about things on the earth. But the One who comes from heaven is greater than all. [32]He tells what he has seen and heard, but no one accepts what he says. [33]The person who accepts what he says has proven that God is true. [34]God sent him, and he tells the things that God says. God gives him the Spirit[d] fully. [35]The Father loves the Son and has given him power over everything. [36]He who believes in the Son has eternal life. But he who does not obey the Son will never have that life. God's anger stays with him."

## JESUS AND A SAMARITAN WOMAN

**4**The Pharisees[d] heard that Jesus was making and baptizing more followers than John. [2](But really Jesus himself did not baptize people. His followers did the baptizing.) Jesus knew that the Pharisees had heard about him. [3]So he left Judea and went

back to Galilee. [4]On the way he had to go through the country of Samaria. [5]In Samaria Jesus came to the town called Sychar. This town is near the field that Jacob gave to his son Joseph. [6]Jacob's well was there. Jesus was tired from his long trip. So he sat down beside the well. It was about noon. [7]A Samaritan[d] woman came to the well to get some water. Jesus said to her, "Please give me a drink." [8](This happened while Jesus' followers were in town buying some food.)

[9]The woman said, "I am surprised that you ask me for a drink. You are a Jew and I am a Samaritan." (Jews are not friends with Samaritans.[n])

## LIVIN' IT!

### CALL ME CRAZY
### JOHN 4:9

*What's he doing!?* his disciples thought. They were only gone a little while, and they came back to find Jesus talking to not only a woman, but a Samaritan woman. In those days, Jews had nothing to do with Samaritans, and women weren't too important, either. But to Jesus, every person was very special.

Jesus did not come to earth to be the most popular person. In fact, his own disciples would have never made anyone's top favorite list. But God doesn't care about what is on the outside of a person. He is deeply concerned with our hearts. Because Jesus shared with a Samaritan woman, a whole town came to know him. We need to see the world through Jesus' eyes. Don't be friends with someone just because they're cool or popular. Everyone needs to know God's love, and you are the perfect person to share it with them!

 **3:25 religious washing** The Jews washed themselves in special ways before eating, before worshiping in the Temple, and at other special times.
**4:9 Jews . . . Samaritans** This can also be translated "Jews don't use things that Samaritans have used."

## Gotta Know!

### Will I become an angel when I get to heaven?

No, because people and angels are two different kinds of God's creations. God made angels before people, and they have qualities that are unique to them. God created them to serve and help people. When we get to heaven, we will actually rule the kingdom alongside Christ. Angels and people will stay different when we get to heaven.

[10]Jesus said, "You don't know what God gives. And you don't know who asked you for a drink. If you knew, you would have asked me, and I would have given you living water."

[11]The woman said, "Sir, where will you get that living water? The well is very deep, and you have nothing to get water with. [12]Are you greater than Jacob, our father? Jacob is the one who gave us this well. He drank from it himself. Also, his sons and flocks drank from this well."

[13]Jesus answered, "Every person who drinks this water will be thirsty again. [14]But whoever drinks the water I give will never be thirsty again. The water I give will become a spring of water flowing inside him. It will give him eternal life."

[15]The woman said to him, "Sir, give me this water. Then I will never be thirsty again. And I will not have to come back here to get more water."

[16]Jesus told her, "Go get your husband and come back here."

[17]The woman answered, "But I have no husband."

Jesus said to her, "You are right to say you have no husband. [18]Really you have had five husbands. But the

man you live with now is not your husband. You told the truth."

[19]The woman said, "Sir, I can see that you are a prophet.[d] [20]Our fathers worshiped on this mountain. But you Jews say that Jerusalem is the place where people must worship."

[21]Jesus said, "Believe me, woman. The time is coming when you will not have to be in Jerusalem or on this mountain to worship the Father. [22]You Samaritans worship what you don't understand. We Jews understand what we worship. Salvation comes from the Jews. [23]The time is coming when the true worshipers will worship the Father in spirit and truth. That time is now here. And these are the

kinds of worshipers the Father wants. [24]God is spirit. Those who worship God must worship in spirit and truth."

[25]The woman said, "I know that the Messiah is coming." (Messiah is the One called Christ.[d]) "When the Messiah comes, he will explain everything to us."

[26]Then Jesus said, "He is talking to you now. I am he."

[27]Just then his followers came back from town. They were surprised

because they saw Jesus talking with a woman. But none of them asked, "What do you want?" or "Why are you talking with her?"

[28]Then the woman left her water jar and went back to town. She said to the people, [29]"A man told me everything I have ever done. Come see him. Maybe he is the Christ!" [30]So the people left the town and went to see Jesus.

[31]While the woman was away, the followers were begging him, "Teacher, eat something!"

[32]But Jesus answered, "I have food to eat that you know nothing about."

[33]So the followers asked themselves, "Did somebody already bring Jesus some food?"

[34]Jesus said, "My food is to do what the One who sent me wants me to do. My food is to finish the work that he gave me to do. [35]You say, 'Four more months to wait before we gather the grain.' But I tell you, open your eyes. Look at the fields that are ready for harvesting now. [36]Even now, the one who harvests the crop is being paid. He is gathering crops for eternal life. So now the one who plants can be happy along with the one who harvests. [37]It is true when we say, 'One person plants, but another

### "Whoever drinks the water i give will never be thirsty again."

*John 4:14*

harvests the crop.' [38]I sent you to harvest a crop that you did not work for. Others did the work, and you get the profit from their work."[n]

[39]Many of the Samaritans in that town believed in Jesus. They believed because of what the woman said: "He told me everything I have ever done." [40]The Samaritans came to Jesus and begged him to stay with them. So he stayed there two days. [41]Many more believed because of the things he said.

## Decode this!

*In the town of Sychar, Jesus spoke to whom at Jacob's well?*

**4:35-38 Look at . . . their work.** As a farmer sends workers to harvest grain, Jesus sends his followers out to bring people to God.

# may joy

**1** JOHN 15:11: I have told you these things so that you can have the same joy I have. I want your joy to be the fullest joy.

**2**

**3** See how long you can keep a smile on your face.

**4**

**5** Prayer Pointer: Take time today to praise God for the hope we have in Jesus.

**6**

**7**

**8** Think of what makes your parents happy and do it.

**9**

**10** ROMANS 15:13: I pray that the God who gives hope will fill you with much joy and peace while you trust in him.

**11** Tell your mom how much you love her.

**12**

**13** Prayer Pointer: Pray for those who are sad or lonely, and ask God to fill them with his joy.

**14**

**15** Study a little longer—school's almost out!

**16**

**17**

**18** Invite friends over for home-made ice cream.

**19** PHILIPPIANS 4:4: Be full of joy in the Lord always. I will say again, be full of joy.

**20**

**21** Play a board game with your brother or sister.

**22**

**23** Prayer Pointer: Ask God to show you ways that you can encourage your parents.

**24**

**25**

**26** ROMANS 12:12: Be joyful because you have hope. Be patient when trouble comes. Pray at all times.

**27**

**28**

**29** Invite the kids in the neighborhood over to play in the sprinklers.

**30**

**31** Cook dinner with your mom.

*Come, let's sing for joy to the Lord. Let's shout praises to the Rock who saves us (Psalm 95:1).*

⁴²They said to the woman, "First we believed in Jesus because of what you told us. But now we believe because we heard him ourselves. We know that this man really is the Savior of the world."

## JESUS HEALS AN OFFICER'S SON

⁴³Two days later, Jesus left and went to Galilee. ⁴⁴(Jesus had said before that

**Q. If you could have one thing right now, what would it be?**

**A. A big screen TV.**

a prophet*ᵈ* is not respected in his own country.) ⁴⁵When Jesus arrived in Galilee, the people there welcomed him. They had seen all the things he did at the Passover*ᵈ* Feast in Jerusalem. They had been at the Passover Feast, too.

⁴⁶Jesus went to visit Cana in Galilee again. This is where Jesus had changed the water into wine. One of the king's important officers lived in the city of Capernaum. This man's son was sick. ⁴⁷The man heard that Jesus had come from Judea and was now in Galilee. He went to Jesus and begged him to come to Capernaum and heal his son. His son was almost dead. ⁴⁸Jesus said to him, "You people must see signs and miracles*ᵈ* before you will believe in me."

⁴⁹The officer said, "Sir, come before my child dies."

⁵⁰Jesus answered, "Go. Your son will live." The man believed what Jesus told him and went home. ⁵¹On the way the man's servants came and met him. They told him, "Your son is well."

⁵²The man asked, "What time did my son begin to get well?"

They answered, "It was about one o'clock yesterday when the fever left him."

⁵³The father knew that one o'clock was the exact time that Jesus had said, "Your son will live." So the man and all the people of his house believed in Jesus.

⁵⁴That was the second miracle that Jesus did after coming from Judea to Galilee.

## JESUS HEALS A MAN AT A POOL

**5** Later Jesus went to Jerusalem for a special Jewish feast. ²In Jerusalem there is a pool with five covered porches. In the Jewish language*ⁿ* it is called Bethzatha.*ⁿ* This pool is near the Sheep Gate. ³Many sick people were lying on the porches beside the pool. Some were blind, some were crippled, and some were paralyzed.*ⁿ* ⁵There was a man lying there who had been sick for

38 years. ⁶Jesus saw the man and knew that he had been sick for a very long time. So Jesus asked him, "Do you want to be well?"

⁷The sick man answered, "Sir, there is no one to help me get into the pool when the water starts moving. I try to be the first one into the water. But when I try, someone else always goes in before I can."

⁸Then Jesus said, "Stand up. Pick up your mat and walk." ⁹And immediately

the man was well. He picked up his mat and began to walk.

The day all this happened was a Sabbath*ᵈ* day. ¹⁰So the Jews said to the man who had been healed, "Today is the Sabbath. It is against our law for you to carry your mat on the Sabbath day."

¹¹But he answered, "The man who made me well told me, 'Pick up your mat and walk.'"

¹²Then they asked him, "Who is the man who told you to pick up your mat and walk?"

¹³But the man who had been healed did not know who it was. There were many people in that place, and Jesus had left.

¹⁴Later, Jesus found the man at the Temple.*ᵈ* Jesus said to him, "See, you are well now. But stop sinning or something worse may happen to you!"

¹⁵Then the man left and went back to the Jews. He told them that Jesus was the one who had made him well.

¹⁶Jesus was doing this on the Sabbath day. So the Jews began to do bad things to him. ¹⁷But Jesus said to them, "My Father never stops working. And so I work, too."

¹⁸This made the Jews try harder to kill

**"Then Jesus said, 'Stand up. Pick up your mat and walk.' And immediately the man was well. He picked up his mat and began to walk."**

*John 5:8*

him. They said, "First Jesus was breaking the law about the Sabbath day. Then he said that God is his own Father! He is making himself equal with God!"

**5:2 Jewish language** Aramaic, the language of the Jews in the first century. **5:2 Bethzatha** Also called Bethsaida or Bethesda, a pool of water north of the Temple in Jerusalem. **5:3 Verse 3** Some Greek copies add "and they waited for the water to move." A few later copies add verse 4: "Sometimes an angel of the Lord came down to the pool and stirred up the water. After the angel did this, the first person to go into the pool was healed from any sickness he had."

## WILD WORLD FACTS

### EWE ASKED

Don't be sheepish. We know you'd like some more facts about sheep, so here they are: Sheep are covered in a thick fleece and have hooves that are split into 2 toes. Some breeds have horns, while others do not. Most live up to 7 years. In addition to eating their meat, we also use sheep to make a variety of needed things like clothing, rugs, leather, lanolin (used for candle wax and makeup), and tennis racquet strings. We even use sheep milk to make certain tasty cheeses like feta and Roquefort. Sheep milk is different from cow milk because it is higher in protein and fat.

### JESUS HAS GOD'S AUTHORITY

19But Jesus said, "I tell you the truth. The Son can do nothing alone. The Son does only what he sees his Father doing. The Son does whatever the Father does. 20The Father loves the Son, and the Father shows the Son all the things he himself does. But the Father will show the Son greater things than this to do. Then you will all be amazed. 21The Father raises the dead and gives them life. In the same way, the Son gives life to those he wants to. 22Also, the Father judges no one. But the Father has given the Son power to do all the judging. 23God did this so that all people will respect the Son the same way they respect the Father. He who does not respect the Son does not respect the Father. The Father is the One who sent the Son.

24"I tell you the truth. Whoever hears what I say and believes in the One who sent me has eternal life. He will not be judged guilty. He has already left death and has entered into life. 25I tell you the truth. The time is coming and is already here when the dead will hear the voice of the Son of God. And those who hear will have life. 26Life comes from the Father himself. So the Father has allowed the Son to give life. 27And the Father has given the Son the power to judge because he is the Son of Man.d

28Don't be surprised at this. A time is coming when all who are dead and in their graves will hear his voice. 29Then they will come out of their graves. Those who did good will rise and have life forever. But those who did evil will rise to be judged guilty.

"My Father never stops working. And so i work, too."
John 5:17

### JESUS IS GOD'S SON

30"I can do nothing alone. I judge only the way I am told, so my judgment is right. I don't try to please myself. I try to please the One who sent me.

31"If I tell people about myself, then they will not accept what I say about myself. 32But there is another who tells about me. And I know that the things he says about me are true.

33"You have sent men to John. And he has told you about the truth. 34But I don't need a man to tell about me. I tell you this so that you can be saved. 35John was like a burning and shining lamp. And you were happy to enjoy his light for a while.

36"But I have a proof about myself that is greater than that of John. The things I do are my proof. These are the things my Father gave me to do. They show that the Father sent me. 37And the Father who sent me has given proof about me himself. You have never heard his voice. You have never seen what he looks like. 38His teaching does not live in you because you don't believe in the One that the Father sent. 39You carefully study the Scripturesd because you think that they give you eternal life. Those are the same Scriptures that tell about me! 40But you refuse to come to me to have that life.

41"I don't want praise from men. 42But I know you—I know that you don't have God's love in you. 43I have come from my Father—I speak for him. But you don't accept me. But when another person comes, speaking only for himself, you will accept him. 44You like to have praise from each other. But you never try to get the praise that comes from the only God. So how can you believe? 45Don't think that I will stand before the Father and say that you are wrong. Moses is the one who says that you are wrong. And he is the one that you hoped would save you. 46If you really believed Moses, you would believe me because Moses wrote about me. 47But you don't believe what Moses wrote. So how can you believe what I say?"

### DECODE THIS!

Jesus healed which member of the king's officer's family?

149

### MORE THAN 5,000 PEOPLE FED

**6** After this, Jesus went across Lake Galilee (or, Lake Tiberias). [2]Many people followed him because they saw the miracles[d] he did to heal the sick. [3]Jesus went up on a hill and there sat down with his followers. [4]It was almost the time for the Jewish Passover[d] Feast.

[5]Jesus looked up and saw a large crowd coming toward him. He said to Philip, "Where can we buy bread for all these people to eat?" [6](Jesus asked Philip this question to test him. Jesus already knew what he planned to do.)

[7]Philip answered, "We would all have to work a month to buy enough bread for each person here to have only a little piece."

[8]Another follower there was Andrew. He was Simon Peter's brother. Andrew said, [9]"Here is a boy with five loaves of barley bread and two little fish. But that is not enough for so many people."

[10]Jesus said, "Tell the people to sit down." This was a very grassy place. There were about 5,000 men who sat down there. [11]Then Jesus took the loaves of bread. He thanked God for the bread and gave it to the people who were sitting there. He did the same with the fish. He gave them as much as they wanted.

[12]They all had enough to eat. When they had finished, Jesus said to his followers, "Gather the pieces of fish and bread that were not eaten. Don't waste anything." [13]So they gathered up the pieces that were left. They filled 12 large baskets with the pieces that were left of the five barley loaves.

[14]The people saw this miracle that Jesus did. They said, "He must truly be the Prophet[n] who is coming into the world."

[15]Jesus knew that the people planned to come and take him by force and make him their king. So he left and went into the hills alone.

### JESUS WALKS ON THE WATER

[16]That evening Jesus' followers went down to Lake Galilee. [17]It was dark now and Jesus had not yet come to them. The followers got into a boat and started across the lake to Capernaum. [18]By now a strong wind was blowing, and the waves on the lake were getting bigger. [19]They rowed the boat about three or four miles. Then they saw Jesus walking on the water, coming toward the boat. The followers were afraid. [20]But Jesus said to them, "Don't be afraid. It is I." [21]Then they were glad to take him into the boat. At once the boat came to land at the place where they wanted to go.

### THE PEOPLE SEEK JESUS

[22]The next day came. Some people had stayed on the other side of the lake. They knew that Jesus had not gone in the boat with his followers but that they had left without him. And they knew that only one boat had been there. [23]But then some boats came from Tiberias. They landed near the place where the people had eaten the bread after the Lord had given thanks. [24]The people saw that Jesus and his followers were not there now. So they got into boats and went to Capernaum. They wanted to find Jesus.

### JESUS, THE BREAD OF LIFE

[25]The people found Jesus on the other side of the lake. They asked him, "Teacher, when did you come here?"

[26]Jesus answered, "Are you looking for me because you saw me do miracles?[d] No! I tell you the truth. You are looking for me because you ate the bread and were satis-fied. [27]Earthly food spoils and ruins. So don't work to get that kind of food. But work to get the food that stays good always and gives you eternal life. The Son of Man[d] will give you that food. God the Father has shown that he is with the Son of Man."

[28]The people asked Jesus, "What are the things God wants us to do?"

[29]Jesus answered, "The work God wants you to do is this: to believe in the One that God sent."

> ## "The work God wants you to do is this: to believe in the One that God sent."
>
> *John 6:29*

[30]So the people asked, "What miracle will you do? If we can see a miracle, then we will believe you. What will you do? [31]Our fathers ate the manna[d] in the desert. This is written in the Scriptures:[d] 'God gave them bread from heaven to eat.'"[n]

[32]Jesus said, "I tell you the truth. Moses was not the one who gave you bread from heaven. But my Father gives you the true bread from heaven. [33]God's bread is the One who comes down from heaven and gives life to the world."

[34]The people said, "Sir, give us this bread always."

[35]Then Jesus said, "I am the bread that gives life. He who comes to me will never be hungry. He who believes in me will never be thirsty. [36]But as I told you before, you have seen me, and still you don't believe. [37]The Father gives me my people. Every one of them will come to me, and I will always accept them. [38]I came down from heaven to do what God wants me to do. I did not come to

## **DECODE THIS!**

### *Where did Jesus walk on water?*

---

⭐ **6:14 Prophet** They probably meant the prophet that God told Moses he would send (Deuteronomy 18:15-19).
**6:31 'God gave . . . eat.'** Quotation from Psalm 78:24.

do what I want to do. [39]I must not lose even one of those that God has given me, but I must raise them up on the last day. This is what the One who sent me wants me to do. [40]Everyone who sees the Son and believes in him has eternal life. I will raise him up on the last day. This is what my Father wants."

[41]The Jews began to complain about Jesus. They complained because he said, "I am the bread that comes down from heaven." [42]The Jews said, "This is Jesus. We know his father and mother. He is only Joseph's son. How can he say, 'I came down from heaven'?"

[43]But Jesus answered, "Stop complaining to each other. [44]The Father is the One who sent me. No one can come to me unless the Father draws him to me. And I will raise him up on the last day. [45]It is written in the prophets,[d] 'God will teach

all the people.'[n] Everyone who listens to the Father and learns from him comes to me. [46]No one has seen the Father except the One who is from God. Only he has seen the Father. [47]I tell you the truth. He who believes has eternal life. [48]I am the bread that gives life. [49]Your ancestors ate the manna in the desert. But still

they died. [50]Here is the bread that comes down from heaven. If anyone eats this bread, he will never die. [51]I am the living bread that came down from heaven. If anyone eats this bread, he will live forever. This bread is my flesh. I will give my flesh so that the people in the world may have life."

[52]Then the Jews began to argue among themselves. They said, "How can this man give us his flesh to eat?"

[53]Jesus said, "I tell you the truth. You must eat the flesh of the Son of Man. And you must drink his blood. If you don't do this, then you won't have real life in you. [54]He who eats my flesh and drinks my blood has eternal life. I will raise him up on the last day. [55]My flesh is true food. My blood is true drink. [56]Whoever eats my flesh and drinks my blood lives in me, and I live in him. [57]The Father sent me. The Father lives, and I live because of the Father. So he who eats me will live because of me. [58]I am not like the bread our ancestors ate. They ate that bread, but still they died. I am the bread that came down from heaven. He who eats this bread will live forever." [59]Jesus said all these things while he was teaching in the synagogue[d] in Capernaum.

## THE WORDS OF ETERNAL LIFE

[60]The followers of Jesus heard this. Many of them said, "This teaching is hard. Who can accept it?"

[61]Jesus knew that his followers were complaining about this. So he said, "Does this teaching bother you? [62]Then will it also bother you to see the Son of

Man[d] going back to the place where he came from? [63]It is not the flesh that gives a person life. It is the spirit that gives life. The words I told you are spirit, and so they give life. [64]But some of you don't believe." (Jesus knew who did not believe. He knew this from the beginning. And he knew who would turn against him.)

## BiBLe BaSiCS
### GOD THE FATHER

God the Father is the Spirit who controls everything that has ever been made. He is the One who made the plan of salvation, and he has shown himself to us through many different names that help us understand his heart better. He loves Jesus and has accepted his death as a payment for the sins of his people. He has given Jesus all rule and power, and he alone will decide when Jesus will come back to earth the second time.

[65]Jesus said, "That is the reason I said, 'If the Father does not let a person come to me, then he cannot come.'"

[66]After Jesus said this, many of his followers left him. They stopped following him.

[67]Jesus asked the 12 followers, "Do you want to leave, too?"

[68]Simon Peter answered Jesus, "Lord, where would we go? You have the words that give eternal life. [69]We believe in you. We know that you are the Holy One from God."

[70]Then Jesus answered, "I chose all 12 of you. But 1 of you is a devil."

[71]Jesus was talking about Judas, the son of Simon Iscariot. Judas was 1 of the 12. But later he was going to turn against Jesus.

"i tell you the truth. He who believes has eternal life. i am the bread that gives life."

*John 6:47-48*

6:45 'God . . . people.' Quotation from Isaiah 54:13.

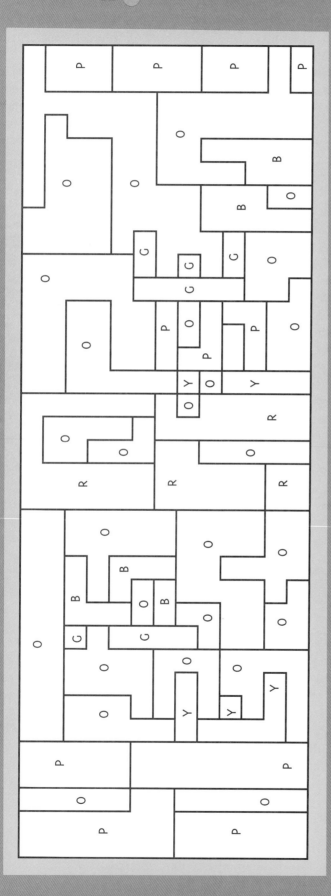

## WHAT WAS THE ANGEL'S EXCITING MESSAGE?

USE THE KEY BELOW TO COLOR EACH BLOCK AND DECODE THE ANSWER!

P= PURPLE
Y= YELLOW
G= GREEN
B= BLUE
R= RED
O= ORANGE

(When you finish, turn the page horizontally to view the answer!)

## JESUS AND HIS BROTHERS

**7** After this, Jesus traveled around Galilee. He did not want to travel in Judea, because the Jews there wanted to kill him. [2]It was time for the Jewish Feast[d] of Shelters. [3]So Jesus' brothers said to him, "You should leave here and go to Judea. Then your followers there can see the miracles[d] you do. [4]Anyone who wants to be well known does not hide what he does. If you are doing these things, show yourself to the world." [5](Even Jesus' brothers did not believe in him.)

[6]Jesus said to his brothers, "The right time for me has not yet come. But any time is right for you. [7]The world cannot hate you. But it hates me, because I tell about the evil things it does. [8]So you go to the feast. I will not go now. The right time for me has not yet come." [9]After saying this, Jesus stayed in Galilee.

[10]So Jesus' brothers left to go to the feast. When they had gone, Jesus went, too. But he did not let people see him. [11]At the feast the Jews were looking for him. They said, "Where is that man?"

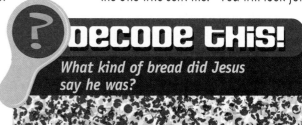

[12]There was a large crowd of people there. Many of them were whispering to each other about Jesus. Some said, "He is a good man."

teach. [15]The Jews were amazed. They said, "This man has never studied in school. How did he learn so much?"

[16]Jesus answered, "The things I teach are not my own. My teaching comes from him who sent me. [17]If anyone chooses to do what God wants, then he will know that my teaching comes from God. He will know that this teaching is not my own. [18]He who teaches his own ideas is trying to get honor for himself. But he who tries to bring honor to the one who sent him—that person speaks the truth. There is nothing false in him. [19]Moses gave you the law,[n] but none of you obey that law. Why are you trying to kill me?"

[20]The people answered, "A demon[d] has come into you. We are not trying to kill you."

[21]Jesus said to them, "I did one miracle,[d] and you are all amazed. [22]Moses gave you the law about circumcision.[d] (But really Moses did not give you circumcision. Circumcision came from our ancestors.) And yet you circumcise a baby on a Sabbath[d] day. [23]This shows that a baby can be circumcised on a Sabbath day to obey the law of Moses. So why are you angry at me for healing a person's whole body on the Sabbath day? [24]Stop judging by the way things look! Be fair, and judge by what is really right."

stop him. Maybe the leaders have decided that he really is the Christ.[d] [27]But we know where this man is from. And when the real Christ comes, no one will know where he comes from."

[28]Jesus was still teaching in the Temple.[d] He cried out, "Yes, you know

> ## "Stop judging by the way things look! Be fair, and judge by what is really right."
>
> *John 7:24*

me, and you know where I am from. But I have not come by my own authority. I was sent by the One who is true. You don't know him. [29]But I know him. I am from him, and he sent me."

[30]When Jesus said this, the people tried to take him. But no one was able to touch him. It was not yet the right time. [31]But many of the people believed in Jesus. They said, "When the Christ comes, will he do more miracles[d] than this man has done?"

## SOME LEADERS TRY TO ARREST JESUS

[32]The Pharisees[d] heard the crowd whispering these things about Jesus. So the leading priests and the Pharisees sent some Temple[d] guards to arrest him. [33]Then Jesus said, "I will be with you a little while longer. Then I will go back to the One who sent me. [34]You will look for

> ## "Lord, where would we go? You have the words that give eternal life. We believe in you. We know that you are the Holy One from God."
>
> *John 6:68-69*

Others said, "No, he fools the people." [13]But no one was brave enough to talk about Jesus openly. They were afraid of the Jews.

## JESUS TEACHES AT THE FEAST

[14]The feast was about half over. Then Jesus went to the Temple[d] and began to

## IS JESUS THE CHRIST?

[25]Then some of the people who lived in Jerusalem said, "This is the man they are trying to kill. [26]But he is teaching where everyone can see and hear him. And no one is trying to

## DECODE THIS!

*What kind of bread did Jesus say he was?*

  **7:19 law** Moses gave God's people the law that God gave him on Mount Sinai (Exodus 34:29-32).

153

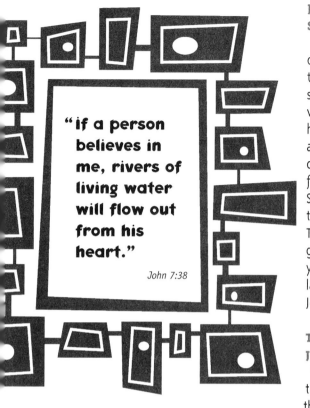

"if a person believes in me, rivers of living water will flow out from his heart."

John 7:38

## JESUS TALKS ABOUT THE SPIRIT

[37]The last day of the feast came. It was the most important day. On that day Jesus stood up and said in a loud voice, "If anyone is thirsty, let him come to me and drink. [38]If a person believes in me, rivers of living water will flow out from his heart. This is what the Scripture[d] says." [39]Jesus was talking about the Holy Spirit.[d] The Spirit had not yet been given because Jesus had not yet been raised to glory. But later, those who believed in Jesus would receive the Spirit.

## THE PEOPLE ARGUE ABOUT JESUS

[40]The people heard these things that Jesus said. Some of them said, "This man really is the Prophet."[n]

[41]Others said, "He is the Christ."[d] Still others said, "The Christ will not come from Galilee. [42]The Scripture[d] says that the Christ will come from David's family. And the Scripture says that the Christ will come from Bethlehem, the town where David lived." [43]So the people did not agree with each other about Jesus. [44]Some of them wanted to arrest him, but no one was able to touch him.

## THE LEADERS WON'T BELIEVE

[45]The Temple[d] guards went back to the leading priests and the Pharisees.[d] The priests and the Pharisees asked, "Why didn't you bring Jesus?"

[46]The Temple guards answered, "The things he says are greater than the words of any man!"

[47]The Pharisees answered, "So Jesus has fooled you too! [48]Have any of the leaders or the Pharisees believed in him? No! [49]But those people, who know nothing about the law, are under God's curse!"

[50]But Nicodemus was there in that group. He was the one who had gone to see Jesus before.[n] Nicodemus said, [51]"Our law does not judge a man without hearing him. We cannot judge him until we know what he has done."

[52]They answered, "Are you from Galilee too? Study the Scriptures.[d] You will learn that no prophet[d] comes from Galilee."

[53]And everyone left and went home.[n]

## THE WOMAN CAUGHT IN ADULTERY

**8** Jesus went to the Mount of Olives.[d] [2]But early in the morning he went back to the Temple.[d] All the people came to Jesus, and he sat and taught them. [3]The teachers of the law and the Pharisees[d] brought a woman there. She had been caught in adultery.[d] They

me, but you will not find me. And you cannot come where I am."

[35]The Jews said to each other, "Where will this man go so we cannot find him? Will he go to the Greek cities where our people live? Will he teach the Greek people there? [36]This man says, 'You will look for me but you will not find me.' He also says, 'You cannot come where I am.' What does this mean?"

**7:40 Prophet** They probably meant the prophet that God told Moses he would send (Deuteronomy 18:15–19).
**7:50 But Nicodemus . . . before** The story about Nicodemus going and talking to Jesus is in John 3:1–21.
**7:53 Verse 53** Some early Greek manuscripts do not contain 7:53–8:11.

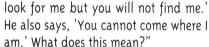

## MARY

She walked into a room full of men. She didn't notice. Her eyes were fixed on Jesus. Mary took the most expensive bottle of perfumed oil she had and poured it on Jesus' head. Then the laughter came. Insults. The men watching her thought it was a waste. They thought she was a fool. But Jesus saw her heart, and there he saw a friend. He said that her service to him was very valuable and would be remembered forever.

Has anyone ever made fun of you for following Christ? Do you ever feel like your service for him is worthless? Remember Mary, who kept her eyes on Jesus and not the world. Remember that God always sees. Always loves. And always rewards those whose hearts belong to him.

forced the woman to stand before the people. ⁴They said to Jesus, "Teacher, this woman was caught having sexual relations with a man who is not her husband. ⁵The law of Moses commands that we kill with stones every woman who does this. What do you say we should do?" ⁶They were asking this to trick Jesus so that they could have some charge against him.

But Jesus knelt down and started writing on the ground with his finger. ⁷They continued to ask Jesus their question. So he stood up and said, "Is there anyone here who has never sinned? The person without sin can throw the first stone at this woman." ⁸Then Jesus knelt down again and wrote on the ground.

⁹Those who heard Jesus began to leave one by one. The older men left first, and then the others. Jesus was left there alone with the woman. She was standing before him. ¹⁰Jesus stood up again and asked her, "Woman, all of those people have gone. Has no one judged you guilty?"

¹¹She answered, "No one has judged me, sir."

Then Jesus said, "So I also don't judge you. You may go now, but don't sin again."

## JESUS IS THE LIGHT OF THE WORLD

¹²Later, Jesus talked to the people again. He said, "I am the light of the world. The person who follows me will never live in darkness. He will have the light that gives life."

¹³But the Pharisees[d] said to Jesus, "When you talk about yourself, you are the only one to say these things are true. We cannot accept these things you say."

¹⁴Jesus answered, "Yes, I am saying these things about myself, but they are true. I know where I came from. And I know where I am going. You don't know where I came from or where I am

going. ¹⁵You judge me the way you would judge any man. I don't judge anyone. ¹⁶But if I judge, my judging is true. When I judge, I am not alone. The Father who sent me is with me. ¹⁷Your own law says that when two witnesses say the same thing, then you must accept what they say. ¹⁸I am one of the witnesses who speaks about myself.

And the Father who sent me is my other witness."

¹⁹They asked, "Where is your father?"

Jesus answered, "You don't know me or my Father. But if you knew me, then you would know my Father, too." ²⁰Jesus said these things while he was teaching in the Temple.[d] He was near the place where the money that the people give is kept. But no one arrested him. The right time for Jesus had not yet come.

## THE PEOPLE MISUNDERSTAND JESUS

²¹Again, Jesus said to the people, "I will leave you. You will look for me, but you will die in your sins. You cannot come where I am going."

²²So the Jews asked, "Will Jesus kill himself? Is that why he said, 'You cannot come where I am going'?"

# Gotta Know!

## Does God ever eat or sleep?

God the Father never sleeps, according to Psalm 121:4, because he is always watching over us. God is spirit and doesn't have a body like us, so he doesn't have a need for food. But when God the Son took the form of a man, Jesus slept and ate just like us. Even after he rose from the dead, he ate fish with his disciples. He also talked about a big wedding feast taking place when we get to heaven, so we will all eat together when we get there.

²³But Jesus said, "You people are from here below. But I am from above. You belong to this world, but I don't belong to this world. ²⁴So I told you that you would die in your sins. Yes, you will die in your sins if you don't believe that I am he."

²⁵They asked, "Then who are you?"

Jesus answered, "I am what I have told you from the beginning. ²⁶I have many things to say about you and to judge you for. But I tell people only the things I have heard from the One who sent me. And he speaks the truth."

²⁷The people did not understand that Jesus was talking to them about the Father. ²⁸So Jesus said to them, "You will lift up the Son of Man.[d] Then you will know that I am he. You will know that

## DECODE THIS!

Jesus is the _____ of the world.

## TOP TEN

### Ways to Earn Money for Missions

1. Save your allowance.
2. Have a car wash.
3. Mow lawns.
4. Write letters to friends asking for support.
5. Bake cakes and cookies to sell.
6. Have a church-wide garage sale.
7. Babysit or be a mother's helper.
8. Clean houses.
9. Sell some of your things on eBay.
10. Ask your class or friends to give.

these things I do are not by my own authority. You will know that I say only what the Father has taught me. 29The One who sent me is with me. I always do what is pleasing to him. So he has not left me alone." 30While Jesus was saying these things, many people believed in him.

### FREEDOM FROM SIN

31So Jesus said to the Jews who believed in him, "If you continue to obey my teaching, you are truly my followers. 32Then you will know the truth. And the truth will make you free."

33They answered, "We are Abraham's children. And we have never been slaves. So why do you say that we will be free?"

34Jesus answered, "I tell you the truth. Everyone who lives in sin is a slave to sin. 35A slave does not stay with a family forever, but a son belongs to the family forever. 36So if the Son makes you free, then you will be truly free. 37I know you are Abraham's children. But you want to kill me because you don't accept my teaching. 38I am telling you what my Father has shown me. But you do what your father has told you."

39They answered, "Our father is Abraham." Jesus said, "If you were really Abraham's children, you would do the things that Abraham did. 40I am a man who has told you the truth which I heard from God. But you are trying to kill me. Abraham did nothing like that. 41So you are doing the things that your own father did."

But they said, "We are not like children who never knew who their father was. God is our Father. He is the only Father we have."

42Jesus said to them, "If God were really your Father, you would love me. I came from God and now I am here. I did not come by my own authority. God sent me. 43You don't understand what I say because you cannot accept my teaching. 44Your father is the devil. You belong to him and want to do what he wants. He was a murderer from the beginning. He was against the truth, for there is no truth in him. He is a liar, and he is like the lies he tells. He is the father of lies. 45But I speak the truth. That is why you don't believe me. 46Can any of you prove that I am guilty of sin? If I am telling the truth, why don't you believe me? 47He who belongs to God accepts what God says. But you don't accept what God says, because you don't belong to God."

### JESUS AND ABRAHAM

48The Jews answered, "We say you are a Samaritan!d We say a demond has come into you. Are we not right?"

49Jesus answered, "I have no demon in me. I give honor to my Father, but you dishonor me. 50I am not trying to get honor for myself. There is One who wants this honor for me, and he is the judge. 51I tell you the truth. If anyone obeys my teaching, he will never die."

52The Jews said to Jesus, "Now we know that you have a demon in you! Even Abraham and the prophetsd died. But you say, 'Whoever obeys my teaching will never die.' 53Do you think that you are greater than our father Abraham? Abraham died. And the prophets died, too. Who do you think you are?"

54Jesus answered, "If I give honor to myself, that honor is worth nothing. The One who gives me honor is my Father. And you say that he is your God. 55But you don't really know him. I know him. If I said I did not know him, then I would be a liar as you are liars. But I do know him, and I obey what he says. 56Your father Abraham was very happy that he would see my day. He saw that day and was glad."

57The Jews said to him, "What? You have never seen Abraham! You are not even 50 years old!"

58Jesus answered, "I tell you the truth. Before Abraham was born, I am!" 59When Jesus said this, the people picked up stones to throw at him. But Jesus hid himself, and then he left the Temple.d

## JESUS HEALS A MAN BORN BLIND

**9** As Jesus was walking along, he saw a man who had been born blind. [2]His followers asked him, "Teacher, whose sin caused this man to be born blind—his own sin or his parents' sin?"

[3]Jesus answered, "It is not this man's sin or his parents' sin that made him be blind. This man was born blind so that God's power could be shown in him. [4]While it is daytime, we must continue doing the work of the One who sent me. The night is coming. And no one can work at night. [5]While I am in the world, I am the light of the world."

[6]After Jesus said this, he spit on the ground and made some mud with it. He put the

mud on the man's eyes. [7]Then he told the man, "Go and wash in the Pool of Siloam." (Siloam means Sent.) So the man went to the pool. He washed and came back. And he was able to see.

[8]Some people had seen this man begging before. They and the man's neighbors said, "Look! Is this the same man who always sits and begs?"

[9]Some said, "Yes! He is the one." But others said, "No, he's not the same man. He only looks like him."

So the man himself said, "I am the man."

[10]They asked, "What happened? How did you get your sight?"

[11]He answered, "The man named Jesus made some mud and put it on my eyes. Then he told me to go to Siloam and wash. So I went and washed and came back seeing."

[12]They asked him, "Where is this man?"

The man answered, "I don't know."

## PHARISEES QUESTION THE HEALING

[13]Then the people took to the Pharisees[d] the man who had been blind. [14]The day Jesus had made mud and healed his eyes was a Sabbath[d] day. [15]So now the Pharisees asked the man, "How did you get your sight?"

He answered, "He put mud on my eyes. I washed, and now I can see."

[16]Some of the Pharisees were saying, "This man does not keep the Sabbath day. He is not from God!"

Others said, "But a man who is a sinner can't do miracles[d] like these." So they could not agree with each other.

[17]They asked the man again, "What do you say about him? It was your eyes he opened."

The man answered, "He is a prophet."[d]

[18]The Jews did not believe that he had been blind and could now see again. So they sent for the man's parents [19]and asked them, "Is this your son? You say that he was born blind. Then how does he see now?"

[20]His parents answered, "We know that this is our son, and we know that he was born blind. [21]But we don't know how he can see now. We don't know who opened his eyes. Ask him. He is old enough to answer for himself." [22]His parents said this because they were afraid of the Jews. The Jews had already decided that anyone who said that Jesus was the Christ[d] would be put out of the synagogue.[d] [23]That is why his parents said, "He is old enough. Ask him."

[24]So for the second time, they called the man who had been blind. They said, "You should give God the glory by telling the truth. We know that this man is a sinner."

[25]He answered, "I don't know if he is a sinner. But one thing I do know. I was blind, and now I can see."

[26]They asked, "What did he do to you? How did he make you see again?"

[27]He answered, "I have already told

## WILD WORLD FACTS

### WORLD HARVEST

In John 12:29, Jesus said that a grain of wheat had to fall to the ground and die in order to grow. The life inside the seed is freed to take root and grow into wheat, which is a very important crop all over the world.

On average, more than 60 million acres of wheat are planted in the United States alone. To get a better picture of what that means, a family of 4 could live for 10 years off the amount of wheat harvested in just one acre of land. And wheat is needed, too. More foods are made with wheat than any other cereal grain. President Bush saw the need for food in Iraq and had the U.S. ship more than 200,000 metric tons of wheat to feed the people.

We need to be like the wheat grain. When we "die" or say "no" to our own desires and obey God instead, we grow spiritually, and he is able to use us to save lives all over the world.

[National Association of Wheat Growers]

## DECODE THIS!

*Jesus healed a blind man's eyes at this spot.*

you that. But you would not listen to me. Why do you want to hear it again? Do you want to become his followers, too?"

[28]Then they insulted him and said, "You are his follower. We are followers of Moses. [29]We know that God spoke to Moses. But we don't even know where this man comes from!"

[30]The man answered, "This is a very strange thing. You don't know where he comes from, and yet he opened my eyes. [31]We all know that God does not listen to sinners. But God listens to anyone who worships and obeys him. [32]Nobody has ever heard of anyone giving sight to a man born blind. [33]If this man were not from God, he could do nothing."

[34]They answered, "You were born full of sin! Are you trying to teach us?" And they threw the man out.

## "Nobody has ever heard of anyone giving sight to a man born blind. if this man were not from God, he could do nothing."

*John 9:32-33*

### SPIRITUAL BLINDNESS

[35]Jesus heard that they had thrown him out. So Jesus found him and said, "Do you believe in the Son of Man?"[d]

[36]He asked, "Who is the Son of Man, sir? Tell me, so I can believe in him!"

[37]Jesus said to him, "You have already seen him. The Son of Man is the one talking with you now."

[38]He said, "Yes, Lord, I believe!" Then the man bowed and worshiped Jesus.

[39]Jesus said, "I came into this world so that the world could be judged. I came so that the blind[n] could see and so that those who see will become blind."

[40]Some of the Pharisees[d] were near Jesus. When they heard him say this, they asked, "What? Are you saying that we are blind, too?"

[41]Jesus said, "If you were really blind, you would not be guilty of sin. But now that you say you can see, your guilt remains."

### THE SHEPHERD AND HIS SHEEP

**10**Jesus said, "I tell you the truth. The man who does not enter the sheepfold by the door, but climbs in some other way, is a thief and a robber. [2]The one who enters by the door is the shepherd of the sheep. [3]The man who guards the door opens it for him. And the sheep listen to the voice of the shepherd. He calls his own sheep, using their names, and he leads them out. [4]He brings all of his sheep out. Then he goes ahead of them and leads them. They follow him because they know his voice. [5]But they will never follow a stranger. They will run away from him because they don't know his voice." [6]Jesus told the people this story, but they did not understand what it meant.

### JESUS IS THE GOOD SHEPHERD

[7]So Jesus said again, "I tell you the truth. I am the door for the sheep. [8]All the people who came before me were thieves and robbers. The sheep did not listen to them. [9]I am the door. The person who enters through me will be saved. He will be able to come in and go out and find pasture. [10]A thief comes to steal and kill and destroy. But I came to give life—life in all its fullness.

[11]"I am the good shepherd. The good shepherd gives his

life for the sheep. [12]The worker who is paid to keep the sheep is different from the shepherd who owns them. So when the worker sees a wolf coming, he runs away and leaves the sheep alone. Then the wolf attacks the sheep and scatters them. [13]The man runs away because he is only a paid worker. He does not really care for the sheep.

[14-15]"I am the good shepherd. I know my sheep, as the Father knows me. And my sheep know me, as I know the Father. I give my life for the sheep. [16]I have other sheep that are not in this flock here. I must bring them also. They will listen to my voice, and there will be one flock and one shepherd. [17]The Father loves me because I give my life. I give my life so that I can take it back again. [18]No one takes it away from me. I give my own life freely. I have the right to give my life, and I have the right to take it back. This is what my Father commanded me to do."

[19]Again the Jews did not agree with each other because of these words Jesus said. [20]Many of them said, "A demon[d] has come into him and made him crazy. Why listen to him?"

[21]But others said, "A man who is crazy with a demon does not say things like this. Can a demon open the eyes of the blind?"

[22]The time came for the Feast[d] of Dedication at Jerusalem. This was during the winter. [23]Jesus was walking in the Temple[d] in Solomon's Porch.[d] [24]The Jews gathered around him and said, "How long will you make us wonder about you? If you are the Christ,[d] then tell us plainly."

### JESUS IS THE SON OF GOD

[25]Jesus answered, "I told you already, but you did not believe. I do miracles[d]

### DECODE THIS!
*A shepherd uses this to call his sheep.*

**9:39 blind** Jesus is talking about people who are spiritually blind, not physically blind.

in my Father's name. Those miracles show who I am. [26]But you don't believe because you are not my sheep. [27]My sheep listen to my voice. I know them, and they follow me. [28]I give them eternal life, and they will never die. And no person can steal them out of my hand. [29]My Father gave my sheep to me. He is greater than all, and no person can steal my sheep out of my Father's hand. [30]The Father and I are one."

[31]Again the Jews picked up stones to kill Jesus. [32]But Jesus said to them, "I have done many good works from the Father. Which of these good works are you killing me for?"

[33]The Jews answered, "We are not killing you for any good work you did. But you say things that are against God. You are only a man, but you say you are the same as God!"

[34]Jesus answered, "It is written in your law that God said, 'I have said you are gods!'[n] [35]This Scripture[d] called those people gods, the people who received God's message. And Scripture is always true. [36]So why do you say that I speak against God because I said, 'I am God's Son'? I am the one God chose and sent into the world. [37]If I don't do what my Father does, then don't believe me. [38]But if I do what my Father does, even though you don't believe in me, believe what I do. Then you will know and understand that the Father is in me and I am in the Father."

[39]They tried to take Jesus again, but he escaped from them.

[40]Then Jesus went back across the Jordan River to the place where John had first baptized. Jesus stayed there, [41]and many people came to him. They said, "John never did a miracle. But everything John said about this man is true." [42]And in that place many believed in Jesus.

## THE DEATH OF LAZARUS

**11**There was a man named Lazarus who was sick. He lived in the town of Bethany, where Mary and her sister Martha lived. [2]Mary is the woman who later put perfume on the Lord and wiped his feet with her hair. Mary's brother was Lazarus, the man who was now sick. [3]So Mary and Martha sent someone to tell Jesus, "Lord, the one you love is sick."

[4]When Jesus heard this he said, "This sickness will not end in death. It is for the glory of God. This has happened to bring glory to the Son of God." [5]Jesus loved Martha and her sister and Lazarus. [6]But when he heard that Lazarus was sick, he stayed where he was for two more days. [7]Then Jesus said to his followers, "Let us go back to Judea."

[8]The followers said, "But Teacher, the Jews there tried to kill you with stones. That was only a short time ago. Now you want to go back there?"

> **"My sheep listen to my voice. I know them, and they follow me. I give them eternal life, and they will never die."**
>
> *John 10:27-28*

[9]Jesus answered, "Are there not 12 hours in the day? If anyone walks in the daylight, he will not stumble because he can see by this world's light. [10]But if anyone walks at night he stumbles because there is no light to help him see."

> **"This sickness will not end in death. It is for the glory of God. This has happened to bring glory to the Son of God.**
>
> *John 11:4*

[11]After Jesus said this, he added, "Our friend Lazarus has fallen asleep. But I am going there to wake him."

[12]The followers said, "But Lord, if he can sleep, he will get well."

[13]Jesus meant that Lazarus was dead. But Jesus' followers thought that he meant Lazarus was really sleeping. [14]So then Jesus said plainly, "Lazarus is dead. [15]And I am glad for your sakes that I was not there so that you may believe. But let us go to him now."

[16]Then Thomas (the one called Didymus) said to the other followers, "Let us go, too. We will die with him."

## JESUS IN BETHANY

[17]Jesus arrived in Bethany. There he learned that Lazarus had already been dead and in the tomb for four days. [18]Bethany was about two miles from Jerusalem. [19]Many Jews had come there to comfort Martha and Mary about their brother.

10:34 'I . . . gods.' Quotation from Psalm 82:6.

²⁰Martha heard that Jesus was coming, and she went out to meet him. But Mary stayed at home. ²¹Martha said to Jesus, "Lord, if you had been here, my brother would not have died. ²²But I know that even now God will give you anything you ask."

²³Jesus said, "Your brother will rise and live again."

> ## "Jesus said, 'Your brother will rise and live again.'"
> *John 11:23*

²⁴Martha answered, "I know that he will rise and live again in the resurrection[n] on the last day."

²⁵Jesus said to her, "I am the resurrection and the life. He who believes in me will have life even if he dies. ²⁶And he who lives and believes in me will never die. Martha, do you believe this?"

²⁷Martha answered, "Yes, Lord. I believe that you are the Christ,[d] the Son of God. You are the One who was coming to the world."

## JESUS CRIES

²⁸After Martha said this, she went back to her sister Mary. She talked to Mary alone. Martha said, "The Teacher is here and he is asking for you." ²⁹When Mary heard this, she got up quickly and went to Jesus. ³⁰Jesus had not yet come into the town. He was still at the place where Martha had met him. ³¹The Jews were with Mary in the house, comforting her. They saw Mary stand and leave quickly. They followed her, thinking that she was going to the tomb to cry there. ³²But Mary went to the place where Jesus was. When she saw him, she fell at his feet and said, "Lord, if you had been here, my brother would not have died."

³³Jesus saw that Mary was crying and that the Jews who came with her were crying, too. Jesus felt very sad in his heart and was deeply troubled. ³⁴He asked, "Where did you bury him?"

"Come and see, Lord," they said.

³⁵Jesus cried.

³⁶So the Jews said, "See how much he loved him."

³⁷But some of them said, "If Jesus healed the eyes of the blind man, why didn't he keep Lazarus from dying?"

## JESUS RAISES LAZARUS

³⁸Again Jesus felt very sad in his heart. He came to the tomb. The tomb was a cave with a large stone covering the entrance. ³⁹Jesus said, "Move the stone away."

Martha said, "But, Lord, it has been four days since he died. There will be a bad smell." Martha was the sister of the dead man.

⁴⁰Then Jesus said to her, "Didn't I tell you that if you believed, you would see the glory of God?"

⁴¹So they moved the stone away from the entrance. Then Jesus looked up and said, "Father, I thank you that you heard me. ⁴²I know that you always hear me. But I said these things because of the people here around me. I want them to believe that you sent me." ⁴³After Jesus said this, he cried out in a loud voice, "Lazarus, come out!" ⁴⁴The dead man came out. His hands and feet were wrapped with pieces of cloth, and he had a cloth around his face.

Jesus said to them, "Take the cloth off of him and let him go."

## THE LEADERS PLAN TO KILL JESUS

⁴⁵There were many Jews who had come to visit Mary. They saw what Jesus did. And many of them believed in him. ⁴⁶But some of them went to the Pharisees.[d] They told the Pharisees what Jesus had done. ⁴⁷Then the leading priests and Pharisees called a meeting of the Jewish council. They asked, "What should we do? This man is doing many miracles.[d] ⁴⁸If we let him continue doing these things, everyone will believe in him. Then the Romans will come and take away our Temple[d] and our nation."

⁴⁹One of the men there was Caiaphas. He was the high priest that year. Caiaphas

11:24 **resurrection** Being raised from death to live again.

## Going Global

### MissionFish

Do you groan when your mom says, "Time to have a yard sale!" Tell her about MissionFish. As you know, yard sale stuff can be sold through eBay. But with MissionFish you can share the proceeds (or a percentage) and support your favorite cause.

Huh? It's easy. You just pick a group that's listed on their website and set a percentage of your sale price to share for each item. When you sell something on eBay, you ship to the winning bidder, and they pay you as usual. But MissionFish receives the donation part and sends your support to your favorite missionary group. (Tell mom, no worries. She will get a tax receipt.)

Don't find that particular missions organization on www.MissionFish.org? It is easy to add them to the site. Share the idea with your family and your church. This yard sale won't get rained out!

said, "You people know nothing! ⁵⁰It is better for one man to die for the people than for the whole nation to be destroyed. But you don't realize this."

⁵¹Caiaphas did not think of this himself. He was high priest that year. So he was really prophesying*d* that Jesus would die for the Jewish nation ⁵²and for God's scattered children. This would bring them all together and make them one.

⁵³That day they started planning to kill Jesus. ⁵⁴So Jesus no longer traveled openly among the Jews. He left there and went to a place near the desert. He went to a town called Ephraim and stayed there with his followers.

⁵⁵It was almost time for the Jewish Passover*d* Feast. Many from the country went up to Jerusalem before the Passover. They went to do the special things to make themselves pure. ⁵⁶The people looked for Jesus. They stood in the Temple and were asking each other, "Is

perfume on Jesus' feet, and then she wiped his feet with her hair. And the sweet smell from the perfume filled the whole house.

⁴Judas Iscariot, one of Jesus' followers, was there. (He was the one who would later turn against Jesus.) Judas said, ⁵"This perfume was worth 300 silver coins.*n* It should have been sold and the money given to the poor." ⁶But Judas did not really care about the poor. He said this because he was a thief. He was the one who kept the money box, and he often stole money from it.

⁷Jesus answered, "Let her alone. It was right for her to save this perfume for today—the day for me to be prepared for burial. ⁸The poor will always be with you, but you will not always have me."

## "She poured the perfume on Jesus' feet, and then she wiped his feet with her hair. And the sweet smell from the perfume filled the whole house." *John 12:3*

he coming to the Feast? What do you think?" ⁵⁷But the leading priests and the Pharisees had given orders about Jesus. They said that if anyone knew where Jesus was, he must tell them. Then they could arrest Jesus.

### JESUS WITH FRIENDS IN BETHANY

**12** Six days before the Passover*d* Feast, Jesus went to Bethany, where Lazarus lived. (Lazarus is the man Jesus raised from death.) ²There they had a dinner for Jesus. Martha served the food. Lazarus was one of the people eating with Jesus. ³Mary brought in a pint of very expensive perfume made from pure nard.*d* She poured the

### THE PLOT AGAINST LAZARUS

⁹A large crowd of Jews heard that Jesus was in Bethany. So they went there to see not only Jesus but also Lazarus. Lazarus was the one Jesus raised from death. ¹⁰So the leading priests made plans to kill Lazarus, too. ¹¹Because of Lazarus many Jews were leaving them and believing in Jesus.

### JESUS ENTERS JERUSALEM

¹²The next day a great crowd in Jerusalem heard that Jesus was coming there. These were the people who had come to the

Passover*d* Feast. ¹³They took branches of palm trees and went out to meet Jesus. They shouted,

"Praise*n* God!
God bless the One who comes in the name of the Lord!
God bless the King of Israel!"

*Psalm 118:25-26*

¹⁴Jesus found a colt and sat on it. This was as the Scripture*d* says,

¹⁵"Don't be afraid, people of Jerusalem!
Your king is coming.
He is sitting on the colt of a donkey." *Zechariah 9:9*

¹⁶The followers of Jesus did not understand this at first. But after Jesus was raised to glory, they remembered that this had been written about him. And they remembered that they had done these things to him.

## BiBLE BASiCS

### WHAT iS HEAVEN?

Before Jesus left his disciples, he wanted them to know that he was going away—but it was for a good reason. He was going to prepare a place for all of God's people to live with him forever. The Bible doesn't give us a ton of clues about heaven, but it does use words that indicate that it's "up," and there will be no more sin, sadness, sickness, or anything else bad. In fact, the Bible says heaven is so incredible that we aren't even able to imagine how great it is. And we get to live there forever with Jesus!

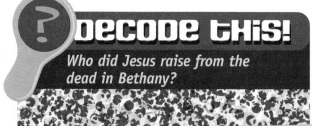

## DECODE THiS!

*Who did Jesus raise from the dead in Bethany?*

12:5 **silver coins** One coin, a denarius, was the average pay for one day's work.
12:13 **Praise** Literally, "Hosanna," a Hebrew word used at first in praying to God for help, but at this time it was probably a shout of joy used in praising God or his Messiah.

## PEOPLE TELL ABOUT JESUS

[17]There had been many people with Jesus when he raised Lazarus from death and told him to come out of the tomb. Now they were telling others about what Jesus did. [18]Many people went out to meet Jesus, because they had heard about this miracle.[d] [19]So the Pharisees[d] said to each other, "You can see that nothing is going right for us. Look! The whole world is following him."

# LIVIN' IT!

## ALL OR NOTHING
## JOHN 12:25

That girl in your class was really mean. Now you have the perfect chance to get back at her by cutting her down in front of your other friends, but you stop. *Jesus probably wouldn't want me to say that,* you think to yourself. *I'm supposed to love my enemies, and pray for them—and only say things that build others up.*

You have a choice. Do what you're dying inside to do—to get even or submit to God and do it his way. That's what God means when he asks us to give up our lives in order to gain them. It feels scary to live the way God wants us to because we're afraid no one is going to help us out. But the truth is, we have to obey God completely if we really want to understand what life is all about and enjoy it. Ask God to help you want to live fully for him.

## JESUS TALKS ABOUT HIS DEATH

[20]There were some Greek people, too, who came to Jerusalem to worship at the Passover[d] Feast. [21]They went to Philip. (Philip was from Bethsaida, in Galilee.) They said, "Sir, we would like to see Jesus." [22]Philip told Andrew. Then Andrew and Philip told Jesus.

[23]Jesus said to them, "The time has come for the Son of Man[d] to receive his glory. [24]I tell you the truth. A grain of wheat must fall to the ground and die. Then it makes many seeds. But if it never dies, it remains only a single seed. [25]The person who loves his life will give up true life. But the person who hates his life in this world will keep true life forever. [26]Whoever serves me must follow me. Then my servant will be with me everywhere I am. My Father will honor anyone who serves me.

[27]"Now I am very troubled. What should I say? Should I say, 'Father, save me from this time'? No, I came to this time so that I could suffer. [28]Father, bring glory to your name!"

Then a voice came from heaven, "I have brought glory to it, and I will do it again."

[29]The crowd standing there heard the voice. They said it was thunder. But others said, "An angel has spoken to him." [30]Jesus said, "That voice was for you, not for me. [31]Now is the time for the world to be judged. Now the ruler of this world will be thrown down. [32]I will be lifted up from the earth. And when this happens, I will draw all people toward me." [33]Jesus said this to show how he would die.

[34]The crowd said, "We have heard from the law that the Christ[d] will live forever. So why do you say, 'The Son of Man must be lifted up'? Who is this 'Son of Man'?"

[35]Then Jesus said, "The light will be with you for a little longer. So walk while you have the light. Then the darkness will not catch you. He who walks in the darkness does not know where he is going. [36]So believe in the light while you still have it. Then you will become sons of light." When Jesus had said this, he left and hid himself from them.

## SOME DON'T BELIEVE IN JESUS

[37]Though Jesus had done many miracles[d] before the people, they still did not believe in him. [38]This was to make clear the full meaning of what Isaiah the prophet[d] said:

"Lord, who believed the things we told them?
Who has seen the Lord's power?"

*Isaiah 53:1*

[39]This is why the people could not believe: Isaiah also said,

[40]"He has blinded their eyes.
He has closed their minds.
This is so that they will not see with their eyes
nor understand in their minds.
This is so they will not
come back to me and be forgiven."

*Isaiah 6:10*

[41]Isaiah said this because he saw Jesus' glory and spoke about him.

[42]But many people believed in Jesus, even many of the leaders. But because of the Pharisees,[d] they did not say that they believed in him. They were afraid that they would be put out of the synagogue.[d] [43]They loved praise from men more than praise from God.

[44]Then Jesus cried out, "He who believes in me is really believing in the One who sent me. [45]He who sees me sees the One who sent me. [46]I have come as light into the world. I came so that whoever believes in me would not stay in darkness.

### "They loved praise from men more than praise from God."
*John 12:43*

[47]"If anyone hears my words and does not obey them, I do not judge him. For I did not come to judge the world, but to save the world. [48]There is a judge for the one who refuses to believe in me and does not accept my words. The word I have taught will be his judge on the last day. [49]The things I taught were not from myself. The Father who sent me told me what to say and what to teach. [50]And I know that eternal life comes from what the Father commands. So whatever I say is what the Father told me to say."

## JESUS WASHES HIS FOLLOWERS' FEET

**13** It was almost time for the Jewish Passover[d] Feast. Jesus knew that it was time for him to leave this world and go back to the Father. He had always loved those who were his own in the world, and he loved them all the way to the end.

[2]Jesus and his followers were at the evening meal. The devil had already persuaded Judas Iscariot to turn against Jesus. (Judas was the son of Simon.) [3]Jesus knew that the Father had given him power over everything. He also knew that he had come from God and was going back to God. [4]So during the meal Jesus stood up and took off his outer clothing. Taking a towel, he wrapped it around his waist. [5]Then he poured water into a bowl and began to wash the followers' feet. He dried them with the towel that was wrapped around him.

[6]Jesus came to Simon Peter. But Peter said to Jesus, "Lord, are you going to wash my feet?"

[7]Jesus answered, "You don't understand what I am doing now. But you will understand later."

[8]Peter said, "No! You will never wash my feet."

Jesus answered, "If I don't wash your feet, then you are not one of my people."

[9]Simon Peter answered, "Lord, after you wash my feet, wash my hands and my head, too!"

[10]Jesus said, "After a person has had a bath, his whole body is clean. He needs only to wash his feet. And you men are clean,[d] but not all of you." [11]Jesus knew who would turn against him. That is why Jesus said, "Not all of you are clean."

[12]When he had finished washing their feet, he put on his clothes and sat down again. Jesus asked, "Do you understand what I have just done for you? [13]You call me 'Teacher' and 'Lord.' And this is right, because that is what I am. [14]I, your Lord and Teacher, have washed your feet. So you also should wash each other's feet. [15]I did this as an example for you. So you should do as I have done for you. [16]I tell you the truth. A servant is not greater than his master. A messenger is not greater than the one who sent him. [17]If you know these things, you will be happy if you do them.

[18]"I am not talking about all of you. I know those I have chosen. But what the Scripture[d] said must happen: 'The man who ate at my table has now turned against me.'[n]

[19]I am telling you this now before it happens. Then when it happens you will believe that I am he. [20]I tell you the truth. Whoever accepts anyone I send also accepts me. And whoever accepts me also accepts the One who sent me."

## JESUS TALKS ABOUT HIS DEATH

[21]After Jesus said this, he was very troubled. He said openly, "I tell you the truth. One of you will turn against me." [22]The followers all looked at each other. They did not know whom Jesus was talking about. [23]One of the followers was sitting[n] next to Jesus. This was the follower Jesus loved. [24]Simon Peter made signs to him to ask Jesus who it was that he was talking about.

[25]That follower leaned closer to Jesus and asked, "Lord, who is it that will turn against you?"

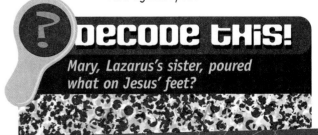

# DECODE THIS!

*Mary, Lazarus's sister, poured what on Jesus' feet?*

13:18 'The man . . . me.' Quotation from Psalm 41:9. 13:23 sitting Literally, "lying." The people of that time ate lying down and leaning on one arm.

[26]Jesus answered, "I will dip this bread into the dish. The man I give it to is the man who will turn against me." So Jesus took a piece of bread. He dipped it and gave it to Judas Iscariot, the son of Simon. [27]As soon as Judas took the bread, Satan entered him. Jesus said to Judas, "The thing that you will do—do it quickly!" [28]None of the men at the table understood why Jesus said this to Judas. [29]He was the one who kept the money box. So some of the followers thought that Jesus was telling Judas to buy what was needed for the

**KIDS SPEAK UP!**

**Q. What do your friends do that really grosses you out?**

**A. My friends like to burp all the time for no reason, and it's really gross.**

feast. Or they thought that Jesus wanted Judas to give something to the poor.

[30]Judas accepted the bread Jesus gave him and immediately went out. It was night.

[31]When Judas was gone, Jesus said, "Now the Son of Man[d] receives his glory. And God receives glory through him. [32]If God receives glory through him, then God will give glory to the Son through himself. And God will give him glory quickly."

[33]Jesus said, "My children, I will be with you only a little longer. You will look for me. And what I told the Jews, I

tell you now: Where I am going you cannot come.

[34]"I give you a new command: Love each other. You must love each other as I have loved you. [35]All people will know that you are my followers if you love each other."

## PETER WILL SAY HE DOESN'T KNOW JESUS

[36]Simon Peter asked Jesus, "Lord, where are you going?"

Jesus answered, "Where I am going you cannot follow now. But you will follow later."

[37]Peter asked, "Lord, why can't I follow you now? I am ready to die for you!"

[38]Jesus answered, "Will you really die for me? I tell you the truth. Before the rooster crows, you will say three times that you don't know me."

## JESUS COMFORTS HIS FOLLOWERS

**14** Jesus said, "Don't let your hearts be troubled. Trust in God. And trust in me. [2]There are many rooms in my Father's house. I would not tell you this if it were not true. I am going there to prepare a place for you. [3]After I go and prepare a place for you, I will come back.

Then I will take you to be with me so that you may be where I am. [4]You know the way to the place where I am going."

[5]Thomas said to Jesus, "Lord, we don't know where you are going. So how can we know the way?"

[6]Jesus answered, "I am the way. And I am

the truth and the life. The only way to the Father is through me. [7]If you really knew me, then you would know my Father, too. But now you do know him, and you have seen him."

[8]Philip said to him, "Lord, show us the Father. That is all we need."

[9]Jesus answered, "I have been with you a long time now. Do you still not know me, Philip? He who has seen me has seen the Father. So why do you say, 'Show us the Father'? [10]Don't you believe that I am in the Father and the Father is in me? The words I say to you don't come from me. The Father lives in me, and he is doing his own work. [11]Believe me when I say that I am in the Father and the Father is in me. Or believe because of the miracles[d] I have done. [12]I tell you the truth. He who believes in me will do the same things that I do. He will do even greater things than these because I am going to the Father. [13]And if you ask for anything in my name, I will do it for you. Then the Father's glory will be shown through the Son. [14]If you ask me for anything in my name, I will do it.

## THE PROMISE OF THE HOLY SPIRIT

[15]"If you love me, you will do the things I command. [16]I will ask the Father, and he will give you another Helper.[n] He will give you this Helper to be with you forever. [17]The Helper is the Spirit[d] of truth. The world cannot accept him because it does not see him or know him. But you know him. He lives with you and he will be in you.

**"Jesus said, 'Don't let your hearts be troubled. Trust in God. And trust in me.'"**

*John 14:1*

## DECODE THIS!

*Jesus said to believe in the light so you could become _____.*

14:16 **Helper** "Counselor," or "Comforter." Jesus is talking about the Holy Spirit.

156

HELP MARY FIND THE WAY TO THE EMPTY TOMB.

[18]"I will not leave you all alone like orphans. I will come back to you. [19]In a little while the world will not see me anymore, but you will see me. Because I live, you will live, too. [20]On that day you will know that I am in my Father. You will know that you are in me and I am in you. [21]He who knows my commands and obeys them is the one who loves me. And my Father will love him who loves me. I will love him and will show myself to him."

[22]Then Judas (not Judas Iscariot) said, "But, Lord, why do you plan to show yourself to us, but not to the world?"

[23]Jesus answered, "If anyone loves me, then he will obey my teaching. My Father will love him, and we will come to him and make our home with him. [24]He who

does not love me does not obey my teaching. This teaching that you hear is not really mine. It is from my Father, who sent me.

[25]"I have told you all these things while I am with you. [26]But the Helper will teach you everything. He will cause you to remember all the things I told you. This Helper is the Holy Spirit whom the Father will send in my name.

[27]"I leave you peace. My peace I give you. I do not give it to you as the world does. So don't let your hearts be troubled. Don't be afraid. [28]You heard me say to you, 'I am going, but I am coming back to you.' If you loved me, you should be happy that I am going back to the Father because he is greater than I am. [29]I have told you this now, before it happens. Then when it happens, you will believe. [30]I will not talk with you much longer. The ruler of this world is coming. He has no power over me. [31]But the world must know that I love the Father. So I do exactly what the Father told me to do.

"Come now, let us go.

## JESUS IS LIKE A VINE

**15** "I am the true vine; my Father is the gardener. [2]He cuts off every branch of mine that does not produce fruit. And he trims and cleans every branch that produces fruit so that it will produce even more fruit. [3]You are already clean[d] because of the words I have spoken to you. [4]Remain in me, and I will remain in you. No branch can produce fruit alone. It must remain in the vine. It is the same with you. You cannot produce fruit alone. You must remain in me.

[5]"I am the vine, and you are the branches. If a person remains in me and I remain in him, then he produces much fruit. But without me he can do nothing. [6]If anyone does not remain in me, then he is like a branch that is thrown away. That branch dies. People pick up dead branches, throw them into the fire, and burn them. [7]Remain in me and follow my teachings. If you do this, then you can ask for anything you want, and it will

## "i am the vine, and you are the branches. if a person remains in me and i remain in him, then he produces much fruit. But without me he can do nothing."

John 15:5

be given to you. [8]You should produce much fruit and show that you are my followers. This brings glory to my Father. [9]I loved you as the Father loved me. Now remain in my love. [10]I have obeyed my Father's commands, and I remain in his love. In the same way, if you obey my commands, you will remain in my love. [11]I have told you these things so that you can have the same joy I have. I want your joy to be the fullest joy.

[12]"This is my command: Love each other as I have loved you. [13]The greatest love a person can show is to die for his friends. [14]You are my friends if you do what I command you. [15]I don't call you servants now. A servant does not know what his master is doing. But now I call you friends because I have made known to you everything I heard from my Father. [16]You did not choose me; I chose you. And I gave you this work, to go and produce fruit. I want you to produce fruit that will last. Then the Father will give you anything you ask for in my name. [17]This is my command: Love each other.

## JESUS WARNS HIS FOLLOWERS

[18]"If the world hates you, remember that it hated me first. [19]If you belonged to the world, then it would love you as

## ?ecode This!

*Jesus told Peter that he would deny Jesus how many times?*

it loves its own. But I have chosen you out of the world. So you don't belong to it. That is why the world hates you. [20]Remember what I told you: A servant is not greater than his master. If people did wrong to me, they will do wrong to you, too. And if they obeyed my teaching, they will obey yours, too. [21]They will do all this to you because of me. They don't know the One who sent me. [22]If I had not come and spoken to them, they would not be guilty of sin. But now they have no excuse for their sin. [23]He who hates me also hates my Father. [24]I did works among them that no one else has ever done. If I had not done those works, they would not be guilty of sin. But now they have seen what I did, and yet they have hated both me and my Father. [25]But this happened so that what is written in their law would be true: 'They hated me for no reason.'[n]

[26]"I will send you the Helper[n] from the Father. He is the Spirit of truth who comes from the Father. When he comes, he will tell about me. [27]And you also must tell people about me because you have been with me from the beginning.

**16** "I have told you these things to keep you from giving up. [2]People will put you out of their synagogues.[d] Yes, the time is coming when whoever kills you will think that he is offering service to God. [3]They will do this because they have not known the Father and they have not known me. [4]I have told you these things now. So when the time comes, you will remember that I warned you.

### THE WORK OF THE HOLY SPIRIT

"I did not tell you these things at the beginning, because I was with you then. [5]Now I am going back to the One who sent me. But none of you asks me, 'Where are you going?' [6]Your hearts are filled with sadness because I have told you these things. [7]But I tell you the

"This is my command: Love each other as I have loved you. The greatest love a person can show is to die for his friends." *John 15:12-13*

truth. It is better for you that I go away. When I go away I will send the Helper[n] to you. If I do not go away, then the Helper will not come. [8]When the Helper comes, he will prove to the people of the world the truth about sin, about being right with God, and about judgment. [9]He will prove to them about sin, because they don't believe in me. [10]He will prove to them that I am right with God, because I am going to the Father. You will not see me anymore. [11]And the Helper will prove to them the truth about judgment, because the ruler of this world is already judged.

[12]"I have many more things to say to you, but they are too much for you now. [13]But when the Spirit[d] of truth comes he will lead you into all truth. He will not speak his own words. He will speak only what he hears and will tell you what is to come. [14]The Spirit of truth will bring glory to me. He will take what I have to say and tell it to you. [15]All that the Father has is mine. That is why I said that the Spirit will take what I have to say and tell it to you.

### SADNESS WILL BECOME HAPPINESS

[16]"After a little while you will not see me. And then after a little while you will see me again."

[17]Some of the followers said to each other, "What does Jesus mean when he says, 'After a little while you will not see me, and then after a little while you will see me again'? And what does he mean when he says, 'Because I am going to the Father'?" [18]They also asked, "What does he mean by 'a little while'? We don't understand what he is saying."

[19]Jesus saw that the followers wanted to ask him about this. So Jesus said to the followers, "Are you asking each other what I meant when I said, 'After a little while you will not see me. And then

## WILD WORLD FACTS

### A CLEAN ENCOUNTER

We use it every day (and hopefully after every time we go to the bathroom!). Soap keeps us and all our stuff clean. So how does it work?

Take a look at a drop of water on the countertop. Notice anything? It beads up because of a property called water tension where the molecules that make up water hold together tightly. Water tension makes it harder to get surface areas wet. Soap's job is to break that surface tension, making the water drop spread out and wet the surface better. When the soap contains the right chemicals, it is able to loosen, emulsify (disperse through water) and hold soil loosely until it can be washed away.

When Jesus washed the disciples' feet, he did it as a sign for us. We need to keep our hearts clean by repenting of sin, and we also need to serve one another.

15:25 'They . . . reason.' These words could be from Psalm 35:19 or Psalm 69:4. 15:26; 16:7 Helper "Counselor," or "Comforter." Jesus is talking about the Holy Spirit.

after a little while you will see me again'? ²⁰I tell you the truth. You will cry and be sad, but the world will be happy. You will be sad, but your sadness will become joy. ²¹When a woman gives birth to a baby, she has pain, because her time has come. But when her baby is born, she forgets the pain. She forgets because she is so happy that a child has been born into the world. ²²It is the same with you. Now you are sad. But I will see you again and you will be happy. And no one will take away your joy. ²³In that day you will not ask me for anything. I tell you the truth. My Father will give you anything you ask for in my name. ²⁴You have never asked for anything in my name. Ask and you will receive. And your joy will be the fullest joy.

## VICTORY OVER THE WORLD

²⁵"I have told you these things, using words that hide the meaning. But the time will come when I will not use words like that to tell you things. I will speak to you in plain words about the Father. ²⁶In that day you will ask the Father for things in my name. I am saying that I will not need to ask the Father for you. ²⁷No! The Father himself loves you. He loves you because you have loved me. And he loves you because you have believed that I came from God. ²⁸I came from the Father into the

world. Now I am leaving the world and going back to the Father."

²⁹Then the followers of Jesus said, "You are speaking clearly to us now. You are not using words that are hard to understand. ³⁰We can see now that you know all

things. You can answer a person's question even before he asks it. This makes us believe that you came from God."

³¹Jesus answered, "So now you believe? ³²Listen to me. A time is coming when you will be scattered. Each of you will be scattered to his own home. That time

is now here. You will leave me. I will be alone. But I am never really alone. Why? Because the Father is with me.

³³"I told you these things so that you can have peace in me. In this world you will have trouble. But be brave! I have defeated the world!"

## JESUS PRAYS FOR HIS FOLLOWERS

**17** After Jesus said these things he looked toward heaven. Jesus prayed, "Father, the time has come. Give glory to your Son so that the Son can give glory to you. ²You gave the Son power over all people so that the

> **"i told you these things so that you can have peace in me. in this world you will have trouble. But be brave! i have defeated the world!"**
>
> *John 16:33*

Son could give eternal life to all those people you have given to him. ³And this is eternal life: that men can know you, the only true God, and that men can know Jesus Christ, the One you sent. ⁴I finished the work you gave me to do. I

## Favorite Game Websites

1. Candystand.com
2. funbrain.com
3. Lego.com
4. iknowthat.com
5. PBSKids.org
6. Yahooligans.Yahoo.com
7. Postopia.com
8. Toomunchfun.com
9. thekidzpage.com
10. Netives.com

brought you glory on earth. ⁵And now, Father, give me glory with you. Give me the glory I had with you before the world was made.

⁶"You gave me some men from the world. I have shown them what you are like. Those men belonged to you, and you gave them to me. They have obeyed your teaching. ⁷Now they know that everything you gave me comes from you. ⁸I gave these men the teachings that you gave me. They accepted those teachings. They know that I truly came from you. ⁹I pray for them now. I am not praying for the people in the world. But I am praying for those men you gave me, because they are yours. ¹⁰All I have is yours, and all you have is mine. And my glory is shown through these men. ¹¹Now I am coming to you. I will not stay in the world now. But these men are still in the world. Holy Father,

keep them safe. Keep them safe by the power of your name (the name you gave me), so that they will be one, the same as you and I are one. [12]While I was with them, I kept them safe. I kept them safe by the power of your name—the name you gave me. I protected them. And only one of them, the one who is going to hell, was lost. He was lost so that what was said in the Scripture[d] would happen.

[13]"I am coming to you now. But I pray these things while I am still in the world. I say these things so that these

you gave me. I gave them this glory so that they can be one, the same as you and I are one. [23]I will be in them and you will be in me. So they will be completely one. Then the world will know that you sent me. And the world will know that you loved these people the same as you loved me.

[24]"Father, I want these people that you have given me to be with me in every place I am. I want them to see my glory. This is the glory you gave me because you loved me before the world was made. [25]Father, you are the One who is

it you are looking for?"

[5]The men answered, "Jesus from Nazareth."

Jesus said, "I am Jesus." (Judas, the one who turned against Jesus, was standing there with them.) [6]When Jesus said, "I am Jesus," the men moved back and fell to the ground.

[7]Jesus asked them again, "Who is it you are looking for?"

They said, "Jesus of Nazareth."

[8]Jesus said, "I told you that I am he. So if you are looking for me, then let these other men go." [9]This happened so that the words Jesus said before might come true: "I have not lost any of the men you gave me."

[10]Simon Peter had a sword. He took out the sword and struck the servant of the high priest, cutting off his right ear. (The servant's name was Malchus.) [11]Jesus said to Peter, "Put your sword back. Shall I not drink of the cup[n] the Father has given me?"

> ## "Then the world will know that you [God] sent me."
> John 17:23

men can have my joy. I want them to have all of my joy. [14]I have given them your teaching. And the world has hated them. The world hated these men, because they don't belong to the world, the same as I don't belong to the world. [15]I am not asking you to take them out of the world. But I am asking that you keep them safe from the Evil One. [16]They don't belong to the world, the same as I don't belong to the world. [17]Make them ready for your service through your truth. Your teaching is truth. [18]I have sent them into the world, the same as you sent me into the world. [19]I am making myself ready to serve. I do this for them so that they can truly be ready for your service.

[20]"I pray for these men. But I am also praying for all people who will believe in me because of the teaching of these men. [21]Father, I pray that all people who believe in me can be one. You are in me and I am in you. I pray that these people can also be one in us, so that the world will believe that you sent me. [22]I have given these people the glory that

good. The world does not know you, but I know you. And these people know that you sent me. [26]I showed them what you are like. And again I will show them what you are like. Then they will have the same love that you have for me. And I will live in them."

### JESUS IS ARRESTED

**18** When Jesus finished praying, he left with his followers. They went across the Kidron Valley. On the other side there was a garden of olive trees. Jesus and his followers went there.

[2]Judas knew where this place was, because Jesus met there often with his followers. Judas was the one who turned against Jesus. [3]So Judas led a group of soldiers to the garden. Judas also brought some guards from the leading priests and the Pharisees.[d] They were carrying torches, lanterns, and weapons.

[4]Jesus knew everything that would happen to him. Jesus went out and asked, "Who is

### JESUS IS BROUGHT BEFORE ANNAS

[12]Then the soldiers with their commander and the Jewish guards arrested Jesus. They tied him [13]and led him first to Annas. Annas was the father-in-law of Caiaphas, the high priest that year. [14]Caiaphas was the one who had told the Jews that it would be better if one man died for all the people.

### PETER SAYS HE DOESN'T KNOW JESUS

[15]Simon Peter and another one of Jesus' followers went along after Jesus. This follower knew the high priest. So he went with Jesus into the high priest's courtyard. [16]But Peter waited outside near the door. The follower who knew

**DECODE THIS!**

*What plant was Jesus compared to?*

18:11 cup Jesus is talking about the bad things that will happen to him. Accepting these things will be very hard, like drinking a cup of something that tastes very bitter.

the high priest came back outside. He spoke to the girl at the door and brought Peter inside. [17]The girl at the door said to Peter, "Aren't you also one of that man's followers?"

Peter answered, "No, I am not!"

[18]It was cold, so the servants and guards had built a fire. They were standing around it and warming themselves. Peter was standing with them, warming himself.

### THE HIGH PRIEST QUESTIONS JESUS

[19]The high priest asked Jesus questions about his followers and his teaching. [20]Jesus answered, "I have spoken openly to everyone. I have always taught in synagogues[d] and in the Temple,[d] where

The servant said, "Didn't I see you with him in the garden?"

[27]Again Peter said it wasn't true. Just then a rooster crowed.

### JESUS IS BROUGHT BEFORE PILATE

[28]Then they led Jesus from Caiaphas' house to the Roman governor's palace. It was early in the morning. The Jews would not go inside the palace. They did not want to make themselves unclean,[n] because they wanted to eat the Passover[d] meal. [29]So Pilate went outside to them. He asked, "What charges do you bring against this man?"

[30]They answered, "He is a criminal. That is why we brought him to you."

[31]Pilate said to them, "Take him yourselves and judge him by your own law."

"You say that I am a king. That is true. I was born for this: to tell people about the truth. That is why I came into the world. And everyone who belongs to the truth listens to me."

[38]Pilate said, "What is truth?" After he said this, he went out to the Jews again. He said to them, "I can find nothing to charge against this man. [39]But it is your custom that I free one prisoner to you at the time of the Passover. Do you want me to free this 'king of the Jews'?"

[40]They shouted back, "No, not him! Let Barabbas go free!" (Barabbas was a robber.)

**19** Then Pilate ordered that Jesus be taken away and whipped. [2]The soldiers used some thorny branches to make a crown. They put this crown on Jesus' head and put a purple robe around him. [3]Then they came to Jesus many times and said, "Hail, King of the Jews!" They hit Jesus in the face.

## "i was born for this: to tell people about the truth. That is why i came into the world."

*John 18:37*

all the Jews come together. I never said anything in secret. [21]So why do you question me? Ask the people who heard my teaching. They know what I said."

[22]When Jesus said this, one of the guards standing there hit him. The guard said, "Is that the way you answer the high priest?"

[23]Jesus answered him, "If I said something wrong, then say what was wrong. But if what I said is true, why do you hit me?"

[24]Then Annas sent Jesus to Caiaphas, the high priest. Jesus was still tied.

### PETER SAYS AGAIN HE DOESN'T KNOW JESUS

[25]Simon Peter was standing and warming himself. They said to him, "Aren't you one of that man's followers?"

Peter denied it and said, "No, I am not."

[26]One of the servants of the high priest was there. This servant was a relative of the man whose ear Peter had cut off.

They answered, "But we are not allowed to put anyone to death." [32](This happened so that what Jesus had said about how he would die would come true.)

[33]Then Pilate went back inside the palace. He called Jesus to him and asked, "Are you the king of the Jews?"

[34]Jesus said, "Is that your own question, or did others tell you about me?"

[35]Pilate answered, "I am not a Jew. It was your own people and their leading priests who brought you before me. What have you done wrong?"

[36]Jesus said, "My kingdom does not belong to this world. If it belonged to this world, my servants would fight so that I would not be given over to the Jews. But my kingdom is from another place."

[37]Pilate said, "So you are a king!"

Jesus answered,

[4]Again Pilate came out and said to them, "Look! I am bringing Jesus out to you. I want you to know that I find nothing I can charge against him." [5]Then Jesus came out, wearing the crown of thorns and the purple robe. Pilate said to the Jews, "Here is the man!"

[6]When the leading priests and the guards saw Jesus they shouted, "Kill him on a cross! Kill him on a cross!"

But Pilate answered, "Take him and nail him to a cross yourselves. I find nothing I can charge against him."

[7]The Jews answered, "We have a law that says he should die, because he said he is the Son of God."

[8]When Pilate heard this, he was even more afraid. [9]He went back inside the palace and asked Jesus, "Where are you from?" But Jesus did not answer him.

---

**DECODE THIS!**

*Jesus prayed that his followers would be safe from whom?*

---

⭐ **18:28 unclean** Going into a non-Jewish place would make them unfit to eat the Passover Feast, according to Jewish law.

# JUNE EVANGELISM

*I am proud of the Good News. It is the power God uses to save everyone who believes (Romans 1:16).*

**1**

**2** MARK 16:15: Jesus said to the followers, "Go everywhere in the world. Tell the Good News to everyone."

**3** Go swimming!

**4**

**5** Prayer Pointer: Ask God to bring someone into your life who needs to hear the Good News, and pray for wisdom to know how to tell them.

**6**

**7** Glue seashells to picture frames, and give them away as gifts.

**8**

**9**

**10** JOHN 20:29: Then Jesus told him, "You believe because you see me. Those who believe without seeing me will be truly happy."

**11**

**12** See how long you can hold your breath under water.

**13**

**14** Prayer Pointer: Ask God to raise up people who will go into the world to preach the gospel.

**15**

**16** Set up a lemonade stand with your brothers and sisters, and give the money to missions.

**17**

**18** Acts 20:24: I want to finish the work that the Lord Jesus gave me—to tell people the Good News about God's grace.

**19**

**20**

**21** Ask your neighbors if you can help them mow their lawn or water their flowers.

**22**

**23** Tell your memory verse to your siblings.

**24** Prayer Pointer: Pray for physical and spiritual protection for God's missionaries.

**25**

**26** Tell your dad how proud you are of him and how much you love him.

**27** Colossians 4:5: Be wise in the way you act with people who are not believers. Use your time in the best way you can.

**28**

**29** Pick flowers and take them to someone who needs to be cheered up.

**30** Prayer Pointer: Pray for the people in your life who don't know God to repent and believe him.

**31**

[10]Pilate said, "You refuse to speak to me? Don't you know that I have power to set you free and power to have you killed on a cross?"

[11]Jesus answered, "The only power you have over me is the power given to you by God. The man who gave me to you is guilty of a greater sin."

[12]After this, Pilate tried to let Jesus go free. But the Jews cried out, "Anyone who makes himself king is against Caesar. If you let this man go free, you are not Caesar's friend."

[13]Pilate heard what the Jews were saying. So he brought Jesus out to the place called The Stone Pavement. (In the Jewish language[n] the name is Gabbatha.) Pilate sat down on the judge's seat there. [14]It was about six o'clock in the morning on Preparation[d]

## GET CONNECTED

### REMEMBER

You wake up. Go to school. Play with friends. Do homework. Eat meals. Go to sleep again. Your life is crowded with lots of activities. And it's easy to go from one thing to the next until the day is over, without ever once remembering that God is with you.

God doesn't want to be a part of just your devotional time, although that time is needed. He wants to be with you in every part of your day. Turn your thoughts to God, and invite him into your day. Let him know what you're thinking, and keep his words in your heart. You'll discover an incredible friendship that will last forever.

> **"The only power you have over me is the power given to you by God."** *John 19:11*

Day of Passover[d] week. Pilate said to the Jews, "Here is your king!"

[15]They shouted, "Take him away! Take him away! Kill him on a cross!"

Pilate asked them, "Do you want me to kill your king on a cross?"

The leading priests answered, "The only king we have is Caesar!"

[16]So Pilate gave Jesus to them to be killed on a cross.

### JESUS IS KILLED ON A CROSS

The soldiers took charge of Jesus. [17]Carrying his own cross, Jesus went out to a place called The Place of the Skull. (In the Jewish language[n] this place is called Golgotha.) [18]There they nailed Jesus to the cross. They also put two other men on crosses, one on each side of Jesus with Jesus in the middle. [19]Pilate wrote a sign and put it on the cross. It

read: "JESUS OF NAZARETH, THE KING OF THE JEWS." [20]The sign was written in the Jewish language, in Latin, and in Greek. Many of the Jews read the sign, because this place where Jesus was killed was near the city. [21]The leading Jewish priests said to Pilate, "Don't write, 'The King of the Jews.' But write, 'This man said, I am the King of the Jews.'"

[22]Pilate answered, "What I have written, I have written!"

[23]After the soldiers nailed Jesus to the cross, they took his clothes. They divided them into four parts. Each soldier got one part. They also took his long shirt. It was all one piece of cloth, woven from top to bottom. [24]So the soldiers said to each other, "We should not tear this into parts. We should throw lots[d] to see who will get it." This happened to give full meaning to the Scripture:[d]

> "They divided my clothes among
>      them.
>   And they threw lots[d] for my
>      clothing."     *Psalm 22:18*

So the soldiers did this.

[25]Jesus' mother stood near his cross.

His mother's sister was also standing there, with Mary the wife of Clopas, and Mary Magdalene. [26]Jesus saw his mother. He also saw the follower he loved standing there. He said to his mother, "Dear woman, here is your son." [27]Then he said to the follower, "Here is your mother." From that time on, this follower took her to live in his home.

### JESUS DIES

[28]After this, Jesus knew that everything had been done. To make the Scripture[d] come true, he said, "I am thirsty."[n] [29]There was a jar full of vinegar there, so the soldiers soaked a sponge in it. Then they put the sponge on a branch of a hyssop plant and lifted it to Jesus' mouth. [30]Jesus tasted the vinegar. Then he said, "It is finished." He bowed his head and died.

[31]This day was Preparation[d] Day. The next day was a special Sabbath[d] day. The Jews did not want the bodies to stay on the cross on the Sabbath day. So they asked Pilate to order that the legs of the men be broken[n] and the bodies be taken away. [32]So the soldiers came and broke the legs of the first man on the cross beside Jesus. Then they broke the legs of the man on the other cross beside Jesus. [33]But when the soldiers came to Jesus, they saw that he was already dead. So they did not break his legs. [34]But one of

19:13, 17 **Jewish language** Aramaic, the language of the Jews in the first century. 19:28 **"I am thirsty."** Read Psalms 22:15; 69:21. 19:31 **broken** The breaking of the men's bones would make them die sooner.

the soldiers stuck his spear into Jesus' side. At once blood and water came out. 35(The one who saw this happen has told about it. The things he says are true. He knows that he tells the truth. He told about it so that you also can believe.) 36These things happened to make the Scripture come true: "Not one of his bones will be broken."[n] 37And another Scripture said, "They will look at the one they have stabbed."[n]

## JESUS IS BURIED

38Later, a man named Joseph from Arimathea asked Pilate if he could take the body of Jesus. (Joseph was a secret follower of Jesus, because he was afraid of the Jews.) Pilate gave his permission. So Joseph came and took Jesus' body away. 39Nicodemus went with Joseph. Nicodemus was the man who earlier had come to Jesus at night. He brought

ever been buried. 42The men laid Jesus in that tomb because it was near, and the Jews were preparing to start their Sabbath[d] day.

> "The things he says are true. He knows that he tells the truth. He told about it so that you also can believe." *John 19:35*

## JESUS' TOMB IS EMPTY

**20** Early on the first day of the week, Mary Magdalene went to the tomb. It was still dark. Mary saw that the large stone had been moved away from the tomb. 2So Mary ran to Simon Peter and the other follower (the

faster than Peter. So the other follower reached the tomb first. 5He bent down and looked in. He saw the strips of linen cloth lying there, but he did not go in. 6Then following him came Simon Peter. He went into the tomb and saw the strips of linen lying there. 7He also saw the cloth that had been around Jesus' head. The cloth was folded up and laid in a different place from the strips of linen. 8Then the other follower, who had reached the tomb first, also went in. He saw and believed. 9(These followers did not yet understand from the Scriptures[d] that Jesus must rise from death.)

## JESUS APPEARS TO MARY MAGDALENE

10Then the followers went back home. 11But Mary stood outside the tomb, crying. While she was still crying, she bent down and looked inside the tomb. 12She saw two angels dressed in white. They were sitting where Jesus' body had been, one at the head and one at the feet.

13They asked her, "Woman, why are you crying?"

She answered, "They have taken away my Lord. I don't know where they have put him." 14When Mary said this, she turned around and saw Jesus standing there. But she did not know that it was Jesus.

15Jesus asked her, "Woman, why are you crying? Whom are you looking for?"

Mary thought he was the gardener. So she said to him, "Did you take him away, sir? Tell me where you put him, and I will get him."

16Jesus said to her, "Mary."

Mary turned toward Jesus and said in

# Gotta Know!

## What do missionaries really do?

Missionaries are people who tell others about the Good News of Jesus. All of God's people are missionaries in a way, since we all need to tell non-believers God's truth. But some people are called by God to make it the focus of their work. They may remain at home, but many move to other countries around the world so they can reach people who have never heard the gospel. Often they offer a service to the people, such as teaching English or providing medicine or food. As they meet basic needs, people are open to what they have to say about Jesus. They rely on people like us back at home to provide the money they need to keep spreading God's Word.

about 75 pounds of spices. This was a mixture of myrrh[d] and aloes.[d] 40These two men took Jesus' body and wrapped it with the spices in pieces of linen cloth. (This is how the Jews bury people.) 41In the place where Jesus was killed, there was a garden. In the garden was a new tomb where no one had

one Jesus loved). Mary said, "They have taken the Lord out of the tomb. We don't know where they have put him."

3So Peter and the other follower started for the tomb. 4They were both running, but the other follower ran

SPREAD THE GOOD NEWS!

# DECODE THIS!

*What weapon did Simon Peter use to cut off the servant's ear?*

19:36 "Not one . . . broken." Quotation from Psalm 34:20. The idea is from Exodus 12:46; Numbers 9:12.
19:37 "They . . . stabbed." Quotation from Zechariah 12:10.

# JESUS IS RISEN!

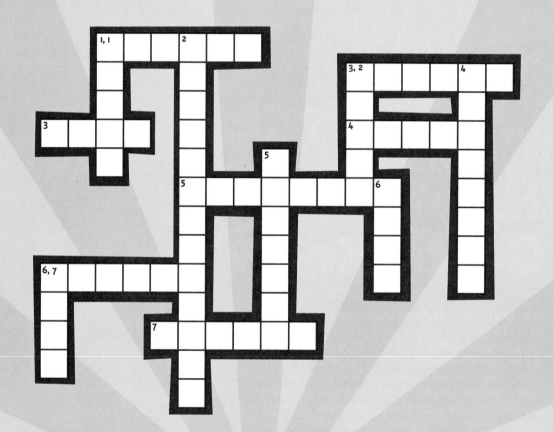

## ACROSS

1. Triumphant ride
2. Answered with vinegar
3. Peter's sin
4. Angel's message
5. Jesus' conclusion
6. Clean hands, bad heart
7. Jesus' home

## DOWN

1. Jesus said _____ my blood.
2. Nailed sign
3. Days in death
4. Christ's family status
5. Impossible happens
6. Price Jesus paid
7. Type of branch fans waved

## WILD WORLD FACTS

### SEEING IS BELIEVING

Thomas wouldn't believe Jesus had risen from the dead until he saw Jesus alive with his own 2 eyes. So when Jesus appeared to him, how did Thomas see Jesus?

Our eyes are somewhat round in shape and hold just the right tools to help us see. The cornea is the clear outside part of our eye where light enters. Light goes past the iris (the colored part) and through the lens, which is made of protein. The lens, like on a camera, sends the image to the back of the eyeball, where the retina is located. Special cells on the retina send the messages through the optic nerve to the brain to tell us what the eyes are seeing.

Thomas believed that Jesus was God because he saw him with his own 2 eyes, but Jesus said that we who believe in him without seeing are even more blessed!

[BrainPOP: Senses]

the Jewish language," "Rabboni." (This means Teacher.)

[17] Jesus said to her, "Don't hold me. I have not yet gone up to the Father. But go to my brothers and tell them this: 'I am going back to my Father and your Father. I am going back to my God and your God.'"

[18] Mary Magdalene went and said to the followers, "I saw the Lord!" And she told them what Jesus had said to her.

### JESUS APPEARS TO HIS FOLLOWERS

[19] It was the first day of the week. That evening the followers were together. The doors were locked, because they were afraid of the Jews. Then Jesus came and stood among them. He said, "Peace be with you!" [20] After he said this, he showed them his hands and his side. The followers were very happy when they saw the Lord.

[21] Then Jesus said again, "Peace be with you! As the Father sent me, I now send you." [22] After he said this, he breathed on them and said, "Receive the Holy Spirit.[d] [23] If you forgive anyone his sins, they are forgiven. If you don't forgive them, they are not forgiven."

### JESUS APPEARS TO THOMAS

[24] Thomas (called Didymus) was not with the followers when Jesus came. Thomas was 1 of the 12. [25] The other followers told Thomas, "We saw the Lord."

But Thomas said, "I will not believe it until I see the nail marks in his hands. And I will not believe until I put my finger where the nails were and put my hand into his side."

[26] A week later the follow-

ers were in the house again. Thomas was with them. The doors were locked, but Jesus came in and stood among them. He said, "Peace be with you!" [27] Then he said to Thomas, "Put your finger here. Look at my hands. Put your hand here in my side. Stop doubting and believe."

[28] Thomas said to him, "My Lord and my God!"

[29] Then Jesus told him, "You believe because you see me. Those who believe without seeing me will be truly happy."

### WHY JOHN WROTE THIS BOOK

[30] Jesus did many other miracles[d] before his followers that are not written in this book. [31] But these are written so that you can believe that Jesus is the Christ,[d] the Son of God. Then, by believing, you can have life through his name.

### JESUS APPEARS TO SEVEN FOLLOWERS

**21** Later, Jesus showed himself to his followers by Lake Galilee." This is how it happened: [2] Some of the followers

> "'Peace be with you!' After he said this, he showed them his hands and his side. The followers were very happy when they saw the Lord."
> John 20:19-20

were together. They were Simon Peter, Thomas (called Didymus), Nathanael from Cana in Galilee, the two sons of Zebedee, and two other followers. [3] Simon Peter said, "I am going out to fish."

The other followers said, "We will go with you." So they went out and got

### DECODE THIS!

*What was the name of the criminal set free at Jesus' trial?*

 20:16 Jewish language  Aramaic, the language of the Jews in the first century.
21:1 Lake Galilee  Literally, "Sea of Tiberias."

**167**

into the boat. They fished that night but caught nothing.

⁴Early the next morning Jesus stood on the shore. But the followers did not know that it was Jesus. ⁵Then he said to them, "Friends, have you caught any fish?"

They answered, "No."

⁶He said, "Throw your net into the water on the right side of the boat, and you will find some." So they did this. They caught so many fish that they could not pull the net back into the boat.

⁷The follower whom Jesus loved said to Peter, "It is the Lord!" When Peter heard him say this, he wrapped

**"There are many other things that Jesus did. if every one of them were written down, i think the whole world would not be big enough for all the books that would be written."**

John 21:25

big fish. There were 153. Even though there were so many, the net did not tear. ¹²Jesus said to them, "Come and eat." None of the followers dared ask him, "Who are you?" They knew it was the Lord. ¹³Jesus came and took the bread and gave it to them. He also gave them the fish.

¹⁴This was now the third time Jesus showed himself to his followers after he was raised from death.

### JESUS TALKS TO PETER

¹⁵When they finished eating, Jesus said to Simon Peter, "Simon son of John do you love me more than these?"

He answered, "Yes, Lord, you know that I love you."

Jesus said, "Take care of my lambs."

¹⁶Again Jesus said, "Simon son of John do you love me?"

He answered, "Yes, Lord, you know that I love you."

Jesus said, "Take care of my sheep."

¹⁷A third time he said, "Simon son of John do you love me?"

Peter was hurt because Jesus asked him the third time, "Do you love me?" Peter said, "Lord, you know everything. You know that I love you!"

He said to him, "Take care of my sheep. ¹⁸I tell you the truth. When you were younger, you tied your own belt and went where you wanted. But when you are old, you will put out your hands and someone else will

tie them. They will take you where you don't want to go." ¹⁹(Jesus said this to show how Peter would die to give glory to God.) Then Jesus said to Peter, "Follow me!"

²⁰Peter turned and saw that the follower Jesus loved was walking behind them. (This was the follower who had leaned against Jesus at the supper and had said, "Lord, who will turn against you?") ²¹When Peter saw him behind them he asked Jesus, "Lord, what about him?"

²²Jesus answered, "Perhaps I want him to live until I come back. That should not be important to you. You follow me!"

²³So a story spread among the brothers that this follower would not die. But Jesus did not say that he would not die. He only said, "Perhaps I want him to live until I come back. That should not be important to you."

²⁴That follower is the one who is telling these things. He is the one who has now written them down. We know that what he says is true.

²⁵There are many other things that Jesus did. If every one of them were written down, I think the whole world would not be big enough for all the books that would be written.

### KIDS SPEAK UP!

**Q. What foods have you mixed and eaten?**

**A. I have mixed mustard, potatoes, corn, and peas together and eaten it.**

his coat around himself. (Peter had taken his clothes off.) Then he jumped into the water. ⁸The other followers went to shore in the boat, dragging the net full of fish. They were not very far from shore, only about 100 yards. ⁹When the followers stepped out of the boat and onto the shore, they saw a fire of hot coals. There were fish on the fire, and there was bread.

¹⁰Then Jesus said, "Bring some of the fish that you caught."

¹¹Simon Peter went into the boat and pulled the net to the shore. It was full of

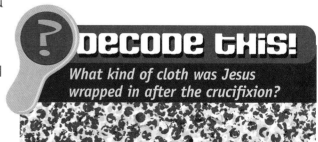

### DECODE THIS!

*What kind of cloth was Jesus wrapped in after the crucifixion?*

Peter preaches to the non-Jews.

Acts 1:8 is called the Great Commission.

The Holy Spirit comes with flames of fire to believers meeting in Jerusalem.

# THE ACTS
## OF THE APOSTLES

Saul (a Pharisee) changes his name to Paul.

The Good News of Jesus spreads.

Written by Luke and picks up where his Gospel left off.

Stephen is the first ever to die for Christ.

## LUKE WRITES ANOTHER BOOK

**1** To Theophilus,
The first book I wrote was about everything that Jesus did and taught. [2]I wrote about the whole life of Jesus, from the beginning until the day he was taken up into heaven. Before this, Jesus talked to the apostles[d] he had chosen. With the help of the Holy Spirit,[d] Jesus told them what they should do. [3]After his death, he showed himself to them and proved in many ways that he was alive. The apostles saw Jesus during the 40 days after he was raised from death. He spoke to them about the kingdom of God. [4]Once when he was eating with them, he told them not to leave Jerusalem. He said, "The Father has made you a promise which I told you about before. Wait here to receive this promise. [5]John baptized people with water, but in a few days you will be baptized with the Holy Spirit."

## JESUS IS TAKEN UP INTO HEAVEN

[6]The apostles[d] were all together. They asked Jesus, "Lord, are you at this time going to give the kingdom back to Israel?"

> ## "John baptized people with water, but in a few days you will be baptized with the Holy Spirit."
> *Acts 1:5*

[7]Jesus said to them, "The Father is the only One who has the authority to decide dates and times. These things are not for you to know. [8]But the Holy Spirit[d] will come to you. Then you will receive power. You will be my witnesses—in Jerusalem, in all of Judea, in Samaria, and in every part of the world."

[9]After he said this, as they were watching, he was lifted up. A cloud hid him from their sight. [10]As he was going, they were looking into the sky. Suddenly, two men wearing white clothes stood beside them. [11]They said, "Men of Galilee, why are you standing here looking into the sky? You saw Jesus taken away from you into heaven. He will come back in the same way you saw him go."

## A NEW APOSTLE IS CHOSEN

[12]Then they went back to Jerusalem from the Mount of Olives.[d] (This mountain is about half a mile from Jerusalem.) [13]When they entered the city, they went to the upstairs room where they were staying. Peter, John, James, Andrew, Philip, Thomas, Bartholomew, Matthew, James son of Alphaeus, Simon (known as the Zealot[d]), and Judas son of James were there. [14]They all continued praying together. Some women, including Mary the mother of Jesus, and Jesus' brothers were also there with the apostles.

[15]During this time there was a meeting of the believers. (There were about 120 of them.) Peter stood up and said, [16-17]"Brothers, in the Scriptures[d] the Holy Spirit[d] said through David that something must happen. The Spirit was talking about Judas, one of our own group, who served together with us. The Spirit said that Judas would lead men to arrest Jesus. [18](Judas bought a field with the money he got for his evil act. But Judas fell to his death, his body burst open, and all his intestines poured out. [19]Everyone in Jerusalem learned about this. This is why they named the field Akeldama. In their language Akeldama means "field of blood.") [20]In the book of Psalms, this is written:

'May his place be empty.
    Leave no one to live in it.'
*Psalm 69:25*

And it is also written:
'Let another man replace him
        as leader.'    *Psalm 109:8*

[21-22]"So now a man must join us and become a witness of Jesus' being raised from death. He must be one of the men who were part of our group during all the time the Lord Jesus was with us. He must have been with us from the time John began to baptize

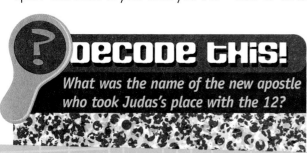

**DECODE THIS!**
*What was the name of the new apostle who took Judas's place with the 12?*

### Places to Serve

1. **A nursing home**
2. **Inner-city missions**
3. **Soup kitchen**
4. **Children's home (or adoption agency)**
5. **Vacation Bible School**
6. **Children's hospital**
7. **Youth group**
8. **Physically or mentally challenged kids**
9. **Overseas missions**
10. **Your home!**

people until the day when Jesus was taken up from us to heaven."

²³They put the names of two men before the group. One was Joseph Barsabbas, who was also called Justus. The other was Matthias. ²⁴⁻²⁵The apostles prayed, "Lord, you know the minds of everyone. Show us which one of these two you have chosen to do this work. Judas turned away from it and went where he belongs. Lord, show us which one should take his place as an apostle!"ᵈ ²⁶Then they used lotsᵈ to choose between them, and the lots showed that Matthias was the one. So he became an apostle with the other 11.

## THE COMING OF THE HOLY SPIRIT

**2** When the day of Pentecostᵈ came, they were all together in one place. ²Suddenly a noise came from heaven. It sounded like a strong wind blowing. This noise filled the whole house where they were sitting. ³They saw something that looked like flames of fire. The flames were separated and stood over each person there. ⁴They were all filled with the Holy Spirit,ᵈ and they began to speak differ-

> **"i keep the Lord before me always. Because he is close by my side, i will not be hurt."**
>
> *Acts 2:25*

ent languages. The Holy Spirit was giving them the power to speak these languages.

⁵There were some religious Jews staying in Jerusalem who were from every country in the world. ⁶When they heard this noise, a crowd came together. They were all surprised, because each one heard them speaking in his own language. ⁷They were completely amazed at this. They said, "Look! Aren't all these men that we hear speaking from Galilee?ⁿ ⁸But each of us hears them in his own language. How is this possible? We are from different places: ⁹Parthia, Media, Elam, Mesopotamia, Judea, Cappadocia, Pontus, Asia, ¹⁰Phrygia, Pamphylia, Egypt, the areas of Libya near Cyrene, Rome ¹¹(both Jews and those who had become Jews), Crete and Arabia. But we hear these men telling in our own languages about the great things God has done!" ¹²They were all amazed and confused. They asked each other, "What does this mean?"

¹³But others were making fun of them, saying, "They have had too much wine."

## PETER SPEAKS TO THE PEOPLE

¹⁴But Peter stood up with the 11 apostles.ᵈ In a loud voice he spoke to the crowd: "My fellow Jews, and all of you who are in Jerusalem, listen to me. Pay attention to what I have to say. ¹⁵These men are not drunk, as you think; it is only nine o'clock in the morning! ¹⁶But Joel the prophetᵈ wrote about what is happening here today:

¹⁷'God says: In the last days
    I will give my Spiritᵈ freely to all
        kinds of people.
Your sons and daughters will
        prophesy.ᵈ
    Your old men will dream dreams.
    Your young men will see visions.
¹⁸At that time I will give my Spirit
        even to my servants, both men
        and women.
    And they will prophesy.

¹⁹I will show miraclesᵈ
    in the sky and on the earth:
    blood, fire and thick smoke.
²⁰The sun will become dark.
    The moon will become red as
        blood.
    And then the great and glorious
        day of the Lord will come.
²¹Then anyone who asks the Lord
        for help
    will be saved.'        *Joel 2:28-32*

²²"Men of Israel, listen to these words: Jesus from Nazareth was a very special man. God clearly showed this to you by the miracles,ᵈ wonders, and signs God did through him. You all know this, because it happened right here among you. ²³Jesus was given to you, and you killed him. With the help of evil men you nailed him to a cross. But God knew all this would happen. This was God's plan which he had made long ago. ²⁴God raised Jesus from death. God set him free from the pain of death. Death could not hold him. ²⁵For David said this about him:

'I keep the Lord before me always.
    Because he is close by my side,
    I will not be hurt.
²⁶So I am glad, and I rejoice.
    Even my body has hope.
²⁷This is because you will not leave me
        in the grave.
    You will not let your Holy One rot.
²⁸You will teach me God's way to live.
    Being with you will fill me
        with joy.'        *Psalm 16:8-11*

²⁹"Brothers, I can tell you truly about David, our ancestor. He died and was buried. His grave is still here with us today. ³⁰David was a prophetᵈ and knew what God had said. God had promised David that he would make a person from David's family a king just as he was."ⁿ ³¹David knew this

2:7 **from Galilee** The people thought men from Galilee could speak only their own language. 2:30 **God . . . was** See 2 Samuel 7:13; Psalm 132:11.

**171**

# WHO'S WHO?

AS USUAL, THE DISCIPLES ARE A LITTLE CONFUSED.
CAN YOU HELP THEM STRAIGHTEN OUT THEIR NAMES?

*In case you're counting, 2 disciples share the same name as 2 others, leaving 10 different names.

1. SAMJE _____
2. REPTE _____
3. STOHAM _____
4. NDARWE _____
5. ARTBHOOLMEW _____
6. NJHO _____
7. TTMAWHE _____
8. SADUJ _____
9. PIIPHL _____
10. NSMIO _____

before it happened. That is why he said:

'He was not left in the grave.
His body did not rot.'

David was talking about the Christ[d] rising from death. [32]So Jesus is the One who God raised from death! And we are all witnesses to this. [33]Jesus was lifted up to heaven and is now at God's right side. The Father has given the Holy Spirit[d] to Jesus as he promised. So now Jesus has poured out that Spirit. This is what you see and hear. [34]David was not the one who was lifted up to heaven. But he said:

'The Lord said to my Lord:
Sit by me at my right side,
[35]    until I put your enemies
       under your control.'[n]

Psalm 110:1

[36]"So, all the people of Israel should know this truly: God has made Jesus both Lord and Christ. He is the man you nailed to the cross!"

[37]When the people heard this, they were sick at heart. They asked Peter and the other apostles, "What shall we do?"

> ## "Change your hearts and lives and be baptized, each one of you, in the name of Jesus Christ for the forgiveness of your sins."
>
> Acts 2:38

[38]Peter said to them, "Change your hearts and lives and be baptized, each one of you, in the name of Jesus Christ for the forgiveness of your sins. And you will receive the gift of the Holy Spirit. [39]This promise is for you. It is also for your children and for all who are far away. It is for everyone the

Lord our God calls to himself."

[40]Peter warned them with many other words. He begged them, "Save yourselves from the evil of today's people!" [41]Then those people who accepted what Peter said were baptized. About 3,000 people were added to the number of believers that day. [42]They spent their time learning the apostles' teaching. And they continued to share, to break bread,[n] and to pray together.

# LIVIN' IT!

## SLICE OF HEAVEN
### ACTS 2:44

Do you ever wonder what heaven's going to be like? We get a small glimpse of it here in Acts, when God first poured out his Holy Spirit on the believers at Pentecost. Everyone lived together, worked together, and shared everything they had.

Can you imagine what it would be like at your house if you and your brothers and sisters had the same attitude? No more arguing. No more yelling, "That's mine!" Peace and love would fill your hearts. Sound like a crazy dream?

Jesus says he wants us all to have the same purpose and love in our hearts. We are to work to be peacemakers. And we are called to share all that we have. What we have is not our own anyway; everything is a gift from God. We can always share without worry because God promises to provide everything we really need at the right time.

## THE BELIEVERS SHARE

[43]The apostles[d] were doing many miracles[d] and signs. And everyone felt great respect for God. [44]All the believers stayed together. They shared everything. [45]They sold their land and the things they owned. Then they divided the money and gave it to those people who needed it. [46]The believers met together in the Temple[d] every day. They all had the same purpose. They broke bread in their homes, happy to share their food with joyful hearts. [47]They praised God, and all the people liked them. More and more people were being saved every day; the Lord was adding those people to the group of believers.

## PETER HEALS A CRIPPLED MAN

**3** One day Peter and John went to the Temple.[d] It was three o'clock in the afternoon. This was the time for the daily prayer service. [2]There, at the Temple gate called Beautiful Gate, was a man who had been crippled all his life. Every day he was carried to this gate to beg. He would ask for money from the people going into the Temple. [3]The man saw Peter and John going into the Temple and asked them for money. [4]Peter and John looked straight at him and said, "Look at us!" [5]The man looked at them; he thought they were going to give him some money. [6]But Peter said, "I don't have any silver or gold, but I do have something else I can give you: By the power of Jesus Christ from Nazareth—stand up and walk!" [7]Then Peter took the

## DECODE THIS!

*What was the name of the gate where Peter healed a man?*

2:35 until . . . control Literally, "until I make your enemies a footstool for your feet." 2:42 break bread This may mean a meal as in verse 46, or the Lord's Supper, the special meal Jesus told his followers to eat to remember him (Luke 22:14-20).

173

man's right hand and lifted him up. Immediately the man's feet and ankles became strong. [8]He jumped up, stood on his feet, and began to walk. He went into the Temple with them, walking and jumping, and praising God. [9-10]All the people recognized him. They knew he was the crippled man who always sat by the Beautiful Gate begging for money. Now they saw this same man walking and praising God. The people were amazed. They could not understand how this could happen.

## PETER SPEAKS TO THE PEOPLE

[11]The man was holding on to Peter and John. All the people were amazed and ran to Peter and John at Solomon's Porch.[d] [12]When Peter saw this, he said to them, "Men of Israel, why are you surprised? You are looking at us as if it were our own power that made this man walk. Do you think this happened because we are good? No! [13]The God of Abraham, Isaac and Jacob, the God of our ancestors, gave glory to Jesus, his servant. But you gave him up to be killed. Pilate decided to let him go free. But you told Pilate you did not want Jesus. [14]He was pure and good, but you said you did not want him. You told Pilate to give you a murderer[n] instead of Jesus. [15]And so you killed the One

> "He will give you Jesus, the One he chose to be the Christ."
>
> Acts 3:20

## LIVIN' IT!

### THE PERFECT GIFT
### ACTS 3:6

Some people can sing. Others dance. Some are really smart, while others are hilarious. And then there are those people who don't seem to have any real talent or gift to offer at all. Maybe you feel that way, or you know someone who does. Peter and John, Jesus' famous disciples, could even relate.

As they passed by a crippled man who begged them for help, they admitted that they didn't have money or anything natural to offer the man. But what they could give him was power from God. When they restored his legs, his whole soul was healed.

No matter what your gifts are (or aren't), God can use you to do mighty things for his kingdom when you allow his Spirit to work through your life. Remember that there is nothing better you can bring to the world than the message of hope and love found in Christ Jesus.

who gives life! But God raised him from death. We are witnesses to this. [16]It was the power of Jesus that made this crippled man well. This happened because we trusted in the power of Jesus. You can see this man, and you know him. He was made completely well because of trust in Jesus. You all saw it happen!

[17]"Brothers, I know you did those things to Jesus because you did not understand what you were doing. Your leaders did not understand either. [18]God said this would happen. He said through the prophets[d] that his Christ[d] would suffer and die. And now

God has made these things come true in this way. [19]So you must change your hearts and lives! Come back to God, and he will forgive your sins. [20]Then the Lord will give you times of spiritual rest. He will give you Jesus, the One he chose to be the Christ. [21]But Jesus must stay in heaven until the time comes when all things will be made right again. God told about this time long ago when he spoke through his holy prophets. [22]Moses said, 'The Lord your God will give you a prophet like me. He will be one of your own people. You must obey everything he tells you. [23]Anyone who does not obey him will die, separated from God's people.'[n] [24]Samuel, and all the other prophets who spoke for God after Samuel, told about this time now. [25]You have received what the prophets talked about. You have received the agreement God made with your ancestors. He said to your father Abraham, 'Through your descendants[d] all the nations on the earth will be blessed.'[n] [26]God has raised up his servant and sent him to you first. He sent Jesus to bless you by turning each of you away from doing evil things."

## PETER AND JOHN AT THE COUNCIL

[4] While Peter and John were speaking to the people, a group of men came up to them. There were Jewish priests, the captain of the soldiers that guarded the Temple,[d] and some Sadducees.[d] [2]They were upset because the two apostles[d] were teaching the people. Peter and John were preaching that people will rise from death through the power of Jesus. [3]The

3:14 murderer Barabbas, the man the Jews asked Pilate to let go free instead of Jesus (Luke 23:18). 3:22-23 'The Lord . . . people.' Quotation from Deuteronomy 18:15, 19. 3:25 'Through . . . blessed.' Quotation from Genesis 22:18; 26:24.

174

Jewish leaders grabbed Peter and John and put them in jail. It was already night, so they kept them in jail until the next day. ⁴But many of those who heard Peter and John preach believed the things they said. There were now about 5,000 men in the group of believers.

⁵The next day the Jewish leaders, the older Jewish leaders, and the teachers of the law met in Jerusalem. ⁶Annas the high priest, Caiaphas, John, and Alexander were there. Everyone from the high priest's family was there. ⁷They made Peter and John stand before them. The Jewish leaders asked them: "By what power or authority did you do this?"

¹³The Jewish leaders saw that Peter and John were not afraid to speak. They understood that these men had no special training or education. So they were amazed. Then they realized that Peter and John had been with Jesus. ¹⁴They saw the crippled man standing there beside the two apostles. They saw that the man was healed. So they could say nothing against them. ¹⁵The Jewish leaders told them to leave the meeting. Then the leaders talked to each other about what they should do. ¹⁶They said, "What shall we do with these men? Everyone in Jerusalem knows that they have done a great miracle!ᵈ We cannot say it is not true. ¹⁷But we must warn

**"Jesus is your holy Servant. He is the One you made to be the Christ."**

*Acts 4:27*

⁸Then Peter was filled with the Holy Spirit.ᵈ He said to them, "Rulers of the people and you older leaders, ⁹are you questioning us about a good thing that was done to a crippled man? Are you asking us who made him well? ¹⁰We want all of you and all the Jewish people to know that this man was made well by the power of Jesus Christ from Nazareth! You nailed him to a cross, but God raised him from death. This man was crippled, but he is now well and able to stand here before you because of the power of Jesus! ¹¹Jesus is

'the stoneⁿ that you builders did
    not want.
    It has become the cornerstone.'ᵈ
                        *Psalm 118:22*

¹²Jesus is the only One who can save people. His name is the only power in the world that has been given to save people. And we must be saved through him!"

them not to talk to people anymore using that name. Then this thing will not spread among the people."

¹⁸So they called Peter and John in again. They told them not to speak or to teach at all in the name of Jesus. ¹⁹But Peter and John answered them, "What do you think is right? What would God want? Should we obey you or God? ²⁰We cannot keep quiet. We must speak about what we have seen and heard." ²¹⁻²²The Jewish leaders could not find a way to punish them because all the people were praising God for what had been done. (This miracle was a proof from God. The man who was healed was more than 40 years old!) So the Jewish leaders warned the apostles again and let them go free.

**THE BELIEVERS' PRAYER**

²³Peter and John left the meeting of Jewish leaders and went to their own group. They told them everything that the leading priests and the older Jewish leaders had said to them. ²⁴When the believers heard this, they prayed to God with one purpose. They prayed, "Lord, you are the One who made the sky, the earth, the sea, and everything in the world. ²⁵Our father David was your servant. With the help of the Holy Spiritᵈ he said:

'Why are the nations so angry?
    Why are the people making
        useless plans?
²⁶The kings of the earth prepare
        to fight.
    Their leaders make plans together
against the Lord
    and against his Christ.'ᵈ *Psalm 2:1-2*

²⁷These things really happened when Herod, Pontius Pilate, the non-Jewish people, and the Jewish people all came together against Jesus here in Jerusalem. Jesus is your holy Servant. He is the One you made to be the Christ. ²⁸These people made your plan happen; it happened because of your power and your will. ²⁹And now, Lord, listen to what they are saying. They are trying to make us afraid! Lord, we are your servants. Help us to speak your word without fear. ³⁰Help us to be brave by showing us your power; make sick people well, give proofs, and make miraclesᵈ happen by the power of Jesus, your holy servant."

³¹After they had prayed, the place where they were meeting was shaken. They were all filled with the Holy Spirit,ᵈ and they spoke God's word without fear.

⭐ 4:11 **stone** A symbol meaning Jesus.

**? DECODE THIS!**
*Jesus is compared to what kind of stone?*

## THE BELIEVERS SHARE

[32]The group of believers were joined in their hearts, and they had the same spirit. No person in the group said that the things he had were his own. Instead, they shared everything. [33]With great power the apostles[d] were telling people that the Lord Jesus was truly raised from death. And God blessed all the believers very much. [34]They all received the things they needed. Everyone that owned fields or houses sold them. They brought the money [35]and gave it to the apostles. Then each person was given the things he needed.

[36]One of the believers was named Joseph. The apostles called him Barnabas. (This name means "one who encourages.") He was a Levite, born in Cyprus. [37]Joseph owned a field. He sold it, brought the money, and gave it to the apostles.

## ANANIAS AND SAPPHIRA

**5** A man named Ananias and his wife Sapphira sold some land. [2]But he gave only part of the money to the apostles.[d] He secretly kept some of it for himself. His wife knew about this, and she agreed to it. [3]Peter said, "Ananias, why did you let Satan rule your heart? You lied to the Holy Spirit.[d] Why did you keep part of the money you received for the land for yourself? [4]Before you sold the land, it belonged to you. And even after you sold it, you could have used the money any way you wanted. Why did you think of doing this? You lied to God, not to men!" [5-6]When Ananias heard this, he fell down and died. Some young men came in, wrapped

up his body, carried it out, and buried it. And everyone who heard about this was filled with fear.

[7]About three hours later his wife came in. She did not know what had happened. [8]Peter said to her, "Tell me how much money you got for your field. Was it this much?"

Sapphira answered, "Yes, that was the price."

[9]Peter said to her, "Why did you and your husband agree to test the Spirit of the Lord? Look! The men who buried your husband are at the door! They will carry you out." [10]At that moment Sapphira fell down by his feet and died. The young men came in and saw that she was dead. They carried her out and buried her beside her husband. [11]The whole church and all the others who heard about these things were filled with fear.

## PROOFS FROM GOD

[12]The apostles[d] did many signs and miracles[d] among the people. And they would all meet together on Solomon's Porch.[d] [13]None of the others dared to stand with them. All the people were

saying good things about them. [14]More and more men and women believed in the Lord and were added to the group of believers. [15]As Peter was passing by, the people brought their sick into the streets. They put their sick on beds and mats so at least Peter's shadow might fall on them. [16]Crowds came from all the towns around Jerusalem. They brought their sick and those who were bothered by evil spirits. All of them were healed.

## THE APOSTLES OBEY GOD

[17]The high priest and all his friends (a group called the Sadducees[d]) became very jealous. [18]They took the apostles[d] and put them in jail. [19]But during the night, an angel of the Lord opened the doors of the jail. He led the apostles outside and said, [20]"Go and stand in the Temple.[d] Tell the people everything about this new life." [21]When the apostles heard this, they obeyed and went into the Temple. It was early in the morning, and they began to teach.

The high priest and his friends arrived. They called a meeting of the Jewish leaders and all the important older men of the Jews. They sent some men to the jail to bring the apostles to them. [22]When the men went to the jail,

> **"The apostles did many signs and miracles among the people."**
>
> *Acts 5:12*

they could not find the apostles. So they went back and told the Jewish leaders about this. [23]They said, "The jail was closed and locked. The guards were standing at the doors. But when we opened the doors, the jail was empty!" [24]Hearing this, the captain of the Temple guards and the leading priests were confused. They wondered,

"What will happen because of this?"

[25] Then someone came and told them, "Listen! The men you put in jail are standing in the Temple. They are teaching the people!" [26] Then the captain and his men went out and brought the apostles back. But the soldiers did not use force, because they were afraid that the people would kill them with stones.

[27] The soldiers brought the apostles to the meeting and made them stand before the Jewish leaders. The high priest questioned them. [28] He said, "We gave you strict orders not to go on teaching in that name. But look what you have done! You have filled Jerusalem with your teaching. You are trying to make us responsible for this man's death."

[29] Peter and the other apostles answered, "We must obey God, not men! [30] You killed Jesus. You hung him on a cross. But God, the same God our ancestors had, raised Jesus up from death! [31] Jesus is the One whom God raised to be on his right side. God made Jesus our Leader and Savior. God did this so that all Jews could change their hearts and lives and have their

> **"God has given the Spirit to all who obey him."**
>
> *Acts 5:32*

sins forgiven. [32] We saw all these things happen. The Holy Spirit[d] also proves that these things are true. God has given the Spirit to all who obey him."

[33] When the Jewish leaders heard this, they became very angry and wanted to kill them. [34] A Pharisee[d] named

Gamaliel stood up in the meeting. He was a teacher of the law, and all the people respected him. He ordered the apostles to leave the meeting for a little while. [35] Then he said to them, "Men of Israel, be careful of what you are planning to do to these men! [36] Remember when Theudas appeared? He said that he was a great man, and about 400 men joined him. But he was killed. And all his followers were scattered. They were able to do nothing. [37] Later, a man named Judas came from Galilee at the time of the registration.[n] He led a group of followers, too. He was also killed, and all his followers were scattered. [38] And so now I tell you: Stay away from these men. Leave them alone. If their plan comes from men, it will fail. [39] But if it is from God, you will not be able to stop them. You might even be fighting against God himself!"

The Jewish leaders agreed with what Gamaliel said. [40] They called the apostles in again. They beat the apostles and told them not to speak in the name of Jesus again. Then they let them go free. [41] The apostles left the meeting full of joy because they were given the honor of suffering disgrace for Jesus. [42] The apostles did not stop teaching people. Every day in the Temple and in people's homes they continued to tell the Good News—that Jesus is the Christ.[d]

### SEVEN MEN ARE CHOSEN

**6** More and more people were becoming followers of Jesus. But during this same time, the Greek-speaking followers had an argument with the other Jewish followers. The Greek-speaking Jews said that their widows were not getting their share of the food that was given out every day. [2] The 12 apostles[d] called the whole group of followers together. They said, "It is not right for us to stop our work of teaching God's word in order to serve tables. [3] So, brothers, choose seven of your own men. They must be men who are good. They must be full of wisdom and full of the Spirit.[d] We will put them in charge of this work. [4] Then we can use all our time to pray and to teach the word of God."

[5] The whole group liked the idea. So they chose these seven men: Stephen (a man with great faith and full of the Holy Spirit), Philip,[n] Procorus, Nicanor,

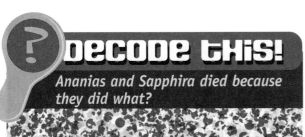

## DECODE THIS!

*Ananias and Sapphira died because they did what?*

⭐ **5:37 registration** Census. A counting of all the people and the things they own. **6:5 Philip** Not the apostle named Philip.

Timon, Parmenas, and Nicolas (a man from Antioch who had become a Jew). [6]Then they put these men before the apostles. The apostles prayed and laid their hands on[n] the men.

[7]The word of God was reaching more and more people. The group of followers in Jerusalem became larger and larger. A great number of the Jewish priests believed and obeyed.

## ROCK ON

Rocks on the earth are like the outer crust of bread on a sandwich and are made from different minerals. People who study rocks are called petrologists, and they have grouped rocks into 3 different kinds: igneous, sedimentary, and metamorphic. Igneous rocks come from cooled lava that came from the earth's core. Sedimentary rocks are made from other rocks and animal remains. Metamorphic rocks are igneous or sedimentary rocks that have been changed in form by really high heat.

When God says that he is our rock and our refuge, he's telling us that he is the very stuff that holds all of life. He is strong, firm, and never changes!

[Yahooligans]

## STEPHEN IS ARRESTED

[8]Stephen was richly blessed by God. God gave him the power to do great miracles[d] and signs among the people. [9]But some Jews were against him. They belonged to a synagogue[d] of Free Men[n] (as it was called). (This synagogue was also for Jews from Cyrene and from Alexandria.) Jews from Cilicia and Asia were also with them. They all came and argued with Stephen.

[10]But the Spirit[d] was helping him to speak with wisdom. His words were so strong that they could not argue with him. [11]So they paid some men to say, "We heard him say things against Moses and against God!"

[12]This upset the people, the older Jewish leaders, and the teachers of the law. They came to Stephen, grabbed him and brought him to a meeting of the Jewish leaders. [13]They brought in some men to tell lies about Stephen. They said, "This man is always saying things against this holy place and the law of Moses. [14]We heard him say that Jesus from Nazareth will destroy this place. He also said that Jesus will change the things that Moses told us to do." [15]All the people in the meeting were watching Stephen closely. His face looked like the face of an angel.

## STEPHEN'S SPEECH

**7**The high priest said to Stephen, "Are these things true?"

[2]Stephen answered, "Brothers and fathers, listen to me. Our glorious God appeared to Abraham, our ancestor. Abraham was in Mesopotamia before he lived in Haran. [3]God said to Abraham, 'Leave your country and your relatives. Go to the land I will show you.'[n] [4]So Abraham left the country of Chaldea and went to live in Haran. After Abraham's father died, God sent him to this place where you now live. [5]God did not give Abraham any of this land, not even a foot of it. But God promised that he would give him and his descendants[d] this land. (This was before Abraham had any descendants.) [6]This is what God said to him: 'Your descendants will be strangers in a land they don't own. The people there will make them slaves. And they will do cruel things to them for 400 years. [7]But I will punish the nation where they are slaves. Then your descendants will leave that land. Then they will worship me in this place.'[n] [8]God made an agreement with Abraham; the sign for this agreement was circumcision.[d] And so when Abraham had his son Isaac, Abraham circumcised him when he was eight days old. Isaac also circumcised his son Jacob. And Jacob did the same for his sons, the 12 ancestors[n] of our people.

[9]"These sons became jealous of Joseph. They sold him to be a slave in Egypt. But God was with him. [10]Joseph had many troubles there, but God saved him from all those troubles. The king of Egypt liked Joseph and respected him because of the wisdom that God gave him. The king made him governor of Egypt. He put Joseph in charge of all the people in his palace. [11]"Then all the land of Egypt and of

## DECODE THIS!

Who helped Stephen speak strong words of wisdom?

6:6 laid their hands on Here, doing this showed that these men were given a special work of God. 6:9 Free Men Jews who had been slaves or whose fathers had been slaves, but were now free. 7:3 'Leave . . . you' Quotation from Genesis 12:1. 7:6-7 'Your descendants . . . place.' Quotation from Genesis 15:13-14 and Exodus 3:12. 7:8 12 ancestors Important ancestors of the Jews; the leaders of the 12 Jewish tribes.

# Gotta Know!

### What's the fastest way to become friends again after a fight?

Be the first one to say you're sorry, and ask your friend to forgive you. Even if she was the one who started it, you should still apologize for letting the issue come between you and for not showing love the way Christ wants. When she sees you let your guard down, she will be more likely to talk the problem out without fighting. True forgiveness and love will bring you back together again.

Canaan became so dry that nothing would grow there. This made the people suffer very much. The sons could not find anything to eat. [12]But when Jacob heard that there was grain in Egypt, he sent his sons, our ancestors, there. This was their first trip to Egypt. [13]Then they went there a second time. This time, Joseph told his brothers who he was. And the king learned about Joseph's family. [14]Then Joseph sent some men to invite Jacob, his father, to come to Egypt. He also invited all his relatives (75 persons altogether). [15]So Jacob went down to Egypt, where he and his sons died. [16]Later their bodies were moved to Shechem and put in a grave there. (It was the same grave that Abraham had bought in Shechem from the sons of Hamor for a sum of money.)

[17]"The number of people in Egypt grew large. There were more and more of our people there. (The promise that God made to Abraham was soon to come true.) [18]Then a new king began to rule Egypt. He did not know who Joseph was. [19]This king tricked our people and was cruel to our ancestors.

He forced them to put their babies outside to die. [20]This was the time when Moses was born. He was a fine child. For three months Moses was cared for in his father's house. [21]When they put Moses outside, the king's daughter took him. She raised him as if he were her own son. [22]The Egyptians taught Moses all the things they knew. He was a powerful man in the things he said and did.

[23]"When Moses was about 40 years old, he thought it would be good to visit his brothers, the people of Israel. [24]Moses saw an Egyptian doing wrong to a Jew. So he defended the Jew and punished the Egyptian for hurting him. Moses killed the Egyptian. [25]Moses thought that his fellow Jews would understand that God was using him to save them. But they did not understand. [26]The next day, Moses saw two Jewish men fighting. He tried to make peace between them. He said, 'Men, you are brothers! Why are you hurting each other?' [27]The man who was hurt-

ing the other man pushed Moses away. He said, 'Who made you our ruler and judge? [28]Are you going to kill me as you killed the Egyptian yesterday?'"

[29]When Moses heard him say this, he left Egypt. He went to live in the land of Midian where he was a stranger. While Moses lived in Midian, he had two sons.

[30]"After 40 years Moses was in the desert near Mount Sinai. An angel appeared to him in the flames of a burning bush. [31]When Moses saw this, he was amazed. He went near to look closer at it. Moses heard the Lord's voice. [32]The Lord said, 'I am the God of your ancestors. I am the God of Abraham, Isaac and Jacob.'" Moses began to shake with fear and was afraid to look. [33]The Lord said to him, 'Take off your sandals. You are standing on holy ground. [34]I have seen the troubles my people have suffered in Egypt. I have heard their cries. I have come down to save them. And now, Moses, I am sending you back to Egypt.'"

[35]"This Moses was the same man the Jews said they did not want. They had said to him, 'Who made you our ruler and judge?'" Moses is the same man God sent to be a ruler and savior, with the help of an angel. This was the angel Moses saw in the burning bush. [36]So Moses led the people out of Egypt. He worked miracles[d] and signs in

"i have seen the troubles my people have suffered in Egypt. i have heard their cries. i have come down to save them."

*Acts 7:34*

7:27-28 'Who . . . yesterday?' Quotation from Exodus 2:14.  7:32 'I am . . . Jacob.' Quotation from Exodus 3:6.  7:33-34 'Take . . . Egypt.' Quotation from Exodus 3:5-10.  7:35 'Who . . . judge?' Quotation from Exodus 2:14.

Egypt, at the Red Sea,[d] and then in the desert for 40 years. [37]This is the same Moses that said to the Jewish people: 'God will give you a prophet[d] like me. He will be one of your own people.'[n]

## "You received the law of Moses, which God gave you through his angels."

*Acts 7:53*

[38]This is the same Moses who was with the gathering of the Jews in the desert. He was with the angel that spoke to him at Mount Sinai, and he was with our ancestors. He received commands from God that give life, and he gave those commands to us.

[39]"But our fathers did not want to obey Moses. They rejected him. They wanted to go back to Egypt again. [40]They said to Aaron, 'Moses led us out of Egypt. But we don't know what has happened to him. So make us gods who will lead us.'[n] [41]So the people made an idol that looked like a calf. Then they brought sacrifices to it. The people were proud of what they had made with their own hands! [42]But God turned against them. He did not try to stop them from worshiping the sun,

moon and stars. This is what is written in the book of the prophets: God says,

'People of Israel, you did not bring
   me sacrifices and offerings
   while you traveled in the desert
   for 40 years.
[43]But now you will have to carry
   with you
   the tent to worship the false god
     Molech[d]
   and the idols of the star god
     Rephan that you made to
     worship.
This is because I will send you away
   beyond Babylon.'    *Amos 5:25-27*

[44]"The Holy Tent[d] where God spoke to our fathers was with the Jews in the desert. God told Moses how to make this Tent. He made it like the plan God showed him. [45]Later, Joshua led our fathers to capture the lands of the other nations. Our people went in, and God drove the other people out. When our people went into this new land, they took with them this same Tent. They received this Tent from their fathers and kept it until the time of David. [46]God was very pleased with David. He asked God to let him build a house for him, the God of Jacob. [47]But Solomon was the one who built the Temple.[d]

[48]"But the Most High does not live in

houses that men build with their hands. This is what the prophet says:
[49]'Heaven is my throne.
   The earth is my footstool.
So do you think you can build a
    house for me? says the Lord.
   There is no place where I need to
    rest.
[50]Remember, I made all these things!'"

*Isaiah 66:1-2*

[51]Stephen continued speaking: "You stubborn Jewish leaders! You have not given your hearts to God! You won't listen to him! You are always against what the Holy Spirit[d] is trying to tell you. Your ancestors were like this, and you are just like them! [52]Your fathers tried to hurt every prophet who ever lived. Those prophets said long ago that the Righteous One would come. But your fathers killed them. And now you have turned against the Righteous One and killed him. [53]You received the law of Moses, which God gave you through his angels. But you don't obey it!"

### STEPHEN IS KILLED

[54]When the leaders heard Stephen saying all these things, they became very angry. They were so mad that

7:37 'God . . . people.' Quotation from Deuteronomy 18:15. 7:40 'Moses . . . us.' Quotation from Exodus 32:1.

# REAL SUPER HEROES

## PAUL

He started off with the name "Saul" and was the biggest killer of Christians in the region. Saul thought Christians were lying and needed to be punished. But Jesus stopped him on the road with a blinding light and told him that he was fighting the wrong enemy.

From there his name was changed to Paul, and he became just as eager to help Christians as he had been eager to hurt them in the past. He took the Good News all over Europe so everyone could learn about Jesus. God used Paul in huge ways to grow his kingdom, and through him wrote more of the New Testament than any other person.

It's never too late to admit we're wrong and turn from our sinful ways. Like Paul, we should repent when God shows us our sin. God will forgive us and use us in cool ways, too.

# BiBLe Basics

## What is salvation?

You hear a lot about salvation, but what exactly does it mean? It simply means to be saved from something bad. So what are Christians saved from? We are being rescued from the punishment that our sins deserve. The Bible says that when we sin just one time, we deserve to die. Jesus, who is perfect, died in our place, though. By trusting him to forgive us, we are saved from spiritual death, and we gain a place in heaven.

they were grinding their teeth at Stephen. [55]But Stephen was full of the Holy Spirit.[d] He looked up to heaven and saw the glory of God. He saw Jesus standing at God's right side. [56]He said, "Look! I see heaven open. And I see the Son of Man[d] standing at God's right side!"

[57]Then they all shouted loudly. They covered their ears with their hands and all ran at Stephen. [58]They took him out of the city and threw stones at him until he was dead. The men who told lies against Stephen left their coats with a young man named Saul. [59]While they were throwing stones, Stephen prayed, "Lord Jesus, receive my spirit!" [60]He fell on his knees and cried in a loud voice, "Lord, do not hold this sin against them!" After Stephen said this, he died.

**8** Saul agreed that the killing of Stephen was a good thing.

## TROUBLE FOR THE BELIEVERS

[2-3]Some religious men buried Stephen. They cried very loudly for him. On that day people began trying to hurt the church in Jerusalem and make it suffer.

Saul was also trying to destroy the church. He went from house to house. He dragged out men and women and put them in jail. All the believers, except the apostles,[d] went to different places in Judea and Samaria. [4]And everywhere they were scattered, they told people the Good News.[d]

## PHILIP PREACHES IN SAMARIA

[5]Philip[n] went to the city of Samaria and preached about the Christ.[d] [6]The people there heard Philip and saw the miracles[d] he was doing. They all listened carefully to the things he said. [7]Many of these people had evil spirits in them. But Philip made the evil spirits leave them. The spirits made a loud noise when they came out. There were also many weak and crippled people there. Philip healed them, too. [8]So the people in that city were very happy.

[9]But there was a man named Simon in that city. Before Philip came there, Simon had practiced magic. He amazed all the people of Samaria with his magic. He bragged and called himself a great man. [10]All the people—the least important and the most important—paid attention to what Simon said. They said, "This man has the power of God, called 'the Great Power'!" [11]Simon had amazed them with his magic tricks so long that the people became his followers. [12]But Philip told

them the Good News[d] about the kingdom of God and the power of Jesus Christ. Men and women believed Philip and were baptized. [13]Simon himself believed and was baptized. He stayed very close to Philip. When he saw the miracles and the very powerful things that Philip did, Simon was amazed.

[14]The apostles[d] were still in Jerusalem. They heard that the people of Samaria had accepted the word of God. So they sent Peter and John to them. [15]When Peter and John arrived, they prayed that the Samaritan believers might receive the Holy Spirit.[d] [16]These people had been baptized in the name of the Lord Jesus. But the Holy Spirit had not

> "When he saw the miracles and the very powerful things that Philip did, Simon was amazed."
>
> *Acts 8:13*

## DECODE THIS!

*How was Stephen killed?*

8:5 **Philip** Not the apostle named Philip.

yet entered any of them. [17]Then, when the two apostles began laying their hands on[n] the people, they received the Holy Spirit.

[18]Simon saw that the Spirit was given to people when the apostles laid their hands on them. So he offered the apostles money. [19]He said, "Give me also this power so that when I lay my hands on a person, he will receive the Holy Spirit."

[20]Peter said to him, "You and your money should both be destroyed! You thought you could buy God's gift with money. [21]You cannot share with us in this work. Your heart is not right before God. [22]Change your heart! Turn away from this evil thing you have done. Pray to the Lord. Maybe he will forgive you for thinking this. [23]I see that you are full of bitter jealousy and ruled by sin."

[24]Simon answered, "Both of you pray for me to the Lord. Pray that the things you have said will not happen to me!"

[25]Then the two apostles told the people the things they had seen Jesus do. And after the apostles had given the message of the Lord, they went back to Jerusalem. On the way, they went through many Samaritan towns and preached the Good News to the people.

### PHILIP TEACHES AN ETHIOPIAN

[26]An angel of the Lord spoke to Philip.[n] The angel said, "Get ready and go south. Go to the road that leads down to Gaza from Jerusalem—the desert road." [27]So Philip got ready and went. On the road he saw a man from Ethiopia, a eunuch.[d] He was an important officer in the service of Candace, the queen of the

> **"A bright light from heaven suddenly flashed around him."**
>
> *Acts 9:3*

Ethiopians. He was responsible for taking care of all her money. He had gone to Jerusalem to worship, and [28]now he was on his way home. He was sitting in his chariot and reading from the book of Isaiah, the prophet.[d] [29]The Spirit[d] said to Philip, "Go to that chariot and stay near it."

[30]So Philip ran toward the chariot. He heard the man reading from Isaiah, the prophet. Philip asked, "Do you understand what you are reading?"

[31]He answered, "How can I understand? I need someone to explain it to me!" Then he invited Philip to climb in and sit with him. [32]The verse of Scripture[d] that he was reading was this:

"He was like a sheep being led to be killed.

He was quiet, as a sheep is quiet while its wool is being cut.
He said nothing.

[33] He was shamed and was treated unfairly.
He died without children to continue his family.
His life on earth has ended."

*Isaiah 53:7-8*

[34]The officer said to Philip, "Please tell me, who is the prophet talking about? Is he talking about himself or about someone else?" [35]Philip began to speak. He started with this same Scripture and told the man the Good News[d] about Jesus.

[36]While they were traveling down the road, they came to some water. The officer said, "Look! Here is water! What is stopping me from being baptized?" [37][n]
[38]Then the officer commanded the chariot to stop. Both Philip and the officer went down into the water, and Philip baptized him. [39]When they came up out of the water, the Spirit of the Lord took Philip away; the officer never saw him again. The officer continued on his way home, full of joy. [40]But Philip appeared in a city called Azotus and preached the Good News in all the towns on the way from Azotus to Caesarea.

### SAUL IS CONVERTED

**9** In Jerusalem Saul was still trying to frighten the followers of the Lord by saying he would kill them. So he went to the high priest [2]and asked him to write letters to the synagogues[d] in the city of Damascus. Saul wanted the high priest to give him the authority to find people in Damascus who were followers of Christ's Way. If he found any there, men or women, he would arrest them and bring them back to Jerusalem.

[3]So Saul went to Damascus. As he came near the city, a bright light from heaven suddenly flashed around him. [4]Saul fell to the ground. He heard a voice saying to him, "Saul, Saul! Why are you doing things against me?"

[5]Saul said, "Who are you, Lord?"

The voice answered, "I am Jesus. I am the One you are trying to hurt. [6]Get up now and go into the city. Someone there will tell you what you must do."

[7]The men traveling with Saul stood there, but they said nothing. They heard the voice, but they saw no one. [8]Saul got up from the ground. He opened his eyes, but he could not see. So the men with Saul took his hand and led him into Damascus. [9]For three days

**8:17 laying their hands on** Here, doing this showed that these men were given a special work of God.
**8:26 Philip** Not the apostle named Philip. **8:37 Verse 37** Some late copies of Acts add verse 37: "Philip answered, 'If you believe with all your heart, you can.' The officer said, 'I believe that Jesus Christ is the Son of God.'"

**DECODE THIS!**
*Philip teaches a eunuch from this African country.*

# THE PAUL PUZZLE

Through the guidance of the Holy Spirit, Paul wrote more of the New Testament than any other author. So how well do you know this spiritual giant? Test your knowledge and see!
Score 9-10: Congrats! You know your stuff! Score 7-8: Advanced! You know more than most, but have a few things to learn. Score 5-6: Average! Paul pulled a few fast ones on you! Score 4 or below: Beginner—but take heart! You have a lot of fun facts to learn about Paul and his God!

1. Paul's name was originally
   a. John.
   b. Paulus.
   c. Silas.
   d. Saul.

2. Before he became a Christian, Paul was known for
   a. his good deeds.
   b. his love for Christians.
   c. his hatred for Christians.
   d. his money.

3. Paul was blind for how long?
   a. 1 year
   b. 1 day
   c. 3 days
   d. 1 month

4. Which of the following didn't happen to Paul?
   a. He was thrown in prison.
   b. He was beaten and stoned.
   c. He was shipwrecked.
   d. He was burned.

5. In which of the following places did Paul preach?
   a. Iconium
   b. Berea
   c. Athens
   d. Rome
   e. All of the above

6. How did Paul preach the gospel?
   a. By healing the sick
   b. By explaining the truth
   c. By writing letters
   d. All of the above

7. God worked all of these miracles through Paul, except
   a. casting out demons.
   b. escaping prison.
   c. making an evil man blind.
   d. creating money.

8. The book of the Bible that tells us most about Paul's life is
   a. Matthew.
   b. Romans.
   c. Acts.
   d. Revelation.

9. The word that best describes Paul is
   a. bold.
   b. shy.
   c. funny.
   d. laid-back.

10. Paul compared the Christian life to
    a. a circus.
    b. a prison.
    c. a race.
    d. a fairy tale.

ANSWER KEY: 1. D; 2. C; 3. C; 4. D; 5. E; 6. D; 7. D; 8. C; 9. A; 10. C

Saul could not see, and he did not eat or drink.

[10]There was a follower of Jesus in Damascus named Ananias. The Lord spoke to Ananias in a vision, "Ananias!"

Ananias answered, "Here I am, Lord."

[11]The Lord said to him, "Get up and go to the street called Straight Street. Find the house of Judas.[n] Ask for a man named Saul from the city of Tarsus. He is there now, praying. [12]Saul has seen a vision. In it a man named Ananias comes to him and lays his hands on him. Then he sees again."

[13]But Ananias answered, "Lord, many people have told me about this man and the terrible things he did to your people in Jerusalem. [14]Now he has come here to Damascus. The leading priests have given him the power to arrest everyone who worships you."

[15]But the Lord said to Ananias, "Go! I have chosen Saul for an important work. He must tell about me to non-Jews, to kings, and to the people of Israel. [16]I will show him how much he must suffer for my name."

[17]So Ananias went to the house of Judas. He laid his hands on Saul and said, "Brother Saul, the Lord Jesus sent me. He is the one you saw on the road on your way here. He sent me so that you can see again and be filled with the Holy Spirit."[d] [18]Immediately, something that looked like fish scales fell from Saul's eyes. He was able to see again! Then Saul got up and was baptized. [19]After eating some food, his strength returned.

"He sent me so that you can see again and be filled with the Holy Spirit."

*Acts 9:17*

## SAUL PREACHES IN DAMASCUS

Saul stayed with the followers of Jesus in Damascus for a few days. [20]Soon he began to preach about Jesus in the synagogues,[d] saying, "Jesus is the Son of God!"

[21]All the people who heard him were amazed. They said, "This is the man who was in Jerusalem. He was trying to destroy those who trust in this name! He came here to do the same thing. He came here to arrest the followers of Jesus and take them back to the leading priests."

[22]But Saul became more and more powerful. His proofs that Jesus is the Christ[d] were so strong that the Jews in Damascus could not argue with him.

## SAUL ESCAPES FROM DAMASCUS

[23]After many days, the Jews made plans to kill Saul. [24]They were watching the city gates day and night. They

wanted to kill him, but Saul learned about their plan. [25]One night some followers of Saul helped him leave the city. They lowered him in a basket through an opening in the city wall.

## SAUL IN JERUSALEM

[26]Then Saul went to Jerusalem. He tried to join the group of followers, but they were all afraid of him. They did not believe that he was really a follower. [27]But Barnabas accepted Saul and took him to the apostles.[d] Barnabas told them that Saul had seen the Lord on the road. He explained how the Lord had spoken to Saul. Then he told them how boldly Saul had preached in the name of Jesus in Damascus.

[28]And so Saul stayed with the followers. He went everywhere in Jerusalem, preaching boldly in the name of Jesus. [29]He would often talk and argue with the Jews who spoke Greek. But they were trying to kill him. [30]When the brothers learned about this, they took Saul to Caesarea. From there they sent him to Tarsus.

[31]The church everywhere in Judea, Galilee, and Samaria had a time of peace. With the help of the Holy Spirit,[d] the group became stronger. The believers showed that they respected the Lord by the way they lived. Because of this, the group of believers grew larger and larger.

DECODE THIS!

*Peter healed this woman who was always doing good deeds.*

9:11 Judas This is not either of the apostles named Judas.

> **"God has heard your prayers. He has seen what you give to the poor. And God remembers you."** *Acts 10:4*

## PETER HEALS AENEAS

³²As Peter was traveling through all the area, he visited God's people who lived in Lydda. ³³There he met a paralyzed man named Aeneas. Aeneas had not been able to leave his bed for the past eight years. ³⁴Peter said to him, "Aeneas, Jesus Christ heals you. Stand up and make your bed!" Aeneas stood up immediately. ³⁵All the people living in Lydda and on the Plain of Sharon saw him. These people turned to the Lord.

## BIBLE BASICS

### WHAT IS A DISCIPLE?

Another name for disciple is "a learner." A disciple is anyone who follows the teachings of Jesus, not only by studying Jesus' words, but also by following them with his life. Jesus spent an extra amount of time with 12 men he chose specifically to be his disciples. But the Bible also uses the same word to describe others who obeyed Jesus' teachings, including women. (Check out Acts 9:36.)

## PETER IN JOPPA

³⁶In the city of Joppa there was a follower named Tabitha. (Her Greek name, Dorcas, means "a deer.") She was always doing good and helping the poor. ³⁷While Peter was in Lydda, Tabitha became sick and died. Her body was washed and put in a room upstairs. ³⁸The followers in Joppa heard that Peter was in Lydda. (Lydda is near Joppa.) So they sent two men to Peter.

They begged him, "Hurry, please come to us!" ³⁹Peter got ready and went with them. When he arrived, they took him to the upstairs room. All the widows stood around Peter, crying. They showed him the shirts and coats that Tabitha had made when she was still alive. ⁴⁰Peter sent everyone out of the room. He kneeled and prayed. Then he turned to the body and said, "Tabitha, stand up!" She opened her eyes, and when she saw Peter, she sat up. ⁴¹He gave her his hand and helped her up. Then he called the saints[d] and the widows into the room. He showed them Tabitha; she was alive! ⁴²People everywhere in Joppa learned about this, and many believed in the Lord. ⁴³Peter stayed in Joppa for many days with a man named Simon who was a leatherworker.

## PETER AND CORNELIUS

**10** At Caesarea there was a man named Cornelius. He was an officer in the Italian group of the Roman army. ²Cornelius was a religious man. He and all the other people who lived in his house worshiped the true God. He gave much of his money to the poor and prayed to God often. ³One afternoon about three o'clock, Cornelius saw a vision clearly. In the vision an angel of God came to him and said, "Cornelius!"

⁴Cornelius stared at the angel. He became afraid and said, "What do you want, Lord?"

The angel said, "God has heard your prayers. He has seen what you give to the poor. And God remembers you. ⁵Send some men now to Joppa to bring

back a man named Simon. Simon is also called Peter. ⁶Simon is staying with a man, also named Simon, who is a leatherworker. He has a house beside the sea." ⁷Then the angel who spoke to Cornelius left. Cornelius called two of his servants and a soldier. The soldier was a religious man who worked for Cornelius. ⁸Cornelius explained everything to these three men and sent them to Joppa.

⁹The next day as they came near Joppa, Peter was going up to the roof[f] to pray. It was about noon. ¹⁰Peter was hungry and wanted to eat. But while the food was being prepared, he had a vision. ¹¹He saw heaven opened and something coming down. It looked like a big sheet being lowered to earth by its four corners. ¹²In it were all kinds of animals, reptiles, and birds. ¹³Then a voice said to Peter, "Get up, Peter; kill and eat."

¹⁴But Peter said, "No, Lord! I have never eaten food that is unholy or unclean."[d]

¹⁵But the voice said to him again, "God has made these things clean. Don't call them 'unholy'!" ¹⁶This happened three times. Then the sheet was taken back to heaven.

¹⁷While Peter was wondering what this vision meant, the men Cornelius sent had found Simon's house. They were standing at the gate. ¹⁸They asked, "Is Simon Peter staying here?"

¹⁹Peter was still thinking about the vision. But the Spirit[d] said to him, "Listen! Three men are looking for you. ²⁰Get up and go downstairs. Go with them and don't ask questions. I have sent them to you."

²¹So Peter went down to the men. He said, "I am the man you are looking

**10:9 roof** In Bible times houses were built with flat roofs. The roof was used for drying things such as flax and fruit. And it was used as an extra room, as a place for worship and as a place to sleep in the summer.

for. Why did you come here?"

²²They said, "A holy angel spoke to Cornelius, an army officer. He is a good man; he worships God. All the Jewish people respect him. The angel told Cornelius to ask you to his house so that he can hear what you have to say." ²³Peter asked the men to come in and spend the night.

The next day Peter got ready and went with them. Some of the brothers from Joppa joined him. ²⁴On the following day they came to Caesarea. Cornelius was waiting for them. He had called together his relatives and close friends. ²⁵When Peter entered, Cornelius met him. He fell at Peter's feet and worshiped him. ²⁶But Peter helped him up, saying, "Stand up! I too am only a man." ²⁷Peter went on talking with Cornelius as they went inside. There Peter saw many people together. ²⁸He said, "You people understand that it is against our Jewish law for a Jew to associate with or visit anyone who is not a Jew. But God has shown me that I should not call any person 'unholy' or 'unclean.' ²⁹That is why I did not argue when I was asked to come here. Now, please tell me why you sent for me."

³⁰Cornelius said, "Four days ago, I was praying in my house. It was at this same time—three o'clock in the afternoon. Suddenly, there was a man standing before me wearing shining clothes. ³¹He said, 'Cornelius! God has heard your prayer. He has seen what you give to the poor. And God remembers you. ³²So send some men to Joppa and ask Simon Peter to come. Peter is staying in the house of a man, also named Simon, who is a leatherworker. His house is beside the sea.' ³³So I sent for you immediately, and it was very good of you to come. Now we are all

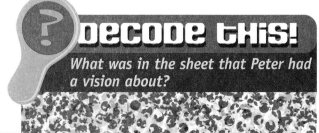

## KIDS SPEAK UP!

**Q. Is there something you think you just can't live without?**

**A. TV**

here before God to hear everything the Lord has commanded you to tell us."

### PETER'S SPEECH

³⁴Peter began to speak: "I really understand now that to God every person is the same. ³⁵God accepts anyone who worships him and does what is right. It is not important what country a person comes from. ³⁶You know that God has sent his message to the people of Israel. That message is the Good News$^d$ that peace has come through Jesus Christ. Jesus is the Lord of all people! ³⁷You know what has happened all over Judea. It began in Galilee after John$^n$ preached to the people about baptism. ³⁸You know about Jesus from

Nazareth. God made him the Christ$^d$ by giving him the Holy Spirit$^d$ and power. You know how Jesus went everywhere doing good. He healed those who were ruled by the devil, for God was with Jesus. ³⁹We saw all the things that Jesus did in Judea and in Jerusalem. But they killed him by nailing him to a cross. ⁴⁰Yet, on the third day, God raised Jesus to life and caused him to be seen. ⁴¹But he was not seen by all the people. Only the witnesses that God had already chosen saw him, and we are those witnesses. We ate and drank with him after he was raised from death. ⁴²He told us to preach to the people and to tell them that he is the one whom God chose to be the judge of the living and the dead. ⁴³Everyone who believes in Jesus will be forgiven. God will forgive his sins through Jesus. All the prophets$^d$ say this is true."

### NON-JEWS RECEIVE THE HOLY SPIRIT

⁴⁴While Peter was still saying this, the Holy Spirit$^d$ came down on all those who were listening. ⁴⁵The Jewish believers who came with Peter were amazed that the gift of the Holy Spirit had been given even to the non-Jewish people. ⁴⁶These Jewish believers heard them speaking in different

## ? DECODE THIS!

**What was in the sheet that Peter had a vision about?**

10:37 **John** John the Baptist, who preached to people about Christ's coming (Matthew 3, Luke 3).

> **"Never lose your faith. Always obey the Lord with all your hearts."** *Acts 11:23-24*

languages and praising God. Then Peter said, [47]"Can anyone keep these people from being baptized with water? They have received the Holy Spirit just as we did!" [48]So Peter ordered that they be baptized in the name of Jesus Christ. Then they asked Peter to stay with them for a few days.

## PETER RETURNS TO JERUSALEM

**11** The apostles[d] and the believers in Judea heard that non-Jewish people had accepted God's teaching too. [2]But when Peter came to Jerusalem, some Jewish believers argued with him. [3]They said, "You went into the homes of people who are not Jews and are not circumcised![d] You even ate with them!"

[4]So Peter explained the whole story to them. [5]He said, "I was in the city of Joppa. While I was praying, I had a vision. In the vision, I saw something which looked like a big sheet coming down from heaven. It was being lowered to earth by its four corners. It came down very close to me, and [6]I looked inside it. I saw animals, wild beasts, reptiles, and birds. [7]I heard a voice say to me, 'Get up, Peter. Kill and eat.' [8]But I said, 'No, Lord! I have never eaten anything that is unholy or unclean.'[d] [9]But the voice from heaven answered again, 'God has made these things clean. Don't call them unholy!' [10]This happened three times. Then the whole thing was taken back to heaven. [11]Right then three men came to the house where I was staying. They were sent to me from Caesarea. [12]The Spirit[d] told me

to go with them without doubting. These six believers here also went with me. We went to the house of Cornelius. [13]He told us about the angel he saw standing in his house. The angel said to him, 'Send some men to Joppa and invite Simon Peter to come. [14]He will speak to you. The things he will say will save you and all your family.' [15]When I began my speech, the Holy Spirit came on them just as he came on us at the beginning. [16]Then I remembered the words of the Lord. He said, 'John baptized in water, but you will be baptized in the Holy Spirit!' [17]God gave to them the same gift that he gave to us who believed in the Lord Jesus Christ. So could I stop the work of God? No!"

[18]When the Jewish believers heard this, they stopped arguing. They praised God and said, "So God is allowing the non-Jewish people also to turn to him and live."

## THE GOOD NEWS COMES TO ANTIOCH

[19]Many of the believers were scattered by the terrible things that happened after Stephen was killed. Some of them went to places as far away as Phoenicia, Cyprus, and Antioch. They were telling the message to others, but only to Jews. [20]Some of these believers were men from Cyprus and Cyrene. When they came to Antioch, they spoke also to Greeks, telling them the Good News[d] about the Lord Jesus. [21]The Lord was helping the believers. And a large group of people believed and turned to the Lord.

[22]The church in Jerusalem heard about all of this, so they sent Barnabas to Antioch. [23-24]Barnabas was a good man, full of the Holy Spirit[d] and full of faith. When he reached Antioch and saw how God had blessed the people, he was glad. He encouraged all the believers in Antioch. He told them, "Never lose your faith. Always obey the Lord with all your hearts." Many people became followers of the Lord.

[25]Then Barnabas went to the city of Tarsus to look for Saul. [26]When he found Saul, he brought him to Antioch. And for a whole year Saul and Barnabas met with the church. They taught many people there. In Antioch the followers were called Christians for the first time.

[27]About that time some prophets[d]

## GET CONNECTED

### SECRET GUIDE

Want to know what really makes you different from non-believers? You actually have the Spirit of God living inside of you, and they do not. We may often forget that we have this incredible helper everywhere we go—though he doesn't forget. The Holy Spirit lives inside of us to help us see our sin and get rid of it, as well as to understand what the Bible is really saying to us. He even helps us pray.

Take time to thank the Spirit for his work in you, and ask him to help you pay better attention to his directions.

came from Jerusalem to Antioch. [28]One of them was named Agabus. He stood up and spoke with the help of the Holy Spirit. He said, "A very hard time is coming to the whole world. There will be no food for people to eat." (This happened when Claudius ruled.) [29]The followers all decided to help their brothers who lived in Judea. Each one planned to send them as much as he could. [30]They gathered the money and gave it to Barnabas and Saul, who brought it to the elders[d] in Judea.

## HEROD AGRIPPA HURTS THE CHURCH

**12** During that same time King Herod began to do terrible things to some who belonged to the church. [2]He ordered James, the brother of John, to be killed by the sword. [3]Herod saw that the Jews liked this, so he decided to arrest Peter, too. (This happened during the time of the Feast[d] of Unleavened Bread.) [4]After Herod arrested Peter, he put him in jail and handed him over to be guarded by 16 soldiers. Herod planned to bring Peter before the people for trial after the Passover[d] Feast. [5]So Peter was kept in jail. But the church kept on praying to God for him.

## PETER LEAVES THE JAIL

[6]The night before Herod was to bring him to trial, Peter was sleeping. He was between two soldiers, bound with two chains. Other soldiers were guarding the door of the jail. [7]Suddenly, an angel of the Lord stood there. A light shined in the room. The angel touched Peter on the side and

> "The angel said, 'Hurry! Get up!' And the chains fell off Peter's hands."
>
> Acts 12:7

woke him up. The angel said, "Hurry! Get up!" And the chains fell off Peter's hands. [8]The angel said to him, "Get dressed and put on your sandals." And so Peter did this. Then the angel said, "Put on your coat and follow me." [9]So the angel went out, and Peter followed him. Peter did not know if what the angel was doing was real. He thought he might be seeing a vision. [10]They went past the first and the second guard. They came to the iron gate that separated them from the city. The gate opened itself for them. They went through the gate and walked down a street. And the angel suddenly left him.

[11]Then Peter realized what had happened. He thought, "Now I know that the Lord really sent his angel to me. He rescued me from Herod and from all the things the Jewish people thought would happen."

[12]When he realized this, he went to the home of Mary. She was the mother of John. (John was also called Mark.) Many people were gathered there, praying. [13]Peter knocked on the outside door. A servant girl named Rhoda came to answer it. [14]She recognized Peter's voice, and she was very happy. She even forgot to open the door. She ran inside and told the group, "Peter is at the door!"

[15]They said to her, "You are crazy!" But she kept on saying that it was true. So they said, "It must be Peter's angel."

[16]Peter continued to knock. When they opened the door, they saw him and were amazed. [17]Peter made a sign with his hand to tell them to be quiet. He explained how the Lord led him out of the jail. And he said, "Tell James and the other believers what happened." Then he left to go to another place.

[18]The next day the soldiers were very upset. They wondered what had happened to Peter. [19]Herod looked everywhere for Peter but could not find him. So he questioned the guards and ordered that they be killed.

## THE DEATH OF HEROD AGRIPPA

Later Herod moved from Judea and went to the city of Caesarea, where he stayed for a while. [20]Herod was very angry with the people of Tyre and Sidon. But the people of those cities all came in a group to Herod. They were able to get Blastus, the king's personal servant, on their side. They asked Herod for peace because their country got its food from his country.

[21]On a chosen day Herod put on his royal robes. He sat on his throne and made a speech to the people. [22]They shouted, "This is the voice of a god, not a man!" [23]Herod did not give the glory to God. So an angel of the Lord caused him to become sick. He was eaten by worms and died.

[24]God's message continued to spread and reach more and more people.

[25]After Barnabas and Saul finished

their task in Jerusalem, they returned to Antioch. John, also called Mark, was with them.

## BARNABAS AND SAUL ARE CHOSEN

**13** In the church at Antioch there were these prophets[d] and teachers: Barnabas, Simeon (also called Niger), Lucius (from the city of Cyrene), Manaen (who had grown up with Herod, the ruler) and Saul. [2]They were all worshiping the Lord and giving up eating.[n] The Holy Spirit[d] said to them, "Give Barnabas and Saul to me to do a special work. I have chosen them for it."

[3]So they gave up eating and prayed. They laid their hands on[n] Barnabas and Saul and sent them out.

## BARNABAS AND SAUL IN CYPRUS

[4]Barnabas and Saul were sent out by the Holy Spirit.[d] They went to the city of Seleucia. From there they sailed to the island of Cyprus. [5]When they came to Salamis, they preached the Good News[d] of God in the Jewish synagogues.[d] John Mark was with them to help.

[6]They went across the whole island to Paphos. In Paphos they met a Jew who was a magician. His name was Bar-Jesus. He was a false prophet,[d] [7]who always stayed close to Sergius Paulus, the governor. Sergius Paulus was a smart man. He asked Barnabas and Saul to come to him, because he wanted to hear the message of God. [8]But Elymas, the magician, was against them. (Elymas is the name for Bar-Jesus in the Greek language.) He tried to stop the governor from believing in Jesus. [9]But Saul was filled with the Holy Spirit. (Saul's other name was Paul.) He looked straight at Elymas [10]and said, "You son of the devil! You are an enemy of everything that is right! You are full of evil tricks and lies. You are always trying to change the Lord's truths into lies! [11]Now the Lord will touch you, and you will be blind. For a time you will not be able to see anything—not even the light from the sun."

Then everything became dark for Elymas. He walked around, trying to find someone to lead him by the hand. [12]When the governor saw this, he believed. He was amazed at the teaching about the Lord.

## PAUL AND BARNABAS LEAVE CYPRUS

[13]Paul and those with him sailed away from Paphos. They came to Perga, in Pamphylia. But John Mark left them and returned to Jerusalem. [14]They continued their trip from Perga and went to Antioch, a city in Pisidia. On the Sabbath[d] day they went into the synagogue[d] and sat down. [15]The law of Moses and the writings of the prophets[d] were read. Then the leaders of the synagogue sent a message to Paul and Barnabas: "Brothers, if you have any message that will encourage the people, please speak!"

[16]Paul stood up. He raised his hand and said, "Men of Israel and you other people who worship God, please listen! [17]The God of the people of Israel chose our ancestors. He made the people great during the time they lived in Egypt. He brought them out of that country with great power. [18]And he was patient with them for 40 years in the desert. [19]God destroyed seven nations in the land of Canaan and gave the land to his people. [20]All

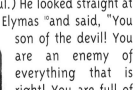

## WILD WORLD FACTS

### THE DIRT ON WORMS

Herod made a bad mistake. He allowed the people to call him their god. Because of his pride, God caused him to be eaten by worms and die.

In addition to helping the decay process along, worms are helpful in other ways, too. When they burrow down into the earth, they mix topsoil with subsoil and leave a slimy film that contains nitrogen, an important food for plants. There are 2,700 kinds of worms, most of which need food, moisture, and oxygen to grow. With no eyes, legs, or arms, most earthworms are 90-300 millimeters long, but one earthworm found in South Africa measured 22 feet! If you want to find a worm, you don't have to look for long. More than 1 million earthworms live in a single acre of land!

[Worm Facts]

## DECODE THIS!

**What happened to Herod when he died?**

★ **13:2 giving up eating** This is called "fasting." The people would give up eating for a special time of prayer and worship to God. It was also done to show sadness. **13:3 laid their hands on** Here, this was a sign to show that these men were given a special work of God.

189

this happened in about 450 years.

"After this, God gave them judges until the time of Samuel the prophet. <sup>21</sup>Then the people asked for a king. God gave them Saul son of Kish. Saul was from the tribe<sup>d</sup> of Benjamin. He was king for 40 years. <sup>22</sup>After God took him away, God made David their king. This is what God said about him: 'I have found David son of Jesse. He is the kind of man I want. He will do all that I want him to do.' <sup>23</sup>So God has

> **"You can have forgiveness of your sins through Jesus."**
> *Acts 13:38-39*

leaders did not realize that Jesus was the Savior. They did not understand the words that the prophets wrote, which are read every Sabbath<sup>d</sup> day. But they made them come true when they said Jesus was guilty. <sup>28</sup>They could not find any real reason for Jesus to die, but they asked Pilate

Jesus from death. We read about this also in Psalm 2:
> 'You are my Son.
> Today I have become your
> Father.' *Psalm 2:7*

<sup>34</sup>God raised Jesus from death. He will never go back to the grave and become dust. So God said:
> 'I will give you the holy and sure blessings
> that I promised to David.'
> *Isaiah 55:3*

<sup>35</sup>But in another place God says:
> 'You will not let your Holy One rot in the grave.' *Psalm 16:10*

<sup>36</sup>David did God's will during his lifetime. Then he died and was buried with his fathers. And his body did rot in the grave! <sup>37</sup>But the One God raised from death did not rot in the grave. <sup>38-39</sup>Brothers, you must understand what we are telling you: You can have forgiveness of your sins through Jesus. The law of Moses could not free you from your sins. But everyone who believes is free from all sins through him. <sup>40</sup>Be careful! Don't let what the prophets said happen to you:
> <sup>41</sup>'Listen, you people who doubt!
> You can wonder, and then die.
> I will do something in your lifetime that will amaze you.
> You won't believe it even when you are told about it!'"
> *Habakkuk 1:5*

# Gotta Know!

## Why is God a jealous God?

God is the only One who has the right to be jealous—wanting all of our hearts—because he alone is worthy to receive our respect and love. Because he is who he is, the Creator and Sustainer of the whole universe, he deserves all our love. When we give it to someone or something else, he is acting rightly to want us back for himself. If you picture a husband and wife, you know that it is right for them to love only each other and wrong if one of them gives their love to someone else. Loving God, just like loving one's spouse, is the right way. To do anything else hurts the beauty of life as God intended it.

brought one of David's descendants<sup>d</sup> to Israel to be their Savior.<sup>d</sup> That descendant is Jesus. And God promised to do this. <sup>24</sup>Before Jesus came, John<sup>n</sup> preached to all the people of Israel. He told them about a baptism of changed hearts and lives. <sup>25</sup>When he was finishing his work, he said, 'Who do you think I am? I am not the Christ.<sup>d</sup> He is coming later. I am not worthy to untie his sandals.'

<sup>26</sup>"Brothers, sons in the family of Abraham, and you non-Jews who worship God, listen! The news about this salvation has been sent to us. <sup>27</sup>Those who live in Jerusalem and their

to have him killed. <sup>29</sup>They did to him all that the Scriptures<sup>d</sup> had said. Then they took him down from the cross and laid him in a tomb. <sup>30</sup>But God raised him up from death! <sup>31</sup>After this, for many days, the people who had gone with Jesus from Galilee to Jerusalem saw him. They are now his witnesses to the people. <sup>32</sup>We tell you the Good News<sup>d</sup> about the promise God made to our ancestors. <sup>33</sup>We are their children, and God has made this promise come true for us. God did this by raising

<sup>42</sup>While Paul and Barnabas were leaving the synagogue, the people asked them to tell them more about these

**13:24 John** John the Baptist, who preached to people about Christ's coming (Matthew 3, Luke 3).

**190**

things on the next Sabbath. 43 After the meeting, many Jews followed Paul and Barnabas from that place. With the Jews there were many who had changed to the Jewish religion and worshiped God. Paul and Barnabas were persuading them to continue trusting in God's kindness.

44 On the next Sabbath day, almost all the people in the city came to hear the word of the Lord. 45 Seeing the crowd, the Jews became very jealous. They said insulting things and argued against what Paul said. 46 But Paul and Barnabas spoke very boldly. They said, "We must speak the message of God to you first. But you refuse to listen. You are judging yourselves not worthy of having eternal life! So we will now go to the people of other nations! 47 This is what the Lord told us to do. The Lord said:

'I have made you a light for the non-Jewish nations.
You will show people all over the world the way to be saved.'"

*Isaiah 49:6*

48 When the non-Jewish people heard Paul say this, they were happy. They gave honor to the message of the Lord. And many of the people believed the message. They were the ones chosen to have life forever.

49 And so the message of the Lord was spreading through the whole country. 50 But the Jews stirred up some of the important religious women and the leaders of the city against Paul and Barnabas. They started trouble against Paul and Barnabas and drove them out of their area. 51 So Paul and Barnabas shook the dust off their feet[n] and went to Iconium. 52 But the followers were filled with joy and the Holy Spirit.[d]

### PAUL AND BARNABAS IN ICONIUM

**14** In Iconium, Paul and Barnabas went as usual to the Jewish synagogue.[d] They spoke so well that a great many Jews and Greeks believed. 2 But some of the Jews who did not believe excited the non-Jewish people and turned them against the believers. 3 But Paul and Barnabas stayed in Iconium a long time and spoke bravely for the Lord. The Lord showed that their message about his grace was true by giving them the power to work miracles[d] and signs. 4 But some of the people in the city agreed with the Jews. Others believed the apostles.[d] So the city was divided.

> **"He is the One who made the sky, the earth, the sea, and everything that is in them."**
>
> *Acts 14:15*

5 Some non-Jewish people, some Jews, and some of their rulers wanted to harm Paul and Barnabas by killing them with stones. 6 When Paul and Barnabas learned about this, they went to Lystra and Derbe, cities in Lycaonia, and to the areas around those cities. 7 They announced the Good News[d] there, too.

### PAUL IN LYSTRA AND DERBE

8 In Lystra there sat a man who had been born crippled; he had never walked. 9 This man was listening to Paul speak. Paul looked straight at him and saw that the man believed God could heal him. 10 So he cried out, "Stand up on your feet!" The man jumped up and began walking around. 11 When the crowds saw what Paul did, they shouted in their own Lycaonian language. They said, "The gods have become like men! They have come down to us!" 12 And the people began to call Barnabas "Zeus."[n] They called Paul "Hermes,"[n] because he was the main speaker. 13 The temple of Zeus was near the city. The priest of this temple brought some bulls and flowers to the city gates. The priest and the people wanted to offer a sacrifice to Paul and Barnabas. 14 But when the apostles,[d] Barnabas and Paul, understood what they were about to do, they tore their clothes in anger. Then they ran in among the people and shouted, 15 "Men, why are you doing these things? We are only men, human beings like you! We are bringing you the Good News.[d] We are telling you to turn away from these worthless things and turn to the true living God. He is the One who made the sky, the earth, the sea, and everything that is in them. 16 In the past, God let all the nations do what they wanted. 17 Yet he did things to prove he is real: He shows kindness to you. He gives you rain from heaven and crops at the right times. He gives you food and fills your hearts with joy." 18 Even with these words, they were barely able to keep the crowd from offering sacrifices to them.

19 Then some Jews came from Antioch and Iconium. They persuaded the people to turn against Paul. And so they threw stones at Paul and dragged him out of town. They thought that

**? DECODE THIS!**

*Who traveled with Paul on many of his journeys?*

**13:51 shook . . . feet** A warning. It showed that they were finished talking to these people. **14:12 "Zeus"** The Greeks believed in many gods. Zeus was their most important god. **14:12 "Hermes"** The Greeks believed he was a messenger for the other gods.

they had killed him. ²⁰But the followers gathered around him, and he got up and went back into the town. The next day, he and Barnabas left and went to the city of Derbe.

## THE RETURN TO ANTIOCH IN SYRIA

²¹Paul and Barnabas told the Good News^d in Derbe and many became followers. Paul and Barnabas returned to Lystra, Iconium, and Antioch. ²²In those cities they made the followers of Jesus stronger. They helped them to stay in the faith. They said, "We must suffer many things to enter God's kingdom." ²³They chose elders^d for

> ## "Paul and Barnabas told the Good News."
> *Acts 14:21*

each church, by praying and giving up eating.^n These elders were men who had trusted the Lord. So Paul and Barnabas put them in the Lord's care. ²⁴Then they went through Pisidia and came to Pamphylia. ²⁵They preached the message in Perga, and then they went down to Attalia. ²⁶And from there they sailed away to Antioch. This is where the believers had put them into God's care and had sent them out to do this work. And now they had finished the work. ²⁷When they arrived in Antioch, they gathered the church together. Paul and Barnabas told them all about what God had done with them. They told how God had made it possible for the non-Jews to believe! ²⁸And they stayed there a long time with the followers.

## THE MEETING AT JERUSALEM

**15** Then some men came to Antioch from Judea. They began teaching the non-Jewish brothers: "You cannot be saved if you are not circumcised.^d Moses taught us to do this." ²Paul and Barnabas were against this teaching and argued with the men about it. So the group decided to send Paul, Barnabas, and some other men to Jerusalem. There they could talk more about this with the apostles^d and elders.^d

³The church helped the men leave on the trip. They went through the countries of Phoenicia and Samaria, telling all about how the non-Jewish people had turned to God. This made all the believers very happy. ⁴When they arrived in Jerusalem, the apostles, the elders, and the church welcomed them. Paul, Barnabas, and the others told about all the things that God had done with them. ⁵But some of the believers who had belonged to the Pharisee^d group came forward. They said, "The non-Jewish believers must be circumcised. We must tell them to obey the law of Moses!"

⁶The apostles and the elders gathered to study this problem. ⁷There was a long debate. Then Peter stood up and said to them, "Brothers, you know what happened in the early days. God chose me from among you to preach the Good News^d to the non-Jewish people. They heard the Good News from me, and they believed. ⁸God, who knows the thoughts of all men, accepted them. He showed this to us by giving them the Holy Spirit,^d just as he did to us. ⁹To God, those people are not different from us. When they believed, he made their hearts pure. ¹⁰So now why are you testing God? You are putting a heavy load around the necks of the non-Jewish brothers. It is a load that neither we nor our fathers were able to carry. ¹¹But we believe that we and they too will be saved by the grace of the Lord Jesus!"

¹²Then the whole group became quiet.

They listened to Paul and Barnabas speak. Paul and Barnabas told about all the miracles^d and signs that God did through them among the non-Jewish people. ¹³After they finished speaking, James spoke. He said, "Brothers, listen to me. ¹⁴Simon has told us how God showed his love for the non-Jewish people. For the first time he has accepted them and made them his people. ¹⁵The words of the prophets^d agree with this too:
¹⁶'After these things I will return.

The kingdom of David is like a
fallen tent.

## Things to Pray for Others

1. Wisdom for your parents
2. Your siblings' relationship with God
3. Thanks for God's good gifts
4. Patience and wisdom for your teachers
5. Praising God for who he is
6. Protection for his missionaries around the world
7. To raise up new missionaries
8. Your pastor and his family
9. The president and our government leaders
10. Everyone who doesn't know Jesus as Savior

---

 14:23 **giving up eating** This is called "fasting." The people would give up eating for a special time of prayer and worship to God. It was also done to show sadness.

But I will rebuild it.
    And I will again build its
      ruins.
    And I will set it up.
[17]Then those people who are left
    alive may ask the Lord
    for help.
    And all people from
      other nations may
      worship me,
  says the Lord.
    And he will make it
      happen.
[18]   And these things have been
    known for a long time.'

*Amos 9:11-12*

[19]"So I think we should not bother the non-Jewish brothers who have turned to God. [20]Instead, we should write a letter to them. We should tell them these things: Do not eat food that has been offered to idols. (This makes the food unclean.[d]) Do not take part in any kind of sexual sin. Do not taste blood. Do not eat animals that have been strangled. [21]They should not do these things, because there are still men in every city who teach the law of Moses. For a long time the words of Moses have been read in the synagogue[d] every Sabbath[d] day."

### LETTER TO NON-JEWISH BELIEVERS

[22]The apostles,[d] the elders,[d] and the whole church decided to send some of their men with Paul and Barnabas to Antioch. They chose Judas Barsabbas and Silas, who were respected by the believers. [23]They sent the following letter with them:

From the apostles and elders, your brothers.

To all the non-Jewish brothers in Antioch, Syria and Cilicia:

Dear Brothers,

[24]We have heard that some of our men have come to you and said things that trouble and upset you. But we did not tell them to do this! [25]We have all agreed to choose some men and send them to you. They will be with our dear friends Barnabas and Paul— [26]men who have given their lives to serve our Lord Jesus Christ. [27]So we have sent Judas and Silas with them. They will tell you the same things. [28]It has pleased the Holy Spirit[d] that you should not have a heavy load to carry, and we agree. You need to do only these things: [29]Do not eat any food that has been offered to idols. Do not taste blood. Do not eat any animals that have been strangled. Do not take part in any kind of sexual sin. If you stay away from these things, you will do well.

Good-bye.

[30]So the men left Jerusalem and went to Antioch. There they gathered the church and gave them the letter. [31]When they read it, they were very happy because of the encouraging letter. [32]Judas and Silas were also prophets,[d] who said many things to encourage the believers and make them stronger. [33]After some time Judas and Silas were sent off in peace by the believers. They went back to those who had sent them. [34] [n]

[35]But Paul and Barnabas stayed in Antioch. They and many others preached the Good News[d] and taught the people the message of the Lord.

### PAUL AND BARNABAS SEPARATE

[36]After some time, Paul said to Barnabas, "We preached the message of the Lord in many towns. We should go back to all those towns to visit the believers and see how they are doing." [37]Barnabas wanted to take John Mark with them too. [38]But John Mark had left them at Pamphylia; he did not continue with them in the work. So Paul did not think it was a good idea to take him. [39]Paul and Barnabas had a serious argument about this. They separated and went different ways. Barnabas

> **"Do not eat food that has been offered to idols."**
> *Acts 15:20*

## DECODE THIS!

*What did Paul preach to the nations?*

15:34 **Verse 34** Some Greek copies add verse 34: ". . . but Silas decided to remain there."

193

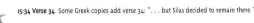

sailed to Cyprus and took Mark with him. ⁴⁰But Paul chose Silas and left. The believers in Antioch put Paul into the Lord's care. ⁴¹And he went through Syria and Cilicia, giving strength to the churches.

## TIMOTHY GOES WITH PAUL AND SILAS

**16** Paul came to Derbe and Lystra. A follower named Timothy was there. Timothy's mother was Jewish and a believer. His father was a Greek. ²The brothers in Lystra and Iconium respected Timothy and said good things about him. ³Paul wanted Timothy to travel with him. But all the Jews living in that area knew that Timothy's father was Greek. So Paul circumcised[d] Timothy to please the Jews. ⁴Paul and the men with him traveled from town to town. They gave the decisions made by the apostles[d] and elders[d] in Jerusalem for the people to obey. ⁵So the churches became stronger in the faith and grew larger every day.

## PAUL IS CALLED OUT OF ASIA

⁶Paul and the men with him went through the areas of Phrygia and Galatia. The Holy Spirit[d] did not let them preach the Good News[d] in the country of Asia. ⁷When they came near the country of Mysia, they tried to go into Bithynia. But the Spirit of Jesus did not let them. ⁸So they passed by Mysia and went to Troas. ⁹That night Paul had a vision. In the vision, a man from Macedonia came to him. The man stood there and begged, "Come over to Macedonia. Help us!" ¹⁰After Paul had seen the vision, we immediately prepared to leave for Macedonia. We understood that God had called us to tell the Good News to those people.

## LYDIA BECOMES A CHRISTIAN

¹¹We left Troas in a ship, and we sailed straight to the island of Samothrace. The next day we sailed to Neapolis.[n] ¹²Then we went by land to Philippi, the leading city in that part of Macedonia. It is also a Roman colony.[n] We stayed there for several days. ¹³On the Sabbath[d] day we went outside the city gate to the river. There we thought we would find a special place for prayer. Some women had gathered there, so we sat down and talked with them. ¹⁴There was a woman named Lydia from the city of Thyatira. Her job was selling purple cloth. She worshiped the true God. The Lord opened her mind to pay attention to what Paul was saying. ¹⁵She and all the people in her house were baptized. Then Lydia invited us to her home. She said, "If you think I am truly a believer in the Lord, then come stay in my house." And she persuaded us to stay with her.

## PAUL AND SILAS IN JAIL

¹⁶Once, while we were going to the place for prayer, a servant girl met us. She had a special spirit[n] in her. She earned a lot of money for her owners by telling fortunes. ¹⁷This girl followed Paul and us. She said loudly, "These men are servants of the Most High God! They are telling you how you can be saved!" ¹⁸She kept this up for many days. This bothered Paul, so he turned and said to the spirit, "By the power of Jesus Christ, I command you to come out of her!" Immediately, the spirit came out.

¹⁹The owners of the servant girl saw this. These men knew that now they

---

---

> **"So the churches became stronger in the faith and grew larger every day."** *Acts 16:5*

---

16:11 **Neapolis** City in Macedonia. It was the first city Paul visited on the continent of Europe. 16:12 **Roman colony** A town begun by Romans with Roman laws, customs and privileges. 16:16 **spirit** This was a spirit from the devil. It caused her to say she had special knowledge.

could not use her to make money. So they grabbed Paul and Silas and dragged them before the city rulers in the marketplace. ²⁰Here they brought Paul and Silas to the Roman rulers and said, "These men are Jews and are making trouble in our city. ²¹They are teaching things that are not right for us as Romans to do."

²²The crowd joined the attack against them. The Roman officers tore the clothes of Paul and Silas and had them beaten with rods again and again. ²³Then Paul and Silas were thrown into jail. The jailer was ordered to guard them carefully. ²⁴When he heard this order, he put them far inside the jail. He pinned down their feet between large blocks of wood.

²⁵About midnight Paul and Silas were praying and singing songs to God. The other prisoners were listening to them. ²⁶Suddenly, there was a big earthquake. It was so strong that it shook the foundation of the jail. Then all the doors of the jail broke open. All the prisoners were freed from their chains. ²⁷The jailer woke up and saw that the jail doors were open. He thought that the prisoners had already escaped. So he got his sword and was about to kill himself.ⁿ ²⁸But Paul shouted, "Don't hurt yourself! We are all here!"

²⁹The jailer told someone to bring a light. Then he ran inside. Shaking with fear, he fell down before Paul and Silas. ³⁰Then he brought them outside and said, "Men, what must I do to be saved?"

³¹They said to him, "Believe in the Lord Jesus and you will be saved—you and all the people in your house." ³²So Paul and Silas told the message of the

Lord to the jailer and all the people in his house. ³³At that hour of the night the jailer took Paul and Silas and washed their wounds. Then he and all his people were baptized immediately. ³⁴After this the jailer took Paul and Silas home and gave them food. He and his family were very happy because they now believed in God.

³⁵The next morning, the Roman officers sent the police to tell the jailer, "Let these men go free!"

³⁶The jailer said to Paul, "The officers have sent an

> "The crowd joined the attack against them. The Roman officers tore the clothes of Paul and Silas and had them beaten with rods again and again."
>
> *Acts 16:22*

order to let you go free. You can leave now. Go in peace."

³⁷But Paul said to the police, "They beat us in public without a trial, even though we are Roman citizens.ⁿ And they threw us in jail. Now they want to make us go away quietly. No! Let them come themselves and bring us out!"

³⁸The police told the Roman officers what Paul said. When the

officers heard that Paul and Silas were Roman citizens, they were afraid. ³⁹So they came and told Paul and Silas they were sorry. They took Paul and Silas out of jail and asked them to leave the city. ⁴⁰So when they came out of the jail, they went to Lydia's house. There they saw some of the believers and encouraged them. Then they left.

## PAUL AND SILAS IN THESSALONICA

**17** Paul and Silas traveled through Amphipolis and Apollonia and came to Thessalonica. In that city there was a Jewish synagogue.ᵈ ²Paul went into the synagogue as he always did. On each Sabbathᵈ day for three weeks, Paul talked with the Jews about the Scriptures.ᵈ ³He explained and proved that the Christᵈ must die and then rise from death. He said, "This Jesus I am telling you about is the Christ." ⁴Some of the Jews were convinced and joined Paul and Silas. Many of the Greeks who worshiped the true God and many of the important women joined them.

⁵But the Jews became jealous. They got some evil men from the marketplace, formed a mob and started a riot. They ran to Jason's house, looking for Paul and Silas. The men wanted to bring Paul and Silas out to the people. ⁶But they did not find them. So they dragged Jason and some other believers to the leaders of the city. The people were yelling, "These men have made trouble everywhere in the world. And now they have come here too! ⁷Jason is keeping them in his house. All of them do things against the laws of Caesar.ᵈ They say that there is another king called Jesus."

**DECODE THIS!**
*What color of cloth did Lydia sell?*

16:27 **kill himself** He thought the leaders would kill him for letting the prisoners escape.
16:37 **Roman citizens** Roman law said that Roman citizens must not be beaten before they had a trial.

# JULY OBEDIENCE

**1**

**2** PRAYER POINTER: Pray today for your teachers to have wisdom and patience with your class. Pray that they would get extra strength from God.

**3**

**4** Bake a cake to celebrate our country's birthday.

**5** EPHESIANS 6:1: Children, obey your parents the way the Lord wants. This is the right thing to do.

**6**

**7** Write your governor or senators and tell them you appreciate their work.

**8**

**9**

**10** Visit a police station and thank the officers for their service.

**11** PRAYER POINTER: Thank God for the people in your life who teach you and help you know him better.

**12**

**13** Tell your memory verse to your dad.

**14** I PETER 2:17: Show respect for all people. Love the brothers and sisters of God's family. Respect God. Honor the king.

**15**

**16**

**17** Draw a picture of what your country means to you.

**18**

**19** PRAYER POINTER: Pray for our president, his family, and our soldiers who are protecting our country.

**20**

**21** Go to a history museum with friends from school.

**22** HEBREWS 13:7: Remember your leaders. They taught God's message to you. Remember how they lived and died, and copy their faith.

**23**

**24**

**25** Write a note to your last teacher, and tell them they did a good job.

**26**

**27** PRAYER POINTER: Ask God to help you want to obey your parents and honor them.

**28**

**29**

**30** Hebrews 5:9: And he became our perfect high priest. He gives eternal salvation to all who obey him.

**31** Ask your parents what God has been teaching them lately.

*If you love me, you will do the things I command (John 14:15).*

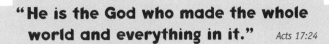

> **"He is the God who made the whole world and everything in it."** *Acts 17:24*

⁸When the people and the leaders of the city heard these things, they became very upset. ⁹They made Jason and the others put up a sum of money. Then they let the believers go free.

## PAUL AND SILAS GO TO BEREA

¹⁰That same night the believers sent Paul and Silas to Berea. There Paul and Silas went to the Jewish synagogue.ᵈ ¹¹These Jews were better than the Jews in Thessalonica. They were eager to hear the things Paul and Silas said. These Jews in Berea studied the Scripturesᵈ every day to find out if these things were true. ¹²So, many of them believed. Many important Greek men and women also believed. ¹³But when the Jews in Thessalonica learned that Paul was preaching the word of God in Berea, they came there, too. They upset the people and made trouble. ¹⁴So the believers quickly sent Paul away to the coast. But Silas and Timothy stayed in Berea. ¹⁵The men who took Paul went with him to Athens. Then they carried a message from Paul back to Silas and Timothy. It said, "Come to me as soon as you can."

## PAUL IN ATHENS

¹⁶Paul was waiting for Silas and Timothy in Athens. He was troubled because he saw that the city was full of idols. ¹⁷In the synagogue,ᵈ he talked with the Jews and the Greeks who worshiped the true God. He also talked every day with people in the marketplace.

¹⁸Some of the Epicurean and Stoic philosophersⁿ argued with him. Some of them said, "This man doesn't know what he is talking about. What is he trying to say?" Paul was telling them the Good Newsᵈ of Jesus' rising from death. They said, "He seems to be telling us about some other gods." ¹⁹They got Paul and took him to a meeting of

**Q. What do you own that you would never want to share with your friends?**

**A. My dog. I love my dog and would not want to share him with anyone.**

the Areopagus.ⁿ They said, "Please explain to us this new idea that you have been teaching. ²⁰The things you are saying are new to us. We want to know what this teaching means." ²¹(All the people of Athens and those from other countries always used their time talking about all the newest ideas.)

²²Then Paul stood before the meeting of the Areopagus. He said, "Men of Athens, I can see that you are very religious in all things. ²³I was going through your city, and I saw the things you worship. I found an altar that had these words written on it: ᴛᴏ ᴀ ɢᴏᴅ ᴡʜᴏ ɪs ɴᴏᴛ ᴋɴᴏᴡɴ. You worship a god that you don't know. This is the God I am telling you about! ²⁴He is the God who made the whole world and everything in it. He is the Lord of the land and the sky. He does not live in temples that men build! ²⁵This God is the One who gives life, breath, and everything else to people. He does not need any help from them. He has everything he needs. ²⁶God began by making one man. From him came all the different people who live everywhere in the world. He decided exactly when and where they must live. ²⁷God wanted them to look for him and perhaps search all around for him and find him. But he is not far from any of us: ²⁸'We live in him. We walk in him. We are in him.' Some of your own poets have said: 'For we are his children.' ²⁹We are

### KIDS SPEAK UP!

## ? DECODE THIS!

*Who was thrown into jail with Paul by Roman officers?*

⭐ **17:18 Epicurean and Stoic philosophers** Philosophers were those who searched for truth. Epicureans believed that pleasure, especially pleasures of the mind, were the goal of life. Stoics believed that life should be without feelings of joy or grief. **17:19 Areopagus** A council or group of important leaders in Athens. They were like judges.

God's children. So, you must not think that God is like something that people imagine or make. He is not like gold, silver, or rock. ³⁰In the past, people did not understand God, but God ignored this. But now, God tells everyone in the world to change his heart and life. ³¹God has decided on a day that he will judge all the world. He will be fair. He will use a man to do this. God chose that man long ago. And God has proved this to everyone by raising that man from death!"

³²When the people heard about Jesus being raised from death, some of them laughed. They said, "We will hear more about this from you later." ³³So Paul went away from them. ³⁴But some of the people believed Paul and joined him. One of those who believed was Dionysius, a member of the Areopagus. Also a woman named Damaris and some others believed.

### PAUL IN CORINTH

**18** Later, Paul left Athens and went to Corinth. ²Here he met a Jew named Aquila. Aquila was born in the country of Pontus. But Aquila and his wife, Priscilla, had recently moved to Corinth from Italy. They left Italy because Claudius" commanded that all Jews must leave Rome. Paul went to visit Aquila and Priscilla. ³They were tentmakers, just as he was. He stayed with them and worked with them. ⁴Every Sabbath⁴ day he talked with the Jews and Greeks in the synagogue.⁴ Paul tried to persuade these people to believe in Jesus.

⁵Silas and Timothy came from Macedonia and joined Paul in Corinth. After this, Paul used all his time telling people the Good News.⁴ He showed the Jews that Jesus is the Christ.⁴ ⁶But they would not accept Paul's teaching and said some evil things. So he shook off the dust from his clothes." He said to them, "If you are not saved, it will be your own fault! I have done all I can do! After this, I will go only to non-Jewish people!" ⁷Paul left the synagogue and moved into the home of Titius Justus. It was next to the synagogue. This man worshiped the true God. ⁸Crispus was the leader of that synagogue. He and all the people living in his house believed in the Lord. Many others in Corinth also listened to Paul. They too believed and were baptized.

⁹During the night, Paul had a vision. The Lord said to him, "Don't be afraid! Continue talking to people and don't be quiet! ¹⁰I am with you. No one will hurt you because many of my people are in this city." ¹¹Paul stayed there for a year and a half, teaching God's word to the people.

### PAUL IS BROUGHT BEFORE GALLIO

¹²Gallio became the governor of the country of Southern Greece. At that time, some of the Jews came together against Paul and took him to the court. ¹³They said to Gallio, "This man is teaching people to worship God in a way that is against our law!"

¹⁴Paul was about to say something, but Gallio spoke to the Jews. Gallio said, "I would listen to you Jews if you were complaining about a crime or some wrong. ¹⁵But the things you are saying are only questions about words and names—arguments about your own law. So you must solve this problem yourselves. I don't want to be a judge of these things!" ¹⁶Then Gallio made them leave the court.

¹⁷Then they all grabbed Sosthenes. (Sosthenes was now the leader of the synagogue.⁴) They beat him there before the court. But this did not bother Gallio.

18:2 **Claudius** The emperor (ruler) of Rome, A.D. 41–54. 18:6 **shook . . . clothes** This was a warning. It showed that Paul was finished talking to the Jews.

## PAUL RETURNS TO ANTIOCH

[18]Paul stayed with the believers for many more days. Then he left and sailed for Syria. Priscilla and Aquila went with him. At Cenchrea, Paul cut off his hair.[n] This showed that he had made a promise to God. [19]Then they went to Ephesus, where Paul left Priscilla and Aquila. While Paul was there, he went into the synagogue[d] and talked with the Jews. [20]When they asked him to stay with them longer, he refused. [21]He left them, but he said, "I will come back to you again if God wants me to." And so he sailed away from Ephesus.

[22]Paul landed at Caesarea. Then he went and gave greetings to the church in Jerusalem. After that, Paul went to Antioch. [23]He stayed there for a while and then left and went through the countries of Galatia and Phrygia. He traveled from town to town in these countries, giving strength to all the followers.

## APOLLOS IN EPHESUS AND CORINTH

[24]A Jew named Apollos came to Ephesus. He was born in the city of Alexandria. He was an educated man who knew the Scriptures[d] well. [25]He had been taught about the Lord. He was always very excited when he spoke and taught the truth about Jesus. But the only baptism that Apollos knew about was the baptism that John[n] taught. [26]Apollos began to speak very boldly in the synagogue,[d] and Priscilla and Aquila heard him. So they took him to their home and helped him better understand the way of God. [27]Now Apollos wanted to

go to the country of Southern Greece, so the believers helped him. They wrote a letter to the followers there, asking them to accept him. These followers had believed in Jesus because of God's grace. When Apollos went there, he helped them very much. [28]He argued very strongly with the Jews before all the people. Apollos clearly proved that the Jews were wrong. Using the Scriptures, he proved that Jesus is the Christ.[d]

## PAUL IN EPHESUS

**19** While Apollos was in Corinth, Paul was visiting some places on the way to Ephesus. There he found some followers. [2]Paul asked them, "Did you receive the Holy Spirit[d] when you believed?"

They said, "We have never even heard of a Holy Spirit!"

[3]So he asked, "What kind of baptism did you have?"

They said, "It was the baptism that John[n] taught."

[4]Paul said, "John's baptism was a baptism of changed hearts and lives. He told people to believe in the One who would come after him. That One is Jesus."

[5]When they heard this, they were baptized in the name of the Lord Jesus. [6]Then Paul laid his hands on them,[n] and the Holy Spirit came upon them. They began speaking different languages and prophesying.[d] [7]There were about 12 men in this group.

[8]Paul went into the synagogue[d] and spoke out boldly for three months. He talked with the Jews and persuaded them to accept the things he said about the kingdom of God. [9]But some of the Jews became stubborn and refused to

believe. These Jews said evil things about the Way of Jesus. All the people heard these things. So Paul left them and took the followers with him. He went to a place where a man named Tyrannus had a school. There Paul talked with people every day [10]for two years. Because of his work, every Jew and Greek in the country of Asia heard the word of the Lord.

## THE SONS OF SCEVA

[11]God used Paul to do some very special miracles.[d] [12]Some people took handkerchiefs and clothes that Paul had used and put them on the sick. When they did this, the sick were healed and evil spirits left them.

[13-14]But some Jews also were traveling around and making evil spirits go out of people. The seven sons of Sceva were doing this. (Sceva was a leading Jewish priest.) These Jews tried to use the name of the Lord Jesus to force the evil spirits out. They would say, "By

> **"John's baptism was a baptism of changed hearts and lives. He told people to believe in the One who would come after him. That One is Jesus."** Acts 19:4

the same Jesus that Paul talks about, I order you to come out!"

[15]But one time an evil spirit said to these Jews, "I know Jesus, and I know about Paul, but who are you?"

[16]Then the man, who had the evil spirit in him, jumped on these Jews.

## Decode this!

*What profession did Paul's friends Priscilla and Aquila have?*

18:18 cut . . . hair Jews did this to show that the time of a special promise to God was finished. 18:25; 19:3 John John the Baptist, who preached to people about Christ's coming (Matthew 3, Luke 3). 19:6 laid his hands on them Here, doing this was a sign to show that Paul had God's authority or power to give these people special powers of the Holy Spirit.

He was much stronger than all of them. He beat them and tore their clothes off, so they ran away from the house. [17]All the people in Ephesus, Jews and Greeks, learned about this. They were filled with fear. And the people gave great honor to the Lord Jesus. [18]Many of the believers began to confess openly and tell all the evil things they had done. [19]Some of them had used magic. These believers brought their magic books and burned them before everyone. Those books were worth about 50,000 silver coins.[n]

[20]So in a powerful way the word of the Lord kept spreading and growing.

## PAUL PLANS A TRIP

[21]After these things, Paul made plans to go to Jerusalem. He planned to go through the countries of Macedonia and Southern Greece, and then on to Jerusalem. He said, "After I have been to Jerusalem, I must also visit Rome." [22]Paul sent Timothy and Erastus, two of his helpers, ahead to Macedonia. He himself stayed in Asia for a while.

## TROUBLE IN EPHESUS

[23]But during that time, there was some serious trouble in Ephesus about the Way of Jesus. [24]There was a man named Demetrius, who worked with silver. He made little silver models that looked like the temple of the goddess Artemis.[n] The men who did this work made much money. [25]Demetrius had a meeting with these men and some others who did the same kind of work. He told them, "Men, you know that we make a lot of money from our busi-

ness. [26]But look at what this man Paul is doing! He has convinced and turned away many people in Ephesus and in almost all of Asia! He says the gods that men make are not real. [27]There is a danger that our business will lose its good name. But there is also another danger: People will begin to think that the temple of the great goddess Artemis is not important! Her greatness will be destroyed. And Artemis is the goddess that everyone in Asia and the whole world worships."

> "So in a powerful way the word of the Lord kept spreading and growing."
>
> Acts 19:20

[28]When the men heard this, they became very angry. They shouted, "Artemis, the goddess of Ephesus, is great!" [29]The whole city became confused. The people grabbed Gaius and Aristarchus. (These two men were from Macedonia and were traveling with Paul.) Then all the people ran to the theater. [30]Paul wanted to go in

and talk to the crowd, but the followers did not let him. [31]Also, some leaders of Asia were friends of Paul. They sent him a message, begging him not to go into the theater. [32]Some people were shouting one thing, and some were shouting another. The meeting was completely confused. Most of the people did not know why they had come together. [33]The Jews put a man named Alexander in front of the people. Some of them had told him what to do. Alexander waved his hand because he wanted to explain things to the people. [34]But when they saw that Alexander was a Jew, they all began shouting the same thing. They continued shouting for two hours: "Great is Artemis of Ephesus!"

[35]Then the city clerk made the crowd be quiet. He said, "Men of Ephesus, everyone knows that Ephesus is the city that keeps the temple of the great goddess Artemis. All people know that we also keep her holy stone[n] that fell from heaven. [36]No one can say that this is not true. So you should be quiet. You must stop and think before you do anything. [37]You brought these men here, but they have not said anything evil against our goddess. They have not stolen anything from her temple. [38]We have courts of law, and there are judges. Do Demetrius and the men who work with him have a charge against anyone? They should go to the courts! That is where they can argue with each other! [39]Is there something else you want to talk about? It can be decided at the regular town meeting of the people. [40]I say this because some people might see

# Gotta Know!

## Why do some countries not let Christians in?

Some countries have governments that do not like Christian teachings because God's truth shows that their ways are wrong. They do not want the people in their country to become Christians, or they might lose their power. So they try to keep Christians from coming inside to share the Good News of God's love. However, God's Word will not be stopped. Christians have to get creative, but they can find ways into even the most closed countries and share the news the people need to hear.

this trouble today and say that we are rioting. We could not explain this because there is no real reason for this meeting." ⁴¹After the city clerk said these things, he told the people to go home.

## PAUL IN MACEDONIA AND GREECE

**20** When the trouble stopped, Paul sent for the followers to come to him. He encouraged them and then told them good-bye. Paul left and went to the country of Macedonia. ²He said many things to strengthen the followers in the different places on his way through Macedonia. Then he went to Southern Greece. ³He stayed there three months. He was ready to sail for Syria, but some Jews were planning something against him. So Paul decided to go

> **"Paul went down to Eutychus. He knelt down and put his arms around him. He said, 'Don't worry. He is alive now.'"** *Acts 20:10*

back through Macedonia to Syria. ⁴Some men went with him. They were Sopater son of Pyrrhus, from the city of Berea; Aristarchus and Secundus,

from the city of Thessalonica; Gaius, from Derbe; and Timothy; and Tychicus and Trophimus, two men from the country of Asia. ⁵These men went first, ahead of Paul, and waited for us at Troas. ⁶We sailed from Philippi after the Feast*ᵈ* of Unleavened Bread and we met them in Troas five days later. We stayed there seven days.

## PAUL'S LAST VISIT TO TROAS

⁷On the first day of the week,*ⁿ* we all met together to break bread.*ⁿ* Paul spoke to the group. Because he was planning to leave the next day, he kept on talking till midnight. ⁸We were all together in a room upstairs, and there were many lamps in the room. ⁹A young man named Eutychus was sitting in the window. As Paul continued talking, Eutychus was falling into a deep sleep. Finally, he went sound asleep and fell to the ground from the third floor. When they picked him up, he was dead. ¹⁰Paul went down to Eutychus. He knelt down and put his arms around him. He said, "Don't worry. He is alive

now." ¹¹Then Paul went upstairs again, broke bread, and ate. He spoke to them a long time, until it was early morning. Then he left. ¹²They took the young man home alive and were greatly comforted.

## THE TRIP FROM TROAS TO MILETUS

¹³We sailed for the city of Assos. We went first, ahead of Paul. He wanted to join us on the ship there. Paul planned it this way because he wanted to go to Assos by land. ¹⁴When he met us at Assos, we took him aboard and went to Mitylene. ¹⁵The next day, we sailed from Mitylene and came to a place near Chios. The next day, we sailed to Samos. A day later, we reached Miletus. ¹⁶Paul had already decided not to stop at Ephesus. He did not want to stay too long in the country of Asia. He was hurrying to be in Jerusalem on the day of Pentecost,*ᵈ* if that was possible.

## THE ELDERS FROM EPHESUS

¹⁷Now from Miletus Paul sent to Ephesus and called for the elders*ᵈ* of the church. ¹⁸When they came to him, he said, "You know about my life from the first day I came to Asia. You know the way I lived all the time I was with you. ¹⁹The Jews plotted against me. This troubled me very much. But you know that I always served the Lord. I never thought of myself first, and I often cried. ²⁰You know I preached to you, and I did not hold back anything that would help you. You know that I

**DECODE THIS!**

*Who was the silversmith in Ephesus who made goddess models?*

**20:7 first day of the week** Sunday, which for the Jews began at sunset on our Saturday. But if in this part of Asia a different system of time was used, then the meeting was on our Sunday night.
**20:7 break bread** Probably the Lord's Supper, the special meal that Jesus told his followers to eat to remember him (Luke 22:14-20).

taught you in public and in your homes. 21I warned both Jews and Greeks to change their lives and turn to God. And I told them all to believe in our Lord Jesus. 22But now I must obey the Holy Spirit[d] and go to Jerusalem. I don't know what will happen to me there. 23I know only that in every city the Holy Spirit tells me that troubles and even jail wait for me. 24I don't care about my own life. The most important thing is that I complete my mission. I want to finish the work that the Lord Jesus gave me—to tell people the Good News[d] about God's grace.

25"And now, I know that none of you will ever see me again. All the time I was with you, I was preaching the kingdom of God. 26So today I can tell you one thing that I am sure of: If any of you should be lost, I am not responsible. 27This is because I have told you everything God wants you to know. 28Be careful for yourselves and for all the people God has given you. The Holy Spirit gave you the work of caring for this flock. You must be like shepherds to the church of God.[n] This is the church that God bought with his own death. 29I know that after I leave, some men will come like wild wolves and try to destroy the flock. 30Also, men from your

own group will rise up and twist the truth. They will lead away followers after them. 31So be careful! Always remember this: For three years I never stopped warning each of you. I taught you night and day. I often cried over you.

32"Now I am putting you in the care of God and the message about his grace. That message is able to give you strength, and it will give you the blessings that God has for all his holy people. 33When I was with you, I never wanted anyone's money or fine clothes. 34You know that I always worked to take care of my own needs and the needs of those who were with me. 35I showed you in all things that you should work as I did and help the weak. I taught you to remember the words of Jesus. He said, 'It is more blessed to give than to receive.'"

36When Paul had said this, he knelt down with all of them and prayed. 37-38And they all cried because Paul had said that they would never see him again. They put their arms around him and kissed him. Then they went with him to the ship.

## PAUL GOES TO JERUSALEM

**21** We all said good-bye to them and left. We sailed straight to Cos island. The next day, we reached Rhodes, and from Rhodes we went to Patara. 2There we found a ship that was going to Phoenicia. We went aboard and sailed away. 3We sailed near the island of Cyprus. We could see it to the north, but we sailed on to Syria. We stopped at Tyre because the ship needed to unload its cargo there. 4We found some followers in Tyre, and we stayed with them for seven days. Through the Holy Spirit[d] they warned Paul not to go to Jerusalem.

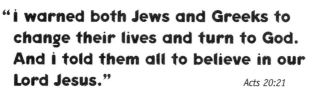

> "i warned both Jews and Greeks to change their lives and turn to God. And i told them all to believe in our Lord Jesus."
>
> *Acts 20:21*

## Ways to Live Unlike the World

1. Say things that build each other up.
2. Obey your parents with a happy heart.
3. Serve your brothers and sisters.
4. See the value in every person.
5. Put others' needs before your own.
6. Answer an angry person with soft, kind words.
7. Forgive others when wronged.
8. Tell others about Jesus.
9. Stay away from every evil or wrong.
10. Always tell the truth.

5When we finished our visit, we left and continued our trip. All the followers, even the women and children, came outside the city with us. We all knelt down on the beach and prayed. 6Then we said good-bye and got on the ship. The followers went back home. 7We continued our trip from Tyre and arrived at Ptolemais. We greeted the believers there and stayed with them for a day. 8We left Ptolemais and went to the city of Caesarea. There we went into the home of Philip and stayed

 **20:28 of God** Some Greek copies say, "of the Lord."

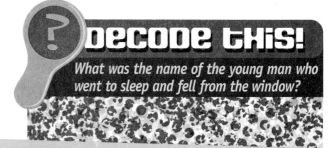

## DECODE THIS!

*What was the name of the young man who went to sleep and fell from the window?*

CAN YOU HELP PAUL FIND HIS WAY TO MACEDONIA TO PREACH THE GOOD NEWS?

with him. Philip had the work of telling the Good News.[d] He was one of the seven helpers.[n] [9]He had four unmarried daughters who had the gift of prophesying.[d] [10]After we had been there for some time, a prophet named Agabus arrived from Judea. [11]He came to us and borrowed Paul's belt. Then he used the belt to tie his own hands and feet. He said, "The Holy Spirit says, 'This is how the Jews in Jerusalem will tie up the man who wears this belt. Then they will give him to the non-Jewish people.'"

[12]We all heard these words. So we and the people there begged Paul not to go to Jerusalem. [13]But he said, "Why are you crying and making me so sad? I am ready to be tied up in Jerusalem. And I am ready to die for the Lord Jesus!"

[14]We could not persuade him to stay away from Jerusalem. So we stopped begging him and said, "We pray that what the Lord wants will be done."

[15]After this, we got ready and started on our way to Jerusalem. [16]Some of the followers from Caesarea went with us. They took us to the home of Mnason, a man from Cyprus. Mnason was one of the first followers. They took us to his home so that we could stay with him.

Q. Why are bubbles always round?

A. The air blown into them is shaped like a circle.

**"We pray that what the Lord wants will be done."**

*Acts 21:14*

### PAUL VISITS JAMES

[17]In Jerusalem the believers were glad to see us. [18]The next day, Paul went with us to visit James. All the elders[d] were there, too. [19]Paul greeted them and told them everything that God had done among the non-Jewish people through him. [20]When they heard this, they praised God. Then they said

to Paul, "Brother, you can see that many thousands of Jews have become believers. But they think it is very important to obey the law of Moses. [21]These Jews have heard about your teaching. They heard that you tell the Jews who live among non-Jews to leave the law of Moses. They heard that you tell them not to circumcise[d] their children and not to obey Jewish customs. [22]What should we do? The Jewish believers here will learn that you have come. [23]So we will tell you what to do: Four of our men have made a promise to God. [24]Take these men with you and share

in their cleansing ceremony.[n] Pay their expenses. Then they can shave their heads.[n] Do this and it will prove to everyone that what they have heard about you is not true. They will see that you follow the law of Moses in your own life. [25]We have already sent a letter to the non-Jewish believers. The letter said: 'Do not eat food that has been offered to idols. Do not taste blood. Do not eat animals that have been strangled. Do not take part in any kind of sexual sin.'"

[26]Then Paul took the four men with him. The next day, he shared in the cleansing ceremony. Then he went to the Temple.[d] Paul announced the time when the days of the cleansing ceremony would be finished. On the last day an offering would be given for each of the men.

[27]The seven days were almost over. But some Jews from Asia saw Paul at the Temple. They caused all the people to be upset, and they grabbed Paul. [28]They shouted, "Men of Israel, help us! This is the man who goes everywhere teaching things that are against the law of Moses, against our people, and against this Temple. And now he has brought some Greek men into the Temple. He has made this holy place unclean!"[d] [29](The Jews said this because they had seen Trophimus with Paul in Jerusalem. Trophimus was a man from Ephesus. The Jews thought that Paul had brought him into the Temple.)

[30]All the people in Jerusalem became very upset. They ran and took Paul and dragged him out of the Temple. The Temple doors were closed immediately. [31]The people were about to kill

**DECODE THIS!**
*Paul learned about ancestral law from this teacher.*

**21:8 helpers** The seven men chosen for a special work described in Acts 6:1-6. **21:24 cleansing ceremony** The special things Jews did to end the Nazirite promise. **21:24 shave their heads** The Jews did this to show that their promise was finished.

 204

Paul. Now the commander of the Roman army in Jerusalem learned that there was trouble in the whole city. [32]Immediately he ran to the place where the crowd was gathered. He brought officers and soldiers with him, and the people saw them. So they stopped beating Paul. [33]The commander went to Paul and arrested him. He told his soldiers to tie Paul with two chains. Then he asked, "Who is this man? What has he done wrong?" [34]Some in the crowd were yelling one thing, and some were yelling another. Because of all this confusion and shouting, the commander could not learn what had happened. So he ordered the soldiers to take Paul to the army building. [35-36]The whole mob was following them. When the soldiers came to the steps, they had to carry Paul. They did this because the people were ready to hurt him. They were shouting, "Kill him!"

[37]The soldiers were about to take Paul into the army building. But he spoke to the commander, "May I say something to you?"

The commander said, "Do you speak Greek? [38]I thought you were the Egyptian who started some trouble against the government not long ago. He led 4,000 killers out to the desert."

[39]Paul said, "No, I am a Jew from Tarsus in the country of Cilicia. I am a citizen of that important city. Please, let me speak to the people."

[40]The commander gave permission, so Paul stood on the steps. He waved with his hand so that the people would be quiet. When there was silence, Paul spoke to them in the Jewish language.[n]

## PAUL SPEAKS TO THE PEOPLE

**22** Paul said, "Brothers and fathers, listen to me! I will make my defense to you." [2]When the Jews heard him speaking the Jewish language,[n] they became very quiet. Paul said, [3]"I am a Jew. I was born in Tarsus in the country of Cilicia. I grew up in this city. I was a student of Gamaliel.[n] He carefully taught me everything about the law of our ancestors. I was very serious about serving God, just as are all of you here today. [4]I hurt the people who followed the Way of Jesus. Some of them were even killed. I arrested men and women and put them in jail. [5]The high priest and the whole council of older Jewish leaders can tell you that this is true. These leaders gave me letters to the Jewish brothers in Damascus. So I was going there to arrest these people and bring them back to Jerusalem to be punished.

[6]"But something happened to me on my way to Damascus. It was about noon when I came near Damascus. Suddenly a bright light from heaven flashed all around me. [7]I fell to the ground and heard a voice saying, 'Saul, Saul, why are you doing things against me?' [8]I asked, 'Who are you, Lord?' The voice said, 'I am Jesus from Nazareth. I am the One you are trying to hurt.' [9]The men who were with me did not understand the voice. But they saw the light. [10]I said, 'What shall I do, Lord?' The Lord answered, 'Get up and go to Damascus. There you will be told about all the things I have planned for you to do.' [11]I could not see, because the bright light had made me blind. So the men led me into Damascus.

[12]"There a man named Ananias came to me. He was a religious man; he obeyed the law of Moses. All the Jews who lived there respected him. [13]Ananias came to me, stood by me, and said, 'Brother Saul, see again!' Immediately I was able to see him. [14]Ananias told me, 'The God of our fathers chose you long ago. He chose you to know his plan. He chose you to see the Righteous One and to hear words from him. [15]You will be his witness to all people. You will tell them about the things you have seen and heard. [16]Now, why wait any longer? Get up, be baptized, and wash

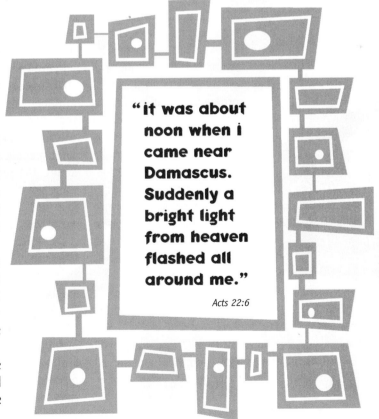

"it was about noon when i came near Damascus. Suddenly a bright light from heaven flashed all around me."

*Acts 22:6*

---

 **21:40; 22:2 Jewish language** Aramaic, the language of the Jews in the first century. **22:3 Gamaliel** A very important teacher of the Pharisees, a Jewish religious group (Acts 5:34).

your sins away. Do this, trusting in him to save you.'

[17]"Later, I returned to Jerusalem. I was praying in the Temple,[d] and I saw a vision. [18]I saw the Lord saying to me, 'Hurry! Leave Jerusalem now! The people here will not accept the truth about me.' [19]But I said, 'Lord, they know that in every synagogue[d] I put the believers in jail and beat them. [20]They also know that I was there when Stephen, your witness, was killed. I stood there and agreed that they should kill him. I even held the coats of the men who were killing him!' [21]But the Lord said to me, 'Leave now. I will send you far away to the non-Jewish people.'"

[22]The crowd listened to Paul until he said this. Then they began shouting, "Kill him! Get him out of the world! A man like this should not be allowed to live!" [23]They shouted and threw off their coats.[n] They threw dust into the air.[n]

[24]Then the commander ordered the soldiers to take Paul into the army building and beat him. The commander wanted to make Paul tell why the people were shouting

against him like this. [25]So the soldiers were tying him up, preparing to beat him. But Paul said to an officer there, "Do you have the right to beat a Roman citizen[n] who has not been proven guilty?"

[26]When the officer heard this, he went to the commander and told him about it. The officer said, "Do you know what you are doing? This man is a Roman citizen!"

[27]The commander came to Paul and said, "Tell me, are you really a Roman citizen?"

He answered, "Yes."

[28]The commander said, "I paid a lot of money to become a Roman citizen."

But Paul said, "I was born a citizen."

[29]The men who were preparing to question Paul moved away from him immediately. The commander was frightened because he had already tied Paul, and Paul was a Roman citizen.

## PAUL SPEAKS TO JEWISH LEADERS

[30]The next day the commander decided to learn why the Jews were accusing Paul. So he ordered the leading priests and the Jewish council to meet. The commander took Paul's chains off. Then he brought Paul out and stood him before their meeting.

**23** Paul looked at the Jewish council and said, "Brothers, I have lived my life in a good way before God up to this day." [2]Ananias,[n] the high priest, heard this and told the men who were standing near Paul to hit him on his mouth. [3]Paul said to Ananias, "God will hit you too! You are like a wall that has been painted white! You sit there and judge me, using the law of Moses. But you are telling them

to hit me, and that is against the law." [4]The men standing near Paul said to him, "You cannot talk like that to God's high priest! You are insulting him!"

[5]Paul said, "Brothers, I did not know

> ## "Get up, be baptized, and wash your sins away. Do this, trusting in him to save you."  *Acts 22:16*

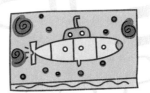

this man was the high priest. It is written in the Scriptures,[d] 'You must not curse a leader of your people.'"[n]

[6]Some of the men in the meeting were Sadducees,[d] and others were Pharisees.[d] So Paul shouted to them, "My brothers, I am a Pharisee and my father was a Pharisee! I am on trial here because I hope that people will rise from death!"

[7]When Paul said this, there was an argument between the Pharisees and the Sadducees. The group was divided. [8](The Sadducees believe that after people die, they cannot live again. The Sadducees also teach that there are no angels or spirits. But the Pharisees believe in them all.) [9]So there was a great uproar. Some of the teachers of the law, who were Pharisees, stood up and argued, "We find nothing wrong with this man! Maybe an angel or a spirit did speak to him."

[10]The argument was beginning to turn into a fight. The commander was afraid that the Jews would tear Paul to pieces. So the commander told the soldiers to go down and take Paul

> # BiBLe BasiCS
>
> ## WHaT IS a CHRiStian?
>
> The word *Christian* means "belonging to Christ" and includes any person who believes that Jesus—the Son of God—came to earth, lived a perfect life, was killed on a cross, rose again, and now lives in heaven. They trust that Jesus' work on the cross will save them from the judgment their sins deserve. They enjoy friendship with God now, and they will spend eternity in heaven with him. They love God and want to obey him.

---

 **22:23 threw off their coats** This showed that the Jews were very angry at Paul. **22:23 threw dust into the air** This showed even greater anger. **22:25 Roman citizen** Roman law said that Roman citizens must not be beaten before they had a trial. **23:2 Ananias** This is not the same man named Ananias in Acts 22:12. **23:5 'You . . . people.'** Quotation from Exodus 22:28.

away and put him in the army building.

¹¹"The next night the Lord came and stood by Paul. He said, "Be brave! You have told people in Jerusalem about me. You must do the same in Rome also."

¹²In the morning some of the Jews made a plan to kill Paul. They made a promise that they would not eat or drink anything until they had killed him. ¹³There were more than 40 Jews who made this plan. ¹⁴They went and talked to the leading priests and the older Jewish leaders. They said, "We have made a promise to ourselves that we will not eat or drink until we have killed Paul! ¹⁵So this is what we want you to do: Send a message to the commander to bring Paul out to you. Tell him you want to ask Paul more questions. We will be waiting to kill him while he is on the way here."

¹⁶But Paul's nephew heard about this plan. He went to the army building and told Paul about it. ¹⁷Then Paul called one of the officers and said, "Take this young man to the commander. He has a message for him."

¹⁸So the officer brought Paul's nephew to the commander. The officer said, "The prisoner, Paul, asked me to bring this young man to you. He wants to tell you something."

¹⁹The commander led the young man to a place where they could be alone. The commander asked, "What do you want to tell me?"

²⁰The young man said, "The Jews have decided to ask you to bring Paul down to their council meeting tomorrow. They want you to think that they are going to ask him more questions. ²¹But don't believe them! There are more than 40 men who are hiding and waiting to kill Paul. They have all made a promise not to eat or drink until they have killed him! Now they are waiting

"in the morning some of the Jews made a plan to kill Paul. They made a promise that they would not eat or drink anything until they had killed him."

*Acts 23:12*

for you to agree."

²²The commander sent the young man away. He said to him, "Don't tell anyone that you have told me about their plan."

**PAUL IS SENT TO CAESAREA**

²³Then the commander called two officers. He said to them, "I need some men to go to Caesarea. Get 200 soldiers ready. Also, get 70 horsemen and 200 men with spears. Be ready to leave at nine o'clock tonight. ²⁴Get some horses for Paul to ride. He must be taken to Governor Felix safely." ²⁵And he wrote a letter that said:

²⁶From Claudius Lysias.

To the Most Excellent Governor Felix: Greetings.

²⁷The Jews had taken this man, and they planned to kill him. But I learned that he is a Roman citizen, so I went with my soldiers and saved him. ²⁸I wanted to know

why they were accusing him. So I brought him before their council meeting. ²⁹I learned that the Jews said Paul did some things that were wrong. But these charges were about their own laws. And no charge was worthy of jail or death. ³⁰I was told that some of the Jews were planning to kill Paul. So I sent him to you at once. I also told those Jews to tell you what they have against him.

³¹So the soldiers did what they were told. They took Paul and brought him to the city of Antipatris that night. ³²The next day the horsemen went with Paul to Caesarea. But the other soldiers went back to the army building in Jerusalem. ³³The horsemen came to Caesarea and gave the letter to the governor. Then they turned Paul over to him. ³⁴The governor read the letter. Then he asked Paul, "What area are you from?" He learned that Paul was from Cilicia. ³⁵He said, "I will hear your case when those who are against you come here too." Then the governor gave orders for Paul to be kept under guard in the palace. (This building had been built by Herod.)

**THE JEWS ACCUSE PAUL**

**24** Five days later Ananias, the high priest, went to the city of Caesarea. With him were some of the older Jewish leaders and a lawyer named Tertullus. They had come to make charges against Paul before the governor. ²Paul was called into the meeting, and Tertullus began to accuse him, saying: "Most Excellent

**DECODE THIS!**
*The commander sent Paul to Governor Felix in what area?*

Felix! Our people enjoy much peace because of you, and many wrong things in our country are being made right through your wise help. ³We accept these things always and in every place. And we are thankful for them. ⁴But I do not want to take any more of your time. I beg you to be kind and listen to our few words. ⁵This man is a troublemaker. He makes trouble among the Jews everywhere in the world. He is a leader of the Nazarene[d] group. ⁶Also, he was trying to make the Temple[d] unclean,[d] but we stopped him.[n] ⁸You can decide if all these things are true. Ask him some questions yourself." ⁹The other Jews agreed and said that all of this was true.

¹⁰The governor made a sign for Paul to speak. So Paul said, "Governor Felix, I know that you have been a judge over this nation for a long time. So I am happy to defend myself before you. ¹¹I went to worship in Jerusalem only 12 days ago. You can learn for yourself that this is true. ¹²Those who are accusing me did not find me arguing with anyone in the

## WHAT STINKS?

Jesus said we shouldn't throw pearls before pigs. And when you take a close look at piggish behavior, it's easy to see why. Although pigs can be clean and cute creatures if they are bathed, most often they are not. In order to keep cool and protect themselves from sun and insects, pigs wallow in mud—as well as their own waste, since pig breeders don't move them around much. So when you mix mud, water, and poop, you get one stinky pig!

Of course, Jesus wasn't talking about literal pigs. He meant that we shouldn't give God's precious truth to people who will only make fun of it or ignore it. But God can still work in their hearts, so we need to pray for them and ask God to lift them out of their dirty sin and make them clean and new.

[Yahooligans: Ask Earl]

in the books of the Prophets.[d] ¹⁵I have the same hope in God that they have—the hope that all people, good and bad, will be raised from death. ¹⁶This is why I always try to do what I believe is right before God and men.

¹⁷"I was away from Jerusalem for several years. I went back there to bring money to my people and to offer sacrifices. ¹⁸I was doing this when they found me in the Temple. I had finished

when I stood before them: 'You are judging me today because I believe that people will rise from death!'"

²²Felix already understood much about the Way of Jesus. He stopped the trial and said, "When commander Lysias comes here, I will decide about your case." ²³Felix told the officer to keep Paul guarded. But he told the officer to give Paul some freedom and to let his friends bring what he needed.

> ## "i have the same hope in God that they have—the hope that all people, good and bad, will be raised from death."
>
> Acts 24:15

Temple. I was not stirring up the people. And I was not making trouble in the Temple or in the synagogues[d] or in the city. ¹³They cannot prove the things they are saying against me now. ¹⁴But I will tell you this: I worship the God of our ancestors as a follower of the Way of Jesus. The Jews say that the Way of Jesus is not the right way. But I believe everything that is taught in the law of Moses and that is written

the cleansing ceremony. I had not made any trouble; no people were gathering around me. ¹⁹But some Jews from the country of Asia were there. They should be here, standing before you. If I have really done anything wrong, they are the ones who should accuse me. ²⁰Or ask these Jews here if they found any wrong in me when I stood before the Jewish council in Jerusalem. ²¹But I did say one thing

### PAUL SPEAKS TO FELIX AND HIS WIFE

²⁴After some days Felix came with his wife, Drusilla, who was a Jew. He asked for Paul to be brought to him. He listened to Paul talk about believing in Christ Jesus. ²⁵But Felix became afraid when Paul spoke about things like right living, self-control, and the time when God will judge the world. He said, "Go away now. When I have

**24:6 Verse 6** Some Greek copies add 6b-8a: "And we wanted to judge him by our own law. ⁷ But the officer Lysias came and used much force to take him from us. ⁸ And Lysias commanded his people to come to you to accuse us."

more time, I will call for you." ²⁶At the same time Felix hoped that Paul would give him some money. So he sent for Paul often and talked with him.

²⁷But after two years, Porcius Festus became governor. Felix was no longer governor, but he had left Paul in prison to please the Jews.

## PAUL ASKS TO SEE CAESAR

**25** Three days after Festus became governor, he went from Caesarea to Jerusalem. ²There the leading priests and the important Jewish leaders made charges against Paul before Festus. ³They asked Festus to do something for them; they wanted him to send Paul back to Jerusalem. (They had a plan to kill Paul on the way.) ⁴But Festus answered, "No! Paul will be kept in Caesarea. I will return there soon myself. ⁵Some of your leaders should go with me. They can accuse the man there in Caesarea, if he has really done something wrong."

⁶Festus stayed in Jerusalem another eight or ten days. Then he went back to Caesarea. The next day he told the soldiers to bring Paul before him. Festus was seated on the judge's seat ⁷when Paul came into the room. The Jews who had come from Jerusalem stood around him. They started making serious charges against Paul. But they could not prove any of them. ⁸This is what Paul said to defend himself: "I have done nothing wrong against the Jewish law, against the Temple,ᵈ or against Caesar!"ᵈ

⁹But Festus wanted to please the Jews. So he asked Paul, "Do you want to go to Jerusalem? Do you want me to

judge you there on these charges?"

¹⁰Paul said, "I am standing at Caesar's judgment seat now. This is where I should be judged! I have done nothing wrong to the Jews; you know this is true. ¹¹If I have done something wrong and the law says I must die, I do not ask to be saved from death. But if these charges are not true, then no one can give me to them. No! I want Caesar to hear my case!"

¹²Festus talked about this with the people who advised him. Then he said, "You have asked to see Caesar; so you will go to Caesar!"

## PAUL BEFORE KING AGRIPPA

¹³A few days later King Agrippa and Bernice came to Caesarea to visit Festus. ¹⁴They stayed there for some time, and Festus told the king about Paul's case. Festus said, "There is a man that Felix left in prison. ¹⁵When I went to Jerusalem, the leading priests and the older Jewish leaders there made charges against him. They wanted me to sentence him to death. ¹⁶But I answered, 'When a man is accused of a crime, Romans do not hand him over just to please someone. The man must be allowed to face his accusers and defend himself against their charges.' ¹⁷So these Jews came here to Caesarea for the trial. And I did not waste time. The next day I sat on the judge's seat and commanded that the man be brought in. ¹⁸The Jews stood up and accused him. But they did not accuse him of any serious

crime as I thought they would. ¹⁹The things they said were about their own religion and about a man named Jesus. Jesus died, but Paul said that he is still alive. ²⁰I did not know much about these things; so I did not ask questions. But I asked Paul, 'Do you want to go to Jerusalem and be judged there?' ²¹But he asked to be kept in Caesarea. He wants a decision from the Emperor." So I ordered that Paul be held until I could send him to Caesarᵈ in Rome."

²²Agrippa said to Festus, "I would like to hear this man, too."

Festus said, "Tomorrow you will hear him!"

²³The next day Agrippa and Bernice appeared. They dressed and acted like very important people. Agrippa and Bernice, the army leaders, and the important men of Caesarea went into the judgment room. Then Festus ordered the soldiers to bring Paul in. ²⁴Festus said, "King Agrippa and all who are gathered here with us, you see this man. All the Jewish people, here and in Jerusalem, have complained to me about him. They shout that he should not live any longer. ²⁵When I judged him, I could find nothing wrong. I found no reason to order his death. But he asked to be judged by Caesar. So I decided to send him. ²⁶But I have nothing definite to write the Emperor about him. So I have brought him before all of you—especially you, King Agrippa. I hope that you can question him and give me something to write. ²⁷I think it is foolish to send a prisoner to Caesar

> ### "Jesus died, but Paul said that he is still alive."
> *Acts 25:19*

**DECODE THIS!**

*The name of the king who listened to Paul's trial was _____.*

⭐ **25:21 Emperor** The ruler of the Roman Empire, which was almost all the world.

without telling what the charges are against him."

## PAUL DEFENDS HIMSELF

**26** Agrippa said to Paul, "You may now speak to defend yourself."

Then Paul raised his hand and began to speak. ²He said, "King Agrippa, I will answer all the charges that the Jews make against me. I think it is a

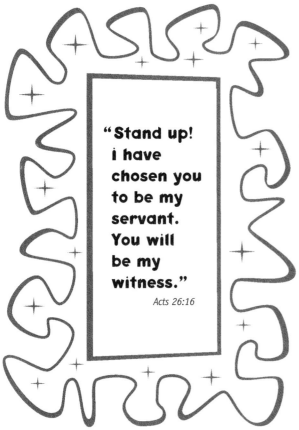

"Stand up!
i have
chosen you
to be my
servant.
You will
be my
witness."

*Acts 26:16*

blessing that I can stand here before you today. ³I am very happy to talk to you, because you know so much about all the Jewish customs and the things that the Jews argue about. Please listen to me patiently.

⁴"All the Jews know about my whole life. They know the way I lived from the beginning in my own country and later in Jerusalem. ⁵They have known me for a long time. If they want to,

they can tell you that I was a good Pharisee.ᵈ And the Pharisees obey the laws of the Jewish religion more carefully than any other group of Jewish people. ⁶Now I am on trial because I hope for the promise that God made to our ancestors. ⁷This is the promise that the 12 tribesᵈ of our people hope to receive. For this hope the Jews serve God day and night. My king, the Jews have accused me because I hope for this same promise! ⁸Why do any of you people think it is impossible for God to raise people from death?

⁹"I too thought I ought to do many things against Jesus from Nazareth. ¹⁰And in Jerusalem I did many things against God's people. The leading priests gave me the power to put many of them in jail. When they were being killed, I agreed that it was a good thing. ¹¹In every synagogue,ᵈ I often punished them. I tried to make them say evil things against Jesus. I was so angry against them that I even went to other cities to find them and punish them.

¹²"One time the leading priests gave me permission and the power to go to Damascus. ¹³On the way there, at noon, I saw a light from heaven. The light was brighter than the sun. It flashed all around me and the men who were traveling with me. ¹⁴We all fell to the ground. Then I heard a voice speaking to me in the Jewish language.ⁿ The voice said, 'Saul, Saul, why are you doing things against me? You are only

hurting yourself by fighting me.' ¹⁵I said, 'Who are you, Lord?' The Lord said, 'I am Jesus. I am the One you are trying to hurt. ¹⁶Stand up! I have chosen you to be my servant. You will be my witness—you will tell people the things that you have seen and the things that I will show you. This is why I have come to you today. ¹⁷I will not let your own people hurt you. And I will keep you safe from the non-Jewish people too. These are the people I am sending you to. ¹⁸I send you to open their eyes that they may turn away from darkness to the light. I send you that they may turn away from the power of Satan and turn to God. Then their sins can be forgiven and they can have a place with those people who have been made holy by believing in me.'

¹⁹"King Agrippa, after I had this vision from heaven, I obeyed it. ²⁰I began telling people that they should change their hearts and lives and turn to God. I told them to do things to show that they really had changed. I told this first to those in Damascus, then in Jerusalem and in every part of Judea, and also to the non-Jewish people. ²¹This is why the Jews took me and were trying to kill me in the Temple.ᵈ ²²But God helped me and is still helping me today. With God's help I am standing here today and telling all people what I have seen. But I am saying nothing new. I am saying what Moses and the prophetsᵈ said would happen. ²³They said that the Christᵈ would die and be the first to rise from death. They said that the Christ would bring light to the Jewish and non-Jewish people."

★ 26:14 **Jewish language** Aramaic, the language of the Jews in the first century.

210

**DECODE THIS!**

*What happened on Paul's sea journey to Rome?*

## PAUL TRIES TO PERSUADE AGRIPPA

[24]While Paul was saying these things to defend himself, Festus said loudly, "Paul, you are out of your mind! Too much study has driven you crazy!"

[25]Paul said, "Most Excellent Festus, I am not crazy. My words are true. They are not the words of a foolish man. [26]King Agrippa knows about these things. I can speak freely to him. I know that he has heard about all of these things. They did not happen off in a corner. [27]King Agrippa, do you believe what the prophets[d] wrote? I know you believe!"

[28]King Agrippa said to Paul, "Do you think you can persuade me to become a Christian in such a short time?"

[29]Paul said, "Whether it is a short or a long time, I pray to God that not only you but every person listening to me today would be saved and be like me—except for these chains I have!"

[30]Then King Agrippa, Governor Festus, Bernice, and all the people sitting with them stood up [31]and left the room. They were talking to each other. They said, "There is no reason why this man should die or be put in jail." [32]And Agrippa said to Festus, "We

Aristarchus, a man from the city of Thessalonica in Macedonia, went with us. [3]The next day we came to Sidon. Julius was very good to Paul. He gave Paul freedom to go visit his friends, who took care of his needs. [4]We left Sidon and sailed close to the island of Cyprus because the wind was blowing against us. [5]We went across the sea by Cilicia and Pamphylia. Then we came to the city of Myra, in Lycia. [6]There the officer found a ship from Alexandria that was going to Italy. So he put us on it.

[7]We sailed slowly for many days. We had a hard time reaching Cnidus because the wind was blowing against us. We could not go any farther that way. So we sailed by the south side of the island of Crete near Salmone. [8]We sailed along the coast,

the officer did not believe Paul. Instead, the officer believed what the captain and owner of the ship said. [12]And that harbor was not a good place for the ship to stay for the winter. So most of the men decided that the ship should leave. The men hoped we could go to Phoenix. The ship could stay there for the winter. (Phoenix was a city on the island of Crete. It had a harbor which faced southwest and northwest.)

### THE STORM

[13]Then a good wind began to blow from the south. The men on the ship thought, "This is the wind we wanted, and now we have it!" So they pulled up the anchor. We sailed very close to the island of Crete. [14]But then a very strong wind named the "Northeaster" came from the island. [15]This wind took the ship and carried it away. The ship could not sail against it. So we stopped trying and let the wind blow us. [16]We went below a small island named Cauda. Then we were able to bring in the lifeboat, but it was very hard to do. [17]After the men took the lifeboat in, they tied ropes around the

> **"But God helped me and is still helping me today. With God's help i am standing here today and telling all people what i have seen."**
>
> Acts 26:22

could let this man go free, but he has asked Caesar[d] to hear his case."

## PAUL SAILS FOR ROME

**27** It was decided that we would sail for Italy. An officer named Julius, who served in the Emperor's[n] army, guarded Paul and some other prisoners. [2]We got on a ship and left. The ship was from the city of Adramyttium and was about to sail to different ports in the country of Asia.

but the sailing was hard. Then we came to a place called Safe Harbors, near the city of Lasea.

[9]But we had lost much time. It was now dangerous to sail, because it was already after the Day of Cleansing.[n] So Paul warned them, [10]"Men, I can see there will be a lot of trouble on this trip. The ship and the things in the ship will be lost. Even our lives may be lost!" [11]But the captain and the owner of the ship did not agree with Paul. So

ship to hold it together. The men were afraid that the ship would hit the sandbanks of Syrtis.[n] So they lowered the sail and let the wind carry the ship. [18]The next day the storm was blowing us so hard that the men threw out some of the cargo. [19]A day later they threw out the ship's equipment. [20]For many days we could not see the sun or the stars. The storm was very bad. We lost all hope of staying alive—we thought we would die.

27:1 **Emperor** The ruler of the Roman Empire, which was almost all the world. 27:9 **Day of Cleansing** An important Jewish holy day in the fall of the year. This was the time of year that bad storms happened on the sea. 27:17 **Syrtis** Shallow area in the sea near the Libyan coast.

## Gotta Know!

### Will we always live with our parents?

It might seem like you'll be with them forever, but that's not the expected course of events. You're really only with your parents a short time. After your teen years, you either get a job or go to college. From that point on, most people move out from their parents' home and get a place of their own. You are no longer under your parents' authority, but you should continue to show them honor and respect all your life.

<sup>21</sup>The men had gone without food for a long time. Then one day Paul stood up before them and said, "Men, I told you not to leave Crete. You should have listened to me. Then you would not have all this trouble and loss. <sup>22</sup>But now I tell you to cheer up. None of you will die! But the ship will be lost. <sup>23</sup>Last night an angel from God came to me. This is the God I worship. I am his. <sup>24</sup>God's angel said, 'Paul, do not be afraid! You must stand before Caesar.<sup>d</sup> And God has given you this promise: He will save the lives of all those men sailing with you.' <sup>25</sup>So men, be cheerful! I trust in God. Everything will happen as his angel told me. <sup>26</sup>But we will crash on an island."

<sup>27</sup>On the fourteenth night we were floating around in the Adriatic Sea.<sup>n</sup> The sailors thought we were close to land. <sup>28</sup>They threw a rope into the water with a weight on the end of it. They found that the water was 120 feet deep. They went a little farther and threw the rope in again. It was 90 feet deep. <sup>29</sup>The sailors were afraid that we would hit the rocks, so they threw four anchors into the water. Then they prayed for daylight to come. <sup>30</sup>Some of the sailors wanted to leave the ship, and they lowered the lifeboat. These sailors wanted the other men to think that they were throwing more anchors from the front of the ship.

<sup>31</sup>But Paul told the officer and the other soldiers, "If these men do not stay in the ship, your lives cannot be saved!" <sup>32</sup>So the soldiers cut the ropes and let the lifeboat fall into the water.

<sup>33</sup>Just before dawn Paul began persuading all the people to eat something. He said, "For the past 14 days you have been waiting and watching. You have not eaten. <sup>34</sup>Now I beg you to eat something. You need it to stay alive. None of you will lose even one hair off your heads." <sup>35</sup>After he said this, Paul took some bread and thanked God for it before all of them. He broke off a piece and began eating. <sup>36</sup>All the men felt better. They all started eating too. <sup>37</sup>(There were 276 people on the ship.) <sup>38</sup>We ate all we wanted. Then we began making the ship lighter by throwing the grain into the sea.

### THE SHIP IS DESTROYED

<sup>39</sup>When daylight came, the sailors saw land. They did not know what land it was, but they saw a bay with a beach. They wanted to sail the ship to the beach, if they could. <sup>40</sup>So they cut the ropes to the anchors and left the anchors in the sea. At the same time, they untied the ropes that were holding the rudders. Then they raised the front sail into the wind and sailed toward the beach. <sup>41</sup>But the ship hit a sandbank. The front of the ship stuck there and could not move. Then the big waves began to break the back of the ship to pieces.

<sup>42</sup>The soldiers decided to kill the prisoners so that none of them could swim away and escape. <sup>43</sup>But Julius, the officer, wanted to let Paul live. He did not allow the soldiers to kill the prisoners. Instead he ordered everyone who could swim to jump into the water and swim to land. <sup>44</sup>The rest used wooden boards or pieces of the ship. And this is how all the people made it safely to land.

### PAUL ON THE ISLAND OF MALTA

**28** When we were safe on land, we learned that the island was called Malta. <sup>2</sup>It was raining and very cold. But the people who lived there were very good to us. They made us a fire and welcomed all of us. <sup>3</sup>Paul gathered a pile of sticks for the fire. He was putting them on the fire when a poisonous snake came out because of the heat and bit him on the hand. <sup>4</sup>The people living on the island saw the snake hanging from Paul's hand. They said to each other, "This man must be a murderer! He did not die in the sea, but Justice<sup>n</sup> does not want him to live."

> **"An angel from God came to me. This is the God I worship. I am his."** *Acts 27:23*

<sup>27:27</sup> **Adriatic Sea** The sea between Greece and Italy, including the central Mediterranean. <sup>28:4</sup> **Justice** The people thought there was a god named Justice who would punish bad people.

God's got a plan to save us!

Paul's longest letter.

Written by Paul, the former persecutor, during his third big mission trip.

# The Letter of Paul the Apostle to the ROMANS

Rome was the greatest city in the world.

Phoebe, one of the first Christian believers, delivered this letter to Rome.

Over one million people lived in Rome.

Key words: Good News!

⁵But Paul shook the snake off into the fire. He was not hurt. ⁶The people thought that Paul would swell up or fall down dead. The people waited and watched him for a long time, but nothing bad happened to him. So they changed their minds about Paul. Now they said, "He is a god!"

⁷There were some fields around there owned by a very important man on the island. His name was Publius. He welcomed us into his home and was very good to us. We stayed in his house for three days. ⁸Publius' father was very sick with a fever and dysentery.ⁿ But Paul went to him and prayed. Then he put his hands on the man and healed him. ⁹After this, all the other sick people on the island came to Paul, and he healed them, too. ¹⁰⁻¹¹The people on the island gave us many honors. We stayed there three months. When we were ready to leave, they gave us the things we needed.

## "Paul spoke to them all day long, explaining the kingdom of God to them."

*Acts 28:23*

### PAUL GOES TO ROME

We got on a ship from Alexandria. The ship had stayed on the island during the winter. On the front of the ship was the sign of the twin gods.ⁿ ¹²We stopped at Syracuse for three days and then left. ¹³From there we sailed to Rhegium. The next day a wind began to blow from the southwest, so we were able to leave. A day later we came to Puteoli. ¹⁴We found some believers there, and they asked us to stay with them for a week. Finally, we came to Rome. ¹⁵The believers in Rome heard that we were there. They came out as far as the Market of Appiusⁿ and the Three Innsⁿ to meet us. When Paul saw them, he was encouraged and thanked God.

### PAUL IN ROME

¹⁶Then we arrived at Rome. There, Paul was allowed to live alone. But a soldier stayed with him to guard him.

¹⁷Three days later Paul sent for the Jewish leaders there. When they came together, he said, "Brothers, I have done nothing against our people. I have done nothing against the customs of our fathers. But I was arrested in Jerusalem and given to the Romans. ¹⁸The Romans asked me many questions. But they could find no reason why I should be killed. They wanted to let me go free, ¹⁹but the Jews there did not want that. So I had to ask to come to Rome to have my trial before Caesar.ᵈ But I have no charge to bring against my own people. ²⁰That is why I wanted to see you and talk with you. I am bound with this chain because I believe in the hope of Israel."

²¹The Jews answered Paul, "We have received no letters from Judea about you. None of our Jewish brothers who have come from there brought news about you or told us anything bad about you. ²²We want to hear your ideas. We know that people everywhere are speaking against this religious group."

²³Paul and the Jews chose a day for a meeting. On that day many more of the Jews met with Paul at the place he was staying. Paul spoke to them all day long, explaining the kingdom of God to them. He tried to persuade them to believe these things about Jesus. He used the law of Moses and the writings of the prophetsᵈ to do this. ²⁴Some of the Jews believed what Paul said, but others did not. ²⁵So they argued, and the Jews were ready to leave. But Paul said one more thing to them: "The Holy Spiritᵈ spoke the truth to your fathers through Isaiah the prophet. He said, ²⁶'Go to this people and say:

You will listen and listen, but you
    will not understand.
  You will look and look, but you
      will not learn.
²⁷For these people have become
    stubborn.
  They don't hear with their ears.
  And they have closed their eyes.
Otherwise, they might really
    understand
  what they see with their eyes
  and hear with their ears.
They might really understand in
    their minds.
If they did this, they would come
    back to me and be forgiven.'

*Isaiah 6:9-10*

²⁸"I want you Jews to know that God has also sent his salvation to the non-Jewish people. They will listen!" ²⁹ⁿ

³⁰Paul stayed two full years in his own rented house. He welcomed all people who came and visited him. ³¹He preached about the kingdom of God and taught about the Lord Jesus Christ. He was very bold, and no one tried to stop him from speaking.

**28:8 dysentery** A sickness like diarrhea. **28:10-11 twin gods** Statues of Castor and Pollux, gods in old Greek tales. **28:15 Market of Appius** A town about 27 miles from Rome. **28:15 Three Inns** A town about 30 miles from Rome. **28:29 Verse 29** Some late Greek copies add verse 29: "After Paul said this, the Jews left. They were arguing very much with each other."

## DECODE THIS!

*While on the island of Malta, Paul was bitten on the hand by what?*

# LIVIN' IT!

## BRAVE HEART
## ROMANS 1:16

The moment has come. Your friends, who don't believe in Jesus, finally ask, "What's all the Christian stuff you believe? Why are you always going to church? Do you really believe all that made-up junk?"

You might get nervous. Maybe feel angry. Most likely a little afraid. What will they think? God says in Romans 1:16 not to worry about what others think of your faith. Be bold and tell them exactly why you believe Jesus is the Son of God and why you believe what you do. God says his truth is so powerful it can change even the hardest hearts. You may be really surprised by how they respond. Remember, when you are sharing your faith, you don't need to be embarrassed. You alone have the words of hope that can save your friends' lives. So speak up!

**1** From Paul, a servant of Christ Jesus. God called me to be an apostle[d] and chose me to tell the Good News.[d] ²God promised this Good News long ago through his prophets.[d] That promise is written in the Holy Scriptures.[d] ³⁻⁴The Good News is about God's Son, Jesus Christ our Lord. As a man, he was born from the family of David. But through the Spirit[d] of holiness he was appointed to be God's Son with great power by rising from death. ⁵Through Christ, God gave me the special work of an apostle. This was to lead people of all nations to believe and obey. I do this work for Christ. ⁶And you who are in Rome are also called to belong to Jesus Christ.

⁷This letter is to all of you in Rome whom God loves and has called to be his holy people.

May God our Father and the Lord Jesus Christ show you kindness and give you peace.

## A PRAYER OF THANKS

⁸First I want to say that I thank my God through Jesus Christ for all of you. I thank God because people everywhere in the world are talking about your great faith. ⁹⁻¹⁰God knows that every time I pray I always mention you. God is the One I serve with my whole heart by telling the Good News[d] about his Son. I pray that I will be allowed to come to you, and this will happen if God wants it. ¹¹I want very much to see you, to give you some spiritual gift to make you strong. ¹²I mean that I want us to help each other with the faith that we have. Your faith will help me, and my faith will help you. ¹³Brothers, I want you to know that I planned many times to come to you. But this has not been possible. I wanted to come so that I could help you grow spiritually. I wanted to help you as I have helped the other non-Jewish people.

¹⁴I must serve all people—Greeks and non-Greeks, the wise and the foolish. ¹⁵That is why I want so much to preach the Good News to you in Rome.

¹⁶I am proud of the Good News. It is the power God uses to save everyone who believes—to save the Jews first, and also to save the non-Jews. ¹⁷The Good News shows how God makes people right with himself. God's way of making people right with him begins and ends with faith. As the Scripture[d] says, "The person who is made right with God by faith will live forever."[n]

## ALL PEOPLE HAVE DONE WRONG

¹⁸God's anger is shown from heaven against all the evil and wrong things that people do. By their own evil lives they hide the truth. ¹⁹God shows his anger because everything that may be known about God has been made clear. Yes, God has clearly shown them everything that may be known about him. ²⁰There are things about God that people cannot see—his eternal power and all the things that make him God. But since the beginning of the world those things have been easy to understand. They are made clear by what God has made. So people have no excuse for the bad things they do. ²¹They knew God. But they did not give glory to God, and they did not thank him. Their thinking became useless. Their foolish minds were filled with darkness. ²²They said they were wise, but they became fools. ²³They gave up the glory of God who lives forever. They traded that glory for the worship of idols made to look like earthly people. They traded God's glory for things that look like birds, animals, and snakes.

²⁴People were full of sin, wanting only to do evil. So God let them go their sinful way. They became full of sexual sin, using their bodies wrongly with each other. ²⁵They traded the truth of God for a lie and worshiped and served things that were made by man. But they did

1:17 "The person . . . forever." Quotation from Habakkuk 2:4.

## DECODE THIS!

*Who wrote the book of Romans?*

not worship and serve the God who made those things. God should be praised forever. Amen.

[26]Because people did those things, God left them and let them do the shameful things they wanted to do. Women stopped having natural sex and started having sex with other women. [27]In the same way, men stopped having natural sex and began wanting each other. Men did shameful things with other men. And in their bodies they received the punishment for those wrongs.

[28]People did not think it was important to have a true knowledge of God. So God left them and allowed them to have their own worthless thinking. And so those people do the things that they should not do. [29]They are filled with every kind of sin, evil, selfishness, and hatred. They are full of jealousy, murder, fighting, lying, and thinking the worst about each other. They gossip [30]and say evil things about each other. They hate God. They are rude and conceited and brag about themselves. They invent ways of doing evil. They do not obey their parents. [31]They are foolish, they do not keep their promises, and they show no kindness or mercy to other people. [32]They know God's law says that those who live like this should die. But they continue to do these evil things. And they also feel that those who do these things are doing right.

### YOU PEOPLE ALSO ARE SINFUL

**2** If you think that you can judge others, then you are wrong. You too are guilty of sin. You judge people, but you do the same bad things they do. So when you judge them, you are really judging yourself guilty. [2]God judges those who do wrong things. And we know that God's judging is right. [3]You judge those

who do wrong, but you do wrong yourselves. Do you think you will be able to escape the judgment of God? [4]God has been very kind to you, and he has been patient with you. God has been waiting for you to change. But you think nothing of his kindness. Perhaps you do not understand that God is kind to you so that you will change your hearts and lives. [5]But you are hard and stubborn and refuse to change. So you are making your own punishment greater and greater on the day God shows his anger. On that day all people will see God's right judgments. [6]God will reward or punish every person for what he has done. [7]Some people live for God's glory, for honor, and for life that has no end. They live for those things by always continuing to do good. God will give life forever to them. [8]But other people are selfish and refuse to follow truth. They follow evil. God will give them his punishment and anger. [9]He will give trouble and suffering to everyone who does evil—to the Jews first and also to the non-Jews. [10]But God will give glory, honor, and peace to everyone who does good—to the Jews first and also to the non-Jews. [11]For God judges all people in the same way.

[12]People who have God's law and those who have never heard of the law are all the same when they sin. Those who do not have the law and are sinners will be lost. And, in the same way, people who have the law and are sinners will be judged by the law. [13]Hearing the law does not make people right with God. The law makes people right with God only if they obey what the law says. [14](The non-Jews do not have the law. But when they freely do things that the law commands, then they are the law for themselves. This is true even though they do not have the law. [15]They show that in their hearts they know what is right and wrong, just as the law commands. And they also show this by the way they feel about right and wrong. Sometimes their thoughts tell them they did wrong. And sometimes their thoughts tell them they did right.) [16]All these things will happen on the day when God will judge the secret thoughts of people's hearts. The Good News[d] that I preach says that God will judge everyone through Christ Jesus.

### THE JEWS AND THE LAW

[17]What about you? You call yourself a Jew. You trust in the law of Moses and brag that you are close to God. [18]You

## GET CONNECTED

### THE CURE

If your friend had a terrible disease and was about to die, and you had the medicine that would cure him, would you give it to him? Of course!

Right now, all around us, the world is dying. People don't know or believe in Jesus, and they are headed for eternal life in hell apart from God. But we have the cure. We can tell them that God has made a way to beat eternal death—by trusting in his Son. We don't need to be scared or embarrassed by telling them the truth because we know if they listen, their very lives will be saved. Who do you need to share with today? Pray for them, and tell them God's truth in love.

## DECODE THIS!
*God does what to all people in the same way?*

know what God wants you to do. And you know the things that are important because you have learned the law. [19]You think you are a guide for the blind and a light for those who are in darkness. [20]You think you can show foolish people what is right and teach those who know nothing. You have the law; so you think you know everything and have all truth. [21]You teach other people. So why don't you teach yourself? You tell others not to steal. But you yourselves steal. [22]You say that others must not take part in adultery.[d] But you yourselves are guilty of that sin. You hate idols. But you steal from temples. [23]You brag about having God's law. But you bring shame to God by breaking his law. [24]It is written in the Scriptures:[d] "The non-Jews speak against God's name because of you Jews."[n]

[25]If you follow the law, then your circumcision[d] has meaning. But if you break the law, then it is as if you were never circumcised. [26]The non-Jews are not circumcised. But if they do what the law says, then it is as if they were circumcised. [27]You Jews have the written law and circumcision, but you break the law. So those who are not circumcised in their bodies, but still obey the law, will show that you are guilty.

[28]A person is not a true Jew if he is only a Jew in his physical body. True circumcision is not only on the outside of the body. [29]A person is a true Jew only if he is a Jew inside. True circumcision is done in the heart by the Spirit,[d] not by the written law. Such a person gets praise from God, not from other people.

**3** So, do Jews have anything that other people do not have? Is there

---

# LIVIN' IT!

## A COMMON PROBLEM
## ROMANS 3:23

Have you ever wondered why the Bible makes such a fuss about sin? Sure, there are those people in the world who murder, or kidnap, or do some other major thing—but some people seem to be pretty good. They may mess up once in awhile, but by comparison, they are sweet and nice and don't seem like the kind of people God would consider as complete sinners, deserving of death.

But he does. Romans 3:23 says plainly that every person is a sinner who deserves death. So we can quit trying to *earn* God's love and forgiveness—it simply can't be done. The good news, though, is that Jesus takes away the guilt of our sins if we repent and believe in his promise.

---

anything special about being circumcised? [2]Yes, of course, there is in every way. The most important thing is this: God trusted the Jews with his teachings. [3]It is true that some Jews were not faithful to God. But will that stop God from doing what he promised? [4]No! God will continue to be true even when every person is false. As the Scriptures[d] say:

"So your words may be shown to be right.
You are fair when you judge me."
*Psalm 51:4*

[5]When we do wrong, that shows more clearly that God is right. So can we say that God is wrong to punish us? (I am talking as men might talk.) [6]No! If God could not punish us, then God could not judge the world.

[7]A person might say, "When I lie, it really gives God glory, because my lie shows God's truth. So why am I judged

a sinner?" [8]It would be the same to say, "We should do evil so that good will come." Some people find fault with us and say that we teach this. Those who say such things about us are wrong, and they should be punished.

## ALL PEOPLE ARE GUILTY

[9]So are we Jews better than others? No! We have already said that Jews and non-Jews are the same. They are all guilty of sin. [10]As the Scriptures[d] say:
"There is no one without sin. None!
[11] There is no one who understands.
There is no one who looks to God for help.
[12]All have turned away.
Together, everyone has become evil.
None of them does anything good."
*Psalm 14:1-3*
[13]"Their throats are like open graves.
They use their tongues for telling lies."
*Psalm 5:9*
"Their words are like snake's poison."
*Psalm 140:3*
[14] "Their mouths are full of cursing and hate."
*Psalm 10:7*
[15]"They are always ready to kill people.
[16] Everywhere they go they cause ruin and misery.
[17]They don't know how to live in peace."
*Isaiah 59:7-8*
[18] "They have no fear of or respect for God."
*Psalm 36:1*
[19]The law commands many things. We know that those commands are for those who are under the law. This stops all excuses and brings the whole world under God's judgment, [20]because no one can be made right with God by following the law. The law only shows us our sin.

## HOW GOD MAKES PEOPLE RIGHT

[21]But God has a way to make people right with him without the law. And God has now shown us that way which the

---

2:24 "The non-Jews . . . Jews." Quotation from Isaiah 52:5; Ezekiel 36:20.

law and the prophets[d] told us about. [22]God makes people right with himself through their faith in Jesus Christ. This is true for all who believe in Christ, because all are the same. [23]All people have sinned and are not good enough for God's glory. [24]People are made right with God by his grace, which is a free gift. They are made right with God by being made free from sin through Jesus Christ. [25]God gave Jesus as a way to forgive sin through faith. And all of this is because of the blood of Jesus' death. This showed that God always does what is right and fair. God was right in the past when he was patient and did not punish people for their sins. [26]And God gave Jesus to show today that God does what is right. God did this so that he could judge rightly and also make right any person who has faith in Jesus.

[27]So do we have a reason to brag about ourselves? No! And why not? It is the way of faith that stops all bragging, not the way of following the law. [28]A person is made right with God through faith, not through what he does to follow the law. [29]Is God only the God of the Jews? Is he not also the God of the non-Jews? [30]Of course he is, for there is only one God. He will make Jews right with him by their faith. And he will also make non-Jews right with him through their faith. [31]So do we destroy the law by following the way of faith? No! Faith causes us to be what the law truly wants.

## THE EXAMPLE OF ABRAHAM

**4** So what can we say about Abraham,[n] the father of our people? What did he learn about faith? [2]If Abraham was made right by the things he did, then he had a reason to brag. But he could not brag before God. [3]The Scripture[d] says, "Abraham believed God. And that faith made him right with God."[n]

[4]When a person works, his pay is not given to him as a gift. He earns the pay he gets. [5]But a person cannot do any work that will make him right with God. So he must trust in God. Then God accepts his faith, and that makes him right with God. God is the One who can make even those who are evil right in his sight. [6]David said the same thing. He said that a person is truly blessed when God does not look at what he has done but accepts him as good:

[7]"Happy are they
whose sins are forgiven,
whose wrongs are pardoned.
[8]Happy is the person
whom the Lord does not consider
guilty."                    *Psalm 32:1-2*

[9]Is this blessing only for those who are circumcised?[d] Or is it also for those who are not circumcised?

We have already said that God accepted Abraham's faith, and that faith made him right with God. [10]So how did this happen? Did God accept Abraham before or after he was circumcised? God accepted him before his circumcision. [11]Abraham was circumcised later to show that God accepted him. His circumcision was proof that he was right with God through faith before he was circumcised. So Abraham is the father of all those who believe but are not circumcised. He is the father of all believers who are accepted as being right with God. [12]And Abraham is also the father of those who have been circumcised. But it is not their circumcision that makes him their father. He is their father only if they live following the faith that our father Abraham had before he was circumcised.

## GOD KEEPS HIS PROMISE

[13]Abraham[n] and his descendants[d] received the promise that they would get the whole world. But Abraham did not receive that promise through the law. He received it because he was right with God through his faith. [14]If people could receive what God promised by following the law, then faith is worthless. And God's promise to Abraham is worthless, [15]because the law can only bring God's anger. But if there is no law, then there is nothing to disobey.

[16]So people receive God's promise by having faith. This happens so that the promise can be a free gift. And if the promise is a free gift, then all of Abraham's children can have that promise. The promise is not only for those people that live under the law of Moses. It is for anyone who lives with faith like

---

## LIVIN' IT!

### HAPPY ENDINGS
### ROMANS 3:24

Because God is perfect, he can't mix with even the smallest sin. A price must be paid to forgive the sin. That's why everyone needs a Savior. Jesus, who was fully God and fully man, is the only One who has ever lived a perfect life—which is why his death made the perfect sacrifice for our sins.

God's gift of forgiveness is absolutely free through Jesus. We must simply repent from our sins and believe that Jesus has the power to forgive us. Then we trust that God has done what he promised to do: forgive us. We become a part of his family and can know for sure that we have a place in heaven.

---

## DECODE THIS!

*How does God make people right with him?*

---

**4:1, 13 Abraham** Most respected ancestor of the Jews. Every Jew hoped to see Abraham.
**4:3 "Abraham . . . God."** Quotation from Genesis 15:6.

# 10 TOP TEN

## Favorite Bible Songs

1. Heaven Is a Wonderful Place
2. Onward Christian Soldiers
3. Shout to the Lord
4. Jesus Loves Me
5. Amazing Grace
6. The Crayon Song
7. Holy, Holy, Holy
8. When I Survey
9. I Can Only Imagine
10. I Love You, Lord

Abraham. He is the father of us all. [17]As it is written in the Scriptures:[d] "I am making you a father of many nations."[n] This is true before God. Abraham believed in God—the God who gives life to the dead and decides that things will happen that have not yet happened.

[18]There was no hope that Abraham would have children. But Abraham believed God and continued hoping. And that is why he became the father of many nations. As God told him, "Your descendants will also be too many to count."[n] [19]Abraham was almost 100 years old, much past the age for having children. Also, Sarah could not have children. Abraham thought about all this. But his faith in God did not become weak. [20]He never doubted that God would keep his promise. Abraham never stopped believing. He grew stronger in his faith and gave praise to God. [21]Abraham felt sure that God was able to do the thing that God promised. [22]So, "God accepted Abraham's faith, and that made him right with God."[n] [23]Those words ("God accepted Abraham's faith") were written not only for Abraham. [24]They were written also for us. God will accept us also because we believe. We believe in the One who raised Jesus our Lord from death. [25]Jesus was given to die for our sins. And he was raised from death to make us right with God.

## RIGHT WITH GOD

**5** We have been made right with God because of our faith. So we have peace with God through our Lord Jesus Christ. [2]Through our faith, Christ has brought us into that blessing of God's grace that we now enjoy. And we are happy because of the hope we have of sharing God's glory. [3]And we also have joy with our troubles because we know that these troubles produce patience. [4]And patience produces character, and character produces hope. [5]And this hope will never disappoint us, because God has poured out his love to fill our hearts. God gave us his love through the Holy Spirit,[d] whom God has given to us.

[6]Christ died for us while we were still weak. We were living against God, but at the right time, Christ died for us. [7]Very few people will die to save the life of someone else. Although perhaps for a good man someone might possibly die. [8]But Christ died for us while we were still sinners. In this way God shows his great love for us.

[9]We have been made right with God by the blood of Christ's death. So through Christ we will surely be saved from God's anger. [10]I mean that while we were God's enemies, God made friends with us through the death of his Son. Surely, now that we are God's friends, God will save us through his Son's life. [11]And not only that, but now we are also very happy in God through our Lord Jesus Christ. Through Jesus we are now God's friends again.

## ADAM AND CHRIST

[12]Sin came into the world because of what one man did. And with sin came death. And this is why all men must die—because all men sinned. [13]Sin was in the world before the law of Moses. But God does not judge people guilty of sin if there is no law. [14]But from the time of Adam to the time of Moses, everyone had to die. Adam died because he sinned by not obeying God's command. But even those who did not sin in the same way had to die.

Adam was like the One who was coming in the future. [15]But God's free gift is not like Adam's sin. Many people died because of the sin of that one man. But the grace that they received from God was much greater. Many people received God's gift of life by the grace of the one man, Jesus Christ. [16]After Adam sinned once, he was judged guilty. But the gift of God is different. God's free gift came after many sins. And the gift makes people right with God. [17]One man sinned, and so death ruled all people because of that one man. But now some people accept God's full grace and the great gift of being made right with him. They will surely have true life and rule through the one man, Jesus Christ.

[18]So one sin of Adam brought the punishment of death to all people. But in the same way, one good act that Christ did makes all people right with God.

 4:17 "I . . . nations." Quotation from Genesis 17:5. 4:18 "Your . . . count." Quotation from Genesis 15:5. 4:22 "God . . . God." Quotation from Genesis 15:6.

219

And that brings true life for all. [19]One man disobeyed God, and many became sinners. But in the same way, one man obeyed God, and many will be made right. [20]The law came to make people have more sin. But when people had more sin, God gave them more of his grace. [21]Sin once used death to rule us. But God gave people more of his grace so that grace could rule by making people right with him. And this brings life forever through Jesus Christ our Lord.

## BiBLe BasiCS

### wHat is sin?

The word *sin* means to "miss the mark"—just like when you practice shooting a target and miss the bull's-eye. When we do, say, or think anything that goes against what God wants us to do, we have sinned. We have also sinned if God does want us to do something (like tell others about Jesus), but we don't do it. The first is called a sin of "commission," and the second is a sin of "omission," but either way, sin is simply disobeying God.

### DEAD TO SIN BUT ALIVE IN CHRIST

**6** So do you think that we should continue sinning so that God will give us more and more grace? [2]No! We died to our old sinful lives. So how can we continue living with sin? [3]Did you forget that all of us became part of Christ when we were baptized? We shared his death in our baptism. [4]So when we were baptized, we were buried with Christ and shared his death. We were buried with him so that we could live a new life, just as Christ was raised from death by the wonderful power of the Father.

[5]Christ died, and we have been joined with Christ by dying too. So we will also be joined with him by rising from death as he did. [6]We know that our old life died with Christ on the cross. This was so that our sinful selves would have no power over us, and we would not be slaves to sin. [7]Anyone who has died is made free from sin's control.

[8]If we died with Christ, we know that we will also live with him. [9]Christ was raised from death. And we know that he cannot die again. Death has no power over him now. [10]Yes, when Christ died, he died to defeat the power of sin one time—enough for all time. He now has a new life, and his new life is with God. [11]In the same way, you should see yourselves as being dead to the power of sin and alive with God through Christ Jesus.

[12]So, do not let sin control you in your life here on earth. You must not be ruled by the things your sinful self makes you want to do. [13]Do not offer the parts of your body to serve sin. Do not use your bodies as things to do evil with, but offer yourselves to God. Be like people who have died and now live. Offer the parts of your body to God to be used for doing good. [14]Sin will not be your master, because you are not under law but under God's grace.

### SLAVES OF RIGHTEOUSNESS

[15]So what should we do? Should we sin because we are under grace and not under law? No! [16]Surely you know that when you give yourselves like slaves to obey someone, then you are really slaves of that person. The person you obey is your master. You can follow sin, or obey God. Sin brings spiritual

death. But obeying God makes you right with him. [17]In the past you were slaves to sin—sin controlled you. But thank God, you fully obeyed the things that were taught to you. [18]You were made free from sin, and now you are slaves to goodness. [19]I use this example because this is hard for you to understand. In the past you offered the parts of your body to be slaves to sin and evil. You lived only for evil. In the same way now you must give yourselves to be slaves of goodness. Then you will live only for God.

[20]In the past you were slaves to sin, and goodness did not control you. [21]You did evil things, and now you are ashamed of them. Those things only bring death. [22]But now you are free from sin and have become slaves of God. This brings you a life that is only for God. And this gives you life forever. [23]When someone sins, he earns what sin pays—death. But God gives us a free gift—life forever in Christ Jesus our Lord.

### AN EXAMPLE FROM MARRIAGE

**7** Brothers, all of you understand the law of Moses. So surely you know that the law rules over a person only while he is alive. [2]For example, a woman must stay married to her husband as long as he is alive. But if her husband dies, then she is free from the law of marriage. [3]But if she marries another man while her husband is still alive, the law says she is guilty of adultery.[d] But if her husband dies, then the woman is free from the law of marriage. So if she marries another man after her husband dies, she is not guilty of adultery.

[4]In the same way, my brothers, your old selves died, and you became free from the law through the body of Christ. Now you belong to someone else. You belong to the One who was raised from death. We belong to Christ so that we can be used in service to

God. [5]In the past, we were ruled by our sinful selves. The law made us want to do sinful things. And those sinful things we wanted to do controlled our bodies, so that the things we did were only bringing us death. [6]In the past, the law held us like prisoners. But our old selves died, and we were made free from the law. So now we serve God in a new way, not in the old way with written rules. Now we serve God in the new way, with the Spirit.[d]

## OUR FIGHT AGAINST SIN

[7]You might think that I am saying that sin and the law are the same thing. That is not true. But the law was the only way I could learn what sin meant. I would never have known what it means to want something wrong if the law had not said, "You must not want to take your neighbor's things."[n] [8]And sin found a way to use that command and cause me to want every kind of wrong thing. So sin came to me because of that command. But without the law, sin has no power. [9]I was alive without the law before I knew the law. But when the law's command came to me, then sin began to live. [10]And I died because of sin. The command was meant to bring life, but for me that command brought death. [11]Sin found a way to fool me by using the command. Sin used the command to make me die.

[12]So the law is holy, and the command is holy and right and good. [13]Does this mean that something that is good brought death to me? No! Sin used something that is good to bring death to me. This happened so that I could see what sin is really like. The command was used to show that sin is something very evil.

## THE WAR WITHIN MAN

[14]We know that the law is spiritual. But I am not spiritual. Sin rules me as if I were its slave. [15]I do not understand the things I do. I do not do the good things I want to do. And I do the bad things I hate to do. [16]And if I do not want to do the bad things I do, then that means that I agree that the law is good. [17]But I am not really the one who is doing these bad things. It is sin living in me that does these things. [18]Yes, I know that nothing good lives in me— I mean nothing good lives in the part of me that is earthly and sinful. I want to do the things that are good. But I do not do them. [19]I do not do the good things that I want to do. I do the bad things that I do not want to do. [20]So if I do things I do not want to do, then I am not the one doing those things. It is sin living in me that does those bad things.

[21]So I have learned this rule: When I want to do good, evil is there with me. [22]In my mind, I am happy with God's law. [23]But I see another law working in my body. That law makes war against the law that my mind accepts. That other law working in my body is the law of sin, and that law makes me its prisoner. [24]What a miserable man I am! Who will save me from this body that brings me death? [25]God will. I thank him for saving me through Jesus Christ our Lord!

So in my mind I am a slave to God's law. But in my sinful self I am a slave to the law of sin.

## LIFE IN THE SPIRIT

**8** So now, those who are in Christ Jesus are not judged guilty. [2]I am not judged guilty because in Christ Jesus the law of the Spirit[d] that brings life made me free. It made me free from the law that brings sin and death. [3]The law was without power, because the law was made weak by our sinful selves. But God did what the law could not do. He sent his own Son to earth with the same human life that others use for sin. He sent his Son to be an offering to pay for sin. So God used a human life to destroy sin. [4]He did this so that we could be right as the law said we must be. Now we do not live following our sinful selves, but we live following the Spirit.

[5]Those who live following their sinful selves think only about things that their sinful selves want. But those who

### Decode this!

*Trouble produces patience; patience produces character; character produces* _____

7:7 "You . . . things." Quotation from Exodus 20:13, 15–17.

221

# BIBLE TRIVIA

## ACROSS:

1. A link to God
2. First book of the NT
3. Another word for love
4. Rejected Jesus and the resurrection
5. Worth selling all you have to buy it
6. What Christians are
7. Another word for believer

## DOWN:

1. Loving it is evil
2. What we owe God
3. It was with God and was God
4. Ministering spirits
5. Don't let the sun go down on it
6. What Satan is
7. Another word for disciple

live following the Spirit are thinking about the things that the Spirit wants them to do. [6]If a person's thinking is controlled by his sinful self, then there is death. But if his thinking is controlled by the Spirit, then there is life and peace. [7]This is true because if a person's thinking is controlled by his sinful self, then he is against God. He refuses to obey God's law. And really he is not able to obey God's law. [8]Those people who are ruled by their sinful selves cannot please God.

[9]But you are not ruled by your sinful selves. You are ruled by the Spirit, if that Spirit of God really lives in you. But if anyone does not have the Spirit of Christ, then he does not belong to Christ. [10]Your body will always be dead because of sin. But if Christ is in you, then the Spirit gives you life, because Christ made you right with God. [11]God raised Jesus from death. And if God's Spirit is living in you, then he will also give life to your bodies that die. God is the One who raised Christ from death. And he will give life through his Spirit that lives in you.

[12]So, my brothers, we must not be ruled by our sinful selves. We must not live the way our sinful selves want. [13]If you use your lives to do the wrong things your sinful selves want, then you will die spiritually. But if you use the Spirit's help to stop doing the wrong things you do with your body, then you will have true life.

[14]The true children of God are those who let God's Spirit lead them. [15]The Spirit that we received is not a spirit that makes us slaves again to fear. The Spirit that we have makes us children of God. And with that Spirit we say, "Father, dear Father."[n] [16]And the Spirit himself joins with our spirits to say that we are God's children. [17]If we are God's children, then we will receive the blessings God has for us. We will receive these things from God together with Christ. But we must suffer as Christ suffered, and then we will have glory as Christ has glory.

## OUR FUTURE GLORY

[18]We have sufferings now. But the sufferings we have now are nothing compared to the great glory that will be given to us. [19]Everything that God made is waiting with excitement for the time when God will show the world who his children are. The whole world wants very much for that to happen. [20]Everything that God made was changed to become useless. This was not by its own wish. It happened because God wanted it. But there was this hope: [21]that everything God made would be set free from ruin. There was hope that everything God made would have the freedom and glory that belong to God's children.

[22]We know that everything God made has been waiting until now in pain, like a woman ready to give birth. [23]Not only the world, but we also have been waiting with pain inside us. We have the Spirit[d] as the first part of God's promise. So we are waiting for God to finish making us his own children. I mean we are waiting for our bodies to be made free. [24]We were saved, and we have this hope. If we see what we are waiting for, then that is not really hope. People do not hope for some-thing they already have. [25]But we are hoping for something that we do not have yet. We are waiting for it patiently.

[26]Also, the Spirit helps us. We are very weak, but the Spirit helps us with our weakness. We do not know how to pray as we should. But the Spirit himself speaks to God for us, even begs God for us. The Spirit speaks to God with deep feelings that words cannot explain. [27]God can see what is in people's hearts. And he knows what is in the mind of the Spirit, because the Spirit speaks to God for his people in the way that God wants.

[28]We know that in everything God works for the good of those who love

### TALK IT OUT
### ROMANS 8:26

Prayer is kind of a weird thing. You're supposed to talk to someone you can't see and someone you barely understand. What on earth are you supposed to say?

Don't worry. God knows your heart, so you might as well tell him whatever's on it. But God also gives you help that you might not even know about. When you belong to Jesus, he puts his Holy Spirit inside you to help you understand God's Word better and to live the right kind of life. The Holy Spirit also prays for you. Even adults often don't know how to pray in a particular situation, but the Holy Spirit—who is God—knows God the Father's heart and knows exactly what to say. We can't hear his words, but we can trust God's promise that he is at work in us praying to God the right things we need to pray.

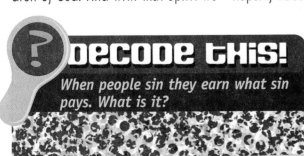

### DECODE THIS!

When people sin they earn what sin pays. What is it?

8:15 "Father, dear Father." Literally, "Abba, Father." Jewish children called their fathers "Abba."

him. They are the people God called, because that was his plan. [29]God knew them before he made the world. And God decided that they would be like his Son. Then Jesus would be the firstborn[n] of many brothers. [30]God planned for them to be like his Son. And those he planned to be like his Son, he also called. And those he called, he also made right with him. And those he made right, he also glorified.

## GOD'S LOVE IN CHRIST JESUS

[31]So what should we say about this? If God is with us, then no one can defeat us. [32]God let even his own Son suffer for us. God gave his Son for us all. So with Jesus, God will surely give us all things. [33]Who can accuse the people that God has chosen? No one! God is the One who makes them right. [34]Who can say that God's people are guilty? No one! Christ Jesus died, but that is not all. He was also raised from death. And now he is on God's right side and is begging God for us. [35]Can anything separate us from the love Christ has for us? Can troubles or problems or sufferings? If we have no food or clothes, if we are in danger, or even if death comes—can any of these things separate us from Christ's love? [36]As it is written in the Scriptures:[d]

"For you we are in danger of death
    all the time.
People think we are worth no
    more than sheep to be killed."

*Psalm 44:22*

[37]But in all these things we have full victory through God who showed his love for us. [38-39]Yes, I am sure that nothing can separate us from the love God has for us. Not death, not life, not angels, not ruling spirits, nothing now,

## THE ULTIMATE GLUE
### ROMANS 8:38

Do you ever wonder what the future holds for you? What will you look like when you are grown? Where will you live? What will you do? There are a lot of things that can change any moment in a person's life. But there is one thing that will always stay the same: God's love for you.

The Bible says that absolutely nothing in this life or this world will ever be able to separate God's love from his children. We are his, and there's nothing sin, Satan, or others can do to stop it! No matter what comes our way in this life, God will see to it that we are never taken from his hand. What an incredible thing to know you will always be loved!

nothing in the future, no powers, nothing above us, nothing below us, or anything else in the whole world will ever be able to separate us from the love of God that is in Christ Jesus our Lord.

## GOD AND THE JEWISH PEOPLE

**9** I am in Christ, and I am telling you the truth. I do not lie. My feelings are ruled by the Holy Spirit,[d] and they tell me that I am not lying. [2]I have great sorrow and always feel much sadness for the Jewish people. [3]I wish I could help my Jewish brothers, my people. I would even wish that I were cursed and cut off from Christ if that would help them. [4]They are the people of Israel. They were God's chosen children. They have the glory of God and the agreements that God

made between himself and his people. God gave them the law of Moses and the right way of worship. And God gave his promises to them. [5]They are the descendants[d] of our great ancestors, and they are the earthly family of Christ. Christ is God over all. Praise him forever!" Amen.

[6]I do not mean that God failed to keep his promise to them. But only some of the people of Israel are truly God's people.[n] [7]And only some of Abraham's[n] descendants are true children of Abraham. But God said to Abraham: "The descendants I promised you will be from Isaac."[n] [8]This means that not all of Abraham's descendants are God's true children. Abraham's true children are those who become God's children because of the promise God made to Abraham. [9]God's promise to Abraham was this: "At the right time I will return, and Sarah will have a son."[n] [10]And that is not all. Rebekah also had sons. And those sons had the same father, our father Isaac. [11-12]But before the two boys were born, God told Rebekah, "The older will serve the younger."[n] This was before the boys had done anything good or bad. God said this before they were born so that the one chosen would be chosen because of God's own plan. He was chosen because he was the one God wanted to call, not because of anything he did. [13]As the Scripture[d] says, "I loved Jacob, but I hated Esau."[n]

[14]So what should we say about this? Is God unfair? In no way. [15]God said to Moses, "I will show kindness to anyone I want to show kindness. I will show mercy to anyone I want to show

**8:29 firstborn** Here this probably means that Christ was the first in God's family to share God's glory. **9:5 Christ . . . forever!** This can also mean, "May God, who rules over all things, be praised forever!" **9:6 God's people** Literally, "Israel," the people God chose to bring his blessings to the world. **9:7 Abraham** Most respected ancestor of the Jews. Every Jew hoped to see Abraham. **9:7 "The descendants . . . Isaac."** Quotation from Genesis 21:12. **9:9 "At . . . son."** Quotation from Genesis 18:10, 14. **9:11-12 "The older . . . younger."** Quotation from Romans 25:23. **9:13 "I . . . Esau."** Quotation from Malachi 1:2-3.

## DECODE THIS!

*Those who are in Christ Jesus are not judged _____.*

# CHECK MATE

God tells us that we tend to become like the people we hang around. So what kind of friends do you have? Take this quiz to see if your friends are more likely to pull you up or pull you down.

**1.** Your closest friends
a. say they are Christians.
b. say and act like they are Christians.
c. don't claim to be Christians.

**2.** When you are with them, you usually talk about
a. sports.
b. TV.
c. other people.
d. God.
e. none of the above.

**3.** They go to church
a. all the time.
b. as often as they can.
c. rarely.
d. never.

**4.** The way they speak to their parents
a. honors and respects them.
b. makes their parents look silly.
c. disrespects them.
d. makes each seem like another kid.

**5.** If the teacher corrects them, they are most likely to
a. argue.
b. cry.
c. get angry.
d. obey.

**6.** If you get in a fight, your best friend will
a. tattle on you.
b. forgive you.
c. remember what you did wrong for a long time.
d. talk bad about you to others.

**7.** If you asked your friends to pray for you, they would
a. laugh.
b. look embarrassed.
c. say they will do it later.
d. pray for you right then.

**8.** Your best friend is _____ toward his/her siblings.
a. mean
b. ignorant
c. loving
d. competitive

**9.** You're sad. Your best friend is likely to
a. go play with someone in a good mood.
b. give you a hug.
c. try to make you laugh.
d. make fun of you.

**10.** You and your friend want to play different games. Your friend will most likely
a. insist on getting his/her way.
b. want to play his/her game first, then yours.
c. offer to play your game first.
d. leave.

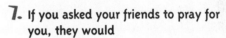

# Gotta Know!

## Why did God make sin?

God did not create sin. He created angels and people with the ability to choose between right and wrong. By creating creatures who could choose to love or not love God, he allowed sin to happen when they chose their own way instead of God's. Likewise, God does not ever *make* anyone sin. But he allows us to sin, if that's what we choose. The responsibility is ours, not God's.

mercy."[n] [16]So God will choose the one he decides to show mercy to. And his choice does not depend on what people want or try to do. [17]The Scripture says to the king of Egypt: "I made you king so I might show my power in you. In this way my name will be talked about in all the earth."[n] [18]So God shows mercy where he wants to show mercy. And he makes stubborn the people he wants to make stubborn.

[19]So one of you will ask me: "If God controls the things we do, then why does he blame us for our sins? Who can fight his will?" [20]Do not ask that. You are only human. And human beings have no right to question God. An object cannot tell the person who made it, "Why did you make me like this?" [21]The man who makes a jar can make anything he wants to make. He can use the same clay to make different things. He can make one thing for special use and another thing for daily use.

[22]It is the same way with what God has done. God wanted to show his anger and to let people see his power. But God patiently stayed with those people he was angry with—people who were ready to be destroyed. [23]God waited with patience so that he could make known his rich glory. He wanted to give that glory to the people who receive his mercy. He has prepared these people to have his glory, and [24]we are those people whom God called. He called us from the Jews and from the non-Jews. [25]As the Scripture says in Hosea:

"I will say, 'You are my people'
    to those I had called 'not my
    people.'
And I will show my love
    to those people I did not love."
                                *Hosea 2:1, 23*

[26]"Now it is said to Israel,
    'You are not my people.'
But later they will be called
    'children of the living God.'"
                                *Hosea 1:10*

[27]And Isaiah cries out about Israel:
"There are so many people of Israel.
    They are like the grains of sand
    by the sea.
But only a few of them will be saved.
[28]  For the Lord will quickly and
    completely punish the people
    on the earth."    *Isaiah 10:22-23*

[29]It is as Isaiah said:
"The Lord of heaven's armies
    allowed a few of our descendants
    to live.
Otherwise we would have been
    completely destroyed
    like the cities of Sodom and
    Gomorrah."[n]          *Isaiah 1:9*

[30]So what does all this mean? It means this: the non-Jews were not trying to make themselves right with God. But they were made right with God because of their faith. [31]And the people of Israel tried to follow a law to make themselves right with God. But they did not succeed, [32]because they tried to make themselves right by the things they did. They did not trust in God to make them right. They fell over the stone that causes people to fall. [33]As it is written in the Scripture:

"I will put in Jerusalem a stone that
    causes people to stumble.
It is a rock that makes them fall.
Anyone who trusts in him will not be
    disappointed."  *Isaiah 8:14; 28:16*

**10** Brothers, the thing I want most is for all the Jews to be saved. That is my prayer to God. [2]I can say this about them: They really try to follow God. But they do not know the right way. [3]They did not know the way that God makes people right with him. And they tried to make themselves right in their own way. So they did not accept God's way of making people right. [4]Christ ended the law, so that everyone who believes in him may be right with God.

[5]Moses writes about being made right by following the law. He says, "A person who does these things will have life

## "God shows mercy where he wants to show mercy." *Romans 9:18*

forever because of them."[n] [6]But this is what the Scripture says about being made right through faith: "Don't say to yourself, 'Who will go up into heaven?'" (That means, "Who will go up to heaven to get Christ and bring him down to earth?") [7]"And do not say, 'Who will go down into the world below?'" (That means, "Who will go down to get Christ and bring him up from death?") [8]This is what the Scripture

## DECODE THIS!

*God can see what is in people's*

**9:15** "I . . . mercy." Quotation from Exodus 33:19. **9:17** "I . . . earth." Quotation from Exodus 9:16. **9:29 Sodom and Gomorrah** Two cities that God destroyed because the people were so evil. **10:5** "A person . . . them." Quotation from Leviticus 18:5.

# AUGUST SELF-CONTROL

**1** Play a game of checkers with your younger sister, and let her win.

**2**

**3** Go shopping with your mom to pick out school clothes.

**4** PRAYER POINTER: Ask the Holy Spirit to fill you with his fruit.

**5**

**6** GALATIANS 5:16: So I tell you: Live by following the Spirit. Then you will not do what your sinful selves want.

**7**

**8** Go all day without watching TV.

**9** Make a list of all the things you want to do this coming school year.

**10**

**11** PRAYER POINTER: Pray that you and your friends will make decisions each day that bring glory to God.

**12**

**13** Call everyone from school, and have a party before school starts.

**14**

**15** GALATIANS 5:22-23: But the Spirit gives love, joy, peace, patience, kindness, goodness, faithfulness, gentleness, self-control.

**16**

**17** Write a story about your adventures this past summer.

**18**

**19** Prayer Pointer: Pray for you and your siblings to find joy in putting each other first.

**20**

**21** Lie on a blanket at night, and count shooting stars.

**22** 2 PETER 1:6: To your knowledge, add self-control; and to your self-control, add the ability to hold on; and to your ability to hold on, add service for God.

**23**

**24**

**25** See how many fireflies you can catch and put in a jar.

**26**

**27**

**28** PRAYER POINTER: Pray for the members in your church to grow in love for one another.

**29** Rent a funny movie, and watch it with your family.

**30**

**31**

The only temptations that you have are the temptations that all people have. But you can trust God. He will not let you be tempted more than you can stand (1 Corinthians 10:13).

## Gotta Know!

### Why do Christian friends do mean things sometimes?

Your Christian friends, just like you, are sinners. They belong to Jesus and can enjoy his forgiveness when they repent, but they still have a sin nature, and their jealousy or greed or whatever sin will eventually come out in the course of your friendship. God is still working in their hearts, too, so you have to be patient. Jesus says that no matter how many times people sin against us, we should forgive them because God always forgives us.

says: "God's teaching is near you; it is in your mouth and in your heart."[n] That is the teaching of faith that we tell. [9]If you use your mouth to say, "Jesus is Lord," and if you believe in your heart that God raised Jesus from death, then you will be saved. [10]We believe with our hearts, and so we are made right with God. And we use our mouths to say that we believe, and so we are saved. [11]As the Scripture says, "Anyone who trusts in him will never be disappointed."[n] [12]That Scripture says "anyone" because there is no difference between Jew and non-Jew. The same Lord is the Lord of all and gives many blessings to all who trust in him. [13]The Scripture says, "Anyone who asks the Lord for help will be saved."[n]

[14]But before people can trust in the Lord for help, they must believe in him.

And before they can believe in the Lord, they must hear about him. And for them to hear about the Lord, someone must tell them. [15]And before someone can go and tell them, he must be sent. It is written, "How beautiful is the person who comes to bring good news."[n]

[16]But not all the Jews accepted the good news. Isaiah said, "Lord, who believed what we told them?"[n] [17]So faith comes from hearing the Good News.[d] And people hear the Good News when someone tells them about Christ.

[18]But I ask: Didn't people hear the Good News? Yes, they heard—as the Scripture says:

"Their message went out through all
    the world.
It goes everywhere on
    earth."        *Psalm 19:4*

[19]Again I ask: Didn't the people of Israel understand? Yes, they did understand. First, Moses says:

"I will use those who are not a nation
    to make you jealous.
I will use a nation that does not
    understand to make you
    angry."        *Deuteronomy 32:21*

[20]Then Isaiah is bold enough to say:

"I was found by those who were not
    asking me for help.
I made myself known to people
    who were not looking for me."
                        *Isaiah 65:1*

[21]But about Israel God says,

"All day long I stood ready to accept
    people who disobey and are
    stubborn."        *Isaiah 65:2*

### GOD SHOWS MERCY TO ALL PEOPLE

**11** So I ask: Did God throw out his people? No! I myself am an Israelite. I am from the family of Abraham, from the tribe[d] of Benjamin. [2]God chose the Israelites to be his people before they were born. And God did not leave his people. Surely you know what the Scripture[d] says about Elijah, how he prayed to God against the people of Israel. Elijah said, [3]"They

10:8 **Verses 6-8** Quotations from Deuteronomy 9:4; 30:12-14; Psalm 107:26. 10:11 "Anyone . . . disappointed." Quotation from Isaiah 28:16. 10:13 "Anyone . . . saved." Quotation from Joel 2:32. 10:15 "How . . . news." Quotation from Isaiah 52:7. 10:16 "Lord . . . them?" Quotation from Isaiah 53:1.

## REAL SUPER HEROES

## MOSES

God was with him from the very beginning. From the time he floated in the basket and Pharaoh's daughter found him, through the time he was raised in Pharaoh's court, Moses was saved for a very special reason: to save and lead his own people, the Israelites, out of bondage.

Armed with a staff, Moses told Pharaoh to let Israel leave. God showed Pharaoh, through Moses and 10 terrible plagues, that he meant business. God freed the Israelites, and Moses led them through the parted Red Sea into the wilderness to prepare them for God's promised land.

Have you ever thought that God put you in your specific family, with your parents, for a reason? God is right now building you into the kind of person he wants you to be so that you, too, can lead others closer to God.

have killed your prophets,[d] and they have destroyed your altars. I am the only prophet left. And now they are trying to kill me, too."[n] [4]But what answer did God give Elijah? He said, "But I have left 7,000 people in Israel. Those 7,000 have never bowed down before Baal."[n] [5]It is the same now. There are a few people that God has chosen by his grace. [6]And if God chose them by grace, then it is not for the things they have done. If they could be made God's people by what they did, then God's gift of grace would not really be a gift.

[7]So this is what has happened: The people of Israel tried to be right with God. But they did not succeed. But the ones God chose did become right with him. The others became hard and refused to listen to God. [8]As it is written in the Scriptures:[d]

"God gave the people a dull mind so they could not understand."

*Isaiah 29:10*

"God closed their eyes so they could not see,
and God closed their ears so they could not hear.
This continues until today."

*Deuteronomy 29:4*

[9]And David says:
"Let their own feasts trap them and cause their ruin.
Let their feasts cause them to sin and be paid back.
[10]Let their eyes be closed so they cannot see.
Let their backs be forever weak from troubles." *Psalm 69:22-23*

[11]So I ask: When the Jews fell, did that fall destroy them? No! But their mistake brought salvation to the non-Jews. This took place to cause the Jews to be jeal-ous. [12]The Jews' mistake brought rich blessings for the world. And what the Jews lost brought rich blessings for the non-Jewish people. So surely the world will get much richer blessings when enough Jews become the kind of people God wants.

[13]Now I am speaking to you who are not Jews. I am an apostle[d] to the non-Jews. So while I have that work, I will do the best I can. [14]I hope I can make my own people jealous. That way, maybe I can help some of them to be saved. [15]God turned away from the Jews. When that happened, God became friends with the other people in the world. So when God accepts the Jews, then surely that will bring to them life after death. [16]If the first piece of bread is offered to God, then the whole loaf is made holy. If the roots of a tree are holy, then the tree's branches are holy too.

[17]Some of the branches from an olive tree have been broken off, and the branch of a wild olive tree has been joined to that first tree. You non-Jews are the same as that wild branch, and you now share the strength and life of the first tree, the Jews. [18]So do not brag about those branches that were broken off. You have no reason to brag. Why? You do not give life to the root. The root gives life to you. [19]You will say, "Branches were broken off so that I could be joined to their tree." [20]That is true. But those branches were broken off because they did not believe. And you continue to be part of the tree only because you believe. Do not be proud, but be afraid. [21]If God did not let the natural branches of that tree stay, then he will not let you stay if you don't believe.

[22]So you see that God is kind, but he can also be very strict. God punishes those who stop following him. But God

## Going Global

**24-7 Prayer**

24-7 Prayer exists to transform the world through a movement of Christ-centered and mission-minded prayer. It is not an organization, but a network of like-minded people. It all began "by accident" with a church on the south coast of England, and the idea has snowballed from there. In September 1999, a bunch of young people got the crazy idea of trying to pray non-stop for a month.

In one room they prayed without ceasing in one-hour shifts for several weeks, inspired by the example of the 18th-century Moravians who had a great impact on men (such as John Wesley) through their model of "laus perennis" (unbroken prayer). From there the prayer meeting has spread into many age groups, denominations, and nations.

Hundreds of non-stop prayer meetings now link up at www.24-7prayer.com to form a unique chain of prayer. Check out the link for Operation World. To get your church group involved, just follow the easy instructions given there!

## DECODE THIS!

*Anyone who calls on the Lord will be*

11:3 "They . . . too." Quotation from 1 Kings 19:10, 14. 11:4 "But . . . Baal." Quotation from 1 Kings 19:18.

is kind to you, if you continue following in his kindness. If you do not continue following him, you will be cut off from the tree. ²³And if the Jews will believe in God again, then God will accept the Jews back again. God is able to put them back where they were. ²⁴It is not natural for a wild branch to be part of a good tree. But you non-Jews are like a branch cut from a wild olive tree. And you were joined to a good olive tree. But those Jews are like a branch that grew from the good tree. So surely they can be joined to their own tree again.

²⁵I want you to understand this secret truth, brothers. This truth will help you understand that you do not know everything. The truth is this: Part of Israel has been made stubborn. But that will change when many non-Jews have come to God. ²⁶And that is how all Israel will be saved. It is written in the Scriptures:

"The Savior will come from Jerusalem;
    he will take away all evil from the
        family of Jacob." ⁿ
²⁷And I will make this agreement with
        those people
    when I take away their sins."

*Isaiah 59:20-21; 27:9*

²⁸The Jews refuse to accept the Good News,ᵈ so they are God's enemies. This has happened to help you non-Jews. But the Jews are still God's chosen people, and God loves them very much. He loves them because of the promises he made to their ancestors. ²⁹God never changes his mind about the people he calls and the things he gives them. ³⁰At one time you refused to obey God. But now you have received mercy, because those people refused to obey. ³¹And now the Jews refuse to obey, because God showed mercy to you. But this happened so that they also can receive mercy from God. ³²All people have refused to obey God. God has given

them all over to their stubborn ways, so that God can show mercy to all.

## PRAISE TO GOD

³³Yes, God's riches are very great! God's wisdom and knowledge have no end! No one can explain the things God decides. No one can understand God's ways. ³⁴As the Scriptureᵈ says,

"Who has known the mind of the
        Lord?
    Who has been able to give the
        Lord advice?"  *Isaiah 40:13*
³⁵"No one has ever given God anything
    that he must pay back."  *Job 41:11*
³⁶Yes, God made all things. And everything continues through God and for God. To God be the glory forever! Amen.

## GIVE YOUR LIVES TO GOD

**12** So brothers, since God has shown us great mercy, I beg you to offer your lives as a living sacrifice to him. Your offering must be only for God and pleasing to him. This is the spiritual way for you to worship. ²Do not change yourselves to be like the people of this world. But be changed within by a new way of thinking. Then you will be able to decide what God wants for you. And you will be able to know what is good and pleasing to God and what is perfect. ³God has given me a special gift. That is why I have something to say to everyone among you. Do not think that you are better than you are. You must see yourself as you really are. Decide what you are by the amount of faith God has given you. ⁴Each one of us has a body, and that body has many parts. These parts all have different uses. ⁵In the same way, we are many, but in Christ we are all one body. Each one is a part of that body. And each part belongs to all the other parts. ⁶We all have different gifts. Each gift came because of the grace that God gave us. If one has the gift of prophecy,ᵈ he should use that gift with the faith he has. ⁷If one has the gift of serving, he

## PANTS ON FIRE

You knew you had done it. But when your parents asked, you just didn't tell the truth. You lied, and with the lie your heart pounded, your palms sweated, and you probably felt like you were going to die.

You're not alone. Most people have the same kind of response when they tell lies on purpose. That's what made John Larson, a medical student, develop the first lie-detector test in 1921. By placing sensors on the body, medical instruments could report any changes in breathing, pulse, blood pressure, and sweat. These changes reveal the stress that comes from lying.

Peter didn't need a lie-detector test when Ananias and Sapphira lied about the money they had given. God knew their hearts, and he judged them for their sin. (Read Acts 5:1-11.) God also knows our hearts, and he says that we must always speak the truth.

[About: Police Technology and Forensics]

**DECODE THIS!**
*If your enemy is hungry, what should you do?*

11:26 Jacob Father of the 12 family groups of Israel, the people God chose to be his people.

should serve. If one has the gift of teaching, he should teach. [8]If one has the gift of encouraging others, he should encourage. If one has the gift of giving to others, he should give freely. If one has the gift of being a leader, he should try hard when he leads. If one has the gift of showing kindness to others, that person should do so with joy.

[9]Your love must be real. Hate what is evil. Hold on to what is good. [10]Love each other like brothers and sisters. Give your brothers and sisters more honor than you want for yourselves. [11]Do not be lazy but work hard. Serve the Lord with all your heart. [12]Be joyful because you have hope. Be patient when trouble comes. Pray at all times. [13]Share with God's people who need help. Bring strangers in need into your homes.

> ## "Do not be lazy but work hard. Serve the Lord with all your heart."
>
> Romans 12:11

[14]Wish good for those who do bad things to you. Wish them well and do not curse them. [15]Be happy with those who are happy. Be sad with those who are sad. [16]Live together in peace with each other. Do not be proud, but make friends with those who seem unimportant. Do not think how smart you are.

[17]If someone does wrong to you, do not pay him back by doing wrong to him. Try to do what everyone thinks is right. [18]Do your best to live in peace with everyone. [19]My friends, do not try to punish others when they wrong you. Wait for God to punish them with his

anger. It is written: "I am the One who punishes; I will pay people back,"[n] says the Lord. [20]But you should do this:

"If your enemy is hungry, feed him;
    if your enemy is thirsty, give him
      a drink.
Doing this will be like pouring
    burning coals on his head."

*Proverbs 25:21-22*

[21]Do not let evil defeat you. Defeat evil by doing good.

## CHRISTIANS SHOULD OBEY THE LAW

**13** All of you must obey the government rulers. No one rules unless God has given him the power to rule. And no one rules now without that power from God. [2]So if anyone is against the government, he is really against what God has commanded. And so he brings punishment on himself. [3]Those who do right do not have to fear the rulers. But people who do wrong must fear them. Do you want to be unafraid of the rulers? Then do what is right, and the ruler will praise you. [4]He is God's servant to help you. But if you do wrong, then be afraid. The ruler has the power to punish; he is God's servant to punish those who do wrong. [5]So you must obey the government. You must obey not only because you might be punished, but because you know it is the right thing to do.

[6]And this is also why you pay taxes. Rulers are working for God and give their time to their work. [7]Pay everyone, then, what you owe him. If you owe any kind of tax, pay it. Show respect and honor to them all.

## LOVING OTHERS

[8]Do not owe people anything. But you will always owe love to each other. The person who loves others has obeyed all the law. [9]The law says, "You must not be guilty of adultery.[d]

You must not murder anyone. You must not steal. You must not want to take your neighbor's things."[n] All these commands and all others are really only one rule: "Love your neighbor as you love yourself."[n] [10]Love never hurts a neighbor. So loving is obeying all the law.

[11]I say this because we live in an important time. Yes, it is now time for you to wake up from your sleep. Our salvation is nearer now than when we first believed. [12]The "night"[n] is almost finished. The "day"[n] is almost here. So we should stop doing things that belong to darkness and take up the weapons used for fighting in the light. [13]Let us live in a right way, like people who belong to the day. We should not have wild parties or get drunk. There should be no sexual sins of any kind, no fighting or

## LIVIN' IT!

### FIT FOR ROYALTY
### ROMANS 13:14

So what does it look like to be a Christian? It looks like someone who has given his or her life to the Lord Jesus. How can we give our lives when we're still living? God says that we should obey God in everything we do, say, and even think. That means asking him for help to live a holy (or separate) life from the world. Ask him to help you see the sin areas in your heart so you can repent and live more like Jesus would.

When you understand what an incredible gift it is to be God's friend—his own child—you will want to do what pleases him. It brings us joy to bring God joy. So stop sinning, and start acting like the child of the King that you are!

12:19 **"I . . . back"** Quotation from Deuteronomy 32:35. 13:9 **"You . . . things."** Quotation from Exodus 20:13-15, 17. 13:9 **"Love . . . yourself."** Quotation from Leviticus 19:18. 13:12 **"night"** This is used as a symbol of the sinful world we live in. This world will soon end. 13:12 **"day"** This is used as a symbol of the good time that is coming, when we will be with God.

231

jealousy. ¹⁴But clothe yourselves with the Lord Jesus Christ. Forget about satisfying your sinful self.

## DO NOT CRITICIZE OTHER PEOPLE

**14** Do not refuse to accept into your group someone who is weak in faith. And do not argue with him about opinions. ²One person believes that he can eat all kinds of food.ⁿ But if another man's faith is weak, then he believes he can eat only vegetables. ³The one who knows that he can eat any kind of food must not feel that he is better than the one who eats only vegetables. And the person who eats only vegetables must not think that the one who eats all foods is wrong. God has accepted him. ⁴You cannot judge another man's servant. His own master decides if he is doing well or not. And the Lord's servant will do well because the Lord helps him do well.

⁵One person thinks that one day is more important than another. And someone else thinks that every day is the same. Each one should be sure in his own mind. ⁶The person who thinks one day is more important than other days is doing that for the Lord. And the one who eats all kinds of food is doing that for the Lord. Yes, he gives thanks to God for that food. And the man who refuses to eat some foods does that for the Lord, and he gives thanks to God. ⁷For we do not live or die for ourselves. ⁸If we live, we are living for the Lord. And if we die, we are dying for the Lord. So living or dying, we belong to the Lord. ⁹That is why Christ died and rose from death to live again. He did this so that he would be Lord over both the dead and the living. ¹⁰So why do you judge your brother in Christ? And why do you think that you are better than he is? We will all stand before God, and he will judge us all. ¹¹Yes, it is written in the Scriptures:ᵈ

### THE REAL JUDGE
### ROMANS 14:13

Isn't it just a lot more fun to find the sins or problems in other people than it is to find it in yourself? It makes us feel better about our own faults when others mess up, and we're often quick to judge them, or look down on them, because of their problems.

The real problem is us, though. God doesn't want us to try to find fault in everyone else (although we do keep out a watchful eye for false teachings). *God* is in charge of them. He wants us to pay close attention to our own lives and the areas where sin may be growing, so he can help us obey him better. So if you see someone in sin, search your own heart for the same problem. Then ask God to help you and the other person to obey the truth.

"Everyone will bow before me;
    everyone will say that I am God.
As surely as I live, these things will
    happen, says the Lord."

*Isaiah 45:23*

¹²So each of us will have to answer to God for what he has done.

## DO NOT CAUSE OTHERS TO SIN

¹³So we should stop judging each other. We must make up our minds not to do anything that will make a Christian brother sin. ¹⁴I am in the Lord Jesus, and I know that there is no food that is wrong to eat. But if a person believes that something is wrong, then that thing is wrong for him. ¹⁵If you hurt your brother's faith because of something you eat, then you are not really following the way of love. Do not

destroy his faith by eating food that he thinks is wrong. Christ died for him. ¹⁶Do not allow what you think is good to become what others say is evil. ¹⁷In the kingdom of God, eating and drinking are not important. The important things are living right with God, peace, and joy in the Holy Spirit.ᵈ ¹⁸Anyone who serves Christ by living this way is pleasing God and will be accepted by other people.

¹⁹So let us try to do what makes peace and helps one another. ²⁰Do not let the eating of food destroy the work of God. All foods are all right to eat, but it is wrong to eat food that causes someone else to sin. ²¹It is better not to eat meat or drink wine or do anything that will cause your brother to sin.

²²Your beliefs about these things should be kept secret between you and God. A person is blessed if he can do what he thinks is right without feeling guilty. ²³But if he eats something without being sure that it is right, then he is wrong because he did not believe that it was right. And if he does anything without believing that it is right, then it is a sin.

**15** We who are strong in faith should help those who are weak. We should help them with their weaknesses, and not please only ourselves. ²Let each of us please his neighbor for his good, to help him be stronger in faith. ³Even Christ did not live to please himself. It was as the Scripturesᵈ said: "When people insult you, it hurts me."ⁿ ⁴Everything that was written in the past was written to teach us, so that we could have hope. That hope comes from the patience and encouragement that

### DECODE THIS!

*Who should those who are strong in faith help?*

14:2 all . . . food The Jewish law said there were some foods Jews should not eat. When Jews became Christians, some of them did not understand they could now eat all foods. 15:3 "When . . . me." Quotation from Psalm 69:9.

232

the Scriptures give us. [5]Patience and encouragement come from God. And I pray that God will help you all agree with each other the way Christ Jesus wants. [6]Then you will all be joined together, and you will give glory to God the Father of our Lord Jesus Christ. [7]Christ accepted you, so you should accept each other. This will bring glory to God. [8]I tell you that Christ became a servant of the Jews. This was to show that God's promises to the Jewish ancestors are true. [9]And he also did this so that the non-Jews could give glory to God for the mercy he gives to them. It is written in the Scriptures:

"So I will praise you among the
    non-Jewish people.
I will sing praises to your name."

Psalm 18:49

[10]The Scripture also says,

"Be happy, you non-Jews, together
    with God's people."

Deuteronomy 32:43

[11]Again the Scripture says,

"All you non-Jews, praise the Lord.
All you people, sing praises
    to him."    Psalm 117:1

[12]And Isaiah says,

"A new king will come from Jesse's
    family.[n]
He will come to rule over the
    non-Jews;
and the non-Jews will have hope
    because of him."    Isaiah 11:10

[13]I pray that the God who gives hope will fill you with much joy and peace while you trust in him. Then your hope will overflow by the power of the Holy Spirit.[d]

## PAUL TALKS ABOUT HIS WORK

[14]My brothers, I am sure that you are full of goodness. I know that you have all the knowledge you need and that you are able to teach each other. [15]But I have written to you very openly about some things that I wanted you to remember. I did this because God gave me this special gift: [16]to be a minister of

Christ Jesus to the non-Jewish people. I served God by teaching his Good News,[d] so that the non-Jewish people could be an offering that God would accept—an offering made holy by the Holy Spirit.[d]

[17]So I am proud of what I have done for God in Christ Jesus. [18]I will not talk about anything I did myself. I will talk only about what Christ has done through me in leading the non-Jewish people to obey God. They have obeyed God because of what I have said and done. [19]And they have obeyed God because of the power of miracles[d] and the great things they saw, and the power of the Holy Spirit. I preached the Good News from Jerusalem all the way around to Illyricum. And so I have finished that part of my work. [20]I always want to preach the Good News in places where people have never heard of Christ. I do this because I do not want to build on the work that someone else has already started. [21]But it is written in the Scriptures:[d]

"Those who were not told about him
    will see,
and those who have not heard
    about him will understand."

Isaiah 52:15

## PAUL'S PLAN TO VISIT ROME

[22]That is why many times I was stopped from coming to you. [23]Now I have finished my work here. Since for many years I have wanted to come to you, [24]I hope to visit you on my way to Spain. I will enjoy being with you, and you can help me on my trip. [25]Now I am going to Jerusalem to help God's people. [26]The believers in Macedonia and Southern Greece were happy to give their money to help the poor among God's people at Jerusalem. [27]They were happy to do this, and really they owe it to them. These non-Jews have shared in the Jews' spiritual blessings. So they should use their material possessions to help the Jews. [28]I must be sure that the poor in Jerusalem get the money that has been given for them. After I do this, I will leave for Spain and stop and visit you. [29]I know that when I come to you, I will bring Christ's full blessing.

[30]Brothers, I beg you to help me in my work by praying for me to God. Do this because of our Lord Jesus and the love that the Holy Spirit[d] gives us. [31]Pray that

## WILD WORLD FACTS

### BLOOD WORK

Have you ever wondered why God talks so much about blood in the Bible? He says that life is in the blood—and it's true. Without blood, we couldn't live.

Our blood is made up of 4 parts: red cells, white cells, platelets, and plasma. The red cells carry oxygen and carbon dioxide around our bodies to keep us alive. They also contain a red chemical called hemoglobin, making blood look red. The white cells fight infection, while the platelets help clot the blood whenever we get a cut. Plasma is the liquid part that carries the other stuff around.

God said that somebody perfect had to die in order to forgive sins. Jesus shed his own blood for us so we could be forgiven.

[Yahooligans: Ask Earl]

---

 15:12 **Jesse's family** Jesse was the father of David, king of Israel. Jesus was from their family.

I will be saved from the non-believers in Judea. And pray that this help I bring to Jerusalem will please God's people there. [32]Then, if God wants me to, I will come to you. I will come with joy, and together you and I will have a time of rest. [33]The God who gives peace be with you all. Amen.

## GREETINGS TO THE CHRISTIANS

**16** I recommend to you our sister Phoebe. She is a helper[n] in the church in Cenchrea. [2]I ask you to accept her in the Lord in the way God's people should. Help her with anything she needs because she has helped me and many other people too.

[3]Give my greetings to Priscilla and Aquila, who work together with me in Christ Jesus. [4]They risked their own lives to save my life. I am thankful to them, and all the non-Jewish churches are thankful to them as well. [5]Also, greet for me the church that meets at their house.

Greetings to my dear friend Epenetus. He was the first person in the country of Asia to follow Christ. [6]Greetings to Mary, who worked very hard for you. [7]Greetings to Andronicus and Junias, my relatives, who were in prison with me. The apostles feel they are very important. They were believers in Christ before I was. [8]Greetings to Ampliatus, my dear friend in the Lord. [9]Greetings to Urbanus. He is a worker together with me for Christ. And greetings to my dear friend Stachys. [10]Greetings to Apelles. He was tested and proved that he truly loves Christ. Greetings to all those who are in the family of Aristobulus. [11]Greetings to Herodion, my relative. Greetings to all those in the family of Narcissus who

belong to the Lord. [12]Greetings to Tryphena and Tryphosa. Those women work very hard for the Lord. Greetings to my dear friend Persis. She also has worked very hard for the Lord. [13]Greetings to Rufus who is a special person in the Lord. Greetings to his mother, who has been a mother to me also. [14]Greetings to Asyncritus, Phlegon, Hermes, Patrobas, Hermas, and all the brothers who are with them. [15]Greetings to Philologus and Julia, Nereus and his sister, and Olympas. And greetings to all God's people with them. [16]Greet each other with a holy kiss. All of Christ's churches send greetings to you.

[17]Brothers, I ask you to look out for those who cause people to be against each other and who upset other people's faith. They are against the true teaching you learned. Stay away from them. [18]For such people are not serving our Lord Christ. They are only doing what pleases themselves. They use fancy talk and fine words to fool the minds of those who do not know about evil. [19]All the believers have heard that you obey. So I am very happy because of you. But I want you to be wise in what is good and innocent in what is evil.

[20]The God who brings peace will soon defeat Satan and give you power over him.

The grace of our Lord Jesus be with you.

[21]Timothy, a worker together with me, sends greetings, as well as Lucius, Jason, and Sosipater, my relatives.

[22]I am Tertius, and I am writing this letter

from Paul. I send greetings to you in the Lord.

[23]Gaius is letting me and the whole church here use his home. He also sends greetings to you, as do Erastus and our brother Quartus. Erastus is the city treasurer here. [24] [n]

[25]Glory to God! God is the One who can make you strong in faith by the Good News[d] that I tell people and by the message about Jesus Christ. The message about Christ is the secret truth that was hidden for long ages past, but is now made known. [26]It has been made clear through the writings of the prophets.[d] And by the command of the eternal God it is made known to all nations, that they might believe and obey.

[27]To the only wise God be glory forever through Jesus Christ! Amen.

16:1 **helper** Literally, "deaconess." This might mean the same as one of the special women helpers in 1 Timothy 3:11.
16:24 **Verse 24** Some Greek copies add verse 24: "The grace of our Lord Jesus Christ be with all of you. Amen."

Paul gives help to a church with problems.

Fun to memorize: "The Love Chapter" (1 Corinthians 13)

# THE FIRST LETTER OF PAUL THE APOSTLE TO THE

# CORINTHIANS

About two-thirds of the people in Corinth were slaves.

Paul wrote to Christians in Corinth while he was in Ephesus.

Corinth was a key city in Greece with 2 seaports.

**1** From Paul. I was called to be an apostle[d] of Christ Jesus because that is what God wanted. Also from Sosthenes, our brother in Christ.

²To the church of God in Corinth, to those people who have been made holy in Christ Jesus. You were called to be God's holy people with all people everywhere who trust in the name of the Lord Jesus Christ—their Lord and ours:

³Grace and peace to you from God our Father and the Lord Jesus Christ.

## PAUL GIVES THANKS TO GOD

⁴I always thank my God for you because of the grace that God has given you in Christ Jesus. ⁵In Jesus you have been blessed in every way, in all your speaking and in all your knowledge. ⁶The truth about Christ has been proved in you. ⁷So you have every gift from God while you wait for our Lord Jesus Christ to come again. ⁸Jesus will keep you strong until the end. He will keep you strong, so that there will be no wrong in you on the day our Lord Jesus Christ comes again. ⁹God is faithful. He is the One who has called you to share life with his Son, Jesus Christ our Lord.

## PROBLEMS IN THE CHURCH

¹⁰I beg you, brothers, in the name of our Lord Jesus Christ. I beg that all of you agree with each other, so that you will not be divided into groups. I beg that you be completely joined together by having the same kind of thinking and the same purpose. ¹¹My brothers, some people from Chloe's family have told me that there are arguments among you. ¹²This is what I mean: One of you says, "I follow Paul"; another says, "I follow Apollos"; another says, "I follow Peter"; and another says, "I follow Christ." ¹³Christ cannot be divided into

> ### "Jesus will keep you strong until the end."
>
> *1 Corinthians 1:8*

different groups! Did Paul die on the cross for you? No! Were you baptized in the name of Paul? No! ¹⁴I am thankful that I did not baptize any of you except Crispus and Gaius. ¹⁵I am thankful, because now no one can say that you were baptized in my name. ¹⁶(I also baptized the family of Stephanas. But I do not remember that I myself baptized any others.) ¹⁷Christ did not give me the work of baptizing people. He gave me the work of preaching the Good News,[d] and he sent me to preach the Good News without using words of worldly wisdom. If I used worldly wisdom to tell the Good News, the cross[n] of Christ would lose its power.

## CHRIST IS GOD'S POWER AND WISDOM

¹⁸The teaching about the cross seems foolish to those who are lost. But to us who are being saved it is the power of God. ¹⁹It is written in the Scriptures:[d]

> "I will cause the wise men to lose their wisdom.
> I will make the wise men unable to understand."  *Isaiah 29:14*

²⁰Where is the wise person? Where is the educated person? Where is the philosopher[n] of our times? God has made the wisdom of the world foolish. ²¹The world did not know God through its own wisdom. So God chose to use the message that sounds foolish to save those who believe it. ²²The Jews ask for miracles[d] as proofs. The Greeks want wisdom. ²³But we preach Christ on the cross. This is a big problem to the Jews. And it seems foolish to the non-Jews. ²⁴But Christ is the power of God and the wisdom of God to those people God has called—Jews and Greeks. ²⁵Even the foolishness of God is wiser than men. Even the weakness of God is stronger than men.

²⁶Brothers, look at what you were when God called you. Not many of you were wise in the way the world judges wisdom. Not many of you had great influence. Not many of you came from

## GET CONNECTED

### REAL CONVERSATION

When you see your friend, do you immediately start talking? Do you keep talking and talking and talking so that your friend can never answer? If you do, it will be very hard to ever know what your friend thinks or feels. Yet that's exactly what most of us do when we pray.

God says that we need to be still and remember who he is. He says that he speaks in a still, small voice—which means we must take time to be quiet so he can speak to our hearts. We know his voice because it matches what we learn in the Bible. His peace will help us know what to do in life.

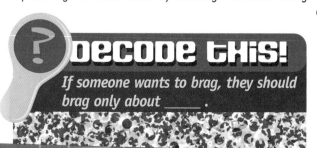

## DECODE THIS!

*If someone wants to brag, they should brag only about _____.*

---

⭐ **1:17 cross** Paul uses the cross as a picture of the gospel, the story of Christ's death and rising from death to pay for men's sins. The cross, or Christ's death, was God's way to save men.
**1:20 philosopher** Philosophers were those who searched for truth.

important families. [27]But God chose the foolish things of the world to shame the wise. He chose the weak things of the world to shame the strong. [28]And he chose what the world thinks is not important. He chose what the world hates and thinks is nothing. He chose these to destroy what the world thinks is important. [29]God did this so that no man can brag before him. [30]It is God who has made you part of Christ Jesus. Christ has become wisdom for us from God. Christ is the reason we are right with God and have freedom from sin; Christ is the reason we are holy. [31]So, as the Scripture[d] says, "If a person brags, he should brag only about the Lord."[n]

## THE MESSAGE OF CHRIST'S DEATH

**2** Dear brothers, when I came to you, I did not come as a proud man. I preached God's truth, but not with fancy words or a show of great learning. [2]I decided that while I was with you I would forget about everything except Jesus Christ and his death on the cross. [3]When I came to you, I was weak and shook with fear. [4]My teaching and my speaking were not with wise words that persuade people. But the proof of my teaching was the power that the Spirit[d] gives. [5]I did this so that your faith would be in God's power, not in the wisdom of a man.

## GOD'S WISDOM

[6]Yet I speak wisdom to those who are mature. But this wisdom is not from this world or of the rulers of this world. (These rulers are losing their power.) [7]But I speak God's secret wisdom, which he has kept hidden. God planned this wisdom for our glory, before the world began. [8]None of the rulers of this world understood it. If they had, they would not have killed the Lord of glory on a cross. [9]But as it is written in the Scriptures:[d]

"No one has ever seen this.
No one has ever heard about it.
No one has ever imagined
what God has prepared for those
who love him."      *Isaiah 64:4*

[10]But God has shown us these things through the Spirit.[d]

The Spirit knows all things, even the deep secrets of God. [11]It is like this: No one knows the thoughts that another person has. Only a person's spirit that lives in him knows his thoughts. It is the same with God. No one knows the thoughts of God. Only the Spirit of God knows God's thoughts. [12]We did not receive the spirit of the world, but we received the Spirit that is from God. We received this Spirit so that we can know all that God has given us. [13]When we speak, we do not use words taught to us by the wisdom that men have. We use words taught to us by the Spirit. We use spiritual words to explain spiritual things. [14]A person who is not spiritual does not accept the gifts that come from the Spirit of God. That person thinks they are foolish. He cannot understand the Spirit's gifts, because they can only be judged spiritually. [15]But the spiritual person is able to judge all things. Yet no one can judge him. The Scripture says:

[16]"Who has known the mind of
the Lord?
Who has been able to teach
him?"      *Isaiah 40:13*

But we have the mind of Christ.

## FOLLOWING MEN IS WRONG

**3** Brothers, in the past I could not talk to you as I talk to spiritual people. I had to talk to you as I would to people of the world—babies in Christ. [2]The teaching I gave you was like milk, not solid food. I did this because you were not ready for solid food. And even now you are not ready. [3]You are still not spiritual. You have jealousy and arguing among you. This shows that you are not spiritual. You are acting like people of the world. [4]One of you says, "I follow Paul," and another says, "I follow Apollos." When you say things like this, you are acting like worldly people.

[5]Is Apollos important? No! Is Paul important? No! We are only servants of God who helped you believe. Each one of us did the work God gave us to do. [6]I planted the seed of the teaching in you, and Apollos watered it. But God is the One who made the seed grow. [7]So the one who plants is not important, and the one who waters is not important. Only God is important, because he is the One who makes things grow.

## LIVIN' IT!

### JOIN THE TEAM!
### 1 CORINTHIANS 3:6

Helping other people come to Jesus might seem to be an impossible task. And really it is, if you're doing it on your own.

The great news about God's kingdom is that it's a team effort. God uses each of us in different ways right where we are to help tell others about Jesus. You don't have to tell everything you know about God to someone you just met, if it doesn't seem to fit your conversation. Ask God to help you always be prepared to say just the right thing when the time comes. He promises to give us wisdom right when we need it. Then God will have another Christian share a little bit more with that person. In God's perfect timing, he will change that person's heart and draw her to himself.

1:31 "If . . . Lord." Quotation from Jeremiah 9:24.

## TO FIND THE
# HIDDEN MESSAGE,
## COLOR ONLY THE BLOCKS THAT CONTAIN VOWELS.

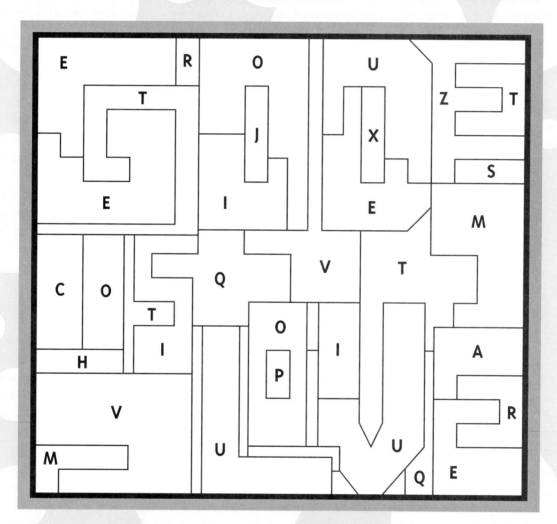

**WRITE THE MESSAGE BELOW.**

_____

# LIVIN' IT!

## BUFF BODIES
### 1 CORINTHIANS 3:16

If you had built a temple for God, you wouldn't let it go to ruin, would you? No! You'd keep it in tip-top shape. God says that our bodies are actually his temple where his spirit lives. God wants us to show self-control and discipline when taking care of our bodies by exercising, resting, and eating the right foods. We are better able to serve him when we are in shape.

Of course, staying in shape requires as much spiritual discipline as it does exercise. In other words, we need to work our spiritual muscles by refusing to sin and doing the will of God instead. Then our bodies and our hearts will make a good home for God's Spirit, and he will be able to do his good work in and through us.

8 The one who plants and the one who waters have the same purpose. And each will be rewarded for his own work. 9 We are workers together for God. And you are like a farm that belongs to God.

And you are a house that belongs to God. 10 Like an expert builder I built the foundation of that house. I used the gift that God gave me to do this. Others are building on that foundation. But everyone should be careful how he builds. 11 The foundation has already been built. No one can build any other foundation. The foundation that has already been laid is Jesus Christ. 12 Anyone can build on that foundation, using gold, silver, jewels, wood, grass, or straw. 13 But the work that each person does will be clearly seen, because the Day[n] will make it plain. That Day will appear with fire, and the fire will test every man's work. 14 If the building that a man puts on the foundation still stands, he will get his reward. 15 But if his building is burned up, he will suffer loss. The man will be saved, but it will be as if he escaped from a fire.

16 You should know that you yourselves are God's temple. God's Spirit[d] lives in you. 17 If anyone destroys God's temple, God will destroy him, because God's temple is holy. You yourselves are God's temple.

18 Do not fool yourselves. If anyone among you thinks he is wise in this world, he should become a fool. Then he can become truly wise, 19 because the wisdom of this world is foolishness to God. It is written in the Scriptures,[d] "He catches wise men in their own clever traps."[n] 20 It is also written in the Scriptures, "The Lord knows what people think. He knows they are just a puff of wind."[n] 21 So you should not brag about men. All things are yours: 22 Paul, Apollos and Peter; the world, life, death, the present, and the future—all these things are yours. 23 And you belong to Christ, and Christ belongs to God.

## APOSTLES OF CHRIST

4 This is what people should think about us: We are servants of Christ. We are the ones God has trusted with his secret truths. 2 A person who is trusted with something must show that he is worthy of that trust. 3 I do not care if I am judged by you or if I am judged by any human court. I do not even judge myself. 4 I know of no wrong that I have done. But this does not make me innocent. The Lord is the One who judges me. 5 So do not judge before the right time; wait until the Lord comes. He will bring to light things that are now hidden in darkness. He will make known the secret purposes of people's hearts. Then God will give everyone the praise he should get.

6 Brothers, I have used Apollos and myself as examples. I did this so that you could learn from us the meaning of the words, "Follow only what is written in the Scriptures."[d] Then you will not be proud of one man and hate another. 7 Who says that you are better than others? Everything you have was given to you. And if this is so, why do you brag as if you got these things by your own power?

8 You think you have everything you need. You think you are rich. You think you have become kings without us. I wish you really were kings! Then we could be kings together with you. 9 But it seems to me that God has given me and the other apostles[d] the last place. We are like men sentenced to die. We are like a show for the whole world to see—angels and people. 10 We are fools for Christ's sake. But you think you are very wise in Christ. We are weak, but you think you are strong. You receive honor, but we are hated. 11 Even now we still do not have enough to eat or drink or enough

## DECODE THIS!

*Who did Paul send to help the people of Corinth?*

3:13 **Day** The day Christ will come to judge all people and take his people home to live with him.
3:19 **"He . . . traps."** Quotation from Job 5:13.  3:20 **"The Lord . . . wind."** Quotation from Psalm 94:11.

clothes. We are often beaten. We have no homes. [12]We work hard with our own hands for our food. People curse us, but we bless them. They hurt us, and we accept it. [13]They say evil things against us, but we say only kind things to them. Even today, we are treated as though we are the garbage of the world—the dirt of the earth.

[14]I am not trying to make you feel ashamed. I am writing this to give you a warning as if you were my own dear children. [15]For though you may have 10,000 teachers in Christ, you do not have many fathers. Through the Good News[d] I became your father in Christ Jesus. [16]So I beg you, please be like me. [17]That is why I am sending Timothy to you. He is my son in the Lord. I love Timothy, and he is faithful. He will help you remember the way I live in Christ Jesus. This way of life is what I teach in all the churches everywhere.

[18]Some of you have become proud, thinking that I will not come to you again. [19]But I will come very soon if the Lord wants me to. Then I will see what those who are proud can do, not what they say. [20]I want to see this because the kingdom of God is not talk but power. [21]Which do you want: that I come to you with punishment, or that I come with love and gentleness?

## WICKEDNESS IN THE CHURCH

**5** Now, it is actually being said that there is sexual sin among you. And it is of such a bad kind that it does not happen even among those who do not know God. A man there has his father's wife. [2]And still you are proud of yourselves! You should have been filled with sadness. And the man who did that sin should be put out of your group. [3]My body is not there with you, but I am with you in spirit. And I have already judged the man who did that sin. I judged him just as I would if I were really there. [4]Meet together as the people of our Lord Jesus. I will be with you in spirit, and you will have the power of our Lord Jesus with you. [5]Then give this man to Satan, so that his sinful self[n] will be destroyed. And then his spirit can be saved on the day of the Lord.

[6]Your bragging is not good. You know the saying, "Just a little yeast makes the whole batch of dough rise." [7]Take out all the old yeast so that you will be a new batch of dough. And you really are new dough without yeast. For Christ, our Passover[d] lamb, was killed to cleanse us. [8]So let us continue our feast, but not with the bread that has the old yeast. That old yeast is the yeast of sin and wickedness. But let us eat the bread that has no yeast. This is the bread of goodness and truth.

[9]I wrote to you in my letter that you should not associate with those who take part in sexual sin. [10]But I did not mean that you should not associate with the sinful people of this world. People of the world do take part in sexual sin, or they are selfish and they cheat each other, or they worship idols. But to get away from them you would have to leave this world. [11]I am writing to tell you that the person you must not associate with is this: anyone who calls himself a brother in Christ but who takes part in sexual sin, or is selfish, or worships idols, or lies about others, or gets drunk, or cheats people. Do not even eat with someone like that.

[12-13]It is not my business to judge those who are not part of the church. God will judge them. But you must judge the people who are part of the church. The Scripture[d] says, "You must get rid of the evil person among you."[n]

## REAL SUPER HEROES

# ABRAHAM

You might think that Abraham must have been a great man for God to pick him to become the father of Israel, God's chosen people. But he was just an ordinary guy. God, however, made his life spectacular because Abraham did whatever God said.

When God told Abraham to leave his family and homeland to go to the place where God had for him, he obeyed. Even though he hadn't grown up in a family that served God, he trusted that God would keep his promise. True to his word, God blessed Abraham with more descendants than he could count, with Jesus eventually coming through his bloodline.

It doesn't matter who you are or where you come from, either. God is able to bless your life in amazing ways when you give it to him.

## JUDGING PROBLEMS AMONG CHRISTIANS

**6** When one of you has something against a brother in Christ, why do you go to the judges in the law courts? Those people are not right with God. So why do you let them decide who is right? You should be ashamed! Why do you not let God's people decide who is right? ²Surely you know that God's people will judge the world. So if you are to judge the world, then surely you are able to judge small things as well. ³You know that in the future we will judge angels. So surely we can judge things in this life. ⁴So if you have disagreements that must be judged, why do you take them to those who are not part of the church? They mean nothing to the church. ⁵I say this to shame you. Surely there is someone among you wise enough to judge a complaint between two brothers in Christ. ⁶But now one brother goes to court against another brother. And you let men who are not believers judge their case!

⁷The lawsuits that you have against each other show that you are already defeated. It would be better for you to let someone wrong you! It would be better for you to let someone cheat you! ⁸But you yourselves do wrong and cheat! And you do this to your own brothers in Christ!

⁹⁻¹⁰Surely you know that the people who do wrong will not receive God's kingdom. Do not be fooled. These people will not receive God's kingdom: those who sin sexually, or worship idols, or take part in adultery,ᵈ or men who have sexual relations with other men, or steal, or are selfish, or get drunk, or lie about others, or cheat. ¹¹In the past, some of you were like that. But you were washed clean. You were made holy. And you were made right with God in the name of the Lord Jesus Christ and by the Spirit of our God.

### USE YOUR BODIES FOR GOD'S GLORY

¹²"I am allowed to do all things." But all things are not good for me to do. "I am allowed to do all things." But I must not do those things that will make me their slave. ¹³"Food is for the stomach, and the stomach for food." Yes. But God will destroy them both. The body is not for sexual sin. The body is for the Lord, and the Lord is for the body. ¹⁴By God's power God raised the Lord Jesus from death. And God will also raise us from death. ¹⁵Surely you know that your bodies are parts of Christ himself. So I must never take parts of Christ and join them to a prostitute!ᵈ ¹⁶It is written in the Scriptures,ᵈ

"The two people will become one body."ⁿ So you should know that a man who joins himself with a prostitute becomes one with her in body. ¹⁷But the one who joins himself with the Lord is one with the Lord in spirit.

¹⁸So run away from sexual sin. Every other sin that a man does is outside his body. But the one who sins sexually sins against his own body. ¹⁹You should know that your body is a temple for the Holy Spirit.ᵈ The Holy Spirit is in you. You have received the Holy Spirit from God. You do not own yourselves. ²⁰You were bought by God for a price. So honor God with your bodies.

### ABOUT MARRIAGE

**7** Now I will discuss the things you wrote to me about. It is good for a man not to marry. ²But sexual sin is a danger. So each man should have his own wife. And each woman should have her own husband. ³The husband should give his wife all that she should have as his wife. And the wife should give her husband all that he should have as her husband. ⁴The wife does not have power over her own body. Her husband has the power over her body. And the husband does not have power over his own body. His wife has the power over his body. ⁵Do not refuse to give your bodies to each other. But you might both agree to stay away from sexual relations for a time. You might do this so that you can give your time to prayer. Then come together again. This is so that Satan cannot tempt you in your weakness. ⁶I say this to give you permission. It is not a command. ⁷I wish everyone were like me. But each person has his own gift from

KIDS SPEAK UP!

Q. What have you put up your nose?

A. One time I stuck a carrot up my nose.

---

6:16 "The two . . . body." Quotation from Genesis 2:24.

**DECODE THIS!**

*Your body is God's temple, and you should run away from _____.*

# Gotta Know!

## Why is it so hard to be myself around my friends?

**Many people find it hard to be themselves because they don't like who they are, and they are afraid that other people won't like them, either, if they find out who they really are. Relax! God made you in a special way. No one can do the things that God has created you specifically to do and to be. So what if you are a little quirky? Everybody is—and it's the differences in us that make us interesting. Thank God for making you the way you are, and ask him for courage to be yourself.**

God. One has one gift, another has another gift.

[8]Now for those who are not married and for the widows I say this: It is good for them to stay single as I am. [9]But if they cannot control their bodies, then they should marry. It is better to marry than to burn with sexual desire.

[10]Now I give this command for the married people. (The command is not from me; it is from the Lord.) A wife should not leave her husband. [11]But if she does leave, she must not marry again. Or she should go back to her husband. Also the husband should not divorce his wife.

[12]For all the others I say this (I am saying this, not the Lord): A brother in Christ might have a wife who is not a believer. If she will live with him, he must not divorce her. [13]And a woman might have a husband who is not a believer. If he will live with her, she must not divorce him. [14]The husband who is not a believer is made holy through his believing wife. And the wife who is not a believer is made holy through her believing husband. If this were not true, then your children would not be clean.[d] But now your children are holy.

[15]But if the person who is not a believer decides to leave, let him leave. When this happens, the brother or sister in Christ is free. God called us to a life of peace. [16]Wives, maybe you will save your husband; and husbands, maybe you will save your wife. You do not know now what will happen later.

## LIVE AS GOD CALLED YOU

[17]But each one should continue to live the way God has given him to live—the way he was when God called him. This is a rule I make in all the churches. [18]If a man was already circumcised[d] when he was called, he should not change his circumcision. If a man was without circumcision when he was called, he should not be circumcised. [19]It is not important if a man is circumcised or not circumcised. The important thing is obeying God's commands. [20]Each one should stay the way he was when God called him. [21]If you were a slave when God called you, do not let that bother you. But if you can be free, then become free. [22]The person who was a slave when the Lord called him is free in the Lord. He belongs to the Lord. In the same way, the one who was free when he was called is now Christ's slave. [23]You all were bought for a price. So do not become slaves of men. [24]Brothers, in your new life with God each one of you should continue the way you were when you were called.

## QUESTIONS ABOUT GETTING MARRIED

[25]Now I write about people who are not married. I have no command from the Lord about this, but I give my opinion. And I can be trusted, because the Lord has given me mercy. [26]This is a time of trouble. So I think that it is good for you to stay the way you are. [27]If you have a wife, then do not try to become free from her. If you are not married, then do not try to find a wife. [28]But if you decide to marry, this is not a sin. And it is not a sin for a girl who has never married to get married. But those who marry will have trouble in this life. And I want you to be free from this trouble.

[29]Brothers, this is what I mean: We do not have much time left. So starting now, those who have wives should use their time to serve the Lord as if they had no wives. [30]Those who are sad should live as if they are not sad. Those who are happy should live as if they are not happy. Those who buy things should live as if they own nothing. [31]Those who use the things of the world should live as if those things are not important to them. You should live like this, because this world, the way it is now, will soon be gone.

> **"The person who was a slave when the Lord called him is free in the Lord."** *1 Corinthians 7:22*

[32]I want you to be free from worry. A man who is not married is busy with the Lord's work. He is trying to please the Lord. [33]But a man who is married is busy with things of the world. He is trying to please his wife. [34]He must think about two things—pleasing his wife and pleasing the Lord. A woman who is not married or a girl who has never married is busy with the Lord's work.

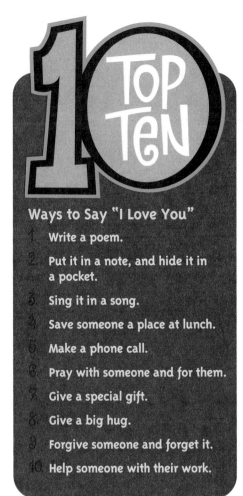

**TOP TEN**

## Ways to Say "I Love You"

1. Write a poem.
2. Put it in a note, and hide it in a pocket.
3. Sing it in a song.
4. Save someone a place at lunch.
5. Make a phone call.
6. Pray with someone and for them.
7. Give a special gift.
8. Give a big hug.
9. Forgive someone and forget it.
10. Help someone with their work.

She wants to give herself fully—body and soul—to the Lord. But a married woman is busy with things of the world. She is trying to please her husband. ³⁵I am saying this to help you. I am not trying to limit you. But I want you to live in the right way. And I want you to give yourselves fully to the Lord without giving your time to other things.

³⁶A man might think that he is not doing the right thing with the girl he is engaged to. The girl might be almost past the best age to marry. So he might feel that he should marry her. He should do what he wants. They should get married. It is no sin. ³⁷But another

man might be more sure in his mind. There may be no need for marriage, so he is free to do what he wants. If he has decided in his own heart not to marry, he is doing the right thing. ³⁸So the man who marries his girl does right. And the man who does not marry does even better.

³⁹A woman must stay with her husband as long as he lives. If the husband dies, she is free to marry any man she wants. But she must marry in the Lord. ⁴⁰The woman is happier if she does not marry again. This is my opinion, and I believe that I have God's Spirit.

## ABOUT FOOD OFFERED TO IDOLS

**8** Now I will write about meat that is sacrificed to idols. We know that "we all have knowledge." Knowledge puffs you up with pride, but love builds up. ²Whoever thinks he knows something does not yet know anything as he should. ³But he who loves God is known by God.

⁴So this is what I say about eating meat sacrificed to idols: We know that an idol is really nothing in the world. And we know that there is only one God. ⁵It is really not important if there are things called gods, in heaven or on earth. (And there are many things that people call "gods" and "lords.") ⁶But for us there is only one God. He is our Father. All things came from him, and we live for him. And there is only one Lord—Jesus Christ. All things were made through Jesus, and we also have life through him.

⁷But not all people know this. Until now, some people have had the habit of worshiping idols. So now when they eat meat, they still feel as if it belongs to an idol. They are not sure that it is right to eat this meat.

When they eat it, they feel guilty. ⁸But food will not make us closer to God. Refusing to eat does not make us less pleasing to God. And eating does not make us better in God's sight.

⁹But be careful with your freedom. Your freedom may cause those who are weak in faith to fall into sin. ¹⁰You have "knowledge," so you might eat in an idol's temple.ᵗ Someone who is weak in faith might see you eating there. This would encourage him to eat meat sacrificed to idols. But he really thinks it is wrong. ¹¹So this weak brother is ruined because of your "knowledge." And Christ died for this brother. ¹²When you sin against your brothers in Christ like this and cause them to do what they feel is wrong, you are also sinning against Christ. ¹³So if the food I eat makes my brother fall into sin, I will never eat meat again. I will stop eating meat, so that I will not cause my brother to sin.

## PAUL IS LIKE THE OTHER APOSTLES

**9** I am a free man. I am an apostle.ᵈ I have seen Jesus our Lord. You people are all an example of my work in the Lord. ²Others may not accept me as an apostle, but surely you accept me. You are proof that I am an apostle in the Lord.

³Some people want to judge me. So this is the answer I give them: ⁴Do we not have the right to eat and drink? ⁵Do we not have the right to bring a believing wife with us when we travel? The other apostles, the Lord's brothers, and Peter all do this. ⁶And are Barnabas and I the only ones who must work to earn our living? ⁷No soldier ever serves in the army and pays his own salary. No one ever plants a vineyard without eating some of the grapes himself. No person takes care of a flock of sheep without drinking some of the milk himself.

**DECODE THIS!**

*Knowledge puffs you up with _____ .*

8:10 **idol's temple** Building where a false god is worshiped.

[8]This is not only what men think. God's law says the same thing. [9]Yes, it is written in the law of Moses: "When an ox is working in the grain, do not cover its mouth and keep it from eating."[n] When God said this, was he thinking only about oxen? No. [10]He was really talking about us. Yes, that Scripture[d] was written for us. The one who plows and the one who works in the grain should hope to get some of the grain for their work. [11]We planted spiritual seed among you. So we should be able to harvest from you some things for this life. Surely this is not asking too much. [12]Other men have the right to get something from you. So surely we have this right, too. But we do not use this right. No, we put up with everything ourselves so that we will not stop anyone from obeying the Good News[d] of Christ. [13]Surely you know that those who work at the Temple[d] get their food from the Temple. And those who serve at the altar get part of what is offered at the altar. [14]It is the same with those who tell the Good News. The Lord has commanded that those who tell the Good News should get their living from this work.

[15]But I have not used any of these rights. And I am not writing this now to get anything from you. I would rather die than to have my reason for bragging taken away. [16]Telling the Good News is not my reason for bragging. Telling the Good News is my duty—something I must do. And how bad it will be for me if I do not tell the Good News. [17]If I preach because it is my own choice, I should get a reward. But I have no choice. I must tell the Good News. I am only doing the duty that was given to me. [18]So what reward do I get? This is my reward: that when I tell the Good News I can offer it freely. In this way I do not use my right to be paid in my work for the Good News.

[19]I am free. I belong to no man. But I make myself a slave to all people. I do this to help save as many people as I can. [20]To the Jews I became like a Jew. I did this to help save the Jews. I myself am not ruled by the law. But to those who are ruled by the law I became like a person who is ruled by the law. I did this to help save those who are ruled by the law. [21]To those who are without the law I became like a person who is without the law. I did this to help save those people who are without the law. (But really, I am not without God's law—I am ruled by Christ's law.) [22]To those who are weak, I became weak so that I could help save them. I have become all things to all people. I did this so that I could save some of them in any way possible. [23]I do all this because of the Good News. I do it so that I can share in the blessings of the Good News.

[24]You know that in a race all the runners run. But only one gets the prize. So run like that. Run to win! [25]All those who compete in the games use strict training. They do this so that they can win a crown. That crown is an earthly thing that lasts only a short time. But our crown will continue forever. [26]So I do not run without a goal. I fight like a boxer who is hitting something—not just the air. [27]It is my own body that I hit. I make it my slave. I do this so that I myself will not be rejected after I have preached to others.

## DON'T BE LIKE THE JEWS

**10** Brothers, I want you to know what happened to our ancestors who followed Moses. They were all under the cloud, and they all went through the sea. [2]They were all baptized as followers of Moses in the cloud and in the sea. [3]They all ate the same spiritual food. [4]And they all drank the

---

## A LIGHT THOUGHT

## WILD WORLD FACTS

When God spoke into the darkness and created light, what exactly did he do? He created energy! Light is a form of traveling energy that comes in waves (like the ocean) that are so small we can't see them with our eyes. What our eyes do see are the effects of those waves, which carry all the colors of the rainbow. But when all the colors are combined, we simply see white light, like we see in a light bulb or from the sun. The smaller the waves of light or the shorter the wavelength, the stronger the light is. In fact, gamma rays, the strongest form of light, can cut through almost anything, including metal.

## DECODE THIS!

*In a race, all the runners run, but how many get the prize?*

9:9 "When an ox . . . eating." Quotation from Deuteronomy 25:4.

same spiritual drink. They drank from that spiritual rock that was with them. That rock was Christ. [5]But God was not pleased with most of them. They died in the desert.

[6]And these things that happened are examples for us. They should stop us from wanting evil things as those people did. [7]Do not worship idols, as some of them did. It is written in the Scriptures:[d] "The people sat down to eat and drink. Then they got up and sinned sexually."[n] [8]We should not take part in sexual sins, as some of them did. In one day 23,000 of them died because of their sins. [9]We should not test the Lord as some of them did. They were killed by snakes. [10]And do not complain as some of them did. They were killed by the angel that destroys.

[11]The things that happened to those people are examples. And they were written down to be warnings for us. For we live in a time when all these things of the past have reached their goal. [12]So anyone who thinks he is standing strong should be careful not to fall. [13]The only temptations that you have are the temptations that all people have. But you can trust God. He will not let you be tempted more than you can stand. But when you are tempted, God will also give you a way to escape that temptation. Then you will be able to stand it.

[14]So, my dear friends, stay away from worshiping idols. [15]I am speaking to you, as to intelligent people; judge for yourselves what I say. [16]We give thanks for the cup of blessing.[n] It is a sharing in the blood of Christ's death. And the bread that we break is a sharing in the body of Christ. [17]There is one loaf of bread. And we are many people. But we all share from that one loaf. So we are really one body.

[18]Think about the people of Israel: Do not those who eat the sacrifices share in the altar? [19]I do not mean that the food sacrificed to an idol is something important. And I do not mean that an idol is anything at all. [20]But I say that what is sacrificed to idols is offered to demons,[d] not to God. And I do not want you to share anything with demons. [21]You cannot drink the cup of the Lord and the cup of demons, too. You cannot share in the Lord's table and the table of demons, too. [22]Do we want to make the Lord jealous? We are not stronger than he is, are we?

## HOW TO USE CHRISTIAN FREEDOM

[23]"We are allowed to do all things." Yes. But all things are not good for us to do. "We are allowed to do all things." Yes. But not all things help others grow stronger. [24]No one should try to do what will help only himself. He should try to do what is good for others.

[25]Eat any meat that is sold in the meat market. Do not ask questions about the meat to see if it is something you think is wrong to eat. [26]You can eat it, "because the earth and everything on it belong to the Lord."[n]

[27]Someone who is not a believer may invite you to eat with him. If you want to go, eat anything that is put before you. Do not ask questions to see if it is something you think might be wrong to eat. [28]But if anyone says to you, "That food was offered to idols," then do not eat it. Do not eat it because of that person who told you and because eating it would be something that might be thought wrong. [29]I don't mean that you think it is wrong. But the other person might think it is wrong. My own freedom should not be judged by what someone else thinks. [30]I eat the meal with thankfulness. And I do not want to be criticized because of something I thank God for.

[31]So if you eat, or if you drink, or if you do anything, do everything for the glory of God. [32]Never do anything that might make others do wrong—Jews, Greeks, or God's church. [33]I do the same thing. I try to please everybody in

## LIVIN' IT!

**SECRET STATUES**
**1 CORINTHIANS 10:14**

Did you know that most people are idol worshipers? It may sound crazy, but it's true—even for some Christians. The tricky part about idol worship is that it's not always easy to spot. Sure, if someone has made a little statue out of wood or stone and bows down to it, you can be sure they're idol worshipers. But what about us? Do we have anything in our lives that we think is so important that it takes the place of God in our lives?

Before you answer, think about your TV habits. Or maybe how much time you spend on the computer or with friends. Then think about how much time you spend with God. Get the picture? It's easy to put things before God because we are naturally bent to sin. But God wants our love first. We need to work hard to keep anything from becoming more important than God and his will for us.

10:7 "The people . . . sexually." Quotation from Exodus 32:6. 10:16 cup of blessing The cup of the fruit of the vine that Christians thank God for and drink at the Lord's Supper. 10:26 "because . . . Lord" Quotation from Psalms 24:1; 50:12; 89:11.

every way. I am not trying to do what is good for me. I try to do what is good for the most people. I do this so that they can be saved.

**11** Follow my example, as I follow the example of Christ.

## BEING UNDER AUTHORITY

[2]I praise you because you remember me in everything. You follow closely the teachings that I gave you. [3]But I want you to understand this: The head of every man is Christ. And the head of a woman is the man.[n] And the head of Christ is God. [4]Every man who prophesies[d] or prays with his head covered brings shame to his head. [5]But every woman who prays or prophesies should have her head covered. If her head is not covered, she brings shame to her head. She is the same as a woman who has her head shaved. [6]If a woman does not cover her head, it is the same as cutting off all her hair. But it is shameful for a woman to cut off her hair or to shave her head. So she should cover her head. [7]But a man should not cover his head, because he is made like God and is God's glory. But woman is man's glory. [8]Man did not come from woman, but woman came from man. [9]And man was not made for woman. Woman was made for man. [10]So that is why a woman should have her head covered with something to show that she is under authority. And also she should do this because of the angels.

[11]But in the Lord the woman is important to the man, and the man is important to the woman. [12]This is true because woman came from man, but also man is born from woman. Really, everything comes from God. [13]Decide this for yourselves: Is it right for a woman to pray to God without something on her head? [14]Even nature itself teaches you that wearing long hair is shameful for a man. [15]But wearing long

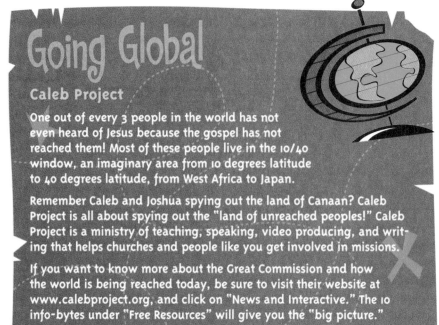

## Going Global

### Caleb Project

One out of every 3 people in the world has not even heard of Jesus because the gospel has not reached them! Most of these people live in the 10/40 window, an imaginary area from 10 degrees latitude to 40 degrees latitude, from West Africa to Japan.

Remember Caleb and Joshua spying out the land of Canaan? Caleb Project is all about spying out the "land of unreached peoples!" Caleb Project is a ministry of teaching, speaking, video producing, and writing that helps churches and people like you get involved in missions.

If you want to know more about the Great Commission and how the world is being reached today, be sure to visit their website at www.calebproject.org, and click on "News and Interactive." The 10 info-bytes under "Free Resources" will give you the "big picture."

You *can* make a difference through your prayers and giving!

hair is a woman's honor. Long hair is given to the woman to cover her head. [16]Some people may still want to argue about this. But I would add that neither we nor the churches of God accept any other practice.

## THE LORD'S SUPPER

[17]In the things I tell you now I do not praise you. Your meetings hurt you more than they help you. [18]First, I hear that when you meet together as a church you are divided. And I believe some of this. [19](It is necessary for there to be differences among you. That is the way to make it clear which of you are really doing right.) [20]When you all come together, you are not really eating the Lord's Supper.[n] [21]This is because when you eat, each person eats without waiting for the others. Some people do not get enough to eat, while others have too much to drink. [22]You can eat and drink in your own homes! It seems that you think God's church is not important. You embarrass those who are poor. What should I tell you?

Should I praise you for doing this? I do not praise you.

[23]The teaching that I gave you is the same teaching that I received from the Lord: On the night when Jesus was handed over to be killed, he took bread [24]and gave thanks for it. Then he broke the bread and said, "This is my body; it is for you. Do this to remember me." [25]In the same way, after they ate, Jesus took the cup. He said, "This cup shows the new agreement from God to his people. This new agreement begins with the blood of my death. When you drink this, do it to remember me." [26]Every time you eat this bread and drink this cup, you show others about the Lord's death until he comes.

[27]So a person should not eat the bread or drink the cup of the Lord in a way that is not worthy of it. If he does he is sinning against the body and the blood of the Lord. [28]Everyone should look into his own heart before he eats the bread and drinks the cup. [29]If someone eats the bread and drinks the cup without recognizing the body,

**11:3 the man** This could also mean "her husband." **11:20 Lord's Supper** The meal Jesus told his followers to eat to remember him (Luke 22:14-20).

then he is judged guilty by eating and drinking. [30]That is why many in your group are sick and weak. And many have died. [31]But if we judged ourselves in the right way, then God would not judge us. [32]But when the Lord judges us, he punishes us to show us the right way. He does this so that we will not be destroyed along with the world.

[33]So my brothers, when you come together to eat, wait for each other. [34]If anyone is too hungry, he should eat at home. Do this so that your meeting together will not bring God's judgment on you. I will tell you what to do about the other things when I come.

## GIFTS FROM THE HOLY SPIRIT

**12** Now, brothers, I want you to understand about spiritual gifts. [2]You remember the lives you lived before you were believers. You let yourselves be influenced and led away to worship idols—things that have no life. [3]So I tell you that no one who is speaking with the help of God's Spirit says, "Jesus be cursed." And no one can say, "Jesus is Lord," without the help of the Holy Spirit.[d]

[4]There are different kinds of gifts; but they are all from the same Spirit. [5]There are different ways to serve; but all these ways are from the same Lord. [6]And there are different ways that God works in people; but all these ways are from the same God. God works in us all in everything we do. [7]Something from the Spirit can be seen in each person, to help everyone. [8]The Spirit gives one person the ability to speak with wisdom. And the same Spirit gives another the ability to speak with knowledge. [9]The same Spirit gives faith to one person. And that one Spirit gives another gifts of healing. [10]The Spirit gives to another person the power to do miracles,[d] to another the ability to prophesy.[d] And he gives to another the

ability to know the difference between good and evil spirits. The Spirit gives one person the ability to speak in different kinds of languages and to another the ability to interpret those languages. [11]One Spirit, the same Spirit, does all these things. The Spirit decides what to give each person.

## THE BODY OF CHRIST

[12]A person's body is only one thing, but it has many parts. Yes, there are many parts to a body, but all those parts make only one body. Christ is like that too. [13]Some of us are Jews, and some of us are Greeks. Some of us are slaves, and some of us are free. But we were all baptized into one body through one Spirit.[d] And we were all made to share in the one Spirit.

[14]And a person's body has more than one part. It has many parts. [15]The foot might say, "I am not a hand. So I am not part of the body." But saying this would not stop the foot from being a part of the body. [16]The ear might say, "I am not an eye. So I am not part of the body." But saying this would not make the ear stop being a part of the body. [17]If the whole body were an eye, the body would not be able to hear. If the whole body were an ear, the body would not be able to smell anything. [18-19]If each part of the body were the same part, there would be no body. But truly God put the parts in the body as he wanted them. He

made a place for each one of them. [20]And so there are many parts, but only one body.

[21]The eye cannot say to the hand, "I don't need you!" And the head cannot say to the foot, "I don't need you!" [22]No! Those parts of the body that seem to be weaker are really very important. [23]And the parts of the body that we think are not worth much are the parts that we give the most care to. And we give special care to the parts of the body that we want to hide. [24]The more beautiful parts of our body need no

## LIVIN' IT!

**UNWRAP YOUR GIFTS
1 CORINTHIANS 12:7**

You've probably heard that you were made the way you are for a reason. God chose your eye color, hair, skin, family—everything about you for a reason. But did you know that when you became a Christian, you got something else that's really cool? God gave you his Holy Spirit, who has now given you a special gift that is uniquely yours to use for his kingdom.

Just as there are many parts of the human body, there are many parts of Christ's body. You need to ask God to show you which part you are. Find out what your strengths are and what you love to do, whether it's serving others, teaching, encouraging, or something else. No one else can do the work that God has planned for you to do. So enjoy who you are and the incredible gifts that come from being God's child!

## ? DECODE THIS!

*The church, just like the body, is made of many different _____ .*

special care. But God put the body together and gave more honor to the parts that need it. ²⁵God did this so that our body would not be divided. God wanted the different parts to care the same for each other. ²⁶If one part of the body suffers, then all the other parts suffer with it. Or if one part of our body is honored, then all the other parts share its honor.

²⁷All of you together are the body of Christ. Each one of you is a part of that body. ²⁸And in the church God has given a place first to apostles,ᵈ second to prophets,ᵈ and third to teachers. Then God has given a place to those who do miracles,ᵈ those who have gifts of healing, those who can help others, those who are able to lead, and those who can speak in different languages. ²⁹Not all are apostles. Not all are prophets. Not all are teachers. Not all do miracles. ³⁰Not all have gifts of healing. Not all speak in different languages. Not all interpret those languages. ³¹But you should truly want to have the greater gifts.

## LOVE

And now I will show you the best way of all.

**13** I may speak in different languages of men or even angels. But if I do not have love, then I am only a noisy bell or a ringing cymbal. ²I may have the gift of prophecy;ᵈ I may understand all the secret things of God and all knowledge; and I may have faith so great that I can move mountains. But even with all these things, if I do not have love, then I am nothing. ³I may give everything I have to feed the poor. And I may even give my body as an offering to be burned. But I gain

nothing by doing these things if I do not have love.

⁴Love is patient and kind. Love is not jealous, it does not brag, and it is not proud. ⁵Love is not rude, is not selfish, and does not become angry easily. Love does not remember wrongs done against it. ⁶Love is not happy with evil, but is happy with the truth. ⁷Love patiently accepts all things. It always trusts, always hopes, and always continues strong.

⁸Love never ends.

There are gifts of prophecy,ᵈ but they will be ended. There are gifts of speaking in different languages, but those gifts will end. There is the gift of knowledge, but it will be ended. ⁹These things will end, because this knowledge and these prophecies we have are not complete. ¹⁰But when perfection comes, the things that are not complete will end. ¹¹When I was a child, I talked like a child; I thought like a child; I made plans like a child. When I became a man, I stopped those childish ways. ¹²It is the same with us. Now we see as if we are

looking into a dark mirror. But at that time, in the future, we shall see clearly. Now I know only a part. But at that time I will know fully, as God has known me. ¹³So these three things continue forever: faith, hope and love. And the greatest of these is love.

## SPIRITUAL GIFTS

**14** Love, then, is what you should try for. And you should truly want to have the spiritual gifts. And the gift you should want most is to be able to prophesy.ᵈ ²I will explain why. One who has the gift of speaking in a different language is not speaking to people. He is speaking to God. No one understands him—he is speaking secret things through the Spirit.ᵈ ³But one who prophesies is speaking to people. He gives people strength, encouragement, and comfort. ⁴The one who speaks in a different language is helping only himself. But the one who prophesies is helping the whole church. ⁵I would like all of you to have the gift of speaking in different kinds of languages. But more, I want you to prophesy. The person who prophesies is greater than the one who can only speak in different languages—unless someone is there who can explain what he says. Then the whole church can be helped.

⁶Brothers, will it help you if I come to you speaking in different languages? No! It will help you only if I bring you a new truth or some knowledge, or some prophecy, or some teaching. ⁷It is the same as with non-living things that make sounds—like a flute or a harp. If different musical notes are not made

## BIBLE BASICS

### WHAT IS LOVE?

A lot of songwriters these days think they know what love is, but God gives us the straight scoop. Love is not just a feeling. It is the result of God living in our hearts (because God himself is love), and it shows itself through action. To love others means to put their needs before our own. Check out 1 Corinthians 13, the great love chapter. Paul tells us loud and clear what love does, and what it does not.

## DECODE THIS!

Faith, hope, and love continue forever. Which is the greatest?

## FIND AS MANY WORDS AS YOU CAN THAT DESCRIBE LOVE.

```
T P A T I E N T R E
H K L R P R E S K I
O H I U O U G S I N
U G I S F T I S N M
G O F T L O F E D E
H H O P E V T R W T
T U H F O R E V E R
F M A T I L O N T U
U B S E R V A N T T
L L G T J E S U S H
O E S H A P P Y E L
```

clear, you will not know what song is being played. Each note must be played clearly for you to be able to understand the tune. [8]And in a war, if the trumpet does not sound clearly, the soldiers will not know it is time to prepare for fighting. [9]It is the same with you. The words you speak with your tongue must be clear. Unless you speak clearly, no one can understand what you are saying. You will be talking in the air! [10]It is true that there are many kinds of speech in the world. And they all have meaning. [11]So unless I understand the meaning of what someone says to me, I am a stranger to him, and he is a stranger to me. [12]It is the same with you. You want spiritual gifts very much. So try most to have the gifts that help the church grow stronger.

[13]The one who has the gift of speaking in a different language should pray that he can also interpret what he says. [14]If I pray in a different language, my spirit is praying, but my mind does nothing. [15]So what should I do? I will pray with my spirit, but I will also pray with my mind. I will sing with my spirit, but I will also sing with my mind. [16]You might be praising God with your spirit. But a person there without understanding cannot say "Amen"[n] to your prayer of thanks. He does not know what you are saying. [17]You may be thanking God in a good way, but the other person is not helped.

[18]I thank God that my gift of speaking in different kinds of languages is greater than any of yours. [19]But in the church meetings I would rather speak five words that I understand than thousands of words in a different language. I would rather speak with my understanding, so that I can teach others.

[20]Brothers, do not think like children. In evil things be like babies. But in your thinking you should be like full-grown men. [21]It is written in the Scriptures:[d]

"I will use strange words and
    foreign languages
to speak to these people.
But even then they will not listen."

*Isaiah 28:11-12*

That is what the Lord says.

[22]So the gift of speaking in different kinds of languages is a proof for those who do not believe, not for those who believe. And prophecy is for people who believe, not for those who do not believe. [23]Suppose the whole church meets together and everyone speaks in different languages. If some people come in who are without understanding or do not believe, they will say you are crazy. [24]But suppose everyone is prophesying and someone comes in who does not believe or is without understanding. If everyone is prophesying, his sin will be shown to him, and he will be judged by all that he hears. [25]The secret things in his heart will be made known. So he will bow down and worship God. He will say, "Truly, God is with you."

## MEETINGS SHOULD HELP THE CHURCH

[26]So, brothers, what should you do? When you meet together, one person has a song. Another has a teaching. Another has a new truth from God. Another speaks in a different language, and another person interprets that language. The purpose of all these things should be to help the church grow strong. [27]When you meet together, if anyone speaks in a different language, then it should be only two, or not more than three, who speak. They should speak one after the other. And someone else should interpret what they say. [28]But if there is no interpreter, then anyone who speaks in a different language should be quiet in the church meeting. He should speak only to himself and to God.

[29]And only two or three prophets[d] should speak. The others should judge what they say. [30]And if a message from God comes to another person who is sitting, then the first speaker should stop. [31]You can all prophesy one after the other. In this way all the people can be taught and encouraged. [32]The spirits of prophets are under the control of the prophets themselves. [33]God is not a

### LIVIN' IT!

#### THE REAL THING
#### 1 CORINTHIANS 13

Both Christians and non-Christians alike say they know what love is. The way God defines it, though, makes all other kinds of love seem fake or shallow. First of all, God says that he himself is love. When you break it down into parts you can better understand, love becomes the actions you find here in 1 Corinthians 13.

You'll notice that it doesn't mention anything about feelings. God's kind of love is unchanging and much deeper than emotions that come and go. Go on and read through all of chapter 13. Then put your own name in where the word "love" appears. Do you love God and others this way? If not, ask God right now to change your heart and help you love others the way he wants you to.

### DECODE THIS!

*Who died for our sins?*

14:16 "Amen" When a person says "Amen," it means he agrees with the things that were said.

258

God of confusion but a God of peace. This is true in all the churches of God's people. [34]Women should keep quiet in the church meetings. They are not allowed to speak. They must be under control. This is also what the law of Moses says. [35]If there is something the women want to know, they should ask their own husbands at home. It is shameful for a woman to speak in the church meeting. [36]Did God's teaching come from you? Or are you the only ones who have received that teaching?

[37]If anyone thinks that he is a prophet or that he

## THE GOOD NEWS ABOUT CHRIST

**15** Now, brothers, I want you to remember the Good News[d] I brought to you. You received this Good News, and you continue strong in it. [2]And you are saved by this Good News. But you must continue believing what I told you. If you do not, then you believed for nothing.

[3]I passed on to you what I received. And this was the most important: that Christ died for our sins, as the Scriptures[d] say; [4]that he was buried and

## WILD WORLD FACTS

### ONE SCARY OUTFIT

The Bible says that Satan and evil people are like wolves in sheep's clothing. So what makes wolves so scary?

Wolves travel together in groups called packs, with anywhere from 6 to 30 wolves in a pack. They have 42 teeth (compared to our 32) and huge molars. They also have extremely powerful jaws that are able to crush their prey in just a few bites. Fortunately for humans, wolves prefer to eat animals like deer, moose, elk, caribou, and other large, hoofed animals. On average, wolves eat about 15-20 deer per year.

Wolves are beautiful to watch, but they are also very dangerous. When you see them at the zoo, remember God's warning that our enemy, Satan, wants to harm us just like wolves go after their prey—so always stay on guard.

[International Wolf Center]

has a spiritual gift, then he should understand that what I am writing to you is the Lord's command. [38]If that person does not know this, then he is not known by God.

[39]So my brothers, you should truly want to prophesy. And do not stop people from using the gift of speaking in different kinds of languages. [40]But let everything be done in a way that is right and orderly.

was raised to life on the third day as the Scriptures say; [5]and that he showed himself to Peter and then to the twelve apostles.[d] [6]After that, Jesus showed himself to more than 500 of the believ-ers at the same time. Most of them are still living today. But some have died. [7]Then Jesus showed himself to James and later to all the apostles. [8]Last of all he showed himself to me—as to a person not born at the normal time. [9]All the other apostles are greater than I am. This is because I persecuted the church of God. And this is why I am not even good enough to be called an apostle. [10]But God's grace has made me what I am. And his grace to me was not wasted. I worked harder than all the other apostles. (But I was not really the one working. It was God's grace that was with me.) [11]So then it is not important if I preached to you or if the other apostles preached to you. We all preach the same thing, and this is what you believed.

## WE WILL BE RAISED FROM DEATH

[12]It is preached that Christ was raised from death. So why do some of you say that people will not be raised from death? [13]If no one will ever be raised from death, then Christ was not raised from death. [14]And if Christ was not raised, then our preaching is worth nothing. And your faith is worth nothing. [15]And also, we will be guilty of lying about God. Because we have preached about him by saying that he raised Christ from death. And if people are not raised from death, then God never raised Christ from death. [16]If the dead are not raised, Christ has not been raised either. [17]And if Christ has not been raised, then your faith is for noth-ing; you are still guilty of your sins. [18]And also, those in Christ who have already died are lost. [19]If our hope in Christ is for this life only, we should be pitied more than anyone else in the world.

[20]But Christ has truly been raised from death—the first one and proof that those who are asleep in death will also be raised. [21]Death comes to everyone because of what one man did. But the

rising from death also happens because of one man. ²²In Adam all of us die. In the same way, in Christ all of us will be made alive again. ²³But everyone will be raised to life in the right order. Christ was first to be raised. When Christ comes again, those who belong to him will be raised to life. ²⁴Then the end will come. Christ will destroy all rulers, authorities, and powers. And he will give the kingdom to God the Father. ²⁵Christ must rule until God puts all enemies under Christ's control. ²⁶The last enemy to be destroyed will be death. ²⁷The Scripture[d] says, "God put all things under his control."[n] When it says that "all things" are put under him, it is clear that this does not include God himself. God is the one putting everything under Christ's control. ²⁸After everything has been put under Christ, then the Son himself will be put under God. God is the One who put all things under Christ. And Christ will be put under God, so that God will be the complete ruler over everything.

²⁹If the dead are never raised, then what will people do who are baptized for those who have died? If the dead are not raised at all, why are people baptized for them?

³⁰And what about us? Why do we put ourselves in danger every hour? ³¹I die every day. That is true, brothers, just as it is true that I brag about you in Christ Jesus our Lord. ³²If I fought wild animals in Ephesus only for human reasons, I have gained nothing. If the dead are not raised, then, "Let us eat and drink, because tomorrow we will die."[n]

³³Do not be fooled: "Bad friends will ruin good habits." ³⁴Come back to your right way of thinking and stop sinning. I say this to shame you—some of you do not know God.

## WHAT KIND OF BODY WILL WE HAVE?

³⁵But someone may ask, "How are the dead raised? What kind of body will they have?" ³⁶Those are stupid questions. When you plant something, it must die in the ground before it can live and grow. ³⁷And when you plant it, what you plant does not have the same "body" that it will have later. What you plant is only a seed, maybe wheat or something else. ³⁸But God gives it a body that he has planned for it. And God gives each kind of seed its own body. ³⁹All things made of flesh are not the same kinds of flesh: People have one kind of flesh, animals have another kind, birds have another, and fish have another. ⁴⁰Also there are heavenly bodies and earthly bodies. But the beauty of the heavenly bodies is one kind. The beauty of the earthly bodies is another kind. ⁴¹The sun has one kind of beauty. The moon has another beauty, and the stars have another. And each star is different in its beauty.

⁴²It is the same with the dead who are raised to life. The body that is "planted" will ruin and decay. But that body is raised to a life that cannot be destroyed. ⁴³When the body is "planted," it is without honor. But it is raised in glory. When the body is "planted," it is weak. But when it is raised, it has power. ⁴⁴The body that is "planted" is a physical body. When it is raised, it is a spiritual body.

There is a physical body. And there is also a spiritual body. ⁴⁵It is written in the Scriptures:[d] "The first man became a living person."[n] But the last Adam became a spirit that

**LIVIN' IT!**

GOOD WORK!
1 CORINTHIANS 15:58

Do you ever get tired of doing the right thing? Does it feel like no one notices when you do it right, but only when you do it wrong?

Don't be discouraged. Your Father in heaven knows what is going on in your heart all the time, and he sees you right where you are. You may think you are just being kind to your younger brother, but God sees it as work done for his honor. You may think you're just helping your mom clean the house, but God sees an obedient heart that brings pleasure to him. Nothing that you do for the Lord is ever a waste. God sees and remembers it all, and he will reward you now with a closer friendship with him and later in heaven, too. So keep up the good work!

gives life. ⁴⁶The spiritual man did not come first. It was the physical man who came first; then came the spiritual. ⁴⁷The first man came from the dust of the earth. The second man came from heaven. ⁴⁸People belong to the earth. They are like the first man of earth. But those people who belong to heaven are like the man of heaven. ⁴⁹We were made like the man of earth. So we will also be made like the man of heaven.

⁵⁰I tell you this, brothers: Flesh and blood cannot have a part in the kingdom of God. A thing that will ruin cannot have a part in something that never ruins. ⁵¹But listen, I tell you this secret: We will not all die, but we will

15:27 "God put . . . control." Quotation from Psalm 8:6.  15:32 "Let us . . . die." Quotation from Isaiah 22:13; 56:12.  15:45 "The first . . . person." Quotation from Genesis 2:7.

**DECODE THIS!**

*Bad friends will ruin what?*

all be changed. ⁵²It will only take a second. We will be changed as quickly as an eye blinks. This will happen when the last trumpet sounds. The trumpet will sound and those who have died will be raised to live forever. And we will all be changed. ⁵³This body that will ruin must clothe itself with something that will never ruin. And this body that dies must clothe itself with something that will never die. ⁵⁴So this body that ruins will clothe itself with that which never ruins. And this body that dies will clothe itself with that which never dies. When this happens, then this Scripture will be made true:

"Death is destroyed forever in
victory."                    *Isaiah 25:8*
⁵⁵"Death, where is your victory?
Death, where is your power to
hurt?"                    *Hosea 13:14*
⁵⁶Death's power to hurt is sin. The power of sin is the law. ⁵⁷But we thank God! He gives us the victory through our Lord Jesus Christ.

⁵⁸So my dear brothers, stand strong. Do not let anything change you. Always give yourselves fully to the work of the Lord. You know that your work in the Lord is never wasted.

### THE GIFT FOR OTHER BELIEVERS

**16** Now I will write about the collection of money for God's people. Do the same thing that I told the Galatian churches to do: ²On the first day of every week, each one of you should put aside as much money as you can from what you are blessed with. You should save it up, so that you will not have to collect money after I come. ³When I arrive, I will send some men to take your gift to Jerusalem. These will be men who you all agree should go. I will send them with letters of introduction. ⁴If it seems good for me

to go also, these men will go along with me.

### PAUL'S PLANS

⁵I plan to go through Macedonia. So I will come to you after I go through there. ⁶Maybe I will stay with you for a time. I might even stay all winter. Then you can help me on my trip, wherever I go. ⁷I do not want to come to see you now, because I would have to leave to go other places. I hope to stay a longer time with you if the Lord allows it. ⁸But I will stay at Ephesus until Pentecost.ᵈ ⁹I will stay, because a good opportunity for a great and growing work has been given to me now. And there are many people working against me.

¹⁰Timothy might come to you. Try to make him feel comfortable with you. He is working for the Lord just as I am. ¹¹So none of you should refuse to accept Timothy. Help him on his trip in peace, so that he can come back to me. I am expecting him to come back with the brothers.

Q. What would you do if you were the President?

A. I would close school forever.

¹²Now about our brother Apollos: I strongly encouraged him to visit you with the other brothers. But he was sure that he did not want to go now. But when he has the opportunity, he will go to you.

> **"Always give yourselves fully to the work of the Lord. You know that your work in the Lord is never wasted."**
>
> *1 Corinthians 15:58*

### PAUL ENDS HIS LETTER

¹³Be careful. Continue strong in the faith. Have courage, and be strong. ¹⁴Do everything in love. ¹⁵You know that the family of Stephanas were the first believers in Southern Greece. They have given themselves to the service of God's people. I ask you, brothers, ¹⁶to follow the leading of people like these and anyone else who works and serves with them.

¹⁷I am happy that Stephanas, Fortunatus, and Achaicus have come. You are not here, but they have filled your place. ¹⁸They have given rest to my spirit and to yours. You should recognize the value of men like these.

¹⁹The churches in the country of Asia send greetings to you. Aquila and Priscilla greet you in the Lord. Also the church that meets in their house greets you. ²⁰All the brothers here send greetings. Give each other a holy kiss when you meet.

²¹I am Paul, and I am writing this greeting with my own hand.

²²If anyone does not love the Lord, then let him be separated from God—lost forever!

Come, O Lord!

²³The grace of the Lord Jesus be with you. ²⁴My love be with all of you in Christ Jesus.

False teachers say that Paul is proud, sloppy looking, and lying.

Unsolved mystery: What is Paul's "painful problem"?

Titus delivers the second letter to the believers in Corinth.

Paul answers those who accuse him.

# THE SECOND LETTER of PAUL THE APOSTLE TO THE CORINTHIANS

Paul tells them about his daring basket escape in Damascus.

**1** From Paul, an apostle[d] of Christ Jesus. I am an apostle because that is what God wanted.

Also from Timothy our brother in Christ. To the church of God in Corinth, and to all of God's people in the whole country of Southern Greece:

[2]Grace and peace to you from God our Father and the Lord Jesus Christ.

### PAUL GIVES THANKS TO GOD

[3]Praise be to the God and Father of our Lord Jesus Christ. God is the Father who is full of mercy. And he is the God of all comfort. [4]He comforts us every time we have trouble, so

that we can comfort others when they have trouble. We can comfort them with the same comfort that God gives us. [5]We share in the many sufferings of Christ. In the same way, much comfort comes to us through Christ. [6]If we have troubles, it is for your comfort and salvation. If we have comfort, then you also have comfort. This helps you to accept patiently the same sufferings that we have. [7]Our hope for you is strong. We know that you share in our sufferings. So we know that you also share in the comfort we receive.

> ## "it happened so that we would trust in God, who raises people from death."
> *2 Corinthians 1:9*

[8]Brothers, we want you to know about the trouble we suffered in the country of Asia. We had great burdens there that were greater than our own strength. We even gave up hope for life. [9]Truly, in our own hearts we believed that we would die. But this happened so that we would not trust in ourselves. It happened so that we would trust in God, who raises people from death. [10]God saved us from these great dangers of death. And he will continue to save us. We have put our hope in him, and he will save us again. [11]And you can help us with your prayers. Then many people will give thanks for us— that God blessed us because of their many prayers.

### THE CHANGE IN PAUL'S PLANS

[12]This is what we are proud of, and I can say with all my heart that it is true: In all the things we have done in the world, we have done everything with an honest and pure heart from God. And this is even more true in what we have done with you. We did this by God's grace, not by the kind of wisdom the world has. [13]For we write to you only what you can read and understand. And I hope that [14]as you have understood some things about us, you may come to know everything about us. Then you can be proud of us, as we will be proud of you on the day our Lord Jesus Christ comes again.

[15]I was very sure of all this. That is why I made plans to visit you first. Then you could be blessed twice. [16]I planned to visit you on my way to Macedonia. Then I planned to visit you again on my way back. I wanted to get help from you for my trip to Judea. [17]Do you think that I made these plans without really thinking? Or maybe you think I make plans as the world does, so that I say "Yes, yes," and at the same time "No, no."

[18]But if you can believe God, then you can believe that what we tell you is never both "Yes" and "No." [19]The Son of God, Jesus Christ, that Silas and Timothy and I preached to you, was not "Yes" and "No." In Christ it has always been "Yes." [20]The "Yes" to all of God's promises is in Christ. And that is why we say "Amen"[n] through Christ to the glory of God. [21]And God is the One who makes you and us strong in Christ. God made us his chosen people. [22]He put his mark on us to show that we are his. And he put his Spirit[d] in our hearts to be a guarantee for all he has promised.

[23]I tell you this, and I ask God to be my witness that this is true: The reason I did not come back to Corinth was that I did not want to punish or hurt you. [24]I do not mean that we are trying to control your faith. You are strong in faith. But we are workers with you for your own happiness.

**2** So I decided that my next visit to you would not be another visit to make you sad. [2]If I make you sad, who will make me happy? Only you can make me happy—you whom I made sad. [3]I wrote you a letter for this reason: that when I came to you I would not be made sad by the people who should make me happy. I felt sure of all of you. I felt sure that you would share my joy. [4]When I wrote to you before, I was very troubled and unhappy in my heart. I wrote with many tears. I did not write

## decode this!

*Who comforts us every time we have trouble?*

to make you sad, but to let you know how much I love you.

### FORGIVE THE SINNER

⁵Someone there among you has caused sadness. He caused this not to me, but to all of you—I mean he caused sadness to all in some way. (I do not want to make it sound worse than it really is.) ⁶The punishment that most of you gave him is enough for him. ⁷But now you should forgive him and comfort him. This will keep him from having too much sadness and giving up completely. ⁸So I beg you to show him that you love him. ⁹This is why I wrote to you. I wanted to test you and see if you obey in everything. ¹⁰If you forgive someone, I also forgive him. And what I have forgiven—if I had anything to forgive—I forgave it for you, and Christ was with me. ¹¹I did this so that Satan would not win anything from us. We know very well what Satan's plans are.

### PAUL'S CONCERN IN TROAS

¹²I went to Troas to preach the Good News*d* of Christ. The Lord gave me a good opportunity there. ¹³But I had no peace because I did not find my brother Titus there. So I said good-bye and went to Macedonia.

### VICTORY THROUGH CHRIST

¹⁴But thanks be to God, who always leads us in victory through Christ. God uses us to spread his knowledge everywhere like a sweet-smelling perfume. ¹⁵Our offering to God is this: We are the sweet smell of Christ among those who are being saved and among those who are being lost. ¹⁶To those who are lost, we are the smell of death that brings death. But to those who are being saved, we are the smell of life that brings life. So who is able to do this work? ¹⁷We do not sell the word of God for a profit as many other people do. But in Christ we speak the truth before God. We speak as men sent from God.

### SERVANTS OF THE NEW AGREEMENT

**3** Are we starting to brag about ourselves again? Do we need letters of introduction to you or from you, like some other people? ²You yourselves are our letter, written on our hearts. It is known and read by everyone. ³You show that you are a letter from Christ that he sent through us. This letter is not written with ink, but with the Spirit*d* of the living God. It is not written on stone tablets.* It is written on human hearts.

⁴We can say this, because through Christ we feel sure before God. ⁵I do not mean that we are able to say that we can do this work ourselves. It is God who makes us able to do all that we do. ⁶God made us able to be servants of a new agreement from himself to his people. This new agreement is not a written law. It is of the Spirit. The written law brings death, but the Spirit gives life.

⁷The law that brought death was written in words on stone. It came with God's glory. Moses' face was so bright with glory that the people of Israel could not continue to look at his face. And that glory later disappeared. ⁸So surely the new way that brings the Spirit has even more glory. ⁹That law judged people guilty of sin, but it had glory. So surely the new way that makes people right with God has much greater glory. ¹⁰That old law had glory. But it really loses its glory when it is compared to the much greater glory of this new way. ¹¹If that law which disappeared came with glory, then this new way which continues forever has much greater glory.

¹²We have this hope, so we are very brave. ¹³We are not like Moses. He put a covering over his face so that the people of Israel would not see it. The glory was disappearing, and Moses did not want them to see it end. ¹⁴But their minds were closed. Even today that same covering hides the meaning when they read the old agreement. That covering is taken away only through Christ. ¹⁵But even today, when they read the law of Moses, there is a covering over their minds. ¹⁶But when a person changes and follows the Lord, that covering is taken away. ¹⁷The Lord is the Spirit. And where the Spirit of the Lord is, there is freedom. ¹⁸Our faces, then, are not covered. We all show the Lord's glory, and we are being changed to be like him. This change in us brings more and more glory. And it comes from the Lord, who is the Spirit.

3:3 **stone tablets** Meaning the law of Moses that was written on stone tablets (Exodus 24:12; 25:16).

## PREACHING THE GOOD NEWS

**4** God, with his mercy, gave us this work to do. So we don't give up. [2]But we have turned away from secret and shameful ways. We use no trickery, and we do not change the teaching of God. We teach the truth plainly. This is how we show everyone who we are. And this is how they can know in their hearts what kind of people we are before God. [3]The Good News[d] that we preach may be hidden. But it is hidden only to those who are lost. [4]The devil who rules this world has blinded the minds of those who do not believe. They cannot see the light of the Good News—the Good News about the glory of Christ, who is exactly like God. [5]We do not preach about ourselves. But we preach that Jesus Christ is Lord; and we preach that we are your servants for Jesus. [6]God once said, "Let the light shine out of the darkness!" And this is the same God who made his light shine in our hearts. He gave us light by letting us know the glory of God that is in the face of Christ.

## SPIRITUAL TREASURE IN CLAY JARS

[7]We have this treasure from God. But we are only like clay jars that hold the treasure. This shows that this great power is from God, not from us. [8]We have troubles all around us, but we are not defeated. We do not know what to do, but we do not give up. [9]We are persecuted, but God does not leave us. We are hurt sometimes, but we are not destroyed. [10]We carry the death of Jesus in our own bodies, so that the life of Jesus can also be seen in our bodies. [11]We are alive, but for Jesus we are always in danger of death. This is so that the life of Jesus can be seen in our bodies that die. [12]So death is working in us, but life is working in you.

[13]It is written in the Scriptures,[d] "I believed, so I spoke."[n] Our faith is like this,

## LIVIN' IT!

### JARS OF CLAY
### 2 CORINTHIANS 4:7

Do you remember how God made Adam? He was the only part of creation that God made from the dust. Second Corinthians 4:7 reminds us where we came from—that our physical bodies are like jars of clay. In other words, the fingers and toes and eyes that we have now won't last. But inside our "jars of clay" lie the Holy Spirit and the hope for our future.

We don't need to find joy or peace or security from the material things we have—even our own bodies—because they won't last. But God and his Word will live forever. And because of him our souls will also live on. We will be given new bodies that will not die. We should live each day knowing that this life is short, but the next is forever. So build up spiritual treasures in heaven that last forever!

too. We believe, and so we speak. [14]God raised the Lord Jesus from death. And we know that God will also raise us with Jesus. God will bring us together with you, and we will stand before him. [15]All these things are for you. And so the grace of God is being given to more and more people. This will bring more and more thanks to God for his glory.

## LIVING BY FAITH

[16]So we do not give up. Our physical body is becoming older and weaker, but our spirit inside us is made new every day. [17]We have small troubles for a while now, but they are helping us gain an eternal glory. That

glory is much greater than the troubles. [18]So we set our eyes not on what we see but on what we cannot see. What we see will last only a short time. But what we cannot see will last forever.

**5** We know that our body—the tent we live in here on earth—will be destroyed. But when that happens, God will have a house for us to live in. It will not be a house made by men. It will be a home in heaven that will last forever. [2]But now we are tired of this body. We want God to give us our heavenly home. [3]It will clothe us, and we will not be naked. [4]While we live in this body, we have burdens, and we complain. We do not want to be naked. We want to be clothed with our heavenly home. Then this body that dies will be fully covered with life. [5]This is what God made us for. And he has given us the Spirit[d] to be a guarantee for this new life.

[6]So we always have courage. We know that while we live in this body, we are away from the Lord. [7]We live by what we believe, not by what we can see. [8]So I say that we have courage. And we really want to be away from this body and be at home with the Lord. [9]Our only goal is to please God. We want to please him whether we live here or there. [10]For we must all stand before Christ to be judged. Each one will receive what he should get—good or bad—for the things he did when he lived in the earthly body.

## BECOMING FRIENDS WITH GOD

[11]We know what it means to fear the Lord. So we try to help people accept the truth. God knows what we really are. And I hope that in your hearts you know, too. [12]We are not trying to prove ourselves to

## DECODE THIS!

God uses us to spread his knowledge like a sweet-smelling _____.

4:13 "I . . . spoke." Quotation from Psalm 116:10.

## SOMETHING'S FISHY

**WILD WORLD FACTS**

What do Peter, James, John, and a lot of other followers of Jesus have in common? They were fishermen before they became disciples. Fishing can be a career, or it can be something to do for fun. If you ever fish, Fishingworld.com suggests these 5 tips:

- Decide which kind of fish you want to catch, and pick the correct bait to use.

- Look for fish around rocks, weeds, and pilings because fish like shade.

- Choose fishing tackle that fits your size (nothing too heavy or hard to use).

- Fish in the early morning and late evening, just at sunrise or sunset.

- Be quiet! Fish can feel vibrations.

Even if fishing is not your thing, God still says we should be fishermen. But don't worry. You don't have to handle the slimy stuff. He wants us to "catch" people's hearts, to bring them to Jesus.

you again. But we are telling you about ourselves, so you will be proud of us. Then you will have an answer for those who are proud about things that can be seen. They do not care about what is in the heart. [13]If we are out of our minds, it is for God. If we have our right mind, then it is for you. [14]The love of Christ controls us. Because we know that One died for all. So all have died. [15]Christ died for all so that those who live would not continue to live for themselves. He died for them and was raised from death so that they would live for him.

[16]From this time on we do not think of anyone as the world does. It is true that in the past we thought of Christ as the world thinks. But we no longer think of him in that way. [17]If anyone belongs to Christ, then he is made new. The old things have gone; everything is made new! [18]All this is from God. Through Christ, God made peace between us and himself. And God gave us the work of bringing everyone into peace with him. [19]I mean that God was in Christ, making peace between the world and himself. In Christ, God did not hold the world guilty

of its sins. And he gave us this message of peace. [20]So we have been sent to speak for Christ. It is as if God is calling to you through us. We speak for Christ when we beg you to be at peace with God. [21]Christ had no sin. But God made him become sin. God did this for us so that in Christ we could become right with God.

**6** We are workers together with God. So we beg you: Do not let the grace that you received from God be for nothing. [2]God says,

"I heard your prayers at the right time,
and I gave you help on the day
of salvation."      *Isaiah 49:8*

I tell you that the "right time" is now. The "day of salvation" is now.

[3]We do not want anyone to find anything wrong with our work. So we do nothing that will be a problem for anyone. [4]But in every way we show that we are servants of God: in accepting many hard things, in troubles, in difficulties, and in great problems. [5]We are beaten and thrown into prison. Men become upset and fight us. We work hard, and sometimes we get no sleep or food. [6]We show that we are servants of God by living a pure life, by our understanding, by our patience, and by our kindness. We show this by the Holy Spirit,[d] by true love, [7]by speaking the truth, and by God's power. We use our right living to defend ourselves against everything. [8]Some people honor us, but other people shame us. Some people say good things about us, but other people say bad things. Some people say we are liars, but we speak the truth. [9]We are not known, but we are well-known. We seem to be dying, but look—we continue to live. We are punished, but we are not killed. [10]We have much sadness, but we are always rejoicing. We are poor, but we are making many people rich in faith. We have nothing, but really we have everything.

[11]We have spoken freely to you in Corinth. We have opened our hearts to you.

## GET CONNECTED

### BOUND TO WIN

Have you ever run in a 3-legged race? You have to tie your leg with someone else's and together run to the finish line. Find a good match to win, but a bad match only makes you fall.

The Bible says that we shouldn't tie ourselves up with non-believers, for the same reason. It's not that we can't be friends with non-Christians; they just shouldn't be our best friends or people that we marry. Because they don't trust in Jesus for their salvation, they won't encourage us to keep on in our faith. Their doubt and bad decisions can trip us up and distract us from the prize. We can pray for them and love them, but our closest friends need to share our love for Christ.

# september HUMILITY

**1** Matthew 20:27: If one of you wants to become first, then he must serve the rest of you like a slave.

**2** Ask your grandmother what her favorite memory is.

**3**

**4** Prayer Pointer: Ask God to show you if you have any pride or if you are not depending on God for strength in any area of your life.

**5**

**6** Let your brothers and sisters have their way all day today.

**7** 1 Peter 3:4: Your beauty should come from within you—the beauty of a gentle and quiet spirit. This beauty will never disappear, and it is worth very much to God. **8**

**9**

**10** Make a collage from magazine clippings that show what you like about school.

**11**

**12** Prayer Pointer: Ask God to give you a humble heart like Jesus has.

**13**

**14** JAMES 4:6: But God gives us even more grace, as the Scripture says, "God is against the proud, but he gives grace to the humble."

**15**

**16**

**17** Ask your friends how you can best pray for them.

**18**

**19**

**20** Prayer Pointer: Praise Jesus for being willing to come to earth as a person just to save us from our sins.

**21** Clean your room without being asked.

**22** Philippians 2:3: When you do things, do not let selfishness or pride be your guide. Be humble and give more honor to others than to yourselves.

**23**

**24**

**25**

**26** Help your brothers and sisters with their chores.

**27**

**28** Prayer Pointer: Ask God to guard his people against pride and to help us put others before ourselves.

**29**

**30** Rub your mom's shoulders.

Do what is right to other people. Love being kind to others. And live humbly, trusting your God (Micah 6:8).

[12]Our feelings of love for you have not stopped. It is you that have stopped your feelings of love for us. [13]I speak to you as if you were my children. Do to us as we have done—open your hearts to us.

## WARNING ABOUT NON-CHRISTIANS

[14]You are not the same as those who do not believe. So do not join yourselves to them. Good and bad do not belong together. Light and darkness cannot share together. [15]How can Christ and Belial, the devil, have any agreement? What can a believer have together with a non-believer? [16]The temple of God cannot have any agreement with idols. And we are the temple of the living God. As God said: "I will live with them and walk with them. And I will be their God. And they will be my people."[n]

[17]"Leave those people,
    and make yourselves pure, says
        the Lord.
Touch nothing that is unclean,[d]
    and I will accept you."

*Isaiah 52:11; Ezekiel 20:34, 41*

[18]"I will be your father,
    and you will be my sons and
        daughters,
    says the Lord All-Powerful."

*2 Samuel 7:14; 7:8*

**7** Dear friends, we have these promises from God. So we should make ourselves pure—free from anything that makes body or soul unclean. We should try to become perfect in the way we live, because we respect God.

## PAUL'S JOY

[2]Open your hearts to us. We have not done wrong to anyone. We have not ruined the faith of any person, and we have cheated no one. [3]I do not say this to blame you. I told you before that we love you so much that we would live or die with you. [4]I feel very sure of you. I am very proud of you. You give me

much comfort. And in all of our troubles I have great joy.

[5]When we came into Macedonia, we had no rest. We found trouble all around us. We had fighting on the outside and fear on the inside. [6]But God comforts those who are troubled. And God comforted us when Titus came. [7]We were comforted by his coming and also by the comfort that you gave him. Titus told us about your wish to see me. He told us that you are very sorry for what you did. And he told me about your great care for me. When I heard this, I was much happier.

[8]Even if the letter I wrote you made you sad, I am not sorry I wrote it. I know it made you sad, and I was sorry for that. But it made you sad only for a short time. [9]Now I am happy, but not because you were made sad. I am happy because your sorrow made you change your hearts. You became sad in the way God wanted you to. So you were not hurt by us in any way. [10]Being sorry

in the way God wants makes a person change his heart and life. This leads to salvation, and we cannot be sorry for that. But the kind of sorrow the world has will bring death. [11]"You had the kind of sorrow God wanted you to have. Now see what this sorrow has brought you: It has made you very serious. It made you want to prove that you were not wrong. It made you angry and afraid. It made you want to see me. It made you care. It made you want the right thing to be done. You proved that you were not guilty in any part of the problem. [12]I wrote that letter, but not because of the one who did the wrong. And it was not written because of the person who was hurt. But I wrote the letter so that you could see, before God, the great care that you have for us. [13]That is why we were comforted.

We were very comforted. And we were even happier to see that Titus was so

### Going Global

#### Christian Blind Mission

Hello everyone. I'm Chris, the CBM Mole. As you know, moles have poor eyesight. That's why I have been helping Christian Blind Mission. CBM is a worldwide Christian service that exists to help cure and prevent blindness, deafness, and other disabilities. Did you know that 250 million children around the world are showing signs of vitamin A deficiency? When it becomes severe, it can permanently blind a child in a matter of days.

Last year, CBM supported over 1,000 relief projects, providing medical, educational, and rehabilitation services to almost 10 million needy people in 108 developing countries on 4 continents. I hope you will visit our site at www.cbmuk.org.uk/home.shtm and encounter God's great compassion for those suffering from disabilities. You'll learn how to build a "tower of help" at your church or school. And you will see the possibilities of hope given out in the name of Jesus.

### ? DECODE THIS!

*If you want to give, your gift will be _____ .*

6:16 "I . . . people." Quotation from Leviticus 26:11–12; Jeremiah 32:38; Ezekiel 37:27.

happy. All of you made him feel much better. [14]I bragged to Titus about you. And you showed that I was right. Everything that we said to you was true. And you have proved that what we bragged about to Titus is true. [15]And his love for you is stronger when he remembers that you were all ready to obey. You welcomed him with respect and fear. [16]I am very happy that I can trust you fully.

## CHRISTIAN GIVING

**8** And now, brothers, we want you to know about the grace that God gave the churches in Macedonia. [2]They have been tested by great troubles. And they are very poor. But they gave much because of their great joy. [3]I can tell you that they gave as much as they were able. They gave even more than they could afford. No one told them to do it. [4]But they asked us again and again—they begged us to let them share in this service for God's people. [5]And they gave in a way that we did not expect: They first gave themselves to the Lord and to us. This is what God wants. [6]So we asked Titus to help you finish this special work of grace. He is the one who started this work. [7]You are rich in everything—in faith, in speaking, in knowledge, in truly wanting to help, and in the love you learned from us. And so we want you to be rich also in this gift of giving.

[8]I am not commanding you to give. But I want to see if your love is true love. I do this by showing you that others really want to help. [9]You know the grace of our Lord Jesus Christ. You know that Christ was rich, but for you he became poor. Christ did this so that by his being poor you might become rich.

[10]This is what I think you should do: Last year you were the first to want to give. And you were the first who gave. [11]So now finish the work that you started. Then your "doing" will be equal to your "wanting to do." Give from what you have. [12]If you want to give, your gift will be accepted. Your gift will be judged by what you have, not by what you do not have. [13]We do not want you to have troubles while other people are at ease. We want everything to be equal. [14]At this time you have plenty. What you have can help others who are in need. Then later, when they have plenty, they can help you when you are in need. Then all will be equal. [15]As it is written in the Scriptures,[d] "The person who gathered more did not have too much. The person who gathered less did not have too little."[n]

## TITUS AND HIS COMPANIONS

[16]I thank God because he gave Titus the same love for you that I have. [17]Titus accepted what we asked him to do. He wanted very much to go to you. This was his own idea. [18]We are sending with him the brother who is praised by all the churches. This brother is praised because of his service in preaching the Good News.[d] [19]Also, this brother was chosen by the churches to go with us when we deliver this gift of money. We are doing this service to bring glory to the Lord and to show that we really want to help.

[20]We are being careful so that no one will criticize us about the way we are handling this large gift. [21]We are trying to do what is right. We want to do what the Lord accepts as right and also what people think is right.

[22]Also, we are sending with them our brother who is always ready to help. He has proved this to us in many ways. And he wants to help even more now because he has much faith in you.

[23]Now about Titus—he is my partner who is working with me to help you. And about the other brothers—they are sent from the churches, and they bring glory to Christ. [24]So show these men that you really have love. Show them why we are proud of you. Then all the churches can see it.

## HELP FOR FELLOW CHRISTIANS

**9** I really do not need to write to you about this help for God's people. [2]I know that you want to help. I have been bragging about this to the people in Macedonia. I have told them that you in Southern Greece have been ready to give since last year. And your wanting to give has made most of them here ready to give also. [3]But I am sending the brothers to you. I do not want our bragging about you in this to be for nothing. I want you to be ready, as I said you would be. [4]If any of the people

## LIVIN' IT!

**JOYFUL GIVERS**
**2 CORINTHIANS 9:7**

Picture this: You have been saving up for weeks to buy the latest video game. You've earned just about what you need, when you go to Sunday school where a missionary shares with the class about the poor children in his area who need money just to eat and have clothes to wear. What will you do?

Jesus says that we should give some of our money (called a tithe) back to the church each time we earn it. But he also encourages us to give more than what we simply "owe" God. He wants us to have hearts that love to give . . . and give happily. If our first concern is to build up God's kingdom and not serve ourselves, then we will be happy to give when we see the need. By giving, we protect ourselves from making material things too important, and we also bless others in the process.

8:15 "The person . . . little." Quotation from Exodus 16:18.

### PUMP IT UP

Who's your favorite athlete? How do you think they got to be so great? Without question, they had a good coach—but that's not all. They had to listen to what the coach said and then obey.

Do you want to be a strong Christian? Then listen to God and obey what he says. He is our Coach, and he knows what we need to succeed. We cannot become what he intends us to be if we do not listen or obey. Practicing obedience in the small and big ways strengthens our spiritual muscles for success in life.

from Macedonia come with me and find that you are not ready, we will be ashamed. We will be ashamed that we were so sure of you. (And you will be ashamed, too!) [5]So I thought that I should ask these brothers to go to you before we come. They will finish getting in order the gift you promised. Then the gift will be ready when we come, and it will be a gift you wanted to give—not a gift that you hated to give.

[6]Remember this: The person who plants a little will have a small harvest. But the person who plants a lot will have a big harvest. [7]Each one should give, then, what he has decided in his heart to give. He should not give if it makes him sad. And he should not give if he thinks he is forced to give. God loves the person who gives happily. [8]And God can give you more blessings than you need. Then you will always have plenty of everything. You will have enough to give to every good work. [9]It is written in the Scriptures:[d]

"He gives freely to the poor.
    The things he does are right and
        will continue forever."

*Psalm 112:9*

[10]God is the One who gives seed to the farmer. And he gives bread for food. And God will give you all the seed you

> ## "The person who plants a little will have a small harvest. But the person who plants a lot will have a big harvest."
> *2 Corinthians 9:6*

need and make it grow. He will make a great harvest from your goodness. [11]God will make you rich in every way so that you can always give freely. And your giving through us will cause many to give thanks to God. [12]This service that

you do helps the needs of God's people. It is also bringing more and more thanks to God. [13]This service you do is a proof of your faith. Many people will praise God because of it. They will praise God because you follow the Good News[d] of Christ—the gospel you say you believe. They will praise God because you freely share with them and with all others. [14]And when they pray, they will wish they could be with you. They will feel this because of the great grace that God has given you. [15]Thanks be to God for his gift that is too wonderful to explain.

### PAUL DEFENDS HIS MINISTRY

**10** I, Paul, am begging you with the gentleness and the kindness of Christ. Some people say that I am easy on you when I am with you and strict when I am away. [2]They think that we live in a worldly way. I plan to be very strict against them when I come. I beg you that when I come I will not need to use that same strictness with you. [3]We do live in the world. But we do not fight in the same way that the world fights. [4]We fight with weapons that are different from those the world uses. Our weapons have power from God. These weapons can destroy the enemy's strong places. We destroy men's arguments. [5]And we destroy every proud thing that raises itself against the knowledge of God. We

capture every thought and make it give up and obey Christ. [6]We are ready to punish anyone there who does not obey. But first we want you to obey fully.

[7]You must look at the facts before you. If anyone feels sure that he belongs to Christ, then he must remember that we belong to Christ just as he does. [8]It is true that we brag freely about the authority the Lord gave us. But he gave us this authority to strengthen you, not to hurt you. So I will not be ashamed of the bragging we do. [9]I don't want you to think that I am trying to scare you with my letters. [10]Some people say, "Paul's letters are powerful and sound important. But when he is with us, he is weak. And his speaking is nothing." [11]They should know this: We are not there with you now, so we say these things in letters. But when we are there with you, we will show the same authority that we show in our letters.

[12]We do not dare to put ourselves in the same group with those who think that they are very important. We do not compare ourselves to them. They use themselves to measure themselves, and they judge themselves by what they themselves are. This shows that they know nothing. [13]But we will not brag about things outside the work that was given us to do. We will limit our bragging to the work that God gave us. And

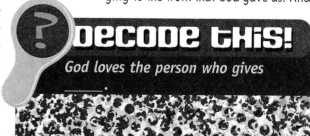

## DECODE THIS!
*God loves the person who gives _____.*

# THE LORD'S SUPPER

The preparations are almost made. Unscramble these words to set the scene for the Lord's Supper.

1. **CPU**  ___ ___ ___

2. **DOBLO**  ___ ___ ___ ___ ___

3. **RDEBA**  ___ ___ ___ ___ ___

4. **NEIW**  ___ ___ ___ ___

5. **EVTLWE**  ___ ___ ___ ___ ___ ___

6. **SJUAD**  ___ ___ ___ ___ ___

7. **HMYSN**  ___ ___ ___ ___ ___

8. **YDBO**  ___ ___ ___ ___

9. **SSOAEPVR**  ___ ___ ___ ___ ___ ___ ___ ___

10. **WLBO**  ___ ___ ___ ___

this work includes our work with you. [14]We are not bragging too much. We would be bragging too much if we had not already come to you. But we have come to you with the Good News[d] of Christ. [15]We limit our bragging to the work that is ours. We do not brag in the work other men have done. We hope that your faith will continue to grow. And we hope that you will help our work to grow much larger. [16]We want to tell the Good News in the areas beyond your city. We do not want to brag about work that has already been done in another man's area. [17]But, "If a person brags, he should brag only about the Lord."[n] [18]It is not the one who says he is good who is accepted but the one that the Lord thinks is good.

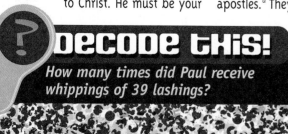

Q. If you could visit a movie star, who would it be?

A. Hilary Duff

## PAUL AND THE FALSE APOSTLES

**11** I wish you would be patient with me even when I am a little foolish. But you are already doing that. [2]I am jealous over you. And this jealousy comes from God. I promised to give you to Christ. He must be your only husband. I want to give you to Christ to be his pure bride. [3]But I am afraid that your minds will be led away from your true and pure following of Christ. This might happen just as Eve was tricked by the snake with his evil ways. [4]You are very patient with anyone who comes to you and preaches a different Jesus than the one we preached. You are very willing to accept a spirit or Good News that is different from the Spirit[d] and Good News[d] that you received from us.

[5]I do not think that those "great apostles" are any better than I am. [6]I may not be a trained speaker, but I do have knowledge. We have shown this to you clearly in every way.

[7]I preached God's Good News to you without pay. I made myself unimportant to make you important. Do you think that was wrong? [8]I accepted pay from other churches. I took their money so that I could serve you. [9]If I needed something when I was with you, I did not trouble any of you. The brothers who came from Macedonia gave me all that I needed. I did not allow myself to depend on you in any way. And I will never depend on you. [10]No one in Southern Greece will stop me from bragging about that. I say this with the truth of Christ in me. [11]And why do I not depend on you? Do you think it is because I do not love you? No. God knows that I love you.

[12]And I will keep on doing what I am doing now. I will continue because I want to stop those people from having a reason to brag. They would like to say that the work they brag about is the same as ours. [13]Such men are not true apostles.[d] They are workers who lie. And they change themselves to look like apostles of Christ. [14]This does not surprise us. Even Satan changes himself to look like an angel of light.[n] [15]So it does not surprise us if Satan's servants also make themselves look like servants who work for what is right. But in the end they will be punished for the things they do.

## PAUL TELLS ABOUT HIS SUFFERINGS

[16]I tell you again: No one should think that I am a fool. But if you think that I am a fool, then accept me as you would accept a fool. Then I can brag a little, too. [17]I brag because I feel sure of myself. But I am not talking as the Lord would talk. I am bragging like a fool. [18]Many people are bragging about their lives in the world. So I will brag, too. [19]You are wise, so you will gladly be patient with fools! [20]You are even patient with someone who orders you around and uses you! You are patient with those who trick you, or think they are better than you, or hit you in the face! [21]It is shameful to me to say this, but we were too "weak" to do those things to you!

But if anyone else is brave enough to brag, then I also will be brave and brag. (I am talking like a fool.) [22]Are they Hebrews?[n] So am I. Are they Israelites? So am I. Are they from Abraham's family? So am I. [23]Are they serving Christ? I am serving him more. (I am crazy to talk like this.) I have worked much harder than they. I have been in prison more often. I have been hurt more in beatings. I have been near death many times. [24]Five times the Jews have given me their punishment of 39 lashes with a whip. [25]Three different times I was beaten with rods. One time they tried to kill me with stones. Three times I was in ships that were wrecked, and one of those times I spent the night and the next day in the sea. [26]I have gone on many travels. And I have been in danger from rivers, from thieves, from my own people, the Jews, and from those who are not Jews. I have been in

## DECODE THIS!

*How many times did Paul receive whippings of 39 lashings?*

10:17 "If a person . . . Lord." Quotation from Jeremiah 9:24. 11:14 angel of light Messenger from God. The devil fools people so that they think he is from God. 11:22 Hebrews A name for the Jews that some Jews were very proud of.

# LIVIN' IT!

## HOLY HELPER
## 2 CORINTHIANS 12:9

Well, becoming a Christian seemed easy enough. Just prayed a prayer and that was that. But living a life that obeys God is quite another story. We seem to want to do exactly the opposite of what God wants us to do most of the time. Being good is just hard work!

Actually, being good is just impossible on our own. But Jesus didn't leave us here all alone. He is right here beside us, his Holy Spirit lives in us, and he will give us the strength we need to understand his ways and to follow them. The apostle Paul says we should really be excited about our weaknesses, because they make us depend on Jesus to be strong for us. So go ahead. Admit you need his help. He'll be glad to show you what incredible things you can do with him supplying your strength.

danger in cities, in places where no one lives, and on the sea. And I have been in danger with false brothers. ²⁷I have done hard and tiring work, and many times I did not sleep. I have been hungry and thirsty. Many times I have been without food. I have been cold and without clothes. ²⁸Besides all this, there is on me every day the load of my concern for all the churches. ²⁹I feel weak every time someone is weak. I feel upset every time someone is led into sin.

³⁰If I must brag, I will brag about the things that show I am weak. ³¹God knows that I am not lying. He is the God and Father of the Lord Jesus Christ, and he is to be praised forever. ³²When I was in Damascus, the governor under King Aretas wanted to arrest me. So he put guards around the city. ³³But my friends put me in a basket. Then they put the basket through a hole in the wall and lowered me down. So I escaped from the governor.

## A SPECIAL BLESSING IN PAUL'S LIFE

**12** I must continue to brag. It will do no good, but I will talk now about visions and revelations* from the Lord. ²I know a man in Christ who was taken up to the third heaven. This happened 14 years ago. I do not know whether the man was in his body or out of his body. But God knows. ³⁻⁴And I know that this man was taken up to paradise.* I don't know if he was in his body or away from his body. But he heard things he is not able to explain. He heard things that no man is allowed to tell. ⁵I will brag about a man like that. But I will not brag about myself, except about my weaknesses. ⁶But if I wanted to brag about myself, I would not be a fool. I would not be a fool, because I would be telling the truth. But I will not brag about myself. I do not want people to think more of me than what they see me do or hear me say.

⁷But I must not become too proud of the wonderful things that were shown to me. So a painful problem* was given to me. This problem is a messenger from Satan. It is sent to beat me and keep me from being too proud. ⁸I begged the Lord three times to take this problem away from me. ⁹But the Lord said to me, "My grace is enough for you. When you are weak, then my power is made perfect in you." So I am very happy to brag about my weaknesses. Then Christ's power can live in me. ¹⁰So I am happy when I have weaknesses, insults, hard times, sufferings, and all kinds of troubles. All these things are for Christ. And I am happy, because when I am weak, then I am truly strong.

## PAUL'S LOVE FOR THE CHRISTIANS

¹¹I have been talking like a fool. But you made me do it. You are the ones who

 12:1 **revelations** Revelation is making known a truth that was hidden. 12:3-4 **paradise** A place where good people go when they die. 12:7 **painful problem** Literally, "thorn in the flesh."

# REAL SUPER HEROES

# JOSEPH

Joseph should have been angry at least. After all, his 11 other brothers had sold him into slavery because they didn't like him, and then they lied to their father about it. On top of that, Joseph had spent many years in jail because someone had accused him of doing something he didn't do. But Joseph wasn't angry. Instead, he was filled with love.

Joseph knew God controlled every moment in his life. Even though his brothers had done an evil thing, God turned it into something good. Joseph became one of the top rulers in the land and was able to save his people from famine.

God promises that everything works out for good for those who love and trust him. We never have to worry, even when life disappoints us. God is in control, and he will work it out.

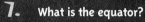

# WHAT IN THE WORLD?!

1. Which country is located north of America?
   a. Mexico
   b. Russia
   c. Spain
   d. Canada

2. How many continents are there?
   a. 1
   b. 3
   c. 6
   d. 7

3. Israel would be considered a part of:
   a. the Middle East
   b. Asia
   c. South America
   d. Australia

4. True or False: The Philippines are a group of islands.
   ■ T  ■ F

5. Where is the capital of the United States?
   a. Hawaii
   b. Texas
   c. Maine
   d. Washington D.C.

6. Which of these countries is not in Europe?
   a. France
   b. Italy
   c. America
   d. Germany

We know God wants us to take his good news all over the world, but how well do we know what's out there? Test your geography knowledge with the following quiz and see.

Score of 9-10: Congratulations! You're a world scholar.
Score 8-9: Great job! You're an expert geographer.
Score 6-7: Not bad! You're an amateur, so keep studying.
Score 4-5: You're a beginner. Take time each day to learn a new country.
Score 3 or below: Get to know God's world better!

7. What is the equator?
   a. a math problem
   b. something you ride up and down
   c. someone who rides horses
   d. an invisible line dividing the northern and southern hemispheres

8. True or False: Africa is a country.
   ■ T  ■ F

9. Which of the following countries is not in Asia?
   a. China
   b. Thailand
   c. Guatemala
   d. Japan

10. Which of the following countries is in South America?
    a. Switzerland
    b. Rwanda
    c. Canada
    d. Columbia

ANSWER KEY: 1.D; 2.D; 3.A; 4.T; 5.D; 6.C; 7.D; 8.F; 9.C; 10.D

> **"Test yourselves to see if you are living in the faith."** *2 Corinthians 13:5*

should say good things about me. I am worth nothing, but those "great apostles" are not worth any more than I am! [12]When I was with you, I did what proves that I am an apostle[d]—signs, wonders, and miracles.[d] And I did these things with much patience. [13]So you received everything that the other churches have received. Only one thing was different: I was not a burden to you. Forgive me for this!

[14]I am now ready to visit you the third time. And I will not be a burden to you. I want nothing from you, I only want you. Children should not have to save up to give to their parents. Parents should save to give to their children. [15]So I am happy to give everything I have for you. I will even give myself for you. If I love you more, will you love me less?

[16]It is clear that I was not a burden to you. But you think that I was tricky and used lies to catch you. [17]Did I cheat you by using any of the men I sent to you? No, you know I did not. [18]I asked Titus to go to you. And I sent our brother with him. Titus did not cheat you, did he? No, you know that Titus and I did the same thing and with the same spirit.

[19]Do you think that we have been defending ourselves to you all this time? We have been speaking in Christ and before God. You are our dear friends. And everything that we do is to make you stronger. [20]I do this because I am afraid that when I come, you will not be what I want you to be. And I am afraid that I will not be what you want me to be. I am afraid that among you there may be arguing, jealousy, anger, selfish fighting, evil talk, gossip, pride, and confusion. [21]I am afraid that when I come to you again, my God will make me ashamed before you. I may be saddened by many of those who have sinned. I may be saddened because they have not changed their hearts and have not turned away from their sexual sins and from the shameful things they have done.

### FINAL WARNINGS AND GREETINGS

**13** I will come to you for the third time. And remember, "Every case must be proved by two or three witnesses."[n] [2]When I was with you the second time, I gave a warning to those who had sinned. Now I am away from you, and I give a warning to all the others. When I come to you again, I will not be easy with them. [3]You want proof that Christ is speaking through me. My proof is that he is not weak among you, but he is powerful. [4]It is true that he was weak when he was killed on the cross. But he lives now by God's power. It is true that we are weak in Christ. But for you we will be alive in Christ by God's power.

[5]Look closely at yourselves. Test yourselves to see if you are living in the faith. You know that Christ Jesus is in you—unless you fail the test. [6]But I hope you will see that we ourselves have not failed the test. [7]We pray to God that you will not do anything wrong. It is not important to see that we have passed the test. But it is important that you do what is right, even if it seems that we have failed. [8]We cannot do anything against the truth, but only for the truth. [9]We are happy to be weak, if you are strong. And we pray that you will grow stronger and stronger. [10]I am writing this while I am away from you. I am writing so that when I come I will not have to be harsh in my use of authority. The Lord gave me this authority to use to make you stronger, not to destroy you.

[11]Now, brothers, I say good-bye. Try to be perfect. Do what I have asked you to do. Agree with each other, and live in peace. Then the God of love and peace will be with you.

## Ways to Bless Your Brother

1. **Stop bothering him.**
2. **Pray for him.**
3. **Make his bed.**
4. **Have a surprise party for him with his friends.**
5. **Let him have an extra turn on the computer.**
6. **Include him with your friends.**
7. **Say something nice.**
8. **Smile at him more.**
9. **Write an encouraging note, and put it in his backpack.**
10. **Let him win once in awhile.**

[12]Give each other a holy kiss when you greet each other. [13]All of God's holy people send greetings to you.

[14]The grace of the Lord Jesus Christ, the love of God, and the fellowship of the Holy Spirit[d] be with you all.

## DECODE THIS!

*Paul asked the people of Corinth to agree with each other and live in _____.*

  13:1 "Every . . . witnesses." Quotation from Deuteronomy 19:15.

Paul uses extra big handwriting in this letter.

Paul scolds Peter for being a hypocrite.

Famous passage: Fruit of the Spirit in chapter 5.

# THE LETTER OF PAUL THE APOSTLE TO THE

# GALATIANS

Galatia is in modern-day western Turkey.

Paul is upset with the Galatians for being foolish and getting tricked.

Blessing comes through faith not law.

## WILD WORLD FACTS

### FROM STORM TO STILL

A terrible storm had blown up while they were in their small fishing boat, and the disciples were afraid. Storms were the fisherman's worst enemy.

So what causes storms? The strong storms—like thunderstorms, hurricanes, and tornadoes—happen when warm air near the earth moves upward into cooler air temperatures very quickly (even up to 100 miles per hour). At any point during the day, there are an average of over 2,000 thunderstorms happening somewhere around the world. Each kind of storm can cause hail, lightning, or tornadoes. They can also cause a lot of problems for a small boat, which is why the disciples were worried. But Jesus wasn't. He is God, and he's in charge of even the weather. So he told the wind and the waves—and us, too—"Peace, be still."

[Yahooligans]

**1** From Paul, an apostle.$^d$
I was not chosen to be an apostle by men. I was not sent from men. It was Jesus Christ and God the Father who made me an apostle. God is the One who raised Jesus from death. $^2$This letter is also from all the brothers who are with me.

To the churches in Galatia.$^n$

$^3$I pray that God our Father and the Lord Jesus Christ will be good to you and give you peace. $^4$Jesus gave himself for our sins to free us from this evil world we live in. This is what God the Father wanted. $^5$The glory belongs to God forever and ever. Amen.

### THE ONLY GOOD NEWS

$^6$A short time ago God called you to follow him. He called you by his grace that came through Christ. But now I am amazed at you! You are already turning away and believing something different than the Good News.$^d$ $^7$Really, there is no other Good News. But some people are confusing you and want to change the Good News of Christ. $^8$We preached to you the Good News. So if we ourselves, or even an angel from heaven, preach to you something different than the Good News, he should be condemned! $^9$I said this before. Now I say it again: You have already accepted the Good News. If anyone tells you another way to be saved, he should be condemned!

$^{10}$Do you think I am trying to make people accept me? No! God is the One I am trying to please. Am I trying to please men? If I wanted to please men, I would not be a servant of Christ.

### PAUL'S AUTHORITY IS FROM GOD

$^{11}$Brothers, I want you to know that the Good News$^d$ I preached to you was not made by men. $^{12}$I did not get it from men, nor did any man teach it to me. Jesus Christ showed it to me.

$^{13}$You have heard about my past life. I belonged to the Jewish religion. I hurt the church of God very much and tried to destroy it. $^{14}$I was becoming a leader in the Jewish religion. I did better than most other Jews of my age. I tried harder than anyone else to follow the old rules. These rules were the customs handed down by our ancestors.

$^{15}$But God had special plans for me even before I was born. So he called me through his grace that I might $^{16}$tell the Good News about his Son to the non-Jewish people. So God showed me about his Son. When God called me, I did not get advice or help from any man. $^{17}$I did not go to Jerusalem to see those who were apostles$^d$ before I was. But, without waiting, I went away to Arabia and later went back to Damascus.

$^{18}$After three years I went to Jerusalem to meet Peter and stayed with him for 15 days. $^{19}$I met no other apostles, except James, the brother of the Lord. $^{20}$God knows that these things I write are not lies. $^{21}$Later, I went to the areas of Syria and Cilicia.

$^{22}$In Judea the churches in Christ had never met me. $^{23}$They had only heard this about me: "This man was trying to hurt us. But now he is preaching the same faith that he once tried to destroy." $^{24}$And these believers praised God because of me.

### OTHER APOSTLES ACCEPTED PAUL

**2** After 14 years, I went to Jerusalem again, this time with Barnabas. I also took Titus with me. $^2$I went because God showed me that I should go. I met with those men who were the leaders of the believers. When we were alone, I told them the Good News$^d$ that I preach to the non-Jewish people. I did not want my past work and the work I am now doing to be wasted. $^3$Titus was with me. But

### DECODE THIS!

Who did Paul get his authority from?

 **1:2 Galatia** Probably the same country where Paul preached and began churches on his first missionary trip. Read the book of Acts, chapters 13 and 14.

269

# Gotta Know!

## Will my parents still be my parents when we get to heaven?

**You will know who your parents are, and they will know you. It will be like a fantastic reunion. But in heaven, families will no longer be broken into small groups like they are here on earth. In heaven, we will all be one large family, with Jesus as the head of it.**

Titus was not forced to be circumcised,[d] even though he was a Greek. 4We talked about this problem because some false brothers had come into our group secretly. They came in like spies to find out about the freedom we have in Christ Jesus. They wanted to make us slaves. 5But we did not agree with anything those false brothers wanted! We wanted the truth of the Good News to continue for you.

6Those men who seemed to be important did not change the Good News that I preach. (It doesn't matter to me if they were "important" or not. To God all men are the same.) 7But these leaders saw that God had given me special work, just as he had to Peter. God gave Peter the work of telling the Good News to the Jews. But God gave me the work of telling the Good News to the non-Jewish people. 8God gave Peter the power to work as an apostle[d] for the Jewish peo-ple. But he also gave me the power to work as an apostle for those who are not Jews. 9James, Peter, and John, who seemed to be the leaders, saw that God had given me this special grace. So they accepted Barnabas and me. They said, "Paul and Barnabas, we agree that you should go to the people who are not Jews. We will go to the Jews." 10They asked us to do only one thing—to remember to help the poor. And this was something that I really wanted to do.

## PAUL SHOWS THAT PETER WAS WRONG

11When Peter came to Antioch, I was against him because he was wrong. 12This is what happened: When Peter first came to Antioch, he ate with the non-Jewish people. But then some Jewish men were sent from James. When they arrived, Peter stopped eating with the non-Jewish people and separated himself from them. He was afraid of the Jews who believe that all non-Jewish people must be circumcised.[d] 13So Peter was a hypocrite.[d] The other Jewish believers joined with him and were hypocrites, too. Even Barnabas was influenced by what these Jewish believers did. 14I saw what they did. They were not following the truth of the Good News.[d] So I spoke to Peter in front of them all. I said: "Peter, you are a Jew, but you are not living like a Jew. You are living like the non-Jewish people. So why do you now try to force the non-Jewish people to live like Jews?"

15We were not born as non-Jewish "sinners," but we were born as Jews. 16Yet we know that a person is not made right with God by following the law. No! It is trusting in Jesus Christ that makes a person right with God. So we, too, have put our faith in Christ Jesus, that we might be made right with God. And we are right with God because we trusted in Christ—not because we followed the law. For no one can be made right with God by following the law.

17We Jews came to Christ to be made right with God. So it is clear that we were sinners too. Does this mean that Christ makes us sinners? No! 18But I would really be wrong to begin teaching again those things of the Law of Moses that I gave up. 19I stopped living for the law. It was the law that put me to death. I died to the law so that I can now live for God. I was put to death on the cross with Christ. 20I do not live anymore—it is Christ living in me. I still live in my body, but I live by faith in the Son of God. He loved me and gave himself to save me. 21This gift is from God, and it is very important to me. If the law could make us right with God, then Christ did not have to die.

## BLESSING COMES THROUGH FAITH

**3** You people in Galatia were told very clearly about the death of Jesus Christ on the cross. But you were very

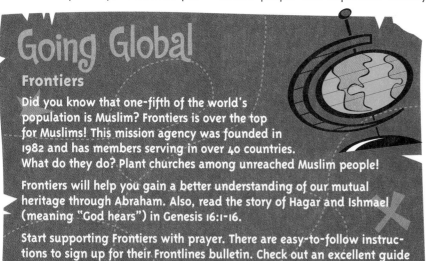

## Going Global

### Frontiers

Did you know that one-fifth of the world's population is Muslim? Frontiers is over the top for Muslims! This mission agency was founded in 1982 and has members serving in over 40 countries. What do they do? Plant churches among unreached Muslim people!

Frontiers will help you gain a better understanding of our mutual heritage through Abraham. Also, read the story of Hagar and Ishmael (meaning "God hears") in Genesis 16:1-16.

Start supporting Frontiers with prayer. There are easy-to-follow instructions to sign up for their Frontlines bulletin. Check out an excellent guide on "How to Pray for Muslims" at www.30-days.net/islam/praying.

foolish. You let someone trick you. [2]Tell me this one thing: How did you receive the Holy Spirit?[d] Did you receive the Spirit by following the law? No! You received the Spirit because you heard the Good News[d] and believed it. [3]You began your life in Christ by the Spirit. Now do you try to continue it by your own power? That is foolish. [4]You have experienced many things. Were all those experiences wasted? I hope not! [5]Does God give you the Spirit because you follow the law? No! Does God work miracles[d] among you because you follow the law? No! God gives you his Spirit and works miracles among you because you heard the Good News and believed it.

[6]The Scriptures[d] say the same thing about Abraham: "Abraham believed God, and God accepted Abraham's faith, and that faith made him right with God."[n] [7]So you should know that the true children of Abraham are those who have faith. [8]The Scriptures told what would happen in the future. They said that God would make the non-Jewish people right through their faith. This Good News was told to Abraham beforehand, as the Scripture says: "All nations will be blessed through you."[n] [9]Abraham believed this, and because he believed, he was blessed. It is the same today. All who believe today are blessed just as Abraham was blessed. [10]But those who depend on following the law to make them right are under a curse because the Scriptures say, "Anyone will be cursed who does not always obey what is written in the Book of the Law!"[n] [11]So it is clear that no one can be made right with God by the law. The Scriptures say, "He who is right with God by faith will live." [12]The law does not use faith. It says, "A person who does these things will live forever because of them."[n] [13]So the law put a curse on us, but Christ took away that curse. He changed places with us and put himself under that curse. It is written in the Scriptures, "Everyone whose body is displayed on a tree[n] is cursed." [14]Christ did this so that God's blessing promised to Abraham might come to the non-Jews. This blessing comes through Jesus Christ. Jesus died so that we could have the Spirit that God promised and receive this promise by believing.

### THE LAW AND THE PROMISE

[15]Brothers, let me give you an example: Think about an agreement that a person makes with another person. After that agreement is accepted by both people, no one can stop that agreement or add anything to it. [16]God made promises to Abraham and his descendant.[d] God did not say, "and to your descendants." That would mean many people. But God said, "and to your descendant." That means only one person; that person is Christ. [17]This is what I mean: God had an agreement with Abraham and promised to keep it. The law, which came 430 years later, cannot change God's promise to Abraham. [18]Can following the law give us what God promised? No! If this is so, it is not God's promise that brings us the blessings. Instead God freely gave his blessings to Abraham through the promise he had made.

**Bugs to Collect**

1. **Monarch butterfly**
2. **Praying mantis**
3. **Rhinoceros beetle**
4. **Walking stick**
5. **Luna moth**
6. **Katydid**
7. **Cicada**
8. **Ladybug**
9. **Firefly**
10. **Fuzzy caterpillars**

## LIVIN' IT!

**OUT OF THE BOX**
**GALATIANS 3:28**

Look around you. You can probably put each kid in your class into some sort of group. You've got the cool kids, the smart kids, the funny kids, the shy kids . . . and the list goes on. Maybe you like the group you're in, and maybe you don't. But the fact remains, in this world people are judged by how they look, act, and think.

But God does not want his children to act or think like the world. When he looks at us, he sees his beautiful creation living exactly how he wanted us to be. No one is better than the other, no matter what they look like or what talents they have. In Jesus we are all the same—loved the same, valued the same, and worth everything to God. It really doesn't matter how other people see you. What matters is what God thinks—and he thinks you're pretty incredible!

## DECODE THIS!
**Who did Paul challenge in Antioch?**

 3:6 "Abraham . . . God." Quotation from Genesis 15:6. 3:8 "All . . . you." Quotation from Genesis 12:3. 3:10 "Anyone . . . Law!" Quotation from Deuteronomy 27:26. 3:12 "A person . . . them." Quotation from Leviticus 18:5. 3:13 displayed on a tree Deuteronomy 21:22-23 says that when a person was killed for doing wrong, his body was hung on a tree to show shame. Paul means that the cross of Jesus was like that.

# GET CONNECTED

## DADDY

Some children don't have parents. Their parents have either died or left them because they were unable to care for them. They live in orphanages where adults take care of them until a family comes along who wants to adopt them and make them a part of their family.

Did you know that, if you are a Christian, the Bible says you are adopted? Your parents and siblings on earth stay the same, but God himself has brought you into his family, the body of Christ. You now belong to him, and he has become your "Abba" or heavenly Daddy. He loves you even more than your earthly parents and will fulfill every promise because you are his.

¹⁹So what was the law for? The law was given to show the wrong things people do. It continued until the special descendant of Abraham came. God's promise was about this descendant. The law was given through angels who used Moses for a mediator" to give the law to men. ²⁰But a mediator is not needed when there is only one side. And God is only one.

## THE PURPOSE OF THE LAW OF MOSES

²¹Does this mean that the law is against God's promises? Never! If there were a law that could give men life, then we could be made right by following that law. ²²But this is not true, because the Scriptures$^d$ showed that the whole world is bound by sin. This was so that the promise would be given through faith. And it is given to people who believe in Jesus Christ.

²³Before this faith came, we were all held prisoners by the law. We had no freedom until God showed us the way of faith that was coming. ²⁴So the law was our master until Christ came. After Christ came, we could be made right with God through faith. ²⁵Now the way of faith has come, and we no longer live under the law.

²⁶⁻²⁷You were all baptized into Christ, and so you were all clothed with Christ. This shows that you are all children of God through faith in Christ Jesus. ²⁸Now, in Christ, there is no difference between Jew and Greek. There is no difference between slaves and free men. There is no difference between male and female. You are all the same in Christ Jesus. ²⁹You belong to Christ. So you are Abraham's descendants.$^d$ You get all of God's blessings because of the promise that God made to Abraham.

**4** I want to tell you this: While the one who will inherit his father's property is still a child, he is no different from a slave. It does not matter that the child owns everything. ²While he is a child, he must obey those who are chosen to care for him. But when the child reaches the age set by his father, he is free. ³It is the same for us. We were once like children. We were slaves to the useless rules of this world. ⁴But when the right time came, God sent his Son. His Son was born of a woman and lived under the law. ⁵God did this so that he could buy freedom for those who were under the law. His purpose was to make us his children.

⁶And you are God's children. That is why God sent the Spirit of his Son into your hearts. The Spirit$^d$ cries out, "Father, dear Father."$^n$ ⁷So now you are not a slave; you are God's child, and God will give you what he promised, because you are his child.

## PAUL'S LOVE FOR THE CHRISTIANS

⁸In the past you did not know God. You were slaves to gods that were not real. ⁹But now you know the true God. Really, it is God who knows you. So why do you turn back to those weak and useless rules you followed before? Do you want to be slaves to those things again? ¹⁰You still follow teachings about special days, months, seasons, and years. ¹¹I am afraid

3:19 **mediator** A person who helps one person talk to or give something to another person.
4:6 **"Father, dear Father"** Literally, "Abba, Father." Jewish children called their fathers "Abba."

# REAL SUPER HEROES

## JOSHUA

Talk about guts. Joshua had them—but he was brave because he knew what kind of God he served. Back when Israel first saw the Promised Land and they sent spies in to check it out, Joshua and Caleb were the only ones who believed God was strong enough to defeat the bad people inside the land. As a result, they were the only 2 from the original group of Israelites to get to enter the land.

As Joshua took God's people into the Promised Land, he told them to decide whom they would serve. He made it clear how important it was for each person to submit to God. Joshua served God his whole life.

It's important for you to decide whom you will serve, too. It doesn't matter what your parents or friends believe— you must have your own relationship with God.

# LIVIN' IT!

## OLD HABITS DIE HARD
## GALATIANS 5:1

What were they thinking? These Christian Jews had heard the Good News that Jesus had paid the price for their sins. They had accepted his gift with gratitude. But as each day passed, they began to forget that their salvation was a gift. Old habits of following the law to get God to like them started to pop up again.

The apostle Paul had to remind them—and us—with strong words. If God saved us by grace through Jesus and not because we did anything right, then we continue to grow in him by trusting in God's goodness. It's not like we're saved and then we have to work hard the rest of our lives to make God like us. He loves us completely now. His love never changes. So stop trying to earn God's approval. You already have it in Jesus. Now go out and enjoy his love by sharing it with the world!

for you. I fear that my work for you has been wasted.

<sup>12</sup>Brothers, I was like you; so I beg you to become like me. You were very good to me before. <sup>13</sup>You remember that I came to you the first time because I was sick. That was when I preached the Good News<sup>d</sup> to you. <sup>14</sup>Though my sickness was a trouble for you, you did not hate me or make me leave. But you welcomed me as an angel from God, as if I were Jesus Christ himself! <sup>15</sup>You were very happy then. Where is that joy now? I remember that you would have taken out your eyes and given them to me if that were possible. <sup>16</sup>Now am I your enemy because I tell you the truth?

<sup>17</sup>"Those people" are working hard to persuade you. But this is not good for you. They want to persuade you to turn against us. They want you to follow only them. <sup>18</sup>It is good for people to show interest in you, but only if their purpose is good. This is always true. It is true when I am with you and when I am away. <sup>19</sup>My little children, again I feel pain for you as a mother feels when she gives birth. I will feel this until you truly become like Christ. <sup>20</sup>I wish I could be with you now. Then maybe I could change the way I am talking to you. Now I do not know what to do about you.

## THE EXAMPLE OF HAGAR AND SARAH

<sup>21</sup>Some of you people still want to be under the law of Moses. Tell me, do you know what the law says? <sup>22</sup>The Scriptures<sup>d</sup> say that Abraham had two sons. The mother of one son was a slave woman. The mother of the other son was a free woman. <sup>23</sup>Abraham's son from the slave woman was born in the normal human way. But the son from the free woman was born because of the promise God made to Abraham.

<sup>24</sup>This makes a picture for us. The two women are like the two agreements between God and men. One agreement is the law that God made on Mount Sinai." The people who are under this agreement are like slaves. The mother named Hagar is like that agreement. <sup>25</sup>She is like Mount Sinai in Arabia and is a picture of the earthly Jewish city of Jerusalem. This city is a slave, and all its people, the Jews, are slaves to the law. <sup>26</sup>But the heavenly Jerusalem which is above is like the free woman. She is our mother. <sup>27</sup>It is written in the Scriptures:

"Be happy, Jerusalem.
You are like a woman who never gave birth to children.
Start singing and shout for joy.
You never felt the pain of giving birth to children.
But you will have more children than the woman who has a husband." *Isaiah 54:1*

<sup>28</sup>My brothers, you are God's children because of his promise, as Isaac was then. <sup>29</sup>The son who was born in the normal way treated the other son badly. It is the same today. <sup>30</sup>But what does the Scripture say? "Throw out the slave woman and her son! The son of the free woman will receive everything his father has. But the son of the slave woman will receive nothing."<sup>n</sup> <sup>31</sup>So, my brothers, we are not children of the slave woman. We are children of the free woman.

## BIBLE BASICS

### WHAT IS THE FRUIT OF THE SPIRIT?

Galatians 5:22-23 spells it out simply as "love, joy, peace, patience, kindness, goodness, faithfulness, gentleness, and self-control." Basically, God's kind of fruit is the attitude we have in our hearts toward God and others—the attitude that shows Jesus is in control of our lives. Without the Holy Spirit living and ruling inside us, we would not have this kind of fruit. He's the One who grows these right attitudes in our hearts.

## DECODE THIS!

*We have freedom now because who made us free?*

**4:17 Those people** They are the false teachers who were bothering the believers in Galatia (Galatians 1:7).
**4:24 Mount Sinai** Mountain in Arabia where God gave his laws to Moses (Exodus 19 and 20).
**4:30 "Throw . . . nothing."** Quotation from Genesis 21:10.

UNSCRAMBLE THESE FRUIT OF THE SPIRIT, AND THEN COLOR THEM IN!

BUT THE SPIRIT GIVES _____, _____, _____,
ELOV        YJO        EPCAE

_____, _____, _____, _____,
AINCTPEE    ESDNKNSSI    OSGDNOSE    ATUSILFFNSEH

_____, AND _____.
ELESGTNSNE        FLSE-TNCORLO

GALATIANS 5:22

---

 LIVIN' IT!

FREE ADVICE
## GALATIANS 5:13

Have you ever wanted to skip childhood and just be an adult? Then you could stay up as late as you wanted, make your own decisions, do whatever you wanted. Sound nice? But maybe you haven't thought about the responsibility that comes with freedom. Like having to work to pay bills, feeding and taking care of others, and keeping the house clean.

The Galatian Christians were having a problem with their new freedom in Jesus. They were so excited that they were free from the law, they thought they could sin and do whatever they wanted, and it wouldn't matter. Paul said that our freedom from the law is not an excuse to sin. It is, however, a great reason to want to obey God out of grateful hearts instead of doing it because we have to.

### KEEP YOUR FREEDOM

**5** We have freedom now because Christ made us free. So stand strong. Do not change and go back into the slavery of the law. [2]Listen! I am Paul. I tell you that if you go back to the law by being circumcised,[d] then Christ is no good for you. [3]Again, I warn every man: If you allow yourselves to be circumcised, then you must follow all the law. [4]If you try to be made right with God through the law, then your life with Christ is over—you have left God's grace. [5]But we hope to be made right with God through faith, and we wait for this hope anxiously with the Spirit's[d] help. [6]When we are in Christ Jesus, it is not important if we are circumcised or not. The important thing is faith—the kind of faith that works through love.

[7]You were running a good race. You were obeying the truth. Who stopped you from following the true way? [8]Whatever way he used did not come from the One who chose you. [9]Be careful! "Just a little yeast makes the whole batch of dough rise." [10]But I trust in the Lord that you will not believe those different ideas. Someone is confusing you with such ideas. And he will be punished, whoever he is.

[11]My brothers, I do not teach that a man must be circumcised. If I teach circumcision, then why am I still being treated badly? If I still taught circumcision, my preaching about the cross would not be a problem. [12]I wish the people who are bothering you would castrate[n] themselves!

⭐ 5:12 **castrate** To cut off part of the male sex organ. Paul uses this word because it is similar to "circumcision." Paul wanted to show that he is very upset with the false teachers.

# LIVIN' IT!

[13] My brothers, God called you to be free. But do not use your freedom as an excuse to do the things that please your sinful self. Serve each other with love. [14] The whole law is made complete in this one command: "Love your neighbor as you love yourself."[n] [15] If you go on hurting each other and tearing each other apart, be careful! You will completely destroy each other.

## THE SPIRIT AND HUMAN NATURE

[16] So I tell you: Live by following the Spirit.[d] Then you will not do what your sinful selves want. [17] Our sinful selves want what is against the Spirit. The Spirit wants what is against our sinful selves. The two are against each other. So you must not do just what you please. [18] But if you let the Spirit lead you, you are not under the law.

[19] The wrong things the sinful self does are clear: being sexually unfaithful, not being pure, taking part in sexual sins, [20] worshiping false gods, doing witchcraft,[d] hating, making trouble, being jealous, being angry, being selfish, making people angry with each other, causing divisions among people, [21] having envy, being drunk, having wild and wasteful parties, and doing other things like this. I warn you now as I warned you before: Those who do these things will not be in God's kingdom. [22] But the Spirit gives love, joy, peace, patience, kindness, goodness, faithfulness, [23] gentleness, self-control. There is no law that says these things are wrong. [24] Those who belong to Christ Jesus have crucified their own sinful selves. They have given up their old selfish feelings and the evil things they wanted to do. [25] We get our new life from the Spirit. So we should follow the Spirit. [26] We must not be proud. We must not make trouble with each other. And we must not be jealous of each other.

## HELP EACH OTHER

**6** Brothers, someone in your group might do something wrong. You who are spiritual should go to him and help make him right again. You should do this in a gentle way. But be careful! You might be tempted to sin, too. [2] Help each other with your troubles. When you do this, you truly obey the law of Christ. [3] If anyone thinks that he is important when he is really not important, he is only fooling himself. [4] He should not compare himself with others. Each person should judge his own actions. Then he can be proud for what he himself has done. [5] Each person must be responsible for himself.

[6] Anyone who is learning the teaching of God should share all the good things he has with his teacher.

## LIFE IS LIKE PLANTING A FIELD

[7] Do not be fooled: You cannot cheat God. A person harvests only what he plants. [8] If he plants to satisfy his sinful self, his sinful self will bring him eternal death. But if he plants to please the Spirit,[d] he will receive eternal life from the Spirit. [9] We must not become tired of doing good. We will receive our harvest of eternal life at the right time. We must not give up! [10] When we have the opportunity to help anyone, we should do it. But we should give special attention to those who are in the family of believers.

## PAUL ENDS HIS LETTER

[11] I am writing this myself. See what large letters I use. [12] Some men are trying to force you to be circumcised.[d] They do these things so that the Jews will accept them. They are afraid that they will be treated badly if they follow only the cross of Christ." [13] Those who are circumcised do not obey the law themselves, but they want you to be circumcised. Then they can brag about what they forced you to do. [14] I hope I will never brag about things like that. The cross of our Lord Jesus Christ is my only reason for bragging. Through the cross of Jesus my world was crucified and I died to the world. [15] It is not important if a man is circumcised or not circumcised. The important thing is being the new people God has made. [16] Peace and mercy to those who follow this rule—to all of God's people.

[17] So do not give me any more trouble. I have scars on my body. These show[n] I belong to Christ Jesus.

[18] My brothers, I pray that the grace of our Lord Jesus Christ will be with your spirit. Amen.

**DECODE THIS!**

*We must not become tired of doing what?*

**5:14 "Love . . . yourself."** Quotation from Leviticus 19:18. **6:12 cross of Christ** Paul uses the cross as a picture of the gospel, the story of Christ's death and rising from death to pay for men's sins. The cross, or Christ's death, was God's way to save men. **6:17 These show** Many times Paul was beaten and whipped by people who were against him because he was teaching about Christ. The scars were from these beatings.

How to dress in God's armor!

Ephesus is home for the Temple of Diana, one of the 7 wonders of the ancient world.

## THE LETTER OF PAUL THE APOSTLE TO THE

# EPHESIANS

Directions for husbands, wives, kids, and parents.

Paul writes with encouragement from a jail cell (again).

Finally—a letter from Paul that does not address problems!

God unites his people.

**1** From Paul, an apostle[d] of Christ Jesus. I am an apostle because that is what God wanted.

To God's holy people living in Ephesus, believers in Christ Jesus.

[2]Grace and peace to you from God our Father and the Lord Jesus Christ.

## SPIRITUAL BLESSINGS IN CHRIST

[3]Praise be to the God and Father of our Lord Jesus Christ. In Christ, God has given us every spiritual blessing in heaven. [4]In Christ, he chose us before the world was made. In his love he chose us to be his holy people—people without blame before him. [5]And before the world was made, God decided to make us his own children through Jesus Christ. That was what he wanted and what pleased him. [6]This brings praise to God because of his wonderful grace. God gave that grace to us freely, in Christ, the One he loves. [7]In Christ we are set free by the blood of his death. And so we have forgiveness of sins because of God's rich grace. [8]God gave us that grace fully and freely. God, with full wisdom and understanding, [9]let us know his secret purpose. This

was what God wanted, and he planned to do it through Christ. [10]His goal was to carry out his plan when the right time came. He planned that all things in heaven and on earth would be joined together in Christ as the head.

[11]In Christ we were chosen to be God's people. God had already chosen us to be his people, because that is what he wanted. And God is the One who makes everything agree with what he decides and wants. [12]We are the first people who hoped in Christ. And we were chosen so that we would bring praise to God's glory. [13]So it is with you. You heard the true teaching—the Good News[d] about your salvation. When you heard it, you believed in Christ. And in Christ, God put his special mark on you by giving you the Holy Spirit[d] that he had promised. [14]That Holy Spirit is the guarantee that we will get what God promised for his people. This will bring full freedom to the people who belong to God, to bring praise to God's glory.

## PAUL'S PRAYER

[15-16]That is why I always remember you in my prayers and always thank God for you. I have always done this since the time I heard about your faith in the Lord Jesus and your love for all God's people. [17]I always pray to the God of our Lord Jesus Christ—to the glorious Father. I pray that he will give you a spirit that will make you wise in the knowledge of God—the knowledge that he has shown you. [18]I pray that you will have greater understanding in your heart. Then you will know the hope that God has chosen to give us. I pray that you will know that the blessings God has promised

## BIBLE BASICS

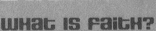

### WHAT IS FAITH?

The Bible says that faith is a gift from God (Ephesians 2). Faith helps us know for sure that everything God has told us in his Word is true and will happen. Not only does faith show itself by our believing, but also through our lives when we stop living for ourselves and start obeying God. God says it is impossible to please him without faith. But if we have trouble believing, we can always ask him for help, and he will give us more faith.

## 10 TOP TEN

### Ways to Bless Your Sister

1. Tell her she's pretty.
2. Share your dessert.
3. Let her go first.
4. Let her borrow your clothes.
5. Ask her how she's feeling.
6. Pray for and with her.
7. Write her an encouraging note.
8. Help her with her homework.
9. Play with her outside.
10. Help her with her chores.

his holy people are rich and glorious. [19]And you will know that God's power is very great for us who believe. That power is the same as the great strength [20]God used to raise Christ from death and put him at his right side in heaven. [21]God made Christ more important than all rulers, authorities, powers, and kings. Christ is more important than anything in this world or in the next world. [22]God put everything under his power. And God made him the head over everything for the church. [23]The church is Christ's body. The church is filled with Christ, and Christ fills everything in every way.

## DECODE THIS!

*What made God decide to make us his children?*

## FROM DEATH TO LIFE

**2** In the past your spiritual lives were dead because of your sins and the things you did wrong against God. [2] Yes, in the past you lived the way the world lives. You followed the ruler of the evil powers that are above the earth. That same spirit is now working in those who refuse to obey God. [3] In the past all of us lived like them. We lived trying to please our sinful selves. We did all the things our bodies and minds wanted. We should have suffered God's anger because of the way we were. We were the same as all other people.

[4] But God's mercy is great, and he loved us very much. [5] We were spiritually dead because of the things we did wrong against God. But God gave us new life with Christ. You have been saved by God's grace. [6] And he raised us up with Christ and gave us a seat with him in the heavens. He did this for those of us who are in Christ Jesus. [7] He did this so that for all future time he could show the very great riches of his grace. He shows that grace by being kind to us in Christ Jesus. [8] I mean that you have been saved by grace because you believe. You did not save yourselves. It was a gift from God. [9] You cannot brag that you are saved by the work you have done. [10] God has made us what we are. In Christ Jesus, God made us new people so that we would do good works. God had planned in advance those good works for us. He had planned for us to live our lives doing them.

## ONE IN CHRIST

[11] You were born non-Jews. You are the people the Jews call "uncircumcised."[n] Those who call you "uncircumcised" call themselves "circumcised."[d] (Their circumcision is only something they themselves do on their bodies.) [12] Remember that in the past you were without Christ. You were not citizens of Israel. And you had no part in the agreements[n] with the promise that God made to his people. You had no hope, and you did not know God. [13] Yes, at one time you were far away from God. But now in Christ Jesus you are brought near to God through the blood of Christ's death. [14] Because of Christ we now have peace. Christ made both Jews and non-Jews one people. They were separated as if there were a wall between them. But Christ broke down that wall of hate by giving his own body. [15] The Jewish law had many commands and rules. But Christ ended that law. Christ's purpose was to make the two groups of people become one new people in him. By doing this Christ would make peace. [16] Through the cross Christ ended the hatred between the two groups. And after Christ made the two groups to be one body, he wanted to bring them back to God. Christ did this with his death on the cross. [17] Christ came and preached peace to you non-Jews who were far away from God. And he preached peace to those Jews who were near to God. [18] Yes, through Christ we all have the right to come to the Father in one Spirit.[d]

[19] So now you non-Jews are not visitors or strangers. Now you are citizens together with God's holy people. You belong to God's family. [20] You believers are like a building that God owns. That building was built on the foundation of the apostles[d] and prophets.[d] Christ Jesus himself is the most important stone[n] in that building. [21] That whole building is joined together in Christ. And Christ

**2:11 uncircumcised** People not having the mark of circumcision as the Jews have. **2:12 agreements** The agreements that God gave to his people in the Old Testament. **2:20 most important stone** Literally, "cornerstone." The first and most important stone in a building.

makes it grow and become a holy temple in the Lord. [22]And in Christ you, too, are being built together with the Jews. You are being built into a place where God lives through the Spirit.

## PAUL'S WORK FOR THE NON-JEWS

**3** So I, Paul, am a prisoner of Christ Jesus. I am a prisoner for you who are not Jews. [2]Surely you know that God gave me this work through his grace to help you. [3]God let me know his secret plan. He showed it to me. I have already written a little about this. [4]And if you read what I wrote, then you can see that I truly understand the secret truth about the Christ.[d] [5]People who lived in other times were not told that secret truth. But now, through the Spirit,[d] God has shown that secret truth to his holy apostles[d] and prophets.[d] [6]This is that secret truth: that the non-Jews will receive what God has for his people, just as the Jews will. The non-Jews are together with the Jews as part of the same body. And they share together in the promise that God made in Christ Jesus. The non-Jews have all of this because of the Good News.[d]

[7]By God's special gift of grace, I became a servant to tell that Good News. God gave me that grace through his power. [8]I am the least important of all God's people. But God gave me this gift—to tell the non-Jewish people the Good News about the riches of Christ. Those riches are too great to understand fully. [9]And God gave me the work of telling all people about the plan for God's secret truth. That secret truth has been hidden in God since the beginning of time. God is the One who created everything. [10]His purpose was that through the church all the rulers and powers in the heavenly world will now know God's wisdom, which has so many forms. [11]This agrees with the purpose God had since the beginning of time. And God carried out his plan through Christ Jesus our Lord. [12]In Christ we can come before God with freedom and without fear. We can do this through faith in Christ. [13]So I ask you not to become discouraged because of the sufferings I am having for you. My sufferings bring honor to you.

## THE LOVE OF CHRIST

[14]So I bow in prayer before the Father. [15]Every family in heaven and on earth gets its true name from him. [16]I ask the Father in his great glory to give you the power to be strong in spirit. He will give you that strength through his Spirit.[d] [17]I pray that Christ will live in your hearts because of your faith. I pray that your life will be strong in love and be built on love. [18]And I pray that you and all God's holy people will have the power to understand the greatness of Christ's love. I pray that you can understand

## LIVIN' IT!

### PRAYER'S POWER SOURCE
### EPHESIANS 3:20

Suddenly something comes up, and you need help. The problem is so big you're not even sure how to pray about it, or how God could possibly straighten things out. What do you do? Well, you could worry—but that won't help things. God even tells us not to worry but, instead, to bring everything to him in prayer. You know why?

God is a big God. He is bigger than our problems, and even bigger than our imaginations. We can't even begin to understand how powerful he really is. So when he says he can help us, believe him! Take whatever's on your heart to his throne. Then let him have it. Stop worrying, and wait for God to act. Trust that he will answer in the way that is the very best for you—whether it's the way you wanted or not.

## REAL SUPER HEROES

# RUTH

Ruth and Naomi's husbands had died. Neither had any children left. Common sense would have told young Ruth to leave Naomi, her mother-in-law, go home, and find another husband. But she didn't. She loved Naomi and Naomi's God so much that she would stick with Naomi no matter what it cost her.

God saw Ruth's loyalty and kindness and blessed both her and Naomi. He provided a husband for her, who gave her everything she and Naomi needed to live. Her life became a beautiful picture of how God cares for his children and provides for them in incredible ways when they look to him for help.

What kind of friend are you? Do you stick around, even when things aren't going well? Remember Ruth and her loyalty. Then ask God to help you and your friends to stay close to him.

how wide and how long and how high and how deep that love is. [19]Christ's love is greater than any person can ever know. But I pray that you will be able to know that love. Then you can be filled with the fullness of God.

[20]With God's power working in us, God can do much, much more than anything we can ask or think of. [21]To him be glory in the church and in Christ Jesus for all time, forever and ever. Amen.

### THE UNITY OF THE BODY

**4** I am in prison because I belong to the Lord. God chose you to be his people. I tell you now to live the way God's people should live. [2]Always be humble and gentle. Be patient and accept each other with love. [3]You are joined together with peace through the Spirit.[d] Do all you can to continue together in this way. Let peace hold you together. [4]There is one body and one Spirit. And God called you to have one hope.

## Going Global

### Habitat for Humanity

So you think you need to be able to use a power drill to help Habitat for Humanity build houses? Started by former President Jimmy Carter, Habitat has built more than 125,000 houses in more than 80 countries.

You will find other ways to be a part of this work at www.habitat.org. It's true! No matter your age, gender, creed, race, or nationality there is a place for you within Habitat for Humanity where your efforts can make a difference. Check out another link—www.habitat.org/ccyp/youth.html— where you'll discover ideas for kids ages 5-7, 7-10, and 10-12 to get involved: Make welcome cards, paint window boxes, and tons more!

in the Scriptures,[d]
"When he went up to the heights,
he led a parade of captives.
And he gave gifts to people."

*Psalm 68:18*

[9]When it says, "He went up," what does it mean? It means that he first came

to men—he made some to be apostles,[d] some to be prophets,[d] some to go and tell the Good News,[d] and some to have the work of caring for and teaching God's people. [12]Christ gave those gifts to prepare God's holy people for the work of serving. He gave those gifts to make the body of Christ stronger. [13]This work must continue until we are all joined together in the same faith and in the same knowledge about the Son of God. We must become like a mature person—we must grow until we become like Christ and have all his perfection.

[14]Then we will no longer be babies. We will not be tossed about like a ship that the waves carry one way and then another. We will not be influenced by every new teaching we hear from men who are trying to fool us. Those men make plans and try any kind of trick to fool people into following the wrong path. [15]No! We will speak the truth with love. We will grow up in every way to be

# Gotta Know!

### How do I know my friends really like me?

**You could spend countless hours worrying about what other people think about you, but it won't help much. Draw your strength from God. Know how God feels about you—that he loves you more than you can imagine! Then be strong in who you are as a child of God. When you do that, you are able to love others whether or not they return your love. In time, you will know which people will make the best friends.**

[5]There is one Lord, one faith, and one baptism. [6]There is one God and Father of everything. He rules everything. He is everywhere and in everything.

[7]Christ gave each one of us a special gift. Each one received what Christ wanted to give him. [8]That is why it says

down to the earth. [10]So Jesus came down, and he is the same One who went up. He went up above all the heavens. Christ did that to fill everything with himself. [11]And Christ gave gifts

## DECODE THIS!

*God gave a gift of what to save us through faith?*

## iT HOLDS WATER

### WiLD WORLD FACTS

Jesus said that when Christians serve other people—even just by giving a cup of cold water to drink—we are doing it for him. So why is it important that we drink water?

More than half of our bodies (50-65 percent) are made of water! Our blood is 83 percent water, muscle is 75 percent, and bones are 22 percent! We have to have water in our bodies in order to keep them at the right temperature, as well as to carry all the food and oxygen to the places they need to go. Water even keeps our joints and organs safe—which is why we need to drink at least 8 8-ounce glasses of water a day (an average can of coke is 12 ounces). When we're thirsty, it's a sign we haven't been drinking enough, and our body is dehydrated. So drink up! And get a cup of cool water for your friend, too.

[Yahooligans: Ask Earl]

like Christ, who is the head. <sup>16</sup>The whole body depends on Christ. And all the parts of the body are joined and held together. Each part of the body does its own work. And this makes the whole body grow and be strong with love.

### THE WAY YOU SHOULD LIVE

<sup>17</sup>In the Lord's name, I tell you this. I warn you: Do not continue living like those who do not believe. Their thoughts are worth nothing. <sup>18</sup>They do not understand. They know nothing, because they refuse to listen. So they cannot have the life that God gives. <sup>19</sup>They have lost their feeling of shame. And they use their lives for doing evil. More and more they want to do all kinds of evil things. <sup>20</sup>But the things you learned in Christ were not like this. <sup>21</sup>I know that you heard about him, and you are in him; so you were taught the truth. Yes, the truth is in Jesus. <sup>22</sup>You were taught to leave your old self—to stop living the evil way you lived before. That old self becomes worse and worse because people are fooled by the evil things they want to do. <sup>23</sup>But you were taught to be made new in your hearts. <sup>24</sup>You were taught to become a new person. That new person is made to be like

God—made to be truly good and holy. <sup>25</sup>So you must stop telling lies. Tell each other the truth because we all belong to each other in the same body." <sup>26</sup>When you are angry, do not sin. And do not go on being angry all day. <sup>27</sup>Do not give the devil a way to defeat you. <sup>28</sup>If a person is stealing, he must stop stealing and start working. He must use his hands for doing something good. Then he will have something to share with those who are poor.

<sup>29</sup>When you talk, do not say harmful things. But say what people need—words that will help others become stronger. Then what you say will help those who listen to you. <sup>30</sup>And do not make the Holy Spirit<sup>d</sup> sad. The Spirit is God's proof that you belong to him. God gave you the Spirit to show that God will make you free when the time comes. <sup>31</sup>Do not be bitter or angry or mad. Never shout angrily or say things to hurt others. Never do anything evil. <sup>32</sup>Be kind and loving to each other. Forgive each other just as God forgave you in Christ.

### LIVING IN THE LIGHT

**5** You are God's children whom he loves. So try to be like God. <sup>2</sup>Live a life of love. Love other people just as Christ loved us. Christ gave himself for us—he was a sweet-smelling offering and sacrifice to God.

<sup>3</sup>But there must be no sexual sin among you. There must not be any kind of evil or greed. Those things are not right for God's holy people. <sup>4</sup>Also, there must be no evil talk among you. You must not speak foolishly or tell evil jokes. These things are not right for you. But you should be giving thanks to God. <sup>5</sup>You can be sure of this: No one will have a place in the kingdom of Christ and of God if he does sexual sins, or does evil things, or is greedy. Anyone who is greedy is serving a false god.

## LIVIN' iT!

### WHO'S YOUR DADDY?
### EPHESIANS 5:8

Imagine a family that is very rich, the father being one of the most important people in the land. Then picture his son, dressed in rags, sitting by the roadside begging people for food. What's wrong with the picture? The son doesn't seem to know who he is, or what kind of dad he has.

Sadly, many Christians are like the son by the road. They don't understand that because they belong to Jesus, they are loved by God as much as Jesus is. In Jesus, they have every spiritual gift they need to defeat sin and live like the children of God they are. Don't make their mistake. Know who your heavenly Father is. Because of who he is, you know who you are. Now that you know you're a child of the King, act like it.

 4:25 Tell . . . body. Quotation from Zechariah 8:16.

# SECRET TRUTHS

## CAN YOU UNSCRAMBLE THESE WORDS TO FIND THE SECRET BEHIND SUCCESSFUL KIDS?

ILCHDRNE , YBOE YOUR ARPNEST

THE WAY EHT DORL STWAN . THIS

SI THE TIRGH GNIHT TO DO .

**EPHESIANS 6:1**

ANSWER KEY: Children, obey your parents the way the Lord wants. This is the right thing to do.

[6]Do not let anyone fool you by telling you things that are not true. These things will bring God's anger on those who do not obey him. [7]So have no part with them. [8]In the past you were full of darkness, but now you are full of light in the Lord. So live like children who belong to the light. [9]Light brings every kind of goodness, right living, and truth. [10]Try to learn what pleases the Lord. [11]Do not do the things that people in darkness do. That brings nothing good. But do good things to show that the things done in darkness are wrong. [12]It is shameful even to talk about what those people do in secret.

[13]But the light makes all things easy to see. [14]And everything that is made easy to see can become light. This is why it is said:

"Wake up, sleeper!
Rise from death,
and Christ will shine on you."

[15]So be very careful how you live. Do not live like those who are not wise. Live wisely. [16]I mean that you should use every chance you have for doing good, because these are evil times. [17]So do not be foolish with your lives. But learn what the Lord wants you to do. [18]Do not be drunk with wine. That will ruin you spiritually. But be filled with the Spirit.[d] [19]Speak to each other with psalms, hymns, and spiritual songs. Sing and make music in your hearts to the Lord. [20]Always give thanks to God the Father for everything, in the name of our Lord Jesus Christ.

### WIVES AND HUSBANDS

[21]Be willing to obey each other. Do this because you respect Christ.

[22]Wives, be under the authority of your husbands, as of the Lord. [23]The husband is the head of the wife, as Christ is the head of the church. The church is Christ's body—Christ is the Savior of the body. [24]The church is under the authority of Christ. So it is the same with you wives. You should be under the authority of your husbands in everything.

[25]Husbands, love your wives as Christ loved the church. Christ died for the church [26]to make it belong to God. Christ used the word to make the church clean by washing it with water. [27]Christ died so that he could give the church to himself like a bride in all her beauty. He died so that the church could be pure and without fault, with no evil or sin or any other wrong thing in it. [28]And husbands should love their wives in the same way. They should love their wives as they love

## DECODE THIS!

*Don't lie. Tell the truth, and don't give the _____ a way to defeat you.*

# LIVIN' IT!

**ATTENTION!!**
**EPHESIANS 6:10**

Smell the dust. Listen for sounds. Did you hear that? It sounds like the enemy—yes, you are a soldier, and we are at war. Of course, the battle we fight is not with Black Hawks or scud missiles; it is with the spiritual armor that God gives us to fight Satan, his demons, and our own sin.

What kind of weapons do we have in our arsenal? God gives us the belt of truth, a breastplate of righteousness, protective shoes of the Good News, a shield of faith, a helmet of salvation, and a sword of the Spirit. Armed with God's righteousness and truth, we are able to say "No!" to Satan's plans for us and others. So get ready by learning and knowing God's Word. Be ready to fight. But don't worry about the battles. God has already won the war.

their own bodies. The man who loves his wife loves himself. [29]No person ever hates his own body, but feeds and takes care of it. And that is what Christ does for the church, [30]because we are parts of his body. [31]The Scripture says, "So a man will leave his father and mother and be united with his wife. And the two people will become one body."[n] [32]That secret truth is very important—I am talking about Christ and the church. [33]But each one of you must love his wife as he loves himself. And a wife must respect her husband.

## CHILDREN AND PARENTS

**6** Children, obey your parents the way the Lord wants. This is the right thing to do. [2]The command says, "Honor your father and mother."[n] This is the first command that has a promise with it. [3]The promise is: "Then everything will be well with you, and you will have a long life on the earth."[n]

[4]Fathers, do not make your children angry, but raise them with the training and teaching of the Lord.

## SLAVES AND MASTERS

[5]Slaves, obey your masters here on earth with fear and respect. And do that with a heart that is true, just as you obey Christ. [6]You must do more than obey your masters to please them only while they are watching you. You must obey them as you are obeying Christ. With all your heart you must do what God wants. [7]Do your work, and be happy to do it. Work as if you were serving the Lord, not as if you were serving only men. [8]Remember that the Lord will give a reward to everyone, slave or free, for doing good.

[9]Masters, in the same way, be good to your slaves. Do not say things to scare them. You know that the One who is your Master and their Master is in heaven. And that Master treats everyone alike.

## WEAR THE FULL ARMOR OF GOD

[10]Finally, be strong in the Lord and in his great power. [11]Wear the full armor of God. Wear God's armor so that you can fight against the devil's evil tricks. [12]Our fight is not against people on earth. We are fighting against the rulers and authorities and the powers of this world's darkness. We are fighting against the spiritual powers of evil in the heavenly world. [13]That is

why you need to get God's full armor. Then on the day of evil you will be able to stand strong. And when you have finished the whole fight, you will still be standing. [14]So stand strong, with the belt of truth tied around your waist. And on your chest wear the protection of right living. [15]And on your feet wear the Good News[d] of peace to help you stand strong. [16]And also use the shield of faith. With that you can stop all the burning arrows of the Evil One. [17]Accept God's salvation to be your helmet. And take the sword of the Spirit[d]—that sword is the teaching of God. [18]Pray in the Spirit at all times. Pray with all kinds of prayers, and ask for everything you need. To do this you must always be ready. Never give up. Always pray for all God's people.

[19]Also pray for me. Pray that when I speak, God will give me words so that I can tell the secret truth of the Good News without fear. [20]I have the work of speaking that Good News. I am doing that now, here in prison. Pray that when I preach the Good News I will speak without fear, as I should.

## FINAL GREETINGS

[21]I am sending to you Tychicus, our brother whom we love. He is a faithful servant of the Lord's work. He will tell you everything that is happening with me. Then you will know how I am and what I am doing. [22]That is why I am sending him. I want you to know how we are. I am sending him to encourage you.

[23]Peace and love with faith to you from God the Father and the Lord Jesus Christ. [24]God's grace to all of you who love our Lord Jesus Christ with love that never ends.

## DECODE THIS!

*Children should ____ their parents as the Lord wants them to.*

5:31 "So . . . body." Quotation from Genesis 2:24. 6:2 "Honor . . . mother." Quotation from Exodus 20:12; Deuteronomy 5:16. 6:3 "Then . . . earth." Quotation from Exodus 20:12; Deuteronomy 5:16.

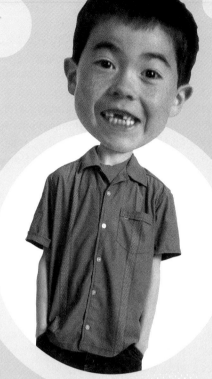

A military town named after Alexander the Great's father: King Philip.

# THE LETTER OF PAUL THE APOSTLE TO THE

# PHILIPPIANS

Paul writes a cheery note thanking the believers for their gifts.

Philippi was home to Lydia, a purple fabric seller.

A big earthquake helps Paul and Silas get out of jail the first time they went to Philippi.

Serve others with joy.

## BIBLE Basics

### WHAT IS GOSSIP?

Gossip is spreading news or information about someone else that could hurt the way other people look at them. Even if the facts are true, it is not the Christian's place to say bad things about others. The Bible warns us against this sin because every word that comes out of our mouths should honor God and build up the people around us, not tear them down. If we have a problem with someone, it is our job to go directly to that person and work it out.

**1** From Paul and Timothy, servants of Jesus Christ.

To all of God's holy people in Christ Jesus who live in Philippi. And to your elders[d] and deacons.[d]

[2]Grace and peace to you from God our Father and the Lord Jesus Christ.

### PAUL'S PRAYER

[3]I thank God every time I remember you. [4]And I always pray for all of you with joy. [5]I thank God for the help you gave me while I preached the Good News.[d] You helped from the first day you believed until now. [6]God began doing a good work in you. And he will continue it until it is finished when Jesus Christ comes again. I am sure of that.

[7]And I know that I am right to think like this about all of you. I am sure because I have you in my heart. All of you share in God's grace with me. You share in God's grace with me while I am in prison, while I am defending the Good News, and while I am proving the truth of the Good News. [8]God knows that I want to see you very much. I love all of you with the love of Christ Jesus.

[9]This is my prayer for you: that your love will grow more and more; that you will have knowledge and understanding with your love; [10]that you will see the difference between good and bad and choose the good; that you will be pure and without wrong for the coming of Christ; [11]that you will do many good things with the help of Christ to bring glory and praise to God.

### PAUL'S TROUBLES HELP THE WORK

[12]Brothers, I want you to know that what has happened to me has helped to spread the Good News.[d] [13]I am in prison because I am a believer in Christ. All the palace guards and everyone else knows this. [14]I am still in prison, but most of the believers feel better about it now. And so they are much braver about telling the Good News about Christ.

[15]It is true that some preach about Christ because they are jealous and bitter. But others preach about Christ because they want to help. [16]They preach because they have love, and they know that God gave me the work of defending the Good News. [17]But others preach about Christ because they are selfish. Their reason for preaching is wrong. They want to make trouble for me in prison.

[18]But I do not care if they make trouble for me. The important thing is that they are preaching about Christ. They should do it for the right reasons. But I am happy even if they do it for wrong reasons. And I will continue to be happy. [19]You are praying for me, and the Spirit of Jesus Christ helps me. So I know that this trouble will bring my freedom. [20]The thing I want and hope for is that I will not fail Christ in anything. I hope that I will have the courage now, as always, to show the greatness of Christ in my life here on earth. I want to do that if I die or if I live. [21]To me the only important thing about living is Christ. And even death would be profit for me. [22]If I continue living in the body, I will be able to work for the Lord. But what should I choose—living or dying? I do not know. [23]It is hard to choose between the two. I want to leave this life and be with Christ. That is much better. [24]But you need me here in my body. [25]I know that you need me, and so I know that I will stay with you. I will help you grow and have joy in your faith. [26]You will be very happy in Christ Jesus when I am with you again.

[27]Be sure that you live in a way that brings honor to the Good News of Christ. Then whether I come and visit you or am away from you, I will hear good things about you. I will hear that you continue strong with one purpose and that you work together as a team for the faith of the Good News. [28]And you will not be afraid of those who are against you. All of these things are proof from God that you will be saved and that your enemies will be lost. [29]God gave you the honor both of believing in Christ and suffering for Christ. Both these things bring glory to Christ. [30]When I was with you, you saw the struggles I had. And you hear about the struggles I am having now. You yourselves are having the same kind of struggles.

**2** Does your life in Christ give you strength? Does his love comfort you? Do we share together in the Spirit?[d] Do you have mercy and kindness? [2]If so, make me very happy by having the same thoughts, sharing the same love, and having one mind and purpose. [3]When you do things, do not let selfishness or pride be your guide. Be humble and give more honor to others than to yourselves. [4]Do not be interested only in your own life, but be interested in the lives of others.

### DECODE THIS!

Paul prayed that the Philippians would have their _____ grow.

# GET CONNECTED

## ALIEN INVASION

Imagine your older brother or sister coming home from school and asking about your day. They offer to make you a snack and let you watch TV in their room. Then, without being asked, they do your chores so you won't have to do them. You would probably think a UFO had come and switched out an alien for your sibling. Life just doesn't work that way.

But with Jesus, it does. Even though he's the King, he came to earth to serve. Even though he really was more important than us, he didn't think about that. He just loved us, instead. When you look at your brothers, sisters, parents, and friends, try to see them the way Jesus does. Look for ways to put their needs first, and show them what God's love looks like in action.

### BE UNSELFISH LIKE CHRIST

[5] In your lives you must think and act like Christ Jesus.
[6] Christ himself was like God in everything.
He was equal with God.
But he did not think that being equal with God was something to be held on to.
[7] He gave up his place with God and made himself nothing.
He was born to be a man and became like a servant.
[8] And when he was living as a man, he humbled himself and was fully obedient to God.
He obeyed even when that caused his death—death on a cross.
[9] So God raised Christ to the highest place.
God made the name of Christ greater than every other name.
[10] God wants every knee to bow to Jesus—
everyone in heaven, on earth, and under the earth.
[11] Everyone will say, "Jesus Christ is Lord"
and bring glory to God the Father.

### BE THE PEOPLE GOD WANTS YOU TO BE

[12] My dear friends, you have always obeyed. You obeyed God when I was with you. It is even more important that you obey now while I am not with you. Keep on working to complete your salvation, and do it with fear and trembling. [13] Yes, God is working in you to help you want to do what pleases him. Then he gives you the power to do it.

[14] Do everything without complaining or arguing. [15] Then you will be innocent and without anything wrong in you. You will be God's children without fault. But you are living with crooked and mean people all around you. Among them you shine like stars in the dark world. [16] You offer to them the teaching that gives life. So when Christ comes again, I can be happy because my work was not wasted. I ran in the race and won.

[17] Your faith makes you offer your lives as a sacrifice in serving God. Perhaps I will have to offer my own blood with your sacrifice. But if that happens, I will be happy and full of joy with all of you. [18] You also should be happy and full of joy with me.

### TIMOTHY AND EPAPHRODITUS

[19] I hope in the Lord Jesus to send Timothy to you soon. I will be happy to learn how you are. [20] I have no other person like Timothy. He truly cares for you. [21] Other people are interested only in their own lives. They are not interested in the work of Christ Jesus. [22] You know the kind of person Timothy is. You know that he has served with me in telling the Good News,[d] as a son serves his father. [23] I plan to send him to you quickly when I know what will happen to me. [24] I am sure that the Lord will help me to come to you soon.

[25] Epaphroditus is my brother in Christ. He works and serves with me in the army of Christ. When I needed help, you sent him to me. I think now that I must send

## LIVIN' IT!

### BORN TO SERVE
### PHILIPPIANS 2:3

In today's world, people put a lot of importance on serving themselves. They say things like, "Work hard to make yourself number one. If you don't take care of yourself, no one will." But Jesus wants us to follow his example. Even though he was more important than anyone else, he made up his mind to become a servant to everyone else.

We need to see others the same way. Look for ways to build up others instead of just yourself. Trust God to help you become the person you were meant to be, without trying to make it happen on your own. True humility is a heart issue; it's an attitude that comes from knowing you don't have to make yourself look important. (You already are as a child of the King.) Now it's your joy to be able to serve others—just like Jesus did—to help them come to know him better.

him back to you ²⁶because he wants very much to see all of you. He is worried because you heard that he was sick. ²⁷Yes, he was sick, and nearly died. But God helped him and me too, so that I would not have more sadness. ²⁸So I want very much to send him to you. When you see him, you can be happy. And I can stop worrying about you. ²⁹Welcome him in the Lord with much joy. Give honor to people like Epaphroditus. ³⁰He should be honored because he almost died for the work of Christ. He put his life in danger so that he could help me. This was help that you could not give me.

## THE IMPORTANCE OF CHRIST

**3** My brothers, be full of joy in the Lord. It is no trouble for me to write the same things to you again, and it will help you to be more ready. ²Be careful of those who do evil. They are like dogs. They demand to cut*ⁿ* the body. ³But we are the ones who are truly circumcised.*ᵈ* We worship God through his Spirit.*ᵈ* We are proud to be in Christ Jesus. And we do not trust in ourselves or anything we can do.

# LIVIN' IT!

**WHAT A JOY!**
**PHILIPPIANS 3:1**

Want to know how to spot a Christian who really has a close friendship with God? You'll see it on his face. You'll hear it in her speech. Joy in the Lord is his strength and the one quality that amazes everyone else. But when Paul says that we should always be joyful, he doesn't mean that we should be happy all the time. There are times of sadness in every life.

Joy goes deeper than happiness. Even in hard times, we still know that, in the end, things will get better. One day we will be with Jesus, and even in the difficult times, Jesus is right by our side. Knowing that Jesus is still in control and loves us—even when everything seems to be going wrong—brings us a joy that never goes away.

⁴Even if I am able to trust in myself, still I do not. If anyone thinks that he has a reason to trust in himself, he should know that I have greater reason for trusting in myself. ⁵I was circumcised eight days after my birth. I am from the people of Israel and the tribe*ᵈ* of Benjamin. I am a Hebrew, and my parents were Hebrews. The law of Moses was very important to me. That is why I became a Pharisee.*ᵈ* ⁶I was so enthusiastic that I tried to hurt the church. No one could find fault with the way I obeyed the law of Moses. ⁷At one time all these things were important to me. But now I think those things are worth nothing because of Christ. ⁸Not only those things, but I think that all things are worth nothing compared with the greatness of knowing Christ Jesus my Lord. Because of Christ, I have lost all those things. And now I know that all those things are worthless trash. This allows me to have Christ ⁹and to belong to him. Now that I belong to Christ, I am right with God and this being right does not come from my following the law. It comes from God through faith. God uses my faith in Christ to make me right with him. ¹⁰All I want is to know Christ and the power of his rising from death. I want to share in Christ's sufferings and become like him in his death. ¹¹If I have those things, then I have hope that I myself will be raised from death.

## CONTINUING TOWARD OUR GOAL

¹²I do not mean that I am already as God wants me to be. I have not yet reached that goal. But I continue trying to reach it and to make it mine. Christ wants me to do that. That is the reason Christ made me his. ¹³Brothers, I know that I have not yet reached that goal. But there is one thing I always do: I forget the things that are past. I try as hard as I can to reach the goal that is before me. ¹⁴I keep trying to reach the goal and get the prize. That prize is mine because God called me through Christ to the life above.

### "My brothers, be full of joy in the Lord." *Philippians 3:1*

¹⁵All of us who have grown spiritually to be mature should think this way, too. And if there are things you do not agree with, God will make them clear to you. ¹⁶But we should continue following the truth we already have.

¹⁷Brothers, all of you should try to follow my example and to copy those who live the way we showed you. ¹⁸Many people

# BiBLe BASiCS
## WHY iS THE resUrrection imPORTANT?

Without the resurrection, Jesus would be dead. If he were still dead, he wouldn't be God, and none of his teachings would be worth anything. Basically, we would have no hope at all. But because he rose from the dead, we know that he has power over death—eternal death without God—and so do we if we are completely trusting in him. We know that he truly is the Christ, and everything he has said about our lives now and in the future will come true.

**3:2 cut** The word in Greek is like the word "circumcise," but it means "to cut completely off."

live like enemies of the cross of Christ. I have often told you about them, and it makes me cry to tell you about them now. ¹⁹The way they live is leading them to destruction. Instead of serving God, they do whatever their bodies want. They do shameful things, and they are proud of it. They think only about earthly things. ²⁰But our homeland is in heaven, and we are waiting for our Savior, the Lord Jesus Christ, to come from heaven. ²¹He will change our simple bodies and make them like his own glorious body. Christ can do this by his power. With that power he is able to rule all things.

## LIVIN' IT!

### CHANGE YOUR MIND
### PHILIPPIANS 4:8

Did you know that before you do anything, you've thought about it first in your mind? In fact, the real battle against sin and becoming more like Jesus starts first in your brain.

If we let wrong ideas into our heads and don't fight them with the truth of the Bible, we will begin to think wrongly and then act wrongly. Philippians 4:8 reminds us what kind of thoughts we need to keep in our minds—whatever is true, honorable, right, pure, beautiful, and respected. If you notice that you're worried, or angry, or having thoughts that you know wouldn't please God, go to God immediately and tell him. Ask him to help you get control of what you're thinking. Memorize Bible verses (like this one) that will help you fight wrong ideas. Then let God's Word change your mind for the good!

## WHAT THE CHRISTIANS ARE TO DO

**4** My dear brothers, I love you and want to see you. You bring me joy and make me proud of you. Continue following the Lord as I have told you. ²I ask Euodia and Syntyche to agree in the Lord. ³And because you serve faithfully with me, my friend, I ask you to help these women to do this. They served with me in telling people the Good News.ᵈ They served together with Clement and others who worked with me. Their names are written in the book of life.ⁿ

⁴Be full of joy in the Lord always. I will say again, be full of joy. ⁵Let all men see that you are gentle and kind. The Lord is coming soon. ⁶Do not worry about anything. But pray and ask God for everything you need. And when you pray, always give thanks. ⁷And God's peace will keep your hearts and minds in Christ Jesus. The peace that God gives is so great that we cannot understand it.

⁸Brothers, continue to think about the things that are good and worthy of praise. Think about the things that are true and honorable and right and pure and beautiful and respected. ⁹And do what you learned and received from me. Do what I told you and what you saw me do. And the God who gives peace will be with you.

## PAUL THANKS THE CHRISTIANS

¹⁰I am very happy in the Lord that you have shown your care for me again. You continued to care about me, but there was no way for you to show it. ¹¹I am telling you this, but it is not because I need anything. I have learned to be satisfied with the things I have and with everything that happens. ¹²I know how to live when I am poor. And I know how to live when I have plenty. I have learned the secret of being happy at any time in everything that happens. I have learned to be happy when I have enough to eat and when I do not have enough to eat. I have learned to be happy when I have all that I need and when I do not have the things I need. ¹³I can do all things through Christ because he gives me strength.

¹⁴But it was good that you helped me when I needed help. ¹⁵You people in Philippi remember when I first preached the Good Newsᵈ there. When I left Macedonia, you were the only church that gave me help. ¹⁶Several times you sent me things I needed when I was in Thessalonica. ¹⁷Really, it is not that I want to receive gifts from you. But I want you to have the good that comes from giving. ¹⁸And now I have everything, and more. I have all I need because Epaphroditus brought your gift to me. Your gift is like a sweet-smelling sacrifice offered to God. God accepts that sacrifice, and it pleases him. ¹⁹My God will use his wonderful riches in Christ Jesus to give you everything you need. ²⁰Glory to our God and Father forever and ever! Amen.

²¹Greet each of God's people in Christ. God's people who are with me send greetings to you. ²²All of God's people greet you. And those believers from the palace of Caesarᵈ greet you, too.

²³The grace of the Lord Jesus Christ be with you all.

4:3 **book of life** God's book that has the names of all God's chosen people (Revelation 3:5; 21:27).

## DECODE THIS!

*Paul tried to reach the goal and the _____.*

Colosse was a small business center famous for glossy black wool.

Only Christ can save people.

Paul tells the church in Colosse to watch out for man-made religion.

THE LETTER
OF PAUL THE
APOSTLE TO THE

# COLOSSIANS

Key verse: "Think only about the things in heaven, not the things on earth" (3:2).

Thought to be the most Christ-centered book of the Bible.

**1** From Paul, an apostle[d] of Christ Jesus. I am an apostle because that is what God wanted.

Also from Timothy, our brother.

[2] To the holy and faithful brothers in Christ that live in Colosse. Grace and peace from God our Father.

[3] In our prayers for you we always thank God, the Father of our Lord Jesus Christ. [4] We thank God because we have heard about the faith you have in Christ Jesus and the love you have for all of God's people. [5] You have this faith and love because of your hope, and what you hope for is saved for you in heaven. You learned about this hope when you heard the true teaching, the Good News[d] [6] that was told to you. Everywhere in the world that Good News is bringing blessings and is growing. This has happened with you, too, since you heard the Good News and understood the truth about the grace of God. [7] You learned about God's grace from Epaphras, whom we love. Epaphras works together with us, and is a faithful servant of Christ for us. [8] He also told us about the love you have from the Holy Spirit.[d]

[9] Since the day we heard this about you, we have continued praying for you. We ask God that you will know fully what God wants. We pray that you will also have great wisdom and understanding in spiritual things. [10] Then you will live the kind of life that honors and pleases the Lord in every way. You will produce fruit in every good work and grow in the knowledge of God. [11] Then God will strengthen you with his own great power. And you will not give up when troubles come, but you will be patient. [12] Then you will joyfully give thanks to the Father. He has made you able to have all that he has prepared for his people who live in the light. [13] God made us free from the power of darkness, and he brought us into the kingdom of his dear Son. [14] The Son paid for our sins, and in him we have forgiveness.

### THE IMPORTANCE OF CHRIST

[15] No one has seen God, but Jesus is exactly like him. Christ ranks higher than all the things that have been made. [16] Through his power all things were made—things in heaven and on earth, things seen and unseen, all powers, authorities, lords, and rulers. All things were made through Christ and for Christ. [17] Christ was there before anything was made. And all things continue because of him. [18] He is the head of the body. (The body is the church.) Everything comes from him. And he is the first one who was raised from death. So in all things Jesus is most important. [19] God was pleased for all of himself to live in Christ. [20] And through Christ, God decided to bring all things back to himself again—things on earth and things in heaven. God made peace by using the blood of Christ's death on the cross.

[21] At one time you were separated from God. You were God's enemies in your minds because the evil deeds you did were against God. [22] But now Christ has made you God's friends again. He did this by his death while he was in the body, that he might bring you into God's presence. He brings you before God as people who are holy, with no wrong in you, and with nothing that God can judge you guilty of. [23] And Christ will do this if you continue to believe in the Good News[d] you heard. You must continue strong and sure in your faith. You must not be moved away from the hope that Good News gave you. That same Good News has been told to everyone in the world. I, Paul, help in preaching that Good News.

### PAUL'S WORK FOR THE CHURCH

[24] I am happy in my sufferings for you. There are many things that Christ must still suffer through his body, the church. I am accepting my part of these things

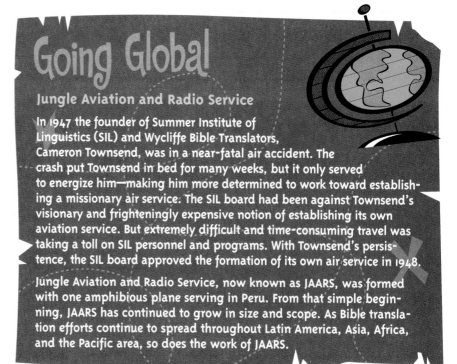

## Going Global

### Jungle Aviation and Radio Service

In 1947 the founder of Summer Institute of Linguistics (SIL) and Wycliffe Bible Translators, Cameron Townsend, was in a near-fatal air accident. The crash put Townsend in bed for many weeks, but it only served to energize him—making him more determined to work toward establishing a missionary air service. The SIL board had been against Townsend's visionary and frighteningly expensive notion of establishing its own aviation service. But extremely difficult and time-consuming travel was taking a toll on SIL personnel and programs. With Townsend's persistence, the SIL board approved the formation of its own air service in 1948.

Jungle Aviation and Radio Service, now known as JAARS, was formed with one amphibious plane serving in Peru. From that simple beginning, JAARS has continued to grow in size and scope. As Bible translation efforts continue to spread throughout Latin America, Asia, Africa, and the Pacific area, so does the work of JAARS.

### DECODE THIS!

*What will God do to help you not give up when trouble comes?*

that must be suffered. I accept these sufferings in my body. I suffer for his body, the church. ²⁵I became a servant of the church because God gave me a special work to do that helps you. My work is to tell fully the teaching of God. ²⁶This teaching is the secret truth that was hidden since the beginning of time. It was hidden from everyone, but now it is made known to God's holy people. ²⁷God decided to let his people know this rich and glorious truth which he has for

> **"Be strong in the faith, just as you were taught. And always be thankful."**
> *Colossians 2:7*

all people. This truth is Christ himself, who is in you. He is our only hope for glory. ²⁸So we continue to preach Christ to all men. We use all wisdom to warn and to teach everyone. We are trying to bring each one into God's presence as a mature person in Christ. ²⁹To do this, I work and struggle, using Christ's great strength that works so powerfully in me.

**2** I want you to know that I am trying very hard to help you. And I am trying to help those in Laodicea and others who have never seen me. ²I want them to be strengthened and joined together with love. I want them to be rich in the strong belief that comes from understanding. I mean I want you to know fully God's secret truth. That truth is Christ himself. ³And in him all the treasures of wisdom and knowledge are safely kept.

⁴I say this so that no one can fool you by arguments that seem good, but are false. ⁵I am not there with you, but my heart is with you. I am happy to see your good lives and your strong faith in Christ.

## CONTINUE TO LIVE IN CHRIST

⁶As you received Christ Jesus the Lord, so continue to live in him. ⁷Keep your roots deep in him and have your lives built on him. Be strong in the faith, just as you were taught. And always be thankful.

⁸Be sure that no one leads you away with false ideas and words that mean nothing. Those ideas come from men. They are the worthless ideas of this world. They are not from Christ. ⁹All of God lives in Christ fully (even when Christ was on earth). ¹⁰And in him you have a full and true life. He is ruler over all rulers and powers.

¹¹In Christ you had a different kind of circumcision.ᵈ That circumcision was not done by hands. I mean, you were made free from the power of your sinful self. That is the kind of circumcision Christ does. ¹²When you were baptized, you were buried with Christ and you were raised up with Christ because of your faith in God's power. That power was shown when he raised Christ from death. ¹³You were spiritually dead because of your sins and because you were not free from the power of your sinful self. But God made you alive with Christ. And God forgave all our sins. ¹⁴We owed a debt because we broke God's laws. That debt listed all the rules we failed to follow. But God forgave us that debt. He took away that debt and nailed it to the cross.

¹⁵God defeated the spiritual rulers and powers. With the cross God won the victory and defeated them. He showed the world that they were powerless.

## DON'T FOLLOW PEOPLE'S RULES

¹⁶So do not let anyone make rules for you about eating and drinking or about a religious feast, a New Moonᵈ Festival, or a Sabbathᵈ day. ¹⁷In the past, these things were like a shadow of what was to come. But the new things that were coming are found in Christ. ¹⁸Some enjoy acting as if they were humble and love to worship angels. They are always talk-

### Ways to Encourage Your Father

1. Give him a hug before he leaves for work.
2. Tell him thanks for his hard work.
3. Ask him about his day.
4. Ask him if he has any prayer requests, and pray for them.
5. Weed the flower bed without being asked.
6. Take out the trash.
7. Help your mom make his favorite meal.
8. Put a note in his briefcase that says you love him.
9. Ask him about his childhood and special memories.
10. Buy a verse-a-day calendar.

ing about the visions they have seen. Do not let them tell you that you are wrong. They are full of foolish pride because of their human way of thinking. [19]They do not keep themselves under the control of Christ, the head. The whole body depends on Christ. Because of him all the parts of the body care for each other and help each other. This strengthens the body and holds it together. And so the body grows in the way God wants.

[20]You died with Christ and were made free from the worthless rules of the world. So why do you act as if you still belong to this world? I mean, why do you follow rules like these: [21]"Don't eat this," "Don't taste that," "Don't touch that thing"? [22]These rules are talking about earthly things that are gone as soon as they are used. They are only man-made commands and teachings. [23]These rules seem to be wise. But they are only part of a man-made religion. They make people pretend not to be proud and make them punish their bodies. But they do not really control the evil desires of the sinful self.

> **"Children, obey your parents in all things. This pleases the Lord."**
>
> *Colossians 3:20*

### YOUR NEW LIFE IN CHRIST

**3** You were raised from death with Christ. So aim at what is in heaven, where Christ is sitting at the right hand of God. [2]Think only about the things in heaven, not the things on earth. [3]Your old sinful self has died, and your new life is kept with Christ in God. [4]Christ is your life. When he comes again, you will share in his glory.

**DECODE THIS!**

Be strong in _____ and always be thankful.

[5]So put all evil things out of your life: sexual sinning, doing evil, letting evil thoughts control you, wanting things that are evil, and always selfishly wanting more and more. This really means living to serve a false god. [6]These things make God angry." [7]In your evil life in the past, you also did these things.

[8]But now put these things out of your life: anger, bad temper, doing or saying things to hurt others, and using evil words when you talk. [9]Do not lie to each other. You have left your old sinful life and the things you did before. [10]You have begun to live the new life. In your new life you are being made new. You are becoming like the One who made you. This new life brings you the true knowledge of God. [11]In the new life there is no difference between Greeks and Jews. There is no difference between those who are circumcised[d] and those who are not circumcised, or people that are foreigners, or Scythians." There is no difference between slaves and free people. But Christ is in all believers. And Christ is all that is important.

[12]God has chosen you and made you his holy people. He loves you. So always do these things: Show mercy to others; be kind, humble, gentle, and patient. [13]Do not be angry with each other, but forgive each other. If someone does wrong to you, then forgive him. Forgive each other because the Lord forgave you. [14]Do all these things; but most important, love each other. Love is what holds you all together in perfect unity. [15]Let the peace that Christ gives control your thinking. You were all called together in one body" to have peace. Always be thankful. [16]Let the teaching of Christ

## LIVIN' IT!

**IT ADDS UP
COLOSSIANS 3:16**

Some people think of the Bible kind of like a calculator. Why should you have to learn to add and subtract when you could just use a calculator? Or, why should you have to memorize God's Word when you can just go to your Bible and look it up when you need it?

Truth is, we need to be able to add and subtract all throughout the day. We can't always run to get our calculators. Likewise, every day holds new challenges for us. We need to know God's Word so well that it becomes a part of us. We actually start thinking like God does. And when that difficult time pops up, we're ready to handle it the right way. God's Word not only directs our lives, but we can use what we know to encourage others in the right way, too.

live in you richly. Use all wisdom to teach and strengthen each other. Sing psalms, hymns, and spiritual songs with thankfulness in your hearts to God. [17]Everything you say and everything you do should all be done for Jesus your Lord. And in all you do, give thanks to God the Father through Jesus.

### YOUR NEW LIFE WITH OTHER PEOPLE

[18]Wives, be under the authority of your husbands. This is the right thing to do in the Lord.

[19]Husbands, love your wives, and be gentle to them.

[20]Children, obey your parents in all things. This pleases the Lord.

[21]Fathers, do not nag your children. If you are too hard to please, they may want to stop trying.

[22]Slaves, obey your masters in all things. Do not obey just when they are watching you, to gain their favor. But

3:6 **These . . . angry** Some Greek copies add: "against the people who do not obey God."
3:11 **Scythians** The Scythians were known as very wild and cruel people.
3:15 **body** The spiritual body of Christ, meaning the church or his people.

# OCTOBER FAITH

**1** Draw a picture of how you see heaven.

**2** LUKE 17:6: The Lord said, "If your faith is as big as a mustard seed, then you can say to this mulberry tree, 'Dig yourself up and plant yourself in the sea!' And the tree will obey you."

**3**

**4** Invite friends to go on a hayride to a pumpkin patch.

**5** Prayer Pointer: Thank God for his gift of faith and helping you to understand the truth.

**6**

**7** Help your dad rake the yard.

**8**

**9**

**10** ROMANS 15:2: Let each of us please his neighbor for his good, to help him be stronger in faith.

**11** Taste a pomegranate.

**12**

**13** Prayer Pointer: Ask God to increase your faith and the faith of your family and friends.

**14**

**15** Learn how to make pumpkin pie.

**16**

**17** EPHESIANS 2:8: I mean that you have been saved by grace because you believe. You did not save yourselves. It was a gift from God.

**18**

**19** Go for a walk, and collect leaves of every color.

**20**

**21** Make a scarecrow with your brothers and sisters.

**22** Prayer Pointer: Pray for God to help people to understand the Good News all over the world.

**23**

**24** Go for a nature walk with your parents, and tell them about your friends.

**25**

**26**

**27** 2 CORINTHIANS 5:7: We live by what we believe, not by what we can see.

**28**

**29** Take blankets to a homeless shelter.

**30**

**31** Tell your pastor you are praying for him.

Faith means being sure of the things we hope for. And faith means knowing that something is real even if we do not see it (Hebrews 11:1).

serve them honestly, because you respect the Lord. ²³In all the work you are doing, work the best you can. Work as if you were working for the Lord, not for men. ²⁴Remember that you will receive your reward from the Lord, which he promised to his people. You are serving the Lord Christ. ²⁵But remember that anyone who does wrong will be punished for that wrong. And the Lord treats everyone the same.

**4** Masters, give the things that are good and fair to your slaves. Remember that you have a Master in heaven.

## BiBLe BasiCS

### WHAT DOES IT MEAN TO BAPTIZE?

The word *baptize* means "to dip or immerse." Christians in the New Testament baptized one another with water to show, through an outward symbol, what was going on inside the person's heart. It forms a picture of the life, death, and resurrection of Jesus, as well as the cleansing work of the Holy Spirit as the believer is forgiven and raised to new life in Christ.

### WHAT THE CHRISTIANS ARE TO DO

²Continue praying and keep alert. And when you pray, always thank God. ³Also pray for us. Pray that God will give us an opportunity to tell people his message. Pray that we can preach the secret truth that God has made known about Christ. I am in prison because I preach this truth. ⁴Pray that I can speak in a way that will make it clear as I should.

⁵Be wise in the way you act with people who are not believers. Use your time in the best way you can. ⁶When you talk, you should always be kind and wise. Then you will be able to answer everyone in the way you should.

### NEWS ABOUT THE PEOPLE WITH PAUL

⁷Tychicus is my dear brother in Christ. He is a faithful minister and servant with me in the Lord. He will tell you all the things that are happening to me. ⁸That is why I am sending him. I want you to know how we are. I am sending him to encourage you. ⁹I send him with Onesimus. Onesimus is a faithful and dear brother in Christ. He is one of your group. They will tell you all that has happened here.

¹⁰Aristarchus greets you. He is a prisoner with me. And Mark, the cousin of Barnabas, also greets you. (I have already told you what to do about Mark. If he comes, welcome him.) ¹¹Jesus, who is called Justus, also greets you. These are the only Jewish believers who work with me for the kingdom of God.

They have been a comfort to me.

¹²Epaphras also greets you. He is a servant of Jesus Christ. And he is from your group. He always prays for you. He prays that you will grow to be spiritually mature and have everything that God wants for you. ¹³I know that he has worked hard for you and the people in Laodicea and in Hierapolis. ¹⁴Demas and our dear friend Luke, the doctor, greet you.

¹⁵Greet the brothers in Laodicea. And greet Nympha and the church that meets in her house. ¹⁶After this letter is read to you, be sure that it is also read to the church in Laodicea. And you read the letter that I wrote to Laodicea. ¹⁷Tell Archippus, "Be sure to do the work the Lord gave you."

¹⁸I, Paul, greet you and write this with my own hand. Remember me in prison. God's grace be with you.

## GET CONNECTED

### MAKING WRONGS RIGHT

You knew it was wrong, and you did it anyway. But the Holy Spirit who lives inside of you won't leave you alone. You've got to make things right again with God and your parents, but you're scared. What should you do?

Pray. Confess it to God, and ask for forgiveness. Then ask God to show you the right time to tell your parents. If you just can't speak, write it down. Remember, punishments only last a short time. But the separation from God and your parents that you feel in your heart will remain until you deal with your sin. Your parents will appreciate your honesty and will help you recover from your mistake.

Paul
encourages
new Christians.

Paul wears 2
hats while in
Thessalonica:
tentmaker and
church leader.

# THE FIRST LETTER OF PAUL THE APOSTLE TO THE

# THESSALONIANS

Timothy is sent by Paul
to check on the new
church. His report: They
are enduring great
troubles, but want to
know, "When is Jesus
coming back?"

Thessalonica
is the capital and
largest city in
Macedonia (population
200,000).

Paul's visit is
very short—run
out of town
by a riot!

**1** From Paul, Silas, and Timothy. To the church in Thessalonica, the church in God the Father and the Lord Jesus Christ. May God's grace and peace be yours.

## THE FAITH OF THE THESSALONIANS

²We always remember you when we pray and thank God for all of you. ³When we pray to God our Father, we always thank him for the things you have done because of your faith. And we thank him for the work you have done because of your love. And we thank him that you continue to be strong because of your hope in our Lord Jesus Christ.

⁴Brothers, God loves you. And we know that he has chosen you to be his. ⁵We brought the Good News⁴ to you. But we did not use only words. We brought the Good News with power, with the Holy Spirit,⁴ and with sure knowledge that it is true. Also you know how we lived when we were with you. We lived that way to help you. ⁶And you became like us and like the Lord. You suffered much, but still you accepted the teaching with the joy that comes from the Holy Spirit. ⁷So you became an example to all the believers in Macedonia and Southern Greece. ⁸The Lord's teaching spread from you in Macedonia and Southern Greece. And your faith in God has become known everywhere. So we do not need to say anything about your faith. ⁹People everywhere are telling about the good way you accepted us when we were there with you. They tell about how you stopped worshiping idols and changed to serving the living and true God. ¹⁰And you changed to wait for God's Son to come from heaven. God raised that Son from death. He is Jesus, who saves us from God's angry judgment that is sure to come.

## PAUL'S WORK IN THESSALONICA

**2** Brothers, you know that our visit to you was not a failure. ²Before we came to you, we suffered in Philippi. People there insulted us. You know about that. And when we came to you, many people were against us. But our God helped us to be brave and to tell you his Good News.⁴ ³Our message was a message to encourage you. We were not trying to lie. We had no evil plan. We were not trying to trick you. ⁴But we speak the Good News because God tested us and trusted us to do it. When we speak, we are not trying to please men. But we are trying to please God, who tests our hearts. ⁵You know that we never tried to influence you by saying nice things about you. We were not trying to get your money. We had no selfishness to hide from you. God knows that this is true. ⁶We were not looking for praise from you or anyone else. We are apostles⁴ of Christ. When we were with you, we could have used our authority to make you do things.

⁷But we were very gentle with you. We were like a mother caring for her little children. ⁸Because we loved you, we were happy to share God's Good News with you. But not only that, we were also happy to share even our own lives with you. ⁹Brothers, I know that you remember how hard we worked. We worked night and day so that we would not burden any of you while we preached God's Good News to you.

¹⁰When we were with you, we lived in a holy and right way, without fault. You know that this is true, and God knows that this is true. ¹¹You know that we treated each of you as a father treats his own children. ¹²We strengthened you, we comforted you, and we told you to live good lives for God. It is God who calls you to his glorious kingdom.

¹³Also, we always thank God because of the way you accepted his message. You heard his message from us, and you accepted it as the word of God, not the words of men. And it really is God's message. And that message works in you who believe. ¹⁴Brothers, you have been like God's churches in Christ that are in Judea.⁴ God's people suffered bad things from the other Jews there. And you suffered the same bad things from the people of your own country. ¹⁵Those Jews killed both the Lord Jesus and the prophets.⁴ And they forced us to leave that country. They do not please God. They are against all people. ¹⁶They try to stop us from teaching the non-Jews so that they may be saved. But those Jews are adding more and more sins to the sins they already have. The anger of God has come to them at last.

## PAUL WANTS TO VISIT THEM AGAIN

¹⁷Brothers, we were separated from you for a short time, but our thoughts were still with you. We wanted very much to see you, and tried very hard to do so. ¹⁸I, Paul, tried to come many times, but Satan stopped us. ¹⁹For you are our hope, our joy, and the crown we will be proud of when our Lord Jesus Christ comes. ²⁰Truly you are our glory and our joy.

**3** We could not come to you, but it was very hard to wait any longer. So we decided to stay in Athens alone ²and send Timothy to you. Timothy is our brother, who works with us for God. He helps us tell people the Good News⁴ about Christ. We sent Timothy to strengthen and comfort you in your faith. ³We sent him so that none of you would be upset by these troubles we have now. You yourselves know that we must have these troubles. ⁴Even when we were with you, we told you that we all would have to suffer. And you know that it has happened the way we said. ⁵This is why I sent Timothy to you, so that I could

**DECODE THIS!**

*Who will come from heaven with a loud voice and a trumpet call?*

**2:14 Judea** The Jewish land where Jesus lived and taught and where the church first began.

# LIVIN' IT!

## WALK THE TALK
### 1 THESSALONIANS 4:12

Did you know that you can tell another person the Good News without even saying a word?

God's Word says that we are to be smart in the way we act toward other people who don't know him. We need to remember that the way we talk to one another and about one another, the way we love others, the way we forgive, and the way we spend our time says a lot more about what's really in our hearts than just what we say. People who don't know God will see that our lives are different and better when we obey what God says in his Word. Then they can ask us why we are the way we are, and we can tell them everything that Jesus has done to save us. It's much easier for them to believe us when our words match the way we behave.

know about your faith. I sent him when I could not wait any longer. I was afraid that the devil had tempted you, and then our hard work would have been wasted. ⁶But Timothy now has come back to us from you and has brought us good news about your faith and love. He told us that you always remember us in a good way. He told us that you want to see us just as much as we want to see you. ⁷So, brothers, we are comforted about you, because of your faith. We have much trouble and suffering, but still we are comforted. ⁸For our life is really full if you stand strong in the Lord. ⁹We have so much joy before our God because of you, and we thank him for you. But we cannot thank him enough for all the joy we feel. ¹⁰And we continue praying with all our heart for you night and day. We pray that we can see you again and give you all the things you need to make your faith strong.

¹¹We pray that our God and Father and our Lord Jesus will prepare the way for us to come to you. ¹²We pray that the Lord will make your love grow more and more for each other and for all people. We pray that you will love others as we love you and ¹³that your hearts will be made strong. Then you will be holy and without fault before our God and Father when our Lord Jesus comes with all his holy people.

## A LIFE THAT PLEASES GOD

**4** Brothers, now I have some other things to tell you. We taught you how to live in a way that will please God. And you are living that way. Now we ask you and encourage you in the Lord Jesus to live that way more and more. ²You know what we told you to do by the authority of the Lord Jesus. ³God wants you to be holy and to stay away from sexual sins. ⁴He wants each one of you to learn how to take a wife" in a way that is holy and honorable. ⁵Don't use your body for sexual sin. The people who do

⭐ **4:4 learn . . . wife** This might also mean "learn to control your own body."

---

# GAMES & QUIZZES

## HAPPY THOUGHTS

## ACROSS
1. Being sure of our future
2. Kindness instead of judgment
3. Happens when we repent
4. We win it with Christ
5. God is _____
6. God's riches at Christ's expense
7. What God is to Christians

## DOWN
1. Our gift through Jesus
2. No lie: it's God's Word
3. What Christ paid for us
4. What Christ's blood does
5. God's gift in our weakness
6. Another word for vow
7. Feeling calm

not know God use their bodies for that. [6]So do not wrong your brother or cheat him in this way. The Lord will punish people who do those things. We have already told you and warned you about that. [7]God called us to be holy and does not want us to live in sin. [8]So the person who refuses to obey this teaching is refusing to obey God, not man. And God is the One who gives us his Holy Spirit.[d]

[9]We do not need to write to you about having love for your brothers and sisters in Christ. God has already taught you to love each other. [10]And truly you do love the brothers in all of Macedonia. Brothers, now we encourage you to love them more and more.

[11]Do all you can to live a peaceful life. Take care of your own business. Do your own work. We have already told you to do these things. [12]If you do, then people who are not believers will respect you. And you will not have to depend on others for what you need.

## THE LORD'S COMING

[13]Brothers, we want you to know about those who have died. We do not want you to be sad as others who have no hope. [14]We believe that Jesus died and that he rose again. So, because of Jesus, God will bring together with Jesus those who have died. [15]What we tell you now is the Lord's own message. We who are living now may still be living when the Lord comes again. We who are living at that time will be with the Lord, but not before those who have already died. [16]The Lord himself will come down from heaven. There will be a loud command with the voice of the archangel[n] and with the trumpet call of God. And those who have died and were in Christ will rise first. [17]After that, those who are still alive at that time will be gathered up with them. We will be taken up in the clouds to meet the Lord in the air. And we will be with the Lord forever. [18]So comfort each other with these words.

## BE READY FOR THE LORD'S COMING

**5** Now, brothers, we do not need to write to you about times and dates. [2]You know very well that the day the Lord comes again will be a surprise like a thief that comes in the night. [3]People will say, "We have peace and we are safe." At that time they will be destroyed quickly, as pains come quickly to a woman having a baby. And those people will not escape. [4]But you, brothers, are not living in darkness. And so that day will not surprise you like a thief. [5]You are all people who belong to the light. You belong to the day. We do not belong to the night or to darkness. [6]So we should not be like other people. We should not be sleeping, but we should be awake and have self-control. [7]Those who sleep, sleep at night. Those who get drunk, get drunk at night. [8]But we belong to the day; so we should control ourselves. We should wear faith and love to protect us. And the hope of salvation should be our helmet. [9]God did not choose us to suffer his anger, but to have salvation through our Lord Jesus Christ. [10]Jesus died for us so that we can live together with him. It is not important if we are alive or dead when Jesus comes. [11]So comfort each other and give each other strength, just as you are doing now.

## FINAL INSTRUCTIONS AND GREETINGS

[12]Now, brothers, we ask you to respect those people who work hard with you, who lead you in the Lord and teach you. [13]Respect them with a very special love because of the work they do with you.

Live in peace with each other. [14]We ask you, brothers, to warn those who do not work. Encourage the people who are afraid. Help those who are weak. Be patient with every person. [15]Be sure that no one pays back wrong for wrong. But always try to do what is good for each other

## BIBLE BASICS

### WHAT IS PRAYER?

Prayer is simply talking to God and listening to him. It is an attitude of your heart and mind that welcomes Jesus to be a part of every moment in your day and help you live the life he wants for you. Prayer can take the form of words, where you praise God, confess sin, give thanks, or make requests. Or you can be quiet and remember the words of God, letting the Holy Spirit pray through you and draw you closer to God's heart. The Bible says that we should always be in prayer to God.

and for all people.

[16]Always be happy. [17]Never stop praying. [18]Give thanks whatever happens. That is what God wants for you in Christ Jesus.

[19]Do not stop the work of the Holy Spirit.[d] [20]Do not treat prophecy[d] as if it were not important. [21]But test everything. Keep what is good. [22]And stay away from everything that is evil.

[23]We pray that God himself, the God of peace, will make you pure, belonging only to him. We pray that your whole self—spirit, soul, and body—will be kept safe and be without wrong when our Lord Jesus Christ comes. [24]The One who calls you will do that for you. You can trust him.

[25]Brothers, please pray for us.

[26]Give all the brothers a holy kiss when you meet. [27]I tell you by the authority of the Lord to read this letter to all the brothers.

[28]The grace of our Lord Jesus Christ be with you.

## DECODE THIS!

*Keep what is good and stay away from everything _____.*

---

★ **4:16 archangel** The leader among God's angels or messengers.

Silas, Timothy, and Paul **get** together in Corinth and write this letter to their **friends**.

The Thessalonians are still strong for Christ, yet suffering.

How did this church get started? Read all about the men who were called **trouble makers** in Acts 17:1-10.

# THE SECOND LETTER OF PAUL THE APOSTLE TO THE

# THESSALONIANS

**Paul** sends this message: Get back to work! You can't just quit your jobs because you think Jesus is coming!

Oh, the problems of being a new Christian!

**1** From Paul, Silas, and Timothy. To the church in Thessalonica in God our Father and the Lord Jesus Christ.

[2] Grace and peace to you from God the Father and the Lord Jesus Christ.

### PAUL TALKS ABOUT GOD'S JUDGMENT

[3] We must always thank God for you. And we should do this because it is right. It is right because your faith is growing more and more. And the love that every one of you has for each other is also growing. [4] So we brag about you to the other churches of God. We tell them about the way you continue to be strong and have faith. You are being treated badly and are suffering many troubles, but you continue with strength and faith.

[5] This is proof that God is right in his judgment. God wants you to be worthy of his kingdom. Your suffering is for that kingdom. [6] And God will do what is right. He will give trouble to those who trouble you. [7] And he will give peace to you people who are troubled and to us also. God will give us this help when the Lord Jesus is shown to us from heaven with his powerful angels. [8] He will come from heaven with burning fire to punish those who do not know God. He will punish those who do not obey the Good News[d] of our Lord Jesus Christ. [9] Those people will be punished with a destruction that continues forever. They will not be allowed to be with the Lord, and they will be kept away from his great power. [10] This will happen on the day when the Lord Jesus comes to receive glory with his holy people. And all the people who have believed will be amazed at Jesus. You will be in that group of believers because you believed what we told you. [11] That is why we always pray for you.

## WILD WORLD FACTS

### FRUITLESS EFFORT

One minute the fig tree was alive and well. The next minute, it was dead. It wasn't bearing fruit, so Jesus spoke the word and it shriveled up (see Matthew 21:18-22).

So how do you know when a plant is really dead? After all, they often seem to die in the winter, only to return in spring, right? Well, even scientists have a hard time knowing for sure when a plant is truly dead. Mainly, a plant is considered a goner when the cells that carry water and nutrients from the soil to the rest of the plant stop working. The tricky part is the seed. In itself, it doesn't have to keep feeding to live. It can actually lie dormant—not doing anything at all—for many years. The best way even for scientists to know if a plant is alive is simply to plant it and see if it grows.

Jesus caused the fig tree to wither because it wasn't bearing fruit. As people who belong to Jesus, we should be bearing the fruit of his Spirit in our lives so we can be a part of his work on earth. Ask him to help you bear his fruit so you're ready at the right time.

**[NewScientist.com]**

We ask our God to help you live the good way that he called you to live. The goodness you have makes you want to do good, and the faith you have makes you work. We pray that with his power God will help you do these things more and more. [12] We pray all this so that the name of our Lord Jesus Christ can have glory in you. And you can have glory in him. That glory comes from the grace of our God and the Lord Jesus Christ.

### EVIL THINGS WILL HAPPEN

**2** Brothers, we have something to say about the coming of our Lord Jesus Christ. We want to talk to you about that time when we will meet together with him. [2] Do not become easily upset in your thinking or afraid if you hear that the day of the Lord has already come. Someone may say this in a prophecy[d] or in a message. Or you may read it in a letter that someone tells you came from us. [3] Do not let any person fool you in any way. That day of the Lord will not come until the turning away from God happens. And that day will not come until the Man of Evil appears. He belongs to hell. [4] He is against anything called God or anything that people worship. And the Man of Evil puts himself above anything called God or anything that people worship. And that Man of Evil even goes into God's Temple[d] and sits there. Then he says that he is God.

[5] I told you when I was with you that all this would happen. Do you not remember? [6] And you know what is stopping that Man of Evil now. He is being stopped now so that he will appear at the right time. [7] The secret power of evil is already working in the world now.

## DECODE THIS!

*Who was the second letter to the church of Thessalonica from?*

# LIVIN' IT!

## REMEMBER
## 2 THESSALONIANS 3:1

Every now and then some of them may come to your church and tell you wild stories about faraway places. Sometimes you might even see their pictures on a bulletin board. But more often, we forget about the missionaries that are working—even now as you read this article—to help other people know about Jesus.

God tells us in his Word that we need to remember our missionaries and help them do their job by praying for them. We need to pray for their protection, that they will be able to explain the gospel clearly, and that God would open up the hearts of those who hear them. Ask your parents to help you pick a special missionary for each week or month of the year, and lift them and their needs to God in prayer.

But there is one who is stopping that power. And he will continue to stop it until he is taken out of the way. ⁸Then that Man of Evil will appear. And the Lord Jesus will kill him with the breath that comes from his mouth and will destroy him with the glory of his coming. ⁹The Man of Evil will come by the power of Satan. He will have great power, and he will do many different false miracles,ᵈ signs, and wonders. ¹⁰He will use every kind of evil to trick those who are lost. They are lost because they refused to love the truth. (If they loved the truth, they would be saved.) ¹¹But they refused to love the truth; so God sends them something powerful that leads them away from the truth. He sends them that power so they will believe something that is not true. ¹²So all those who do not believe

the truth will be judged guilty. They did not believe the truth, and they enjoyed doing evil.

## YOU ARE CHOSEN FOR SALVATION

¹³Brothers, the Lord loves you. God chose you from the beginning to be saved. So we must always thank God for you. You are saved by the Spiritᵈ that makes you holy and by your faith in the truth. ¹⁴God used the Good Newsᵈ that we preached to call you to be saved. He called you so that you can share in the glory of our Lord Jesus Christ. ¹⁵So, brothers, stand strong and continue to believe the teachings we gave you. We taught you those things in our speaking and in our letter to you.

¹⁶⁻¹⁷We pray that the Lord Jesus Christ himself and God our Father will comfort you and strengthen you in every good thing you do and say. God loved us. Through his grace he gave us a good hope and comfort that continues forever.

## PRAY FOR US

**3** And now, brothers, pray for us. Pray that the Lord's teaching will continue to spread quickly. And pray

that people will give honor to that teaching, just as happened with you. ²And pray that we will be protected from bad and evil people. (Not all people believe in the Lord.)

³But the Lord is faithful. He will give you strength and protect you from the Evil One. ⁴The Lord makes us feel sure that you are doing the things we told you. And we know that you will continue to do those things. ⁵We pray that the Lord will lead your hearts into God's love and Christ's patience.

## THE DUTY TO WORK

⁶Brothers, by the authority of our Lord Jesus Christ we command you to stay away from any believer who refuses to work. People who refuse to work are not following the teaching that we gave them. ⁷You yourselves know that you should live as we live. We were not lazy when we were with you. ⁸And when we ate another person's food, we always paid for it. We worked and worked so that we would not be a trouble to any of you. We worked night and day. ⁹We had the right to ask you to help us. But we worked to take care of ourselves so that we would be an example for you to follow. ¹⁰When we were with you, we gave you this rule: "If anyone will not work, he will not eat."

¹¹We hear that some people in your group refuse to work. They do nothing. And they busy themselves in other

# Gotta Know!
## Is God ever mad?

Yes. In fact, he is mad every day at the sin he sees in the world. Just like in Noah's day, God grows disgusted with the evil doings of the people who don't believe in him. And one day, God will stop being patient and judge the world. But believers never need to worry. Because of Jesus, God is not mad at us any more. He still hates our sin and works in our hearts to remove it, but he will not judge us. We are completely forgiven and loved in Jesus.

people's lives. ¹²We command those people to work quietly and earn their own food. In the Lord Jesus Christ we beg them to do this. ¹³Brothers, never become tired of doing good.

¹⁴If anyone does not obey what we tell you in this letter, then remember who he is. Do not associate with him. Then maybe he will feel ashamed. ¹⁵But do not treat him as an enemy. Warn him as a brother.

## GET THE CONNECTION

To be friends, you have to know one another and stay in touch on a regular basis. Prayer is the tool God gives us to stay in touch with him. It isn't anything fancy. It's just talking to God and listening to his Spirit talk back to us through the Bible.

God isn't interested in you saying a bunch of words. He wants to hear straight from your heart how you really feel and what you truly need. You don't need to try to be super spiritual. Just be real. Admit and repent of your sins. And speak to your heavenly Father like you would to your best friend who loves you—because that's who God is.

### FINAL WORDS

¹⁶We pray that the Lord of peace will give you peace at all times and in every way. May the Lord be with all of you.

¹⁷I am Paul, and I end this letter now in my own handwriting. All my letters have this to show they are from me. This is the way I write.

¹⁸May our Lord Jesus Christ show all of you his grace.

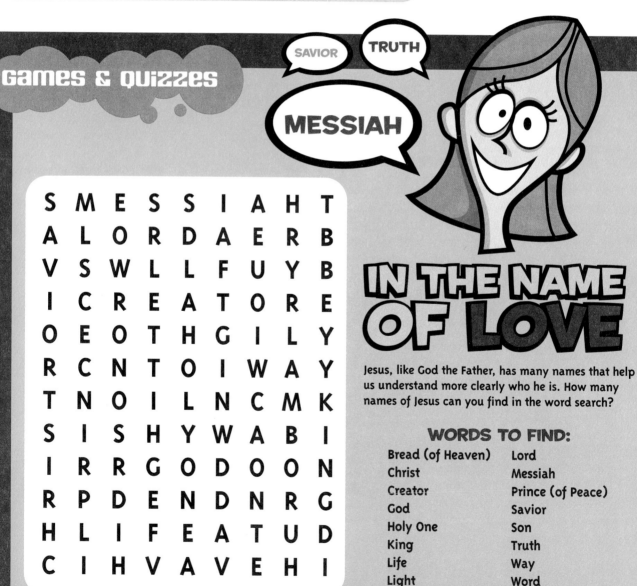

# GAMES & QUIZZES

# IN THE NAME OF LOVE

Jesus, like God the Father, has many names that help us understand more clearly who he is. How many names of Jesus can you find in the word search?

## WORDS TO FIND:

Bread (of Heaven)
Christ
Creator
God
Holy One
King
Life
Light
Lord
Messiah
Prince (of Peace)
Savior
Son
Truth
Way
Word

Advice **to** a Young Preacher

After spending 2 years in Corinth with Paul, Timothy is promoted to head pastor in Ephesus.

THE FIRST LETTER OF PAUL THE APOSTLE TO

# TIMOTHY

Did you know Timothy's mother's name was Eunice?

Timothy's new job description: Get rid of false teaching, lead worship, and be a good example.

**1** From Paul, an apostle[d] of Christ Jesus, by the command of God our Savior and Christ Jesus our hope.

[2]To Timothy, a true son to me because you believe.

Grace, mercy, and peace from God the Father and Christ Jesus our Lord.

## WARNING AGAINST FALSE TEACHING

[3]I want you to stay in Ephesus. I asked you to do that when I went into Macedonia. Some people there in Ephesus are teaching false things. Stay there

is for people to have love. To have this love they must have a pure heart, they must do what they know is right, and they must have true faith. [6]Some people have wandered away from these things. They talk about things that are worth nothing. [7]They want to be teachers of the law, but they do not know what they are talking about. They do not even understand what they say they are sure about. [8]We know that the law is good if a man uses it right. [9]We also know that the law is not made for good men. The law is made for people who are against the law and for those who refuse to follow the law. It is for people who are against God and are sinful, who are not holy and have no religion, who kill their fathers and mothers, who murder, [10]who take part in sexual sins, men who have sexual relations with other men, those who sell slaves, who tell lies, who speak falsely, and who do anything against the true teaching of God. [11]That teaching is part of the Good News[d] that God gave me to tell. That glorious Good News is from the blessed God.

## THANKS FOR GOD'S MERCY

[12]I thank Christ Jesus our Lord because he trusted me and gave me this work of serving him. And he gives me strength. [13]In the past I spoke against Christ and persecuted him and did all kinds of things to hurt him. But God showed mercy to me because I did not know what I was doing. I did those things when I did not believe. [14]But the grace of our Lord was fully given to me. And with that grace came the faith and love that are in Christ Jesus.

[15]What I say is true, and you should fully accept it: Christ Jesus came into the world to save sinners. And I am the worst of those sinners. [16]But I was given mercy. I was given mercy so that in me Christ Jesus could show that he has patience without limit. And he showed his patience with me, the worst of all sinners. Christ wanted me to be an example for those who would believe in him and have life forever. [17]Honor and glory to the King that rules forever! He cannot be destroyed and cannot be seen. Honor and glory forever and ever to the only God. Amen.

[18]Timothy, you are like a son to me. I am giving you a command that agrees with the prophecies[d] that were given about you in the past. I tell you this so that you can follow those prophecies and fight the good fight of faith. [19]Continue to have faith and do what you know is right. Some people have not done this. Their faith has been destroyed. [20]Hymenaeus and Alexander are men who have done that. I have given them to Satan so that they will learn not to speak against God.

## SOME RULES FOR MEN AND WOMEN

**2** First, I tell you to pray for all people. Ask God for the things people need, and be thankful to him. [2]You should pray for kings and for all who have authority. Pray for the leaders so that we can have quiet and peaceful lives—lives full of worship and respect for God. [3]This is good, and it pleases God our Savior. [4]God wants all people to be saved. And he wants everyone to know the truth. [5]There is only one God. And there is only one way that people can reach God. That way is through Jesus Christ, who is also a man. [6]Jesus gave himself to pay for the sins of all people. Jesus is proof that God wants all people to be saved. And that proof came at the right time. [7]That is why I was chosen to tell the Good News[d] and was chosen to be an apostle.[d] (I am telling the truth. I am not lying.) I was chosen to

## BIBLE BASICS

### WHO ARE GENTILES?

Gentiles are simply everyone who isn't a Jew. From the beginning, the Jewish people were to stay pure and not marry other people who didn't believe the same way they did. They later came to think that God's plan of salvation would only be for the Jews. Jesus, however, made it clear that his salvation reached across lines to people from every nation and skin color. Both Jews and Gentiles can be a part of God's chosen family if they follow Jesus.

so that you can command them to stop. [4]Tell them not to spend their time on stories that are not true and on long lists of names in family histories. These things only bring arguments; they do not help God's work. God's work is done by faith. [5]The purpose of this command

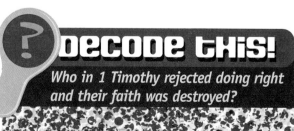

## DECODE THIS!

Who in 1 Timothy rejected doing right and their faith was destroyed?

teach the non-Jewish people to believe and to know the truth.

[8]I want men everywhere to pray. These men who lift up their hands in prayer must be holy. They must not be men who become angry and have arguments.

[9]I also want women to wear clothes that are right for them. They should dress with respect and right thinking. They should not use fancy braided hair or gold or pearls or expensive clothes to make themselves beautiful. [10]But they should make themselves beautiful by doing good deeds. Women who say they worship God should make themselves beautiful in that way.

[11]A woman should learn by listening quietly and being fully ready to obey. [12]I do not allow a woman to teach a man or to have authority over a man. She must remain silent. [13]For Adam was made first; Eve was made later. [14]Also, Adam was not the one who was tricked by the devil. It was the woman who was tricked and became a sinner. [15]But women will be saved through having children. They will be saved if they continue in faith, love, holiness, and self-control.

**KIDS SPEAK UP!**

Q. What's the latest you've ever stayed up?

A. I have stayed up all night and never even went to bed when morning came.

## LEADERS IN THE CHURCH

**3** What I say is true: If anyone wants to become an elder,[d] he is wanting a good work. [2]An elder must be so good that people cannot rightly criticize him. He must have only one wife. He must have self-control and be wise. He must be respected by other people and must be ready to help people by accepting them into his home. He must be a good teacher. [3]He must not drink too much wine, and he must not be a man who likes to fight. He must be gentle and peaceful. He must not love money. [4]He must be a good leader of his own family so that his children obey him with full respect. [5](If a man does not know how to be a leader over his own family, he will not be able to take care of God's church.) [6]But an elder must not be a new believer. A new believer might be too proud of himself. Then he would be judged guilty for his pride just as the devil was. [7]An elder must also have the respect of people who are not in the church. Then he will not be criticized by others and caught in the devil's trap.

## HELPERS IN THE CHURCH

[8]In the same way, deacons[d] must be men that people can respect. They must not say things they do not mean. They must not use their time drinking too much wine, and they must not be men who are always trying to get rich by cheating others. [9]They must follow the faith that God made known to us and always do what they know is right. [10]You should test those men first. If you find nothing wrong in them, then they can serve as deacons. [11]In the same way, the women[n] must have the respect of other people. They must not be women who repeat evil gossip about other people. They must have self-control and be women who can be trusted in everything. [12]Deacons must have only one wife. They must be good leaders of their

children and their own families. [13]Those who serve well as deacons are making an honorable place for themselves. And they will feel very sure of their faith in Christ Jesus.

## THE SECRET OF OUR LIFE

[14]I hope I can come to you soon. But I am writing these things to you now. [15]Then, even if I cannot come soon, you will know about the things that people must do in the family of God. That family is the church of the living God, the support and foundation of the truth. [16]Without doubt, the secret of our life of worship is great:

He was shown to us in a human body,
    proved right by the Spirit,[d]
and seen by angels.

He was preached to the nations,
believed in by the world,
    and taken to heaven in glory.

## A WARNING ABOUT FALSE TEACHERS

**4** The Holy Spirit[d] clearly says that in the later times some people will stop believing the true faith. They will obey spirits that lie and will follow the teachings of demons.[d] [2]Such teachings come from hypocrites,[d] men who cannot see what is right and what is wrong. It is as if their understanding were destroyed by a hot iron. [3]They tell people that it is wrong to marry. And they tell people that there are some foods that must not be eaten. But God made those foods, and the people who believe and who know the truth can eat those foods with thanks. [4]Everything that God made is good. Nothing that God made should be refused if it is accepted with thanks to God. [5]Everything God made is made holy by what God has said and by prayer.

## BE A GOOD SERVANT OF CHRIST

[6]Tell these things to the brothers. This will show that you are a good servant of

3:11 women This might mean the wives of the deacons, or it might mean women who serve in the same way as deacons.

Christ Jesus. You will show that you are made strong by the words of faith and good teaching that you have been following. [7]People tell silly stories that do not agree with God's truth. Do not follow what those stories teach. But teach yourself only to serve God. [8]Training your body helps you in some ways, but serving God helps you in every way. Serving God brings you blessings in this life and in the future life, too. [9]What I say is true, and you should fully accept it. [10]For this is why we work and struggle: We hope in the living God. He is the Savior of all people. And in a very special way, he is the Savior of all who believe in him.

[11]Command and teach these things. [12]You are young, but do not let anyone treat you as if you were not important. Be an example to show the believers how they should live. Show them with your words, with the way you live, with your love, with your faith, and with your pure life. [13]Continue to read the Scriptures[d] to the people, strengthen them, and teach them. Do these things until I come. [14]Remember to use the gift that you have. That gift was given to you through a prophecy[d] when the group of elders[d] laid their hands on[n] you. [15]Continue to do those things. Give your life to doing them. Then everyone can see that your work is progressing. [16]Be careful in your life and in your teaching. Continue to live and teach rightly. Then you will save yourself and those people who listen to you.

## RULES FOR LIVING WITH OTHERS

**5** Do not speak angrily to an older man, but talk to him as if he were your father. Treat younger men like brothers. [2]Treat older women like mothers, and younger women like sisters. Always treat them in a pure way.

[3]Take care of widows who are all alone. [4]But if a widow has children or grandchildren, the first thing they need to learn is to do their duty to their own family. When they do this, they will be repaying their parents or grandparents. That pleases God. [5]If a widow is all alone and without help, then she puts her hope in God and prays night and day for God's help. [6]But the widow who uses her life to please herself is really dead while she is still living. [7]Tell the believers there to do these things so that no one can say they are doing wrong. [8]A believer should take care of his own relatives, especially his own family. If he does not do that, he has turned against the faith. He is worse than a person who does not believe in God.

[9]To be on your list of widows, a woman must be 60 years old or older. She must have been faithful to her husband. [10]She must be known as a woman who has done good works. By this, I mean good works such as raising her children, accepting visitors in her home, washing the feet of God's people, helping those in trouble, and using her life to do all kinds of good deeds.

[11]But do not put younger widows on that list. After they give themselves to Christ, they are often pulled away from him by their physical needs. And then they want to marry again. [12]And they will be judged for not doing what they first promised to do. [13]Also, those younger widows begin to waste their time going from house to house. They begin to gossip and busy themselves with other people's lives. They say things that they should not say. [14]So I want the younger widows to marry, have children, and take care of their homes. If they do this, then no enemy will have any reason to criticize them. [15]But some of the younger widows have already turned away to follow Satan.

[16]If any woman who is a believer has widows in her family, then she should care for them herself. The church should not have to care for them. Then the church will be able to care for the widows who have no living family.

[17]The elders[d] who lead the church well should receive great honor. Those who work hard by speaking and teaching especially should receive great honor. [18]For the Scripture[d] says, "When an ox is working in the grain, do not cover its mouth to keep it from eating."[n] And the Scripture also says, "A worker should be given his pay."[n]

[19]Do not listen to someone who accuses an elder, unless there are two or three other persons who say he did wrong. [20]Tell those who keep on sinning that they are wrong. Do this in front of the whole church so that the others will have a warning.

[21]Before God and Jesus Christ and the chosen angels, I command you to do these things. Be careful to do them

**4:14 laid their hands on** A sign to show that Timothy was being given a special work of God. **5:18 "When . . . eating."** Quotation from Deuteronomy 25:4. **5:18 "A worker . . . pay."** Quotation from Luke 10:7.

**306**

without showing favor to anyone.

²²Think carefully before you lay your hands on" anyone for the Lord's service. Do not share in the sins of others. Keep yourself pure.

²³Timothy, you stop drinking only water and drink a little wine. This will help your stomach, and you will not be sick so often.

²⁴The sins of some people are easy to see even before they are judged. But the sins of others are seen only later. ²⁵So also good deeds are easy to see. But even when they are not easy to see, they cannot stay hidden.

**6** All who are slaves should show full respect to their masters. Then no one will speak against God's name and our teaching. ²Some slaves have masters who are believers. This means they are all brothers. But the slaves should not show their masters any less respect. They should serve their masters even better, because they are helping believers they love.

### FALSE TEACHING AND TRUE RICHES

You must teach and preach these things. ³If anyone has a different teaching, he does not accept the true teaching of our Lord Jesus Christ. And that teaching shows him the true way to serve God. ⁴The person who teaches falsely is full of pride and understands nothing. He is sick with a love for arguing and fighting about words. And that brings jealousy, making trouble, insults, and evil mistrust. ⁵And that also brings arguments from men who have evil minds. They have lost the truth. They think that serving God is a way to get rich.

⁶It is true that serving God makes a person very rich, if he is satisfied with what he has. ⁷When we came into the world, we brought nothing. And when we die, we can take nothing out. ⁸So, if we have food and clothes, we will be satisfied with that. ⁹Those who want to become rich bring temptation to themselves. They are caught in a trap. They begin to want many foolish things that will hurt them, things that ruin and destroy people. ¹⁰The love of money causes all kinds of evil. Some people have left the true faith because they want to get more and more money. But they have caused themselves much sorrow.

### SOME THINGS TO REMEMBER

¹¹But you are a man of God. So you should stay away from all those things. Try to live in the right way, serve God, have faith, love, patience, and gentleness. ¹²Keeping your faith is like running a race. Try as hard as you can to win. Be sure you receive the life that continues forever. You were called to have that life. And you confessed the great truth about Christ in a way that many people heard. ¹³Before God and Christ Jesus I give you a command. Christ Jesus confessed that same great truth when he stood before Pontius Pilate. And God gives life to everything. Now I tell you: ¹⁴Do the things you were commanded to do. Do them without wrong or blame until the time when our Lord Jesus Christ comes again. ¹⁵God will make that happen at the right time. He is the blessed and only Ruler. He is the King of all kings and the Lord of all lords. ¹⁶God is the only One who never dies. He lives in light so bright that men cannot go near it. No one has ever seen God, or can see him. May honor and power belong to God forever. Amen.

¹⁷Give this command to those who are rich with things of this world. Tell them not to be proud. Tell them to hope in God, not their money. Money cannot be trusted, but God takes care of us richly. He gives us everything to enjoy. ¹⁸Tell the rich people to do good and to be rich in doing good deeds. Tell them to be happy to give and ready to share. ¹⁹By doing that, they will be saving a treasure for themselves in heaven. That treasure will be a strong foundation. Their future life can be built on that treasure. Then they will be able to have the life that is true life.

²⁰Timothy, God has trusted you with many things. Keep those things safe. Stay away from people who say foolish things that are not from God. Stay away from those who argue against the truth. They use something they call "knowledge," but it is really not knowledge. ²¹They say that they have that "knowledge," but they have left the true faith.

God's grace be with you.

## BIBLE BASICS

### WHAT ARE PHARISEES AND SADDUCEES?

Jewish people back in Jesus' day had different ways of explaining the Scriptures. Those with these different thoughts were broken down into 2 main groups, the Pharisees and the Sadducees. The Pharisees followed a lot of rules that made them look good on the outside, but their hearts were not obedient to God. The Sadducees were the religious leaders who did not believe in angels or that anyone would ever rise from the dead.

## DECODE THIS!

Do not let anyone treat you as if you are unimportant because you are what?

 **5:22 lay your hands on** A sign of giving authority or power to another person.

This letter was probably the last letter Paul wrote before he died.

Did you know that Timothy was like a son to Paul?

THE SECOND LETTER OF PAUL THE APOSTLE TO

# TIMOTHY

Paul tells Timothy to honor and respect God's Word.

Paul encourages Timothy.

Timothy had a strong Christian family history going back 3 generations!

**1** From Paul, an apostle[d] of Christ Jesus by the will of God. God sent me to tell about the promise of life that is in Christ Jesus.

[2]To Timothy, a dear son to me. Grace, mercy, and peace to you from God the Father and Christ Jesus our Lord.

## ENCOURAGEMENT FOR TIMOTHY

[3]I always remember you in my prayers, day and night. And I thank God for you in these prayers. He is the God my ancestors served. And I serve him, doing what I know is right. [4]I remember that you cried for me. And I want very much to see you so that I can be filled with joy. [5]I remember your true faith. That kind of faith first belonged to your grandmother Lois and to your mother Eunice. And I know that you now have that same faith. [6]That is why I remind you to use the gift God gave you. God gave you that gift when I laid my hands on[n] you. Now let it grow, as a small flame grows into a fire. [7]God did not give us a spirit that makes us afraid. He gave us a spirit of power and love and self-control.

[8]So do not be ashamed to tell people about our Lord Jesus. And do not be ashamed of me. I am in prison for the Lord. But suffer with me for the Good News.[d] God gives us the strength to do that. [9]God saved us and made us his holy people. That was not because of anything we did ourselves but because of what he wanted and because of his grace. That grace was given to us through Christ Jesus before time began. [10]It was not shown to us until our Savior Christ Jesus came. Jesus destroyed death. And through the Good News, he showed us the way to have life that cannot be destroyed. [11]I

## GET CONNECTED

### HOMEWORK

Studying the Bible doesn't have to be difficult. You have a built-in interpreter. God gives you his Spirit to help you understand. Before you begin reading, ask God for his help to understand. Then after you read a passage, you can use some tools to help you know the truth. Ask yourself the who, what, when, where, why, and how questions: Who is speaking? What is really being said? When did this happen? Where did it happen? Why did it happen? And how does it change my life?

Just jot down your answers in a notebook. If you have any questions, write them down, too, and ask a parent or teacher to help you find the answers in God's Word.

was chosen to tell that Good News and to be an apostle[d] and a teacher. [12]And I suffer now because I tell the Good News. But I am not ashamed. I know Jesus, the One I have believed in. And I am sure that he is able to protect what he has trusted me with until that Day.[n] [13]Follow the true teachings you heard from me. Follow them as an example of the faith and love we have in Christ Jesus. [14]Protect the truth that you were given. Protect it with the help of the Holy Spirit[d] who lives in us.

[15]You know that everyone in the country of Asia has left me, even Phygelus and Hermogenes. [16]I pray that the Lord will show mercy to the family of

## A LOYAL SOLDIER OF CHRIST JESUS

**2** Timothy, you are like a son to me. Be strong in the grace that we have in Christ Jesus. [2]You and many others have heard what I have taught. You should teach the same thing to some people you can trust. Then they will be able to teach it to others. [3]Share in the troubles that we have. Accept them like a true soldier of Christ Jesus. [4]A soldier wants to please his commanding officer, so he does not waste his time doing the things that most people do. [5]If an athlete is running a race, he must obey all the rules in order to win. [6]The farmer who works hard should be the first person to get some of the food that he grew. [7]Think about these things that I am saying. The Lord will give you the ability to understand all these things.

> "God did not give us a spirit that makes us afraid. He gave us a spirit of power and love and self-control."
>
> *2 Timothy 1:7*

Onesiphorus. He has often helped me and was not ashamed that I was in prison. [17]When he came to Rome, he looked for me until he found me. [18]I pray that the Lord will allow Onesiphorus to have mercy from the Lord on that Day. You know how many ways Onesiphorus helped me in Ephesus.

[8]Remember Jesus Christ. He is from the family of David. After Jesus died, he was raised from death. This is the Good News[d] that I preach, [9]and I am suffering because of that Good News. I am even bound with chains like a criminal. But God's teaching is not in chains. [10]So I patiently accept all these troubles. I do this so that those whom God has chosen

1:6 laid . . . on A sign to show that Paul had power from God to give Timothy a special blessing. 1:12 Day The day Christ will come to judge all people and take his people to live with him.

317

can have the salvation that is in Christ Jesus. With that salvation comes glory that never ends.

"This teaching is true:

If we died with him,
   then we will also live with him.
[12]If we accept suffering,
   then we will also rule with him.
If we refuse to accept him,
   then he will refuse to accept us.
[13]If we are not faithful,
   he will still be faithful,
   because he cannot be false to
      himself.

## A WORKER PLEASING TO GOD

[14]Continue teaching these things. And warn people before God not to argue about words. Arguing about words does not help anyone, and it ruins those who listen. [15]Do the best you can to be the kind of person that God will

of some people. [19]But God's strong foundation continues to stand. These words are written on that foundation: "The Lord knows those who belong to him." And also these words are written on that foundation, "Everyone who says that he believes in the Lord must stop doing wrong."

[20]In a large house there are things made of gold and silver. But also there are things made of wood and clay. Some things are used for special purposes, and others are made for ordinary jobs. [21]If anyone makes himself clean[d] from evil things, he will be used for special purposes. He will be made holy, and the Master can use him. He will be ready to do any good work.

[22]Stay away from the evil things young people love to do. Try hard to live right and to have faith, love, and peace. Work for these things together with

## Gotta Know!

### Did God plan lives for everybody in the world?

God has specific plans for his people. In Jeremiah 29:11 he says that he knows the plans that he has for us—and they are good plans to bless us and help us know him better. In the New Testament, he lets us know that he already has all the good works picked out that he wants us to do. We just need to ask him to show us what he wants us to do.

accept, and give yourself to him. Be a worker who is not ashamed of his work—a worker who uses the true teaching in the right way. [16]Stay away from those who talk about useless worldly things. That kind of talk will lead a person more and more away from God. [17]Their evil teaching will spread like a sickness inside the body. Hymenaeus and Philetus are men like that. [18]They have left the true teaching. They say that the rising from death of all men has already taken place. And those two men are destroying the faith

those who have pure hearts and who trust in the Lord. [23]Stay away from foolish and stupid arguments. You know that such arguments grow into bigger arguments. [24]And a servant of the Lord must not quarrel! He must be kind to everyone. He must be a good teacher. He must be patient. [25]The Lord's servant must gently teach those who do not agree with him. Maybe God will let them change their hearts so that they can accept the truth. [26]The devil

has trapped them and causes them to do what he wants. But maybe they can wake up and free themselves from the devil's trap.

## THE LAST DAYS

**3** Remember this! There will be many troubles in the last days. [2]In those times people will love only themselves and money. They will brag and be proud. They will say evil things against others. They will not obey their parents. People will not be thankful or be the kind of people God wants. [3]They will not have love for others. They will refuse to forgive others and will speak bad things. They will not control themselves. They will be cruel and will hate what is good. [4]In the

2:19 "The Lord . . . him." Quotation from Numbers 16:5.

### DECODE THIS!

*Timothy's grandmother was _____.*

last days, people will turn against their friends. They will do foolish things without thinking. They will be conceited and proud. They will love pleasure. They will not love God. [5]They will continue to act as if they serve God, but they will not really serve God. Stay away from those people. [6]Some of them go into homes and get control of weak women who are full of sin. They are led to sin by the many evil desires they have. [7]Those women always try to learn new teachings, but they are never able to understand the truth fully. [8]Just as Jannes and Jambres were against Moses, these people are against the truth. They are people whose thinking has been confused. They have failed in trying to follow the faith. [9]But they will not be suc-cessful in what they do. Everyone will see that they are foolish. That is what happened to Jannes and Jambres.

## OBEY THE TEACHINGS

[10]But you know all about me. You know what I teach and the way I live. You know my goal in life. You know my faith, my patience, and my love. You know that I never stop trying. [11]You know how I have been hurt and have suffered. You know all that happened to me in Antioch, Iconium, and Lystra. You know the hurts I suffered in those places. But the Lord saved me from all those troubles. [12]Everyone who wants to live the way God wants, in Christ Jesus, will be hurt. [13]People who are evil and cheat other people will go from bad to worse. They will fool others, but they will also be fooling themselves.

[14]But you should continue following the teachings that you learned. You know that these teachings are true. And you know you can trust those who taught you. [15]You have known the Holy Scriptures[d] since you were a child. The Scriptures are able to make you wise. And that wisdom leads to salvation through faith in Christ Jesus. [16]All Scripture is given by God and is useful for teaching and for showing people what is wrong in their lives. It is useful for correcting faults and teaching how to live right. [17]Using the Scriptures, the person who serves God will be ready

# GAMES & QUIZZES

## SEE HOW MANY BOOKS OF THE NEW TESTAMENT YOU CAN FIND IN THIS PUZZLE.

(Hint: Don't forget to look backwards, too!)

Find all of them, and you'll be the word-search king!

```
P H I L I P P I A N S A G X A R L T M
H P A C D M R T Z Y E V L I G T X Q A
I Q Z D C A H J L K N H O J 3 2 5 R T
L M Z Q D F G J N R V Y A D Z R E F T
E R A R C O L O S S I A N S B I Z Z H
M T E T D A T U R O N O M Y A R R E E
O Z Y S Q U A L E H E B R E W S R E W
N Q B U D A S H U N D L E T R I S P D
O Y C D B O R D I 2 J O H N N G C S H
I C O R I N T H I A N S C H I Z A L P
P H L I S H 2 B O M T A N N E P L E Q
R I Z N O P C F A C S N A I T A L A G
E T S S H V O P E L I Z E N I R D S T
D A S H I N R Q U E K R S U T O P R E
U Q U I Z R I T A S D O A I U G O E T
J A M E S U N H O N H M I M S I S V S
Y O A T H I T S E A D A A L O N A E E
Y G U I S H H Y O I U N E V A I R L S
H A W A N Y I T H S I S N G Q J U A Y
T I T E L I A K E E T H A S B O E T H
O F O R E I N N Y H O U R W H H O I T
M L E L I F S E L P T S N O T N E O O
I A S Y T O K E R E K U L E P M A N M
T K I N G U P L E T T L A R S T H A I
I P E T E R T F T I L A C T S L I N T
N T L H E B L K E A N S B T U I V H 2
A L S T O M N Q P D N O E T I N W O O
M A R K W B Y W 2 R E T I N G I S J N
```

and will have everything he needs to do every good work.

4 Before God and Jesus Christ I give you a command. Christ Jesus is the One who will judge all who are living and all who have died. Jesus has a kingdom, and he is coming again. So I give you this command: ²Preach the Good News.ᵈ Be ready at all times. Tell people what they need to do, tell them when they are wrong, and encourage them. Do these things with great patience and careful teaching. ³The time will come when people will not listen to the true teaching. They will find more and more teachers who are pleasing to them, teachers who say the things they want to hear. ⁴They will stop listening to the truth. They will begin to follow the teaching in false stories. ⁵But you should control yourself at all times. When troubles come, accept them. Do the work of telling the Good News. Do all the duties of a servant of God.

⁶My life is being given as an offering to God. The time has come for me to leave this life. ⁷I have fought the good fight. I have finished the race. I have kept the faith. ⁸Now, a crown is

## WILD WORLD FACTS

### A BITING COMPARISON

Jesus called the Pharisees a brood of vipers. That's quite a biting comparison.

Vipers are extremely poisonous snakes with a bite that is often fatal, even for humans. Not all snakes are dangerous, but they are all cold-blooded carnivores (meat eaters). Venomous snakes have fangs—large, hollow teeth—that are filled with poison. When they bite their prey, they inject the poison through their fangs and either paralyze or kill it. You can often recognize which snakes are poisonous by the triangular shape of their heads. If you ever see one, take 5 steps back slowly, and then turn and run for help.

The Pharisees were like vipers because their bad teaching was causing many people to miss God's truth. We need to guard against anything others say that doesn't agree with God's Word.

[Venomous Snakes]

waiting for me. I will get that crown for being right with God. The Lord is the judge who judges rightly, and he will give me the crown on that Day.ⁿ He will give that crown not only to me but to all those who have waited with love for him to come again.

### PERSONAL WORDS

⁹Do your best to come to me as soon as you can. ¹⁰Demas loved this world too much. He left me and went to Thessalonica. Crescens went to Galatia. And Titus went to Dalmatia. ¹¹Luke is the only one still with me. Get Mark and bring him with you when you come. He can help me in my work here. ¹²I sent Tychicus to Ephesus.

¹³When I was in Troas, I left my coat there with Carpus. So when you come, bring it to me. Also, bring my books, particularly the ones written on parchment.ⁿ

¹⁴Alexander the metalworker did many harmful things against me. The Lord will punish him for the things he did. ¹⁵You should be careful that he does not hurt you too. He fought strongly against our teaching.

¹⁶The first time I defended myself, no one helped me. Everyone left me. I pray that God will forgive them. ¹⁷But the Lord stayed with me. He gave me strength so that I could fully tell the Good Newsᵈ to the non-Jews. The Lord wanted all the non-Jews to hear it. So I was saved from the lion's mouth. ¹⁸The Lord will save me when anyone tries to hurt me. The Lord will bring me safely to his heavenly kingdom. Glory forever and ever be the Lord's. Amen.

### FINAL GREETINGS

¹⁹Greet Priscilla and Aquila and the family of Onesiphorus. ²⁰Erastus stayed in Corinth. And I left Trophimus sick in Miletus. ²¹Try as hard as you can to come to me before winter.

Eubulus sends greetings to you. Also Pudens, Linus, Claudia, and all the brothers in Christ greet you.

²²The Lord be with your spirit. Grace be with you.

## BIBLE BASICS

### WHAT ARE DESCENDANTS?

Descendants are family members who are born to a person and his children. They would include grandchildren, great-grandchildren, and so on. Jews paid close attention to descendants and carefully followed the line of King David, because they knew the promised Messiah would come through his descendants. Jesus was in David's line.

### DECODE THIS!

Timothy's mother was_____.

---

**4:8 Day** The day Christ will come to judge all people and take his people to live with him.
**4:13 parchment** Something like paper made from the skins of sheep and used for writing on.

THE LETTER OF PAUL THE APOSTLE TO

# TITUS

Titus was a Greek believer.

In this very short letter, Titus is given a list of things to do: Choose elders carefully; teach holy living; stay away from arguments.

Paul leaves the church in Crete with instructions to Titus, a trusted friend.

Crete is a large island located 100 miles south-east of Greece.

**1** From Paul, a servant of God and an apostle[d] of Jesus Christ. I was sent to help the faith of God's chosen people. I was sent to help them to know the truth. And that truth shows people how to serve God. ²That faith and that knowledge come from our hope for life forever. God promised that life to us before time began, and God does not lie. ³At the right time God let the world know about that life through preaching. He trusted me with that work, and I preached because God our Savior commanded me to.

⁴To Titus. You are like a true son to me in the faith we share.

Grace and peace to you from God the Father and Christ Jesus our Savior.

### TITUS' WORK IN CRETE

⁵I left you in Crete so that you could finish doing the things that still needed to be done. I left you there also so that you could choose men to be elders[d] in every town. ⁶To be an elder, a man must not be guilty of doing wrong. He must have only one wife. His children must be believers. They must not be known as children who are wild and who do not obey. ⁷An elder has the job of taking care of God's work. So he must not be guilty of doing wrong. He must not be a man who is proud and selfish or who becomes angry quickly. He must not drink too much wine. He must not be a person who likes to fight. And he must not be a person who always tries to get rich by cheating people. ⁸An elder must be ready to help others by accepting them into his home. He must love what is good. He must be wise. He must live right. He must be holy. And he must be able to control himself. ⁹An elder must faithfully fol-

low the truth just as we teach it. He must be able to help people by using true and right teaching. And he must be able to show those who are against the true teaching that they are wrong.

¹⁰There are many people who refuse to obey—people who talk about worthless things and lead others into the wrong way. I am talking mostly about those who say that all non-Jews must be circumcised.[d] ¹¹These people must be stopped from talking. They are destroying whole families by teaching things that they should not teach. They teach them only to cheat people and make money. ¹²Even one of their own prophets from Crete said, "Cretan people are always liars. They are evil animals and lazy people who do nothing but eat." ¹³The words that prophet said are true. So tell those people that they are wrong. You must be strict with them. Then they will become strong in the faith ¹⁴and stop accepting Jewish stories. And they will stop following the commands of others who do not accept the truth. ¹⁵To those who are pure, all things are pure. But to those who are full of sin and do not believe, nothing is pure. The thinking of those people has become evil and their knowledge of what is right has been ruined. ¹⁶They say they know God, but the evil things they do show that they do not accept God. They are terrible people, they refuse to obey, and they are useless for doing anything good.

### FOLLOWING THE TRUE TEACHING

**2** You must tell everyone what they must do to follow the true teaching. ²Teach older men to have self-control, to be serious, and to be wise. They should be strong in faith, strong in love, and strong in patience.

³Also, teach older women to be holy in

### Things to Do When It Rains

1. Stay in bed and sleep.
2. Get blankets and popcorn for a movie day.
3. Paint a picture.
4. Write a poem.
5. Bake cookies for your neighbor.
6. Read your *Magnify*™ Biblezine.™
7. Play with your brother and sister.
8. Help mom clean the house.
9. Put on a play.
10. E-mail a friend.

the way they live. Teach them not to speak against others or have the habit of drinking too much wine. They should teach what is good. ⁴In that way they can teach younger women to love their husbands and children. ⁵They can teach younger women to be wise and pure, to take care of their homes, to be kind, and to obey their husbands. Then no one will be able to criticize the teaching God gave us.

### "He saved us by making us new through the Holy Spirit."
*Titus 3:5*

⁶In the same way, tell young men to be wise. ⁷You should do good deeds to be an example in every way for young men. When you teach, be honest and serious. ⁸And when you speak, speak the truth so that you cannot be criticized. Then anyone who is against you will be

## DECODE THIS!
**Where did Paul leave Titus to do his work?**

## BIBLE BASICS

### WHO OR WHAT IS CHRIST'S BODY?

You know how your body is made up of arms, legs, organs, and a head? Well, God describes the church as Christ's body, and it, too, is made up of many parts. But instead of fingers and toes, each part of his body is made up of the people who trust in him for their salvation. Christ is the head of the church, or the body, and each member has a special role to play in helping the rest of the body function. We must all work together for the whole body to do its work well.

ashamed because there is nothing bad that he can say against us.

⁹And tell slaves to obey their masters at all times. They should try to please them and not argue with them. ¹⁰They should not steal from them. And they should show their masters that they can be trusted. Slaves should do these things so that in everything they do, they will show that the teaching of God our Savior is good.

¹¹That is the way we should live, because God's grace has come. That grace can save every person. ¹²It teaches us not to live against God and not to do the evil things the world wants to do. That grace teaches us to live on earth now in a wise and right way—a way that shows that we serve God. ¹³We should live like that while we are waiting for the coming of our great God and Savior Jesus Christ. He is our great hope, and he will come with glory. ¹⁴He gave himself for us; he died to free us from all evil. He died to make us pure people who belong only to him—people who are always wanting to do good things.

¹⁵Tell everyone these things. You have full authority. So use that authority to strengthen the people and tell them what they should do. And do not let anyone treat you as if you were not important.

### THE RIGHT WAY TO LIVE

**3** Remind the believers to do these things: to be under the authority of rulers and government leaders, to obey them and be ready to do good, ²to speak no evil about anyone, to live in peace with all, to be gentle and polite to all people.

³In the past we were foolish people, too. We did not obey, we were wrong, and we were slaves to many things our bodies wanted and enjoyed. We lived doing evil and being jealous. People hated us and we hated each other. ⁴But then the kindness and love of God our Savior was shown. ⁵He saved us because of his mercy, not because of good deeds we did to be right with God. He saved us through the washing that made us new people. He saved us by making us new through the Holy Spirit.ᵈ ⁶God poured out to us that Holy Spirit fully through Jesus Christ our Savior. ⁷We were made right with God by His grace. And God gave us the Spirit so that we could receive the life that never ends. That is what we hope for.

⁸This teaching is true. And I want you to be sure that the people understand these things. Then those who believe in God will be careful to use their lives for doing good. These things are good and will help all people.

⁹Stay away from those who have foolish arguments, who talk about useless family histories, who make trouble and fight about what the law of Moses teaches. Those things are worth nothing and will not help anyone. ¹⁰If someone causes arguments, then give him a warning. If he continues to cause arguments, warn him again. If he still continues causing arguments, then do not be around him. ¹¹You know that such a person is evil and sinful. His sins prove that he is wrong.

### SOME THINGS TO REMEMBER

¹²I will send Artemas and Tychicus to you. When I send them, try hard to come to me at Nicopolis. I have decided to stay there this winter. ¹³Zenas the lawyer and Apollos will be traveling from there. Do all that you can to help them on their way. Be sure that they have everything they need. ¹⁴Our people must learn to use their lives for doing good deeds. They should do good to those in need. Then our people will not have useless lives.

¹⁵All who are with me greet you. Greet those who love us in the faith.

Grace be with you all.

## LIVIN' IT!

### BE QUIET!
### TITUS 3:9

You've only been in the car a few minutes when your brother begins to work his magic. In a way that only he can, he has bothered you so much that already you're in an all-out argument. *Why can't he just be quiet?* you wonder.

Paul had people like that in the church, so he could understand your frustration. The people in Paul's church were arguing over things about their faith, questioning whether or not what God said was true. Paul told his people—and us, too—not to argue. We really don't have to give an answer to someone just because they said something first. We can speak the truth in love at the right time, and we can also be quiet in order to keep the peace. Ask God to help you stay out of arguments and honor him with all your words.

THE LETTER OF PAUL THE APOSTLE TO

# PHiLEMON

Paul wants Philemon (a Christian) to take back his former slave Onesimus.

Church in Colosse meets in Philemon's home.

Paul instructs a runaway, thieving slave to go back to his master in Colosse.

Look for Paul's use of puns and friendly persuasion.

Onesimus means "useful one."

[1]From Paul, a prisoner of Jesus Christ, and from Timothy, our brother.

To Philemon, our dear friend and worker with us; [2]to Apphia, our sister; to Archippus, a worker with us; and to the church that meets in your home.

[3]Grace and peace to you from God our Father and the Lord Jesus Christ.

### PHILEMON'S LOVE AND FAITH

[4]I remember you in my prayers. And I always thank my God for you. [5]I hear about the love you have for all God's holy people and the faith you have in the Lord Jesus. [6]I pray that the faith you share will make you understand every blessing that we have in Christ. [7]My brother, you have shown love to God's people. You have made them feel happy. This has given me great joy and comfort.

### ACCEPT ONESIMUS AS A BROTHER

[8]There is something that you should do. And because of your love in Christ, I feel free to order you to do it. [9]But because I love you, I am asking you instead. I, Paul, am an old man now, and a prisoner for Christ Jesus. [10]I am asking you a favor for my son Onesimus. He became my son while I was in prison. [11]In the past he was useless to you. But now he has become useful for both you and me.

[12]I am sending him back to you, and with him I am sending my own heart. [13]I wanted to keep him with me to help me while I am in prison for the Good News.[d] By helping me he would be serving you. [14]But I did not want to do anything without asking you first. Then any favor you do for me will be because you want to do it, not because I forced you to do it.

[15]Onesimus was separated from you for a short time. Maybe that happened so that you could have him back forever— [16]not to be a slave, but better than a slave, to be a loved brother. I love him very much. But you will love him even more. You will love him as a man and as a brother in the Lord.

[17]If you think of me as your friend, then accept Onesimus back. Welcome him as you would welcome me. [18]If Onesimus has done anything wrong to you, charge that to me. If he owes you anything, charge that to me. [19]I, Paul, am writing this with my own hand. I will pay back anything Onesimus owes. And I will say nothing about what you owe me for your own life.

[20]So, my brother, I ask that you do this for me in the Lord. Comfort my heart in Christ. [21]I write this letter, knowing that you will do what I ask you and even more.

[22]Also, please prepare a room for me to stay in. I hope that God will answer your prayers and I will be able to come to you.

### FINAL GREETINGS

[23]Epaphras is a prisoner with me for Christ Jesus. He sends greetings to you. [24]And also Mark, Aristarchus, Demas, and Luke send greetings. They are workers together with me.

[25]The grace of our Lord Jesus Christ be with your spirit.

## GET CONNECTED

### EASIER SAID THAN DONE

It's one thing to share your faith and another to live it. We can tell other people how great God is and all about Jesus, but if our lives don't show God's love, people won't believe what we have to say.

Take a look at your life right now. What is important to you? Would nonbelievers see anything different in your life that would make them want to know more about the God you serve? Ask God to help you live an obedient life that honors him. Remember that people are often watching us and what we do, even when we don't know it. The way we live can actually help lead others to know who God is.

## BIBLE BASICS

### WHAT IS A HIGH PRIEST?

In the Old Testament when God set up the rules for his Temple, he allowed only the high priest (something like a pastor today) to enter the Holy Place to ask forgiveness for the people's sins. The people couldn't come close to God themselves; they had to use the high priest. Jesus now has become our High Priest. We can draw near to him and to God the Father any time we want because Jesus brings the perfect sacrifice to God for us—himself.

## ? DECODE THIS!

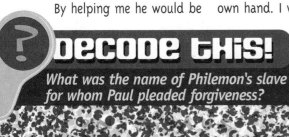

What was the name of Philemon's slave for whom Paul pleaded forgiveness?

An unsolved mystery: Who wrote Hebrews?!

Chapter 11 gives examples of people in the past who became famous for their faith.

# THE LETTER TO THE

# HEBREWS

Be careful! The stranger you turn away from your home might be an angel (13:2).

New Jewish believers in Rome are uncertain they made the right choice.

The message: A better life is found through Christ.

## GOD SPOKE THROUGH HIS SON

**1** In the past God spoke to our ancestors through the prophets.[d] He spoke to them many times and in many different ways. [2]And now in these last days God has spoken to us through his Son. God has chosen his Son to own all things. And he made the world through the Son. [3]The Son reflects the glory of God. He is an exact copy of God's nature. He holds everything together with his powerful word. The Son made people clean from their sins. Then he sat down at the right side of God, the Great One in heaven. [4]The Son became much greater than the angels. And God gave him a name that is much greater than theirs.

[5]This is because God never said to any of the angels,

"You are my Son.
     Today I have become your
          Father."          *Psalm 2:7*

Nor did God say of any angel,
     "I will be his Father,
          and he will be my Son."
                              *2 Samuel 7:14*

[6]And when God brings his firstborn Son into the world, he says,

"Let all God's angels worship
     him."[n]          *Psalm 97:7*

[7]This is what God said about the angels:
     "God makes his angels become like
          winds.
          He makes his servants become like
               flames of fire."          *Psalm 104:4*

[8]But God said this about his Son:
     "God, your throne will last forever
          and ever.
          You will rule your kingdom with
               fairness.
[9]You love what is right and hate evil.
     So God has chosen you to rule
          those with you.
          Your God has given you much
               joy."          *Psalm 45:6-7*

[10]God also says,
     "Lord, in the beginning you made
          the earth.

And your hands made the skies.
[11]They will be destroyed, but you will
     remain.
     They will all wear out like clothes.
[12]You will fold them like a coat.
     And, like clothes, you will change
          them.
But you never change.
     And your life will never end."
                              *Psalm 102:25-27*

[13]And God never said this to an angel:
     "Sit by me at my right side
until I put your enemies under your
     control."[n]          *Psalm 110:1*

[14]All the angels are spirits who serve God and are sent to help those who will receive salvation.

## OUR SALVATION IS GREAT

**2** So we must be more careful to follow what we were taught. Then we will not be pulled away from the truth. [2]The teaching that God spoke through angels was shown to be true. And anyone who did not follow it or obey it received the punishment he earned. [3]The salvation that was given to us is very great. So surely we also will be punished if we live as if this salvation were not important. It was the Lord himself who first told about this salvation. And those who heard him proved to us that this salvation is true. [4]God also proved it by using wonders, great signs, and many kinds of miracles.[d] And he proved it by giving people gifts through the Holy Spirit,[d] just as he wanted.

## CHRIST BECAME LIKE MEN

[5]God did not choose angels to be the rulers of the new world that was coming. It is that future world we have been talking about. [6]It is written somewhere in the Scriptures,[d]

"Why is man important to you?
     Why do you take care of the son of
          man?[n]
[7]For a short time you made him lower
     than the angels.
     But you crowned him with glory
          and honor.
[8]     You put all things under his
          control."          *Psalm 8:4-6*

If God put everything under his control, there was nothing left that he did not rule. But we do not yet see him

## DECODE THIS!

*Who reflects the glory of God and shows exactly what God is like?*

1:6 **"Let . . . him."** These words are found in Deuteronomy 32:43 in the Septuagint, the Greek version of the Old Testament, and in a Hebrew copy among the Dead Sea Scrolls. 1:13 **until . . . control** Literally, "until I make your enemies a footstool for your feet." 2:6 **son of man** This can mean any, but the name "Son of Man" is often used to mean Jesus. When Jesus became a man, he showed what God planned for all people to be.

ruling over everything. ⁹But we see Jesus! For a short time he was made lower than the angels. But now we see him wearing a crown of glory and honor because he suffered and died. Because of God's grace, he died for everyone.

¹⁰God is the One who made all things. And all things are for his glory. God wanted to have many sons share his glory. So God made perfect the One who leads people to salvation. He made Jesus a perfect Savior through Jesus' suffering.

¹¹Jesus, who makes people holy, and those who are made holy are from the same family. So he is not ashamed to call them his brothers. ¹²He says,

"Then, I will tell my fellow Israelites
    about you.
    I will praise you when your
        people meet to worship you."

*Psalm 22:22*

¹³He also says,
    "I will trust in God."            *Isaiah 8:17*
And he also says,
    "I am here. And with me are the
        children that God has given me."

*Isaiah 8:18*

¹⁴These children are people with physical bodies. So Jesus himself became like them and had the same experiences they have. He did this so that, by dying, he could destroy the one who has the power of death. That one is the devil. ¹⁵Jesus became like men and died so that he could free them. They were like slaves all their lives because of their fear of death. ¹⁶Clearly, it is not angels that Jesus helps, but the people who are from Abraham." ¹⁷For this reason Jesus had to be made like his brothers in every way. He became like men so that he could be their merciful and faithful high priest in service to God. Then Jesus could bring forgiveness for their sins. ¹⁸And now he can help those who are tempted. He is able to help because he himself suffered and was tempted.

## JESUS IS GREATER THAN MOSES

**3** So all of you, holy brothers, should think about Jesus. You were all called by God. God sent Jesus to us, and he is the high priest of our faith. ²And Jesus was faithful to God as Moses was. Moses did everything God wanted him to do in God's family. ³A man who is the head of a family receives more honor than others in the family. It is the same with Jesus. Jesus should have more honor than Moses. ⁴Every family has its head, but God is the head of everything. ⁵Moses was faithful in God's family as a servant. He told what God would say in the future. ⁶But Christ is faithful as a Son who is the head of God's family.

---

# LIVIN' IT!

**IN THE FLESH
HEBREWS 2:18**

Jesus was perfect. Never did a single sin his entire life. So you might begin to feel a little helpless with your sin. You may even be afraid to tell Jesus about it because you think he won't understand.

Think again. Jesus never sinned, but he *was* tempted. He went through the same kinds of situations that we face every day—only he always handled them the right way. The Bible says that Jesus came to earth as a human to not only pay for our sins, but also to understand what it was like to be a regular person. Because he was willing to do that, he can understand what we're going through and he knows exactly how to help us. We just need to ask him! You'll be amazed at what he can do.

---

# LIVIN' IT!

**WATCH OUT!
HEBREWS 3:12**

When we're young, most of us have teachable hearts. Our parents and teachers teach us right from wrong and explain what God has said in his Word. As we grow older, we experience more of life, including good and hard times. When the hard times come, we may begin to question whether or not what we were taught as young children really is true.

God says to watch out! It's perfectly fine to ask questions and to look really hard at the Bible to find out what God says. But we must ask God to help us keep hearts that believe in him. Without faith it is impossible to please God. If we see unbelief creeping into our thoughts, we need to turn to God immediately for help. Ask someone you trust who knows the Bible to help explain things better. Then listen to the truth and believe it.

# WHETHER TIMES ARE GOOD OR BAD, WHAT SHOULD YOU DO?

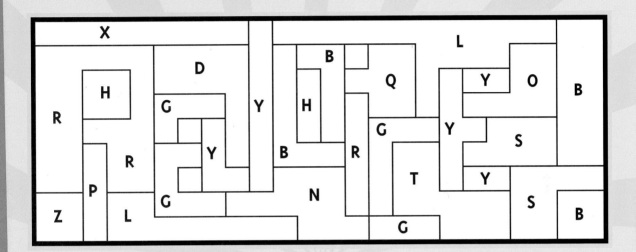

## COLOR ONLY THE FOLLOWING LETTERS THE COLOR GIVEN TO FIND OUT!

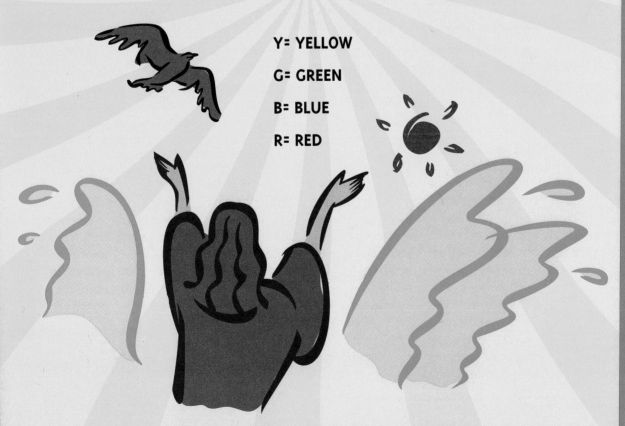

Y= YELLOW

G= GREEN

B= BLUE

R= RED

## HEBREWS 3:7–4:12

And we are God's family if we hold on to our faith and are proud of the great hope we have.

### WE MUST CONTINUE TO FOLLOW GOD

[7]So it is as the Holy Spirit[d] says:
"Today listen to what he says.
[8] Do not be stubborn as in the past when you turned against God.
There you tested God in the desert.
[9] For 40 years in the desert your ancestors saw the things I did.
But they tested me and my patience.
[10]I was angry with them.
I said, 'They are not loyal to me.
They have not understood my ways.'
[11]So I was angry and made a promise.
'They will never enter my land of rest.'"[n] *Psalm 95:7-11*

[12]So brothers, be careful that none of you has an evil, unbelieving heart. This will stop you from following the living

died in the desert. [18]And whom was God talking to when he promised that they would never enter and have his rest? He was talking to those who did not obey him. [19]So we see that they were not allowed to enter and have God's rest because they did not believe.

**4** Now God has left us that promise that we may enter and have his rest. Let us be very careful, then, so that none of you will fail to get that rest. [2]The Good News[d] was preached to us just as it was to them. But the teaching they heard did not help them. They heard it but did not accept it with faith. [3]We who have believed are able to enter and have God's rest. As God has said,

"So I was angry and made a promise.
'They will never enter my land of rest.'" *Psalm 95:11*

But God's work was finished from the time he made the world. [4]Somewhere in the Scriptures[d] he talked about the seventh day of the week: "And on the seventh day God rested from all his

> ### "So brothers, be careful that none of you has an evil, unbelieving heart."
> *Hebrews 3:12*

God. [13]But encourage each other every day. Do this while it is "today."[n] Help each other so that none of you will become hardened because of sin and its tricks. [14]We all share in Christ. This is true if we keep till the end the sure faith we had in the beginning. [15]This is what the Scripture[d] says:

"Today listen to what he says.
Do not be stubborn as in the past when you turned against God." *Psalm 95:7-8*

[16]Who heard God's voice and was against him? It was all those people Moses led out of Egypt. [17]And whom was God angry with for 40 years? He was angry with those who sinned, who

work."[n] [5]And again in the Scripture God said, "They will never enter my land of rest."

[6]It is still true that some people will enter and have God's rest. But those who first heard the way to be saved did not enter. They did not enter because they did not obey. [7]So God planned another day, called "today." He spoke about that day through David a long time later. It is the same Scripture used before:

"Today listen to
what he says.
Do not be
stubborn." *Psalm 95:7-8*

## Ways to Spend Your Saturday

1. Sleep in late.
2. Read your Bible, and practice your memory verses.
3. Help your mom with the housework.
4. Make salt-dough creations and paint them.
5. Invite friends over for midday tea.
6. Go fly a kite.
7. Roller blade, skateboard, or ride your bike.
8. Visit an elderly neighbor.
9. Go fishing with your dad.
10. Bake a treat, and take it to your grandma's.

[8]We know that Joshua[n] did not lead the people into that rest. We know this because God spoke later about another day. [9]This shows that the seventh-day rest[n] for God's people is still coming. [10]For anyone who enters and has God's rest will rest from his work as God did. [11]So let us try as hard as we can to enter God's rest. We must try hard so that no one will be lost by following the example of those who refused to obey.

[12]God's word is alive and working. It is sharper than a sword sharpened on both sides. It cuts all the way into us, where the soul and the spirit are joined.

**Who wears a crown of glory and honor because he suffered and died?**

3:11 rest A place of rest God promised to give his people. 3:13 "today" This word is taken from verse 7. It means that it is important to do these things now. 4:4 "And . . . work." Quotation from Genesis 2:2. 4:8 Joshua After Moses died, Joshua became leader of the Jewish people. Joshua led them into the land that God promised to give them. 4:9 seventh-day rest Literally, "sabbath rest," meaning a sharing in the rest that God began after he created the world.

It cuts to the center of our joints and our bones. And God's word judges the thoughts and feelings in our hearts. [13]Nothing in all the world can be hidden from God. Everything is clear and lies open before him. And to him we must explain the way we have lived.

## JESUS IS OUR HIGH PRIEST

[14]We have a great high priest who has gone into heaven. He is Jesus the Son of God. So let us hold on to the faith we have. [15]For our high priest is able to understand our weaknesses. When he lived on earth, he was tempted in every way that we are, but he did not sin. [16]Let us, then, feel free to come before God's throne. Here there is grace. And we can receive mercy and grace to help us when we need it.

**5** Every high priest is chosen from among men. He is given the work of going before God for them. He must offer gifts and sacrifices for sins. [2]He himself is weak. So he is able to be gentle with those who do not understand and who are doing wrong things. [3]Because he is weak the high priest must offer sacrifices for his own sins. And then he offers sacrifices for the sins of the people.

[4]To be a high priest is an honor. But no one chooses himself for this work. He must be called by God as Aaron[n] was. [5]So also Christ did not choose himself to have the honor of being a high priest. But God chose him. God said to him,

"You are my Son;
today I have become your
Father."            *Psalm 2:7*

[6]And in another Scripture[d] God says,
"You are a priest forever,
a priest like Melchizedek."[n]
            *Psalm 110:4*

# LIVIN' IT!

### ANCHOR'S AWAY
### HEBREWS 6:19

Have you ever seen or been on a boat? When it's time to stop moving, the captain lets down the anchor to keep the boat from getting off course.

We have an anchor, too, as God's people. It's not made out of metal, but out of the truth we find in God's Word. His promise to forgive us and never leave us becomes the anchor our souls need to always keep us close to God's heart.

Sometimes it's hard to believe that someone could love us so much that they'd forgive us again and again and keep on loving us as if we had never done anything wrong. But that's exactly how God feels about us. Even when we can't understand why he would love us, we let down our anchor into his promise and trust that he will do everything he says.

[7]While Jesus lived on earth, he prayed to God and asked God for help. He prayed with loud cries and tears to the One who could save him from death. And his prayer was heard because he left it all up to God. [8]Even though Jesus was the Son of God, he learned to obey by what he suffered. [9]And he became our perfect high priest. He gives eternal salvation to all who obey him. [10]And God made Jesus high priest, a priest like Melchizedek.

## WARNING AGAINST FALLING AWAY

"We have much to say about this. But it is hard to explain because you are so slow to understand. [12]You have had enough time so that by now you should be teachers. But you need someone to teach you again the first lessons of God's message. You still need the teaching that is like milk. You are not ready for solid food. [13]Anyone who lives on milk is still a baby. He knows nothing about right teaching. [14]But solid food is for those who are grown up. They have practiced in order to know the difference between good and evil.

**6** So let us go on to grown-up teaching. Let us not go back over the beginning lessons we learned about Christ. We should not start over again with teaching about turning from acts that lead to death and about believing in God. [2]We should not return to the teaching of baptisms,[n] of laying on of hands,[n] of the raising of the dead and eternal judgment. [3]And we will go on to grown-up teaching if God allows.

[4]Some people cannot be brought back again to a changed life. They were once in God's light. They enjoyed heaven's gift, and they shared in the Holy Spirit.[d] [5]They found out how good God's word is, and they received the powers of his new world. [6]And then they fell away from Christ! It is not possible to keep on bringing them back to a changed life again. For they are nailing the Son of God to a cross again and are shaming him in front of others.

[7]Some people are like land that gets plenty of rain. The land produces a good crop for those who work it, and it receives God's blessings. [8]Other people are like land that grows thorns and

# ? DECODE THIS!

*Be careful that you do not have an evil and _____ heart.*

weeds and is worthless. It is in danger of being cursed by God. It will be destroyed by fire.

[9] Dear friends, we are saying this to you. But we really expect better things from you that will lead to your salvation. [10] God is fair. He will not forget the work you did and the love you showed for him by helping his people. And he will remember that you are still helping them. [11] We want each of you to go on with the same hard work all your lives. Then you will surely get what you hope for. [12] We do not want you to become lazy. Be like those who have faith and patience. They will receive what God has promised.

[13] God made a promise to Abraham. And as there is no one greater than God, he used himself when he swore to Abraham. [14] He said, "I will surely bless you and give you many descendants."[n] [15] Abraham waited patiently for this to happen. And he received what God promised.

[16] People always use the name of someone greater than themselves when they swear. The oath proves that what they say is true. And this ends all arguing about what they say. [17] God wanted to prove that his promise was true. He wanted to prove this to those who would get what he promised. He wanted them to understand clearly

### "We do not want you to become lazy." *Hebrews 6:12*

that his purposes never change. So God proved his promise by also making an oath. [18] These two things cannot change. God cannot lie when he makes a promise, and he cannot lie when he makes an oath. These things encourage us who came to God for safety. They give us strength to hold on to the hope we have been given. [19] We have this hope as an anchor for the soul, sure and strong. It enters behind the curtain

in the Most Holy Place in heaven. [20] Jesus has gone in there ahead of us and for us. He has become the high priest forever, a priest like Melchizedek."

### THE PRIEST MELCHIZEDEK

**7** Melchizedek[n] was the king of Salem and a priest for the Most High God. He met Abraham when Abraham was coming back after defeating the kings. When they met, Melchizedek blessed Abraham. [2] And Abraham gave Melchizedek a tenth of everything he had brought back from the battle. First, Melchizedek's name means "king of

goodness." Also, he is king of Salem, which means "king of peace." [3] No one knows who Melchizedek's father or mother was.[n] No one knows where he came from. And no one knows when he was born or when he died. Melchizedek is like the Son of God;

he continues being a priest forever.

[4] You can see that Melchizedek was very great. Abraham, the great father, gave Melchizedek a tenth of everything that Abraham won in battle. [5] Now the law says that those in the tribe[d] of Levi who become priests must get a tenth from the people. The priests collect it from their own people, even though the priests and the people are both from the family of Abraham. [6] Melchizedek was not from the tribe of Levi. But he got a tenth from Abraham. And he blessed Abraham, the man who had God's promises. [7] And everyone knows that the more important person blesses the less important person. [8] Those priests get a tenth, but they are only men who live and then die. But Melchizedek, who got a tenth from Abraham, continues living, as the Scripture[d] says. [9] It is Levi who gets a tenth from the people. But we might even say that when Abraham paid Melchizedek a tenth, then Levi also paid it. [10] Levi was not yet born. But Levi was in the body of his ancestor Abraham when Melchizedek met Abraham.

[11] The people were given the law[n] based on a system of priests from the tribe of Levi. But they could not be made spiritually perfect through that system of priests. So there was a need for another priest to come. I mean a priest like Melchizedek, not Aaron. [12] And when a different kind of priest comes, the law must be changed, too. [13] We are saying these things about Christ. He belonged to a different tribe. No one from that tribe ever served as a priest at the altar. [14] It is clear that our Lord came from the

## ?ᴅecoᴅe ᴛɦis!
*Hebrews compares the first lessons of God's message to what drink?*

tribe of Judah. And Moses said nothing about priests belonging to that tribe.

## JESUS IS LIKE MELCHIZEDEK

[15]And this becomes even more clear. We see that another priest comes, who is like Melchizedek.[n] [16]He was not made a priest by human rules and laws. He became a priest through the power of his life, which continues forever. [17]In the Scriptures,[d] this is said about him:

"You are a priest forever,
a priest like Melchizedek."

*Psalm 110:4*

[18]The old rule is now set aside because it was weak and useless. [19]The law of Moses could not make anything perfect. But now a better hope has been given to us. And with this hope we can come near to God.

[20]Also, it is important that God made an oath when he made Jesus high priest. When the others became priests, there was no oath. [21]But Christ became a priest with God's oath. God said:

"The Lord has made a promise
and will not change his mind.
'You are a priest forever.'"

*Psalm 110:4*

[22]So this means that Jesus is the guarantee of a better agreement[n] from God to his people.

[23]Also, when one of the other priests died, he could not continue being a priest. So there were many priests. [24]But Jesus lives forever. He will never stop serving as priest. [25]So he is always able to save those who come to God through him. He can do this, because he always lives, ready to help those who come before God.

[26]So Jesus is the kind of high priest that we need. He is holy; he has no sin in him. He is pure and not influenced by sinners. And he is raised above the heavens. [27]He is not like the other priests. They had to offer sacrifices every day, first for their own sins, and then for the sins of the people. But Christ does not need to do that. He offered his sacrifice only once and for all time. Christ offered himself! [28]The law chooses high priests who are men with all their weaknesses. But the word of God's oath came later than the law. It made God's Son to be the high priest. And that Son has been made perfect forever.

## JESUS IS OUR HIGH PRIEST

**8** Here is the point of what we are saying: We do have a high priest who sits on the right side of God's throne in heaven. [2]Our high priest serves in the Most Holy Place. He serves in the true place of worship that was made by God, not by men.

> "But Jesus lives forever. He will never stop serving as priest."
>
> *Hebrews 7:24*

[3]Every high priest has the work of offering gifts and sacrifices to God. So our high priest must also offer something to God. [4]If our high priest were now living on earth, he would not be a priest. I say this because there are already priests here who follow the law by offering gifts to God. [5]The work that they do as priests is only a dim copy of what is in heaven. For when Moses was ready to build the Holy Tent,[d] God warned him: "Be very careful to make everything by the plan I showed you on the mountain."[n] [6]But the priestly work that has been given to Jesus is much greater than the work that was given to the other priests. In the same way, the new agreement that Jesus brought from God to his people is much greater than the old one. And the new agreement is based on promises of better things.

[7]If there was nothing wrong with the first agreement,[n] there would be no need for a second agreement. [8]But God found something wrong with his people. He says:

**7:15 Melchizedek** A priest and king who lived in the time of Abraham. (Read Genesis 14:17-24.) **7:22 agreement** God gives a contract or agreement to his people. For the Jews, this agreement was the law of Moses. But now God has given a better agreement to his people through Christ. **8:5 "Be . . . mountain."** Quotation from Exodus 25:40. **8:7 first agreement** The contract God gave the Jewish people when he gave them the law of Moses.

## REAL SUPER HEROES

# STEPHEN

**Want to see someone cool under pressure? Take a look at Stephen. A dedicated disciple of Jesus, he found himself facing a jury of Jews who lied about him. So what did Stephen do? He witnessed to them. He told them what God had done for his people, starting from the beginning of time, and how Jesus held the only hope for them. They got so mad at him they ordered that he be stoned to death. Again, instead of panicking, Stephen prayed. He asked God to forgive them, and then he asked God to receive his spirit.**

**How did Stephen stay so calm facing death? He knew that Jesus would save him—not in this life, but for the next. He knew that to die meant to be with his Savior. It was his calling—as it is ours—to live and to die in a way that honors Jesus.**

## Gotta Know!

### Why do scientists believe in evolution?

People believe in evolution because they have not opened their hearts to believe or understand God's truth. In their sin, they do not want the world or their own lives to be under God's control. They would rather try to believe that the complex universe came together all by itself. By believing evolution, they feel freed to do whatever they want and not obey God. But God says their judgment will one day come.

"The time is coming, says the Lord,
  when I will make a new
    agreement.
It will be with the people of Israel
  and the people of Judah.
⁹It will not be like the agreement
  I made with their ancestors.
That was when I took them by the
    hand
  to bring them out of Egypt.
But they broke that agreement,
  and I turned away from them,
    says the Lord.
¹⁰In the future I will make this
    agreement
  with the people of Israel, says the
    Lord.
I will put my teachings in their
    minds.
  And I will write them on their
    hearts.
I will be their God,
  and they will be my people.
¹¹People will no longer have to teach
    their neighbors and relatives to
      know the Lord.
This is because all will know me,
  from the least to the most
    important.
¹²I will forgive them for the wicked
    things they did.
  I will not remember their sins
    anymore."            *Jeremiah 31:31-34*
¹³God called this a new agreement, so
he has made the first agreement old.

And anything that is old and worn out
is ready to disappear.

### WORSHIP UNDER THE OLD AGREEMENT

**9** The first agreement*ⁿ* had rules for worship. And it had a man-made place for worship. ²The Holy Tent*ᵈ* was set up for this. The first area in the Tent was called the Holy Place. In it were the lamp and the table with the bread that was made holy for God. ³Behind the second curtain was a room called the Most Holy Place. ⁴In it was a golden altar for burning incense.*ᵈ* Also there was the Holy Box*ᵈ* that held the old agreement. The Holy Box was covered with gold. Inside this Holy Box was a golden jar of manna*ᵈ* and Aaron's rod—the rod that once grew leaves. Also in it were the stone tablets of the old agreement. ⁵Above the Holy Box were the creatures with wings that showed God's glory. The wings of the creatures reached over the lid. But we cannot tell everything about these things now.

⁶Everything in the Tent was made ready

in this way. Then the priests went into the first room every day to do their worship. ⁷But only the high priest could go into the second room, and he did that only once a year. He could never enter the inner room without taking blood with him. He offered that blood to God for himself and for the people's sins. These were sins people did without knowing that they were sinning. ⁸The Holy Spirit*ᵈ* uses this to show that the way into the Most Holy Place was not open. This was while the system of the old Holy Tent was still being used. ⁹This is an example for the present time. It shows that the gifts and sacrifices offered cannot make the worshiper perfect in his heart. ¹⁰These gifts and sacrifices were only about food and drink and special washings. They were rules for the body, to be followed until the time of God's new way.

### WORSHIP UNDER THE NEW AGREEMENT

¹¹But Christ has come as the high priest of the good things we now have. The tent he entered is greater and more perfect. It is not made by men. It does not belong to this world. ¹²Christ

> **"He entered the Most Holy Place and set us free from sin forever."** *Hebrews 9:12*

entered the Most Holy Place only once—and for all time. He did not take with him the blood of goats and calves. His sacrifice was his own blood. He entered the Most Holy Place and set us free from sin forever. ¹³The blood of goats and bulls and the ashes of a cow are sprinkled on the people who are

## DECODE THIS!

*God made a promise to give many descendants to whom?*

9:1 **first agreement** The contract God gave the Jewish people when he gave them the law of Moses.

# november GRATITUDE

*Thank the Lord because he is good. His love continues forever (1 Chronicles 16:34).*

**1** Prayer Pointer: Make a list of all the good things in your life. Tell them to God in prayer, and thank him for his goodness to you.

**2**

**3** Make a turkey out of a pinecone body and construction paper feathers and head.

**4**

**5** I CORINTHIANS 15:57: But we thank God! He gives us the victory through our Lord Jesus Christ.

**6** Ask your parents what they're thankful for.

**7**

**8**

**9** Paint a picture of God's good gifts in your life.

**10** Prayer Pointer: Thank God for picking out your family just for you, and pray that you would all become more thankful for your friendship.

**11**

**12**

**13** EPHESIANS 5:20: Always give thanks to God the Father for everything, in the name of our Lord Jesus Christ.

**14**

**15**

**16** Tell the janitor at school or church how much you appreciate the service.

**17**

**18** Prayer Pointer: Ask God to show you how you can help a needy family this Thanksgiving.

**19**

**20** PHILIPPIANS 4:6: Do not worry about anything. But pray and ask God for everything you need. And when you pray, always give thanks.

**21**

**22**

**23** Write a note to each person in your family that tells them why they're special.

**24**

**25** Prayer Pointer: Pray for those in the world who need food, clothes, and shelter. Ask God to provide for them and to help them become Christians.

**26**

**27** Call a relative you haven't spoken to in awhile, and tell them you're thinking of them.

**28** REVELATION 11:17: We give thanks to you, Lord God All-Powerful. You are the One who is and who was. We thank you because you have used your great power and have begun to rule!

**29**

**30** Give a gift to someone who is not expecting it.

unclean[d] and this makes their bodies clean again.

[14]"How much more is done by the blood of Christ. He offered himself through the eternal Spirit[n] as a perfect sacrifice to God. His blood will make our hearts clean from useless acts. We are made pure so that we may serve the living God. [15]So Christ brings a new agreement from God to his people. Those who are called by God can now receive the blessings that God has promised. These blessings will last forever. They can have those things because Christ died so that the people who lived under the first agreement could be set free from sin.

[16]"When there is a will,[n] it must be proven that the man who wrote that will is dead. [17]A will means nothing while the man is alive. It can be used only after he dies. [18]This is why even the first agreement could not begin without blood to show death. [19]First, Moses told all the people every command in the law. Next he took the blood of calves and mixed it with water. Then he used red wool and a branch of the hyssop plant to sprinkle the blood and water on the book of the law and on all the people. [20]He said, "This is the blood which begins the agreement that God commanded you to obey."[n] [21]In the same way, Moses sprinkled the blood on the Holy Tent[d] and over all the things used in worship. [22]The law says that almost everything must be made clean by blood. And sins cannot be forgiven without blood to show death.

## CHRIST'S DEATH TAKES AWAY SINS

[23]So the copies of the real things in heaven had to be made clean[d] by animal sacrifices. But the real things in heaven need much better sacrifices. [24]For Christ did not go into the Most Holy Place made by men. It is only a copy of the real one. He went into heaven itself. He is there now before God to help us. [25]The high priest enters the Most Holy Place once every year. He

**Q. When did dinosaurs live?**

**A. I think dinosaurs lived a long time ago, like in the Bible days.**

takes with him blood that is not his own blood. But Christ did not go into heaven to offer himself many times. [26]Then he would have had to suffer many times since the world was made. But Christ came only once and for all time. He came at just the right time to take away all sin by sacrificing himself. [27]Everyone must die

once. After a person dies, he is judged. [28]So Christ was offered as a sacrifice one time to take away the sins of many people. And he will come a second time, but not to offer himself for sin. He will come again to bring salvation to those who are waiting for him.

**10** The law is only an unclear picture of the good things coming in the future. It is not a perfect picture of the real things. The people under the law offered the same sacrifices every year. These sacrifices can never make perfect those who come near to worship God. [2]If the law could make them perfect, the sacrifices would have already stopped. The worshipers would be made clean, and they would no longer feel guilty for their sins. [3]These sacrifices remind them of their sins every year, [4]because it is not possible for the blood of bulls and goats to take away sins.

[5]So when Christ came into the world, he said:

"You do not want sacrifices and
offerings.
But you have prepared a body for
me.
[6]You do not ask for burnt offerings
and offerings to take away sins.
[7]Then I said, 'Look, I have come.
It is written about me in the book.
My God, I have come to do what
you want.'"                  *Psalm 40:6-8*

[8]In this Scripture[d] he first said, "You do not want sacrifices and offerings. You do not ask for burnt offerings and offerings to take away sins." (These are all sacrifices that the law commands.) [9]Then he said, "Here I am. I have come to do what you want." So God ends the first system of sacrifices so that he can set up the new system. [10]Jesus Christ did what God wanted him to do. And because of this, we are made holy through the sacrifice of his body. Christ made this sacrifice only once, and for all time.

## DECODE THIS!

*In Hebrews, Jesus is compared to the Old Testament priest named ____.*

**9:14 Spirit** This refers to the Holy Spirit; to Christ's own spirit; or to the spiritual and eternal nature of his sacrifice. **9:16 will** A legal document that shows how a person's money and property are to be distributed at the time of his death. This is the same word in Greek as "agreement" in verse 15. **9:20 "This . . . obey."** Quotation from Exodus 24:8.

"Every day the priests stand and do their religious service. Again and again they offer the same sacrifices. But those sacrifices can never take away sins. [12]But Christ offered one sacrifice for sins, and it is good forever. Then he sat down at the right side of God. [13]And now Christ waits there for his enemies to be put under his power. [14]With one sacrifice he made perfect forever those who are being made holy.

[15]The Holy Spirit[d] also tells us about this. First he says:

[16]"In the future I will make this
agreement[n]
with the people of Israel, says
the Lord.
I will put my teachings in their
hearts.
And I will write them on their
minds."                    *Jeremiah 31:33*

[17]Then he says:

"Their sins and the evil things they
do—
I will not remember anymore."
                            *Jeremiah 31:34*

[18]And when these have been forgiven, there is no more need for a sacrifice for sins.

### CONTINUE TO TRUST GOD

[19]So, brothers, we are completely free to enter the Most Holy Place. We can do this without fear because of the blood of Jesus' death. [20]We can enter through a new way that Jesus opened for us. It is a living way. It leads through the curtain—Christ's body. [21]And we have a great priest over God's house. [22]So let us come near to God with a sincere heart and a sure faith. We have been cleansed and made free from feelings of guilt. And our bodies have been washed with pure water. [23]Let us hold firmly to the hope that we have confessed. We can trust God to do what he promised.

## LIVIN' IT!

### LOOK OUT, NOT IN
### HEBREWS 10:24

Sometimes Christians work so hard to stop doing the wrong things that they forget about actually doing the right things. We are sinful by nature, and we tend to think about ourselves and our needs, forgetting about all the other people around us who are hurting and need help, too.

When we remember that God gives us everything we need to live good lives that please him, then we can stop worrying about ourselves and start helping others. Look at your parents, brothers, sisters, and friends. Think about what they are going through right now. How can you help encourage them in the truth? What can you do to serve them? Ask God for wisdom, and ask your friends how you can help. Your love will help encourage them to do the same for others.

[24]Let us think about each other and help each other to show love and do good deeds. [25]You should not stay away from the church meetings, as some are doing. But you should meet together and encourage each other. Do this even more as you see the Day[n] coming.

[26]If we decide to go on sinning after we have learned the truth, there is no longer any sacrifice for sins. [27]There is nothing but fear in waiting for the judgment and the angry fire that will destroy all those who live against God. [28]Any person who refused to obey the law of Moses was found guilty from the proof given by two or three witnesses. He was put to death without mercy. [29]So what do you think

should be done to a person who does not respect the Son of God? He looks at the blood of the agreement, the blood that made him holy, as no different from other men's blood. He insults the Spirit[d] of God's grace. Surely he should have a much worse punishment. [30]We know that God said, "I will punish those who do wrong. I will repay them."[n] And he also said, "The Lord will judge his people."[n] [31]It is a terrible thing to fall into the hands of the living God.

[32]Remember those days in the past when you first learned the truth. You had a hard struggle with many sufferings, but you continued strong. [33]Sometimes you were hurt and persecuted before crowds of people. And sometimes you shared with those who were being treated that way. [34]You helped the prisoners. And you even had joy when all that you owned was taken from you. You were joyful because you knew that you had something better and more lasting.

[35]So do not lose the courage that you had in the past. It has a great reward. [36]You must hold on, so you can do what God wants and receive what he has promised. [37]For in a very short time,

"The One who is coming will come.
He will not be late.
[38]The person who is right with me
will have life because of his faith.
But if he turns back with fear,
I will not be pleased with him."
                            *Habakkuk 2:3-4*

[39]But we are not those who turn back and are lost. We are people who have faith and are saved.

## DECODE THIS!

*Christ came to take away _____ by sacrificing himself on the cross.*

10:16 **agreement** God gives a contract or agreement to his people. For the Jews, this agreement was the law of Moses. But now God has given a better agreement to his people through Christ. 10:25 **Day** The day Christ will come to judge all people and take his people to live with him. 10:30 "**I . . . them.**" Quotation from Deuteronomy 32:35. 10:30 "**The Lord . . . people.**" Quotation from Deuteronomy 32:36; Psalm 135:14.

**FAITH**

**11** Faith means being sure of the things we hope for. And faith means knowing that something is real even if we do not see it. ²People who lived in the past became famous because of faith.

³It is by faith we understand that the whole world was made by God's command. This means that what we see was made by something that cannot be seen. ⁴It was by faith that Abel offered God a

## GET CONNECTED

### FAITH LIVES

Your group of friends have gotten together and decided that they want to pull a prank on the new kid in school, but you just don't feel right about it inside your heart. What should you do?

God says that his kids need to live by faith—meaning, we need to know what God's Word says is right and true and then follow it. But the Bible doesn't talk about every specific sin. If something happens where we do not have peace in our hearts about it, then we stop what we're doing and go to God in prayer. Ask him for guidance, and look in his Word. Then do what God says by faith.

better sacrifice than Cain did. God said he was pleased with the gifts Abel offered. So God called Abel a good man because of his faith. Abel died, but through his faith he is still speaking.

⁵It was by faith that Enoch was taken to heaven. He never died. He could not be found, because God had taken him away. Before he was taken, the Scripture*d* says that he was a man who truly pleased God. ⁶Without faith no one can please God. Anyone who comes to God must believe that he is real and that he rewards those who truly want to find him.

⁷It was by faith Noah heard God's warnings about things that he could not yet see. He obeyed God and built a large boat to save his family. By his faith, Noah showed that the world was wrong. And he became one of those who are made right with God through faith.

⁸It was by faith Abraham obeyed God's call to go to another place that God promised to give him. He left his own country, not knowing where he was to go. ⁹It was by faith that he lived in the country God promised to give him. He lived there like a visitor who did not belong. He lived in tents with Isaac and Jacob, who had received that same promise from God. ¹⁰Abraham was waiting for the city*n* that has real foundations—the city planned and built by God.

¹¹He was too old to have children, and Sarah was not able to have children. It was by faith that Abraham was made able to become a father. Abraham trusted God to do what he had promised. ¹²This man was so old that he was almost dead. But from him came as many descendants as there are stars in the sky. They are as many as the grains of sand on the seashore that cannot be counted.

¹³All these great men died in faith. They did not get the things that God promised his people. But they saw them coming far in the future and were glad. They said that they were like visitors and strangers on earth. ¹⁴When people say such things, then they show that they are looking for a country that will be their own country. ¹⁵If they had been thinking

about that country they had left, they could have gone back. ¹⁶But those men were waiting for a better country—a heavenly country. So God is not ashamed to be called their God. For he has prepared a city for them.

¹⁷It was by faith that Abraham offered his son Isaac as a sacrifice. God made the promises to Abraham. But God tested him. And Abraham was ready to offer his own son as a sacrifice. ¹⁸God had said, "The descendants I promised you will be from Isaac."*n* ¹⁹Abraham believed that God could raise the dead. And really, it was as if Abraham got Isaac back from death.

²⁰It was by faith that Isaac blessed the future of Jacob and Esau. ²¹It was by faith that Jacob blessed each one of Joseph's sons. He did this while he was dying. Then he worshiped as he leaned on the top of his walking stick.

²²It was by faith that Joseph spoke about the Israelites leaving Egypt while he was dying. He told them what to do with his body.

²³It was by faith that Moses' parents hid him for three months after he was born. They saw that Moses was a beautiful baby. And they were not afraid to disobey the king's order.

²⁴It was by faith that Moses, when he grew up, refused to be called the son of the king of Egypt's daughter. ²⁵He chose to suffer with God's people instead of enjoying sin for a short time. ²⁶He thought that it was better to suffer for the Christ*d* than to have all the treasures of Egypt. He was looking only for God's reward. ²⁷It was by faith that Moses left Egypt. He was not afraid of the king's anger. Moses continued strong as if he could see the God that no one can see. ²⁸It was by faith that Moses prepared the

## DECODE THIS!

*What is something we believe in even if we can't see it?*

**11:10 city** The spiritual "city" where God's people live with him. Also called "the heavenly Jerusalem." (See Hebrews 12:22.) **11:18 "The descendants . . . Isaac."** Quotation from Genesis 21:12.

**330**

Passover[d] and spread the blood on the doors. It was spread so that the one who brings death would not kill the firstborn[d] sons of Israel.

[29]It was by faith that the people crossed the Red Sea as if it were dry land. The Egyptians also tried to do it, but they were drowned.

[30]It was by faith that the walls of Jericho fell. They fell after the people had marched around the walls of Jericho for seven days.

[31]It was by faith that Rahab, the prostitute,[d] welcomed the spies and was not killed with those who refused to obey God.

[32]Do I need to give more examples? I do not have time to tell you about Gideon, Barak, Samson, Jephthah, David, Samuel, and the prophets.[d] [33]Through their faith they defeated kingdoms. They did what was right and received what God promised. They shut the mouths of lions, [34]stopped great fires and were saved from being killed with swords. They were weak, and yet were made strong. They were powerful in battle and defeated other armies. [35]Women received their dead relatives raised back to life. Others were tortured and refused to accept their freedom. They did this so that they could be raised from death to a better life. [36]Some were laughed at and beaten. Others were tied and put into prison. [37]They were killed with stones and they were cut in half. They were killed with swords. Some wore the skins of sheep and goats. They were poor, abused, and treated badly. [38]The world was not good enough for them! They wandered in deserts and mountains, living in caves and holes in the earth.

[39]All these people are known for their faith. But none of them received what God had promised. [40]God planned to give us something better. Then they would be made perfect, but only together with us.

## FOLLOW JESUS' EXAMPLE

**12** So we have many people of faith around us. Their lives tell us what faith means. So let us run the race that is before us and never give up. We should remove from our lives anything that would get in the way. And we should remove the sin that so easily catches us. [2]Let us look only to Jesus. He is the one who began our faith, and he makes our faith perfect. Jesus suffered death on the cross. But he accepted the shame of the cross as if it were nothing. He did this because of the joy that God put before him. And now he is sitting at the right side of God's throne. [3]Think about Jesus. He held on patiently while sinful men were doing evil things against him. Look at Jesus' example so that you will not get tired and stop trying.

## GOD IS LIKE A FATHER

[4]You are struggling against sin, but your struggles have not yet caused you to be killed. [5]You have forgotten his encouraging words for his sons:
"My son, don't think the Lord's discipline of you is worth nothing. And don't stop trying when the Lord corrects you.
[6]The Lord corrects those he loves. And he punishes everyone he accepts as his child."

*Proverbs 3:11-12*

[7]So accept your sufferings as if they were a father's punishment. God does these things to you as a father punishing his sons. All sons are punished by their fathers. [8]If you are never punished (and every son must be punished), you are not true children and not really sons. [9]We have all had fathers here on earth who punished us. And we respected our fathers. So it is even more important that we accept punishment from the Father of our spirits. If we do this, we will have life. [10]Our fathers on earth punished us for a short time. They punished us the way they thought was best. But God punishes us to help us, so that we can become holy as he is. [11]We do not enjoy punishment. Being punished is painful. But later, after we have learned from being punished, we have peace, because we start living in the right way.

## LIVIN' IT!

**ALL YOU'VE GOT
HEBREWS 12:1**

If you wanted to win a race, would you strap on a heavy set of weights? No, you'd make sure you were as light as possible so you could run as fast as you could.

God says that we are in a race, and the prize is Jesus himself. With such an incredible reward up ahead, we need to run with all of our energy and might. We've got to get rid of anything that might weigh us down and keep us from seeking God with all of our heart, soul, mind, and strength.

Does anything get in your way from fully obeying God? Do you have friends, or TV programs, or too many other activities in your life that keep you from the time you need to spend with God? If so, then get rid of them. Run with all your heart so that you'll win.

## BE CAREFUL HOW YOU LIVE

[12]You have become weak. So make yourselves strong again. [13]Live in the right way so that you will be saved and your weakness will not cause you to be lost.

[14]Try to live in peace with all people. And try to live lives free from sin. If anyone's life is not holy, he will never see the Lord. [15]Be careful that no one fails to get God's grace. Be careful that no one becomes like a bitter weed growing among you. A person like that can ruin all of you. [16]Be careful that no one takes part in sexual sin. And be careful that no person is like Esau and never thinks about God. Esau was the oldest son, and he would have received everything from his father. But Esau sold all that for a

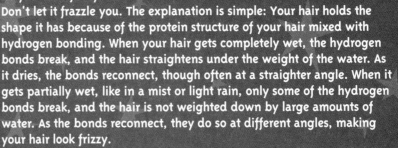

## WILD WORLD FACTS

### FRAZZLED

Do you have frizzy hair?

Don't let it frazzle you. The explanation is simple: Your hair holds the shape it has because of the protein structure of your hair mixed with hydrogen bonding. When your hair gets completely wet, the hydrogen bonds break, and the hair straightens under the weight of the water. As it dries, the bonds reconnect, though often at a straighter angle. When it gets partially wet, like in a mist or light rain, only some of the hydrogen bonds break, and the hair is not weighted down by large amounts of water. As the bonds reconnect, they do so at different angles, making your hair look frizzy.

No matter what your hair looks like, remember that God made you the way you are for a reason. It's okay if you want to fix the frizz or use goop to smooth out your hair—but always remember that having a beautiful heart is way more important to God.

[NewScientist.com]

## IT'S A LOVE THING
## HEBREWS 12:5

When you get in trouble, what's your first reaction? Are you scared? Angry? Sad? As a kid, it might seem like life would be a whole lot better if spankings, time outs, and groundings just never happened.

Truth is, most adults don't like to be disciplined either. We don't like to get caught, and we don't want to get in trouble. Whether you're young or old, one thing remains the same: We are always God's children. He says that he has to discipline us because he loves us. He knows that the only way we'll really happy is when we're obeying him—so he helps us to remember the truth through discipline.

Next time your parents have to discipline you, remember this: It may be painful, but it's an act of love to help you make better choices the next time. Thank them—and God—and pray that you won't make that same mistake again.

single meal. [17]You remember that after Esau did this, he wanted to get his father's blessing. He wanted this blessing so much that he cried. But his father refused to give him the blessing, because Esau could find no way to change what he had done.

[18]You have not come to a mountain that can be touched and that is burning with fire. You have not come to darkness, sadness and storms. [19]You have not come to the noise of a trumpet or to the sound of a voice. When the people of Israel heard the voice, they begged not to have to hear another word. [20]They did not want to hear the command: "If anything, even an animal, touches the mountain, it must be put to death with stones."[n] [21]What they saw was so terrible that Moses said, "I am shaking with fear."[n]

[22]But you have not come to that kind of place. The new place you have come to is Mount Zion.[n] You have come to the city of the living God, the heavenly Jerusalem. You have come to thousands of angels gathered together with joy. [23]You have come to the meeting of God's firstborn[n] children. Their names are written in heaven. You have come

to God, the judge of all people. And you have come to the spirits of good people who have been made perfect. [24]You have come to Jesus, the One who brought the new agreement from God to his people. You have come to the sprinkled blood[n] that has a better message than the blood of Abel.[n]

[25]So be careful and do not refuse to listen when God speaks. They refused to listen to him when he warned them on earth. And they did not escape. Now God is warning us from heaven. So it will be worse for us if we refuse to listen to him. [26]When he spoke before, his voice shook the earth. But now he has promised, "Once again I will shake not only the earth but also the heavens."[n] [27]The words "once again" clearly show us that everything that was made will be destroyed. These are the things that can be shaken. And only the things that cannot be shaken will remain.

[28]So let us be thankful because we have a kingdom that cannot be shaken. We should worship God in a way that pleases him. So let us worship him with respect and fear, [29]because our God is like a fire that burns things up.

**12:20** "If . . . stones." Quotation from Exodus 19:12-13. **12:21** "I . . . fear." Quotation from Deuteronomy 9:19. **12:22 Mount Zion** Another name for Jerusalem, here meaning the spiritual city of God's people. **12:23 firstborn** The first son born in a Jewish family was given the most important place in the family and received special blessings. All of God's children are like that. **12:24 sprinkled blood** The blood of Jesus' death. **12:24 Abel** The son of Adam and Eve, who was killed by his brother Cain (Genesis 4:8). **12:26** "Once . . . heavens." Quotation from Haggai 2:6, 21.

332

**13** Keep on loving each other as brothers in Christ. ²Remember to welcome strangers into your homes. Some people have done this and have welcomed angels without knowing it. ³Do not forget those who are in prison. Remember them as if you were in prison with them. Remember those who are suffering as if you were suffering with them.

⁴Marriage should be honored by everyone. Husband and wife should keep their marriage pure. God will judge guilty those who take part in sexual sins. ⁵Keep your lives free from the love of money. And be satisfied with what you have. God has said,

"I will never leave you;
    I will never forget you."

*Deuteronomy 31:6*

⁶So we can feel sure and say,

"I will not be afraid because the Lord is my helper.
    People can't do anything to me."

*Psalm 118:6*

⁷Remember your leaders. They taught God's message to you. Remember how they lived and died, and copy their faith. ⁸Jesus Christ is the same yesterday, today, and forever.

⁹Do not let all kinds of strange teachings lead you into the wrong way. Your hearts should be strengthened by God's grace, not by obeying rules about foods. Obeying such rules does not help anyone.

¹⁰We have a sacrifice. But the priests who serve in the Holy Tent^d cannot eat from it. ¹¹The high priest carries the blood of animals into the Most Holy Place. There he offers this blood for sins. But the bodies of the animals are burned outside the camp. ¹²So Jesus also suffered outside the city. He died to make his people holy with his own blood. ¹³So let us go to Jesus outside the camp. We should accept the same shame that Jesus had.

> **"i pray that the God of peace will give you every good thing you need so that you can do what he wants."**
>
> *Hebrews 13:20*

¹⁴Here on earth we do not have a city that lasts forever. But we are looking for the city that we will have in the future. ¹⁵So through Jesus let us always offer our sacrifice to God. This sacrifice is our praise, coming from lips that speak his name. ¹⁶Do not forget to do good to others. And share with them what you have. These are the sacrifices that please God.

¹⁷Obey your leaders and be under their authority. These men are watching you because they are responsible for your souls. Obey them so that they will do this work with joy, not sadness. It will not help you to make their work hard.

¹⁸Continue praying for us. We feel sure about what we are doing, because we always want to do the right thing. ¹⁹And I beg you to pray that God will send me back to you soon.

²⁰⁻²¹I pray that the God of peace will give you every good thing you need so that you can do what he wants. God is the One who raised from death our Lord Jesus, the Great Shepherd of the sheep. God raised him because of the blood of his death. His blood began the agreement that God made with his people. And this agreement is eternal. I pray that God, through Christ, will do in us what pleases him. And to Jesus Christ be glory forever and ever. Amen.

²²My brothers, I beg you to listen patiently to this message I have written to encourage you. This letter is not very long. ²³I want you to know that our brother Timothy has been let out of prison. If he arrives soon, we will both come to see you.

²⁴Greet all your leaders and all of God's people. Those from Italy send greetings to you.

²⁵God's grace be with you all.

## Going Global

### New Tribes Mission

New Tribes Mission coordinates missionaries, sent by local churches, to take the gospel to tribal people. (Of the earth's 7,000 ethnic groups, 3,000 are still unreached.) NTM missionaries are planting tribal churches in 18 countries. NTM not only wins new believers, they also translate the Scriptures and train teachers and leaders, who in turn reach out to their own people and to neighboring tribes.

Discover how fun and easy it is to be part of God's plan to take the gospel to every tribe, language, people, and nation. Also check out the great stories and games in "Kidstuff" at the New Tribes Mission's website—www.ntm.org.

## DECODE THIS!

Hebrews instructs us to keep on _____ each other as brothers and sisters.

Key verse:
"If someone says he has faith, but does nothing, his faith is worth nothing" (2:14).

# THE LETTER OF JAMES

One of the oldest books in the New Testament

This letter was sent to Hebrew Christians living outside of Palestine.

Which one of the 4 James in the New Testament is the author?

The "How to Live as a Christian" Guidebook

# LIVIN' IT!

## HAPPY TRIALS
### JAMES 1:2

The first time you read it, you might think it was a mistake. James says that when we have troubles (not if, but when), we should be happy! How can breaking your arm, being made fun of at school, or even losing someone you love be something to be happy about?

Nothing can happen to us that God doesn't allow. And because God is good and he loves us, we know that he is using something bad to make our hearts and lives more beautiful.

In fact, we could never become everything God wants us to be without experiencing pain and disappointment. Even though we know it's coming, we also know we can have joy at the same time because we know God hasn't forgotten us, and he's busy at work in us changing our hearts to become more like his.

**1** From James, a servant of God and of the Lord Jesus Christ. To all of God's people who are scattered everywhere in the world:

Greetings.

## FAITH AND WISDOM

²My brothers, you will have many kinds of troubles. But when these things happen, you should be very happy. ³You know that these things are testing your faith. And this will give you patience. ⁴Let your patience show itself perfectly in what you do. Then you will be perfect and complete. You will have

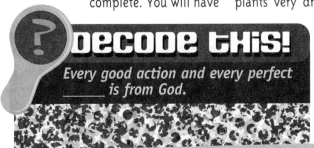

## DECODE THIS!

*Every good action and every perfect _____ is from God.*

everything you need. ⁵But if any of you needs wisdom, you should ask God for it. God is generous. He enjoys giving to all people, so God will give you wisdom. ⁶But when you ask God, you must believe. Do not doubt God. Anyone who doubts is like a wave in the sea. The wind blows the wave up and down. ⁷⁻⁸He who doubts is thinking two different things at the same time. He cannot decide about anything he does. A person like that should not think that he will receive anything from the Lord.

## TRUE RICHES

⁹If a believer is poor, he should be proud because God has made him spiritually rich. ¹⁰If he is rich, he should be proud because God has shown him that he is spiritually poor. The rich person will die like a wild flower in the grass. ¹¹The sun rises and becomes hotter and hotter. The heat makes the plants very dry, and the flower falls off. The flower was beautiful, but now it is dead. It is the same with a rich person. While he is still taking care of his business, he will die.

## TEMPTATION IS NOT FROM GOD

¹²When a person is tempted and still continues strong, he should be happy. After he has proved his faith, God will reward him with life forever. God promised this to all people who love him. ¹³When someone is being tempted, he should not say, "God is tempting me." Evil cannot tempt God, and God himself does not tempt anyone. ¹⁴It is the evil that a person wants that tempts him. His own evil desire leads him away and holds him. ¹⁵This desire causes sin. Then the sin grows and brings death.

## THE SMART START
### JAMES 1:5

Your best friend seems to be turning away from God, and you don't know what to do about it. Your parents are arguing, and you are afraid they'll get divorced. Your brothers and sisters keep fighting with you, and you don't know how to stop it. . . .

All through life we come upon times when we just don't know what we should do. God loves it when we finally understand that we can't control our lives and we turn to him for help. He is in control of everything, and he promises to give us wisdom to understand him and his ways when we ask.

The next time you find yourself wondering what to do, stop whatever you're doing and ask God for wisdom. Search through the Bible to see what he says. And remember that God who has promised to answer your prayer will do what he says.

¹⁶My dear brothers, do not be fooled about this. ¹⁷Every good action and every perfect gift is from God. These good gifts come down from the Creator of the sun, moon, and stars. God does not change like their shifting shadows. ¹⁸God decided to give us life through the word of truth. He wanted us to be the most important of all the things he made.

# GET CONNECTED

## TONGUE-TIED

Sometimes it seems like we just can't help it. Before we even know it, we've opened our mouths and said words that were hurtful or disrespectful, gossiping or complaining. On one hand we love Jesus and tell him so, and then the next minute we're talking badly about others behind their backs.

God says we shouldn't be this way. He warns us that our tongues can really get us into trouble, so we have to work hard to keep them under control. We need to practice the art of keeping our mouths shut. Ask God to change your heart so you only speak the words he wants you to speak.

## LISTENING AND OBEYING

[19] My dear brothers, always be willing to listen and slow to speak. Do not become angry easily. [20] Anger will not help you live a good life as God wants. [21] So put out of your life every evil thing and every kind of wrong you do. Don't be proud but accept God's teaching that is planted in your hearts. This teaching can save your souls.

[22] Do what God's teaching says; do not just listen and do nothing. When you only sit and listen, you are fooling yourselves. [23] A person who hears God's teaching and does nothing is like a man looking in a mirror. [24] He sees his face, then goes away and quickly forgets what he looked like. [25] But the truly happy person is the one who carefully studies God's perfect law that makes people free. He continues to study it. He listens to God's teaching and does not forget what he heard. Then he obeys what God's teaching says. When he does this, it makes him happy.

## THE TRUE WAY TO WORSHIP GOD

[26] A person might think he is religious. But if he says things he should not say, then he is just fooling himself. His "religion" is worth nothing.

[27] Religion that God accepts is this: caring for orphans or widows who need help; and keeping yourself free from the world's evil influence. This is the kind of religion that God accepts as pure and good.

## LOVE ALL PEOPLE

**2** My dear brothers, you are believers in our glorious Lord Jesus Christ. So never think that some people are more important than others. [2] Suppose someone comes into your church meeting wearing very nice clothes and a gold ring. At the same time a poor man comes in wearing old, dirty clothes. [3] You show special attention to the one wearing nice clothes. You say, "Please, sit here in this good seat." But you say to the poor man, "Stand over there," or "Sit on the floor by my feet!" [4] What are you doing? You are making some people more important than others. With evil thoughts you are deciding which person is better.

[5] Listen, my dear brothers! God chose the poor in the world to be rich with faith. He chose them to receive the kingdom God promised to people who love him. [6] But you show no respect to the poor man. And you know that it is the rich who are always trying to control your lives. And they are the ones who take you to court. [7] They are the ones who say bad things against Jesus, who owns you.

[8] One law rules over all other laws. This royal law is found in the Scriptures:[d] "Love your neighbor as you love yourself."[n] If you obey this law, then you are doing right. [9] But if you are treating one person as if he were more important than another, then you are sinning. That royal law proves that you are guilty of breaking God's law. [10] A person might follow all of God's law. But if he fails to obey even one command, he is guilty of breaking all the commands in that law. [11] God said, "You

# LIVIN' IT!

## DOWN TO THE WIRE
### JAMES 2:18

Once there was a man who became famous for his incredible tight-rope-walking stunts across Niagara Falls. Before he began, he asked the crowd if they thought he could make it across. "Sure you can," they shouted. When the crowds saw that he made it, they all cheered. He asked them, "Do you think I can do it carrying another person on my back?" "Of course!" they answered. Then he looked at one man who had answered yes. "So, will you get on my back?" Everyone got quiet. No one wanted to get on.

The story of the tight-rope walker is like our faith. We can say that we believe in Jesus. We can say that he is the King. But until we give him our lives and really do what he's taught us, it's not true faith. Ask God to help you show your faith by how you live.

# DECODE THIS!

What part of your body is compared to a wild animal or fire, wild and untamable?

2:8 "Love . . . yourself." Quotation from Leviticus 19:18.

# Going Global
## Overseas Missionary Fellowship

The middle-aged Chinese man told Hudson Taylor (a missionary from England) that, before accepting Christ as his Savior, he had studied Confucianism, Buddhism, and Taoism. He asked how long the gospel had been known in England. When he was told it had been known for hundreds of years, the man was shocked. "What! For hundreds of years you have had these glad tidings, and only now have come to preach it to us? My father sought after the truth for more than 20 years, and died without finding it. Oh, why did you not come sooner?"

Hudson Taylor founded China Inland Mission in 1865. It is now called Overseas Missionary Fellowship. OMF is a global network of Christians serving throughout East Asia (the world's most unreached continent) in a variety of ministries, including witnessing, starting new churches, teaching English, and training Asian churches to reach out to others.

Interested in being a light to the Buddhist world? Want to learn more about OMF? Find out at www.onebillionwait.org.

must not be guilty of adultery."[dn] The same God also said, "You must not murder anyone."[n] So if you do not take part in adultery, but you murder someone, then you are guilty of breaking all of God's law. [12]You will be judged by the law that makes people free. You should remember this in everything you say and do. [13]Yes, you must show mercy to others, or God will not show mercy to you when he judges you. But the person who shows mercy can stand without fear when he is judged.

## FAITH AND GOOD WORKS

[14]My brothers, if someone says he has faith, but does nothing, his faith is worth nothing. Can faith like that save him? [15]A brother or sister in Christ might need clothes or might need food. [16]And you say to him, "God be with you! I hope you stay warm and get plenty to eat." You say this, but you do not give that person the things he needs. Unless you help him, your words are worth nothing. [17]It is the same with faith. If faith does noth-ing, then that faith is dead, because it is alone.

[18]Someone might say, "You have faith, but I do things. Show me your faith! Your faith does nothing. I will show you my faith by the things I do." [19]You believe there is one God. Good! But the demons[d] believe that, too! And they shake with fear.

[20]You foolish person! Must you be shown that faith that does nothing is worth nothing? [21]Abraham is our father. He was made right with God by the things he did. He offered his son Isaac to God on the altar. [22]So you see that Abraham's faith and the things he did worked together. His faith was made perfect by what he did. [23]This shows the full meaning of the Scripture[d] that says: "Abraham believed God, and God accepted Abraham's faith, and that faith made him right with God."[n] And Abraham was called "God's friend."[n] [24]So you see that a person is made right with God by the things he does. He cannot be made right by faith only.

[25]Another example is Rahab, who was a prostitute.[d] But she was made right with God by something she did: She helped the spies for God's

2:11 "You . . . adultery." Quotation from Exodus 20:14 and Deuteronomy 5:18. 2:11 "You . . . anyone." Quotation from Exodus 20:13 and Deuteronomy 5:17. 2:23 "Abraham . . . God." Quotation from Genesis 15:6. 2:23 "God's friend." These words about Abraham are found in 2 Chronicles 20:7 and Isaiah 41:8.

# REAL SUPER HEROES

# THE KID

Imagine walking for a long way in the hot sun, then standing with thousands of other people to hear Jesus speak all day long. Your stomach is growling, and you remember the lunch your mother packed: 5 small loaves of bread and 2 fish. Nobody else has any food. And then someone shouts, "Does anybody have any food they can give to Jesus?"

Gulp. Would you give your only food away, or secretly keep it for yourself?

This special boy handed it over—all that he had. But in the hands of the Master, his small lunch multiplied and fed the entire crowd around him. It was a small step of faith for the boy, but it had huge results, feeding thousands of stomachs and souls at the same time.

No gift is too small for God. Trust that he will provide for you, and discover the joy of giving.

people. She welcomed them into her home and helped them escape by a different road.

²⁶A person's body that does not have a spirit is dead. It is the same with faith. Faith that does nothing is dead!

## CONTROLLING THE THINGS WE SAY

**3** My brothers, not many of you should become teachers. You know that we who teach will be judged more strictly than others. ²We all make many mistakes. If there were a person who never said anything wrong, he would be perfect. He would be able to control his whole body, too. ³We put bits into the mouths of horses to make them obey us. We can control their whole bodies. ⁴It is the same with ships. A ship is very big, and it is pushed by strong winds. But a very small rudder controls that big ship. The man who controls the rudder decides where the ship will go. The ship goes where the man wants. ⁵It is the same with the tongue. It is a small part of the body, but it brags about doing great things.

A big forest fire can be started with only a little flame. ⁶And the tongue is like a fire. It is a whole world of evil among the parts of our bodies. The tongue spreads its evil through the whole body. It starts a fire that influences all of life. The tongue gets this

fire from hell. ⁷People can tame every kind of wild animal, bird, reptile, and fish, and they have tamed them. ⁸But no one can tame the tongue. It is wild and evil. It is full of poison that can kill. ⁹We use our tongues to praise our Lord and Father, but then we curse people. And God made them like him-

# 10 TOP TEN

## Favorite Ways to Study for Tests

1. With a group of friends
2. Alone in the quiet
3. While eating a bowl of ice cream
4. Right before the test
5. By rewriting your notes
6. By practicing with your parents
7. By using the computer
8. On the sofa with the TV on
9. By rereading the chapter while snuggled up in bed
10. By making up your own practice test

self. ¹⁰Praises and curses come from the same mouth! My brothers, this should not happen. ¹¹Do good and bad water flow from the same spring? ¹²My brothers, can a fig tree make olives? Can a grapevine make figs? No! And a well full of salty water cannot give good water.

## TRUE WISDOM

¹³Is there anyone among you who is truly wise and under-

standing? Then he should show his wisdom by living right. He should do good things without being proud. A wise person does not brag. ¹⁴But if you are selfish and have bitter jealousy in your hearts, you have no reason to brag. Your bragging is a lie that hides the truth. ¹⁵That kind of "wisdom" does not come from God. That "wisdom" comes from the world. It is not spiritual. It is from the devil. ¹⁶Where there is jealousy and self-ishness, there will be confusion and every kind of evil. ¹⁷But the wisdom that comes from God is like this: First, it is pure. Then it is also peaceful, gentle, and easy to please. This wisdom is always ready to help those who are troubled and to do good for others. This wisdom is always fair and honest. ¹⁸When people work for peace in a peaceful way, they receive the good result of their right-living.

## GIVE YOURSELVES TO GOD

**4** Do you know where your fights and arguments come from? They come from the selfish desires that make war inside you. ²You want things, but you do not have them. So you are ready to kill and are jealous of other people. But you still cannot get what you want. So you argue and fight. You do not get what you want because you do not ask God. ³Or when you ask, you do not receive because the reason you ask is wrong. You want things only so that you can use them for your own pleasures.

⁴So, you people are not loyal to God! You should know that loving the world is the same as hating God. So if a per-

> **"Brothers, do not say bad things about each other."**
> *James 4:11*

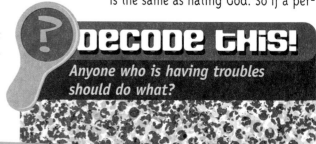

## DECODE THIS!
*Anyone who is having troubles should do what?*

# Gotta Know!

## Why is there war and terrorists who want power?

Check out James 4. The Bible clearly says that we fight each other—in big ways like wars, and smaller ways, like with our siblings—because we want what we do not have. Our desire for those things—whether it's more land, power, glory, or just wanting to be right—drives us to fight whatever or whomever gets in our way.

Other times, we must defend ourselves from what other people want to take from us. Basically, the need for war comes from the result of sin. To experience true peace, we must become satisfied in Jesus and desire only him.

son wants to be a friend of the world, he makes himself God's enemy. ⁵Do you think the Scripture[d] means nothing? It says, "The Spirit[d] that God made to live in us wants us for himself alone."[n] ⁶But God gives us even more grace, as the Scripture says,

"God is against the proud,
but he gives grace to the
humble." *Proverbs 3:34*

⁷So give yourselves to God. Stand against the devil, and the devil will run away from you. ⁸Come near to God, and God will come near to you. You are sinners. So clean sin out of your lives. You are trying to follow God and the world at the same time. Make your thinking pure. ⁹Be sad, cry, and weep! Change your laughter into crying. Change your joy into sadness. ¹⁰Don't be too proud before the Lord, and he will make you great.

### YOU ARE NOT THE JUDGE

¹¹Brothers, do not say bad things about each other. If you say bad things about your brother in Christ or judge him, then you are saying bad things about the law he follows. You are also judging the law he follows. And when you are judging the law, you are not a follower of the law. You have become a judge! ¹²God is the only One who makes laws, and he is the only Judge. He is the only One who can save and destroy. So it is not right for you to judge your neighbor.

### LET GOD PLAN YOUR LIFE

¹³Some of you say, "Today or tomorrow we will go to some city. We will stay there a year, do business, and make money." ¹⁴But you do not know what will happen tomorrow! Your life is like a mist. You can see it for a short time, but then it goes away. ¹⁵So you should say, "If the Lord wants, we will live and do this or that." ¹⁶But now you are proud and you brag. All of this bragging is wrong. ¹⁷And when a person knows the right thing to do, but does not do it, then he is sinning.

### A WARNING TO THE RICH

5 You rich people, listen! Cry and be very sad because of the trouble that will come to you. ²Your riches will rot, and your clothes will be eaten by moths. ³Your gold and silver will rust, and rust will be a proof that you were wrong. It will eat your bodies like fire. You saved your treasure for the last days. ⁴Men worked in your fields, but you did not pay them. They harvested your crops and are crying out against you. Now the Lord of heaven's armies has heard their cries. ⁵Your life on earth was full of rich living. You pleased yourselves with everything you wanted. You made yourselves fat, like an animal ready to be killed. ⁶You showed no mercy to the innocent man. You murdered him. He cannot stand against you.

### BE PATIENT

⁷Brothers, be patient until the Lord comes again. A farmer is patient. He

# GET CONNECTED

## PRAYER PARTNERS

Want to know what real friendship looks like? Read James 5:16. God gives us other Christians in our lives for a reason. A lot of times we think that we need to look spiritual in order to impress them, but when we are fake, we miss the blessing God wants to give us through our friends.

Instead, we need to be honest with each other, especially those we trust. We should confess our sins to them, and ask them to pray for us to help us. In turn, we can pray for our friends or parents that they will stay close to God, too. When we depend upon each other to help us seek God, our friendships grow deep and strong—not only with each other, but also with God.

4:5 "The Spirit . . . alone." These words may be from Exodus 20:5.

waits for his valuable crop to grow from the earth. He waits patiently for it to receive the first rain and the last rain. [8]You, too, must be patient. Do not give up hope. The Lord is coming soon. [9]Brothers, do not complain against each other. If you do

## BiBLe BasiCS

### what is temptation?

You know that feeling you get when your mom puts that plate of cookies on the counter but says you can't have any until after dinner? If only you could just sneak one bite. . . . That's temptation—the urge to do something you know you shouldn't. Temptation isn't a sin, but if you keep thinking about it and end up giving in to it, you have sinned. God says that he gives us the ability to overcome any temptation if we will turn to him and ask for help.

not stop complaining, you will be judged guilty. And the Judge is ready to come! [10]Brothers, follow the example of the prophets[d] who spoke for the Lord. They suffered many hard things, but they were patient. [11]We say they are happy because they were able to do this. You have heard about Job's patience. You know that after all his trouble, the Lord helped him. This shows that the Lord is full of mercy and is kind.

### BE CAREFUL WHAT YOU SAY

[12]My brothers, it is very important that you not use an oath when you make a promise. Don't use the name of heaven, earth, or anything else to prove what you say. When you mean yes, say only "yes." When you mean no, say only "no." Do this so that you will not be judged guilty.

### THE POWER OF PRAYER

[13]If one of you is having troubles, he should pray. If one of you is happy, he should sing praises. [14]If one of you is sick, he should call the church's elders.[d] The elders should pour oil on him[n] in the name of the Lord and pray for him. [15]And the prayer that is said with faith will make the sick person well. The Lord will heal him. And if he has sinned, God will forgive him. [16]Confess your sins to each other and pray for each other. Do this so that God can heal you. When a good man prays, great things happen. [17]Elijah was a man just like us. He prayed that it would not rain. And it did not rain on the land for three and a half years! [18]Then Elijah prayed again. And the rain came down from the sky, and the land grew crops again.

## KIDS SPEAK UP!

Q. What do you think animals dream about?

A. Eating

### SAVING A SOUL

[19]My brothers, one of you may wander away from the truth. And someone may help him come back. [20]Remember this: Anyone who brings a sinner back from the wrong way will save that sinner's soul from death. By doing this, that person will cause many sins to be forgiven.

## WILD WORLD FACTS

### BLOW ME OVER

Did you know that James 1:6 gives you a little science lesson? James tells us that when we doubt (or don't believe) that God can do something that we ask of him, we are like waves of the ocean, blown and tossed by the wind.

Have you ever watched the waves at the beach? It seems like some machine must be turned on in the ocean, keeping them coming, wave after wave. But really, it's the wind. Even deep in the ocean, the wind across the surface of the waters creates ripples. How far and long the wind blows determines the size of the waves. As the wind makes the water rise, gravity pulls it back down—only with momentum. The water pressure from the ocean pushes it back up, creating waves that last all the way until they break on the shore.

[Office of Naval Research]

 **5:14 pour oil on him** Oil was used like medicine, so that is probably how the believers used it.

Nero falsely charged Christians for starting a fire in May, A.D. 64.

The fire totally destroyed a great part of Rome.

The letter was to be read by Jewish believers living in present-day Turkey.

# THE FIRST LETTER OF

# PETER

Written from Rome during Emperor Nero's reign.

Peter wants believers to overcome worry and bitterness with confidence in God.

Encouragement for suffering Christians.

**1** From Peter, an apostle[d] of Jesus Christ.

To God's chosen people who are away from their homes. You are scattered all around the countries of Pontus, Galatia, Cappadocia, Asia, and Bithynia. [2]God planned long ago to choose you by making you his holy people. Making you holy is the Spirit's[d] work. God wanted you to obey him and to be made clean by the blood of the death of Jesus Christ. Grace and peace be yours more and more.

## A LIVING HOPE

[3]Praise be to the God and Father of our Lord Jesus Christ. God has great mercy, and because of his mercy he gave us a new life. He gave us a living hope because Jesus Christ rose from death. [4]Now we hope for the blessings God has for his children. These blessings are kept for you in heaven. They cannot be destroyed or be spoiled or lose their beauty. [5]God's power protects you through your faith, and it keeps you safe until your salvation comes. That salvation is ready to be given to you at the end of time. [6]This makes you very happy. But now for a short time different kinds of troubles may make you sad. [7]These troubles come to prove that your faith is pure. This purity of faith is worth more than gold. Gold can be proved to be pure by fire, but gold will ruin. But the purity of your faith will bring you praise and glory and honor when Jesus Christ comes again. [8]You have not seen Christ, but still you love him. You cannot see him now, but you believe in him. You are filled with a joy that cannot be explained. And that joy is full of glory. [9]Your faith has a goal, to save your souls. And you are receiving that goal—your salvation.

[10]The prophets[d] searched carefully and tried to learn about this salvation. They spoke about the grace that was coming to you. [11]The Spirit[d] of Christ was in the prophets. And the Spirit was telling about the sufferings that would happen to Christ and about the glory that would come after those sufferings. The prophets tried to learn about what the Spirit was showing them. They tried to learn when those things would happen and what the world would be like at that time. [12]It was shown to them that their service was not for themselves. It was for you. They were serving you when they told about the truths you have now heard. The men who preached the Good News[d] to you told you those things. They did it with the help of the Holy Spirit that was sent from heaven. These are truths that even the angels want very much to know about.

## A CALL TO HOLY LIVING

[13]So prepare your minds for service and have self-control. All your hope should be for the gift of grace that will be yours when Jesus Christ comes again. [14]In the past you did not understand, so you did the evil things you wanted. But now you are children of God who obey. So do not live as you lived in the past. [15]But be holy in all that you do, just as God is holy. God is the One who called you. [16]It is written in the Scriptures:[d] "You must be holy, because I am holy."[n]

## BIBLE BASICS

### WHAT DOES IT MEAN TO BE BORN AGAIN?

When we are born, our bodies are alive (our minds, wills, and emotions), but our spirits—the part of us that connects us with God—are dead. When we receive Jesus into our lives and trust him as our Savior, he raises our spirits from the dead. He makes our spirits alive again so we can be friends with his Spirit. To be born again simply means to have "new birth" or "new life." Through God's work, our spirits are actually born again, and we become new people on the inside.

[17]You pray to God and call him Father. And this Father judges each man's work equally. So while you are here on earth, you should live with respect for God. [18]You know that in the past you were living in a worthless way. You got that way of living from the people who lived before you. But you were saved from that useless life. You were bought, but not with something that ruins like gold or silver. [19]You were bought with the precious blood of the death of Christ, who was like a pure and perfect lamb. [20]Christ was chosen before the world was made. But he was shown to the world in these last times for you. [21]You believe in God through Christ. God raised Christ from death and gave him glory. So your faith and your hope are in God.

[22]Now you have made yourselves pure by obeying the truth. Now you can have true love for your brothers. So love each other deeply with all your heart. [23]You have been born again. This new life did not come from something that dies, but

## DECODE THIS!

*The purity of faith is worth more than what?*

 1:16 "You must be . . . holy." Quotation from Leviticus 11:45; 19:2; 20:7.

from something that cannot die. You were born again through God's living message that continues forever. [24]The Scripture says,

"All people are like the grass.
And all their strength is like the flowers of the field.
The grass dies and the flowers fall.
[25]But the word of the Lord will live forever."

*Isaiah 40:6-8*

And this is the word that was preached to you.

## JESUS IS THE LIVING STONE

**2** So then, get rid of all evil and all lying. Do not be a hypocrite.[d] Do not be jealous or speak evil of others. Put all these things out of your life. [2]As newborn babies want milk, you should want the pure and simple teaching. By it you can grow up and be saved. [3]For you have already examined and seen how good the Lord is.

[4]The Lord Jesus is the "stone"[n] that lives. The people of the world did not want this stone. But he was the stone God chose. To God he was worth much. So come to him. [5]You also are like living stones. Let yourselves be used to build a spiritual temple—to be holy priests who offer spiritual sacrifices to God. He will accept those sacrifices through Jesus Christ. [6]The Scripture[d] says:

"I will put a stone in the ground in Jerusalem.
Everything will be built on this important and precious rock.
Anyone who trusts in him will never be disappointed."

*Isaiah 28:16*

[7]This stone is worth much to you who believe. But to the people who do not believe, he is

"the stone that the builders did not want.
It has become the cornerstone."[d]

*Psalm 118:22*

[8]To people who do not believe, he is

"a stone that causes people to stumble.
It is a rock that makes them fall."

*Isaiah 8:14*

They stumble because they do not obey what God says. This is what God planned to happen to them.

[9]But you are chosen people. You are the King's priests. You are a holy nation. You are a nation that belongs to God alone. God chose you to tell about the wonderful things he has done. He called you out of darkness into his wonderful light. [10]At one time you were not God's people. But now you are his people. In the past you had never received mercy. But now you have received God's mercy.

## LIVE FOR GOD

[11]Dear friends, you are like visitors and strangers in this world. So I beg you to stay away from the evil things your bodies want to do. These things fight against your soul. [12]People who do not believe are living all around you. They might say that you are doing wrong. So live good lives. Then they

will see the good things you do, and they will give glory to God on the day when Christ comes again.

## OBEY EVERY HUMAN AUTHORITY

[13]Obey the people who have authority in this world. Do this for the Lord. Obey the king, who is the highest authority.

**WILD WORLD FACTS**

### SCARRED FOR LIFE

Have you ever scraped your leg? The wound didn't last forever, did it? That's because our bodies are wired by God to respond to cuts in a special way. When our skin is injured, our body sends tough, white protein fibers called collagen to the site. Collagen reconnects the torn tissue, while a scab forms over the top to protect it from further damage. Once the skin has healed, the scab falls off. Many times, the new skin is a shiny pink or gray color—what we call scars. Some people are more likely to get scars than others.

Thomas refused to believe that Jesus had risen from the dead until he put his hands on Jesus' wounds and felt his scars. Jesus did appear to Thomas and let him feel his scars so that he—and we—would believe that Jesus lives.

[Yahooligans: Ask Earl]

 2:4 **"stone"** The most important stone in God's spiritual temple or house (his people).

# FOOTWEAR

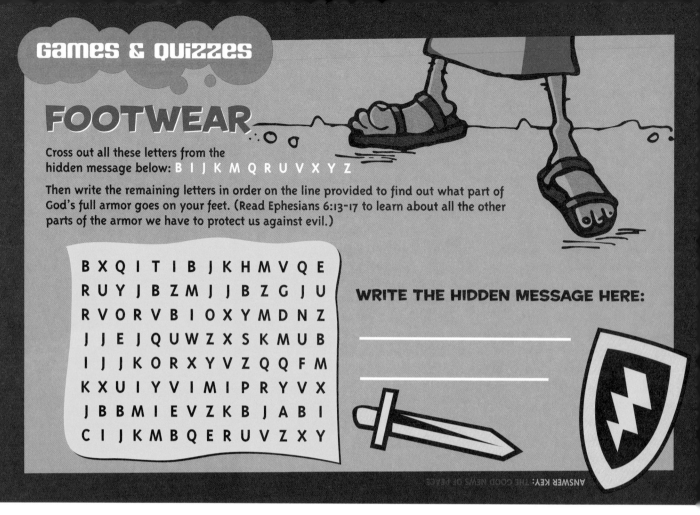

Cross out all these letters from the hidden message below: B I J K M Q R U V X Y Z

Then write the remaining letters in order on the line provided to find out what part of God's full armor goes on your feet. (Read Ephesians 6:13-17 to learn about all the other parts of the armor we have to protect us against evil.)

```
B X Q I T I B J K H M V Q E
R U Y J B Z M J J B Z G J U
R V O R V B I O X Y M D N Z
J J E J Q U W Z X S K M U B
I J J K O R X Y V Z Q Q F M
K X U I Y V I M I P R Y V X
J B B M I E V Z K B J A B I
C I J K M B Q E R U V Z X Y
```

**WRITE THE HIDDEN MESSAGE HERE:**

_____

_____

ANSWER KEY: THE GOOD NEWS OF PEACE

[14]And obey the leaders who are sent by the king. They are sent to punish those who do wrong and to praise those who do right. [15]So when you do good, you stop foolish people from saying stupid things about you. This is what God wants. [16]Live as free men. But do not use your freedom as an excuse to do evil. Live as servants of God. [17]Show respect for all people. Love the brothers and sisters of God's family. Respect God. Honor the king.

> **"Obey the people who have authority in this world."**
>
> 1 Peter 2:13

## FOLLOW CHRIST'S EXAMPLE

[18]Slaves, accept the authority of your masters. Do this with all respect. You should obey masters who are good and kind, and you should obey masters who are bad. [19]A person might have to suffer even when he has done nothing wrong. But if he thinks of God and bears the pain, this pleases God. [20]If you are punished for doing wrong, there is no reason to praise you for bearing punishment. But if you suffer for doing good, and you are patient, then that pleases God. [21]That is what you were called to do. Christ suffered for you. He gave you an example to follow. So you should do as he did.

[22]"He did no sin.
    He never lied." Isaiah 53:9

[23]People insulted Christ, but he did not insult them in return. Christ suffered, but he did not threaten. He let God take care of him. God is the One who judges rightly. [24]Christ carried our sins in his body on the cross. He did this so that we would stop living for sin and start living for what is right. And we are healed because of his wounds. [25]You were like sheep that went the wrong way. But now you have come back to the Shepherd and Protector of your souls.

## WIVES AND HUSBANDS

**3** In the same way, you wives should accept the authority of your husbands. Then, if some husbands have not obeyed God's teaching, they will be persuaded to believe. You will not need to say a word to them. They will be persuaded by the way their wives live.

# LIVIN' IT!

## TRUE BEAUTY
### 1 PETER 3:3-4

Did you know that every group of people around the world has their own ideas about what a beautiful person looks like? Here in America, magazines and TV shows would have us think that young, skinny women and well-built guys are beautiful. Other cultures prefer women to be softer, rounder; some with more make-up, some with less.

So what is beautiful? To God, real beauty is the way you look on the inside. He sees the person who loves him and wants to obey as someone much more gorgeous than the most famous celebrity. A gentle and quiet spirit might not make the headline news here on earth, but it is a cause for celebration in heaven. So don't worry about what you see in the mirror. Instead, ask God to show you what's in your heart. Ask him to make you into a beautiful child of God.

called him her master. And you women are true children of Sarah if you always do what is right and are not afraid.

[7]In the same way, you husbands should live with your wives in an understanding way. You should show respect to them. They are weaker than you. But God gives them the same blessing that he gives you—the grace that gives true life. Do this so that nothing will stop your prayers.

## SUFFERING FOR DOING RIGHT

[8]Finally, all of you should live together in peace. Try to understand each other. Love each other as brothers. Be kind and humble. [9]Do not do wrong to a person to pay him back for doing wrong to you. Or do not insult someone to pay him back for insulting

ing to do good, no one can really hurt you. [14]But you may suffer for doing right. Even if that happens, you are blessed.

"Don't be afraid of the things they fear.
Do not dread those things.
[15]But respect Christ as the holy Lord in your hearts." *Isaiah 8:12-13*

Always be ready to answer everyone who asks you to explain about the hope you have. [16]But answer in a gentle way and with respect. Always feel that you are doing right. Then, those who speak evil of your good life in Christ will be made ashamed. [17]It is better to suffer for doing good than for doing wrong. Yes, it is better, if that is what God wants. [18]Christ himself died for you. And that one death paid for your sins. He was not guilty, but he died for those who are

## "it is not fancy hair, gold jewelry, or fine clothes that should make you beautiful." *1 Peter 3:3*

[2]Your husbands will see the pure lives that you live with your respect for God. [3]It is not fancy hair, gold jewelry, or fine clothes that should make you beautiful. [4]No, your beauty should come from within you—the beauty of a gentle and quiet spirit. This beauty will never disappear, and it is worth very much to God. [5]It was the same with the holy women who lived long ago and followed God. They made themselves beautiful in this way. They accepted the authority of their husbands. [6]Sarah obeyed Abraham, her husband, and

you. But ask God to bless that person. Do this, because you yourselves were called to receive a blessing. [10]The Scripture[d] says,

"A person must do these things
to enjoy life and have many, happy days.
He must not say evil things.
He must not tell lies.
"He must stop doing evil and do good.
He must look for peace and work for it.
[12]The Lord sees the good people.
He listens to their prayers.
But the Lord is against those who do evil."
*Psalm 34:12-16*
[13]If you are always try-

guilty. He did this to bring you all to God. His body was killed, but he was made alive in the spirit. [19]And in the spirit he went and preached to the spirits in prison. [20]These were the spirits who refused to obey God long ago in the time of Noah. God was waiting patiently for them while Noah was building the boat. Only a few people—eight in all—were saved by water. [21]That water is like baptism that now saves you—not the washing of dirt from the body, but the promise made to God from a good heart. And this is because Jesus Christ was raised from death. [22]Now Jesus has gone into heaven and is at God's right side. He rules over angels, authorities, and powers.

## DECODE THIS!

*In 1 Peter Jesus is compared to a _____ that lives.*

## CHANGED LIVES

**4** Christ suffered while he was in his body. So you should strengthen yourselves with the same way of thinking Christ had. The person who has suffered in his body is finished with sin. [2]Strengthen yourselves so that you will live your lives here on earth doing what God wants, not doing the evil things that people want. [3]In the past you wasted too much time doing what the non-believers like to do. You were guilty of sexual sins and had evil desires. You were getting drunk, you had wild and drunken parties, and you did wrong by worshiping idols. [4]Non-believers think it is strange that you do

> ### "Christ suffered while he was in his body." *1 Peter 4:1*

not do the many wild and wasteful things that they do. And so they insult you. [5]But they will have to explain about what they have done. They must explain to God who is ready to judge the living and the dead. [6]The Good News[d] was preached to those who are now dead. By their dying, they were judged like all men. But the Good News was preached

to them so that they could live in the spirit as God lives.

## USE GOD'S GIFTS WISELY

[7]The time is near when all things will end. So keep your minds clear, and control yourselves. Then you will be able to pray. [8]Most importantly, love each other deeply. Love has a way of not looking at others' sins. [9]Open your homes to each other, without complaining. [10]Each of you received a spiritual gift. God has shown you his grace in giving you different gifts. And you are like servants who are responsible for using God's gifts. So be good servants and use your gifts to serve each

other. [11]Anyone who speaks should speak words from God. The person who serves should serve with the strength that God gives. You should do these things so that in everything God will be praised through Jesus Christ. Power and glory belong to him forever and ever. Amen.

## SUFFERING AS A CHRISTIAN

[12]My friends, do not be surprised at the painful things you are now suffering. These things are testing your faith. So do not think that something strange is happening to you. [13]But you should be happy that you are sharing in Christ's

# REAL SUPER HEROES

# THE SAMARITAN WOMAN

Jews normally didn't have anything to do with Samaritans. But Jesus asked the Samaritan woman for some water. The surprised woman asked why he was willing to talk to her. Jesus then told her that he had living water that she could have, and it would keep her from being thirsty ever again. Confused at first, she thought he meant regular water. But after he revealed her many sins, she realized that he was more than just any man. Overjoyed, she ran home to tell everyone the good news. He was the Christ! And she became his first non-Jewish missionary.

The Samaritan woman had committed many bad sins, but Jesus still loved her enough to give her the Good News of salvation. We need to be like her, knowing that our sins are forgiven. And just like she ran back and told the whole town about Jesus, we need to share our faith with the same kind of thankfulness and joy.

sufferings. You will be happy and full of joy when Christ comes again in glory. [14]When people insult you because you follow Christ, then you are blessed. You are blessed because the glorious Spirit,[d]

## LIVIN' IT!

### DON'T FEED THE LIONS
### 1 PETER 5:8

Have you ever watched a program that showed how lions stalk their prey? They crouch down deep in the grass, hidden from view, watching for the weakest animals to wander behind the rest. Then, like a rushing wind, they leap from hiding and land on the poor, surprised animal.

God says that Satan is like a very hungry lion. He is actually watching, waiting to find the weakest part of a Christian's life. He wants to tear us apart, just when we're not expecting it. So we have to be on guard! Let Jesus help you in the areas of life where you are tempted to sin. Ask your parents to help you stay on track. When Satan attacks, you'll be ready for him and through God's Word you will stand firm in your faith.

the Spirit of God, is with you. [15]Do not suffer for murder, theft, or any other crime, nor because you trouble other people. [16]But if you suffer because you are a Christian, then do not be ashamed. You should praise God because you wear that name. [17]It is time for judgment to begin, and it will begin with God's family. If that judging begins with us, what will happen to those people who do not obey the Good News[d] of God? [18]"It is very hard for a good person to be saved.

Then the wicked person and
  the sinner will surely be lost!"[n]

[19]So then those who suffer as God wants them to should trust their souls to him. God is the One who made them, and they can trust him. So they should continue to do what is right.

## THE FLOCK OF GOD

5 Now I have something to say to the elders[d] in your group. I am also an elder. I myself have seen Christ's sufferings. And I will share in the glory that will be shown to us. I beg you to [2]take care of God's flock, his people, that you are responsible for. Watch over it because you want to, not because you are forced to do it. That is how God wants it. Do it because you are happy to serve, not because you want money. [3]Do not be like a ruler over people you are responsible for. Be good examples to them. [4]Then when Christ, the Head Shepherd, comes, you will get a crown. This crown will be glorious, and it will never lose its beauty.

[5]In the same way, younger men should be willing to be under older men. And all of you should be very humble with each other.

"God is against the proud,
  but he gives grace to the
    humble."      *Proverbs 3:34*

[6]So be humble under God's powerful hand. Then he will lift you up when the right time comes. [7]Give all your worries to him, because he cares for you.

[8]Control yourselves and be careful! The devil is your enemy. And he goes around like a roaring lion looking for someone to eat. [9]Refuse to give in to the devil. Stand strong in your faith. You know that your Christian brothers and sisters all over the world are having the same sufferings you have.

[10]Yes, you will suffer for a short time.

> "He will make you strong. He will support you and keep you from falling."      *1 Peter 5:10*

But after that, God will make everything right. He will make you strong. He will support you and keep you from falling. He is the God who gives all grace. He called you to share in his glory in Christ. That glory will continue forever. [11]All power is his forever and ever. Amen.

## FINAL GREETINGS

[12]I wrote this short letter with the help of Silas. I know that he is a faithful brother in Christ. I wrote to comfort and encourage you. I wanted to tell you that this is the true grace of God. Stand strong in that grace.

[13]The church in Babylon sends you greetings. They were chosen the same as you. Mark, my son in Christ, also greets you. [14]Give each other a kiss of Christian love when you meet.

Peace to all of you who are in Christ.

⭐ 4:18 "It . . . lost!" Quotation from Proverbs 11:31 in the Septuagint, the Greek version of the Old Testament.

## DECODE THIS!

*What causes many sins to be forgiven?*

Written by Peter just before his death (between A.D. 64 and A.D. 66).

# THE SECOND LETTER of PETER

Be on guard against false teachers!

Because Christians are blessed they should add goodness, knowledge, self-control, the ability to hold on, service for God, kindness, and love to their faith.

Never mind those who laugh at you . . . Jesus will come again!

**1** From Simon Peter, a servant and apostle[d] of Jesus Christ.

To you who have received a faith as valuable as ours. You received that faith because our God and Savior Jesus Christ is fair and does what is right. [2]Grace and peace be given to you more and more. You will have grace and peace because you truly know God and Jesus our Lord.

## GOD HAS GIVEN US BLESSINGS

[3]Jesus has the power of God. His power has given us everything we need to live and to serve God. We have these things because we know him. Jesus called us by his glory and goodness. [4]Through his glory and goodness, he gave us the very great and rich gifts he promised us. With those gifts you can share in being like God. And so the world will not ruin you with its evil desires.

[5]Because you have these blessings, you should try as much as you can to add these things to your lives: to your faith, add goodness; and to your goodness, add knowledge; [6]and to your knowledge, add self-control; and to your self-control, add the ability to hold on; and to your ability to hold on, add service for God; [7]and to your service for God, add kindness for your brothers and sisters in Christ; and to this kindness, add love. [8]If all these things are in you and are growing, they will help you never to be useless. They will help your knowledge of our Lord Jesus Christ make your lives better. [9]But if anyone does not have these things, he cannot see clearly. He is blind. He has forgotten that he was made clean from his past sins.

[10]My brothers, God called you and chose you to be his. Try hard to show that you really are God's chosen people. If you do all these things, you will never fall. [11]And you will be given a very great welcome into the kingdom of our Lord and Savior Jesus Christ. That kingdom continues forever.

[12]You know these things, and you are very strong in the truth. But I will always help you to remember these things. [13]I think it is right for me to help you remember while I am still living here on earth. [14]I know that I must soon leave this body. Our Lord Jesus Christ has shown me that. [15]I will try the best I can to help you remember these things always. I want you to be able to remember them even after I am gone.

## WE SAW CHRIST'S GLORY

[16]We have told you about the powerful coming of our Lord Jesus Christ. What we told you were not just smart stories that someone invented. But we saw the greatness of Jesus with our own eyes. [17]Jesus heard the voice of God, the Greatest Glory. That was when Jesus received honor and glory from God the Father. The voice said, "This is my Son, and I love him. I am very pleased with him." [18]We heard that voice. It came from heaven while we were with Jesus on the holy mountain.

[19]This makes us more sure about the message the prophets[d] gave. And it is good for you to follow closely what they said. Their message is like a light shining in a dark place. That light shines until the day begins and the morning star rises in your hearts. [20]Most of all, you must understand this: No prophecy in the Scriptures[d] ever comes from the prophet's own interpretation. [21]No prophecy ever came from what a man wanted to say. But men led by the Holy Spirit[d] spoke words from God.

## FALSE TEACHERS

**2** There used to be false prophets[d] among God's people, just as there are now. And you will have some false teachers in your group. They will secretly

> ### "My brothers, God called you and chose you to be his."
> 2 Peter 1:10

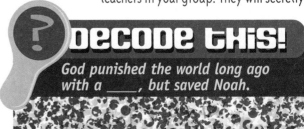

### ? DECODE THIS!

*God punished the world long ago with a _____, but saved Noah.*

## 10 TOP TEN

**Favorite Sundae Toppings**

1. Rainbow sprinkles
2. Banana split
3. Tons of whipped cream
4. Candied cherries
5. Magic Shell® chocolate coating
6. Marshmallows
7. Caramel syrup
8. M&M's®
9. Fresh fruit
10. Nuts

people with him. Noah was a man who preached about being right with God. [6]And God also punished the evil cities of Sodom and Gomorrah.[*] He burned those cities until there was nothing left but ashes. He made those cities an example to show what will happen to those who are against God. [7]But God saved Lot from those cities. Lot, a good man, was troubled because of the dirty lives of evil people. [8](Lot was a good man, but he lived with evil people every day. His good heart was hurt by the evil things that he saw and heard.) [9]And so the Lord knows how to save those who serve him. He will save them when troubles come. And the Lord will hold evil people and punish them, while waiting for the Judgment Day. [10]That punishment is especially for those who live by doing the evil things their sinful selves want, and for those who hate the Lord's authority.

These false teachers do anything they want and brag about it. They are not afraid to say bad things about the glorious angels. [11]The angels are much stronger and more powerful than false teachers. But even the angels do not accuse them with insults before the Lord. [12]But these men say bad things about what they do not understand. They are like animals that act without thinking. These animals are born to be caught and killed. And, like wild animals, these false teachers will be destroyed. [13]They have caused many people to suffer; so they themselves will suffer. That is their pay for what they have done. They take pleasure in doing evil things openly. So they are like dirty spots and stains among you. They bring shame to you in the meals that you eat together. [14]Every time they look at a woman they want her. Their desire for sin is never satisfied. They lead weak people into the trap of sin. They have taught their hearts to be selfish. God will punish them. [15]These false teachers left the right road and lost their way. They followed the way that Balaam went. Balaam was the son of Beor, who loved being paid for doing wrong. [16]But a donkey told Balaam that he was sinning. And the donkey is an animal that cannot talk. But the donkey spoke with a man's voice and stopped the prophet's crazy thinking.

[17]Those false teachers are like rivers that have no water. They are like clouds blown by a storm. A place in the blackest darkness has been kept for them. [18]They brag with words that mean nothing. By their evil desires they lead people into the trap of sin. They lead away people who are just beginning to escape from other people who live in error. [19]They promise them freedom, but they themselves are not free. They are slaves of things that will be destroyed. For a person is a slave of anything that controls him. [20]They were made free from the evil in the world by knowing our Lord and Savior Jesus Christ. But if they return to evil things and those things control them, then it is worse for them than it

> **"They were made free from the evil in the world by knowing our Lord and Savior Jesus Christ."**
>
> 2 Peter 2:20

teach things that are wrong—teachings that will cause people to be lost. They will even refuse to accept the Master, Jesus, who bought their freedom. And so they will quickly destroy themselves. [2]Many will follow their evil ways and say evil things about the Way of truth. [3]Those false teachers only want your money. So they will use you by telling you what is not true. But God has already judged them guilty. And they will not escape the One who will destroy them.

[4]When angels sinned, God did not let them go free without punishment. God sent them to hell and put them in caves of darkness. They are being held there to be judged. [5]And God punished the evil people who lived long ago. He brought a flood to the world that was full of people who were against him. But God saved Noah and seven other

 **2:6 Sodom and Gomorrah** Two cities God destroyed because the people were so evil.

was before. [21]Yes, it would be better for them to have never known the right way. That would be better than to know the right way and then to turn away from the holy teaching that was given to them. [22]What they did is like this true saying: "A dog eats what it throws up."[n] And, "After a pig is washed, it goes back and rolls in the mud."

### JESUS WILL COME AGAIN

**3** My friends, this is the second letter I have written to you. I wrote both letters to you to help your honest minds remember something. [2]I want you to remember the words that the holy prophets[d] spoke in the past. And remember the command that our Lord and Savior gave us through your apostles.[d] [3]It is important for you to understand what will happen in the last days. People will laugh at you. They will live doing the evil things they want to do. [4]They will say, "Jesus promised to come again. Where is he? Our fathers have died. But the world continues the way it has been since it was made." [5]But they do not want to remember what happened long ago. God spoke and made heaven and earth. He made the earth from water and with water. [6]Then the world was flooded and destroyed with water. [7]And that same word of God is keeping heaven and earth that we have now. They are being kept to be destroyed by fire. They are being kept for the Judgment Day and the destruction of all who are against God.

[8]But do not forget this one thing, dear friends: To the Lord one day is as a thousand years, and a thousand years is as one day. [9]The Lord is not slow in doing what he promised—the way some people understand slowness. But God is being patient with you. He does not want anyone to be lost. He wants everyone to change his heart and life.

[10]But the day the Lord comes again will be a surprise, like a thief. The skies will disappear with a loud noise. Everything in the skies will be destroyed by fire. And the earth and everything in it will be burned up.[n] "In that way everything will be destroyed. So what kind of people should you be? You should live holy lives and serve God. [12]You should wait for the day of God and look forward to its coming. When that day comes, the skies will be destroyed with fire, and everything in the skies will melt with heat. [13]But God made a promise to us. And we are waiting for what he promised—a new heaven and a new earth where goodness lives.

[14]Dear friends, we are waiting for this to happen. So try as hard as you can to be without sin and without fault. Try to be at peace with God. [15]Remember that we are saved because our Lord is patient. Our dear brother Paul told you the same thing when he wrote to you with the wisdom that God gave him. [16]Paul writes about this in all his letters. Sometimes there are things in Paul's letters that are hard to understand. And some people explain these things falsely. They are ignorant and weak in faith. They also falsely explain the other Scriptures.[d] But they are destroying themselves by doing that.

[17]Dear friends, you already know about this. So be careful. Do not let those evil people lead you away by the wrong they do. Be careful so that you will not fall from your strong faith. [18]But grow in the grace and knowledge of our Lord and Savior Jesus Christ. Glory be to him now and forever! Amen.

> **"After a pig is washed, it goes back and rolls in the mud."**
>
> *2 Peter 2:22*

## LIVIN' IT!

### THE HOLDUP
### 2 PETER 3:8

What's the worst part about a long trip? Wondering how long it's going to be until you get there!

Ever since Adam and Eve sinned in the garden, God promised that he would send a Savior. Jesus did come—a long time later—to pay the price for our sins. But that's not the end. Jesus promised to come back to earth again one day, to gather all of his people to himself.

Now, 2,000 years later, we're still waiting for Jesus to return. What's the holdup? God says what may seem like a long time to us is not a long time to him. He also says that he will wait until all of his chosen people turn to him before he will return. We don't know when Jesus is coming, but we do need to be ready. Live every day as if it is your last one before Jesus returns.

**DECODE THIS!**

*To the Lord, one day is as a _____ years.*

Written by John, one of the 12 apostles that knew Jesus.

# THE FIRST LETTER OF JOHN

Key verse: We love because God first loved us (4:19).

Probably written in Ephesus after he wrote the Gospel of John

John's message: Love One Another

**1** We write you now about something that has always existed.
We have heard.
We have seen with our own eyes.
We have watched,
and we have touched with our hands. We write to you about the Word[n] that gives life. [2]He who gives life was shown to us. We saw him, and we can give proof about it. And now we tell you that he has life that continues forever. The one who gives this life was with God the Father. God showed him to us. [3]Now we tell you what we have seen and heard because we want you to have fellowship with us. The fellowship we share together is with God the Father and his Son, Jesus Christ. [4]We write this to you so that you can be full of joy with us.

## THE POINT

Uh oh. You messed up again. Good thing you were using a pencil with an eraser. Suddenly, like magic, your wrong marks are erased. But how?

When you run your pencil over your paper, you are actually producing graphite particles. The rough fibers of the paper scrape the pencil lead, and the particles become entangled in the fibers just below the surface of the paper. The eraser is made of rubber, which is a material soft enough to scrub up the graphite from below the paper surface. It, too, gets scraped in the process, causing small pieces of rubber to roll up, with the graphite particles inside. Then you simply blow the mess all away and start over!

God says that when we sin, we can ask for forgiveness. He promises to erase our sins from our souls so that we can start over again.

## LIVIN' IT!

**LOVE IN ACTION**
**1 JOHN 2:3**

Look around you. Do your friends say that they are Christians? If so, do they act like it? Not just going to church, but day-to-day choosing to say and do the things that honor God and not themselves?

Now look at yourself. Would someone from outside your group of friends be able to look at your life and know that you belong to Jesus?

God makes it clear. He doesn't love us because we do the right things. He loved us when we were still sinners. But if we really do love him, then we will want to do what he says. We can't truly love God and feel comfortable ignoring his commands at the same time. Do you think you need to ask God for help to love him better? We all do—so ask him right now to change your heart and help you obey.

### GOD FORGIVES OUR SINS

[5]Here is the message we have heard from God and now tell to you: God is light,[n] and in him there is no darkness at all. [6]So if we say that we have fellowship with God, but we continue living in darkness, then we are liars. We do not follow the truth. [7]God is in the light. We should live in the light, too. If we live in the light, we share fellowship with each other. And when we live in the light, the blood of the death of Jesus, God's Son, is making us clean from every sin.

[8]If we say that we have no sin, we are fooling ourselves, and the truth is not in us. [9]But if we confess our sins, he will forgive our sins. We can trust God. He does what is right. He will make us clean from all the wrongs we have done. [10]If we say that we have not sinned, then we make God a liar. We do not accept God's true teaching.

### JESUS IS OUR HELPER

**2** My dear children, I write this letter to you so that you will not sin. But if anyone does sin, we have Jesus Christ to help us. He is the Righteous One. He defends us before God the Father. [2]Jesus is the way our sins are taken away. And Jesus is the way that all people can have their sins taken away, too.

[3]If we obey what God has told us to do, then we are sure that we truly know God. [4]If someone says, "I know God!" but does not obey God's commands, then he is a liar. The truth is not in him. [5]But if someone obeys God's teaching, then God's love has truly arrived at its goal in him. This is how we know that we are following God: [6]Whoever says that God lives in him must live as Jesus lived.

### THE COMMAND TO LOVE OTHERS

[7]My dear friends, I am not writing a new command to you. It is the same command you have had since the beginning. It is the teaching you have

**DECODE THIS!**

*God is light, and in him there is no _____ at all.*

1:1 **Word** The Greek word is "logos," meaning any kind of communication. It could be translated "message." Here, it means Christ. Christ was the way God told people about himself. 1:5 **light** This word is used to show what God is like. It means goodness or truth.

already heard. [8]But I am writing a new command to you. This command is true; you can see its truth in Jesus and in yourselves. The darkness is passing away, and the true light is already shining.

[9]Someone says, "I am in the light."[n] But if he hates his brother, he is still in the darkness. [10]Whoever loves his brother lives in the light, and there is nothing in him that will cause him to do wrong. [11]But whoever hates his brother is in darkness. He lives in darkness and does not know where he is going. The darkness has made him blind.

[12]I write to you, dear children,
    because your sins are forgiven
        through Christ.
[13]I write to you, fathers,
    because you know the One who
        existed from the beginning.
I write to you, young men,
    because you have defeated the
        Evil One.
[14]I write to you, children,
    because you know the Father.
I write to you, fathers,
    because you know the One who
        existed from the beginning.
I write to you, young men,
    because you are strong;
    the word of God lives in you,
    and you have defeated the
        Evil One.

[15]Do not love the world or the things in the world. If anyone loves the world,

> ## "Do not love the world or the things in the world."
> *1 John 2:15*

the love of the Father is not in him. [16]These are the evil things in the world: wanting things to please our sinful selves, wanting the sinful things we

see, being too proud of the things we have. But none of those things comes from the Father. All of them come from the world. [17]The world is passing away. And everything that people want in the world is passing away. But the person who does what God wants lives forever.

### REJECT THE ENEMIES OF CHRIST

[18]My dear children, the end is near! You have heard that the Enemy of Christ[d] is coming. And now many enemies of Christ are already here. So we know that the end is near. [19]Those enemies of Christ were in our group. But they left us. They did not really belong with us. If they were really part of our group, then they would have stayed with us. But they left. This shows that none of them really belonged with us.

[20]You have the gift[n] that the Holy One gave you. So you all know the truth. [21]Why do I write to you? Do I write because you do not know the truth? No, I write this letter because you do know

the truth. And you know that no lie comes from the truth.

[22]So who is the liar? It is the person who says Jesus is not the Christ. A person who says Jesus is not the Christ is the enemy of Christ. He does not believe in the Father or in his Son. [23]If anyone does not believe in the Son, he does not have the Father. But whoever accepts the Son has the Father, too.

[24]Be sure that you continue to follow the teaching that you heard from the beginning. If you continue in that teaching, you will stay in the Son and in the Father. [25]And this is what the Son promised to us—life forever.

[26]I am writing this letter about those people who are trying to lead you the wrong way. [27]Christ gave you a special gift. You still have this gift in you. So you do not need any other teacher. The gift he gave you teaches you about everything. This gift is true, not false. So continue to live in Christ, as his gift taught you.

[28]Yes, my dear children, live in him. If we do this, we can be without fear on the day when Christ comes back. We will not need to hide and be ashamed when he comes. [29]You know that Christ is righteous. So you know that all who do what is right are God's children.

---

**2:9 light** This word is used to show what God is like. It means goodness or truth.  **2:20 gift** This might mean the Holy Spirit. Or it might mean teaching or truth as in verse 24.

# DECEMBER Peace

**1** Go all day without fighting with your brothers and sisters.

**2**

**3** JOHN 14:27: "I leave you peace. My peace I give you. I do not give it to you as the world does. So don't let your hearts be troubled. Don't be afraid."

**4**

**5** Cut down a Christmas tree with your family.

**6** Prayer Pointer: Ask God to help you not to worry about things, but instead be filled with his peace.

**7**

**8** Write your own Christmas carol.

**9**

**10** Shovel walkways or clean a house to earn money for needy children.

**11** 1 PETER 3:8: Finally, all of you should live together in peace. Try to understand each other. Love each other as brothers. Be kind and humble.

**12** Tell your younger brother or sister how special they are to God.

**13**

**14** Make ornaments with each family member's picture on them.

**15** Prayer Pointer: Ask God to help you and your family to not focus on getting presents this Christmas, but to see and meet other people's needs.

**16**

**17**

**18** Have everyone come over for a Christmas party, but take the gifts to a charity.

**19**

**20** Make breakfast for the family.

**21** JAMES 3:18: When people work for peace in a peaceful way, they receive the good result of their right living.

**22** Make a special gift for your mom and dad.

**23**

**24** Read the nativity story together.

**25** Prayer Pointer: Thank God for coming to earth as a baby, and pray that non-believers would understand what God has done for them.

**26** Go for a long walk and burn off Christmas dinner.

**27** Help your mom clean up the house.

**28**

**29** COLOSSIANS 3:15: Let the peace that Christ gives control your thinking. You were all called together in one body to have peace. Always be thankful.

**30**

**31** Prayer Pointer: Thank God for this past year, and ask him to draw you even closer to his heart in the coming year.

*And God's peace will keep your hearts and minds in Christ Jesus. The peace that God gives is so great that we cannot understand it (Philippians 4:7).*

## WE ARE GOD'S CHILDREN

**3** The Father has loved us so much! He loved us so much that we are called children of God. And we really are his children. But the people in the world do not understand that we are God's children, because they have not known him. [2]Dear friends, now we are children of God. We have not yet been shown what we will be in the future. But we know that when Christ comes again, we will be like him. We will see him as he really is. [3]Christ is pure. And every person who has this hope in Christ keeps himself pure like Christ.

[4]When a person sins, he breaks God's law. Yes, sinning is the same as living against God's law. [5]You know that Christ came to take away sins. There is no sin in Christ. [6]So the person who lives in Christ does not go on sinning. If he goes on sinning, he has never really understood Christ and has never known him.

[7]Dear children, do not let any person lead you the wrong way. Christ is righteous. To be like Christ, a person must do what is right. [8]The devil has been sinning since the beginning. Anyone who continues to sin belongs to the devil. The Son of God came for this purpose: to destroy the devil's work. [9]When God makes someone his child, that person does not go on sinning. The new life God gave that person stays in him. So he is not able to go on sinning, because he has become a child of God. [10]So we can see who God's children are and who the devil's children are. Those who do not do what is right are not children of God. And anyone who does not love his brother is not a child of God.

## WE MUST LOVE EACH OTHER

[11]This is the teaching you have heard from the beginning: We must love each other. [12]Do not be like Cain who belonged to the Evil One. Cain killed his brother. He killed his brother because the things Cain did were evil, and the things his brother did were good.

[13]Brothers, do not be surprised when the people of this world hate you. [14]We know that we have left death and have come into life. We know this because we love our brothers in Christ. Whoever does not love is still in death. [15]Everyone who hates his brother is a murderer." And you know that no murderer has eternal life in him. [16]This is how we know what real love is: Jesus gave his life for us. So we should give our lives for our brothers. [17]Suppose a believer is rich enough to have all that he needs. He sees his brother in Christ who is poor and does not have what he needs. What if the believer does not help the poor brother? Then the believer does not have God's love in his heart. [18]My children, our love should not be only words and talk. Our love must be true love. And we should show that love by what we do.

[19-20]This is the way we know that we belong to the way of truth. When our hearts make us feel guilty, we can still have peace before God. God is greater than our hearts, and he knows everything.

[21]My dear friends, if we do not feel that we are doing wrong, we can be without fear when we come to God. [22]And God gives us the things we ask for. We receive these things because we obey God's commands, and we do what pleases him. [23]This is what God commands: that we believe in his Son, Jesus Christ, and that we love each other, just as he commanded. [24]The person who

obeys God's commands lives in God. And God lives in him. How do we know that God lives in us? We know because of the Spirit[d] whom God gave us.

## WARNING AGAINST FALSE TEACHERS

**4** My dear friends, many false prophets[d] are in the world now. So do not believe every spirit. But test the spirits to see if they are from God. [2]This is how you can know God's Spirit:[d] One spirit says, "I believe that Jesus is the Christ who came to earth and became a man." That Spirit is from God. [3]Another spirit refuses to say this about Jesus. That spirit is not from God but is the spirit of the Enemy of Christ. You have heard that the Enemy of Christ is coming. And now he is already in the world.

[4]My dear children, you belong to God. So you have defeated them because God's Spirit, who is in you, is greater

---

## LiViN' iT!

### REFLECTING LIGHT
### 1 JOHN 4:7-8

She's sitting all alone. She always does. No one at school likes her because she dresses differently. Her face is a little strange. And people prefer to hang out with the popular kids. What should you do?

God says that if we really have his Spirit living inside of us, then it will be obvious by the way we show love to others. If we don't love others, it shows that we don't have the love of God in us. Because God himself is love, he wants us to be like a mirror, reflecting his rays of love into other people's lives. Every single person alive is important. Each was made in God's own image. Each person brings glory to God. When we choose to show love to others, we are doing the very thing we were created to do. It pleases God, and it changes us to become even more like Jesus.

---

3:15 Everyone . . . murderer. If a person hates his brother in Christ, then in his mind he has killed his brother. Jesus taught about this sin to his followers (Matthew 5:21-26).

than the devil, who is in the world. ⁵And they belong to the world. What they say is from the world, and the world listens to them. ⁶But we are from God, and those who know God listen to us. But those who are not from God do not listen to us. That is how we know the Spirit that is true and the spirit that is false.

## LOVE COMES FROM GOD

⁷Dear friends, we should love each other, because love comes from God. The person who loves has become God's child and knows God. ⁸Whoever does not love does not know God, because God is love. ⁹This is how God showed his love to us: He sent his only Son into the world to give us life through him. ¹⁰True love is God's love for us, not our love for God. God sent his Son to be the way to take away our sins.

¹¹That is how much God loved us, dear friends! So we also must love each other. ¹²No one has ever seen God. But if we love each other, God lives in us. If we love each other, God's love has reached its goal. It is made perfect in us.

¹³We know that we live in God and God lives in us. We know this because God gave us his Spirit.ᵈ ¹⁴We have seen that the Father sent his Son to be the Savior of the world. That is what we teach. ¹⁵If someone says, "I believe that Jesus is the Son of God," then God lives in him. And he lives in God. ¹⁶And so we know the love that God has for us, and we trust that love.

God is love. Whoever lives in love lives in God, and God lives in him. ¹⁷If God's love is made perfect in us, then we can be without fear on the day God judges us. We will be without fear, because in this world we are like him. ¹⁸Where God's love is, there is no fear, because God's perfect love takes away fear. It is punishment that makes a person fear. So love is not made perfect in the person who has fear.

¹⁹We love because God first loved us. ²⁰If someone says, "I love God," but hates his brother, he is a liar. He can see his brother, but he hates him. So he cannot love God, whom he has never seen. ²¹And God gave us this command: Whoever loves God must also love his brother.

## FAITH IN THE SON OF GOD

**5** Everyone who believes that Jesus is the Christᵈ is God's child. The person who loves the Father also loves the Father's children. ²How do we know that we love God's children? We know because we love God and we obey his commands. ³Loving God means obeying his commands. And God's commands are not too hard for us. ⁴Everyone who is a child of God has the power to win against the world. It is our faith that wins the victory against the world. ⁵So the one who wins against the world is the person who believes that Jesus is the Son of God. ⁶Jesus Christ is the One who came with water" and with blood." He did not

> ## "We know that we live in God and God lives in us."
>
> *1 John 4:13*

come by water only. He came by both water and blood. And the Spiritᵈ says that this is true. The Spirit is the truth. ⁷So there are three witnesses that tell us about Jesus: ⁸the Spirit, the water, and the blood. These three witnesses agree. ⁹We believe people when they say something is true. But what God says is more important. And he has told us the truth about his own Son. ¹⁰Anyone who believes in the Son of God has the truth that God told us. Anyone who does not believe makes God a liar. He does not believe what

God told us about his Son. ¹¹This is what God told us: God has given us eternal life, and this life is in his Son. ¹²Whoever has the Son has life. But the person who does not have the Son of God does not have life.

## WE HAVE ETERNAL LIFE NOW

¹³I write this letter to you who believe in the Son of God. I write so that you will know that you have eternal life now. ¹⁴We can come to God with no doubts. This means that when we ask God for things (and those things agree with what God wants for us), then God cares about what we say. ¹⁵God listens to us every time we ask him. So we know that he gives us the things that we ask from him.

¹⁶Suppose someone sees his brother in Christ sinning (sin that does not lead to eternal death). That person should pray for his brother who is sinning. Then God will give the brother life. I am talking about people whose sin does not lead to eternal death. There is sin that leads to death. I do not mean that a person should pray about that sin. ¹⁷Doing wrong is always sin. But there is sin that does not lead to eternal death.

¹⁸We know that anyone who is God's child does not continue to sin. The Son of God keeps him safe, and the Evil One cannot hurt him. ¹⁹We know that we belong to God. But the Evil One controls the whole world. ²⁰And we know that the Son of God has come and has given us understanding. Now we can know God, the One who is true. And our lives are in that true God and in his Son, Jesus Christ. He is the true God, and he is eternal life. ²¹So, dear children, keep yourselves away from false gods.

**5:6 water** This probably means the water of Jesus' baptism. **5:6 blood** This probably means the blood of Jesus' death.

## DECODE THIS!
*What is the victory that conquers the world?*

Written by John, who also wrote a Gospel about his time with Jesus

THE SECOND LETTER OF

# JOHN

We should all love each other, but be careful whom you accept in your house.

Do not help false teachers.

Avoid anyone who refuses to say that Jesus Christ came to earth as a man.

¹From the Elder. "

To the chosen lady " and to her children: I love all of you in the truth. " Also, all those who know the truth love you. ²We love you because of the truth—the truth that lives in us and will be with us forever.

³Grace, mercy, and peace will be with us from God the Father and from his Son, Jesus Christ. And may we have these blessings in truth and love.

⁴I was very happy to learn about some of your children. I am happy that they are following the way of truth, as the Father commanded us. ⁵And now, dear lady, I tell you: We should all love each other. This is not a new command. It is the same command we have had from the beginning. ⁶And loving means living the way he commanded us to live. And God's command is this: that you live a life of love. You have heard this command from the beginning.

⁷Many false teachers are in the world now. They refuse to say that Jesus Christ came to earth and became a man. Anyone who refuses to say this is a false teacher and an enemy of Christ. ⁸Be careful! Do not lose the reward that you have worked for. Be careful, so that you will receive your full reward.

⁹A person must continue to follow only the teaching of Christ. If he goes beyond Christ's teaching, then he does not have God. But if he continues following the teaching of Christ, then he has both the Father and the Son. ¹⁰If someone comes to you, but does not bring this teaching, then do not accept him into your house. Do not welcome him. ¹¹If you accept him, you are helping him with his evil work.

¹²I have much to say to you, but I do not want to use paper and ink. Instead, I hope to come visit you. Then we can be together and talk. That will make us very happy. ¹³The children of your chosen sister" send you their love.

1 **Elder** This is probably John the apostle. "Elder" means an older man. It can also mean a special leader in the church (as in Titus 1:5). 1 **lady** This might mean a woman. Or, in this letter, it might mean a church. If it is a church, then "her children" would be the people of the church. 1 **truth** The truth or "Good News" about Jesus Christ that joins all believers together. 13 **sister** Sister of the "lady" in verse 1. This might be another woman or another church.

## GAMES & QUIZZES

# THE PARENT TRAP

It might not seem like it now, but your parents are people just like you! If you let them, they can become your best friends and help you through life. So how well do you know them now? Take this test and see! If you can't answer a question for certain, take it to your parents and get the straight scoop.

What year was your mother born? _____

What was your father's first job? _____

How many siblings do your parents have? _____

What is your mother's maiden name? _____

What is your dad's favorite thing to do on Saturday? _____

What is your mom's favorite hobby? _____

When (if) did your parents become Christians? _____

Why did they choose the church you're in? _____

What encourages your mom the most? Your dad? _____

What is their favorite childhood memory? _____

MOM DAD

CHRISTIAN

Help Christians who teach truth.

John thanks Gaius for helping traveling believers.

Written by John, who also wrote a Gospel about his time with Jesus, 3 letters, and Revelation

# THE THIRD LETTER OF

# JOHN

Diotrephes took over a church in Asia and rejected the teachers sent by John.

> "My dear friend, do not follow what is bad; follow what is good."
>
> 3 John 11

¹From the Elder.*

To my dear friend Gaius whom I love in the truth:*

²My dear friend, I know your soul is doing well. I pray that you are doing fine in every way and that your health is good. ³Some brothers in Christ came and told me about the truth in your life. They said that you are following the way of truth. This made me very happy. ⁴It always gives me the greatest joy when I hear that my children are following the way of truth.

⁵My dear friend, it is good that you continue to help the brothers. You are helping those that you do not even know! ⁶These brothers told the church about the love you have. Please help them to continue their trip. Help them in a way that will please God. ⁷They started out on their trip to serve Christ. They did not accept any help from those who are not believers. ⁸So we should help these brothers. And when we do, we share in their work for the truth.

⁹I wrote a letter to the church. But

# LIVIN' IT!

**TO THE POINT**
3 JOHN 11

It seems like as we get near the end of the Bible, the words get shorter and clearer. The parables are over. The truth is plain before our eyes.

Do you believe in Jesus? Do you trust him to save you from your sins? Do you want to please God? Then do not follow what is bad. Quit thinking that people who dishonor God are cool. Whether it is people, or programs, or your own sinful desires, resist what is wrong. Stand strong in what you believe. Don't let other kids or adults who don't believe get in your way. Prove that you believe by obeying what God says in his Word. Encourage your friends to do the same by living the way God has called you to live.

Diotrephes will not listen to what we say. He always wants to be their leader. ¹⁰When I come, I will talk about what Diotrephes is doing. He lies and says evil things about us. But that is not all he does. He refuses to help those who are working to serve Christ. He also stops those who want to help the brothers and puts them out of the church.

¹¹My dear friend, do not follow what is bad; follow what is good. He who does what is good is from God. But he who does evil has never known God.

¹²Everyone says good things about Demetrius. And the truth agrees with what they say. Also, we say good about him. And you know that what we say is true.

¹³I have many things I want to tell you, but I do not want to use pen and ink. ¹⁴I hope to visit you soon. Then we can be together and talk. ¹⁵Peace to you. The friends here with me send their love. Please give our love to each one of the friends there.

# Gotta Know!

## Does God listen to my prayers?

He does if we have confessed our sins to him. We can't talk to him if we are trying to keep part of our lives to ourselves without letting him have full control. But when we repent, he hears our prayers—whether it's spoken out loud or just thought in our heads. In fact, God even knows our prayers before we pray them, and the Holy Spirit prays for the things that we didn't even know needed prayer. Prayer is the main way God gives us to stay connected to him every moment of the day.

## DECODE THIS!

*Who did John write this 3rd letter to?*

 1 **Elder** This is probably John the apostle. "Elder" means an older man. It can also mean a special leader in the church (as Titus 1:5). 1 **truth** The truth or "Good News" about Jesus Christ that joins all believers together.

369

# THE LETTER of JUDE

Warnings about False Teachers.

Remember how God punished sinners! Remember the unbelievers in Egypt! Remember Sodom and Gomorrah!

Get in shape, and be ready to defend your faith!

Believed to be written by a brother of Jesus (and James).

# LIVIN' IT!

## OUR SAFETY NET
## JUDE 24

By this point, you're getting near to the end of *Magnify™*. Thousands of verses and hundreds of articles have encouraged you to trust God and live the life he wants for you. It's a lot to remember—so much that if you really want to get it, you'll have to go over it again and again.

God's way is so different from the way we think and act naturally that you might think it's just impossible—or something that more "spiritual" kids can do. But he hasn't asked you to do something you can't do. Want to know why? Because in Jude 24, God promises that he himself will keep you from falling. He alone can make you into the person you were meant to be. So rejoice! And keep your eyes on your Father who will make you perfect in his time.

¹From Jude, a servant of Jesus Christ and a brother of James.

To all who have been called by God. God the Father loves you, and you have been kept safe in Jesus Christ.

²All mercy, peace, and love be yours.

## GOD WILL PUNISH SINNERS

³Dear friends, I wanted very much to write to you about the salvation we all share together. But I felt the need to write to you about something else: I want to encourage you to fight hard for the faith that God gave his holy people. God gave this faith once, and it is good for all time. ⁴Some people have secretly entered your group. They have already been judged guilty for the things they are doing. Long ago the prophets[d] wrote about these people. They are against God. They have used the grace of our God in the wrong way—to do sinful things. They refuse to accept Jesus Christ, our only Master and Lord.

⁵I want to remind you of some things that you already know: Remember that the Lord saved his people by bringing them out of the land of Egypt. But later the Lord destroyed all those who did not believe. ⁶And remember the angels who had power but did not keep it. They left their own home. So the Lord has kept these angels in darkness. They are bound with everlasting chains, to be judged on the great day. ⁷Also remember the cities of Sodom and Gomorrah[n] and the other towns around them. They acted as the angels who did not obey God. Their towns were full of sexual sin and men having sexual relations with men. They suffer the punishment of eternal fire, as an example for all to see.

⁸It is the same with these people who have entered your group. They are guided by dreams. They make themselves dirty with sin. They reject God's authority and say bad things against the glorious angels. ⁹Not even the archangel[n] Michael did this. He argued with the devil about who would have the body of Moses. Michael did not dare to accuse the devil with insults. He said, "The Lord punish you." ¹⁰But these people say bad things about what they do not understand. They do understand some things. But they understand them not by thinking, but by feeling, the way dumb animals understand things. And these are the very things that destroy them. ¹¹It will be bad for them. They have followed the way that Cain went. To make money, they have given themselves to doing the wrong that Balaam did. They have fought against God as Korah did. And like Korah, they will be destroyed. ¹²They are like dirty spots in the special meals you share together. They eat with you and have no fear. They take care of only themselves. They are clouds without rain. The wind blows them around. They are trees that have no fruit when it is time and are pulled out of the ground. So they are dead two times. ¹³They are like wild waves in the sea. These people do shameful things in the same way waves make foam. They are like stars that wander in the sky. A place in the blackest darkness has been kept for them forever.

¹⁴Enoch, the seventh descendant[d] from Adam, said this about these people: "Look, the Lord is coming with thousands and thousands of his holy angels. ¹⁵The Lord will judge every person. He is coming to judge everyone and to punish all who are against God. He will punish them for all the evil they have done against him. And he will punish the sinners who are against God. He will punish them for all the evil things they have said against him."

¹⁶These people always complain and blame others. They always do the evil things they want to do. They brag about themselves. The only reason they say good things about other people is to get what they want.

## A WARNING AND THINGS TO DO

¹⁷Dear friends, remember what the apostles[d] of our Lord Jesus Christ said before. ¹⁸They said to you, "In the last times there will be people who laugh about God. They will do only what they want to do—things that are against God." ¹⁹These are the people who divide you. They do only what their sinful selves want. They do not have the Spirit.[d]

²⁰But dear friends, use your most holy faith to build yourselves up strong. Pray with the Holy Spirit. ²¹Keep yourselves in God's love. Wait for the Lord Jesus Christ with his mercy to give you life forever.

²²Show mercy to people who have doubts. ²³Save them. Take them out of the fire. Show mercy mixed with fear to others. Hate even their clothes which are dirty from sin.

## PRAISE GOD

²⁴God is strong and can help you not to fall. He can bring you before his glory without any wrong in you and give you great joy. ²⁵He is the only God. He is the One who saves us. To him be glory, greatness, power, and authority through Jesus Christ our Lord for all time past, now, and forever. Amen.

---

 **7 Sodom and Gomorrah** Two cities God destroyed because they were so evil. **9 archangel** The leader among God's angels or messengers.

Patmos was an island of volcanic rock—a prison for criminals and political offenders.

# THE REVELATION OF JESUS CHRIST

Revelation means "unveiling."

Satan and false prophets will be punished day and night forever and ever!

Written by John while in exile to island of Patmos.

Purpose of John's letter: Christ will win over evil!

# BiBLe BaSiCS
## WHAT IS REVELATION?

The first time you read it, you might think most of the book of Revelation is just really weird. Unlike most of the other books of the New Testament, it is more dreamlike in that God gave John a vision for the future of the church—to give the believers hope. Even though the passages may be difficult to understand, God uses Revelation to let us know that a lot more is going on around us than what we see, and that Jesus is preparing to return one day to take his people home to heaven. We need to be ready!

## JOHN TELLS ABOUT THIS BOOK

**1** This is the revelation[n] of Jesus Christ. God gave this revelation to Jesus, to show his servants what must soon happen. And Jesus sent his angel to show it to his servant John. ²John has told everything that he has seen. It is the truth that Jesus Christ told him; it is the message from God. ³The one who reads the words of God's message is happy. And the people who hear this message and do what is written in it are happy. The time is near when all of this will happen.

## JESUS' MESSAGE TO THE CHURCHES

⁴From John,

To the seven churches in the country of Asia:

Grace and peace to you from the One who is and was and is coming, and from the seven spirits before his throne, ⁵and from Jesus Christ. Jesus is the faithful witness. He is first among those raised from death. He is the ruler of the kings of the earth.

He is the One who loves us. And he is the One who made us free from our sins with the blood of his death. ⁶He made us to be a kingdom of priests who serve God his Father. To Jesus Christ be glory and power forever and ever! Amen.

⁷Look, Jesus is coming with the clouds! Everyone will see him, even those who stabbed him. And all peoples of the earth will cry loudly because of him. Yes, this will happen! Amen.

⁸The Lord God says, "I am the Alpha and the Omega."[n] I am the One who is and was and is coming. I am the All-Powerful."

⁹I am John, and I am your brother in Christ. We are together in Jesus, and we share in these things: in suffering, in the kingdom, and in patience. I was on the island of Patmos[n] because I had preached God's message and the truth about Jesus. ¹⁰On the Lord's day the Spirit[d] took control of me. I heard a loud voice behind me that sounded like a trumpet. ¹¹The voice said, "Write what you see and send that book to the seven churches: to Ephesus, Smyrna, Pergamum, Thyatira, Sardis, Philadelphia, and Laodicea."

¹²I turned to see who was talking to me. When I turned, I saw seven golden lampstands. ¹³I saw someone among the lampstands who was "like a Son of Man."[n] He was dressed in a long robe. He had a gold band around his chest. ¹⁴His head and hair were white like wool, as white as snow. His eyes were like flames of fire. ¹⁵His feet were like bronze that glows hot in a furnace. His voice was like the noise of flooding water. ¹⁶He held seven stars in his right hand. A sharp two-edged sword came out of his mouth. He looked like the sun shining at its brightest time.

¹⁷When I saw him, I fell down at his feet like a dead man. He put his right hand on me and said, "Do not be afraid! I am the First and the Last. ¹⁸I am the One who lives. I was dead, but look: I am alive forever and ever! And I hold the keys of death and where the dead are. ¹⁹So write the things you see, what is now and what will happen later. ²⁰Here is the hidden meaning of the seven stars that you saw in my right hand and the seven golden lampstands that you saw: The seven lampstands are the seven churches. The seven stars are the angels of the seven churches.

## TO THE CHURCH IN EPHESUS

**2** "Write this to the angel of the church in Ephesus:

"The One who holds the seven stars in his right hand and walks among the seven golden lampstands says this to you. ²I know what you do. You work hard, and you never give up. I know that you do not accept evil people. You have tested those who say that they are apostles[d] but really are not. You found that they are liars. ³You continue to serve me. You have suffered troubles for my name, and you have not given up.

⁴"But I have this against you: You have left the love you had in the beginning. ⁵So remember where you were before you fell. Change your hearts and do what you did at first. If you do not change, I will come to you. I will take away your lampstand from its place. ⁶But there is something you do that is right: You hate what the Nicolaitans[n] do, as much as I.

⁷"Every person who has ears should listen to what the Spirit[d] says to the churches. To him who wins the victory I will give the right to eat the fruit from the tree of life. This tree is in the garden of God.

1:1 **revelation** A making known of truth that has been hidden. 1:8 **Alpha and the Omega** The first and last letters in the Greek alphabet. This means "the beginning and the end." 1:9 **Patmos** A small island in the Aegean Sea, near the coast of Asia Minor (modern Turkey). 1:13 **"like . . . Man"** "Son of Man" is a name Jesus called himself. It showed he was God's Son, but he was also a man. 2:6 **Nicolaitans** This is the name of a religious group that followed false beliefs and ideas.

## DECODE THIS!
*Who wrote the book of Revelation?*

## "i will give power to everyone who wins the victory and continues to the end to do what i want."

*Revelation 2:26*

### TO THE CHURCH IN SMYRNA

8"Write this to the angel of the church in Smyrna:

"The One who is the First and the Last says this to you. He is the One who died and came to life again. 9I know your troubles. I know that you are poor, but really you are rich! I know the bad things that some people say about you. They say they are Jews, but they are not true Jews. They are a synagogue[d] that belongs to Satan. 10Do not be afraid of what will happen to you. I tell you, the devil will put some of you in prison to test you. You will suffer for ten days. But be faithful, even if you have to die. If you are faithful, I will give you the crown of life.

11"Everyone who has ears should listen to what the Spirit[d] says to the churches. He who wins the victory will not be hurt by the second death.

faith in me even during the time of Antipas. Antipas was my faithful witness who was killed in your city. Your city is where Satan lives.

14"But I have a few things against you: You have some there who follow the teaching of Balaam. Balaam taught Balak how to cause the people of Israel to sin. They sinned by eating food offered to idols and by taking part in sexual sins. 15You also have some who follow the teaching of the Nicolaitans." 16So change your hearts and lives! If you do not, I will come to you quickly and fight against them with the sword that comes out of my mouth.

17"Everyone who has ears should listen to what the Spirit[d] says to the churches!

"I will give the hidden manna[d] to everyone who wins the victory. I will also give him a white stone with a new name written on

"The Son of God is saying these things. He is the One who has eyes that blaze like fire and feet like shining bronze. He says this to you: 19I know what you do. I know about your love, your faith, your service, and your patience. I know that you are doing more now than you did at first. 20But I have this against you: You let that woman Jezebel do what she wants. She says that she is a prophetess.[d] But she is leading my people away with her teaching. Jezebel leads them to take part in sexual sins and to eat food that is offered to idols. 21I have given her time to change her heart and turn away from her sin. But she does not want to change. 22And so I will throw her on a bed of suffering. And all those who take part in adultery[d] with her will suffer greatly. I will do this now if they do not turn away from the wrongs she does. 23I will also kill her followers. Then all the churches will know that I am the One who knows what people feel and think. And I will repay each of you for what you have done.

24"But others of you in Thyatira have not followed her teaching. You have not learned what some call Satan's deep secrets. This is what I say to you: I will not put any other load on you. 25Only continue the way you are until I come.

26"I will give power to everyone who wins the victory and continues to the end to do what I want. I will give him power over the nations:

# Gotta Know!

## Do animals go to heaven?

The Bible doesn't say whether or not animals go to heaven, so we don't really know for sure. Since they don't have souls like humans, you could easily decide that they must not go to heaven. But with God, there are often surprises. It is possible that when we reach heaven, we'll find all of our beloved pets. Whatever the case, we know that we will be happier than we can imagine when we get there!

### TO THE CHURCH IN PERGAMUM

12"Write this to the angel of the church in Pergamum:

"The One who has the sharp two-edged sword says this to you. 13I know where you live. You live where Satan has his throne. But you are true to me. You did not refuse to tell about your

it. No one knows this new name except the one who receives it.

### TO THE CHURCH IN THYATIRA

18"Write this to the angel of the church in Thyatira:

# Decode this!

*Jesus sends a message in the first part of Revelation to how many churches?*

2:15 **Nicolaitans** This is the name of a religious group that followed false beliefs and ideas.

²⁷'You will make them obey you by punishing them with an iron rod. You will break them into pieces like pottery.'

*Psalm 2:9*

²⁸This is the same power I received from my Father. I will also give him the morning star. ²⁹Everyone who has ears should listen to what the Spirit[d] says to the churches.

## TO THE CHURCH IN SARDIS

**3** "Write this to the angel of the church in Sardis:

"The One who has the seven spirits and the seven stars says this to you. I know what you do. People say that you are alive, but really you are dead. ²Wake up! Make yourselves stronger while you still have something left and before it dies completely. I have found that what you are doing is not good enough for my God. ³So do not forget what you have received and heard. Obey it. Change your hearts and lives! You must wake up, or I will come to you and surprise you like a thief. And you will not know when I will come. ⁴But you have a few there in Sardis who have kept themselves clean. They will walk with me. They will wear white clothes, because they are worthy. ⁵He who wins the victory will be dressed in white clothes like them. I will not take away his name from the book of life. I will say that he belongs to me before my Father and before his angels. ⁶Everyone who has ears should listen to what the Spirit[d] says to the churches.

## TO THE CHURCH IN PHILADELPHIA

⁷"Write this to the angel of the church in Philadelphia:

### COLD FRIES
### REVELATION 3:16

There's nothing quite like fresh, hot French fries. There's also nothing grosser than those same fries about 15 minutes later. They're not cold and definitely not hot—they taste like something with which you'd lace up your shoes.

Some Christians are like those fries. There may have been a time when they were excited about Jesus and did what he wanted—but as time passed, they cooled off. They don't dislike Jesus, but they quit loving him. Jesus describes them as lukewarm, and he says they make him want to vomit!

God wants us to believe him and love him with *all* of our heart, soul, mind, and strength. Anything less than that shows that we have idols in our lives that we need to destroy. When you feel your excitement for God beginning to fade, ask him to relight the fire in your heart that will make you want to give him your all.

"The One who is holy and true says this to you. He holds the key of David. When he opens something, it cannot be closed. And when he closes something, it cannot be opened. ⁸I know what you do. I have put an open door before you, and no one can close it. I know that you have a little strength. But you have followed my teaching. And you were not afraid to speak my name. ⁹Listen! There is a synagogue[d] that belongs to Satan. Those in this synagogue say they are Jews, but they are liars. They are not true Jews. I will

make them come before you and bow at your feet. They will know that I have loved you. ¹⁰You have followed my teaching about not giving up. So I will keep you from the time of trouble that will come to the whole world. This trouble will test those who live on earth.

¹¹"I am coming soon. Continue the way you are now. Then no one will take away your crown. ¹²I will make the one who wins the victory a pillar in the temple of my God. He will never have to leave it. I will write on him the name of my God and the name of the city of my God. This city is the new Jerusalem.ⁿ It comes down out of heaven from my God. I will also write on him my new name. ¹³Every person who has ears should listen to what the Spirit[d] says to the churches.

## TO THE CHURCH IN LAODICEA

¹⁴"Write this to the angel of the church in Laodicea:

"The Amenⁿ is the One who is the faithful and true witness. He is the ruler of all that God has made. He says this to you: ¹⁵I know what you do. You are not hot or cold. I wish that you were hot or cold! ¹⁶But you are only warm—not hot, not cold. So I am ready to spit you out of my mouth. ¹⁷You say you are rich. You think you have become wealthy and do not need anything. But you do not know that you are really miserable, pitiful, poor, blind, and naked. ¹⁸I advise you to buy gold from me—gold made pure in fire. Then you can be truly rich. Buy from me clothes that are white. Then you can cover your shameful nakedness. Buy from me medicine to put on your eyes. Then you can truly see.

---

 **3:12 Jerusalem** This name is used to mean the spiritual city God built for his people. **3:14 Amen** Used here as a name for Jesus, it means to agree fully that something is true.

# A MIGHTY GOD WE SERVE

## ACROSS:
1. Has all power
2. Judges rightly
3. Set apart
4. Knows everything
5. Very strong
6. Living _____
7. Perfect; no sin

## DOWN:
1. Not in a hurry
2. Title of kings
3. 3 persons
4. Everywhere
5. Patriarch
6. In charge
7. Never ending

[19]"I correct and punish those whom I love. So be eager to do right. Change your hearts and lives. [20]Here I am! I stand at the door and knock. If anyone hears my voice and opens the door, I will come in and eat with him. And he will eat with me.

[21]"He who wins the victory will sit with me on my throne. It was the same with me. I won the victory and sat down with my Father on his throne. [22]Everyone who has ears should listen to what the Spirit[d] says to the churches."

## JOHN SEES HEAVEN

**4** After this I looked, and there before me was an open door in heaven. And I heard the same voice that spoke to me before. It was the voice that sounded like a trumpet. The voice said, "Come up here, and I will show you what must happen after this." [2]Then the Spirit[d] took control of me. There before me was a throne in heaven. Someone was sitting on the throne. [3]The One who sat on the throne looked like precious stones, like jasper and carnelian. All around the throne was a rainbow the color of an emerald. [4]Around the throne there were 24 other thrones. There were 24 elders[n] sitting on the 24 thrones. The elders were dressed in white, and they had golden crowns on their heads. [5]Lightning flashes and noises of thunder came from the throne. Before the throne there were seven lamps burning. These lamps are the seven spirits of God. [6]Also before the throne there was something that looked like a sea of glass. It was clear like crystal.

Around the throne, on each side, there were four living things. These living things had eyes all over them, in front and in back. [7]The first living thing was like a lion. The second was like a calf. The third had a face like a man. The fourth was like a flying eagle. [8]Each of these four living things had six wings. The living things were covered all over with eyes, inside and out. Day and night they never stop saying:

"Holy, holy, holy is the Lord God
    All-Powerful.

He was, he is, and he is coming."

[9]These living things give glory and honor and thanks to the One who sits on the throne. He is the One who lives forever and ever. And every time the living things do this, [10]the 24 elders bow down before the One who sits on the throne. The elders worship him who lives forever and ever. They put their crowns down before the throne and say:

[11]"Our Lord and God! You are worthy
    to receive glory and honor
        and power.
You made all things.
    Everything existed and
        was made
    because you
        wanted it."

**5** Then I saw a scroll in the right hand of the One sitting on the throne. The scroll had writing on both sides. It was kept closed with seven seals. [2]And I saw a powerful angel. He called in a loud voice, "Who is worthy to break the seals and open the scroll?" [3]But there was no one in heaven or on earth or under the earth who could open the scroll or look inside it. [4]I cried and cried because there was no one who was worthy to open the scroll or look inside. [5]But one of the elders said to me, "Do not cry! The Lion[n] from the tribe[d] of Judah has won the victory. He is David's descendant.[d] He is able to open the scroll and its seven seals."

[6]Then I saw a Lamb standing in the center of the throne with the four living things around it. The elders were also around the Lamb. The Lamb looked as if he had been killed. He had seven horns and seven eyes. These are the seven spirits of God that were sent into all the world. [7]The Lamb came and took the scroll from the right hand of the One sitting on the throne. [8]After he took the scroll, the four living things and the 24 elders bowed down before the Lamb. Each one of them had a

**4:4 24 elders** Elder means "older." Here the elders probably represent God's people. **5:5 Lion** Here refers to Christ.

## AN ARMY OFFICER

We don't know his name, but Jesus said he had more faith than anyone in Israel. This Roman army officer (sometimes called a centurion) had a servant who was very sick and about to die. So he sent servants to go get Jesus.

But before Jesus reached his house, he sent more servants to tell Jesus that he wasn't worthy enough to have the Son of God come into his house. He knew that Jesus had the power to just say the word, and his servant would be healed. Jesus was amazed by how much this man believed—even when he wasn't Jewish. And Jesus healed his servant.

It's easy to believe things that we can see. But to trust in God, his love, and his power when we can't see him is a lot harder. But remember the army officer's faith. Know that God is in control, and he is real. And he does answer our cries for help.

harp. Also, they were holding golden bowls full of incense.ᵈ These bowls of incense are the prayers of God's holy people. ⁹And they all sang a new song to the Lamb:

"You are worthy to take the scroll
and to open its seals,
because you were killed;
and with the blood of your death
you bought men for God
from every tribe, language,
people, and nation.
¹⁰You made them to be a kingdom of
priests for our God.
And they will rule on the earth."

¹¹Then I looked, and I heard the voices of many angels. The angels were around the throne, the four living things, and the elders. There were thousands and thousands of angels— there were 10,000 times 10,000. ¹²The angels said in a loud voice:

"The Lamb who was killed is worthy
to receive power, wealth, wisdom
and strength,
honor, glory, and praise!"

¹³Then I heard every living thing in heaven and on earth and under the earth and in the sea. I heard every thing in all these places, saying:

"All praise and honor and glory
and power
forever and ever
to the One who sits on the throne
and to the Lamb!"

¹⁴The four living things said, "Amen!" And the elders bowed down and worshiped.

**6** Then I watched while the Lamb opened the first of the seven seals. I heard one of the four living things speak with a voice like thunder. It said, "Come!" ²I looked and there before me was a white horse. The rider on the horse held a bow, and he was given a crown. And he rode out, defeating the enemy. He rode out to win the victory.

³The Lamb opened the second seal.

Then I heard the second living thing say, "Come!" ⁴Then another horse came out. This was a red horse. Its rider was given power to take away peace from the earth. He was given power to make people kill each other. And he was given a big sword.

⁵The Lamb opened the third seal. Then I heard the third living thing say, "Come!" I looked, and there before me was a black horse. Its rider held a pair of scales in his hand. ⁶Then I heard something that sounded like a voice. It

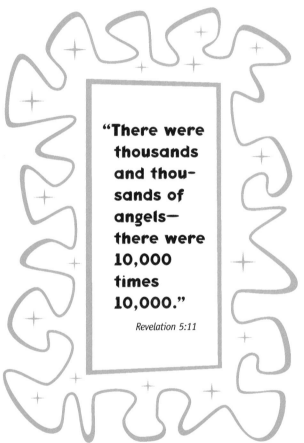

"There were thousands and thousands of angels— there were 10,000 times 10,000."

*Revelation 5:11*

came from where the four living things were. The voice said, "A quart of wheat for a day's pay. And three quarts of barley for a day's pay. And do not damage the olive oil and wine!"

⁷The Lamb opened the fourth seal. Then I heard the voice of the fourth living thing say, "Come!" ⁸I looked, and

there before me was a pale horse. Its rider was named death. Hadesⁿ was following close behind him. They were given power over a fourth of the earth. They were given power to kill people by war, by starving them, by disease, and by the wild animals of the earth.

⁹The Lamb opened the fifth seal. Then I saw some souls under the altar. They were the souls of those who had been killed because they were faithful to God's message and to the truth they had received. ¹⁰These souls shouted in a loud voice, "Holy and true Lord, how long until you judge the people of the earth and punish them for killing us?" ¹¹Then each one of these souls was given a white robe. They were told to wait a short time longer. There were still some of their brothers in the service of Christ who must be killed as they were. They were told to wait until all of this killing was finished.

¹²Then I watched while the Lamb opened the sixth seal. There was a great earthquake. The sun became black like rough black cloth. The full moon became red like blood. ¹³The stars in the sky fell to the earth like figs falling from a fig tree when the wind blows. ¹⁴The sky disappeared. It was rolled up like a scroll. And every mountain and island was moved from its place.

¹⁵Then all people hid in caves and behind the rocks on the mountains. There were the kings of the earth, the rulers, the generals, the rich people

---

⭐ **6:8 Hades** The unseen world where the dead are.

and the powerful people. Everyone, slave and free, hid himself. [16]They called to the mountains and the rocks, "Fall on us. Hide us from the face of the One who sits on the throne. Hide us from the anger of the Lamb! [17]The great day for their anger has come. Who can stand against it?"

### THE 144,000 PEOPLE OF ISRAEL

**7** After this I saw four angels standing at the four corners of the earth. The angels were holding the four winds of the earth. They were stopping the wind from blowing on the land or on the sea or on any tree. [2]Then I saw another angel coming from the east. This angel had the seal of the living God. He called out in a loud voice to the four angels. These were

the four angels that God had given power to harm the earth and the sea. He said to the four angels, [3]"Do not harm the land or the sea or the trees before we put the sign on the people who serve our God. We must put the sign on their foreheads." [4]Then I heard how many people were marked with the sign. There were 144,000. They were from every tribe[d] of the people of Israel.

[5]From the tribe of Judah 12,000 were marked with the sign,

from the tribe of Reuben 12,000,
from the tribe of Gad 12,000,
[6]from the tribe of Asher 12,000,
from the tribe of Naphtali 12,000,
from the tribe of Manasseh 12,000,
[7]from the tribe of Simeon 12,000,
from the tribe of Levi 12,000,
from the tribe of Issachar 12,000,
[8]from the tribe of Zebulun 12,000,
from the tribe of Joseph 12,000,
from the tribe of Benjamin 12,000.

### THE GREAT CROWD

[9]Then I looked, and there was a great number of people. There were so many people that no one could count them. They were from every nation, tribe,[d] people, and language of the earth. They were all standing before the throne and before the Lamb. They wore white robes and had palm branches in their hands. [10]They were shouting in a loud voice, "Salvation belongs to our God, who sits on the throne, and to the Lamb." [11]The elders[n] and the four living things were there. All the angels were standing around them and the throne. The angels bowed down on their faces before the throne and wor-

shiped God. [12]They were saying, "Amen! Praise, glory, wisdom, thanks, honor, power, and strength belong to our God forever and ever. Amen!"

[13]Then one of the elders asked me, "Who are these people in white robes? Where did they come from?"

[14]I answered, "You know who they are, sir."

And the elder said, "These are the people who have come out of the great suffering. They have washed their robes[n] with the blood of the Lamb. Now they are clean and white. [15]And they are before the throne of God. They worship God day and night in his temple. And the One who sits on the throne will protect them. [16]Those people will never be hungry again. They will never be thirsty again. The sun will not hurt them. No heat will burn them. [17]For the Lamb at the center of the throne will be their shepherd. He will lead them to springs of water that give life. And God will wipe away every tear from their eyes."

### THE SEVENTH SEAL

**8** The Lamb opened the seventh seal. Then there was silence in heaven for about half an hour. [2]And I saw the seven angels who stand before God. They were given seven trumpets.

[3]Another angel came and stood at the altar. This angel had a golden pan for incense.[d] The angel was given much incense to offer with the prayers of all God's holy people. The angel put this offering on the golden altar before the throne. [4]The smoke from the incense went up from the angel's hand to God. It went up with the prayers of God's people. [5]Then the angel filled the incense pan with fire from the altar and

## DECODE THIS!

*What was in the right hand of the One sitting on the throne in heaven?*

---

7:11 **elders** Elder means "older." Here the elders probably represent God's people. 7:14 **washed their robes** This means they believed in Jesus so that their sins could be forgiven by Christ's blood.

threw it on the earth. There were flashes of lightning, thunder and loud noises, and an earthquake.

## THE SEVEN ANGELS AND TRUMPETS

⁶Then the seven angels who had the seven trumpets prepared to blow them. ⁷The first angel blew his trumpet. Then hail and fire mixed with blood was poured down on the earth. And a third of the earth and all the green grass and a third of the trees were burned up.

⁸The second angel blew his trumpet. Then something that looked like a big mountain burning with fire was thrown into the sea. And a third of the sea became blood. ⁹And a third of the living things in the sea died, and a third of the ships were destroyed.

¹⁰The third angel blew his trumpet. Then a large star, burning like a torch, fell from the sky. It fell on a third of the rivers and on the springs of water. "The name of the star is Wormwood." And a third of all the water became bitter. Many people died from drinking the water that was bitter.

¹²The fourth angel blew his trumpet. Then a third of the sun and a third of the moon and a third of the stars were hit. So a third of them became dark. A third of the day was without light.

¹³While I watched, I heard an eagle that was flying high in the air. The eagle said with a loud voice, "Trouble! Trouble! Trouble for those who live on the earth! The trouble will begin with the sounds of the trumpets that the other three angels are about to blow."

**9** Then the fifth angel blew his trumpet. And I saw a star fall from the sky to the earth. The star was given the key to the deep hole that leads down to the bottomless pit. ²Then it opened the bottomless pit. Smoke came up from the hole like smoke from a big furnace. The sun and sky became dark because of the smoke from the hole. ³Then locusts*d* came down to the earth out of the smoke. They were given the power to sting like scorpions." ⁴They were told not to harm the grass on the earth or any plant or tree. They could harm only the people who did not have the sign of God on their foreheads. ⁵These locusts were given the power to cause pain to the people for five months. But they were not given the power to kill anyone. And the pain they felt was like the pain that a scorpion gives when it stings a person. ⁶During those days people will look for a way to die, but they will not find it. They will want to die, but death will run away from them.

⁷The locusts looked like horses prepared for battle. On their heads they

**Q. Why do some people have so many freckles?**

**A. I think it's because the sun kissed them a lot.**

wore things that looked like crowns of gold. Their faces looked like human faces. ⁸Their hair was like women's hair, and their teeth were like lions' teeth. ⁹Their chests looked like iron breastplates. The sound their wings made was like the noise of many horses and chariots hurrying into battle. ¹⁰The locusts had tails with stingers like scorpions. The power they had to hurt people for five months was in their tails. "The locusts had a king who was the angel of the bottomless pit. His name in the Hebrew language is Abaddon. In the Greek language his name is Apollyon."

¹²The first great trouble is past. There are still two other great troubles that will come.

¹³The sixth angel blew his trumpet. Then I heard a voice coming from the horns on the golden altar that is before God. ¹⁴The voice said to the sixth angel who had the trumpet, "Free the four angels who are tied at the great river Euphrates." ¹⁵These four angels had been kept ready for this hour and day and month and year. They were freed to kill a third of all people on the earth. ¹⁶I heard how many troops on horses were in their army. There were 200,000,000.

¹⁷In my vision I saw the horses and their riders. They looked like this: They had breastplates that were fiery red, dark blue, and yellow like sulfur. The heads of the horses looked like heads of lions. The horses had fire, smoke, and sulfur coming out of their mouths. ¹⁸A third of all the people on earth were killed by these three terrible things coming out of the horses' mouths: the fire, the smoke, and the sulfur. ¹⁹The horses' power was in their mouths and also in their tails. Their tails were like snakes that have heads to bite and hurt people.

²⁰The other people on the earth were not killed by these terrible things. But they still did not change their hearts and turn away from what they had made with their own hands. They did not stop worshiping demons*d* and idols

---

8:11 **Wormwood** Name of a very bitter plant, used here to give the idea of bitter sorrow. 9:3 **scorpions** A scorpion is an insect that stings with a bad poison. 9:11 **Abaddon . . . Apollyon** Both names mean "Destroyer."

made of gold, silver, bronze, stone, and wood—things that cannot see or hear or walk. [21]These people did not change their hearts and turn away from murder or evil magic, from their sexual sins or stealing.

## THE ANGEL AND THE LITTLE SCROLL

**10** Then I saw another powerful angel coming down from heaven. He was dressed in a cloud and had a rainbow around his head. His face was like the sun, and his legs were like poles of fire. [2]The angel was holding a small scroll open in his hand. He put his right foot on the sea and his left foot on the land. [3]He shouted loudly like the roaring of a lion. When he shouted, the voices of seven thunders spoke. [4]The seven thunders spoke, and I started to write. But then I heard a voice from heaven. The voice said, "Do not write what the seven thunders said. Keep these things secret."

[5]Then the angel I saw standing on the sea and on the land raised his right hand to heaven. [6]He made a promise by the power of the One who lives forever and ever. He is the One who made the skies and all that is in them. He made the earth and all that is in it, and he made the sea and all that is in it. The angel said, "There will be no more waiting! [7]In the days when the seventh angel is ready to blow his trumpet, God's secret plan will be finished. This plan is the Good News[d] God told to his servants, the prophets."[d]

[8]Then I heard the same voice from heaven again. The voice said to me, "Go and take the open scroll that is in the angel's hand. This is the angel that is standing on the sea and on the land."

[9]So I went to the angel and asked him to give me the little scroll. He said to me, "Take the scroll and eat it. It will be sour in your stomach. But in your mouth it will be sweet as honey." [10]So I

> **"Then the angel i saw standing on the sea and on the land raised his right hand to heaven. He made a promise by the power of the One who lives forever and ever."**
>
> *Revelation 10:5-6*

took the little scroll from the angel's hand and I ate it. In my mouth it tasted sweet as honey. But after I ate it, it was sour in my stomach. [11]Then I was told, "You must prophesy[d] again about many peoples, nations, languages, and kings."

## THE TWO WITNESSES

**11** Then I was given a measuring stick like a rod. I was told, "Go and measure the temple[n] of God and the altar, and count the number of people worshiping there. [2]But do not measure the yard outside the temple. Leave it alone. It has been given to the people who are not Jews. They will walk on the holy city for 42 months.

[3]And I will give power to my two witnesses to prophesy[d] for 1,260 days. They will be dressed in rough cloth to show how sad they are."

[4]These two witnesses are the two olive trees and the two lampstands that stand before the Lord of the earth. [5]If anyone tries to hurt the witnesses, fire comes from their mouths and kills their enemies. Anyone who tries to hurt them will die like this. [6]These witnesses have the power to stop the sky from raining during the time they are prophesying. They have power to make the waters become blood. They have power to send every kind of trouble to the earth. They can do this as many times as they want.

[7]When the two witnesses have finished telling their message, the beast will fight against them. This is the beast that comes up from the bottomless pit. He will defeat them and kill them. [8]The bodies of the two witnesses will lie in the street of the great city. This city is named Sodom[n] and Egypt. These names for the city have a special meaning. It is the city where the Lord was killed. [9]Men from every race of people, tribe,[d] language, and nation will look at the bodies of the two witnesses for three and a half days. They will refuse to bury them. [10]People who live on the earth will be happy because these two are dead. They will have parties and send each other gifts. They will do these things because these two prophets brought much suffering to those who live on the earth.

[11]But after three and a half days, God put the breath of life into the two prophets again. They stood on their feet. Everyone who saw them was filled with fear. [12]Then the two prophets heard a loud voice from heaven say, "Come up here!" And they went up into heaven in a cloud. Their enemies watched them go.

## ? DECODE THIS!

*When the Lamb opened the seventh seal, what did the 7 angels have?*

 **11:1 temple** God's house—the place where God's people worship and serve him. Here, John sees it pictured as the special building in Jerusalem where God commanded the Jews to worship him. **11:8 Sodom** City that God destroyed because the people were so evil.

[13]At that same time there was a great earthquake. A tenth of the city was destroyed. And 7,000 people were killed in the earthquake. Those who did not die were very afraid. They gave glory to the God of heaven.

[14]The second great trouble is finished. The third great trouble is coming soon.

## THE SEVENTH TRUMPET

[15]Then the seventh angel blew his trumpet. And there were loud voices in heaven. The voices said:

"The power to rule the world
    now belongs to our Lord and his
    Christ.[d]
And he will rule forever and ever."

[16]Then the 24 elders[n] bowed down on their faces and worshiped God. These are the elders who sit on their thrones before God. [17]They said:

"We give thanks to you, Lord God
    All-Powerful.
    You are the One who is and
    who was.
We thank you because you have used
    your great power
    and have begun to rule!
[18]The people of the world were angry;
    but now is the time for your
    anger.
    Now is the time for the dead to
    be judged.
It is time to reward your servants the
    prophets[d]
    and to reward your holy people,
    all who respect you, great and
    small.
It is time to destroy those who
    destroy the earth!"

[19]Then God's temple[n] in heaven was opened. The Holy Box[d] that holds the agreement that God gave to his people could be seen in his temple. Then there were flashes of lightning, noises, thunder, an earthquake, and a great hailstorm.

---

### Gotta Know!

**Does God do everything for a better life in the future?**

Yes and no. We do receive great rewards in heaven for our obedience and service here on earth. But we also receive incredible benefits right now. When we give our lives to the Lord, we discover our very purpose for being created. Life and relationships make sense, and we experience a deep and lasting joy. We are able to face whatever comes because we feel safe in God's love and protection. Life is wonderful now as it will be in the future.

---

## THE WOMAN AND THE DRAGON

**12** And then a great wonder appeared in heaven: There was a woman who was clothed with the sun. The moon was under her feet. She had a crown of 12 stars on her head. [2]The woman was pregnant. She cried out with pain because she was about to give birth. [3]Then another wonder appeared in heaven: There was a giant red dragon. He had seven heads with seven crowns on each head. He also had ten horns. [4]The dragon's tail swept a third of the stars out of the sky and threw them down to the earth. The dragon stood in front of the woman who was ready to give birth to a baby. He wanted to eat the woman's baby as soon as it was born. [5]The woman gave birth to a son. He will rule all the nations with an iron scepter.[d] But her child was taken up to God and to his throne. [6]The woman ran away into the desert to a place God prepared for her. There she would be taken care of for 1,260 days.

[7]Then there was a war in heaven. Michael[n] and his angels fought against the dragon. The dragon and his angels fought back. [8]But the dragon was not strong enough. He and his angels lost their place in heaven. [9]He was thrown down out of heaven. (The giant dragon is that old snake called the devil or Satan. He leads the whole world the wrong way.) The dragon with his angels was thrown down to the earth.

[10]Then I heard a loud voice in heaven say:

"The salvation and the power and the
    kingdom of our God
    and the authority of his Christ[d]
    have now come.
They have come because the accuser
    of our brothers has been
    thrown out.
    He accused our brothers day and
    night before our God.
[11]And our brothers defeated him
    by the blood of the Lamb's death
    and by the truth they preached.
They did not love their lives so much
    that they were afraid of death.
[12]So be happy, you heavens
    and all who live there!
But it will be terrible for the earth
    and the sea,
    because the devil has come down
    to you!
He is filled with anger.
    He knows that he does not have
    much time."

[13]The dragon saw that he had been thrown down to the earth. So he hunted down the woman who had given birth to the son. [14]But the woman was given

---

### DECODE THIS!

"The power to rule the world now belongs to _____ " (Revelation 11:15).

# HEAVEN RULES

Jesus says that heaven is going to be so awesome that we can't even imagine how great it will be! But he does give us some clues. How many of these words that describe heaven can you find?

```
L L I F E S L E W E J
A B T D L O G S Y O F
N C A I N T P U Y I R
R N G O D D A S L E I
E H A P P I N E S S E
T L T H A E W J R I N
E Y L I M A F O D A D
S T H U T S K Y Y R S
N O I T C E F R E P R
```

## WORDS TO FIND:

| | |
|---|---|
| Eternal life | Jewels |
| Family | Joy |
| Friends | Light |
| God | Perfection |
| Gold | Praise |
| Happiness | Sky |
| Jesus | Up |

the two wings of a great eagle. Then she could fly to the place that was prepared for her in the desert. There she would be taken care of for three and a half years. There she would be away from the snake. ¹⁵Then the snake poured water out of its mouth like a river. He poured the water toward the woman, so that the flood would carry her away. ¹⁶But the earth helped her. The earth opened its mouth and swallowed the river that came from the mouth of the dragon. ¹⁷Then the dragon was very angry at the woman. He went off to make war against all her other children. Her children are those who obey God's commands and have the truth that Jesus taught.

¹⁸And the dragon stood on the seashore.

## THE TWO BEASTS

**13** Then I saw a beast coming up out of the sea. It had ten horns and seven heads. There was a crown on each horn. A name against God was written on each head. ²This beast looked like a leopard, with feet like a bear's feet. He had a mouth like a lion's mouth. The dragon gave the beast all of his power and his throne and great authority. ³One of the heads of the beast looked as if it had been wounded and killed. But this death wound was healed. The whole world was amazed and followed the beast. ⁴People worshiped the dragon because he had given his power to the beast. And they also worshiped the beast. They asked, "Who is as powerful as the beast? Who can make war against him?"

⁵The beast was allowed to say proud words and words against God. He was allowed to use his power for 42 months. ⁶He used his mouth to speak against God. He spoke against God's name, against the place where God lives, and against all those who live in heaven. ⁷He was given power to make war against God's holy people and to defeat them. He was given power over every tribe,ᵈ people, language, and nation. ⁸All who live on earth will worship the beast. These are all the people since the beginning of the world whose names are not written in the Lamb's book of life. The Lamb is the One who was killed.

⁹If anyone has ears, he should listen:
¹⁰If anyone is to be a prisoner,
  then he will be a prisoner.
If anyone is to be killed with the
    sword,
  then he will be killed with the
    sword.
This means that God's holy people must have patience and faith.

¹¹Then I saw another beast coming up out of the earth. He had two horns like a lamb, but he talked like a dragon. ¹²This beast stands before the first beast and uses the same power that the first beast has. He uses this power to make everyone living on earth worship the first beast. The first beast was the one that had the death wound that was healed. ¹³The second one does great miracles.ᵈ He even makes fire come down from heaven to earth while people are watching.

¹⁴This second beast fools those who live on earth. He fools them by the miracles he has been given the power to do. He does these miracles to serve the first beast. The second beast ordered people to make an idol to honor the first beast. This was the one that was wounded by the sword but did not die. ¹⁵The second beast was given power to give life to the idol of the first one. Then the idol could speak and order all who did not worship it to be killed. ¹⁶The second animal also forced all people, small and great, rich and poor, free and slave, to have a mark on their right hand or on their forehead. ¹⁷No one could buy or sell without this mark. This mark is the name of the beast or the number of his name. ¹⁸Whoever has understanding can find the meaning of the number. This requires wisdom. This number is the number of a man. His number is 666.

## THE SONG OF THE SAVED

**14** Then I looked, and there before me was the Lamb. He was standing on Mount Zion.ⁿ There were 144,000 people with him. They all had his

14:1 **Mount Zion** Another name for Jerusalem, here meaning the spiritual city of God's people.

name and his Father's name written on their foreheads. ²And I heard a sound from heaven like the noise of flooding water and like the sound of loud thunder. The sound I heard was like people playing harps. ³And they sang a new song before the throne and before the four living things and the elders." The only ones who could learn the new song were the 144,000 who had been saved from the earth. No one else could learn the song. ⁴These 144,000 are the ones who did not do sinful things with women. They kept themselves pure. They follow the Lamb every place he goes. These 144,000 were saved from among the people of the earth. They are the first people to be offered to God and the Lamb. ⁵They were not guilty of telling lies. They are without fault.

## THE THREE ANGELS

⁶Then I saw another angel flying high in the air. The angel had the eternal Good News$^d$ to preach to those who live on earth—to every nation, tribe,$^d$ language, and people. ⁷The angel said in a loud voice, "Fear God and give him praise. The time has come for God to judge all people. Worship God. He made the heavens, the earth, the sea, and the springs of water."

⁸Then the second angel followed the first angel and said, "She is destroyed! The great city of Babylon is destroyed! She made all the nations drink the wine of her adultery$^d$ and of God's anger."

⁹A third angel followed the first two angels. This third angel said in a loud voice: "It will be bad for the person who worships the beast and his idol and gets the beast's mark on the forehead or on the hand. ¹⁰He will drink the wine of God's anger. This wine is prepared with all its strength in the cup of God's anger. He will be put in pain with burn-

ing sulfur before the holy angels and the Lamb. ¹¹And the smoke from their burning pain will rise forever and ever. There will be no rest, day or night, for those who worship the beast and his idol or who get the mark of his name." ¹²This means that God's holy people must be patient. They must obey God's commands and keep their faith in Jesus.

¹³Then I heard a voice from heaven. It said, "Write this: From now on, the dead who were in the Lord when they died are happy."

**Q. Why can't you win at every game you play?**

**A. You can't be good at everything.**

The Spirit$^d$ says, "Yes, that is true. They will rest from their hard work. The reward of all they have done stays with them."

## THE EARTH IS HARVESTED

¹⁴I looked and there before me was a white cloud. Sitting on the white cloud was One who looked like a Son of Man." He had a gold crown on his head and a sharp sickle" in his hand. ¹⁵Then another angel came out of the temple. This angel called to the One who was sitting

on the cloud, "Take your sickle and gather from the earth. The time to harvest has come. The fruit of the earth is ripe." ¹⁶So the One that was sitting on the cloud swung his sickle over the earth. And the earth was harvested.

¹⁷Then another angel came out of the temple in heaven. This angel also had a sharp sickle. ¹⁸And then another angel came from the altar. This angel has power over the fire. This angel called to the angel with the sharp sickle. He said, "Take your sharp sickle and gather the bunches of grapes from the earth's vine. The earth's grapes are ripe." ¹⁹The angel swung his sickle over the earth. He gathered the earth's grapes and threw them into the great winepress$^d$ of God's anger. ²⁰The grapes were crushed in the winepress outside the city. And blood flowed out of the winepress. It rose as high as the heads of the horses for a distance of 200 miles.

## THE LAST TROUBLES

**15** Then I saw another wonder in heaven. It was great and amazing. There were seven angels bringing seven troubles. These are the last troubles, because after these troubles God's anger is finished.

²I saw what looked like a sea of glass mixed with fire. All of those who had won the victory over the beast and his idol and over the number of his name were standing by the sea. They had harps that God had given them. ³They sang the song of Moses, the servant of God, and the song of the Lamb:

"You do great and wonderful
   things,                    *Psalm 111:2*
Lord God, the God of heaven's
   armies.                    *Amos 3:13*
Everything the Lord does is right
   and true,                  *Psalm 145:17*

---

14:3 **elders** Elder means "older." Here the elders probably represent God's people.  14:14 **Son of Man**  "Son of Man" is a name Jesus called himself. It showed he was God's Son, but he was also a man.
14:14 **sickle** A farming tool with a curved blade. It was used to harvest grain.

King of the nations.
⁴Everyone will respect you, Lord.

*Jeremiah 10:7*

They will honor you.
Only you are holy.
All people will come
and worship you.     *Psalm 86:9-10*

This is because he is a faithful God
who does no wrong.
He is right and fair."

*Deuteronomy 32:4*

⁵After this I saw the temple (the Tent*d* of the Agreement) in heaven. The temple was opened. ⁶And the seven angels bringing the seven troubles came out of the temple. They were dressed in clean, shining linen. They wore golden bands tied around their chests. ⁷Then one of the four living things gave seven golden bowls to the seven angels. The bowls were filled with the anger of God, who lives forever and ever. ⁸The temple was filled with smoke from the glory and the power of God. No one could enter the temple until the seven troubles of the seven angels were finished.

## THE BOWLS OF GOD'S ANGER

**16** Then I heard a loud voice from the temple. The voice said to the seven angels, "Go and pour out the seven bowls of God's anger on the earth."

²The first angel left. He poured out his bowl on the land. Then ugly and painful sores came upon all those who had the mark of the beast and who worshiped his idol.

³The second angel poured out his bowl on the sea. Then the sea became blood like that of a dead man. Every living thing in the sea died.

⁴The third angel poured out his bowl on the rivers and the springs of water. And they became blood. ⁵Then I heard the angel of the waters say to God:

"Holy One, you are the One who is and who was.

You are right to decide to punish these evil people.
⁶They have spilled the blood of your holy people and your prophets.*d*
Now you have given them blood to drink as they deserve."

⁷And I heard the altar say:
"Yes, Lord God All-Powerful,
the way you punish evil people is right and fair."

⁸The fourth angel poured out his bowl on the sun. The sun was given power to burn the people with fire. ⁹They were burned by the great heat, and they cursed the name of God. God is the One who had control over these troubles. But the people refused to change their hearts and lives and give glory to God.

¹⁰The fifth angel poured out his bowl on the throne of the beast. And darkness covered the beast's kingdom. People bit their tongues because of the pain. ¹¹They cursed the God of heaven because of their pain and the sores they had. But they refused to change their hearts and turn away from the evil things they did.

¹²The sixth angel poured out his bowl on the great river Euphrates. The water in the river was dried up. This prepared the way for the kings from the east to come. ¹³Then I saw three evil spirits that looked like frogs. They came out of the mouth of the dragon, out of the mouth of the beast, and out of the mouth of the false prophet.*d* ¹⁴These evil spirits are the spirits of demons.*d* They have power to do miracles.*d* They go out to the kings of the whole world. They go out to gather the kings for battle on the great day of God All-Powerful.

¹⁵"Listen! I will come as a thief comes! Happy is the person who stays awake and keeps his clothes with him. Then he will not have to go without clothes and be ashamed because he is naked."

¹⁶Then the evil spirits gathered the kings together to the place that is called Armageddon*n* in the Hebrew language.

¹⁷The seventh angel poured out his bowl into the air. Then a loud voice

"Then the evil spirits gathered the kings together to the place that is called Armageddon in the Hebrew language."

*Revelation 16:16*

came out of the temple from the throne. The voice said, "It is finished!" ¹⁸Then there were flashes of lightning, noises, thunder, and a big earthquake. This was the worst earthquake that has ever happened since people have been on earth. ¹⁹The great city split into three parts. The cities of the nations were destroyed. And God did not forget to punish Babylon the Great. He gave that city the cup filled with the wine of his terrible anger. [20]Every island disappeared, and there were no more mountains. [21]Giant hailstones fell on people from the sky. The hailstones weighed about 100 pounds each. People cursed God because of the hail. This trouble was a terrible thing.

## THE WOMAN ON THE ANIMAL

**17** One of the seven angels came and spoke to me. This was one of the angels that had the seven bowls. He said, "Come, and I will show you the punishment that will be given to the famous prostitute.[d] She is the one sitting over many waters. [2]The kings of the earth sinned sexually with her. And the people of the earth became drunk from the wine of her sexual sin."

[3]Then the angel carried me away by the Spirit[d] to the desert. There I saw a woman sitting on a red beast. He was covered with names against God written on him. He had seven heads and ten horns. [4]The woman was dressed in purple and red. She was shining with the gold, jewels, and pearls she was wearing. She had a golden cup in her hand. This cup was filled with evil things and the uncleanness of her sexual sin. [5]She had a title written on her forehead. This title has a hidden meaning. This is what was written:

THE GREAT BABYLON
MOTHER OF PROSTITUTES
AND THE EVIL THINGS OF THE EARTH

[6]I saw that the woman was drunk. She was drunk with the blood of God's holy people. She was drunk with the blood of those who were killed because of their faith in Jesus.

When I saw the woman, I was fully amazed. [7]Then the angel said to me, "Why are you amazed? I will tell you the hidden meaning of this woman and the beast she rides—the one with seven heads and ten horns. [8]The beast that you saw was once alive. He is not alive now. But he will be alive and come up out of the bottomless pit and go away to be destroyed. The people who live on earth will be amazed when they see the beast. They will be amazed because he was once alive, is not alive now, but will come again. These are the people whose names have never been written in the book of life since the beginning of the world.

[9]"You need a wise mind to understand this. The seven heads on the beast are the seven hills where the woman sits. They are also seven kings. [10]Five of the kings have already died. One of the kings lives now. And the last king is coming. When he comes, he will stay only a short time. [11]The beast that was once alive but is not alive now is an eighth king. This eighth king also belongs to the first seven kings. And he will go away to be destroyed.

[12]"The ten horns you saw are ten kings. These ten kings have not yet begun to rule. But they will receive power to rule with the beast for one hour. [13]All ten of these kings have the same purpose. And they will give their power and authority to the beast. [14]They will make war against the Lamb. But the Lamb will defeat them, because he is Lord of lords and King of kings. He will defeat them with his chosen and faithful followers—the people that he has called."

[15]Then the angel said to me, "You saw the water where the prostitute sits. These waters are the many peoples, the different races, nations, and languages. [16]The beast and the ten horns you saw will

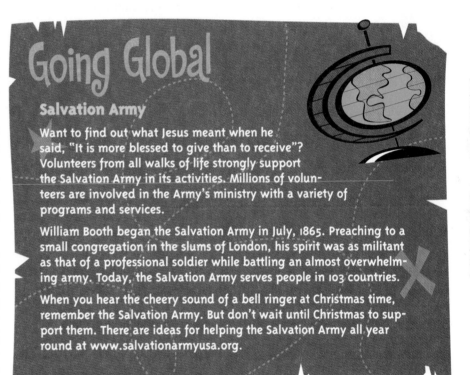

## Going Global

### Salvation Army

Want to find out what Jesus meant when he said, "It is more blessed to give than to receive"? Volunteers from all walks of life strongly support the Salvation Army in its activities. Millions of volunteers are involved in the Army's ministry with a variety of programs and services.

William Booth began the Salvation Army in July, 1865. Preaching to a small congregation in the slums of London, his spirit was as militant as that of a professional soldier while battling an almost overwhelming army. Today, the Salvation Army serves people in 103 countries.

When you hear the cheery sound of a bell ringer at Christmas time, remember the Salvation Army. But don't wait until Christmas to support them. There are ideas for helping the Salvation Army all year round at www.salvationarmyusa.org.

## DECODE THIS!

*What was the name of the woman dressed in purple and red sitting on the red beast?*

hate the prostitute. They will take everything she has and leave her naked. They will eat her body and burn her with fire. [17]God made the ten horns want to carry out his purpose: They agreed to give the beast their power to rule. They will rule until what God has said is completed. [18]The woman you saw is the great city that rules over the kings of the earth."

## BABYLON IS DESTROYED

**18** Then I saw another angel coming down from heaven. This angel had great power. The angel's glory made the earth bright. [2]The angel shouted in a powerful voice:

"The great city of Babylon is destroyed!
    She has become a home for demons.[d]
She has become a city for every evil spirit,
    a city for every unclean[d] and hated bird.
[3]All the peoples of the earth have drunk the strong wine of her sexual sin.
The kings of the earth have sinned sexually with her,
    and the businessmen of the world have grown rich from the great wealth of her luxury."

[4]Then I heard another voice from heaven say:
"Come out of that city, my people,
    so that you will not share in her sins.
    Then you will not receive the terrible things that will happen to her.
[5]The city's sins are piled up as high as the sky.
    God has not forgotten the wrongs she has done.
[6]Give that city the same as she gave to others.
    Pay her back twice as much as she did.

Prepare wine for her that is twice as strong
    as the wine she prepared for others.
[7]She gave herself much glory and rich living.
    Give her that much suffering and sadness.
She says to herself, 'I am a queen sitting on my throne.
    I am not a widow; I will never be sad.'
[8]So these terrible things will come to her in one day:
    death, crying, and great hunger.
She will be destroyed by fire,
    because the Lord God who judges her is powerful."

[9]The kings of the earth who sinned sexually with her and shared her wealth will see the smoke from her burning. Then they will cry and weep because of her death. [10]They will be afraid of her suffering and stand far away. They will say:

"Terrible! How terrible, great city,
    powerful city of Babylon!
Your punishment has come in one hour!"

[11]And the businessmen of the earth will cry and weep for her. They will be sad because now there is no one to buy the

spice, incense,[d] myrrh,[d] frankincense,[d] wine, and olive oil; fine flour, wheat, cattle, sheep, horses, and carriages. They sell the bodies and souls of men. [14]They will say,

"Babylon, the good things you wanted are gone from you.
All your rich and fancy things have disappeared.
    You will never have them again."

[15]The businessmen will be afraid of her suffering and stand far away from her. These are the men who became rich from selling those things to her. The men will cry and be sad. [16]They will say:

"Terrible! How terrible for the great city!

**"Hallelujah! Salvation, glory, and power belong to our God."**
*Revelation 19:1*

things they sell. [12]They sell gold, silver, jewels, pearls, fine linen cloth, purple cloth, silk, and red cloth. They sell all kinds of citron wood and all kinds of things made from ivory, expensive wood, bronze, iron, and marble. [13]They also sell cinnamon,

She was dressed in fine linen,
    purple and red cloth.
She was shining with gold, jewels, and pearls!

## DECODE THiS!
*After Babylon was destroyed, people in heaven rejoiced and said what?*

[17]All these riches have been destroyed in one hour!"

Every sea captain, all those who travel on ships, the sailors, and all the people who earn money from the sea stood far away from Babylon. [18]They saw the smoke from her burning. They said loudly, "There was never a city like this great city!" [19]They threw dust on their heads and cried to show how sad they were. They said:

"Terrible! How terrible for the great city!

All the people who had ships on the sea
became rich because of her wealth!

But she has been destroyed in one hour!

[20]Be happy because of this, heaven!

Be happy, God's holy people and apostles[d] and prophets![d]

God has punished her because of what she did to you."

[21]Then a powerful angel picked up a stone like a large stone for grinding grain. The angel threw the stone into the sea and said:

"That is how the great city of Babylon will be thrown down.

The city will never be found again.

[22]The music of people playing harps and other instruments, flutes and trumpets,
will never be heard in you again.

No workman doing any job
will ever be found in you again.

The sound of grinding grain
will never be heard in you again.

[23]The light of a lamp
will never shine in you again.

The voices of a bridegroom and bride
will never be heard in you again.

Your businessmen were the world's great men.

All the nations were tricked by your magic.

## TOP TEN

### Cool Jobs to Grow Into

1. Parent
2. Big brother or big sister
3. Christian comedian
4. Children's book writer
5. Missionary
6. Politician
7. Movie director
8. Missionary doctor
9. FBI or CIA
10. Pastor

[24]She is guilty of the death
of the prophets and God's holy people
and of all who have been killed on earth."

## PEOPLE IN HEAVEN PRAISE GOD

**19** After this I heard what sounded like a great many people in heaven. They were saying:
"Hallelujah![n]

Salvation, glory, and power belong to our God.

[2] His judgments are true and right.

Our God has punished the prostitute.[d]

She is the one who made the earth evil with her sexual sin.

God has punished the prostitute to pay her for the death of his servants."

[3]Again they said:
"Hallelujah!

She is burning, and her smoke will rise forever and ever."

[4]Then the 24 elders[n] and the four living things bowed down. They worshiped God, who sits on the throne. They said:
"Amen, Hallelujah!"

[5]Then a voice came from the throne:
"Praise our God, all you who serve him!

Praise our God, all you who honor him, both small and great!"

[6]Then I heard what sounded like a great many people. It sounded like the noise of flooding water and like loud thunder. The people were saying:
"Hallelujah!

Our Lord God rules. He is the All-Powerful.

[7]Let us rejoice and be happy
and give God glory!

Give God glory, because the wedding of the Lamb has come.

And the Lamb's bride has made herself ready.

[8]Fine linen was given to the bride for her to wear.

The linen was bright and clean."

(The fine linen means the good things done by God's holy people.)

[9]Then the angel said to me, "Write this: Those who are invited to the wedding meal of the Lamb are happy!" Then the angel said, "These are the true words of God."

[10]Then I bowed down at the angel's feet to worship him. But he said to me, "Do not worship me! I am a servant like you and your brothers who have the truth of Jesus. Worship God! Because the truth about Jesus is the spirit that gives all prophecy."[d]

## THE RIDER ON THE WHITE HORSE

[11]Then I saw heaven open. There before me was a white horse. The rider on the horse is called Faithful and

---

19:1 **Hallelujah** This means "praise God!" 19:4 **24 elders** Elder means "older." Here the elders probably represent God's people.

True. He is right when he judges and makes war. [12]His eyes are like burning fire, and on his head are many crowns. He has a name written on him, but he is the only one who knows the name. No other person knows the name. [13]He is dressed in a robe dipped in blood. His name is the Word of God. [14]The armies of heaven were following him on white horses. They were dressed in fine linen, white and clean. [15]A sharp sword comes out of the rider's mouth. He will use this sword to defeat the nations. He will rule them with a scepter[d] of iron. He will crush out the wine in the winepress[d] of the terrible anger of God All-Powerful. [16]On his robe and on his leg was written this name: "KING OF KINGS AND LORD OF LORDS."

[17]Then I saw an angel standing in the sun. The angel called with a loud voice to all the birds flying in the sky, "Come together for the great feast of God. [18]Come together so that you can eat the bodies of kings and generals and famous men. Come to eat the bodies of the horses and their riders and the bodies of all people—free, slave, small, and great."

[19]Then I saw the beast and the kings of the earth. Their armies were gathered together to make war against the rider on the horse and his army. [20]But the beast was captured and with him the false prophet.[d] This false prophet was the one who did the miracles[d] for the beast. The false prophet had used these miracles to trick those who had the mark of the beast and worshiped his idol. The false prophet and the beast were thrown alive into the lake of fire that burns with sulfur. [21]Their armies were killed with the sword that came out of the mouth of the rider on the horse. All the birds ate the bodies until they were full.

## THE 1,000 YEARS

**20** [1]I saw an angel coming down from heaven. He had the key to the bottomless pit. He also held a large chain in his hand. [2]The angel grabbed the dragon, that old snake who is the devil. The angel tied him up for 1,000 years. [3]Then he threw him into the bottomless pit and closed it and locked it over him. The angel did this so that he could not trick the people of the earth anymore until the 1,000 years were ended. After 1,000 years he must be set free for a short time.

[4]Then I saw some thrones and people sitting on them. They had been given the power to judge. And I saw the souls of those who had been killed because they were faithful to the truth of Jesus and the message from God. They had not worshiped the beast or his idol. They had not received the mark of the beast on their foreheads or on their hands. They came back to life and ruled with Christ for 1,000 years. [5](The others that were dead did not live again until the 1,000 years were ended.) This is the first raising of the dead. [6]Blessed and holy are those who share in this first raising of the dead. The second death has no power over

> "There before me was a white horse. The rider on the horse is called Faithful and True."
>
> *Revelation 19:11*

them. They will be priests for God and for Christ. They will rule with him for 1,000 years.

[7]When the 1,000 years are over, Satan will be set free from his prison. [8]He will go out to trick the nations in all the earth—Gog and Magog. Satan will gather them for battle. There will be so many people that they will be like sand on the seashore. [9]And Satan's army marched across the earth and gathered around the camp of God's people and the city that God loves. But fire came down from heaven and burned them up. [10]And Satan, who tricked them, was thrown into the lake of burning sulfur with the beast and the false prophet.[d] There they will be punished day and night forever and ever.

## PEOPLE OF THE WORLD ARE JUDGED

[11]Then I saw a great white throne and the One who was sitting on it. Earth and sky ran away from him and disappeared. [12]And I saw the dead, great and small, standing before the throne. And the book of life was opened. There were also other books opened. The dead were judged by what they had done, which was written in the books. [13]The sea gave up the dead who were in it. Death and Hades[n] gave up the dead who were in them. Each person was judged by what he had done. [14]And Death and Hades were thrown into the lake of fire. This lake of fire is the second death. [15]And if anyone's name was not found written in the book of life, he was thrown into the lake of fire.

> "The one on the throne said to me: 'it is finished! i am the Alpha and the Omega, the Beginning and the end.'"
>
> *Revelation 21:6*

20:13 **Hades** Where the dead are.

### THE NEW JERUSALEM

**21** Then I saw a new heaven and a new earth. The first heaven and the first earth had disappeared. Now there was no sea. ²And I saw the holy city coming down out of heaven from God. This holy city is the new Jerusalem.ⁿ It was prepared like a bride dressed for her husband. ³I heard a loud voice from the throne. The voice said, "Now God's home is with men. He will live with them, and they will be his people. God himself will be with them and will be their God. ⁴He will wipe away every tear from their eyes. There will be no more death, sadness, crying, or pain. All the old ways are gone."

⁵The One who was sitting on the throne said, "Look! I am making everything new!" Then he said, "Write this, because these words are true and can be trusted."

⁶The One on the throne said to me: "It is finished! I am the Alpha and the Omega,ⁿ the Beginning and the End. I will give free water from the spring of the water of life to anyone who is thirsty. ⁷Anyone who wins the victory will receive this. And I will be his God, and he will be my son. ⁸But those who are cowards, who refuse to believe, who do evil things, who kill, who sin sexually, who do evil magic, who worship idols, and who tell lies—all these will have a place in the lake of burning sulfur. This is the second death."

⁹One of the seven angels came to me. This was one of the angels who had the seven bowls full of the seven last troubles. He said, "Come with me. I will show you the bride, the wife of the Lamb." ¹⁰The angel carried me away by the Spiritᵈ to a very large and high mountain. He showed me the holy city, Jerusalem. It was coming down out of heaven from God. ¹¹It was shining with the glory of God. It was shining bright like a very expensive jewel, like a jasper. It was clear as crystal. ¹²The city had a great high wall with 12 gates. There were 12 angels at the gates. On each gate was written the name of 1 of the 12 tribesᵈ of Israel. ¹³There were three gates on the east, three on the north, three on the south, and three on the west. ¹⁴The walls of the city were built on 12 foundation stones. On the stones were written the names of the 12 apostlesᵈ of the Lamb.

¹⁵The angel who talked with me had a measuring rod made of gold. He had this rod to

### DEEP THOUGHTS

## WILD WORLD FACTS

Revelation 21:1 says that in the new heavens and new earth that God is preparing, there will be no sea. So we better learn about and appreciate all we know about oceans, now!

The Pacific Ocean is the deepest ocean on the earth. The deepest part is called the Mariana Trench, which stretches over 11,000 meters below the water's surface. Even Mount Everest, the world's tallest mountain at 8,848 meters would be swallowed up by such a large gap! The deepest part of the Atlantic Ocean is the Milwaukee Deep, reaching 8,530 meters down. The ocean is an amazing place, like its own world, with its own ecosystem and complex food chain. It holds the smallest plankton and the largest creature (the whale) in the world. Want to learn more? Visit MBGnet.com for more.

[Yahooligans: Ask Earl; MBGnet]

measure the city, its gates, and its wall. ¹⁶The city was built in a square. Its length was equal to its width. The angel measured the city with the rod. The city was 12,000 stadiaⁿ long, 12,000 stadia wide, and 12,000 stadia high. ¹⁷The angel also measured the wall. It was 144 cubitsⁿ high, by man's measurement. That was the measurement the angel was using. ¹⁸The wall was made of jasper. The city was made of pure gold, as pure as glass. ¹⁹The foundation stones of the city walls had every kind of jewel in them. The first cornerstone was jasper, the second was sapphire, the third was chalcedony, the fourth was emerald, ²⁰the fifth was onyx, the sixth was carnelian, the seventh was chrysolite, the eighth was beryl, the ninth was topaz, the tenth was chrysoprase, the eleventh was jacinth, and the twelfth was amethyst. ²¹The 12 gates were 12 pearls. Each gate was made from a single pearl. The street of the city was made of pure gold. The gold was clear as glass.

²²I did not see a temple in the city. The Lord God All-Powerful and the Lamb are the city's temple. ²³The city does not need the sun or the moon to shine on it. The glory of God is its light, and the Lamb is the city's lamp. ²⁴By its light the people of the world will walk. The kings of the earth will bring their glory into it. ²⁵The city's gates will never be shut on any day, because there is no night there. ²⁶The greatness and the honor of the nations will be brought into it. ²⁷Nothing uncleanᵈ will ever enter the city. No one who does shameful things or tells lies will ever

21:2 **new Jerusalem** The spiritual city where God's people live with him. 21:6 **Alpha and the Omega** The first and last letters in the Greek alphabet. This means "the beginning and the end." 21:16 **stadia** One stadion was a distance of about 200 yards. It was one-eighth of a Roman mile. 21:17 **cubits** A cubit is about half a yard, the length from the elbow to the tip of the little finger.

go into it. Only those whose names are written in the Lamb's book of life will enter the city.

**22** Then the angel showed me the river of the water of life. The river was shining like crystal. It flows from the throne of God and of the Lamb ²down the middle of the street of the city. The tree of life was on each side of the river. It produces fruit 12 times a year, once each month. The leaves of the

tree are for the healing of all people. ³Nothing that God judges guilty will be in that city. The throne of God and of the Lamb will be there. And God's servants will worship him. ⁴They will see his face, and his name will be written on their foreheads. ⁵There will never be night again. They will not need the light of a lamp or the light of the sun. The Lord God will give them light. And they will rule like kings forever and ever.

⁶The angel said to me, "These words are true and can be trusted. The Lord is the God of the spirits of the prophets.ᵈ He sent his angel to show his servants the things that must happen soon."

⁷"Listen! I am coming soon! He who obeys the words of prophecy in this book will be happy."

⁸I am John. I am the one who heard and saw these things. When I heard and saw them, I bowed down to worship at the feet of the angel who showed these things to me. ⁹But the angel said to me, "Do not worship me! I am a servant like you and your brothers the prophets. I am a servant like all those who obey the words in this book. Worship God!"

¹⁰Then the angel told me, "Do not keep secret the words of prophecy in this book. The time is near for all this to happen. ¹¹Whoever is doing evil, let him continue to do evil. Whoever is unclean, let him continue to be unclean. Whoever is doing right, let him continue to do right. Whoever is holy, let him continue to be holy."

¹²"Listen! I am coming soon! I will bring rewards with me. I will repay each one for what he has done. ¹³I am the Alpha and the Omega," the First and the Last, the Beginning and the End.

¹⁴"Those who wash their robes" will be blessed. They will have the right to eat the fruit from the tree of life. They may go through the gates into the city. ¹⁵Outside the city are the evil people, those who do evil magic, who sin sexually, who murder, who worship idols, and who love lies and tell lies.

¹⁶"I, Jesus, have sent my angel to tell you these things for the churches. I am the descendantᵈ from the family of David. I am the bright morning star."

¹⁷The Spiritᵈ and the bride say, "Come!" Everyone who hears this should also say, "Come!" If anyone is thirsty, let him come; whoever wishes it may have the water of life as a free gift.

¹⁸I warn everyone who hears the words of the prophecy of this book: If anyone adds anything to these words, God will give him the troubles written about in this book. ¹⁹And if anyone takes away from the words of this book of prophecy, God will take away his share of the tree of life and of the holy city, which are written about in this book.

²⁰Jesus is the One who says that these things are true. Now he says, "Yes, I am coming soon."

Amen. Come, Lord Jesus!

²¹The grace of the Lord Jesus be with all. Amen.

## WILD WORLD FACTS

### GREAT BALL OF FiRE!

Every morning we wake up to its bright light. We rely on it for warmth, light, and all of life. So what exactly is the sun?

The sun is the star located in the center of our solar system about 146 million kilometers from the earth. It is about 109 times larger than the earth, the largest mass in our solar system. Made of burning gases held together by gravity, it releases energy through nuclear fusion, giving us light and heat. Because of its huge size, the sun's gravity is the greatest in the solar system and holds all the planets in orbit.

As powerful as the sun is, God says that when we get to heaven, we won't need a sun. God's own glory will be our light and warmth, because he is all we need.

[Melbourne Planetarium]

## DECODE THiS!

*What does Alpha and Omega mean?*

22:13 **Alpha and the Omega** The first and last letters in the Greek alphabet. This means "the beginning and the end." 22:14 **wash their robes** This means they believed in Jesus so that their sins could be forgiven by Christ's blood.

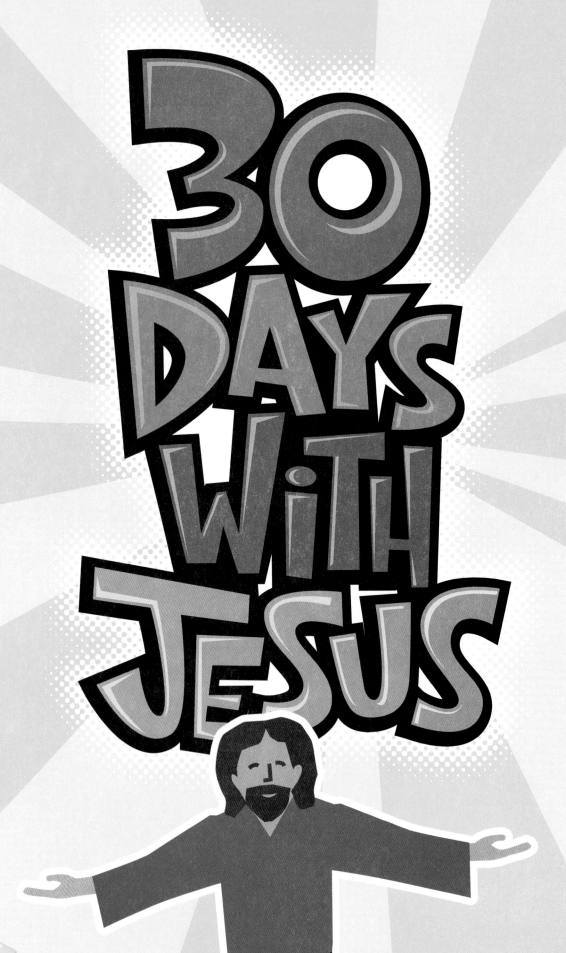

**READ THESE & YOU'LL BE A FISHER OF MEN!**

1. John 1:1-51
2. Luke 2:1-52
3. Mark 1:1-11
4. Luke 4:1-44
5. John 3:1-36
6. Luke 5:1-39
7. John 4:1-54
8. Luke 6:1-49
9. Luke 7:1-50
10. Luke 8:1-56
11. Mark 8:1-38
12. Luke 10:1-42
13. Matthew 5:1-48
14. Matthew 6:1-34
15. Matthew 7:1-29

16. Luke 14:1-35
17. Luke 15:1-32
18. Luke 16:1-31
19. John 8:1-59
20. Luke 17:1-37
21. Luke 18:1-43
22. John 9:1-41
23. Luke 19:1-48
24. Luke 20:1-47
25. John 10:1-42
26. John 11:1-57
27. Mark 13:1-37
28. Luke 22:1-71
29. Matthew 27:1-66
30. Luke 24:1-53

# 60 DAYS

# WITH PAUL

# PRAYER CONCERNS

My List!

Write your prayer concerns on the lines below. Occasionally go
back to these pages and see how God has answered your requests!

# PRAYER CONCERNS

......................................................

......................................................

......................................................

......................................................

......................................................

......................................................

......................................................

......................................................

......................................................

......................................................

......................................................